W9-CBG-911

From Superpower to Besieged Global Power

DATE DUE

MAY 1 1 2014	

BRODART, CO.   Cat. No. 23-221

STUDIES IN SECURITY
AND INTERNATIONAL AFFAIRS

SERIES EDITORS

Gary K. Bertsch
*University Professor of Public and
International Affairs and Director of the
Center for International Trade and Security,
University of Georgia*

Howard J. Wiarda
*Dean Rusk Professor of International Relations
and Head of the Department of International
Affairs, University of Georgia*

SERIES ADVISORY BOARD

Pauline H. Baker
The Fund for Peace

Eliot Cohen
*Paul H. Nitze School of Advanced International
Studies, Johns Hopkins University*

Eric Einhorn
*Center for Public Policy and Administration,
University of Massachusetts, Amherst*

John J. Hamre
*The Center for Strategic and
International Studies*

Josef Joffe
*Hoover Institution, Institute for International
Studies, Stanford University*

Lawrence J. Korb
Center for American Progress

William J. Long
*Sam Nunn School of International Affairs,
Georgia Institute of Technology*

Jessica Tuchman Mathews
Carnegie Endowment for International Peace

Scott D. Sagan
*Center for International Security and
Cooperation, Stanford University*

Lawrence Scheinman
*Monterey Institute of International Studies,
CNS-WDC*

David Shambaugh
*The Elliott School of International Affairs,
George Washington University*

Jessica Stern
*John F. Kennedy School of Government,
Harvard University*

From Superpower to Besieged Global Power

Restoring World Order after the Failure of the Bush Doctrine

EDITED BY *Edward A. Kolodziej and Roger E. Kanet*

The University of Georgia Press | *Athens and London*

© 2008 by the University of Georgia Press
Athens, Georgia 30602
All rights reserved
Set in Electra LH by Graphic Composition, Inc.,
   Bogart, Georgia
Printed and bound by Maple-Vail
The paper in this book meets the guidelines for
permanence and durability of the Committee on
Production Guidelines for Book Longevity of the
Council on Library Resources.

Printed in the United States of America
12 11 10 09 08 C 5 4 3 2 1
12 11 10 09 08 P 5 4 3 2 1

Library of Congress Cataloging-in-Publication Data

From superpower to besieged global power : restoring
world order after the failure of the Bush doctrine / edited
by Edward A. Kolodziej and Roger E. Kanet.
         p. cm. — (Studies in security and international
affairs)
      Includes bibliographical references and index.
      ISBN-13: 978-0-8203-2977-2 (hardcover : alk. paper)
      ISBN-10: 0-8203-2977-0 (hardcover : alk. paper)
      ISBN-13: 978-0-8203-3074-7 (pbk. : alk. paper)
      ISBN-10: 0-8203-3074-4 (pbk. : alk. paper)
      1. United States—Foreign relations—2001– 2. United
States—Military policy. 3. Bush, George W. (George
Walker), 1946—Political and social views. 4. Bush,
George W. (George Walker), 1946—Influence.
5. Great powers—Case studies. 6. United States—
Foreign public opinion. 7. United States—Foreign
relations—Moral and ethical aspects. I. Kolodziej,
Edward A. II. Kanet, Roger E., 1936–
E902.F77 2008
973.93—dc22   2007034024

British Library Cataloging-in-Publication Data available

ACC Library Services
Austin, Texas

Contents

Acronyms

ABM	Antiballistic missile
ACOTA	Africa Contingency Operations Training
ACRI	African Crisis Response Initiative
AENF	Alliance of Eritrea National Forces
AFRICOM	African Command (U.S.)
AGOA	African Growth and Opportunity Act
AMT	Alternate minimum tax
ANP	National Popular Army (Algerian intelligence organization)
AP	Associated Press
APEC	Asia-Pacific Economic Cooperation
ARF	ASEAN Regional Forum
ASEAN	Association of Southeast Asian Nations
ATU	Antiterror unit
BJP	Bharatiya Janata Party (India)
BMD	Ballistic missile defense
BMENA	Broader Middle East and North Africa
CAA	Conference of American Armies
CACM	Central American Common Market
CARICOM	Caribbean Common Market
CBO	Congressional Budget Office
CCP	Chinese Communist Party
CEE	Central and Eastern Europe
CENTCOM	Central Command (U.S.)
CENTO	Central Treaty Organization
CFC	Combined forces command
CFE	Conventional forces in Europe
CFSP	Common Foreign and Security Policy (EU)
CIA	Central Intelligence Agency
CICTC	Committee against Terrorism (OAS)
CIS	Commonwealth of Independent States
CJTF-HOA	Combined Joint Task Force–Horn of Africa

CPA	Coalition Provisional Authority (Iraq)
CTB	Comprehensive test ban
CVID	Complete, verifiable, and irreversible dismantlement
CWC	Chemical Weapons Convention
DCI	Defense Capabilities Initiative (NATO)
DFI	Direct foreign investment
DOD	Department of Defense
DPP	Democratic People's Party (Taiwan)
DPRK	Democratic People's Republic of Korea
DPT	Democratic peace theory
DRS	Department of Intelligence and Security (Algeria)
DRVN	Democratic Republic of Vietnam
EAS	East Asian Summit
EASI	East Asia Security Initiative
EC	European Community
ENP	European Neighborhood Policy (EU)
ESDI	European Security and Defense Identity
ESDP	European Security and Defense Policy (EU)
ESS	European Security Strategy
EU	European Union
EUCOM	European Union (Forces) Command
FBI	Federal Bureau of Investigation
FISA	Federal Intelligence Surveillance Act
FTA	Free trade area
FTAA	Free Trade Area of the Americas
FY	Fiscal year
FYRM	Former Yugoslav Republic of Macedonia
GAP	Grey area phenomenon
GATT	General Agreement on Tariffs and Trade
GDP	Gross domestic product
GIA	Groupe Islamique Armé
GNP	Gross national product
GOP	Grand Old (Republican) Party
GSDF	Ground Self-Defense Force (Japan)
GUAM	Georgia, Ukraine, Azerbaijan, and Moldova
GUUAM	Georgia, Ukraine, Uzbekistan, Azerbaijan, and Moldova
GWOT	Global war on terrorism
HUMINT	Human intelligence
IAEA	International Atomic Energy Agency
IATRA	Inter-American Treaty of Reciprocal Assistance
ICC	International Criminal Court

IDB	Inter-American Development Bank
IED	Improvised explosive device
IFI	International financial institution
IFOR	Implementation Force (Bosnia-Herzegovina)
IGO	International governmental organization
IMET	International military education and training
IMF	International Monetary Fund
INC	Inter-American Naval Conference
ISAF	International Security Assistance Force (NATO)
ISI	Inter-Services Intelligence (Pakistan)
JCATS	Joint Combined Arms Training System
JDA	Japanese Defense Agency
JSA	Justice and Home Affairs (EU)
JSP	Japan Socialist Party
LDP	Liberal Democratic Party (Japan)
LoC	Line of control (Kashmir)
LRA	Lord's Resistance Army (in Uganda)
MCA	Millennium Challenge Account
MEPI	Middle East Partnership Initiative
MERCOSUR	Common Market of the South
MFN	Most favored nation
MINUSTAH	U.N. Mission to Haiti
MLAT	Mutual Legal Assistance Treaty
MOOTW	Military operation other than war
MTCR	Missile Technology Control Regime
NAFTA	North American Free Trade Agreement
NATO	North American Treaty Organization
NDP	National Democratic Party (Egypt)
NEPAD	New Partnership for Africa's Development
NGO	Nongovernmental organization
NMD	National missile defense
NPT	Non-Proliferation Treaty
NRF	NATO Response Force
NSA	National Security Agency
NSC	National Security Council
NSSP	Next steps in strategic partnership (India–U.S.)
OAS	Organization of American States
OAS/CICAD	OAS Drug Abuse Control Commission
ODED	Organization for Democracy and Economic Development (GUAM)
OECD	Organization for Economic Cooperation and Development

OFDI	Outward foreign direct investment
OHR	Operation of the High Representative (Bosnia-Herzegovina)
OIC	Organization of Islamic Countries
ONUMOZ	U.N. Observer Mission in Mozambique
ONUSAL	U.N. Observer Mission in El Salvador
OSCE	Organization for Security and Cooperation in Europe
PAS	Pan-Malaysian Islamic Party
PKK	Kurdistan Workers' Party
PLA	People's Liberation Army (China)
PNE	Peaceful nuclear explosion
PRC	People's Republic of China
PRRI	Revolutionary Government of the Indonesian Republic
PSI	Pan Sahel Initiative
PSI	Proliferation Security Initiative (U.S.)
RMA	Revolution in Military Affairs
RMB	Renminbi
ROK	Republic of Korea
RUF	Revolutionary United Front (Liberia)
R&D	Research and development
SAP	Structural Adjustment Program
SCO	Shanghai Cooperation Organization
SDF	Self-Defense Force (Japan)
SEATO	Southeast Asian Treaty Organization
SES	Single Economic Space (CIS)
SFPR	Stabilization Forces (Bosnia-Herzegovina)
SICOFAA	System of Cooperation among the American Air Forces
SIOP	Single integrated operation plan
SOC	Special Operations Command (U.S.)
SORT	Strategic Offensive (Arms) Reduction Treaty
SOUTHCOM	Southern Command (U.S.)
TEU	Treaty on European Union
TNG	Transitional National Government (Somalia)
TSCTI	Trans-Saharan Counterterrorism Initiative
UIC	Union of Islamic Courts (Somalia)
UMNO	United Malays Nations Organization
UNAVEM	U.N. Mission in Angola
UNCHR	U.N. Commission on Human Rights
UNDCP	U.N. Drug Control Program
UNPKO	U.N. Peacekeeping Operations
USAID	U.S. Agency for International Development

USFK   U.S. forces in Korea
USIA   U.S. Information Agency
USTR   U.S. Trade Representative
VFA   Visiting Forces Agreement (Philippines)
WMD   Weapons of mass destruction
WTO   World Trade Organization
ZOPFAN   Zone of Peace, Freedom and Neutrality

Acknowledgments

This volume owes much to Nancy Cantor, currently president of Syracuse University. As chancellor of the University of Illinois, she initiated a campus-wide competition for research initiatives, aimed particularly at the humanities and social sciences. A proposal to bring together regional experts from around the world to assess the success or failure of the Bush Doctrine and American foreign and security policy was born in response to the chancellor's initiative. Thanks to the generous award of a chancellor's grant, two workshops were mounted and financed, the first in Istanbul in September 2005, the second in Chicago in March 2006.

The editors also wish to thank Professor Robert Rich, chair of the committee that reviewed this proposal, and members of the committee for their confidence in this enterprise. Julian Palmore, director of the Program in Arms Control, Disarmament, and International Security, also merits our appreciation for his help in funding this project.

Planning and organizing these conferences would not have been possible without the assistance of the staff of the Center for Global Studies at the University of Illinois. Special thanks goes to Steve Witt, the associate director, who freed Ed Kolodziej from many of his duties to concentrate on the research for his chapters and to focus on the editorial chores connected with a volume that orchestrated contributions of experts from nine countries. Ms. Beth Bailey, the center's program coordinator, single-handedly organized the Chicago conference long range from Urbana-Champaign, no small feat, and attended to the countless administrative and logistical details that made the second workshop so successful and that produced a rare consensus of the contributors to an edited volume. Along the way, Ms. Lynne Rudasill, librarian of the center, helped in running down citations and fugitive quotations. John Laich updated data presented in chapter 1 and combed the bibliographical references for errors. Ms. Antje H. Kolodziej doubled as editorial assistant and critic for the contributions of the editors to this volume; and Ms. Joan A. Kanet prepared the index.

Special appreciation is extended to Ms. Merrily Shaw, who brought stylistic and editorial order and elegance to the manuscripts submitted to her by the contributors and editors. Merrily has been there for the editors in previous publications. At no small cost to her busy and much preoccupied professional and personal lives, she again volunteered for duty beyond the call—and we owe her a great debt of gratitude and so will the readers for a manuscript that the editors believe is reader friendly. Moreover, we are especially grateful for the interest in the project, which resulted in this volume, of Professors Gary K. Bertsch and Howard J. Wiarda, editors of the new University of Georgia Press series on International Challenges in the Age of Globalization in which this volume will appear. Finally, we appreciate the essential contributions to the publication of this book of Ms. Nancy Grayson, associate director and editor in chief, as well as the production staff, of the University of Georgia Press, notably Ms. M. J. Devaney, who spared the authors countless stylistic gaffes and factual errors.

The consensus of the contributors is summarized in the introduction to this volume. It represents an end product that is truly greater than the sum of the individual parts of this work. That outcome would not have been possible absent the generous contributions of time and expertise of the scholars who enlisted for service in this project. It would simply have been impossible for any one person, however astute and informed, to have conceptual and empirical control of the complex political forces at work in all of the regions of the globe covered by this volume. That informed knowledge and balanced judgment were indispensable ingredients to the success of this intellectual adventure, which we collectively hope will also inform public understanding of the foreign and security policies of major regional actors and that of the United States. The editors are also grateful for the many suggestions and corrections of substance and style offered by the participants. We also profited from the careful reading and constructive suggestions of the two outside evaluators engaged by the University of Georgia Press to assess whether the volume should be published. The editors and contributors are in their debt both for their positive recommendation to publish this work and for their many suggestions to strengthen the manuscript in form and substance. Remaining flaws are decidedly our own.

Finally, the editors are blessed by tolerant and supportive spouses who make these ventures possible and worthwhile.

Edward A. Kolodziej

Roger E. Kanet

Introduction

There's got to be some advantage to being a superpower.

—RICHARD PERLE, former Pentagon official and lobbyist,

quoted in the PBS series *America at a Crossroads*, April 2007,

advocating regime change in Iran, by force if necessary

How This Project Developed

The title of this volume tells it all. That was not the case at the start of this collective enterprise. The editors initially sought to evaluate whether a purported American superpower, alleged to dominate a unipolar world, actually got its way with other actors, state and nonstate. What was not initially questioned was whether the United States was, indeed, a superpower. Conventional wisdom was accepted at face value.

With these assumptions and aims in mind, the editors adopted a method pioneered by Alexander George (1979) that the editors had used successfully in several other edited volumes (e. g., Kolodziej and Kanet 1989, 1996). In this instance we asked regional experts to respond to the same set of questions, that is, to identify the principal actors and issues within a region and to assess whether the United States was getting its say and way in exercising its hard and soft power. Were regional actors acceding, whether by coercion or consent, to American foreign and security preferences? We also thought it would be a good idea to get some fresh perspectives on these questions by recruiting as many recognized foreign scholars as possible, the hope being that we would get a better mix of expert opinion than might be possible from rounding up the usual American suspects.

Over the course of two conferences, commencing in Istanbul in September 2005 at a gathering of international studies associations and capped by a follow-up workshop in Chicago in March 2006, it became increasingly evident that the notion of the United States as a superpower could not stand up to close scrutiny. It was a misleading characterization of U.S. power and of its ability to get others to assent or to submit to its preferences, whether at the margin over specific policy differences, say the means and methods to ferret out and defeat terrorists, or whether over the broader issues of regional and global order and security. It became increasingly clear to the editors and to the contributors that the United States was not a superpower in the sense that other actors were induced either to bandwagon on American preferences or to concede that resistance to American power was a losing game. What became progressively apparent in our deliberations were the material and political constraints limiting American power and the multiple checks either imposed on American power by regional actors or the many and substantial concessions extracted by them from a besieged global power.

To recognize the limits of American power is not to return to the discredited declinist debate of the late 1980s (Kennedy 1987). There is no doubt that the United States is a global power, however much it may be bogged down in the Iraqi and Afghan quagmires, isolated diplomatically, held in low esteem by world opinion (PIPA 2007), increasingly deep in debt, and challenged in world markets. It is the only state capable of projecting its military power around the globe. No other state or group of states, as the chapter by Patrick Morgan makes plain, can defeat the United States in a direct military clash. American economic power and technological leadership remain world class. Its $13 trillion economy dwarfs all others, with Japan a distant second global competitor at $4 trillion (except of course in automotives and electronics). China is moving up fast, but at its present rate it will need at least a generation to match the United States, whose economy will not be standing still in the meantime. American culture, informed by the creativity of its citizens in fashion, music, television, media, and movies, sets the standard for millions around the world, especially the young. America's open system of governance and respect and support for the civil liberties and human rights of its citizens and of peoples everywhere did, at least until recently, command admiration and emulation around the world.

But a superpower it is not.

Why make a big deal of a word? There are several reasons for shaping U.S. policy and purpose to the potentially countervailing and conjoining power of other actors within what is now a global society for the first time in the evolution of the human species (Kolodziej 2007). What counts is the relative power of the United States to influence the thinking and behavior of other states and peoples, not absolute measures of American military and economic capabilities or even subjective calculations of its soft cultural and ideational impact on others. The United States fails the test of a superpower when relative, not absolute, measures are relied on to estimate its power, particularly when that power is weighed in terms of its ability to realize its objectives across the principal regions of the globe.

Exaggerated notions of American power, incorporated into the Bush Doctrine as reflected in such documents as the *National Security Strategy of the United States* of 2002 and 2006 (U.S. White House, Office of the President 2002, 2006), prompt an American global reach that is beyond its grasp. The implicit hubris

and triumphalism accompanying an illusory claim to superpower status in a globalizing world of multiplying, decentralized centers of power foster an ambition
for global dominion. To believe the United States is a superpower without exam-
ining whether there is evidence to support that proposition invites American leaders (and a gullible public) to repeat the mistake of former expansionist powers that
believed that ruling others, with or without their consent, was within their power
to command, and indeed, to make the mistake of believing that that elusive ambition is today within the reach of American power. As this volume argues, the *reach*
of American power should always be calibrated to the scope of its feasible *grasp*.
American aims and policies should be tailored to the limits of American power,
a principle violated more often than not by the Bush administration's grand, but
flawed, design not only to fight an endless global war on terrorism (GWOT) but
also to create a world order that is a mirror image of the United States.

It is ironic that the lesson to be learned from the American Revolution two
centuries ago — that empires don't last even if they make enormous expenditures
of material and human resources — should be rejected by American leaders in
their unreflective embrace of the Bush Doctrine. It is also a lesson that has been
ignored for half a decade now by a majority of American voters through three
national elections held between 2000 and 2006. At this writing it is not clear
whether the loss of control of both houses of Congress by the president's party
will prove a harbinger of change and a repudiation of the imperialist impulse let
loose by the Bush administration. Many still disregard the still recent and relevant
experience of the twentieth century that demonstrates that imperialism and imperial expansion in its many forms — Communist, Fascist, Nazi, or state-based
European and Japanese versions — were fools' errands. These grabs for illegiti-
mate power resulted in tens of trillions of dollars in material destruction and upward of over 100 million deaths — and to no purpose since all these gambles have
since been relegated to the dustbin of history. A population does not become less
resistant to foreign domination, as the Iraqi experience evidences, simply because
the occupying power's announced intentions are ostensibly defined by a commitment to democratic rule and the promotion of human rights.

There is also another reason to jettison the notion of the United States as a
superpower. Those who subscribe to this notion have in recent time gained au-
thoritative control of the material power available to the American state. They
have succumbed to the temptation of believing that the United States, as a superpower, can act alone in displaying and disposing its power; it does not need the
help of others to create a world order responsive to the ideals of the winning coalition of democratic states emerging from the cold war. If one can still speak of a
hegemon in global politics, it does not reside in any one state, but in the prevailing coalition of liberal democratic states, *if its members remain united.* Instead,
the Bush Doctrine rested on the erroneous assumption that the United States,

unlike other powers, did not have to compromise with other states and peoples in negotiating an international order to its liking. This flawed but widely held and deeply embedded assumption of superpower prowess underlying the Bush Doctrine, affirmed by many Americans, generates logically the imperative that international accords that hobble the flexible and opportunistic use of U.S. power to impose its will and writ on resistant allies and recalcitrant adversaries must be ignored, weakened, subjugated to American preferences, or simply undone.

What then results, as recent experience testifies, is that willful American defection from international rules, institutions, laws, and moral standards of conduct invites defection by others, too. Former allies not only have incentive to disavow prevailing international practices, but they also have reason to qualify their support for American policies. As long as the nation-state system remains as the imperfect solution to global rule, states have a responsibility to fashion their foreign and security policies to suit their interests and power. If the aspiring hegemon cannot be trusted to take their interests into account, they will either hide (difficult to do in a globalizing world), refuse to accede to American pressures and blandishments, or move to outright opposition.

Adversaries, some activated for the first time by American expansionist policies, are also mobilized to oppose American interests, some by force as in Iraq or some by seeking nuclear weapons as with Iran and North Korea. Facts on the ground—the combination of rising armed opposition to American power, distancing and defecting allies, and regional states and people just going their own way, unmindful of American power—rob the term "superpower" of much of its meaning when applied to the United States.

Organization of the Volume

In developing the principal thesis of this volume, chapter 1 presents a pure model of the Bush administration's vision of its preferred global order and its strategy to realize its ambitions, based on the errant assumption that the United States is a superpower. The chapter then introduces the Bush Doctrine to the real world. It identifies four structural constraints that bring the American eagle down to earth: the absence of a military strategy equal to the times; the costs of the Iraq war and its negative impact on domestic political support for the occupation; the limited material resources of the United States to support an imperial project; and the rising demands of Americans for increased entitlement spending. Chapter 2 by Patrick Morgan details both the impressive strengths and weaknesses of American military power and critiques the flawed strategies currently being used to cope with the challenges of this century.

Chapters 3 to 14 identify and illuminate the multiple regional bonds entangling the American Gulliver. Chapter 15 uses these findings to develop the fifth structural constraint on U.S. power — the countervailing policies and power of other states and peoples that reduce the United States to a beset global power and strip it of its superpower status. The editors submit that this is one of the principal contributions of the volume to the debate over American power and its implications for global order. This finding has a dual significance. At a policy level, and as the failures of the Bush Doctrine across the principal regions of the globe reveal, basing American power and global strategy on the false assumption of unipolarity and superpower potency has dissipated the human and material resources of the American people, isolated the United States in the world community, delegitimated American power both in domestic and in world opinion, galvanized the opposition of important allies, and mobilized adversaries where none existed before.

Second, and on a larger theoretical plane, the volume also advises abandonment of the widely held notion that states can aspire to imperial, hegemonic, or superpower status. The rise of a world society of increasingly interdependent peoples and states, marked by the decentralization of power across countless state and nonstate actors, including increasingly empowered individuals, frustrates the aspiration of any state to become ascendant. International relations theory itself has to be fundamentally rethought in light of the American experience in the aftermath of the cold war and the folly of American expansion in its wake. The findings of this volume challenge much of contemporary international relations theory and foreign and security policy practice that continue to misleadingly rely on the arcane idiom of hegemony, empire, or rising and declining superpowers to characterize the politics of the world society and of international relations more narrowly — whether reference is made to the United States or new powers, like China and India.

In joining the debate over American foreign and security policy, the editors and most of the contributors to this volume depart from most American foreign policy schools of thought. This volume has no sympathy for current policies and strategies. Specifically rejected is the neocon argument for American aggrandizement. Discarding this position requires little intellectual effort, since grim facts on the ground not only in the Middle East and, specifically, in Iraq but also in every region of the globe, as this volume shows, are a more eloquent critique of this flawed vision of an American global order than words can ever hope to equal. Even many prominent neocons, who were among the most vocal partisans of the Iraq war and American expansion, are now repudiating their former positions either on grounds that they were misunderstood or that the administration's policy was right but ineptly executed.[1]

The editors and the contributors also take issue with critics of the Bush administration's grand strategy either because they advocate a different strategy from the administration's but still insist on pursuing a privileged status and primacy for the

United States in global politics or because they join some neocons in criticizing what they believe is the incompetent execution of the Bush Doctrine's grand design, which they initially defended, to reform the Middle East and democratize the world, expand free markets, and ensure human rights — collective goods to which they subscribe and that, putatively, only the United States is equipped to supply.[2] This book also takes issue with an otherwise probing critique of the Bush Doctrine that suggests that "Bush Doctrine neoconservatism is a variant of realism, specifically balance-of-threat realism" (Alexander 2007, 56). This reductionist interpretation neither gives full credit to the boundless hubris of the Bush Doctrine architects and their revolutionary aims, both to transform domestic and global politics to suit their conceits, nor explains the ruinous squandering of American power in what has proven to be the doctrine's maladroit implementation.

In cutting the United States down to the still formidable size of a global power, chapter 16 recommends a new direction in deploying American power to support U.S. interests and values and those of the liberal, democratic coalition that arose ascendant from the cold war.

First, a tour d'horizon of the regions of the world reveals the fatal flaws of the Bush Doctrine. It should be scrapped.

Second, U.S. efforts to shape world order to suit its preferences should be calibrated to the size and scope of American power. Publicly supported objectives and capabilities should match. The nation's reach should be within its grasp.

Third, American policy must return to showing a respect for the rule of law, domestically and internationally, and for globally recognized moral norms. The defections of the Bush administration from traditional American practices have incurred widespread condemnation and, worse, generated incentives for other states to do likewise. Ironically, but explicably, American power is more formidable and its ability to get its way more likely when the United States binds itself to moral norms, legal strictures, and political accords in cooperation with other like-minded states and peoples. The creation after World War II of a winning coalition of politically liberal, open-market states, dedicated to democratic rule and human rights, testifies to this elemental lesson in global power politics — however much a discredited Bush Doctrine would have us believe otherwise.

Fourth, American power, soft and hard, must be actively and creatively engaged around the world but in concert with other like-minded peoples, dedicated to open, transparent, and accountable government, to free-market practices, and to the protection of civil liberties and human rights. Either the democracies of the world hang together, or they will hang separately by failing to construct a world order that is safer, more prosperous, and legitimate for their citizens and as a legacy for other peoples around the world.

Fifth, and most important of all, the government should make its primary focus and give priority to rebuilding the nation's domestic material power to ensure its continued economic and technological leadership. That imperative generates equally compelling priorities for improving the quality of education at all levels, for renewal of the nation's neglected infrastructure, for the protection of the environment — nationally and globally — and for the repair, maintenance, and expansion of the nation's social welfare safety nets that are prerequisites for the creation of a more perfect union, a union made up of diverse and diverging populations that are the creative human resource indispensable for domestic revival and successful global engagement.

All of this will take time, upward of a generation, to change the thinking of Americans and their leaders about the prospects and promise of American power. American exceptionalism in its form as the first modern nation that has forged peoples of every race, religion, culture, linguistic, and ethnic affiliation into a more perfect union is a positive good — an inspiring ideal that is no less a collective good than security or material progress. Exceptionalism that dons either a conservative or liberal dress to dominate others at home or abroad is likely to be a self-destructive form in a world society of heterogeneous peoples at sixes and sevens, divided against themselves, where power is diffused among proliferating state and especially nonstate actors who want a say about how the world will be governed.

This volume has attempted to clear the ground for a return to a positive formulation of American exceptionalism to fit the times. It has done so by first exposing the bankruptcy of the Bush Doctrine, resting on a specious claim of an American superpower status animated by a boundless hubris, and then by reaffirming the United States as a global power capable of negotiating a global order congenial to American interests and values from a position of strength, bolstered by the rebuilding of its power base at home and by joining these enhanced capabilities with those of other free peoples everywhere to get the world their shared values collectively justify and merit.

The Editors

Notes

1. See the public repudiations of Richard Perle, Kenneth Adelman, and David Frum in "Neo Culpa," *Vanity Fair*, November 3, 2006, and Fukuyama (2006).

2. See, for example, Walt (2005) and Princeton (2006) for those wedded to American primacy. For administration critics who supported the Iraqi war but then turned on the administration for its incompetent management, see the columns of Thomas Friedman in the *New York Times* from 2003 to 2006 and Packer (2005).

▌||||||||||||||||||||||||||||||||||||
▌||||||||||||||||||||||||||||||||||||||||||||||||||||||||||||||||||||||||||||||||||||

PART ONE

American Geopolitical and Military Strategy

CHAPTER ONE

American Power and Global Order

Edward A. Kolodziej

Chapter 1 is divided into two parts. The first presents an ideal or pure "model" of the Bush administration's vision of its preferred global order and of the strategies rationalizing the use of American power to achieve its objectives. The second identifies four constraints that prevent the realization of its global-order preferences. Chapter 15 completes this evaluation of the limits of American power by drawing on the findings of chapters 2 through 14.

The Pure or Ideal Model of Global Order and How to Achieve It: Bush II

Transforming the Power Structures of Global Order

The Bush administration's vision to reform — indeed to revolutionize — global politics and order has both a material and subjective ideological/ideational dimension.[1] Neither can be explained or understood without reference to the other in the actual projection and deployment of American power around the globe. The former pivots principally on American military, economic, and technological capabilities; the latter on the sweeping political and moral claims of the administration that it can legitimately use American power — unilaterally and forcefully if necessary — to get the world it wants.

Quite openly, at the surface of official pronouncements of foreign and security policy, Washington under the Bush administration repeatedly asserts that the United States is uniquely positioned to shape the world to its liking and that the timing is right to do so.

The administration cites three factors that advise the exploitation of this unique historic opportunity to shape global order. First, the American-led coalition of free-market states and peoples is now ascendant. Over the course of a century, it defeated all rivals for global hegemony — Fascism, Nazism and, finally, Communism.

Second, American leadership provides indispensable public goods to other states and peoples. The Bush administration believes the United States furnishes the necessary material resources to ensure global security and sustained economic growth as well as the moral basis for an expanding system of democratic states, fostered by American power and dedicated to freedom, popular rule, and human rights.[2] These public goods are stipulated as prerequisites to ensure the continued ascendancy of a coalition of liberal democracies and to underwrite its claim to legitimately rule the globe. The United States is able to furnish these public goods in its own interests and those of like-minded states as a derivative, purportedly, of its exemplary socioeconomic development, estimable political practices, and undisputed military prowess. Together these attributes simultaneously manifest and demonstrate the validity of the United States as "a single sustainable model for national success: freedom, democracy, and free enterprise" (U.S. White House, Office of the President 2002, Introduction). According to the administration, these values and the institutions through which they are expressed are the foundations of enduring peace and progressively enlarging prosperity for the states and peoples of the world, however diverse and otherwise divided they may appear to be.

Third, within this ruling coalition of dominant free-market states, American power is portrayed by the Bush Doctrine as supreme — a unique power in the evolution of the state system capable of imposing its will and values on the entire global system. No opponent, real or potential, can contest American power where its writ may wish to run. In September 2002, President Bush made this clear in publishing the *National Security Strategy of the United States*. In his introduction the president underlined the disparity in power between the United States and other actors: "The United States enjoys a position of unparalleled military strength and great economic and political influence" (U.S. White House, Office of the President 2002, Introduction).

This stipulation of where power lies in the global order is presented by the Bush Doctrine not simply as an obvious fact of international life and a formidable barrier to potential rivals who might seek to challenge American hegemony (a proposition rejected by this volume). The administration also advances its exaggerated claim to preponderant power as an historic opportunity to achieve an elusive peace that has escaped the nation-state system since its inception and to create the conditions for continuing and growing prosperity on behalf of the world's populations.[3] Where the father heralded but failed to create a new world order, the son is convinced he can succeed.[4] The *National Security* document — hereinafter the Bush Doctrine — is a plan to exploit American power and to harness public will and international support to this grand design.

American power is judged to be sufficient to get the global order the adminis-tration wants. President Bush told the 2002 graduating class at West Point that "as we defend the peace, we also have an historic opportunity to preserve the peace. We have our best chance since the rise of the nation-state in the seventeenth cen-tury to build a world where the great powers compete in peace instead of prepare for war."[5] This positions the United States to use its power to "create a balance of power that favors human freedom: conditions in which all nations and all societ-ies can choose for themselves the rewards and challenges of political and eco-nomic liberty" (U.S. White House, Office of the President 2002, Introduction).

According to the Bush administration's evaluation, previous balance-of-power struggles that led to incessant war are now a thing of the past. First, no state or coalition can presently balance U.S. military power. Second, the United States will continue to outspend other states and outpace them in developing military technology to ensure its continued superiority.[6] No state will be allowed to out-pace the military might of the United States in the foreseeable future. So why try? Rational rivals (if not rogue states) are induced to adapt and incline to American power and bandwagon on its policies and vision of global order. Other democra-cies are invited to increase the weight of the American-created balance of power as an outright, unconditional grant of a public good but not as a necessary condi-tion for the realization of a new global order.

Third, the United States poses no threat to other states. On the contrary, open societies share a common perception of global threats, notably those posed by rogue states with weapons of mass destruction (WMD) or by terrorists who attack the innocent and seek to undermine civil societies around the globe. These fac-tors converge to produce a favorable balance of freedom. As the president con-cluded before his chosen military audience, the West Point graduating class:

> Competition between great nations is inevitable, but armed conflict in our world is
> not. More and more civilized nations find ourselves on the same side — united by
> common dangers of terrorist violence and chaos. America has, and intends to keep,
> military strengths beyond challenge — [applause] — thereby, making the destabilizing
> arms races of other eras pointless, and limiting rivalries to trade and other pursuits of
> peace.[7]

This new and emerging balance of freedom ostensibly reflects the growing convergence of common values across cultures and nations. States "are also in-creasingly united by common values, instead of divided by conflicting ideolo-gies. . . . [T]he tide of liberty is rising."[8] The logic of global power, dominated by the United States, compels states and people to join what is projected as an irreversible global movement favoring American leadership and ideals.

The logic of American power goes much further than inducing other states to bandwagon on American policies. A self-proclaimed benevolent hegemon is obliged to repudiate or relax international constraints that impede its historic mission of peace and prosperity for all states and peoples. The provision of these public goods requires flexibility and quick shifts both in policy and in projecting power to check rivals or to exploit opportunities for advancing this mission. This logic justifies, indeed necessitates, the unraveling or rejection of previous international agreements, if they hinder the exercise or effectiveness of American power.

Among the first acts of the Bush administration was to repudiate the Antiballistic Missile (ABM) treaty with Russia. This move laid the groundwork for the deployment of an ABM system to cope with so-called rogue states aspiring to acquire nuclear weapons — what President Bush characterized in his 2002 State of the Union message as the "axis of evil," comprising Iraq, Iran, and North Korea.[9] Shelved, too, was the Kyoto Protocol to address global warming. The administration charged that in its present form it would seriously weaken American economic growth while excluding developing states, especially China and India as potential American competitors, from the strictures it would impose. If America's economic power were impaired, not only would its ability to meet domestic demands for more jobs and increased GDP be frustrated, but its capacity to ensure global peace and prosperity would presumably also be seriously diminished.

Other international accords that posed obstacles for American national interests also had to be sandbagged. The United States refuses to sign the Comprehensive Test Ban Treaty (CTBT), to join the International Criminal Court (ICC), or to agree to treaties limiting the development of biological and chemical weapons or the use of land mines (rejections dating from the Clinton administration). The rationales for these demurrers are more complex than can be recounted here. What they share is the idea that they would all impose limits on American discretion and flexibility in pursuit of its transformation of global politics and order.

If former great power struggles have been provisionally arrested by American power, the same cannot be said for terrorist groups and for rogue or failed states supporting them. The Bush Doctrine and the war on terror project a global reach that justifies the use of American power, undeterred by the sovereign claims of other states, around the globe. The globe is conceived strategically as a single field of action and the object of U.S. control. The territory of the United States and the American people are also seamlessly woven into an integrated field in which the president can deploy American power. This integrated, global strategic vision makes no distinction in meeting the threat of terrorism at home or abroad. It justifies unchecked presidential authority and power in pursuit of security: the suspension of habeas corpus for those designated by the president as "unlawful enemy combatants," secret foreign prisons run in collusion by cooperating states, rendition of prisoners to home states where they face torture and death, rejection of Geneva Convention prohibitions against torture, the creation of military courts insulated from constitutional protections and judicial review, and illegal and unconstitutional spying on American citizens.

The Bush Doctrine pointedly rejects the strategies of containment and of nuclear and conventional deterrence, so effective during the cold war against state adversaries. Deterrence has been replaced with a strategy of preemptive/preventive war to defeat terrorists. The latter, driven by religious and ideological fervor, are alleged to be inured to deterrent threats. They must be checked and destroyed before they can strike. Waiting to hit back against an elusive adversary, prepared to commit suicide in carrying out his acts of terrorism, is dismissed as a fatal strategy.

The Bush Doctrine privileges the use of force or coercive threats in addressing threats, real or potential, from other states, regimes, and nonstate actors. The mantra repeatedly voiced by the president and his principal advisors is that the option to use force in bargaining with opponents is "never off the table." Preemptive war, a right of all sovereign states, is given pride of place as the first, not last, policy option if another international actor is perceived as threatening the security, vital interests, or grand design for global order of the Bush Administration and if prospects for its successful exercise appear promising. Preemption rapidly morphs into the assertion of a right to preventive war. The United States acted on this right in claiming that the Iraqi regime possessed WMD or was actively seeking them. Worse, there was the danger that these weapons would pass into the hands of terrorist groups.

The Bush administration's belief in the unlimited scope of possible American military action at times, places, and means of its own choosing can be deduced from the following sweeping assertion of the *National Security Strategy of the United States*:

> The United States has long maintained the option of preemptive actions to counter a sufficient threat to our national security. The greater the threat, the greater is the risk of inaction — and the more compelling the case for taking anticipatory action to defend ourselves, even if uncertainty remains as to the time and place of the enemy's attack. To forestall or prevent such hostile acts by our adversaries, the United States will, if necessary, act preemptively (U.S. White House, Office of the President 2002, 15).

The Iraq war puts the United States on record as willing to act preemptively and preventively against another state and to overturn its regime, whether or not intelligence sources can conclusively determine that a foreign threat is evident and imminent. Just the prospect that a state *might* have the capacity to develop

WMD or the possibility that a state or group *might* assist terrorists is sufficient to threaten the triggering of a prompt and overpowering military attack — what the Department of Defense termed a campaign of "shock and awe" in initiating the attack against Iraq in April 2003. Other opponents, notably a nuclear North Korea or an Iranian nuclear wannabe, are put on notice that what happened to Iraq can happen to them if they fail to comply with Washington's policy preferences. Despite White House denials that attacks on these remaining members of the "axis of evil" were being contemplated and planned for, interviews with unidentified Pentagon and executive branch officials contradicted these assurances (Hersh 2006).

Transforming the Legitimacy of Using Force

To reduce the Bush administration's drive to transform global order merely to an exercise of raw power or to view its wanton use of military power simply as an expression of an imperial aspiration underestimates the breadth and depth of its claims to use force, unilaterally, to achieve its global aims. Legitimacy is at the core of its claims in using power whether at home or abroad. Critics who characterize the Bush administration's justification for the use of force in terms of sheer power, much like the Athenian generals in Thucydides' account of the Melian Dialogue, miss the depth of the administration's commitment to the moral — arguably religious — conception of its global mission.[10] Recall that the Athenians rejected any moral justification for their demand to force the Melians to ally with Athens in the war against Sparta for hegemony of the Peloponnesus (Thucydides 1993).[11] Power was its own justification, an imperative imposed on the Athenians by their accounting because of the death struggle with Sparta.

This attribution of a cynical use of power to the Bush administration, however well grounded, falls short of a fully compelling explanation for two reasons. First, there is general agreement by opponents and partisans of the Bush Doctrine that its principal architects genuinely believed (and still do believe) in their ideological portrayal of American power as hegemonic and unchallengeable. Second, and often missed by critics, the Bush Doctrine, in principle, has widespread appeal within American civic culture, even in the face of diminishing public support for the war. From the start of the American Revolution, justified by the Declaration of Independence, through the Civil War, World War I and II, and the cold war, Americans have traditionally supported the use of force in the service of high and estimable moral ends. In creating a world they want, the administration and many Americans are convinced that the United States is providing a collective good — the governance of an unruly world — for the world's populations (Mandelbaum 2005).[12] However much the Right and the Left may disagree on how and for what specific advantage American power should be used, there is an implied principled agreement on the moral superiority of American values and, ipso facto, a privileged claim to the use of force that is not afforded other states.

The Bush Doctrine molds power and morality into a formidable policy instrument. Moral values, as understood by the administration, discipline and justify the use of American material power. As the parsing of the politics and morality of legitimacy in this chapter shows, the moral stance of the administration instills certainty in the minds of American decision makers and underwrites their determination to use American power to elicit or compel changes in the behavior and policies of other actors to achieve the nation's global designs.[13] It is assumed that all people, given a free choice, would adopt the American model, thereby eliminating the need for the United States to topple authoritarian regimes by force to install an open system of rule. Overthrowing an authoritarian regime anticipates the choice that a suppressed population would presumably make if it could — what the French aptly term a policy of *fuite en avant*. A regime acts to produce a desired result, as if the future condition to be realized is endemic in present circumstances that reveal, ironically, that the desired result has already been achieved. Put negatively, this self-fulfilling prophecy can be understood as choosing suicide because of the fear of death.

The president's West Point speech in the spring of 2002 succinctly captures his moral conception of the political mission that remains his lodestar.

> Some worry that it is somehow undiplomatic or impolite to speak the language of right and wrong. I disagree. [Applause.] Different circumstances require different methods, but not different moralities. [Applause.] Moral truth is the same in every culture, in every time, and in every place. . . . There can be no neutrality between justice and cruelty, between the innocent and the guilty. We are in a conflict between good and evil, and America will call evil by name. [Applause.] By confronting evil and lawless regimes, we do not create a problem, we reveal a problem. And we will lead the world in opposing it [sic].[14]

Overturning the Iraqi regime of Saddam Hussein tests the administration's case for its revolutionary justification of the legitimate use of force and, accordingly, its challenge to views widely held by other states and peoples of limits on the use of force, particularly in attacking other states. This position is rejected by the Bush Doctrine as misguided and potentially damaging to U.S. interests and international peace. It fails ostensibly to confront the twin threats of the proliferation of WMD and global terrorism — and the potential merging of these dangers.

The administration's case rests on three moral claims. These challenge widely supported norms proscribing an unprovoked attack on another state or intervention in its domestic affairs, fundamental principles of the nation-state system and, according to some theorists, the foundation of an anarchical but still governable world order (Bull 1977). First, the United States acts on behalf of American security, a right of all states, when confronted by what appears to be a grave threat to the security interests of the nation. Second, the Bush administration insists that it is acting on behalf of the international community. If the United Nations and the Security Council were unable to act to disarm a state's WMD or WMD programs in violation of international accords or to preclude its support of terrorism, then the United States had both a right *and* an obligation to assume that responsibility. Finally, and decisively, armed hostilities are justified, where propitious conditions exist, to install democratic regimes that protect and promote the political liberties and human rights of oppressed peoples. In the wake of disclosures that Iraq neither had WMD nor a program to develop them and that it was neither allied with al Qaeda nor actively engaged in supporting terrorism abroad (not to say at home), then the administration's justification for armed intervention in Iraq shifted exclusively, if ex post facto, to the idea that it was spreading individual freedom and promoting a global order of democratic states. Article 2 of the United Nations Charter that precludes interference in the domestic affairs of other states is relaxed if a regime violates the civil liberties and human rights of its citizens and frustrates their free political expression in choosing their government and its leaders. In this view, the U.N. Charter does not bar either armed humanitarian intervention or the imposition of a democratic regime on a people, albeit in anticipation of their consent, to replace authoritarian rule.

Building Coalitions of the Willing

The Bush administration is also acutely aware that the assertion of an exceptional right by the United States to attack another state is not sufficient to convince other states and peoples, including many Americans, that its invasions of Afghanistan and Iraq were justified. Expanding the scope for the legitimate use of force requires the mobilization of world opinion. Building "coalitions of the willing" is a key element of the Bush administration's rejectionist position to offset United Nations and Security Council refusal to follow U.S. doctrine and intervention schemes. The potentially multiple formation of coalitions of the willing bolsters Washington's case for the unilateral exercise of force. Coalitions, while presented in the *National Security* statement as mechanisms to "augment . . . permanent institutions," like the United Nations, can readily replace them when the latter falter in meeting their American-defined obligations.

As the Bush Doctrine cautions, "International obligations are to be taken seriously. They are not to be undertaken symbolically to rally support for an ideal without furthering its attainment" (U.S. White House 2002, Office of the President, Introduction). The United Nations and its members, including the other four veto powers of the Security Council, must either choose between Washington's stipulations regarding the U.N.'s responsibilities for international security or effectively accede to Washington's pronunciamentos that it has a duty to preempt the authority of the Security Council because of its alleged failure to discharge its charter obligations. This "either-or," "take-it-or-leave-it," "my-way-or-the-highway" approach summarizes the American game plan during the long controversy over U.N. inspections of Iraq's military capabilities and weapons programs and the decision of the United States to attack Iraq, despite Security Council disapproval, before the inspections were completed.

From this vantage point, international institutions do not have the final say about legitimating the use of American power in responding to national and international threats to security. Other states might claim this right, too, but in terms of their ability to project power, only Americans and the American government possess this right, de facto, as the self-proclaimed guarantor of global and national security. International actors are approached in power terms as disaggregated and atomized units and not as collective bodies materially capable or morally competent of frustrating American policy. They provide a pool of potential partners in constructing "coalitions of the willing" to meet the diverse and shifting security requirements of the United States in its purported role as supplier of international security as a collective good. Why submit Washington's policy preferences to tortuously labyrinthine international rules and procedures or hazard the thwarting of its policy preferences to the decisions and self-interests of other powers and intergovernmental organizations, when there are almost always available partners at the ready in a decentralized international system of states who can be induced by threats or blandishments, or both, to align with American power?

These partners have multiple uses. They partially mask the harsh realities of unilateral military moves and Washington's intimidation of recalcitrant opponents and reluctant allies. A rotation in coalitions of the willing also provides useful resources to lighten the burden of American expansion and rule over foreign populations. If international organizations fall short of American needs and demands to alter regimes and state security policies by force or threat, then coalitions of the willing legitimate the use of American power to attack another state, to overturn its regime, and to impose a political framework, guaranteed by American and coalition forces, that installs free, universal suffrage, national elections, and popular rule.

The Bush Doctrine does not imply a rejection of international organizations. If they go along with American preferences, then these organizations can be reintegrated into a rolling "coalition of the willing" whose members change along with their roles and responsibilities, depending on the contingencies of the moment and varying American needs. International institutions are merely reduced to instruments of American designs. Renouncing support or participation in multilateral organizations makes little sense, especially under conditions of growing globalization. The nonmilitary resources of the United States, however large, are still confronted by an increasingly competitive world economy despite U.S. influence in defining the terms of trade and finance of global markets. Without in any way conceding flexibility in unilaterally applying American power, the strategic aim of the administration is to enlist the resources and approval of these organizations, where possible, while reducing these organizations to the status of pliant states. All international actors — states, international governmental organizations (IGOs), and nongovernmental organizations (NGOs) — and the human and material resources they dispose are potentially available components of contingently packaged bundles of capabilities to address Washington's needs and interests of the moment.

Two tactics associated with past imperial powers are evident in Washington's moves to reduce other actors to compliant confederates and thereby create favorable coalitions to support its global reach, while blocking those at home and abroad opposed to its expansion. The first is the tactic of fait accompli — a logical derivative of the administration's strategic doctrine of unilateral initiatives. It has worked with some success in the United Nations and against allies otherwise reluctant to support the Iraqi invasion or other Bush priorities. The Iraqi elections of 2005, first to create a provisional government and then an elected parliament, illustrate this move. The United Nations could scarcely oppose the role cast for it by Washington, that is, to legitimate democratic elections, however imperfect they may have been. In moving toward political reconstruction, the Bush administration could also deflect criticisms for undertaking a unilateral attack on another U.N. member without Security Council approval. Most states, especially those that rely on Middle East oil and fear terrorist threats from these regions, have an interest in bringing stability to Iraq, however much they may have opposed the Iraqi invasion. These cross-cutting constraints — opposition to the U.S. invasion and the need for oil and regional stability in the Middle East — are abundantly reflected in the policies of America's allies, dilemmas of choice imposed by the fait accompli of American occupation of Iraq.

The Clinton administration was also accused of practicing fait accompli politics in bombing Serbia without Security Council approval to protect Kosovars against ethnic cleansing. However, Clinton's actions differed from Bush's. In circumventing an expected Russian veto in the Security Council, Washington relied on NATO to impose sanctions on Serbia. It submitted itself to the consent of its members and resisted calls for the use of ground troops to invade Serbia because there was a lack of unanimous NATO support for such a military strike.

Greece, in particular, was opposed to such an action because it was in the potential line of fire.

The second tactic is the timeless move of divide and rule. The extra twist of the Bush Doctrine is that it has been used more against allies than adversaries as the evidence advanced by the regional chapters in this book suggests. The Bush administration's policy toward its European allies is illustrative. In mobilizing a coalition of the willing for the Iraq invasion, administration officials divided NATO Europe into old and new Europe. Those opposing the United States were castigated as old Europe, principally France and Germany. Neither then–French president Jacques Chirac nor then–German chancellor Gerhard Schroeder would sanction the American intervention in Iraq. Allies opposing Washington's preferences were then attacked and punished. Covertly launched hate campaigns were mounted by the administration and its supporters to vilify defecting allies, to boycott their products, and even to denigrate them and dismiss signals from them, in the wake of the American-led conquest of Iraq, suggesting they were now willing to accommodate the Bush administration and adapt belatedly to an American-imposed fait accompli. Even the asinine and silly — there was nothing too trivial — were invoked into service, as "french fries" in the cafeterias of the U.S. Congress were renamed "freedom fries."

The new Europe presumably includes old Britain, self-selected, small bandwagoning northern states (Denmark and Netherlands but not Belgium), the Mediterranean tier of Spain (until its defection from the "coalition of the willing" in Iraq), Portugal, and Italy, and most especially the new Eastern European members of NATO. The Poles were assigned a symbolic role in the military overthrow of Iraq and a sector to police in post-Hussein Iraq. Washington accords special privileges to members of its willing coalitions. It authorized, for example, the purchase of American fighter aircraft by the Polish government to reward a willing ally, and it granted state dinners to the presidents of Poland and of the Philippines but not to former close allies. American advisors support Philippine military forces to combat local terrorists in parallel with the American global war on terrorism. Unilaterally relaxing the proscriptions of the Non-Proliferation Treaty (NPT), the Bush administration granted India, a former nuclear pariah, access to American nuclear technology for the peaceful development of its energy industry. This concession (still to be approved by a Democratic Congress) would essentially amend the NPT by American fiat. This move is consistent with the corollary to the Bush Doctrine that international agreements have no legal or moral standing if they conflict with what are deemed to be the current imperatives of American national and security interests.

The divide and rule strategy of the Bush administration is not just a reflection of a profound difference of political vision and strategic interest between Europe (old and new) and the United States, as characterized baldly by Robert

Kagan (2003, 1) in his much quoted view that "on major strategic and international questions today, Americans are from Mars and Europeans are from Venus." Kagan contends that "when it comes to setting national priorities, determining threats, defining challenges, and fashioning and implementing foreign and defense policies, the United States and Europe have parted ways" (Kagan 2003, 2). However, the gap between the aspiring coercive American hegemon and the European states and peoples is much deeper and menacing to regional cooperation and global governance than Kagan recognizes.

Within the Bush administration's hegemonic mind-set, Europe, embodied in the European Union (EU), is in reality disaggregated into its twenty-seven component state parts, much as international organizations are. Europe may well act as a unified body in some domains, notably economic affairs, which the *National Security* document tolerates. However, on issues of national, regional, or global security the EU is approached in much the same way as other regions and states. Within the purview of the pure Bush model of global order these regions are composed of juxtaposed, autonomous states or units or, more precisely, a set of states that can be deconstructed in multiple ways by American power to suit prevailing contingencies of policy.

This model reverts essentially to a pre–World War I conception of international relations. It essentially divides European countries into the contesting state actors populating them. Created then is a rich cornucopia of potential members of American-mobilized "coalitions of the willing." Whatever effort preceding administrations may have made to lead the disparate states of the NATO alliance to shared positions on security issues is now relegated to a marginal status as a policy option. "Coalitions of the willing" trump the use of international organizations — whether the United Nations, NATO, or the EU—as a policy option if these groupings impede American global policy.

Domestic Dimensions of Legitimacy

The Bush administration cultivates well-plowed and fertile soil in sowing its conception of legitimate global order among the American people. The Bush Doctrine resonates throughout the history of American civic culture. It well reflects and draws heavily on American exceptionalism. This sense of unique identity and destiny is widely and deeply shared across the American political spectrum. It asserts the superiority of American political practices and rule as well as the unique history of progress and expanding power that defines the United States. The Bush administration is but the latest in a long line of American leaders and presidents to assert these claims. What is new is the assertion that American exceptionalism is, paradoxically, a *universal* model for all states, peoples, and cultures. The victory of the American-led cold war coalition evidences, as noted earlier, the historical validation of American values—the commitment to individual free-dom and democratic rule and the promotion of a national and global economic system based on private ownership and free exchange—and their embodiment in American political and civic practice.

The new strategic doctrine and its implementation as well as the theory of in-ternational politics guiding the use of American hard and soft power rest, however precariously, on these moral claims. President Bush and his spokespersons and his ideological partisans among the public currently display little difficulty in medi-ating between the contradictory assertions of exceptionalism and universalism to justify the projection of American power abroad. They apparently live comfortably within what psychologists might term a permanent state of cognitive dissonance.[15] American leaders, depending on the exigencies of the moment, personal interests, political agendas, electoral posturing, or public moods, alternate with seeming ease between these conflicting claims in generating support for their policies and actions. An important part of the explanation of how American administrations are able to rationalize these conflicting self-representations of American identity, and why, in particular, the Bush Doctrine's call for an invasion of Iraq initially enjoyed widespread congressional and domestic support (until the costs of the war and its incompetent conduct frayed popular will) lies in an understanding of American civic culture and its affirmation of national exceptionalism.

American exceptionalism, as a fundamental determinant of the American psyche and a deeply embedded value of American civic culture, has been much discussed over two centuries (de Tocqueville 1945). It has assumed multiple forms over generations. The pronouncements of successive American presidents are illustrative. President Washington, in warning against entangling alliances, sought to insulate American politics from foreign intervention and corruption; Thomas Jefferson repudiated a Europe ruled by blood and not by ballots; Andrew Jackson elevated the common American to godlike purity and virtue (never mind that he and many Founders were slave holders); Abraham Lincoln's fight for the Union was cast as a struggle for what was best for humanity; Woodrow Wilson and Franklin Delano Roosevelt portrayed American intervention in World Wars I and II as wars to end all wars and to make the world safe for democracies and free markets; President Truman identified American security, economic well-being, and democratic values with their realization globally in the struggle with the So-viet Union (Kolodziej 1966); and Ronald Reagan incorporated the notion of America as the shining "city on the hill" into his public philosophy—a beacon for others to follow. The Bush Doctrine proclaims that other peoples, if given a choice, would adopt America's best practices and thereby enjoy the unparalleled freedoms available to Americans.

There is little need to rehearse this rich and revealing literature (Bukovan-sky 2002; Hartz 1955; Huntington 1981; Ignatieff 2004; T. Smith 2007). What is of interest to this discussion is how American exceptionalism is currently interpreted by the Bush Doctrine and how it is playing out in the expansion of American power. Exceptionalism justifies American rejection of efforts by misguided foreign and domestic critics to enlarge the scope of international law and institutions that Washington believes would be accomplished at the expense of American power, moral status, and global purposes, at the expense of the reform of the international order in an American mode and image. Although the United States was a leader in supporting the Nuremberg and Japanese war crimes trials after World War II, the dominant domestic consensus today is to resist international legal and moral limits on American power in the service of its exceptionalist aspirations. There is, for example, little effective public support for American accession to the ICC. Bush's Washington and much of the American public are convinced that the American Constitution and domestic legal practices and processes afford a more legitimate and effective set of protections for Americans, notably military and civilian public officials, than any foreign body, including, most decidedly, an ICC potentially controlled by enemies of the United States. This is the prevailing mood not only in the executive branch but also in both houses of Congress, evidenced by their joint resistance to the ICC that dates from the Clinton administration and persists today.

Rebuffing the ICC does not preclude ad hoc support for special international tribunals, like those impaneled to try war crimes in Rwanda and the Balkans. This is tantamount to the extension by the administration of its tactic of forming "coalitions of the willing." It supports these fleeting assertions of international law but with no intent to establish precedents that might inhibit the use of American power in the future or expose American civilian and military operatives and political leaders to ICC jurisdiction.

According to the logic of the Bush Doctrine, American exceptionalism, as the justification for the exercise of American power, is seemingly limitless. If American political values and practices are exceptional, then exceptional measures are justified in preserving and promoting them. Preemptive and preventive war is consistent with these claims. Since exceptionalism prevails, Americans and especially their representatives can claim a privileged right to unilaterally, and definitively, define threats to the American political regime and appropriate means and strategies to cope with them. Neither international treaties nor institutions are competent to qualify this claim. Nor can they dilute or diminish national assertion of American interests or hinder the pursuit of American security policies.

Woodrow Wilson, as suggested earlier, can be credited with having been the first to transform American exceptionalism into a universal public good to be enjoyed by all peoples as an outright gift of the American public and to harness American military and economic power to these global objectives of American-dictated world order. Hitherto the virtues of exceptionalism were reserved to Americans. To rationalize American entry into World War I, Wilson rejected the position of traditional realists, like Theodore Roosevelt, who were quite prepared to engage Europe's empire with an American empire of its own, as evidenced by the Spanish American War and efforts to gain concessions from a fading Chinese imperial regime.[16] Reacting to the rise of Europe's imperial systems and adapting U.S. power to its growing global status among the big powers, Wilson advanced the principles of self-determination and democratic rule as the foundation stones of global peace. European empires, led by authoritarian regimes like those of imperialist Germany, purportedly fostered war by frustrating popular will, the sole legitimating agency of all political regimes (de Tocqueville 1945; Bryce 1924). Democratic regimes, based on national self-determination, bolstered the coalition of free peoples and free markets in assuring global peace. A League of Nations would supplant balances of power between imperial powers whose denial of national self-determination and democracy produced ceaseless competition and world war.[17] Empires, the flawed solution to global governance, would be supplanted by a system of nation-states, based on popular will, ruled by freely chosen democratic regimes within internationally recognized borders, and welded together by global market exchanges. Created would be the conditions for perpetual peace and advancing economic growth for all peoples.

The end of imperialism, the principle of national self-determination, and the creation of a world economy of free market exchange also rationalized and legitimated American entry into World War II. These values were affirmed in the Atlantic Charter signed by President Roosevelt and Prime Minister Winston Churchill in 1941 (Graebner 1964, 632–38). These principles, incorporated into the Truman Doctrine and Marshall Plan, subsequently underwrote the rationale and legitimation of American power in the conduct of the cold war — lapses and defections from these principles reflected in interventions around the world that undermined democratic governments, notably throughout Central and Latin America, notwithstanding.[18]

Except for a few prescient scholars (W. Williams 1970, 1991), most observers fail to grasp the fundamentally revolutionary ideology of American culture and its internally driven determination to reform a resistant global order of nation-states to suit American preferences and values. This deeply ingrained driving force of American identity has been enlisted into service by a currently ascendant domestic conservative coalition. The aspiration to transform the international system and global order has been joined to the unprecedented power of the United States. Since the marriage of exceptionalism and universalism is rooted in Wilsonian liberalism, opponents of the administration are disarmed by this cooptation of the values of freedom, democracy, and free markets embodied in Wilsonian internationalism. They are also hoisted on their own petard as advocates of armed humanitarian intervention to prevent large-scale loss of human life and depredations by authoritarian regimes against exposed populations (see, for example, M. Smith 1998 and T. Smith 1994). It is by no means easy to tell in a given argument justifying the invasion of another state whether a moral aim or pragmatic calculation of power serves as the controlling animus for the use of American force. The right to self-determination is, incidentally, the defensive rejoinder repeatedly relied on by China in fending off U.S. attacks on its human rights practices, as the chapter on China describes.

Nation building to implant democratic rule and to create the conditions for sustained economic development within a world market system — liberal causes — are embraced by conservatives. The Wilsonian vision to end wars and make the world safe for democracy and free markets has been transformed into a conservative revolution to reform the world. Wilson's vision was rejected at home, principally by Republican opponents in the Senate, because his design for a new world order failed to cement its foundation in American power and self-interest. Traditional American exceptionalism reasserted itself again in the interwar period as isolation from Europe's conflicts and wars (while the Monroe and Roosevelt Doctrines continued to claim the Western Hemisphere as the American sphere of interest and the justification for its repeated intervention into the affairs of Central and Latin American states).

The conservative revolution unleashed by the Bush administration has reversed the causal arrows in its support of a reformulation of the Wilsonian project. Now American material power is putatively adequate to impose an exceptionalist political culture and model on the world. The flag (American power) is now paraded at home and abroad to discipline the Constitution in the service of expanding executive power. American power, material and presidential, is under the Bush Doctrine fully competent not only to reform resistant powers and peoples abroad but also to marginalize opponents at home who object to American expansionism and presidential assertions of imperial authority.

If the rationale of the Bush administration has turned Wilsonian exceptionalism on its head to justify the creation of a global order in its image, it has also advanced a radical transformation of American constitutional and legal practices to facilitate and fulfill its self-defined global mandate. At the turn of the twentieth century, when the first American overseas empire was created as a consequence of the Spanish–American War, debate in the United States revolved around the question of whether the Constitution followed the flag: that is, whether the protections of civil liberties and democratic practices guaranteed by the Constitution extended to foreigners and enemy combatants, the conduct of war, and the treatment of prisoners captured on the field of battle (Osgood 1953). However much opponents may have differed, they agreed that constitutional limits and the rule of law had to be observed at home. Treaties approved by constitutional procedures and the commitments they entailed were also acknowledged as the rule of law. These normally could not be transgressed or suspended because of hostilities. Traditionally, American support for international law and norms as pronounced by Washington clashed with European claims of imperial insulation from these proscriptions.

The Bush administration mounted a broad attack on these constitutional and legal constraints. On constitutional grounds, the president insists that, in prosecuting a global war on terror of long-term duration, he has inherent authority and a corresponding obligation under the Constitution to use the resources of the United States to prosecute it effectively, wherever the terrorists join the battle — whether at home or abroad. His inherent authority allegedly derives from two sources under article 2 of the Constitution: his offices as chief executive and as commander in chief of the armed forces. Congress can supplement and enhance his authority, as the president insists was the result of the legislative resolution authorizing the use of force to compel Iraqi adherence to international accords. According to the Bush administration, the Congress is precluded from qualifying or hindering the use of the president's authority or the means he chooses to protect Americans.[19] On the score of national security he is the sole executor; he is the judge and jury who decides what is to be done. When Lincoln suspended habeas corpus during the Civil War, he could still rely provisionally on article 1, section 9, of the Constitution that permitted temporary suspension of this right in the case of rebellion.

The Bush Doctrine essentially stipulates that the president's powers are equal in scope to the security threats confronting the United States and the American people. In other words, the administration's self-styled interpretation of these external threats defines the reach of the president's constitutional powers. As threats expand, so also do presidential powers. In pursuit of this limitless claim to presidential power and autonomy, President Bush has signed more signing statements, vastly more than his predecessors combined, that register his refusal to comply with more than 750 legislated directives covering national security policy (Schwarz and Huq, 2007).

Bolstering the implementation of the Bush Doctrine abroad is the president's assertion of the controversial doctrine of the unity of the executive. Under this novel constitutional view, the president can trump Congressional assertions of its powers to limit his power when national security is at stake. Prisoners, including American citizens, may also be held without recourse for remedy under habeas corpus to American courts, a position that was originally asserted by the president and since legislated into law by a Republican controlled Congress. Foreign prisoners can also be rendered to their home countries where incarceration and interrogation practices are less subject to public scrutiny and even more severe than those that have been reported to have occurred under American control. While the administration has condemned the torture and death of prisoners — despite revelations of such practices at prisons in Afghanistan, Guantánamo, and Abu Ghraib — it has at the same time won Congressional approval for the president to define what torture means under article 3 of the Geneva Convention. The Bush administration is on record as supporting a very narrow definition of torture under American law. It is limited to physical bodily injury and death and does not definitively reject psychological injuries, purported religious defamations, or sexual indignities inflicted on prisoners (Bybee 2002). Administration partisans argue that even physical bodily injury and death may be required if national security is at risk, a position that has not been publicly repudiated by the administration (Krauthammer 2005).[20]

It should come as no surprise, then, that the administration would apply this boundless interpretation of its authority to Americans, too, in the conduct of a global war on terror. The public revelation of a widespread national surveillance program covering countless American citizens who might have contacts with terrorist groups is a logical extension of presidential authority, notwithstanding its putative violation of the Federal Intelligence Surveillance Act (FISA) passed by Congress in the 1970s. FISA expressly forbids wiretapping and eavesdropping of any kind on American citizens, absent the issuance of a writ sworn by a special FISA court. Presidential circumvention of FISA rules essentially neutralizes Congress as a coequal branch of government in defining what can or can't be done in the pursuit of national security. Court oversight of this program and of other facets of the administration's conduct of the war on terrorism is equally denied by the administration on the grounds that such oversight falls outside the boundaries of the authority and powers of the judiciary. These unlimited claims of presidential power were aided and abetted by a cowed and compliant Republican Congress before midterm elections of November 2006, which shifted control of both houses of Congress to the opposition Democratic Party. These broad assertions of presidential power to fight the global war on terror are logically embedded in the Bush Doctrine and in the administration's strategic vision of a global war with no national boundaries, not even those of the United States, to limit the field of presidential action. The territory of the United States and its population are integrated into a uniform and unified field of battle that requires the Constitution and the rule of law to be subordinated to the imperative of unfettered use of force and the coercive power of the state in pursuit of presidentially defined security interests.

The Real World Clashes with the Pure Model:
The Limits of American Power

There is the tale of the cockroach who asked the wise owl how he might escape what he viewed as his deplorable lowly status. "Just *think and believe* you're an eagle," advised the owl. Several days later the cockroach returned, complaining that the advice didn't work. "Don't blame me," retorted the owl. "I solved your problem. You figure out how to become an eagle."

In proclaiming the Bush Doctrine in September 2002, the Bush administration, unsatisfied that the United States was simply a global power, announced its intention to soar to eagle superpower heights. Reality, phoenix-like, has since reappeared in the form of five structural constraints that have brought the eagle down to earth: (1) the lack of a coherent and workable military strategy, notably in coping with insurgencies; (2) the rising costs of the Iraq war, material but especially human, and subsequent eroding public support for continued occupation of a country in the midst of civil war provoked by the U.S. invasion; (3) the limited human and material resources of the United States to mount wars, occupy foreign territories, and rule resistant populations whatever the level of public support; and (4) the rising costs of maintaining and enlarging the nation's social welfare safety nets — the opportunity costs of foreign interventions that impact negatively on these entitlement obligations. The analysis below briefly reviews these four constraints. The remaining chapters detail the global scope and regional dimensions of the fifth constraint — the multiple challenges confronting the United States, whatever administration or party is in power, in negotiating a global environment responsive to prevailing national preferences and in impressing these preferences on other states and peoples in regions around the globe.

Failed Strategy

As Patrick Morgan's chapter suggests, the United States is amply prepared to defeat the military of any other state or coalition of states in open combat. Conversely, the technological gap between the United States and other military systems grows in inverse proportion to the capacity of the American military to defeat the insurgency in Iraq or to eliminate definitively the Taliban as a threat in Afghanistan. Quite apart from the criticism that the administration did not allot sufficient numbers of troops to secure the country after the quick defeat of the Iraqi army, American military forces that occupied the country were not prepared for insurgency warfare. As a close observer of the strategic calamity observed, "(T)he vast majority of the soldiers in the field . . . were led by commanders who had been sent to a mission for which they were unprepared by an institution that took away from the Vietnam War only the lesson that it shouldn't get involved in messy counterinsurgencies" (Ricks 2006, 264).

The central principles of counterinsurgency are in counterpoint to those applicable in conventional warfare. The American occupation, tactical and fleeting successes notwithstanding, violated these tenets with impunity: maintaining unity of command was undermined by chronic conflict between civilian and military authorities over the scope of their powers; open borders with opponents, principally Syria and Iran, were unsecured; large caches of military weaponry were seized by insurgents; military commanders "tended to see the Iraqi people as the playing field on which a contest was played against insurgents" (Ricks 2006, 266) rather than seeing the civilian population as a group they should be trying to win over; meeting essential civilian needs — personal security, electricity, water, sanitation — was neglected; the application of combat tactics of conventional warfare to insurgency warfare multiplied combatants; and the urgent requirement of real-time intelligence to separate insurgents from the innocent impelled indiscriminate sweeps of the population, crowded prison conditions (Abu Ghraib et al.), and resultant gratuitous indignities and torture that severely damaged the moral basis for the invasion and swelled Iraqi opposition to the American occupation.[21]

A challenge even more daunting than transforming the mind-set and culture of the American military establishment is the very notion of suppressing insurgencies in the backwash of foreign invasions and the occupation of other states. The clear lesson of the past several centuries, commencing ironically with the American Revolution, is that foreign occupation and empire don't work. It appears almost incomprehensible that the experience of two world wars, a half-century of decolonization, and the cold war, the latter of which undid the Soviet Union as the last and in many ways the most formidable empire, should have been forgotten so quickly and with such calamitous results.

Increasing Costs and Declining Public Support

The human and material costs of the Iraq war are rising with little likelihood that they will decrease in the near term. American casualties continue to mount in Iraq. Since the start of the war, deaths as of July 1, 2007, exceeded 3,500 troops, more than 3,000 more than when President Bush announced "Mission Accomplished" on May 1, 2003.[22] The Pentagon reports wounded at over 25,000 at this writing, many severely with life debilitating injuries.[23] Iraqi civilian casualties are much higher. In July 2005, these were conservatively estimated by a London-based research group to be about 25,000 dead. Of these, approximately 20 percent were women and children. Of the 25,000, almost 40 percent were attributed to

U.S.-led forces (Ewens 2005). This number is undoubtedly much higher today.[24] An Associated Press story, quoting Iraqi officials, cited 150,000 civilian deaths since the invasion (*Seattle Times*, November 10, 2006).[25] There are no presently reliable figures for thousands more Iraqis, who are wounded and physically and psychologically debilitated by the war or displaced as refugees, estimated to be over 700,000. An additional two million have also reportedly have left the country (Institute for the Study of International Migration, March 21, 2007).

Defense spending is also up. The Pentagon's budget for the 2006 fiscal year was projected at $419 billion or about 5 percent of GDP, and for the second year in a row, the defense budget was increased by 5 percent over the previous year, as cuts were made in nondefense areas. Spending for defense is expected to rise annually to $600 billion by the end of the decade. These budgeted figures do not include spending for Iraq and Afghanistan. $25 billion was needed in supplemental funds for fiscal 2005 for these wars. This was in addition to the extra $87 billion passed by Congress in fiscal 2004. An additional $80 billion was requested for fiscal 2006 over the official Pentagon budget for that year. The House Committee on the Budget estimates that the administration will request $170 billion in supplemental funds for the wars in Afghanistan and Iraq in addition to the $500 billion previously requested for the Pentagon in fiscal 2007. Supplemental funds are not counted against the budget limitation imposed by Congress on spending. They are, so to speak, off the books.

The human costs of the Iraq war have been decisive in weakening public support for it. A November 2006 *New York Times* poll reflected public discontent and eroding support for the war. Some 55 percent disapproved of the war, and the same percentage supported either some or total withdrawal of American forces. What is even more significant is the 67 percent of those voting for the House of Representatives in November 2006 cited Iraq as important to their decision. Voter disaffection over the war accounts significantly for the loss of the president's party in both houses of Congress, an outcome for which the president acknowledged full responsibility (*New York Times*, November 9 and 10, 2006).

A Pew Charitable Trust poll in March 2007 found that almost 60 percent of the American public believed the war was not going well and favored congressional legislation that dictated a deadline for troop withdrawals.[26] Public support for the war further eroded a month later as reported in a Gallup poll, which found that seven of ten Americans favored a troop withdrawal from Iraq by April 2008.[27] Meanwhile, the president's approval ratings, which were at stratospheric levels in the wake of 9/11—90 percent—plummeted to a low below 30 in a June 2007 Pew poll.[28]

Adding to this declining support for the president's policies and the Bush Doctrine is Iraqi public opinion, which also wants U.S. forces to leave. A March 2007

ABC poll of 2,212 Iraqi respondents reported that only 26 percent of Iraqis feel safe, down from 63 percent in late 2005. Only 42 percent believe that their lives are better than under the Saddam Hussein regime. Perhaps more disturbing is that more than a half—51 percent—believe it is all right to attack American occupation forces, although (and paradoxically) only a third want American forces to leave immediately.[29]

Limited Resources

Using standard economic measures, a recent detailed analysis by Linda Bilmes and Joseph E. Stiglitz (2006), the latter a Nobel laureate in economics, estimates the real costs of the war to be between $1 and $2 trillion.[30] This number includes not only the direct costs of the war itself but also those associated with death benefits, disability, and long-term health care to survivors, demobilization, loss of productivity of those lost or injured in the war, interest on the debt to pay for the war, and increased cost of oil and energy—to cite just some of the key, constraining assumptions of the study. Down payment on these projected costs covers $357 billion appropriated by Congress by the fall of 2005. Average monthly expenditures for the war now top $7 billion.

The Bush administration also seriously narrowed its room for maneuver in foreign affairs by sharply cutting taxes in 2001. It still insists on making these cuts permanent. The gap between revenues and governmental expenditures has, therefore, ballooned the public debt, moving the country rapidly from surplus in 2000 to accelerating and deepening indebtedness. The Bureau of the Public Debt of the Department of Commerce calculates that the national debt rose to more than $7.3 trillion by the end of 2004. It now approaches $9 trillion in a $13 trillion economy or over 70 percent of GDP.[31] It will continue to rise as a function of continued revenue shortfalls, war expenditures, and relaxed limits on discretionary domestic spending, including Social Security and Medicare, the latter driven upward by a costly and inefficiently administered prescription drug bill passed in 2005.

The Congressional Budget Office (CBO) in 2004 provided a more guarded projection of the deficit over the next decade and its potential negative effects on economic growth. Two Brookings Institution economists who closely follow administration fiscal policies take little comfort from these more optimistic projections. The CBO's lower deficit figures still point to a "staggering decline" in the budget outlook. As they conclude: "Since January 2001, the unified baseline for 2002 and 2011 deteriorated by $8.5 trillion (about $55 billion a week) from a projected surplus of $5.6 trillion to a deficit of $2.9 trillion currently" (Gale and Orszag 2004). This budgetary outlook is likely to get worse before it gets better, since the CBO's projection rests on several problematic assumptions. Its esti-

Table 1. U.S. Trade Deficit on the Current Account, 2002–2006 (in Billions)

Year	2002	2003	2004	2005	2006
Deficit	475	520	668	714	759

Source: U.S. Department of Commerce, Bureau of Economic Analysis, June 15, 2007; U.S. Census, Foreign Trade Statistics, http://www.census.gov/foreign-trade/press-release/current_press_release/excel.html, accessed 24 October 2007.

mates assume that the tax cuts will not be permanent; that the alternative minimum tax (AMT) will be allowed to grow "explosively" (Gale and Orzag 2004); and that discretionary nondefense spending per capita will decline by 8 percent. This would be tantamount to winning the fiscal trifecta.

Absent increased revenues or decreased spending on foreign military operations and welfare, these deficits will continue to grow. Increased taxes, borrowing, or both will be needed to cover legislated entitlements. These solutions will put upward pressure on interest rates. Increases in interest rates have a negative effect on investment and consumption and, accordingly, on economic growth. Americans are already among the lowest savers in the world. Savings rates have been particularly low since 2000. From 2000 to 2003, the American savings rate fell below 2 percent of GDP on the average (U.S. Department of Commerce, Bureau of Economic Analysis 2005). So how will the deficits be financed? Foreign borrowers have until now filled the gap, keeping interest rates at record lows. Whether they will in the future remains problematic absent higher returns on their investment in light of the risks inherent in a galloping U.S. debt. Conversely, if they are willing to buy growing American debt, how will they use their leverage over the American economy and, specifically, over administration economic and security policies?

Before that question is addressed, it is important to recognize that the overall indebtedness of Americans and American corporations is also increasing. This condition of continued high expenditures and a still unquenchable American consumer thirst for imports weakens American competitiveness and, accordingly, the capacity of the federal government to control fiscal policy so that it supports U.S. foreign and domestic programs. Table 1 tracks these trade deficits from 2002 to 2006. They rise from $475 billion in 2002 to $759 billion in 2006. The trade deficit first exceeded $700 billion in 2005 and is expected soon to top $800 billion.

As a consequence of the negative economic and fiscal trends sketched above, U.S. dependency, private and public, on foreign holders of American long- and short-term debt is increasing at an accelerating pace. Table 2 summarizes the rapid rise in governmental and private indebtedness relative to foreign investors from 2002 to 2006. Long-term federal debt held by foreigners rose between one-

Table 2. Foreign Holdings of U.S. Securities, by Type of Security (in Billions)

Type of Security	June 2002	June 2003	June 2004	June 2005	June 2006
Long-Term Debt					
U.S. Treasury	908	1116	1463	1599	1727
U.S. Agency	492	586	623	791	984
Short-Term Debt					
U.S. Treasury	232	269	317	284	253
U.S. Agency	88	97	124	150	147
Total	1720	2068	2527	2824	3111

Source: U.S. Department of the Treasury, Federal Reserve Bank of New York, *Report on Foreign Portfolio Holdings of U. S. Securities*, May 2007, 3. http://www.ustreas.gove/tic/sh12006r.pdf

quarter to one-third of the total, climbing from $1400 billion to $2711 billion from June 2002 to June 2006. In this period, short-term debt increased from $320 billion to $400 billion. In both cases, these are substantial percentage increases by any measure in a very short period of time.

In 2004, Japan held one-third of all U.S. federal debt held by foreigners. China held approximately 20 percent, and its holdings are reportedly rising both in total amount and in the percentage of the debt held by foreign investors (U.S. Department of the Treasury 2005, 7). Chinese reserves now total over $1 trillion, providing Beijing with the potential of enormous leverage over international financial and trade markets, not to mention increasing influence in the developing world as Mingjiang Li's chapter on China describes. Currently, approximately one-quarter of the $9 trillion U.S. debt is held by foreign investors.

Rising Entitlement Expenditures

Spending for domestic welfare and safety nets is likely to increase exponentially rather than decrease in the very near future. Social Security surpluses currently slow the rise in deficits, the so-called Social Security safety box having been raided. It is estimated that the Social Security fund will be in deficit somewhere between the middle of 2010 and 2015. By 2040 the Social Security shortfall in claims over revenues will account roughly for 2.6 percent of GDP. Unless something is done to close this gap in funding, it is expected to reach 4 percent of GDP in 2080 (U.S. Congress, Committee on Ways and Means 2005, 172–83).

The expected rise in Medicare expenditures dwarfs these deficits. As the figure, drawn from Congressional sources, indicates, spending for Medicare as a percentage of GDP is expected to rise from about a little more than 2 percent in 2000 to over 8 percent in 2040.

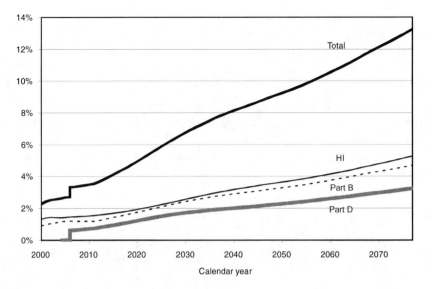

Medicare Expenditures as a Percentage of the Gross Domestic Product.

Source: U.S. Department of Health and Human Services, Board of Trustees, *2005 Annual Report of the Boards of Trustees of the Federal Hospital and Insurance and Federal Supplementary Medical Insurance Trust Funds,* 9.

Conclusions

What are the implications of the four structural constraints on the Bush administration's grand design for global order? They measure the mounting human and material costs of security and, specifically, those associated with the wars in Afghanistan and Iraq, waning public support for the Iraqi occupation, increasing federal indebtedness as a consequence of deep tax cuts matched by increased spending for security and domestic welfare, rising entitlements, particularly for Social Security and Medicare, and increasing foreign indebtedness and dependence.

Taken together, they lower the probability—certainly the sustainability—of American military intervention abroad. They sober estimates, too, of the scope of the political influence that the United States actually possesses to get the world it wants despite the overwhelming military might of American armed forces. There is a discernible and enlarging disconnect between the objective kill power of the American military and the capacity of the American government to rely on these unprecedented capabilities to shape political events abroad, to dictate the kind of Iraq it wants, and to achieve the global order it prefers. As the following chapters recount, the news is bad from all regions of the globe. The need for allies to cope with these challenges grows in inverse proportion to their availability and willingness to help as a consequence of the self-defeating strategies initiated by the Bush Doctrine.

That prudent statesmanship in Washington will recognize constraints on its freedom of action is hardly a certainty. The Bush administration may well continue to throw remaining good power, soft and hard, at bad policies in its quest to shape global order to its liking. Its capacity for denial appears boundless: the catastrophe in Iraq, the devastation of Katrina, the impending costs of global warming, the spread of radical Muslim movements, the rising influence of Iran, yawning budgetary and trade deficits — these are just a sample of the crises confronting Washington, challenges that are currently inflamed by errant administration policies.

One final question is whether Washington will also be checked by rivals at interstate, intrastate, and transnational levels of global politics or whether, indeed, it has been able to enlist some powerful actors in coalitions of the willing to stem the tide of global and regional opposition to American power and purposes. The news from the regions of the world, as the following chapters report, is not good. The message is clear that the Bush Doctrine is a failure and should be shelved and that compromises must be made to position the United States, whatever party is in control in Washington, to negotiate a more favorable global environment than presently exists in the service of American interests, aims, and values.

Notes

1. There is now an avalanche of sources that cover the Bush administration's foreign and security policies. The value added of this volume to these studies is two-fold: it nests the Iraq crisis on which these works are largely focused within a global perspective, thereby providing greater proportion and balance to an understanding of the limits and prospects of the United States as a global power, and it identifies the multiple constraints frustrating and in some limited cases fostering American power by regional actors across the world. Consult, among others, Reus-Smit (2004), Allin and Simon (2004), Andreani (2004), Packer (2005), Ricks (2006), Chandraesekaran (2006b), Woodward (2002, 2006), and Alexander (2007).

2. Even critics of the Bush administration agree that the United States is indispensable as the source of these public goods; see Mandelbaum (2002, 2005).

3. President Bush's speech to the graduating class at West Point, June 1, 2002.

4. The first President Bush declared the creation of a new world order once the first Gulf War was over. This statement can be found at http://64.233.167.104/search?q=cache:_HCK Uy0k47AJ:www.rotten.com/library/bio/presidents/george-hw-bush/+George+Walker+Bush, +New+World+Order&hl=en.

5. President Bush's speech to the graduating class at West Point, June 1, 2002.

6. The gauntlet thrown down by the Bush administration, with broad bipartisan support in Congress, has many of the same features as the failed attempt of the British Empire to

maintain its hegemony of the seas by adopting a two-battleship standard to any challenger, notably Germany, before World War I. See Kennedy (1979, 1980).

7. President Bush's speech to the graduating class at West Point, June 1, 2002.

8. President Bush's speech to the graduating class at West Point, June 1, 2002.

9. http://www.whitehouse.gov/news/releases/2002/01/20020129-11.html.

10. This religious aspect is a theme of Bob Woodward's (2002) first volume on the Bush wars. Hoffmann (2003) makes the point regarding President Bush's commitment to a moral conception of his global war on terror.

11. See also Kagan (2003), who makes the Athenian–Spartan preoccupation with power and imperial rule abundantly clear.

12. See also Mandelbaum (2002), who extends the eulogy to include the triumph of American values over opponents around the globe, a view shared by others, like Thomas Friedman.

13. Bob Woodward's (2002) in-depth study of President Bush underscores the president's moral and religious certainty and fervor.

14. President Bush's speech to the graduating class at West Point, June 2002.

15. Or what Bob Woodward (2006) prefers to call *State of Denial.*

16. Osgood (1953) extensively delineates these differences in rationale.

17. A number of works develop Wilson's transformation of American exceptionalism into a universal solution to war, self-government, and prosperity through global, free markets, including Blum (1956), Levin (1968), and Mandelbaum (2002).

18. Graebner (1964, 730–33) reproduces relevant portions of the Truman Doctrine and Marshall Plan that echo Wilsonian themes of self-determination, democratic government, and free world markets as the foundations for peace and prosperity.

19. Feldman (January 6, 2006) succinctly delineates these presidential claims. Yoo (2005) develops a rationale for these powers. For a trenchant critique of this position, see Cole (2005) and Schwarz and Huq (2007).

20. A retort can be found in Sullivan (December 19, 2005).

21. Ricks (2006) does a superlative job in delineating these shortcomings; see also n. 1.

22. http://icasualties.org/oif\.

23. Ibid.

24. These estimates of Iraqi dead, while very high, are well below those from other sources. See, for example, the website Unknown News (unknownnews.net/casualties.html) which as of May 7, 2007, cites 799,896 dead and 1,529,439 wounded. It also cites a Lancet study of October 2004 to justify these higher totals. Another British-based watchdog group estimates Iraqi civilian deaths as of July 1, 2007, between 66,939 and 73,253 (http://Iraqbodycount .net/database).

25. A Johns Hopkins study, printed in the London journal, *Lancet,* estimated that over 600,000 Iraqis had been killed, a figure disputed by the administration.

26. http://people-press.org/reports/display.php3?ReportID=313.

27. http://www.editorandpublisher.com/eandp/news/article_display.jsp?vnu_content_ id=1003609344.

28. http://people-press.org/reports/display.php3?ReportID=335.

29. *Washington Post*, March 20, 2007, 1.

30. See Joseph Stiglitz's website for the report: www2.gsb.columbia.edu/faculty/jstiglitz/papers.cfm. Citations to other studies estimating the costs of the Iraq war are cited in the Bilmes–Stiglitz report.

31. U.S. National Debt Clock, http://wwww.brillig.com/debtclock/.

CHAPTER TWO

American Military Power and Challenges to International Security

Patrick M. Morgan

This chapter outlines the perspectives and policies the armed forces developed to meet the responsibilities and challenges associated with protecting national security, as well as those associated with the American management of global order and security.[1] It also considers how both the armed forces and their political superiors have contributed to recent American military failures.

The International Strategic Situation

The armed forces operate now in a distinctive security environment, amid considerable debate about how long the features that make it distinctive will endure. Most important is the absence of the intense great-power political competition that generates military rivalries and insecurities. Significant preparations for a possible war figure into only one great-power relationship currently—that of China and the United States over Taiwan—but thus far the threat of military confrontation is due less to the two nations' overall relationship than to a particularly thorny localized dispute. Missing is the security/insecurity mechanism that had been foremost in past international politics—intense, dangerous great-power conflicts and wars (see Jervis 2005, 11–15; Freedman 2006, 9–10). There has been no war among great powers since 1953; chances of one have been declining since 1962 and especially since 1990. (In fact, wars among all governments have become rare and internal wars have declined.) The great powers' threat perception is so subdued that they do little planning for wars with each other.

Another central feature of the current security environment is globalization (Tangredi 2000b). An enormous and controversial phenomenon, it is usually deemed strategically significant for a couple of reasons. First, rising economic interdependence is associated by analysts both with heightened conflict and reduced chances of interstate warfare. Second, and countering the capacity of economic interdependence to limit interstate warfare, globalization is stimulating development and thus putting greater strains on world resources, particularly energy, which, in the past, has provoked interstate warfare. Rising economic interaction also creates a greater need for security and stability, which the United States, more than any other actor, has been providing.

Increased interdependence is also, in part, why disturbing international ripples are generated by domestic internal decay and unrest, failed states and "rogue states," regional conflicts, and any domestic conditions that breed a flow of refugees. The range of system-threatening disturbances now extends beyond states' international behavior to encompass their political nature and their societies' limitations. In addition, nonstate actors have increasingly acquired the power to mount threats; under some circumstances they could be as dangerous as states.

Another feature of today's system is the increasing pressure on countries to acquire or develop weapons of mass destruction (WMD). The international community regards proliferation as threatening in and of itself and also because of parallel proliferation of modern delivery vehicles. Enlarging the concern is possible WMD transfers to terrorists.

Security management in this system is hegemonic in character. In international relations theory hegemony is a structural characteristic, a particular distribution of military strength for wars among states. It is not any specific pattern of security management (though the hegemon's dominant role in that management is assumed) nor does the success or failure of any pattern necessarily affect a given hegemonic structure. In military capabilities, the United States is clearly the hegemon. Somewhat surprising is the disinterest others show in competing for that position; none display the necessary "lean and hungry look." Only the United States maintains a consistently global involvement, perspective, and capability for military action.

This hegemony is not new. As of the early 1990s the United States had accumulated enough relative military power, and relevant other forms of power, that it duplicated its situation back in 1945. It held a hegemonic position then. During the cold war observers and analysts were hypnotized by the concept of bipolarity; in fact, however, the United States maintained its position as dominant state, the one with truly global military reach, throughout the cold war, even though it faced a stiff challenge from a serious, formidable opponent. Currently, it is without such an opponent. Still, as after 1945, such extreme military dominance will be fleeting—various constraints on American military power and limitations on its political influence have already emerged, as this volume makes abundantly clear.

Thus the United States is hardly a neophyte hegemon. However, to call the United States the hegemon is a bit misleading. The true hegemon since 1945 has been a collective — the close association of the Western states (including Japan) for military and other purposes. Disagreements among them remain predominantly tactical. They agree on basic values, main objectives to be pursued in the system, and who belongs in the Western community. They are intent on refashioning the world along Western lines. Never before has there been such a cohesive dominant coalition for so long. The distinctive status of the United States is as leader of that coalition, with a unique global power projection capability.

American-Western hegemony was reaffirmed and reinforced by victory in the cold war, but broad Western objectives were not thereby sufficiently realized, particularly from the perspective of the Bush administration, to make the international system operate properly. Seeking to correct this makes Western states, particularly the United States, revolutionary. The United States, for instance, would transform the world by reforming many nations' political, economic, and social systems. This is also not new in American foreign policy; what has changed is the degree to which force might be used to achieve it.

From a military perspective, American security commitments did not shrink after the cold war. The United States retained virtually all its cold war alliances and other close security associations (with Israel, Saudi Arabia, and others). This underlying continuity is not surprising but was not initially predicted. Many assumed that, when the cold war ended, the profile of the United States would decline, that it would no longer play such a dominant role in world affairs, and that its international activities would subside. However, the American position in the system is the same — it objectives are unchanged, it retains its allies, and it maintains its responsibility for regional security management in much of the world. Hence its militarily relevant commitments have not fundamentally changed.

Also unchanged is its emphasis on military power in pursuing its interests and in carrying out its responsibilities, in comparison with friends, allies, and even potential rivals. Since the disappearance of the European colonial empires, the United States has been consistently more inclined to use force and threats than its friends or other governments.

The Context Provided by Foreign Policy and National Security Strategy

Shaping an overall U.S. military strategy and policy since 1990 has been a complex challenge. The threat environment has greatly changed. Most salient is the dearth of significant military rivals; American military superiority is obvious, which gives the United States a perspective on its possible military conflicts that no country in the history of international politics (since roughly 1500) has ever had. That superiority is augmented by the capabilities of American allies and associates.

The core of U.S. military superiority is the Revolution in Military Affairs (RMA). The RMA marries the information revolution and continuing improvements in reconnaissance, surveillance, and accuracy to produce weapons of much improved speed, accuracy, and range. The military has also made organizational and training shifts and rethought strategy and tactics. These changes are intended to enable the military to best exploit the newly available capabilities (Binnendijk 2002 offers examples).

The RMA is sometimes misunderstood. It is not something the United States has "gone through." Its essence is the embrace of change, the rapid development of new capabilities and adaptations to them. The focus to date has been on improving conventional forces but there is no intrinsic reason why the RMA cannot eventually revolutionize the conduct of other sorts of military conflicts as well.

The idea of the RMA is not that it should provide a significant initial advantage for the lead state, which would then be attained by successive imitators so that that state's initial advantage would be whittled away. Thus far it has been an escalating process of expanded capabilities driven by rapid technological change (Binnendijk 2002 offers examples). Many capabilities showcased in the Gulf War—like speed of target acquisition, the speed and scale of military communications, and weapon accuracy—were out of date by the war on Iraq. Driving such changes is civilian-sector technological innovations, Pentagon R&D spending that outpaces that of the rest of the world combined, and extensive military training. American advantages in these areas are manifest, and no one is attempting to compete. No other government now has the range of security concerns or resources to lead it to do so, and even if it did, it would not have the resources necessary to manage them.

States fearful of this military power are pursuing deterrence through WMD, "asymmetric" war-fighting strategies and resources (defined in Freedman 2006, 53), or selective RMA capabilities for specific objectives such as impeding U.S. military interventions (China, for example, has been seeking the means to threaten U.S. carriers). These are unlikely to work if the United States strives to overcome them. The U.S. military will continue to improve its conventional war-fighting advantages. The limits on this form of American power will be primarily political (international and domestic) in nature.

However, this military superiority may well be increasingly irrelevant. Interstate wars have become rare, great-power wars have disappeared, and the major security problems today arise from failing states, civil wars, irregular warfare, and other low-level threats not readily dealt with via conventional military power. The success of the United States in adapting to the changing nature of its security problems has been quite uneven since the cold war.[2]

Other elements of the strategic situation are even less clear-cut. While the United States remains the most powerful economic actor, the European Union is roughly equivalent in GDP and present trends suggest China will be the largest national economy within decades. The critical issue as far as the strategic situation goes is emerging shifts in the patterns of economic interdependence. Since World War II, building economic interdependence has been a major component of American power. It was a key element in the economic well-being of Western Europe, Japan, and the rest of East Asia during the cold war; at the same time, denying access to the American-dominated world economy, particularly the U.S. economy, was a potent weapon in winning that war. This American advantage is shrinking. The U.S. economy has declining relative influence as competing markets and sources of advanced technology and foreign investment emerge. The power of others in managing the global economic system (and regional systems) is fast expanding, the foremost example being China and its rising influence in East Asia. What the United States uniquely contributes is the security framework and management under which economies operate. Until recently, it stabilized the Middle East. It polices sea lanes, offers intervention capabilities for quelling domestic problems in strategically sensitive places, and protects economically important but militarily weak states. However, misuse of American power in Iraq has somewhat weakened the appeal, domestically and abroad, of this provision of collective security goods, illustrating how limited the benefits can be in the absence of a good overall political-economic strategy.

Other sources of nonmilitary American power and influence are also receding in significance. The components of U.S. "soft power" remain important: its continued global cultural impact, its leadership in the information revolution, its dominance in the flow of news and information, and its predominant influence in the Internet as well as the respect it earns from other countries, the perception of it as relatively benevolent, and so forth. However, these are fleeting assets because many of the components are readily transferable and are proliferating rapidly through U.S. foreign investment, overseas imitation and theft, and the Bush administration's disregard for or clumsy use of them.

Thus assessing American hegemony is difficult for military purposes. Conceptions of it, particularly those offered by neoconservative analysts and the Bush administration, sometimes assume its various components are additive — that each supports and reinforces the others. Often this is not so. Employing one form of power frequently limits or damages another — as when "victory" in Iraq weakened Washington's image and popularity worldwide, and the insurgency damaged U.S. finances. Finding ways to keep differing kinds of power compatible and reinforcing must be a central objective of grand strategy. Lately U.S. foreign policy has been too much influenced by notions that only military power matters or that assertive unilateralism and demonstrated success in U.S. security endeavors will override the disenchantment of other state and nonstate actors.

This error is compounded by the Bush administration's tendency to see U.S. hegemony as inherently benign and beneficial, as unavoidable (it is necessary and nobody else can provide it), and as inevitable given the growth in American power. However, because America is a revolutionary state, society, and culture, its hegemony is often seen as disturbing and threatening. In international politics opposition by other states to any seemingly unconstrained power is unavoidable, and for that reason, American hegemony is also not consistently seen as benign. Its current pattern is also not inevitable; the United States could readily settle for a less extensive and intrusive role. During the cold war it embraced a hegemonic status that drew a good deal on allies and friends and involved some cooperation with enemies.

Hegemonic security management may be impelled by the imperatives of globalization, as rising interdependence increases vulnerability to disturbances almost anywhere. Certainly no other government or collection of governments (such as the European Union) has the ambition, inclinations, and capabilities needed to conduct that management. But the United States should minimize the associated burdens, contain unfavorable reactions to its management, and limit the drain on its resources. Aggressive unilateralism and a too ready resort to military will rarely be best.

Specific Military Steps

The armed forces must proceed by taking American dominance in global and regional security management as a given and by understanding that their related burdens will be shaped by how policy makers specifically define their role over time. They are most likely going to be called on first to play a role in closing the huge gaps between modernized and nonmodern political, economic, and social systems, gaps that, for political, economic, and security reasons, the United States and the West cannot afford to ignore. The question is exactly how their armed forces will be used in this connection, whether they will be asked to isolate and suppress problems arising from the nonmodern world, to intervene against or defeat threatening regimes there, or to assist in interventions to alter those societies and political systems.

Any military force wants a congenial national security strategy, one supplying clear political direction on interests to be militarily sustained and on the priorities involved, backed by the necessary resources. The United States generally operated with such a strategy during the cold war. Since 1990 political leaders have vacillated with respect to American strategic directives — in particular they have changed their minds about what is worth fighting for. At the same time the resources for military efforts and programs, except for the wars in Iraq and Afghanistan, have shrunk. A mismatch now obtains between national strategy and existing military strategy, posture, and capabilities.

The first Bush administration entered the post–cold war era anticipating a significant decline in threats and in American involvements and commitments. The problems it addressed were how to maintain stability and keep American involvement from declining too precipitously as the country sought a peace dividend and put priority on the sagging economy, drugs, crime, and the huge national debt. In turn, the Clinton administration was initially determined to focus on domestic problems, to the frustration of foreign policy officials. And the second Bush administration started off seeking a lower profile and reduced military involvements abroad. During the 1990s, military expenditures and forces experienced cuts on the order of 30 to 40 percent in funds and personnel. There was a modest holiday in new weapons purchases; the services lived mainly off the huge procurement increases ordered in the first Reagan term.

However, no consistent strategic perspective emerged. Instead, each administration adopted an ad hoc approach to world crises. For Bush senior — very late in his administration — that crisis was Somalia, a conflict that turned out badly for his successor. Clinton resisted but could not avoid involvement in Bosnia and the Kosovo crisis, and in 1994 he nearly launched a preemptive attack on North Korea. These were impromptu responses, not products of a consistent and coherent global strategy that took due regard of systemic constraints and the reactions of other actors.

The armed forces, often in league with DOD civilian officials, tried to cope with this situation in several ways. First, they sought to institutionalize constraints on cutting their resources and expanding their responsibilities. Drawing on the cold war practice of defining needed military capabilities by how many wars of what size the United States must be prepared to fight simultaneously, largely on its own, the Pentagon at first insisted that the nation be ready to fight and win two regional wars the size of the Gulf War at the same time, with cuts in forces limited accordingly. The second Bush administration adopted a 1-4-2-1 framework: have forces to defend the homeland (1); deter aggression or military coercion in Europe, Northeast Asia, the rest of Asia, and the Middle East (4); win two simultaneous wars (one at a time) (2); and handle a smaller contingency (1) (L. Davis et al. 2005, 5–6).

These three administrations and the armed forces also insisted on retaining a large strategic deterrence capability. Late in the cold war that meant having roughly twelve thousand strategic nuclear weapons. The first Bush administration and its successor accepted cutting strategic and nonstrategic nuclear weapons significantly, though many of those cut or components of the disassembled weapons were stockpiled so that a large force could be quickly recreated. The Clinton Stockpile Stewardship Program aimed to keep the nuclear stockpile healthy and to sustain the weapons labs. A Pentagon emphasis on nuclear weapons led its officials to sandbag a Clinton administration attempt to revise the Single Integrated Operation Plan (SIOP) and to slash strategic nuclear weapons even further (J. Nolan 1999).

The second Bush administration negotiated cutting, by 2012, to roughly the same level (seventeen hundred to twenty-two hundred strategic nuclear weapons) that earlier agreements had envisioned (although many analysts suggest this is still more weapons than would be needed for any conceivable mission [for example, Wilson and Sokolsky 2002]). However, at the same time the administration discarded various arms control arrangements, such as extensive elucidation of the parties' responsibilities or rigorous verification arrangements, as unnecessary in arms control among friends and because the United States supposedly needed greater flexibility (Levi and O'Hanlon 2005). It also insisted on keeping many "eliminated" missiles and warheads in storage instead of destroying them as under past strategic arms limitation agreements. It also abandoned the Antiballistic Missile (ABM) Treaty, installing initial capabilities for national ballistic missile defense (BMD) at considerable cost. The first goal has been to reinforce power-projection capabilities by testing/developing new nuclear weapons for busting bunkers and other deeply buried installations. The second has been to develop BMD to protect the homeland and American forces fighting abroad and thereby achieve a third goal, to free the United States to attack rogue-state WMD proliferation. The first has been blocked in Congress, the second has yet to emerge at other than the battlefield level, and the third has been shelved by the failure of the Iraq war.

In the 1990s all this sharply limited any major "peace dividend." It was, however, in keeping with the insistence of policy makers on retaining U.S. alliances to prevent regional instability and WMD proliferation and preparing for a possible new Russian threat or states like Iraq. The underlying objective of the armed forces was to prepare for the next "peer competitor" and possible large-scale warfare. The result was a divergence between their view of what to prepare for and what civilian leaders regularly wanted them to do (Barnett 2004, 89–106).

In this context the services and certain Pentagon civilians sought to institutionalize restrictions on using American troops for insurgencies, other unconventional military situations, and humanitarian or political crises (or military operations other than war [MOOTWs]). In the spirit of the Nixon Doctrine,

Reagan's defense secretary, Casper Weinberger, announced elaborate preconditions for entering Vietnam-style conflicts.[3] Then–Joint Chiefs of Staff (JCS) chairman Colin Powell helped the Clinton administration develop restrictive rules along the same lines, with Somalia in mind. Powell had resisted launching the Gulf War, and during the Clinton years he opposed sending American forces to deal with Bosnia and other crises (Daalder and Lindsay 2003, 133–34). The Joint Chiefs were so unhappy with Gen. Wesley Clark for urging that the United States initiate the war with Serbia over their opposition that, despite his successful conduct of it, they ended his career (Halberstam 2002, 478–79). The justification, offered over and over, for all this was that American forces were a unique resource not to be frittered away on minor wars in remote places, counterinsurgency efforts, or peacekeeping but to be saved for fighting conventional wars (Tangredi 2002a and b; Freedman 2006, 5, 54–60). A further goal of the military was to avoid another searing, morale-sapping, prestige-gobbling experience like Vietnam.

The entire effort collapsed in the second Bush administration. This was surprising since the administration was initially committed to the services' point of view. The president and others intended to boost defense spending and procurements, heighten the salience of nuclear weapons, and build BMD. They reiterated their predecessors' commitment to remain ahead of all other nations militarily and were certain that the services had been misused in Bosnia and Kosovo. But with 9/11 Colin Powell's worst nightmare became real. First, top DOD officials insisted on making decisions the services have long wanted reserved to themselves. DOD officials argued that the military needed quicker RMA-inspired reform and more of the "jointness" mandated by the 1985 Goldwater–Nichols Act, things the services had been approaching with more caution than enthusiasm. Remembering how the services had used the Vietnam War to fend off or reverse the McNamara reforms by citing the tradition of leaving wartime operations to them, Defense Secretary Donald Rumsfeld and his associates insisted their wars be used to reinforce reforms.

Thus the Afghanistan War saw extensive use of the Special Forces, which stimulated their enlargement and plans for their increased use in future conflicts. The Special Operations Command is now charged with leading the war on terrorism. The Iraq War has been fought with far fewer forces than the armed forces sought. Military officers had no plan for the occupation but seeing it coming they proposed far more troops than civilian officials would accept. The officials assumed the occupation would be brief. In fact they wished away the need for a lengthy occupation by expecting the Iraqis (and Afghans) to readily govern themselves and by assuming that American corporations, the United States, Europeans and NGOs would readily handle initial reconstruction and peace building (M. Gordon and Trainor 2006). This view shaped the (non)preparation for both postwar situations. While it fit in with military leaders' resistance to being drawn into postwar administration, including order-maintenance, it ignored strong warnings from numerous officers and others in and outside the government that many troops and much time would be involved.

As a result, Iraq became a situation Powell had fought to avoid: a severe internal conflict (eventually a civil war) that has bogged the army down and eroded the morale of officers and enlisted personnel, especially in the reserves, shrunk army combat readiness for a regular war, diverted resources from procurements, training, and readiness, and resulted in failures and atrocities damaging to the armed forces' image and a looming failure that has incited criticism of and recrimination within the military. Military resentment has been palpable, with retired officers calling for the ouster or resignation of the Pentagon leadership. Over time Afghanistan has gone in the same direction for the same reason: unwillingness and therefore lack of preparation to occupy the country and run it, leading to a weak government, a redeveloping insurgency, deteriorating central government control, and the proliferation of suicide attacks, roadside bombs, and other tactics familiar from Iraq. As of 2006 "Statistically it is now as dangerous to serve as an American soldier in Afghanistan as it is in Iraq" (Rohde 2006).

In announcing the "war" on terrorism the administration enlarged potential American military involvements. After the cold war, an "arc of crisis" largely defined future threats. WMD proliferation, state-sponsored terrorism, disintegrating states, refugee flows, vicious human rights situations, and interstate wars seemed most likely in the area from the Balkans through the Middle East and Central Asia into South Asia and Southeast Asia and up through the Philippines, Taiwan, and North Korea. The war on terrorism made the entire area appear much more threatening, requiring larger American involvement.

The assertion that the key to national security was for the United States to undertake the reordering of societies and governments, especially through extensive peace building and/or nation building, stunned the military. Iraq was to be the initial case in point. Thus the first seven pages of the National Military Strategy of March 2006 are devoted to promoting democracy and advancing freedom as the cornerstone of national security.

A minor replica of the cold war was enunciated: here was an enemy with global reach and presence, a conspiracy with deep political roots making regime and societal change the true solution, a national emergency that required expanded government powers, a great crusade on behalf of freedom in which there would be significant recourse to military power. Democratic peace theory morphed into the view that undemocratic systems had to be understood as inherently prone to aggression and war, renewing and intensifying the revolutionary role of the West.

This reversed the view that such endeavors were inappropriate for the services and that American military involvements should shrink. It further expanded the plausible contingencies for which the services were to prepare (the Pentagon has now added an Africa Command). Many officers have been made uneasy by these developments; as the insurgency in Iraq has demonstrated, possible military involvements and responsibilities are almost without limit. U.S. forces were now establishing bases, cooperation arrangements, training programs, and arms transfers in Central Asia and expanding operations in places like Indonesia. In geographical and functional terms the demands made on U.S. forces have sharply increased.

The second Bush administration also revived classic Republican arguments objecting to deterrence and advocating preemptive-preventive war instead, further enlarging potential military operations and leading directly to the war in Iraq. Thus a hegemon facing no significant great-power threat, with unparalleled military advantages and ever more allies and associates, now experiences considerable insecurity, requires a vast military budget, and is stretched thin in combat capabilities.

The armed forces, seeking a posture better suited to their responsibilities, have begun making major adjustments to the strategic situation and the policy context. The core shifts are linked to the ongoing RMA, now termed "the military transformation" (see U.S. Department of Defense, Office of Force Transformation 2003). The RMA has generated huge increases in the conventional military power of smaller units. Since much of the reconnaissance and the destructive effects of conventional weapons can be precisely delivered from great distances, these weapons capabilities are now part of those units. The basic land unit is now the "brigade combat team," packing more punch in its weapons and those on call from far away than a division used to. By 2011 the Army is to have some 43 combat brigades and over 70 support brigades (plus 28 combat and 135 support brigades in the reserves) (U.S. Department of Defense 2006, 43). These smaller units with fewer, more accurate, weapons can be lighter (less armor and artillery), more mobile, and more flexible, with a smaller logistics burden. Naval and air forces are also carrying accurate weapons in smaller units, easing logistics and providing greater flexibility and effectiveness.

There is currently elevated military preparation for irregular warfare, due to the top priority now assigned the war on terrorism and to the demonstrated deficiencies in dealing with the Iraq insurgency. Training for irregular warfare with an emphasis on "jointness" is up, and specialists in such fighting, under the Special Operations Command (SOC), are responsible for conducting the war on terror. The SOC now exceeds fifty thousand and continues to expand, as does the command's budget (Tyson 2006; U.S. Department of Defense 2006). This focus on insurgency and similar threats was late in coming. Numerous analyses stress that both occupation preparations for Iraq as well as the initial responses to the disorder and early violence were woefully inadequate (see M. Gordon and Trainor 2006; Fallows 2006). U.S. forces eventually abandoned the active interaction with the population that counterinsurgency theory highlights and concentrated themselves in compounds and convoy patrols. Typical American responses to the insurgency have been too forceful, with units not properly prepared (see Garfield 2006; F. Hoffman 2006b; M. Gordon and Trainor 2006).

Military adjustments and reforms have culminated in a shift in deployments. Although abroad they remain very high (close to four hundred thousand), over half are related to the wars in Afghanistan and Iraq (Conetta 2006a). Otherwise they have been declining and shifting steadily from Europe toward the Persian Gulf and Central and East Asia. During the cold war many overseas forces were dedicated to stabilizing and dominating specific areas, reassuring allies and friends and deterring attacks on them, sustaining the credibility of particular alliances, and facilitating more U.S. power projection into those areas when necessary. The units served indefinitely where they were located and trained and equipped there for their specific missions. They typically planned and prepared for fighting with the allies where they were based. The allies provided bases, housed stockpiles of American weapons and equipment, and maintained forces for fighting with the Americans to defend themselves.

All this has changed. Forces abroad are now expected to be relatively self-sufficient, not just capable of mounting an initial defense until additional forces arrive. They are no longer being trained and equipped to fight in specific locations but rather are being prepared to undertake operations almost anywhere. Furthermore, they are assigned a wide spectrum of missions, from fighting conventional wars to peacekeeping. Thus U.S. forces in Korea, formerly there to help defend the Republic of Korea (ROK), are now to be available for missions around the region or further away. Units are to come together from the United States or around the world for meeting military contingencies anywhere. The goal is to be able eventually to deliver a brigade combat team anywhere within 96 hours, a division (three brigades) within 120 hours, and a corps (five divisions) within 30 days (Nardulli and McNaugher 2002). Achieving such a response level has become the services' prime preoccupation over the last decade.

Since 2001 the national strategy documents have emphasized the development of highly adaptable and flexible forces, supposedly ready to deal with the unexpected, rather than the strategy of forcing the opponent into an American-style war with American military superiority. However, in the Iraq war as well as in Afghanistan, American forces and military and civilian decision making were at first inflexible and then slow to adapt to the situations they faced. This was particularly evident in the failure to distinguish initial fighting with small, highly mobile units, which went well, from thereafter having to administer a country.

The more extensive forces needed were never provided, and a phase of conflict emerged that has not gone well in either country (see M. Gordon and Trainor 2006; Rohde 2006) and that would have benefited from taking the advice of numerous specialists on reconstruction and peace building (Fallows 2006) and from not stocking much of the early occupation structure in Iraq with political appointees (Chandrasekaran 2006a). In both countries preoccupation with quickly withdrawing U.S. forces, avoiding occupation duties, including maintaining security, and not assuming lengthy reconstruction responsibilities dissipated whatever momentum and good will defeating the opponent had created in the U.S. Army (see International Institute for Strategic Studies 2006).

The Air Force and Navy have been adjusting along similar lines. The Air Force has maintained its traditional focus on advanced fighters for tactical air supremacy; at the same time it is seeking to decrease its dependence on elaborate bases by building more capable combat aircraft and other planes that can use simpler, smaller bases and overcome defenses by stealth and heightened suppression and more drones for reconnaissance and combat. The Navy is developing greater onshore power projection by air and inserting forces ashore, reducing its emphasis on maintaining sea control, since there is no rival in this regard in sight, and instead focusing on defeating or suppressing missiles, air defenses, mines, and other opposition to American access from the sea.

These changes have affected the nature and functions of overseas bases. A three-tiered base structure has replaced large bases that used to house fixed forces for defense and numerous ancillary installations. A few bases or places will serve as hubs for forward deployments and military operations, concentrations of forces, equipment, supplies, and facilities. Britain serves as a hub as do Diego Garcia, Guam, and Japan among others. Smaller permanent or forward operating bases are being established where American forces will be deployed for extended periods to meet ongoing threats. Some are quite substantial; ten to twelve sizeable bases of this sort have been constructed in Iraq to handle U.S. forces there for years (Kaplan 2006), although the likelihood that U.S. forces will be in Iraq in large numbers indefinitely is steadily declining. Others are rudimentary and can be readily closed, like another sixty or so U.S. bases in Iraq or the recently built or refurbished bases in Uzbekistan now being abandoned. Finally, skeletal bases are being established around the world for use in crises. U.S. forces could be sent to such installations on short notice and use the facilities, stockpiles, and so forth located in them, most likely in cooperation with the local government forces that maintain them. Many other overseas installations are being eliminated and the forces sent home.

These changes are adjusting the hierarchy of American alliances somewhat. The "hubs" are central to future military responses almost anywhere, so the allies involved are therefore closely associated with American grand strategy. There will be greater coordination between Britain's and Japan's armed services and U.S. forces in weapons, training, and joint operations as a result. Since U.S. military planning in East Asia emphasizes potential competition and a possible war with China, Japan has accepted greater integration of its forces with American forces, and in a 2005 joint statement with the United States it designated Taiwan as of strategic interest. As the U.S.–Japan alliance has flourished, the China–Japan relationship has correspondingly deteriorated, at least temporarily. In Seoul, the Korean government dislikes hosting forces that could be used anywhere, particularly in a future U.S.–China conflict. This has contributed to the U.S.–ROK alliance being in tatters while the ROK–China relationship has never been better. Other allies are of declining salience to the United States. Germany is the best example in Europe, with U.S. forces shrinking there and emphasis being shifted to smaller bases in Eastern Europe.

The alliances are affected in other ways. During the cold war they mainly supplied reassurance, deterrence, and defense for the allies and secured allied support for the United States. The former functions were primary; as for the latter, allies frequently disagreed with American security policies in other regions, often opposing U.S. military operations and participating unevenly in them. With the disappearance of serious threats to most of the allies, the United States now emphasizes its global security management responsibilities in its national security policy, requesting allied political and military support accordingly. American officials have suggested that the failure of the allies to provide this support diminishes the value and relevance of the alliances. The United States wants allies enlisted in a unified, U.S.-led global security management effort. From the American perspective the alliances merely need to adapt to today's strategic situation.

Since the allies usually resisted participating in "out of area" conflicts, their uneven response now plus their misgivings over U.S. security policies and the caliber of U.S. decision making are consistent with their reaction to U.S. security management during the cold war. Not surprisingly, U.S. frustration also persists. What is new is a reduced allied capacity to be directly helpful in fighting wars. The United States and its allies have long engaged in "burden-sharing" disputes about military operations. But the Gulf War revealed difficulties, due to the RMA, in U.S. and allied forces fighting together. One allied response was to refit their forces to handle crisis interventions beyond their borders by reducing or ending conscription (draftees often could not legally be sent abroad), expanding training, making forces more mobile, and so forth. But the gap has widened. The problem is outdated allied weapons (few precision-guided munitions, no stealth aircraft), intelligence resources, communications, sensors and guidance systems, transportation, and logistics capabilities.

The United States and its allies have also become less militarily useful to each other due to rising disagreement over when and how to use force. While this provoked friction during the cold war, the Iraq War has generated suspicions in both America and Europe that the disagreement is now more deeply rooted. Analysts suggest the problem is not just particular policies but an American divergence from a former Western consensus on how to sensibly manage the global system, a divergence rooted in a populist nationalism that disdains interdependence and other constraints on American freedom of action.

Whatever the reason, alliance specialization patterns are shifting. During the cold war the United States was to provide nuclear and conventional power projection and the allies local conventional defense capabilities. Now the United States fights regular wars while the allies are oriented toward limited interventions for peacekeeping and peace building.

U.S. pressure on its allies to play a more global role in sustaining systemic security is having an effect. Thus in Afghanistan, NATO members are taking more responsibility for trying to militarily suppress a Taliban revival and for maintaining order to shore up the central government. However, the allies are primarily only accepting missions they are comfortable with. NATO is even involved, rather limitedly, in Iraq (it is training Iraqis), Japan has inched into participating in that intervention (taking a few casualties), and the ROK reluctantly supplied the second largest non-American military contingent in Iraq. It is unclear whether this division of labor will continue, will strain some alliances to the breaking point (for example the U.S.–ROK alliance), or lead major allies to develop their own out-of-area security responsibilities independently of the United States.

Other major adjustments in U.S. forces have been made. One is upgrading the caliber, equipment, and preparation of the various reserves and then drawing on the reserves regularly for operations. Another is outsourcing many noncombat activities, thereby freeing more military personnel for combat. Most controversial is using nonmilitary personnel for security-related operations — guarding installations, operating prisons, protecting officials.[4] Over the course of the Iraq War, both outsourcing steps have generated much contention and very likely will be reconsidered as a result.

Impact of the Iraq War

Pentagon civilians ignored the services' resistance to aspects of the military transformation in planning the Iraq War but joined them in expressing distaste for running an elaborate postwar reconstruction (see Daalder and Lindsay 2003). Not wanting to be involved in reconstruction, they therefore did little planning for it, ignored relevant expertise on it, and provided too few troops while insisting on displacing the State Department as the initial managing agency. There was no suitable political context devised to guide the war and its aftermath in terms of national objectives or to deflect probable reactions around the world and in Iraq (see Gray 2005 on American tendencies to downplay the political repercussions of using force). In the anticipated scenario initial military success would evoke broad support from Iraqis, followed by rapid reconstruction run mainly by a new government helped greatly by the international community. Successful installation of democratic government would erode foreign criticism of the war and initiate a political transformation of the Middle East. Pentagon officials refused to give up this political fantasy and avoided most of the burden of running and rebuilding Iraq for months while the country deteriorated (the same took place in Afghanistan).

What has been the impact, and what will the further impact be, on U.S. forces? As with the Vietnam War, the Iraq War will fuel major changes. The war is adding substantially to American combat experience; U.S. armed forces now have the most combat experience in the developed world and they are unmatched in their skill in dealing with many kinds of fighting. If studied carefully, the experience could be exceedingly valuable. The war has already stimulated greater counterinsurgency training. The 2006 Quadrennial Defense Review, for example, has elevated the status of postconflict stability operations, stating that they are as important as war fighting (Noonan 2006). Since 2001 the official national strategy documents have emphasized intrastate warfare as a major mission for American forces. The war has resulted in less R&D for conventional warfare and more for things like land-mine detection and remote detonation, better sensors, and new armor for equipment and personnel. Whether the RMA can have a decisive impact in future subconventional combat and other forms of irregular warfare remains unclear.

In other ways the war has been very damaging and will likely provoke numerous changes. Analysts had suggested that American military supremacy would incite opponents to use "asymmetric warfare" (see Freedman 1998), but they were ignored. In Iraq and the 2006 Israeli incursion into Lebanon modern forces prepared for standard combat found it difficult to deal with the variants of fighting they encountered (Shanker 2006; Freedman 2006, 54–70). Some analysts claim that much of the American emphasis on military reform in the past twenty years has been misplaced, that the military has been preparing for a type of war that is disappearing and provoking countermeasures to its operations for which the services are badly prepared (for example, Barnett 2004, 89–106; Freedman 1998; Freedman 2006). A common view in the peacekeeping literature is that standard combat units cannot readily adopt other, less forcible, approaches. Thus some analysts suggest that the Pentagon really needs a second armed force — a capability for constabulary, counterguerrilla, and policing activities (Barnett 2004; Perito 2004).

There is disagreement as to whether the failure to take occupying Iraq more seriously, and in particular the failure to provide enough troops while at the same time dissolving the Iraq Army, allowed the insurgency to break out or whether Baathists deliberately turned to insurgency as their last resort. Clearly the Pentagon reacted badly to disorder, crime, and other violence during the first months after the seizure of the country. Because the military had to supply forces to fight in Afghanistan as well, the combat units soon displayed signs of being stretched very thin. Those units were less effective in irregular combat situations, and more extensive forces were needed. This eroded the U.S. image of possessing overwhelming military power, while atrocities damaged the reputation of the services and the intelligence community. Any leverage the administration sought to apply elsewhere through victories in Iraq and Afghanistan was sharply curtailed, cramping its strategy for dealing with rogue states and WMD proliferation. Victory in Iraq was to put great pressure on North Korea and Iran to come to terms and make U.S. allies more supportive. Instead, the allies were alienated while U.S. military and political strains undermined the credibility of U.S. threats against other states.

Also undermined was its grand strategy on Islamic fundamentalist terrorism. No vigorous, effective, secular Iraqi democracy has emerged. Terrorist activities mounted from that part of the world have not disappeared. The war has increased civil strife in Iraq, and that strife could end up fragmenting the country and inciting intervention from Iraq's neighbors. This might ultimately destabilize the region, unnerve everyone about disruptions in oil exports, and provoke a greater Western intervention.

The war has degraded equipment, combat readiness, and training in the armed forces, pulling combat units away from training routines and rerouting money intended for new equipment, repairs, and modernization (Conetta 2006a, 2006b). Rotation of units for rest, retraining, reequipping, and full combat readiness is now far below what is appropriate (see Davis et al. 2005). The war has apparently strained the reserves greatly, exacerbating stress on reservists from their prior extended use in crisis interventions. Morale and recruitment difficulties may force the Pentagon to reexamine relying so heavily on the reserves.

Military leaders naturally fear that the war will shrink support for defense spending. Political leaders should anticipate a decline in U.S. ability to use force and a corresponding drop in the credibility of American commitments and threats. As in the past, the chief constraint on American military power has been domestic — American uneasiness over, and rising public opposition to, the burdens of a globalist foreign policy. The war has strained the alliances, reducing their utility in augmenting American military strength and political leverage.

Another result of the wars on terrorism and on Iraq is that they have enlarged the role of the national security complex in foreign and national security decision making. Expansion of the power of the executive branch vis-à-vis Congress, the courts, the media, and the public and expansion of armed forces autonomy is typical in American wars. Reversing this expansion of power may be rendered more complicated in this case by fears of terrorism. This time the influence of the vice president and the Rumsfeld Pentagon was enhanced at the expense of the National Security Advisor, National Security Council (NSC) staff, the State Department, the CIA, and other executive agencies. That alliance dominated planning for the Iraq war and the aftermath, as well as decision making on North Korea and Iran.

In this connection the vice president's office and civilian officials in the Pentagon have created units that operate independently of the intelligence community for analysis and for data mining to support policy-maker preferences. The armed forces have joined civilian officials in a campaign that dates back to the Vietnam War to be the final authority when it comes to intelligence estimates on threats and the assessment of military operations and in an additional campaign since the Gulf War to link surveillance-reconnaissance intelligence more closely to military direction. Thus the Pentagon was not displeased by the demotion and partial dismantling of the CIA and has resisted the intent behind installation of a director of national intelligence, particularly the planned role of that office in tasking national intelligence components, supervising intelligence analysis, and reallocating intelligence assets to meet national priorities. DOD has used the war on terrorism and the power it has been given to deal with threats inside the United States to gain "an unprecedented role in domestic spying," related information gathering, the construction of huge data banks and so forth (Donohue 2006). It has used the war to justify an expanded role in human intelligence (HUMINT) activities abroad, creating teams of special operations officers for operations not subject in the usual way to the authority of U.S. ambassadors (Tyson 2006; Shanker and Shane 2006). It has also used the war to try to supplant the CIA as the dominant organization in covert operations.

Conclusions

Years ago military analysts anticipated that the United States would retain global interests but no longer have a supportive alliance network and overseas base structure, so the Pentagon began planning to project power in other ways if necessary. It anticipated antiaccess threats to the insertion of American forces, retained the Marines at roughly cold war strength and emphasized carriers owing to their flexible power projection. It made serious adjustments to the RMA and the shifting strategic landscape while consistently thinking in global, hegemonic terms.

It was impossible to foresee the emergence of terrorism as the main security threat. The initial post–cold war preoccupation was WMD proliferation by rogue states. It was easier to anticipate American leaders broadening U.S. political-military involvements, even evoking a new crusade, but the Bush administration's conversion to muscular Wilsonian internationalism has nevertheless been a shock. Prior Pentagon planning and preparations would actually have been up to the task if this had taken place on the Pentagon's own terms, fighting conventional wars by using the Pentagon's own, RMA-driven, version of asymmetrical warfare and evading most other sorts of military involvements.

But other involvements intruded. Post-1990 administrations have insisted on them. Civilian officials signed off on war in Iraq, dismissing fears that the result could be disastrous. Iraq may yet work out as the administration hopes, but this seems increasingly unlikely. If Iraq disintegrates and destabilizes the region, there could be strong public resistance for some time to military interventions and hence weakened management of global system security.

If managing security is to be taken seriously it is vital that deterrence and enforcement based on effective power projection be sustained (see Morgan 2003, 172–202; Levi and O'Hanlon 2005, 94–95, 136–38; Freedman 2006). But it is hard to see how this will be adequately provided unless the United States leads the way and the West joins in, with support and participation from much of the world welcomed and actively sought. This means more thoroughly utilizing interdependence and the international community to secure greater collective deterrence, the opposite of what the United States set about doing in 2001–2.

This cannot be done unless U.S. security management employs force sparingly and emphasizes rebuilding, reconstruction, and peace building. In this approach, force would be a crucial component but not dominant. Otherwise, as in Iraq and Afghanistan, American security management may end up reducing security in intervening. Needed is a strategy that blends global and regional security needs and concerns, plus international community values, with suitable American military missions and a politically sustainable conception of American interests and that provides the economic resources required. Learning about such matters from this troubled decade is vital for future success.

Notes

1. Some of the major official sources on these matters are: U.S. Department of Defense, Office of the Secretary of Defense 2006, *Annual Report to Congress: Military Power of the People's Republic of China*; U.S. Department of Defense 2006, *Quadrennial Defense Review Report*; U.S. Department of Defense, Chairman of the Joint Chiefs of Staff 2004, *The National Military Strategy of the United States of America*; U.S. Department of Defense 2005, *The National Defense Strategy of the United States of America*; U.S. White House, Office of the President 2006, *The National Security Strategy of the United States of America 2006*.

2. Analysts point out that irregular warfare is also evolving rapidly, based on experience and the use of new technology; see, for example, F. Hoffman (2006a) and Shanker (2006).

3. It resembled the late 1930s efforts to legislate restrictions on U.S. involvements in other people's wars.

4. This fits with the eroding civil-military distinction reflected in the Patriot Act, Guantánamo Bay incarcerations, and crumbling walls between national security and domestic crime in intelligence.

PART TWO

Regional Limits
of American Power

ASIA

CHAPTER THREE

China

Li Mingjiang

This chapter analyzes China's response to the challenges posed by the United States in the post–cold war era. The first section discusses how Beijing has made economic development a domestic priority and analyzes its perception of U.S. intentions. These are the two major factors that have largely shaped China's overall strategy with the United States, one that is nonconfrontational yet adamant in its defense of China's core interests. The second section analyzes China's strategic moves to safeguard a favorable global as well as regional environment, one that would make any U.S. coercion of China unfeasible. These moves include Beijing's efforts to promote multipolarity in its international dealings, to expand its influence in neighboring regions, and to unify the developing world. The third section discusses China's resolve to defend its sovereignty over Taiwan, which Beijing proclaims as its top national security interest. The fourth section explores Beijing's strategies to prevail over the United States in disputes on human rights, an issue that essentially concerns the domestic political legitimacy of the Chinese Communist Party (CCP). I conclude that, although China is not inclined to openly challenge U.S. primacy in the current international order, it has managed to defend its core interests, which clearly demonstrates the limitations of American power.

China's Views of Itself and the United States

Despite the fact that China has achieved prodigious economic growth in the past three decades, Chinese leaders rightly understand that there is still a long way to go before they fulfill the national dream of restoring China to wealth and strength. The priority for the Chinese leadership is to continue to carry out economic reforms and sustain economic growth for the foreseeable future. China understands very well that the only way to achieve that goal is to go along with the trend of globalization and integrate itself with the outside world, the rules of which are still largely shaped by the United States and its allies. Beijing clearly knows that maintaining a normal relationship with Washington is indispensable to China's modernization drive — China needs American investment, managerial skills, and technologies as well as its market. Also, the Chinese leadership realizes that China is simply too weak to challenge the U.S. supremacy in East Asia and the world. And the cost of openly confronting the United States would be too great for China, given the bandwagoning strategies of other major powers.

China also understands that the United States will need China's cooperation in several important areas: on the U.N. Security Council and in maintaining regional security, checking nuclear proliferation (particularly in North Korea), defeating terrorism, handling Taiwan, trade, and other business interests, controlling transnational crime, protecting the environment, and managing the global energy supply. Beijing also realizes that even if the United States wants to pursue a containment policy against China, as hawkish American politicians and analysts advocate, Washington will have few followers internationally. So, decision makers in Beijing believe that it is possible to maintain at least a working relationship with Washington. In light of these factors, Beijing has adopted a nonconfrontational policy toward the United States while at the same time trying to extract as many economic and security benefits as possible from these bilateral ties. Beijing has repeatedly announced that the guidelines of its U.S. policy are "enhancing trust, reducing trouble, developing cooperation, and avoiding confrontations."

Although crucial to China's future, the United States has not been perceived as a voluntary helping hand. China has much to say about how the United States wields its power. In the eyes of the Chinese, the United States is a hegemonic power that still seeks to preserve and expand its global dominance. U.S. military actions in Kosovo, the development of missile defense, and astronomical military spending are believed to be evidence of an offensive-oriented, neoimperialist, neo-interventionist strategy that the United States has pursued in order to maintain as well as expand its global hegemony (Deng 2001). The invasion of Iraq certainly further enhanced this perception among Chinese leaders and analysts. Despite public pronouncements by American leaders that the United States welcomes a prosperous and strong China, the Chinese tend to believe that the United States is at least partially intent on containing or constraining China (Saunders 2000). Most Chinese analysts think that the United States has adopted a dual strategy of engagement and containment and that it clearly intends to contain China's rise to great-power status (Chen 2003). Top CCP leaders suspect that by interfering in China's domestic affairs, "splitting" China by blocking its reunification with Taiwan, and meddling in affairs in Tibet, the United States is bent on trying to politically "westernize" China. This fear has been aggravated by talk of a "China threat" and of containing China among some U.S. policy makers and strategists in the past decade.

Chinese strategists argue that the recent buildup of substantial U.S. military power in the west Pacific and efforts to strengthen or form strategic alliances with Japan, Australia, and India are part of the U.S. conspiracy to forge a "hidden containment" strategy with which to manipulate China (Lin 2005). They contend that U.S. China policy is increasingly emphasizing the competitive elements of this relation (Medeiros 2006). Beijing is very sensitive to any U.S. move that might structurally restrain China's influence in East Asia. Chinese decision makers doubtless listened with great interest to Secretary of State Condoleezza Rice's proclamation that "I really do believe that the U.S.–Japan relationship, the U.S.–South Korean relationship, the U.S.–Indian relationship, all are important in creating an environment in which China is more likely to play a positive role than a negative role" (Rice 2005). Beijing is equally concerned by the fact that the United States has also in recent years expanded its defense and security ties with some Southeast Asian nations, including Singapore, Thailand, the Philippines, Indonesia, and Vietnam, albeit in the name of antiterrorism.

A string of unfortunate episodes in the 1990s further reinforced the Chinese public's perception of the United States as an assertive and coercive power. These include U.S. contentions of human rights abuse and its denial of Most Favored Nation (MFN) trade status to China, the *Yinhe* incident in which the United States wrongly accused China of proliferating chemical materials in 1993, the U.S. Congress's efforts to block China's bid for the 2000 Olympic Games, NATO's bombing of the Chinese embassy in Belgrade in 1999, and the collision of a U.S. EP-3 spy plane with a Chinese jet fighter in April 2001. Many Chinese regarded these incidents as manifestations of a U.S. anti-China policy in the post–cold war era. President George W. Bush's harsh words toward China early in 2001, when he first entered the White House, particularly his vow to protect Taiwan militarily, further exacerbated Chinese misgivings about U.S. intentions. The tragic events of September 11, 2001, significantly changed the orientation of Sino–U.S. relations due to American need for Chinese support in the war against terrorism, but the feeling that the United States will not volunteer to be a facilitator in China's road to prosperity and strength still widely persists.

The indispensability of the United States to China's modernization and Beijing's perception of U.S. malign intentions have largely determined the Chinese approach to the United States. On the one hand, China has endeavored to pursue a nonconfrontational approach to the United States, delicately trying not to antagonize it. On the other hand, it has kept a wary eye on the United States and has attempted painstakingly to defend its core interests, which include gaining more favorable strategic positions in international politics, preventing Taiwanese independence, and assiduously fending off U.S. interference in China's domestic affairs.

Beijing's Search for Favorable Strategic Positions

Its nonconfrontational attitude toward the United States notwithstanding, Beijing has consistently proposed and insisted on discernibly different notions of sovereignty and human rights and takes a different view from the United States on the use of force, the functionality of security alliances, and the impact of globalization on security (Feigenbaum 2001). Having come to the realization that the United States is partly intent on constraining China, Chinese leaders have adopted a three-prong approach intended to help China enhance its strategic position in global politics: China will promote multipolarity and partnerships with other powers in order to balance U.S. preponderance and increase China's diplomatic maneuverability, use charm diplomacy with its neighbors to consolidate its own backyard, and strengthen relations with the developing world in order to secure political support and thereby counter U.S. pressure. Some scholars have even regarded China as attempting to achieve a "soft balance" through its moves to better position itself, a balance that would constrain U.S. hegemony (Paul 2005).

Promoting Multipolarity

In the early post–cold war years, Beijing believed that the international system was evolving robustly toward multipolarity. This perception subtly changed in light of impressive economic growth during the Clinton administration and the U.S. display of preeminent military capability in several operations. Chinese analysts now think that the international structure of "one superpower, several major powers" will remain in place for quite some time but that the trend toward multipolarity is still inevitable. Given the perception that the United States is partially poised to constrain China, Beijing believes that it is in China's interests to work to transform the current unipolar world to a multipolar one. In a multipolar world China would have greater strategic maneuverability and less vulnerability to U.S. supremacy.

One important step that Beijing has taken to promote multipolarity has been to construct various partnerships with other major powers, including the European Union and its major members, Russia, India, and groups of developing countries. This is part of China's practice of great-power diplomacy, through which it has stressed its commitment to multipolarity and sought to upgrade its international standing. The Sino–Russian strategic partnership is of particular significance in this regard. China and Russia have not only overcome their historical mutual suspicions and distrust but have established and strengthened their strategic partnership in order to "oppose [the] hegemonism and power politics" of the United States (Yan 2000).

The Sino–Russian strategic partnership has been underpinned by several important political documents signed by Beijing and Moscow. In 1997, China and Russia signed a Joint Declaration Regarding a Multi-Polar World and the Establishment of a New International Order (Xinhua News Agency 1997). In 2001, Russia and China signed the Treaty of Good Neighborliness, Friendship, and Cooperation, and in 2005, they signed a joint declaration regarding the international order in the twenty-first century, in which the two countries called for greater adherence to a policy of noninterference in other countries' internal affairs, expressed their opposition to unilateralism and monopolism in international politics, and vowed to strengthen the role of the United Nations (Xinhua News Agency 2005).

Over the past decade, China and Russia have signed over 180 intergovernmental and interstate agreements (Livishin 2006). Summit diplomacy has been an annual feature of the partnership, coupled with regular meetings between ministers of foreign affairs, defense, and energy. Each summoning strong political will, China and Russia successfully solved their border disputes, which had plagued bilateral ties for centuries. In addition to holding joint military exercises with Russia, China has also purchased billions of dollars worth of relatively advanced weapons from the Russians. The all-round improvement in Sino–Russian relations has led observers to conclude that "the two seemingly mismatched giants are drifting into an embrace that could dramatically reshape world relations in coming decades and present a possible counterweight to U.S. global hegemony" (Weir 2003).

China has also pursued a proactive diplomacy toward India, changing Sino–Indian relations from one fraught with suspicion and tension into a "strategic partnership," partly in response to the recent warming up of U.S.–Indian ties that Beijing fears could develop into an implicit alliance against China (Zhang 2005). China and India have shown significant political will in stabilizing their borders. But the goal of China's overtures to India is far more than achieving stable bilateral relations. In 1996, China and India for the first time proposed to establish a constructive cooperative partnership for the twenty-first century. In 2003, then–Indian prime minister Atal Bihari Vajpayee visited Beijing, the culmination of Sino–Indian rapprochement. The two sides signed the Declaration on Principles for Relations and Comprehensive Cooperation and nine other agreements. They vowed to work together to strengthen multipolarity, expressed opposition to interference in others' domestic affairs, and pledged to try to shape a new international political and economic order (Xinhua News Agency 2003). Reaching these goals would have a direct bearing on U.S. external affairs as demonstrated by the Bush administration.

During Chinese Premier Wen Jiabao's visit to India in April 2005, the two countries agreed to establish a strategic partnership. "India and China can together reshape the world order," Indian prime minister Manmohan Singh said at a ceremony for his Chinese counterpart at India's presidential palace (N. George 2005). The two countries also promised to further push bilateral trade to reach $20 billion by 2008 and $30 billion by 2010. Analysts have commented that "Beijing's overtures toward India, though clearly made with the economic opportunities in mind, are also being contemplated with a keen awareness of China's rivalry with the United States" (Sengupta and French 2005).

"Charm Offensive" in Asia

As mentioned above, in the past couple years, the United States has moved to strengthen its security ties with many Southeast Asian nations and built an impressive military presence in Central Asia. Although at this moment these Asian nations have not shown any interest in joining the United States in containing and constraining China, Beijing feels that the U.S. strategic advantage in the region could be inimical to China's economic and security interests at times of crisis. In response to this challenge, China has launched an impressive charm offensive in Southeast Asia. The immediate goal is to strategically reassure Southeast Asia that China's rise does not pose a threat to the region. By building political trust with neighbors and other major players, China is also attempting to "strengthen regional security in favor of China" (J. Wang 2005, 52). The ultimate goal, as observers have argued, is to secure a more advantageous position through which to defuse American dominance in the region (V. Wang 2005).

Taking advantage of its historical and cultural connections in the region, as well as the kudos it earned when it decided not to devalue its currency during the financial crisis of 1997–98, China has pursued an active foreign policy in Southeast Asia. This is most prominently illustrated by its proactive participation in regional economic, political, and security institutions, a participation animated by the belief that China's perspectives and influence may help these multilateral institutions restrain the United States in the region (Shambaugh 2004). From 1995 to 2002, trade between China and Association of Southeast Asian Nations (ASEAN) increased by 19 percent annually, with far greater growth in recent years (Shen 2004). In 2001, China and ASEAN signed a Framework Agreement on Comprehensive Economic Cooperation that serves as the groundwork for the future ASEAN–China free trade area (FTA). Once the FTA is in place, it will link the economies of a total population of two billion and a total GDP of three trillion dollars (McBeth 2003). China also made concessions in its trade arrangements with ASEAN countries by agreeing to the "early harvest package" in which it promised to provide benefits before the FTA was established to ASEAN nations by cutting tariffs on 573 kinds of agricultural and manufactured goods (Ismail

2004). In 2002, the two sides signed the Declaration on the Code of Conduct in the South China Sea and at the ASEAN–China 2003 summit, Beijing signed ASEAN's Treaty of Amity and Cooperation, becoming the first non-ASEAN country to accede to the accord. By signing the two documents, China has formally committed itself to the principles of nonaggression and noninterference and other conflict-resolution mechanisms that have been championed by ASEAN.

China has also waged a diplomatic offensive in Central Asia. In June 2001, China and Russia spearheaded the formation of the Shanghai Cooperation Organization (SCO), a morph of the "Shanghai Five" group created by China in 1994. From its inception, the Shanghai Five focused on antiterrorism and confidence-building among its members. More recently, the SCO has incorporated Mongolia, India, Pakistan, and Iran as observers, expanding its influence to South Asia and West Asia to become the largest international organization spanning Asia and Europe in terms of territory and population. High-level political interactions among members of the SCO are frequent. In addition to working on achieving its original goals of combating religious extremism, terrorism, and ethnic separatism, the SCO is pursuing economic cooperation and is increasingly sensitive to the expansion of U.S. influence in Central Asia. The SCO, under China's and Russia's leadership, has also advocated the so-called Shanghai spirit—that is, the promotion of mutual trust, mutual benefits, equality, coordination, respect for diverse civilizations, and common development. These new principles were effectively countermeasures to the traditional approach the United States has taken in maintaining security alliances (Y. Wang 2005). In July 2005, the SCO, under heavy pressure from Russia and China, called for the United States to set a deadline for withdrawing its military bases from Central Asia. The call was interpreted by many observers as an effort on the part of these countries to "resist U.S. hegemony" inspired by "the Bush administration's claim to enforce the rules of a unipolar world order" (*Boston Globe* 2005).

China's charm offensive in the Asian region is also demonstrated by its conciliatory attitude toward border disputes with its neighbors. Beijing has peacefully concluded border treaties with all of its neighbors except India. The Chinese military has also actively participated in bilateral and multilateral exchange programs and has evinced greater willingness to engage in security dialogues with other Asian nations, which has considerably dissipated regional states' security concerns over China's rise (Shambaugh 2004).

China's diplomatic maneuvers have largely mitigated regional nations' suspicions about China. Its approach has been so successful that some observers have even concluded that Beijing has "created the semblance of a sphere of influence" in Central Asia and Southeast Asia (Vatikiotis 2006). This is perhaps an exaggeration. A more balanced and plausible view is that "over time, China's message of noninterference, cooperative security, and the diminution of the role of the United States that is implied by China's approach will gain in popularity" (Economy 2005). Most nations in the region now see China as "a good neighbor, a constructive partner, a careful listener, and a nonthreatening regional power" (Shambaugh 2004). A recent survey of twenty-two countries, including many Asian nations, revealed that China's influence was perceived more positively than that of the United States (Nye 2005).

Consolidating Unity in the Developing World

In the mid-1990s, as pressure from the United States over human rights, security, and trade mounted, China realized that it needed more friends to answer U.S. challenges. As a result, China began to pay more attention to its diplomacy in the developing world, a traditional political ally of Beijing's that it had neglected to some extent. Beijing also considered that it needed to pursue solidarity with the developing countries in order to better achieve its diplomatic goals, play a bigger role in international politics, and become an independent pole of power in the future multipolar world (Q. Liu 2005). China believed that unity with the developing countries was possible because they agreed with the Chinese on many issues. For instance, they too opposed hegemonism and power politics, strongly objected to foreign meddling in their internal affairs, and desired to establish a more equitable new international political and economic order (Liu and Luo 2001). These views have been proclaimed in many political documents signed by Beijing and other developing countries.

The emphasis of China's diplomacy in the developing world has been Africa. In 2000, China initiated the first China–Africa Cooperation Forum, in which the two sides vowed to push for the establishment of a just and reasonable new international political and economic order. This forum, held every three years, functions as the primary institution cementing Sino–African ties. At the first forum in 2000, China exempted a total of ¥10.5 billion of debt for thirty-one least developed African countries. China also helped train thousands of professionals in African countries in recent years. China has also pushed for more institutionalized cooperation with many countries in Latin America. China engages in regular dialogues with the Rio Group at the foreign minister level. In 1997, China held the first dialogue with the South American Common Market, which was subsequently formalized as regular exchanges and consultations.

China and the developing countries have lent support to each other in fighting Western intervention in such matters as human rights abuse. China, as a permanent member of the U.N. Security Council, has effectively blocked any serious measures to address the massive human rights violations in Darfur in Sudan.

Unlike Western powers and the many international financial institutions under their influence, Beijing does not attach any political strings to its aid programs to developing countries, which cater to many authoritarian leaders in the African continent. In recent years, China's influence in Africa has expanded to such an extent that many African leaders publicly call China their "number one friend" (Eisenman and Kurlantzick 2006).

Beijing's Resolve to Defend Its Sovereignty over Taiwan

China has adamantly insisted that Taiwan has always been and continues to be part of China. The only reason Beijing has not been able to extend its rule over the island since the end of the Chinese civil war in 1949, it maintains, is because of American intervention. As far as Chinese leaders and analysts are concerned, the United States still harbors an insidious desire to use Taiwan to contain or weaken China, and they believe that to that end, Washington has sought to maintain the status quo of "no unification, no independence" and "no war, no peace" across the Taiwan Strait (Sheng 2001, 62). Beijing clearly knows that it still lacks the capability to coerce Taiwan into submission, and it does not expect the United States to help it facilitate a smooth reunification with Taiwan. China's primary goal for the moment is to prevent Washington from moving away from the "one China" policy and to deter Taiwan independence. Despite strong U.S. signals that it will militarily protect Taiwan, Beijing has unequivocally proclaimed that it is prepared to use force if Taiwan declares independence, a position underpinned by the Anti-Secession Law that was passed in 2005 even though the United States expressed its displeasure over the legislation and warned China against passing it. In fact, the modernization of the People's Liberation Army (PLA) has been principally geared toward the contingency of Taiwan independence.

The Chinese government's hard-line position is perhaps an inevitable response to public sentiment, which regards the Taiwan issue as the last vestige of China's century of humiliation at the hands of Western powers. It has been asserted that the "highest degree of consensus" exists among Chinese of all walks of life on Taiwan, and the Chinese people would support their leaders "to do anything necessary to protect the most fundamental national interests" (Chu 1996). According to a poll conducted in December 1995, during the Taiwan Strait crisis, as many as 95 percent of the Chinese public endorsed the means by which their government sought to ensure a strong national defense (Yang, Chen, and Scheb 1997). China's resolve to defend its sovereignty over Taiwan was well illustrated in the crisis of 1995 and 1996.

The crisis, as Beijing has argued, was largely precipitated by Washington's measures to upgrade its relations with Taiwan. In the early 1990s, then–Chinese president Yang Shangkun reportedly warned unequivocally that foreign forces were instigating Taiwan independence and "whoever plays with fire will perish with fire" (*Renmin Ribao* [People's Daily] 1991). In late 1992, when President George Bush announced that the United States planned to sell 150 F-16 jet fighters to Taiwan, Chinese military leaders criticized the civilian leaders' moderate policy on Taiwan and urged them to take a more hawkish stance against advocates of Taiwan independence and American intervention (Garver 1997, 58). In 1994, President Clinton announced that the White House would allow official meetings between more senior officials of the United States and Taiwan, support Taiwan's accession to some international bodies, and permit Taiwan to change the name of its U.S. office from the Coordination Council for North American Affairs to the Taipei Economic and Cultural Representative Office. These steps to upgrade relations with Taiwan resulted in more interactions between senior U.S. and Taiwanese officials (Sheng 2001, 65).

In May 1995, under pressure from the Congress, the White House decided to grant Taiwanese leader Lee Teng-hui a visa to allow him to pay a "private" visit to Cornell University, his alma mater, where he ebulliently touted "the Republic of China on Taiwan." Chinese leaders became furious over this decision, particularly given the fact that the U.S. secretary of state, Warren Christopher, had assured his Chinese counterpart, Qian Qichen, that Washington would not grant such a visa to Lee. Beijing interpreted Lee's visit to the United States as a reflection both of U.S. support for an independent Taiwan and of the Taiwanese leaders' push for de jure independence (Saunders 2000). Coupled with Taiwan's various moves to expand its diplomatic space, conducting, for instance, "vacation diplomacy," "pragmatic diplomacy," and "substantive diplomacy," Beijing realized that if the trend were not curbed, it could well lead to a Taiwan–U.S. conspiracy to push for formal independence (Nathan and Ross 1997, 221).

Lee's visit served as a catalyst for Beijing to unleash its anger with a vengeance. At the same time that it rhetorically bashed Washington and Taipei for these provocative actions, Beijing lodged a formal protest with the U.S. government, recalled its ambassador to the United States, suspended various high-level official visits, and postponed talks on nonproliferation issues with Washington. A number of U.S. companies lost multimillion-dollar business contracts in China to their European counterparts (Sheng 2001, 27).

Soon after Lee Teng-hui concluded his U.S. trip, the PLA conducted a series of military exercises and missile tests in the Taiwan Strait. In late July 1995, the PLA launched six missiles to an area only 50 kilometers from Pengchia Yu Island, which is under Taiwan control and about 150 kilometers north of Taipei. In August, the PLA launched a second round of missiles and artillery in a sea area 136 kilometers north of Taiwan. In October, the PLA conducted military exercises, which involved the air and marine forces in the East China Sea. In November, the PLA conducted an amphibious exercise in the Taiwan Strait, displaying some of its most advanced weapons. In March 1996, Beijing again launched three even larger rounds of missiles and engaged in more military games in the Taiwan Strait. According to some estimates, as many as 40 naval vessels, 260 aircraft, and 150,000 troops took part in all these exercises (Scobell 2003, 177).

These military moves were designed to serve several purposes, principal among them being to signal Beijing's anger over Lee Teng-hui's visit to the United States, to influence Taiwan's March 1996 presidential election, and generally to deter Taiwan from moving toward independence. During the lead-up to the military actions in the Taiwan Strait, the Chinese government conveyed a series of messages to Washington. According to former U.S. assistant secretary of defense Chas Freeman, Chinese government officials told him that China would be willing to sacrifice "millions of men" and "entire cities" to ensure China's territorial integrity. Freeman even suggested that China might be prepared to use nuclear blackmail to forestall U.S. attempts to frustrate PLA moves to safeguard China's national unity (Tyler 1996). Despite the fact that the United States sent two aircraft carriers near the Taiwan Strait to monitor the military exercises, Beijing believed that it had succeeded in sending a clear message to Washington: China was prepared to go to war, even if the United States intervened, to prevent Taiwan from achieving de jure independence from China (Lampton 1997).

China's brinksmanship made it clear that a move toward independence on the part of Taiwan would trigger a war that would involve all three parties and in which none could possibly claim victory regardless of the result of the conflict. After the 1995–96 military exercises and missile firings, many pro-independence politicians in Taiwan, particularly members of the Democratic People's Party (DPP) leadership, began to reconsider their policy and moderate their position (Goldstein 1999, 76). By demonstrating its resolve to use force, Beijing also convinced U.S. decision makers that both countries had good reason to reign in Taiwan's push for independence.

In the aftermath of the crisis, the United States began to readjust its rhetoric and policy toward Taiwan. Many high-level U.S. officials of the Clinton administration, including Secretary of State Warren Christopher, while meeting their Chinese counterparts, noted that the United States fully understood "the seriousness and sensitivity" of visits by Taiwanese leaders to the United States. They also reaffirmed that the United States was committed to the "one China" policy and would put more restrictions on visits to the United States by senior Taiwanese officials (Sheng 2001, 75–77). In a private letter from Clinton to Jiang, the U.S. administration reassured Beijing that it would "oppose or resist efforts by Taiwan to gain independence; would not support the creation of 'two Chinas' or one

China and one separate Taiwan; and would not support Taiwan's admission to the United Nations." This represents the "three no's" policy pronounced for the first time by a U.S. administration (Mann 1999, 330). U.S. reassurance culminated during Clinton's visit to China in 1998, when he publicly announced the "three no's" policy. Ever since, Washington has repeatedly propounded its opposition to Taiwan independence.

In March 2000, Chen Shui-bian, the leader of the pro-independence DPP, won the presidential election. Under pressure from Beijing and Washington, Chen made the "four no's" pledge, stating that provided that the People's Republic of China (PRC) did not attack Taiwan, his administration would not declare Taiwan independence, would not change Taiwan's name from "the Republic of China," would not include the doctrine of special state-to-state relations in the new constitution, and would not promote a referendum on unification or independence.

More recently, in an effort to divert attention from public calls for the president's deposal and to arouse patriotic sentiment among his supporters, the scandal-ridden Chen regime has on several occasions suggested that the Constitution be amended to reflect the status quo of territorial areas under Taiwan's control and that Taiwan seek U.N. membership under the name of "Taiwan." President Chen has also asserted that "Taiwan and China were two separate countries" (Ko 2006). China, as expected, severely denounced Chen's remarks. The United States also sent clear warnings to the Taiwanese leader. A U.S. State Department spokesman repeatedly criticized Chen's remarks, saying that the United States does not support Taiwan independence and opposes unilateral changes to the status quo. The U.S. response was believed to be linked to its hope that China would cooperate on more critical issues, such as the North Korea and Iranian nuclear programs (BBC Monitoring 2006).

Human Rights in Sino–U.S. Relations and China's Strategies

The forceful suppression of the Tiananmen demonstration in 1989 triggered a battle over human rights between China and the United States. International scrutiny of China's human rights became perhaps the most sensitive issue for the ruling elite in Beijing, given the sagging political legitimacy of the CCP government in the reform era. Losing the battle on human rights would entail profound political consequences in the domestic arena. It is thus no wonder that Beijing has fought tenaciously against Washington and its allies to effectively fend off external assaults on China's human rights record. In order to prevail over the United States, Beijing has employed all kinds of tactics, including rhetorically confronting U.S. accusations, splitting the U.S.-led alliance, taking advantage of the U.S. pluralist political system, and consolidating supporters in the third world.

Rebuttal of U.S. Accusations

In the face of strong international pressures on human rights, the Chinese government decided to counter the Western monopoly on human rights discourse. Beijing has vehemently attacked the notion of universality of human rights as advocated by the West. Beijing has firmly maintained that human rights is originally a Western concept and concerns issues that are purely domestic in nature; thus no country should violate the principle of state sovereignty by interfering in other countries' human rights situation. China contends that the treatment of human rights in any country has to be linked to its history, culture, and socioeconomic conditions. Collective rights, such as the well-being of the nation, should take precedence over individual rights. Economic and social rights — for instance, the rights to subsistence and development — are more important than civil and political rights. Beijing has published eight *White Papers* on China's progress in human rights, all of which essentially argue that the improvement in the living standard of the people attests to progress in human rights.

While defending its own rights practice, Beijing also lashed out at the U.S. human rights record. Using different standards (the level of racial and gender equality and of poverty and the number of social crimes), China claimed that its human rights record actually surpassed that of the United States (Xinhua News Agency 1998). Beijing has also published several *White Papers* on human rights in the United States, charging that the U.S. government is responsible for gross domestic violations of human rights, such as failing to guarantee personal safety and political rights and permitting impoverishment, judicial discrimination, social discrimination against ethnic minorities, women, children, and the elderly. Beijing has further noted that the United States treats civilians in other countries violently (Xinhua News Agency 2004).

China also accused the United States of practicing double standards on human rights in the world. Beijing charged that Western criticism of China's human rights is a political tool the West uses to humiliate and weaken the Chinese nation, not a reproach intended to improve its human rights. The Chinese press, under government control, persistently associates U.S. pressure with respect to human rights with the Chinese experience of a "century of humiliation," making the analogy that recent U.S. attacks on the Chinese for violations of human rights is tantamount to earlier Western imperialist aggression against China. This strategy has proved effective and has contributed to surging nationalism in China over the past decade, which has significantly weakened U.S. ideological influence in China. It has been effective largely because "though most Chinese citizens believe there is much to be done to improve their country's human rights, they also agree that it is not the business of the United States or other Western countries to interfere" (Zhou 2005). Beijing's attacks run like this: "The essence of U.S. 'human rights diplomacy' is the pursuit of power politics with the goal of maintaining its dominant role in the world. This has a long history . . . and in this new historical era America still harbors hegemonic ambitions. Under the cloak of 'human rights defender' and the pretext of safeguarding human rights, the United States has run roughshod, bullying the small and the weak with its strength and suppressing the poor with its wealth" (Seymour 1998, 221–22).

Splitting the U.S.-Led Alliance

The United States went to great lengths to construct an international alliance to impose sanctions on China in the aftermath of Tiananmen. To counter the U.S. efforts and sabotage the U.S.-led coalition, the Chinese government has successfully used its traditional strategies of "divide and rule" and "stick and carrot." Soon after Tiananmen, China, in an attempt to gain more international friends, established or normalized diplomatic relations with a number of countries that were not critical of its human rights record, including Singapore, Indonesia, Brunei, Israel, South Korea, and Saudi Arabia.

China also worked on some members of the U.S.-led Western alliance directly. China chose Japan as its first target, when Beijing discerned subtle differences between Tokyo and Washington on the question of sanctions to be imposed on China. The intensification of Beijing's diplomatic activities in Tokyo proved to be effective. By mid-1990, the relationship between China and Japan had already been repaired; high-level visits and meetings were resumed and yen loans were provided. China then worked on the European Community (EC). Beijing effectively used business diplomacy as both a threat and a lure to undermine the Washington–European alliance. For instance, in 1997, at the annual meeting of the U.N. Commission on Human Rights (UNCHR), Denmark introduced a mildly worded resolution concerning political freedom in China. Soon after, the Chinese foreign ministry spokesman declared: "If Denmark insists on doing this, it will end up the biggest loser" (Seymour 1998, 231). The Chinese warning resulted in fewer supporters for the resolution. A Danish businessman confessed: "What happens is that our Chinese trading partners get orders to stop trading with us, and so refrain from handing in new orders[;] . . . no company engaged in China is in any doubt that the political conditions affect trade" (Seymour 1998, 228).

The economic card was perhaps more astutely played by China against France and Germany. In June 1992 China sent its biggest buying delegation ever to Europe, ostensibly with Germany as its particular target. Chancellor Helmut Kohl then led a huge business team to China in November 1993 and signed contracts worth DM7 billion. Japan, fearing a loss of business to other Western countries, was quick to respond, awarding China with more bilateral financial aid and an unprecedented visit by the emperor. The French government also made efforts to regain its share of the Chinese market. Following a political visit by the French foreign minister in April 1994, the French minister of foreign trade, accompanied by some 125 business people, visited China and signed trade agreements worth $2.5 billion.

These were not purely business activities, as then–Chinese premier Li Peng bluntly observed: "If the Europeans adopt more cooperation with China in all areas, not just in economic areas but also in political and other areas, I believe the Europeans can get more orders from China" (Lampton 2001, 112). Toward the end of the 1990s, individual states within the EC began to break away from the practice of coordinating their actions. In recent years, few European countries were even willing to cosponsor draft resolutions on China's human rights in the UNCHR.

Linking Human Rights with Other Issues

Beijing understands that, as a major power, it is an indispensable actor in international politics. Thus, it has tried to squeeze concessions from Washington with respect to human rights in return for its cooperation on other international issues. A good example is the first Gulf War. A little over one year after Tiananmen, the Bush administration lifted the sanctions that had prohibited high-level official contacts with China because it needed China's cooperation in the U.N. Security Council, from which it was seeking authorization to use force to evict the Iraqi invaders from Kuwait (Tucker 2001, 453).

Another incident was the unsuccessful attempt of the United States during the first Clinton administration to use China's MFN status as a political weapon to pressure Beijing on human rights. The first term Clinton administration adopted a very harsh policy on China's human rights, hoping thereby to induce a peaceful evolution in China from communism to democracy. In May 1993, President Clinton issued an executive order, which conditionally offered China MFN trade status for another year but demanded that China show "overall, significant progress" in several areas concerning human rights in order to secure renewal of its MFN status in 1994 (U.S. White House 1993).

Beijing saw the U.S. executive order as a political ultimatum and criticized it as the "hegemonic conduct of a self-styled 'world cop' who tramples upon international law and norms of international relations" (Qian 1993). Instead of working to comply with U.S. demands, Beijing successfully engaged in business diplomacy, targeting U.S. business officials and the business community. In discussions and dealings with U.S. officials and business leaders, Chinese officials persistently stressed the potential market in China. "China will soon be one of the biggest buyers of aircraft[;] . . . there will be rich opportunities for cooperation in the field of oil and natural gas exploration[.] . . . [The] automobile market [is] growing rapidly" and a "huge telecommunications market [is] ripe for exploitation. . . . If you . . . come into the market too late, it will be occupied by others. The Chinese market is a big cake. Come early and you get a big piece" (Foot 2000, 162–23). Chinese officials told their American counterparts straightforwardly that many U.S. allies, including France, Germany, and Canada, were getting contracts from China and "had pulled the rug from under Washington's policy" (Foot 2000, 163).

In early 1994, as the deadline to make a new decision regarding China's MFN status drew close, debates abounded within the Clinton administration as well as among various American interest groups. The business community, sensing the danger of revoking China's MFN status, was "very vociferous" in lobbying the Clinton administration to lift all conditions (Tucker 2001, 460). It also worked on members of Congress, on think tanks, on the media, and on activists at the grassroots level (Sutter 1995, 57–59). The federal economic agencies, reflecting the business community's interests, tried to reverse the administration's policy course. In the words of Assistant Secretary of State Winton Lord, these agencies were actually "attacking the president's own policy" (Tucker 2001, 460).

In March 1994, Secretary of State Christopher visited China to remind the Chinese leaders of the "urgent need" to make further progress on "how the Chinese government treats its people" (Christopher 1994). The Chinese leaders gave Christopher a cold reception and accused the United States of meddling in China's domestic affairs. Chinese premier Li Peng told Christopher bluntly that China would never accept the American concept of human rights, adding, "you've got racism and human rights problems in the United States. . . . So don't come over here and talk to us about our human rights problems" (Mann 1999, 301–2). The Pentagon also became unhappy with Clinton's hard approach to China. It argued that a more accommodating attitude toward Beijing could help solve the North Korean nuclear situation, which was becoming increasingly dangerous in 1993. Also, Pentagon officials believed that talking to their counterparts in the PLA, instead of isolating them, would better serve American strategic interests because they would have a chance that way to learn what the PLA's intentions were.

Obviously, by early 1994, China had done very little to fulfill the criteria as specified in Clinton's executive order. Nevertheless, on May 26, 1994, Clinton announced the unconditional renewal of MFN trading status for China, even though he admitted that China had not made "overall significant progress" in the areas outlined in the executive order. The administration conceded that linking the conferral of MFN trading status to progress in human rights was no longer constructive: "We have reached the end of the usefulness of that policy, and it is time to take a new path toward the achievement of our constant objectives. We need to place our relationship into a larger and more productive framework" (Foot 2000, 165). Beijing concluded that the victory over Clinton's attempt to link trade status to human rights demonstrated the validity of standing firm against U.S. pressures.

Establishing a United Front with the Developing World

In order to address U.S. censure of China's human rights in multilateral settings, China has worked hard to consolidate its ties with the developing world. The developing countries have played a crucial role in assisting Beijing defeat the U.S. assault on China's human rights record in the UNCHR.

China has worked to construct a set of views on human rights among the developing world to oppose those of the United States. For instance, prior to the U.N. Conference on Human Rights in Geneva in 1993, China took great pains to try to influence and manage the Asian regional meeting in Bangkok and thereby soften its outcome. Together with Malaysia, China succeeded in persuading other Asian countries to call for a weakening of the U.N.'s role in human rights. The final document of the meeting took a cultural relativist view on human rights and argued that economic development was a prerequisite to their realization. It also stated that "there should be no interference in any country's internal affairs, and the United Nations should not condemn individual countries' human rights record" (Seymour 1998, 229).

China has also taken advantage of its influential position in the United Nations to weaken the role of the UNCHR by shrinking its already inadequate budget and streamlining the commission's Human Rights Center. To defeat the almost annual U.S. attempt to censure China's human rights record in the commission, China has aggressively lobbied many developing countries. In addition to providing material inducements, Beijing constantly cautions developing countries that "What is happening to China today will happen to any other developing country tomorrow" (Crossette 1996). For many years, Beijing appealed to leaders of the developing world by arguing that the U.S. practice of hegemonism and imperialism was the worst violation of human rights. China's strategy was effective. For instance, at the fifty-seventh meeting of the UNCHR, twenty-two among the twenty-three countries who supported China were developing nations from Asia, Latin America, and Africa.

President George W. Bush, on entering the White House, pledged to adopt a harsher stance on China's human rights, particularly with respect to religious freedom. However, when the United States sponsored a draft resolution to censure China at the UNCHR in 2001, the Bush administration found itself increasingly isolated. It elicited no support from European nations; consequently, China again succeeded in avoiding the debate on its human rights record (Roberts 2003, 631). In 2002, the Bush administration was unable to table a resolution on China because the United States had lost its seat at the commission in the previous year. In 2003, Washington decided not to sponsor a resolution against China, because it needed Chinese cooperation on Iraq, North Korea, and the war on terrorism (Foot 2003). With the backing of the developing world, China has easily defeated all eleven U.S. initiatives at the UNCHR.

Conclusions

China's overall response to U.S. challenges has been reactive and defensive in nature, although one could also argue that there are certain elements of Chinese assertiveness. China has tenaciously defended its core interests — it has guarded itself against a possible U.S. encirclement, curbed Taiwan independence, and fended off U.S. scrutiny of its human rights record. A working Sino–U.S. relationship, fraught with suspicion and friction, has been maintained because of Beijing's willingness to compromise and Washington's need for Beijing's cooperation on a wide range of issues as well as because of Beijing's successful rebuff of U.S. attempts to undermine its core interests.

Beijing's charm offensive has been successful in defusing the "China threat" argument, in building political trust with its neighbors, and in strengthening economic ties in the region. More importantly, it has enabled China to shape a more favorable strategic environment, which will help it to sabotage any possible U.S. attempt to constrain it. Washington could do little about the charm offensive, aimed at winning hearts and minds in the neighboring regions. On the Taiwan issue, China will continue to maintain its hard-line policy and take drastic measures, if necessary, to safeguard its claim of sovereignty over the island. On human rights, Beijing will use all resources available and employ a wide variety of tactics to prevail over Washington.

China's ability to defend its core interests clearly demonstrates the limitations of American power, particularly the impracticability of a coercive China policy as advocated by neocons, members of the so-called blue team in Congress, and some segments of the military establishment. China is too big and too important to be ignored or mistreated. China's large and growing economy, likely to be second only to that of the United States sometime soon, plays an increasingly important role in the well-being of people around the globe. As a permanent member of the U.N. Security Council and a major player in international politics, China is also indispensable on issues concerning world peace and security. Washington needs Chinese support on a whole range of issues, from the North Korean nuclear crisis to peace in the Middle East to the realization of a stable and growing world economy. Resolution or management of these issues and other challenges besetting the peoples and states of the globe will increasingly depend on great-power cooperation between Beijing and Washington.

CHAPTER FOUR

Northeast Asia: South and North Korea and Japan

Davis B. Bobrow

Japan and the two Koreas are part of a security complex whose other members are the United States, Russia, and China. In matters of security, these states grant at least as much importance to external actors other than the United States as to the United States. U.S. policies matter for their direct effects and as they affect the others in the complex and the relationships among them. The security policies of Northeast Asia are influenced by constructed histories of themselves, the other states in the complex, and U.S. geopolitical inclinations (Cumings 1997, 2003; Hughes 2004, 2005; Oberdorfer 2001; Pollack 2005).[1] Each state's policies contain at least potentially contradictory themes, and each uses ambiguity to make those themes synergistic.

Bush II policies most relevant to security policy makers in Northeast Asia deal with the Democratic People's Republic of North Korea (DPRK) as a member of the "axis of evil" and a nuclear proliferator; missile defense; military modernization as well as changes in U.S. force deployments in the Republic of South Korea (ROK) and Japan; and China as a future "peer competitor" and claimant to Taiwan. Other aspects of U.S. policy matter to the extent that they provide or take away from the two Koreas and Japan opportunities and capabilities to influence U.S. policies bearing directly on the Northeast Asian "neighborhood." American military primacy and U.S. interest in the Revolution in Military Affairs (RMA) were recognized well before the Bush II period, and Northeast Asian adaptations to them largely continue policy lines underway before it. The states differ in emphasizing, since the cold war, the reactive (Japan) or initiative-taking (DPRK) "faces" of their security policies, with the ROK transitioning to initiative taking.

In the last two decades, regional changes have posed greater challenges to Japan and the two Koreas than shifts in U.S. military policy or the collapse of bipolarity. These developments include China's rise economically, its emergence as a major actor in international politics, and its ongoing military modernization and the DPRK's nuclear weapons status and missile capabilities (as exemplified by its tests of each in the second half of 2006). In Japan these changes involved the economic torpor that began in the early 1990s and the death, for political purposes, of the antimilitary Japan Socialist Party (JSP), which had been wary of blanket followership of the United States and had taken a relatively favorable view of the DPRK. In South Korea key developments included profound democratization and political elite replacement and the traumas of and recovery from the 1997–98 Asian financial crisis. In North Korea they involved grave economic difficulties and the loss of Russian support as well as falling far behind the ROK in national power and well-being. In Japan and South Korea, the generation inclined to "appreciate" the U.S. provision of security protection has increasingly been succeeded by one more inclined to claim nationalist prerogatives. Non-U.S. members of the security complex, other than the DPRK, have become more involved in emerging regional institutions that America does not control and in some cases does not even belong to (the Asian Political Economic Community [APEC], the Asian Regional Forum [ARF], the Asia-10, and the Shanghai Cooperation Organization [SCO]).

Japan

Japan's security posture has not and does not conform to traditional Western notions of pacifism — that is, no capacity to use force and a rejection of the benefits that come from others displaying or using force on its behalf. Its Peace Constitution's article 9 ("land, sea, and air forces, as well as other war potential, will never be maintained. The right of belligerency of the state will not be recognized") has been subordinated to the right of self-defense in U.N. Charter article 51. Japan in recent decades has one of the world's largest military budgets.

Japan's policy has tried to harmonize several elements. The first is its reliance on the United States for military protection (the U.S.–Japan Security Treaty). In exchange for that protection, Japan grants the United States basing rights, facilitates logistics provision, and agrees to comply with U.S. policy. It hopes thereby to induce the United States to treat it as its key Asian security partner. The second is constraints on its military capabilities (force projection, nonnuclear principles, and, in more recent decades, military budgets at 1 percent of GNP) and on the use of those capabilities (rules of engagement in homeland defense and overseas deployments). The third is an evolving military techno-industrial base enabling Japan to assume a more "normal" major power military posture if and when that seems necessary (Samuels 1994).

The constraints, which derive from Japanese legal and political conventions, forestall some military activities the United States might request. They were supported by public negativism about the military and the use of force, by the desire for good relationships with Asians sensitive to historical Japanese imperialism, and by the conviction that others in Northeast Asia posed no immediate military threat to Japan. The techno-industrial base has grown as a result of military indus-trial cooperation with America, government subsidies, administrative guidance to be at the cutting edge of major military technologies, and the development of civil capabilities convertible to military use (dual-use technologies, flexible pro-duction lines, and the full nuclear fuel cycle).

Japan has sought via these three emphases to avoid both security abandonment by Washington and unwarranted entanglement in its military ventures (Tsuchi-yama 2004). There had long been tension between those who supported a mili-tary posture that made Japan appealing to the United States as a key security contributor and those who supported self-imposed limitations on military capa-bilities and their use. This tension was managed by there being a balance be-tween "normal great power" advocates in the almost continuously ruling Liberal Democratic Party (LDP), on the one hand, and, on the other, the JSP and some smaller parties as well as opponents within the LDP. The balance allowed Japan's government to tolerate U.S. practices violating declared policy limits on use of bases in Japan, reinterpret but not revoke article 9, and preserve independent command and control of its military forces (the Self-Defense Forces [SDF]).

External and domestic challenges in the 1990s eventually led to relaxation, but not elimination, of some self-imposed constraints. After U.S. criticism of Ja-pan's military abstention from the Gulf War, a political consensus emerged that Japan would be harmed if it contributed only money to distant security matters but not "sweat" and "blood." Perceptions of an imminent direct threat rose from the DPRK's development of nuclear and missile programs (evidence of which was made apparent by the 1993–94 crisis and the 1998 incident in which North Korea launched a missile eastward over the home islands). A rising China was seen as posing a future threat. There also were signs of possible shifts in U.S. policy that would advantage China over Japan (President Clinton's reference to China as a "strategic partner"). Yet, notable elements in the U.S. security es-tablishment signaled that such a shift in U.S. policy could be avoided if Japan were to become more of a military contributor, that is, loosen some self-imposed military constraints and provide more support for U.S. military options (the 1995 U.S. Department of Defense "Nye Report"). Domestically, the LDP searched for a way to compensate for poor national economic performance, and the JSP dropped much of its opposition to the U.S.–Japan alliance system before fading away.

The effects of these external stimuli and domestic developments were visible before 2000. New legislation allowed for limited SDF foreign deployments in

U.N.-peacekeeping operations (UNPKO) (the International Peace Cooperation Law of 1992). The 1994 Higuchi Report (Advisory Group on Defense Issues 1994) emphasized possible conflicts in Asia and called for operational strengthening of the U.S.–Japan alliance, greater participation in UNPKOs, more defense industrial cooperation with the United States, and the acquisition of advanced national intelligence capabilities. The 1995 revision of the National Defense Program Outline vaguely expanded the space for possible Japanese military cooperation with the United States to much of the Asia-Pacific and oil transit routes, as did the 1996 U.S.–Japan Joint Declaration and the partially implemented revision of the Japan–U.S. Guidelines for Defense Cooperation the Diet approved in 1999. The 1990s also saw continued explorations of joint missile defense R&D that eventually focused on interceptor technologies (Drohan 1999; Japan Defense Agency 2005, 457–65, 493–500, 504–5).

Japan had thus embarked on an incremental but substantially circumscribed course of "locking in" the U.S. alliance and becoming a more normal military major power, a course abetted by the DPRK's development of a nuclear weapons program. Japan established boundaries by making hedged and vague declaratory policy commitments, by imposing budget limitations, and by severely limiting the ability of the head of government to initiate military operations. Also, the concrete steps that Japan actually took could mostly serve as well for autonomous defense and were accompanied by significant increases in direct participation in security activities with other Asian governments.

Tokyo's preferred presidential candidate won America's 2000 and 2004 elections.[2] In late 2000, the Armitage–Nye report emphasized that Japan was the central pillar of America's Asian security posture and criticized the LDP for sluggishness in stepping up to that military role (IINS 2000).[3] Japan's policy makers viewed the report as signaling what the United States wanted from Japan on military matters, revealing a new U.S. administration that would be less likely to push Japan on economic issues, more supportive of Taiwan, suspicious of China as a rising "peer competitor", and hostile to the DPRK. U.S.–China policy frictions could help Japan remain "the keystone of U.S. involvement in Asia" and "central to America's global strategy" (Przystup 2005, 4). The Bush II administration offered Japan opportunities to bolster the first and third fundamental components of its security policy. Seizing those opportunities would require a domestically acceptable relaxation of the self-imposed restraints component.

The story of Japanese early twenty-first-century security policy features nontrivial incremental relaxations as well as restraints that are still in place, explicit justifications as to why it is necessary to maintain the alliance with the United States, and less explicit ones for the building of a national defense posture to deal independently if necessary with threats from Northeast Asia. The focus of the

Bush II administration on the relaxations and the explicit alliance justifications aided Prime Minister Koizumi in presenting himself at home and abroad as a superbly appreciated, responsive ally of the United States (especially on Iraq).[4] Just as the Japanese government hoped and Armitage–Nye proposed, many governing U.S. elites have come to view Japan as the "U.K. of Asia."

Relaxed constraints grant stronger emergency powers to the prime minister and cabinet to employ the SDF, to use force against military penetrations of areas close to Japan, and to extract cooperation from other Japanese institutions and from civilians. The role the SDF is permitted to play in UNPKOs has been enlarged, as has the role it can play in overseas deployments undertaken in the context of "U.S.-led coalitions" with or without a clear U.N. mandate. The Anti-Terrorism Special Measures Law enabled dispatch to the Indian Ocean to support U.S. actions in Afghanistan and the Law Concerning Special Measure on Humanitarian and Reconstruction Assistance for Iraq has allowed for SDF deployment there (Japan Defense Agency 2005, 509–14, 524–30, 535–37). More generally, the role of the Defense Agency and military personnel in security policy, which had been tightly limited, substantially expanded.

National missile defense (NMD) deployment received cabinet approval in late 2003. Military threats from the DPRK and China became a major explicit subject of the 2005 Defense White Paper. In fall 2004, the Araki Report (Prime Minister's Council on Security and Defense Capabilities 2004) called for heightened military efforts to prevent direct threats to Japan and for cooperation with others outside Japan's territories. It strongly advocated the development of ballistic missile defense, reorienting the Ground Self-Defense Force (GSDF) toward international peacekeeping operations, and further relaxation of the arms export ban. In a more qualified fashion, it proposed considering the acquisition of weapons to destroy DPRK missile capabilities preemptively, thus opening up the possibility that current policy, which authorizes the use of force only to destroy weapons "flying toward Japan, within the territory of Japan, or in the air above the high sea" (Japan Defense Agency 2005, 567), might be changed.[5] Revised National Defense Program Guidelines and a new Mid-Term Defense Plan (for 2005 to 2009) emphasized for the first time the need to acquire force projection and expeditionary capacity equipment (Japan Defense Agency 2005, 451–57, 465–71). In July 2005 accelerated NMD deployment was announced. In late 2005 Japan agreed to jointly develop a new interceptor missile with the United States (and pay one-third of the cost) and in mid-2006 to accelerate PAC-3 deployments to protect U.S. military bases. These and other specific activities, such as its participation in the anti-DPRK Proliferation Security Initiative (PSI) and its embrace of U.S.-style RMA, suggest an intensified and more operational commitment to joint military action with the United States and its allies over a wider geographic space. Bush II officials have welcomed most of these developments, regarding them as strengthening the U.S.–Japan alliance (U.S. Department of State, Security Consultative Committee 2005). Their response to DPRK nuclear weapons testing has been to further emphasize deterrence umbrella commitments to a Japan that is at least as zealous as Washington about imposing sanctions on Pyongyang (unlike other members of the Northeast Asia security complex).

Yet there are other "faces" to recent developments. First, most of them enhance Japan's policy latitude and military capabilities, allowing for an independent, unapologetic security posture. They have been accompanied by domestic practices indicative of greater nationalism and less military self-doubt (e.g., prime ministerial visits to the Yasukuni shrine honoring Japan's war dead and a new war museum there, school textbook revision, and a push for nationalist practices in school ceremonies through "love thy country" legislation).[6] Such "standing tall" also marks Tokyo's drive for permanent membership in the U.N. Security Council and a political push for revising article 9 (*Osamu* 2005). Koizumi successor Shinzo Abe, since succeeded by Yasuo Fakuda, was an outspoken advocate of national pride and military normalization. Important LDP members have even claimed (2002) that the unrevised Constitution does not prohibit Japan from acquiring nuclear weapons. Shortly after the 2006 DPRK nuclear test, important LDP officials called for a national debate on Japan becoming a nuclear weapons state. There also remains considerable ambiguity about Japanese delegation of launch authority to the U.S in planned BMD, and the interdependence of the U.S. and Japanese systems gives Japan, as well as the United States, substantial leverage.[7]

Second, many "normalization" steps are carefully limited. When it deployed troops to Iraq, Japan emphasized that its forces would avoid combat: "Japan will not engage itself in maintaining security. Security enforcement is inseparable from use of military force. Instead, we will . . . combine our economic and technical prowess and dispatch troops for economic reconstruction operations" (Karasaki 2004). Japanese conditions have been that other coalition nations provide force protection for the SDF unit and that it remains under only Japanese command. The general geographical space in which Japan is committed to joint operations with America remains ambiguous and conditional on less than clear situational specifics.[8] Japan has only minimally relaxed its arms export ban; it sells weapons to the United States (or to multinational coalitions in which the United States is involved) and sells equipment for counterterrorism and antipiracy operations (*International Herald Tribune–Asahi Shimbun* 2004). Prime Minister Abe, only a few days after the 2006 DPRK nuclear test, bluntly rejected Japanese entry into the club of nuclear-armed states.

Third, if the Ministry of Finance has its way, budgetary constraints will be put in place making it doubtful that Japan will acquire a robust BMD capability or quickly transform its military.[9] The 2005 defense budget in yen terms was the smallest since 1996 and its share of the General Account budget was the smallest since 2000. Acquisition spending was down from its 1999 peak, and R&D spending went back to its 2001 level (Japan Defense Agency 2005, 484–86).

Fourth, military matters may be subordinated to broader foreign policy preferences. The Koizumi administration took independent normalization initiatives toward the DPRK (Rozman 2002) and did not favor a hard line on Iran (Hiroshi 2005). Newly in office, Prime Minister Abe put nationalist rhetoric aside and chose to give priority to potentially tension-easing summit meetings with his Chinese and South Korean counterparts rather than to a meeting with President Bush. Energy supply imperatives associated with offshore sea zone claims have led to a high level of tension with China and have also been an issue with South Korea (J. Lee 2006).[10] U.S. security officials saw these concerns as merely unwelcome distractions and did not accord them the significance Japanese officials did. Further, some Japanese officials have been disappointed with the at most lukewarm U.S. support for Tokyo's highly desired U.N. Security Council seat and resent Chinese and South Korean opposition to its being given the seat.[11]

Finally, Japan's domestic politics do not permit it to simply conform to the Armitage–Nye and Araki visions, except perhaps with respect to the DPRK. Japan's business community has compelling reasons to shun tense relations with China, whose imports provided about one-third of Japan's real GDP growth by 2003. China is a major host for Japanese outward foreign direct investment (OFDI) and is viewed as the key market for future development and external sales (Hayashi 2004). Some in the business community suspect that "the United States and the West are most advantaged by any schism in Asia" and believe that "though the Japan–U.S. alliance is important to Japan, the basic role that Japan should play through its diplomatic efforts is to foster a vision of 'one Asia'" and that "Japan can actively make its contribution through nonmilitary efforts" (Nakano 2004). Although Japan's defense industry has strongly favored military normalization and relaxing the arms export ban, it plays only a modest role in Japan's economy (Fukuyama and Ramsey 2003). In its early days, the Abe government has both adopted a softer tone toward China, which is welcomed by the business community, and played to domestic sentiment by advocating nationalist civic education and taking a hard line toward the DPRK.

Public opinion has shifted substantially in favor of military normalization as a result of the growing perception that the DPRK and China pose a threat.[12] For Japan's military normalizers, the DPRK is in domestic political terms an ideal enemy — ostensibly irrational, small and poor, an evil hostage taker and keeper, and untrustworthy. Yet the public also has become less enamored of American policies as they affect Japan — without favoring increased military spending. Majorities repeatedly opposed the Iraq deployment (Bobrow 2005a, 2005b). The arduous, lengthy negotiations for realigning U.S. forces based in Japan (including Okinawa), ostensibly concluded in late 2005, show that there has been no decline in citizens' resistance to military relationships with the United States that impinge on their daily lives (Talmadge 2006).

The major political parties do seem inclined to amend article 9 to remove its prohibition of the right to take part in collective defense (as opposed to self-defense). Their disagreement on how restrictive such a right should be contrasts, however, with the consensus to retain the "renunciation of war" language (*Hitoshi* 2005).

In sum, during the Bush II administration, Japan has become more valued by the United States through its revisions in its defense policy. At the same time, it has improved its ability to take an "independent if necessary" security position. Yet, as one Japanese security expert put it, Tokyo still has to maintain a balancing act that convinces Washington that militarily it is doing "the maximum possible" while convincing its public that it is doing "the minimum necessary." Japanese officials have been forthcoming in terms of declarations of intent to pursue military normalization in cooperation with the United States, but those declarations continue to be subject to protracted bilateral bargaining as well as to bargaining at home before they are, usually in a very limited and contingent way, concretely implemented. By fall 2006, Japan's security experts were preparing for U.S. policy to take on more multilateral and diplomatic emphases and possibly come under Democratic Party control. Those scenarios would make it more important for Japan to have harmonious relations with China and the ROK as a means of hedging against the erosion of a militarily based special relationship with Washington and preparing for the possibility that Washington would pay greater attention to economic frictions with the major Asian exporters and their advantageous exchange rates. Japan could have considerable confidence that those changes would be as manageable as were the similar ones that occurred when the Clinton presidency succeeded that of Bush I.

Republic of Korea

The ROK was born with the defeat of imperial Japan and survived due to U.S. willingness to fight a costly war and defend its 38th parallel frontline. Its history features threats from Japan, North Korea, China, and Russia. Not all remembered U.S. behavior provides reassurance—for example, its accepting Japanese domination of the peninsula (the Taft–Katsura agreement early in the twentieth century), its cavalier drawing of the inter-Korean border at the end of World War II, and its declaring shortly before the Korean War that the ROK lay outside its security umbrella. Owing to geography, memory, military realities, and political economy incentives, ROK security policy during and since the cold war centers on simultaneously managing relations with four more powerful states (the United States, China, Japan, and Russia) and with a hostile North Korea. That calls for avoiding destabilizing domestic dissension while mobilizing domestic and external economic resources and political legitimacy to make the ROK more than a pawn in major power relationships.

The cold war solution featured the "armistice system," authoritarian rule centered on military and security services, and state-led economic modernization. Under the armistice system, the South Korean government ceded command and control over the Korean military and over U.S. forces in Korea (USFK) to America (the combined forces command [CFC]), granted those U.S. forces near complete waivers from Korean authorities, and provided material support for U.S. Asian policies (e.g., by sending troops to Vietnam). Authoritarian rule was dominated by military officers, who controlled the Korean government and harshly suppressed domestic dissent. That sort of political system was tolerated and to some extent facilitated by the American and Japanese governments (Nakamura 2006). Modernization was accomplished through export-led growth that was supported by the United States and Japan and through the suppression of labor rights that might hinder an export-led economy or military rule. There still were occasional signs that the U.S. might be weakening its security commitment (e.g., troop cuts in the USFK during the Nixon and Carter administrations) even though the DPRK seemed uninterested in or hostile to reducing security tensions on the peninsula.

As the cold war receded, the ROK become a "tiger" in the "East Asian economic miracle," moved toward democratization by holding a direct presidential election in 1987, and exploited the 1988 Seoul Olympics to initiate its "northern strategy" that sought to normalize relations with the USSR and China in the hope of constraining and isolating the DPRK and decreasing its dependence on the United States and Japan. Until this strategy was successful, prudence would call for retaining the U.S. security umbrella even while reducing the domestic political power of those most associated with the armistice system.

In the midst of the ROK's domestic and international transformation, the North Korean nuclear crisis of 1993–94 occurred. The resulting Clinton administration Agreed Framework with the DPRK cooled the crisis but underscored the ROK's security dependence on the United States and stimulated concerns that Washington would sacrifice the ROK for American interests and make direct deals with North Korea. The sustainability of the U.S. agreement with North Korea seemed doubtful given GOP congressional opposition and continuing DPRK missile programs. The United States had blocked an independent ROK nuclear deterrent while committing to no U.S. nuclear weapons on the peninsula.[13] Finally, while the U.S.–Japan Security Treaty might curb renewed Japanese military assertion, the United States was too eager to have Japan normalize militarily and be central to regional security. Prevailing South (and indeed North) Korean views of their historical experience with Japan make them hypersensitive to any signs that the U.S. supports placing the peninsula's security future in Japan's hands.

Nevertheless, South Korean pride and confidence grew in the mid-1990s as Organization for Economic Cooperation and Development (OECD) membership conveyed international recognition of "graduation" from developing country status. Shortly thereafter, the ROK was hit by the Asian financial crisis (1997–98), a crisis worsened by a U.S.-controlled International Monetary Fund (IMF). South Korea's lessons from that crisis and portents of a U.S.-centered Western hemisphere trade bloc led it to more intensely pursue cooperation and interdependence with other Asians. Before G. W. Bush's election, the democratically elected Korean administration of exdissident Kim Dae-jung committed itself to a "Sunshine Policy" toward the DPRK under which it would attempt to incrementally reduce the level of tension and move toward integration.[14]

The ROK–U.S. relationship was, then, rich in contradictions and concerns before Bush took office (J. Kim 2004). By March 2003, South Korean policy elites found that very senior U.S. officials had a policy mindset "totally out of touch with reality" about the peninsular security situation and one that endangered the ROK. That policy — exemplified most dramatically in the 2002 "axis of evil" speech — seemed to undercut the goal of tension reduction with the DPRK. The preemptive intervention doctrine might leave the ROK out of U.S. decisions to attack North Korea.[15] The U.S. move to reduce its military presence in the ROK suggested the United States was weakening its commitment to defending the ROK. The push for Japan's military and foreign policy normalization could further nationalist and assertive policies by Tokyo. The intermittent emphasis on China as an emerging military threat could make it more difficult for the ROK to secure desired U.S.–China cooperation on the North Korean nuclear issue and have beneficial economic relationships with both China and the United States.

Meanwhile, ROK policy options were being limited by DPRK nuclear and conventional military programs capable of "carrying out massive surprise bombardment against the metropolitan [Seoul] area from its existing positions" and increased procurements of long-range artillery, multiple rocket launchers, and ballistic missiles (ROK Ministry of National Defense 2005, 41; Pollack 2005, 161). ROK policy was further constrained by recurrent incidents in which U.S. troops were seen as flagrantly abusing South Korean citizens and violating the Status of Forces Agreement (SOFA) (e.g., Joo 2005).

The ROK adaptation to regional and international developments has involved a five-part security policy portfolio under President Roh Moo-hyun to replace the armistice system with a peace and prosperity system.[16] That portfolio tries to balance risks of abandonment and entanglement, encourage nationalism and internationalism, and mix an optimistic forecast of ROK international stature with a cautionary recognition of vulnerability. Striking an appropriate balance among the various elements has led to clashing foreign interpretations of ROK policy intentions and ongoing disputes in ROK policy and political party circles. Nevertheless, the overarching aspiration clearly is for the ROK to become an Asian "balancer" (President Roh's term) between the states in the Northeast Asian security complex. From a South Korean perspective, the portfolio was clearly sustainable until the 2006 DPRK nuclear test, although bringing any of its elements to a successful conclusion had remained far from assured even before that. The external security and domestic political costs of abandoning any of its elements, however, were large, clear, and relatively immediate (Ho 2005; Kang 2005). The DPRK test has led to steps by Seoul to bolster some elements (e.g., U.S. presence and commitment) and dampen others (anti-Japanese sentiment) but, even in the face of increased domestic criticism of the current policy, not to decisively revise any of its elements.

One part of the portfolio tries to delay U.S. withdrawals and reassure Washington that the ROK will remain a loyal ally if allowed to be a less subordinate one. The domestically unpopular troop dispatch to Iraq served one declared purpose — "strengthening the alliance between the United States and the ROK to create conditions conducive to resolution of pressing bilateral issues and promote confidence in the ROK" (ROK Ministry of National Defense 2005, 135). The United States might then return some bases, accept smaller support payments for its military presence, and give the ROK a greater voice in wartime command arrangements. The timetable for reducing U.S. forces in Korea has been extended, but the cuts remain planned. An agreement to return a controversial base in central Seoul has been announced, as has an agreement (but only in principle) to reduce ROK payments toward the costs of the USFK. The 2005 defense-ministerial Security Consultative Meeting kept the U.S. nuclear guarantee and wartime command arrangements, leaving a "joint determination" system for future bargaining (Shanker 2005). From the ROK side, that bargaining after the DPRK test has sought more in the way of a U.S. tripwire presence and automatic involvement should North Korea attack and has had at least declaratory policy success.

A second part calls for a more independent and stronger defense capability under the slogan of "cooperative self-reliant defense" (Hwang 2005, 38–39; Noh 2005). The ROK will be "an autonomous party as regards security on the Korean peninsula . . . [through] early expansion of war deterrence capability." This will be accomplished by means of force investments that will enable the establishment of an "independent surveillance and reconnaissance system, development of deep strike capabilities, enhancement of basic forces, and [the] strengthening [of] R&D capabilities." R&D will focus on key elements in the U.S. vision of RMA (C4ISR and PGMSs) (ROK Ministry of National Defense 2005, 99–101, 171–77).

Larger defense budgets admittedly are needed to achieve an "elite high technology force" with greater geographical reach and an independent, national techno-industrial base to equip it. The approved FY 2004 to 2008 Medium Term Expenditure Framework has almost 10 percent annual growth in defense funding, and the Ministry of Defense claims that realizing its objectives only requires increasing the defense budget to 3.2 percent of national GDP over fifteen years from the current 2.8 percent (J. Park 2005). That claim rests on dubious assumptions about real national economic growth, end-item costs, defense industry performance, and the political acceptability of large military modernization costs.

The third portfolio theme mobilizes nationalist sentiment against Japan for domestic political benefit. This emphasis parallels Chinese and DPRK policy lines over disputed islands and sea zones, textbooks, Yasukuni Shrine visits, occupation era grievances, and a permanent member U.N. Security Council seat for Tokyo. It uses and feeds fears that in President Roh's words "Japan is still trying to justify its history of aggression and domination and might move on a path to hegemonism again" (*Korea Herald* 2006). Although Japan's U.N. Security Council bid has been blocked for now, other aspects of the evolution of Japanese security policy can be seen as posing a threat to South Korea. Yet Seoul and Tokyo need to maintain an uneasy balance between their appeals to nationalism and their shared security and economic interests, as was recognized in the fall 2006 Abe-Roh summit.[17] The ROK cannot do much more to restrain unwanted Japanese policies without pushing the United States into choosing one or the other as an ally, a choice that would probably be made in favor of Japan. It can, however, symbolically remind Japan of its distrust by, for example, holding a ROK–Russian joint naval exercise to mark the one hundredth anniversary of the Russo–Japanese War (ROK Ministry of National Defense 2005, 119–20).

A fourth theme calls for close bilateral relations with China, a distancing of itself from a U.S.-led defense of Taiwan, and the development of Asian regional institutions in which China would play a key role (H. Kim 2005).[18] China has become the ROK's largest external trading partner, a major OFDI recipient, and a provider of a substantial trade surplus. Good relations with China are essential for realizing the growth forecasts of the Defense White Paper, managing the DPRK, and imposing limits on Japan. Nevertheless, there are reasons for South Korea to limit the extent to which it relies on China in the future. The Korean Development Bank and the Korean International Trade Association forecast that the ROK sectoral edge would be lost in many areas and that the export advantage could shift to China by 2008 (C. Brown 2005; Barfield and Bolton 2005). ROK trade and investment relationships with the United States will therefore continue to be of great importance — as indicated by the progress made in ROK–U.S. free trade agreement negotiations since they began in the fall of 2006. Good relations with both the United States and China are essential for both the "peace" and "prosperity" planks of the ROK agenda.

The last portfolio theme centers on North Korea and has the ROK seeking to: (1) mix military capability sticks and nonmilitary carrots to avoid war on the peninsula and advance de facto economic integration; (2) persuade others (America, China, Japan, and Russia) to support that approach; (3) block DPRK attempts to isolate the ROK and deal over its head with Washington and Tokyo; and (4) forestall irreversible absorption of North Korea into a foreign state's sphere of influence. The government's emphasizing any single aspect at any one point in time inevitably generates controversy in the ROK. Nevertheless there is substantial domestic consensus that it makes sense to buy time by avoiding crises — and to use it to pursue marginal improvements that "pry open" the DPRK—rather than risking a quick and conclusive resolution. It thus seems advisable to stand aside from or even reject some U.S. proposed policy options that might trigger crises, such as the PSI that would target DPRK shipping, threats like those made in mid-2006 to launch a preventive attack against DPRK missile launch facilities, or, in the aftermath of the nuclear test, the severing of economic ties.

After all, the fundamentals of the DPRK economy and conventional war posture are relatively and, perhaps absolutely, in long-term decline compared to South Korea and most countries of East Asia. Signs that the DPRK has taken steps toward achieving a deliverable nuclear weapons capability only supplement the long-standing fact that the initial impact of conventional DPRK weapons would have disastrous consequences for some 40 percent of the ROK population. North Korea in Seoul's perspective must be treated with great seriousness, but the threat has proven to be manageable and time is on the side of the South. The intermittent Six-Party Talks (all the members of the security complex) about DPRK nuclear programs thus challenge Seoul to keep that negotiating arena alive while forestalling escalatory U.S. responses and distancing itself from threat-centered Japanese positions. Seoul has had to work hard to encourage Washington to be accommodating to the DPRK, to hammer out points on which it can agree with China and Japan, and to insure a major role for itself. Pyongyang has made that increasingly difficult to do without the incumbent politicians in Seoul becoming vulnerable to charges from their domestic opponents that they are gullible targets for exploitation. President Roh has referred in that regard to the DPRK as the "most stubborn country in the world" and the United States as the "most opinionated country in the world" (Kessler 2005; Snyder 2005).

ROK fears of unilateral U.S. escalation abated somewhat with U.S. participation in the talks and the vague agreement of September 2005 under which,
ostensibly, the DPRK would abandon its nuclear program and the United States
would provide it with security assurances and large-scale economic development assistance. The agreement, however, was open to different interpretations,
lacked commitments on the sequences and timing of steps by the parties, and
left unsettled how specifically any regime was to insure U.S.-sought complete,
verifiable, and irreversible dismantlement (CVID) (*New York Times* 2005b; Seo
2005). By mid-2006, no momentum had developed for resolving those matters
and the DPRK clamored for and gained renewed attention by testing missiles. By
fall 2006, that lack of momentum (or even attention by Washington) was even
more evident and the DPRK again drew attention to itself by conducting another
nuclear weapons test. In both cases, the United States initially made noises about
active military measures to deal with a growing DPRK nuclear threat while South
Korean officials questioned that suggestion and the more forceful response options and instead, in tacit agreement with China and Russia, left the U.S. to seek
a revival of the talks.

As in June 2002, when the United States stimulated DPRK admission of its
continuing nuclear program (and noncompliance with the 1994 Agreed Framework), ROK policy makers have worried that elements in the U.S. policy system
want to increase rather than reduce tensions with North Korea (U.S. Treasury
sanctions in late 2005 on financial transactions, suspensions of scheduled food
supplies to the DPRK, the freezing of some North Korean company assets, the
North Korea Human Rights Act of 2004, discussion of preventive strikes, major
military exercises, and accelerated Northeast Asian BMD deployments) (J. Lee
2005a; Sanger 2005). For some ROK officials and experts only vigilant effort will
keep the United States from doing the wrong thing to the DPRK and destabilizing the peninsula.

For the ROK leadership, the multilateral track of the Six-Party Talks proceeded
in harness with bilateral inducements from Seoul, such as the mid-2005 conditional "important proposal" of economic aid to North Korea and the "Korean
Peninsula peace initiative" several months later (Moon 2005). Many of those
offers would increase DPRK economic dependence on the ROK and be conditional on (unclearly defined) DPRK nuclear weapons program reductions short
of full elimination.[19] ROK activism to establish linkages to the DPRK returned
to the unusually high level of 2000 to 2002, a period that had begun with a Clinton administration drive to accommodate North Korea and that had ended with
expressions of overt hostility from the Republican administration. Reactions to
the nuclear test in effect postponed new interdependence initiatives but did not
shut down major ones already in operation. That suggests the consistency of ROK

policy whatever American preferences, and Seoul's willingness to proceed with engagement and crisis limitation in the face of ongoing criticism from influential U.S. and Japanese politicians. As the Bush II administration becomes more of a constrained lame duck, ROK officials can be more confident that the United States will not take military action against the DPRK or succeed in pressuring South Korea to abandon opening to North Korea.

In sum, the DPRK part of the ROK security program has avoided war and increased nonmilitary relationships but has not made either of these a given for the future or forestalled the DPRK from becoming a nuclear weapons state. It has secured enough support from the other participants at the Six-Party Talks to get vague agreements that have at least enabled it to postpone the sort of breakdown in negotiations with the DPRK that would end up severely straining Seoul's relations with either China or the United States. Seoul has not reached robust consensus with the United States and Japan on specific sequences and implementation measures on the nuclear issues but has prevented the formation of a tight U.S.–Japan coalition that might oppose the others in the Six-Party Talks — and thus having to object to or join it. It has managed DPRK moves to bargain bilaterally with the United States about the future of the peninsula, but the DPRK retains the means to try those moves again and again and has done so. Finally, the growing economic and security dependence of the DPRK on China may well be giving Beijing much more lasting influence in the northern part of the peninsula than Seoul would like.

North Korea

In spite of its cultivated nontransparency, several clear and continuing general features of DPRK security policy bear directly on its handling of Bush II policies. For the North Korean leadership, those features have enabled regime and state survival in the face of very harsh odds, and survival has affirmed that external relations of "tense stagnation" can be managed to avoid a "catastrophic phase" of a decisive military showdown (Choi 2005, 257).

First, the military institution and instrument play a predominant role in state and regime preservation. That was true during the Korean War reunification attempt and was reflected in the 1962 Four Military Guidelines — "all soldiers should be trained as cadres, all forces should be modernized, all citizens should be armed, and all territory should be fortified" (Japan Defense Agency 2005, 48). It was reaffirmed in Pyongyang's 1989 response to the collapse of Communism in Eastern Europe and retrospectively in 2005: "the only way to save the country and the people and defend the socialist cause lay in holding fast to the idea and line of attaching importance to the military"; that is, to a "unique Songun [military first] politics" (*Pyongyang Times*, February 12, 2005). That emphasis continues in the extremely large share, by international standards, of North Korean national resources allotted to military matters.

Second, systematic measures are used to limit foreign influence. In the mid-1950s, the Great Leader Kim Il-Sung and his so-called guerrilla faction crushed Soviet and Chinese-supported factions in the Korean Workers' Party. Kim Il-Sung responded to the USSR twentieth Party Congress that denounced the cult of personality by strengthening the cult of personality and rejecting Soviet-advised shifts away from a heavy industry-based economy. More recently, severe limits have been placed on Chinese style "market socialism," inter-Korean family reunification, and contact between the population of North Korea and foreign providers of humanitarian assistance. Openings to the ROK (via, for example, tourism and the Kaesung special economic development zone) are not accessible to domestic society. Chinese appeals to refrain from nuclear weapons testing are rejected.

A third feature noisily denies weakness while creating bargaining options based on that denial, as shown during the famine period of the latter 1990s. The degree of DPRK self-direction is remarkable given severe economic and security dependency, at first on the Soviet Union and then China and the ROK. The key lies in repeatedly asserted commitments to courses of action made credible by their potential Pyrrhic victory consequences. The consequences — such as conventional war on the peninsula, a nuclear exchange, even the prospect of regime collapse and an ensuing flood of refugees into neighboring countries — seem so serious that only a truly committed party would be prepared to expose itself to them. Illustrative signals that North Korea was prepared to tolerate these possible consequences include Kim Jong-Il's proclaimed state of readiness for war (March 1993); words and acts during the first peninsular nuclear crisis (1993–94); the statement that the United States was not the only state that could launch a preemptive nuclear attack (July 2004); the post-2005 Joint Communiqué surge in military exercises, ground to sea missile tests, and redeployment of aircraft to possibly more survivable locations; and asserted rights to test missiles of various ranges (mid-2006) and nuclear weapons (fall 2006).

The bargaining options come from demonstrative rejections of a need to acknowledge weakness while waiting for materially stronger parties to acknowledge their need for DPRK cooperation. The DPRK works hard at generating and retaining a stock of reversible moves it can use to encourage or discourage foreign hopes of accommodation. At least since the early 1990s, it has made agreements to attend international negotiating sessions, to expand negotiating agendas, to sign agreements in principle, and to declare moratoria on weapons and delivery systems. These steps all seem like substantial concessions to foreign concerns. Yet none are irreversible. Meetings can be cancelled, negotiations stymied, agreements reinterpreted, and moratoria ended. Such moves do buy time, discourage sustained foreign pressures (e.g., the 2003 Chinese oil supply cutoff, intended to persuade the DPRK to participate in multilateral talks, lasted only three days), and encourage substantive accommodations by others. The Six-Party Talks are illustrative of the strategy and its benefits. The DPRK threatens to take irreversible steps, such as engage in nuclear weapons tests and transoceanic weapons missile launches, allows those threats to recede, and then makes them again when it needs to. That may not provide security but it does buy time for survival, in itself no mean achievement. Indeed, ambiguity or opaqueness regarding the performance of tested missiles and weapons functions to preserve options in the list of possible future steps even while taking some of them.

A fourth feature identifies the United States as the primary security threat and tries to reduce the peninsular U.S. military presence, split the ROK–U.S. alliance, and threaten U.S. allies and U.S. forces in the ROK and Japan. Mid-1950s proposals for a Far East conference to achieve peaceful reunification called for withdrawal of U.S. forces from the ROK while proposals between 1962 and 1973 called for a peace treaty between the two Koreas that would replace the Armistice Agreement and would be combined with withdrawal. In 2004, DPRK media reemphasized that peace in the region required withdrawal of U.S. forces from the ROK and Japan and, in 2005, called for a Northeast Asian security cooperation process excluding the United States and Japan. Proposals for a bilateral DPRK–U.S. peace treaty first appeared in 1974 and reappeared after the 1994 Agreed Framework and again in mid-2006. Earlier in the 1990s, the DPRK made an attempt at splitting the United States and South Korea by holding prime ministerial talks with the ROK (without the United States) and signing an inter-Korean Agreement on Reconciliation, Non-Aggression, and Exchanges and Cooperation. DPRK calls for direct bilateral talks with the United States leading to security guarantees are a hardy perennial, calls not fully satisfied by the de facto bilateral talks reluctantly participated in by several U.S. administrations (including Bush II).

A fifth feature is that the DPRK persistently pursues nuclear programs with military applications, other forms of weapons of mass destruction (WMD), and extended-range missile delivery systems.[20] A 1950s exploration of nuclear options was stimulated by U.S. consideration of nuclear bombing during the Korean War. In the mid-1960s, the DPRK asked China for nuclear program assistance, a request China denied. In the 1970s, the DPRK was probably aware of a secret ROK nuclear weapons-related program. In about 1980, North Korea began trying to produce plutonium on a substantial scale. Under Soviet pressure, it joined the Non-Proliferation Treaty (NPT) in 1985, but Moscow never provided the several light water reactors expected in return. Arrival of International Atomic Energy Agency (IAEA) inspectors under the NPT was delayed until 1992, and shortly thereafter the CIA estimated that the DPRK could have one to two nuclear weapons. The upshot was the 1993–94 crisis that concluded with the Four-Party Agreed Framework. From the DPRK's perspective, it had gained promises of economic rewards and foreign subsidized reactors in exchange for agreeing to a freeze, specifically on plutonium production at the Yongbyon facility, the dismantlement of which would be deferred until the reactors were completed (with the United States to supply heavy fuel oil in the interim). Yet, a contract for a U.S.-led consortium to build the reactors was not signed until late 1999, only after the 1998 extended range missile test over Japan, the DPRK's declared moratorium on testing such missiles in the early fall of 1999, and the completion of the Four-Party Talks (U.S., DPRK, ROK, China) in 1999 (Oberdorfer 2005; Hassig and Oh 2005; Kogan 2005; ROK Ministry of National Defense 2005, 291–94; and the Nautilus Institute 2006).

United States, Japanese, and ROK sources agree that North Korea undertook a covert program to produce highly enriched uranium suitable for use in nuclear weapons starting in 1998, although U.S. public accusations were not made until October 2002. Shortly after that, DPRK officials told a visiting American delegation that it would allay U.S. concerns in exchange for a legally binding nonaggression treaty including a promise of no attack on their country. Instead, the United States cut off oil shipments, and in short order the DPRK unsealed the Yongbyon facilities, disabled surveillance cameras, expelled IAEA inspectors, withdrew from the NPT, and announced massive processing of spent fuel rods that could yield plutonium for weapons. In October 2003, the IAEA reported that the DPRK had enough plutonium for five to six nuclear weapons, and in July DPRK officials affirmed that to the United States (Sanger 2003). The DPRK declared publicly for the first time in February of 2005 that it had fabricated nuclear weapons and in March proclaimed that it was a nuclear weapons state and should be treated accordingly.

Nevertheless, the DPRK did not conduct an observable nuclear weapons test until October 2006. In the interim, South Korean and U.S. official sources hedged on whether it had any, let alone how many, nuclear weapons (ROK Ministry of National Defense 2005, 44; Pincus 2006). Russian experts seemed to believe that it did not, and they and others suggested that the resistance to comprehensive international inspections might be meant to hide that from the world and avoid exposure to Kim Jong-Il of possibly unwarranted claims by his subordinates (Mikheev 2005; Dwor-Frecault 2005). Even the observed first test raised questions — its low yield left it unclear as to whether the DPRK had a weapon that failed to fully function or a far more sophisticated one that functioned well. Similar lack of clear demonstration of capability by successful and observable tests also has marked the DPRK long-range weapons-capable missile program.

Whatever the actual state of affairs, several conclusions can be drawn about the commitment of the DPRK leadership to nuclear programs and its stance on how to use them. First, the commitment long predates the Bush II presidency, and its (ultimately hollow) threats. Second, there is ample historical reason for North Korea to doubt that moving first to end its nuclear weapons ambitions will subsequently result in its actually receiving power reactors or much else from the United States or others. Third, the image it has created of itself as a country that is capable of posing deliverable nuclear weapons threats has worked, at least for a while, to extract concessionary economic flows from the United States, Japan, and the ROK. The United States and Japan have not acted on the agreement that allows for such concessions for some time, but China and the ROK have. Fourth, signs associated with but not conclusively demonstrating nuclear weapons and long-range delivery capability have not and probably will not result in harsh U.S. military retaliation — regardless of which American party holds the presidency.

The Bush II years have given DPRK officials even more reason to conclude that a nuclear-armed image provides an extremely valuable lever for constraining U.S. policy. From the "axis of evil" of the 2002 Bush inaugural, the United States moved to offering written assurance not to attack North Korea (November 2003) and to proposing a "permanent peace mechanism" linked to CVID in which the "five other parties . . . would pledge to provide security assurances to North Korea" (February 2004) (Xia 2005). By July 2005, the United States declared that it had "absolutely no intention" of launching a military attack and would recognize the DPRK as a sovereign state, had changed its position regarding rewards, no longer insisting that they would come after CVID but instead agreeing to something closer to the DPRK's demand for simultaneity of program constraints and rewards ("words for words and actions for actions"), and had accepted the plan under which the ROK would provide an early economic aid package (Yardley and Buckley 2005; J. Lee 2005d, 2005e). In the Joint Communiqué a few months later the United States affirmed that "it has . . . no intention to attack or invade . . . with conventional or nuclear weapons." Almost a year later, with no CVID progress, the administration rejected a forceful response to possible DPRK long-range and shorter-range missile threats, although it did initially hype their imminence and gravity. This pattern repeated itself in a more abbreviated time span after the nuclear weapons test.

From the North Korean perspective, the six-party process has worked to embed the United States in diplomacy, where a hard, rigid line would isolate it from China and the ROK, and has shifted the focus from disarming the DPRK to denuclearizing a region that might be broader than the peninsula itself. Without acceding to any specific reductions or additional postponements, Pyongyang, with the 2006 missile and weapons tests, induced others to woo it assiduously to return to the talks, that is, to give others including China and the ROK a face-saving, diplomatic option in the wake of progressing DPRK WMD programs. Those same demonstrative nuclear acts led at least some others in the regional security complex (including members of Republican circles in the United States) to press the United States to enter into the bilateral talks the DPRK had long wanted. Nevertheless, those gains do not guarantee that the DPRK's fundamental security problems with the United States, Japan, China, or the ROK will be resolved. Hawks are not an extinct species in the United States and Japan, although they may be less able in the terminal phase of the Bush II presidency to dominate or sabotage policy than previously.

The six-party mechanism yielded another agreement in February 2007 that claimed to be a breakthrough on DPRK disarmament and, indeed, on cooperative security in Northeast Asia. Besides setting up a host of working groups to address issues important for one or more of the participating regimes, the only concrete steps several months later were that the United States had substantially lifted the bank sanctions affecting the DPRK, that the ROK had resumed economic aid to North Korea, and subsequently that the DPRK had taken steps toward an IAEA-certified shutdown of its Yongbyon facility. It remains unclear when, if ever, the DPRK will make major progress toward CVID. By entering into the agreement, the DPRK has made major progress toward securing what amount to security guarantees from the United States, enhanced the chances for concessional economic flows from the ROK, reduced frictions with China, and isolated Japan's chauvinistic leadership fixated on the abductee issue. That has been done without giving up a single nuclear weapon or gram of weapons material and without an unprecedented imminent increase in national transparency.

The North Korean WMD programs have served the DPRK well, allowing it to avoid political-military catastrophe and convince several others in the Northeast Asian security complex to temper the sanctioning and isolation the Republican administration of the United States only now seems prepared to discard. WMD programs then merit being perpetuated in some form while the long game continues — and long it will be. It would take twenty or more years to complete full CVID from whenever it starts and ten or so years to build a new foreign-supplied reactor (Moon 2005). The DPRK will then repeatedly face decisions about how much and how unambiguously it should call international attention to its WMD achievements and limitations. Yet experience to date provides it with no rival options for securing regime-bolstering gains and avoiding regional and global insignificance. Nor does North Korea's experience suggest that nuclear-capacity demonstrations short of war will trigger additional sustained, irreversible punishments from others in the security complex.

Conclusions

The Northeast Asian security complex is in a period of significant adaptation to changed circumstances. For Japan and the ROK, policy lines that de facto reduce reliance on the United States seem increasingly desirable if managed so as to retain a significant U.S. shield as long as possible. That combination makes ambiguity unavoidable about the future of their alliances with the United States. Ambiguity has certain attractions given the need to cope with a rising China and, at least relatively, a declining United States. The fog enables these countries to put off making choices that might offend Beijing or Washington and clouds the intentions behind Seoul's and Tokyo's military enhancements. There is not so much a simple rejection of the United States as the hegemonic power in the region as there is a recognition that it lacks the means and will reliably to impose regional order and provide protection. That is of course exactly what North Korea has demonstrated.

Yet China seems no more able, willing, and acceptable as the order maker than the United States. Does that mean that the Northeast Asian complex will break down into hot war? Pessimists would point to the rise of nationalist themes in the domestic politics of the members of the complex, arms buildups, and alleged DPRK "craziness." Alternatively, muted optimists would point to the tendency of most governments in the complex most of the time to strategize over extended futures and pursue hedged and balanced policies. The risks of breakdown through miscalculation seem limited by a high level of exchange of information, major economic flows, and the uncertainty of what subcoalitions would form if hot conflicts broke out. For the members of the complex, change may well be recognized as inevitable and in some ways desirable — but best left to ripen slowly with intervals during which it can be absorbed and shaped. Responses to the North Korean nuclear test as well as the recent Six-Party Agreement and the future steps it lays out support that assessment.

Notes

1. I draw on off-the-record interviews with Japanese and South Korean officials and analysts, as well as numerous unclassified but not-for-citation-or-quotation papers by them. All responsibility for the interpretations presented here is mine. Special thanks for research assistance go to Art Maxwell, as well as to Huiping Xie and Chad Serena.

2. Koizumi advisor Yukio Okamoto on the 2004 election: "A new Democratic administration could deem Beijing a strategic economic partner, just like with the Clinton administration. If so . . . priority now focused on building mutual trust and . . . cooperation to realize the U.S.–Japan security arrangement . . . will likely shift away" (Karasaki 2004).

3. Armitage became the number two State Department official, and member Michael Green assumed Japan and broader Asian responsibilities at the National Security Council.

4. In March 2003, Koizumi supported imminent U.S. use of force against Iraq. In July, he defeated a no-confidence vote in the Diet and a filibuster, which allowed him to secure approval for sending SDF units to Iraq. The deployment did not take place until 2004 after cabinet approval of a plan in December 2003. Withdrawal was completed in 2006.

5. The president of Japan's National Defense Academy held it "no longer realistic to stick to the defense-only principle" (Suzuki 2004).

6. China and the ROK unsurprisingly have responded with official and unofficial protests that Japan is "trying hard to deny, dilute, and even sanitize history" ("China Accuses Japan of Denying History," *Daily Yomiuri*, August 4, 2005, 3). On Yasukuni, see Nelson (2003).

7. The Japanese parliament arguably has agreed to Japanese Defense Agency (JDA) authority to launch without permission from the prime minister or the cabinet (World in Brief: Tokyo, *Washington Post*, July 23, 2005). On BMD interdependence, see "U.S. Wants Japan to Share Missile Defense Radar Data," *Daily Yomiuri Online*, July 20, 2005 (www.Yomiuri .co.jp). Aspects of the U.S.–East Asia basing realignment also create greater interdependence.

8. The Far East clause (article 6) of the Japan–U.S. Security Treaty limiting the area for which U.S. forces based in Japan can be used ostensibly remains in force (*International Herald Tribune–Asahi Shimbun* 2004b). In early 2006, Japan was only considering a law requiring local governments to allow U.S. forces to use ports and airports for Taiwan or Korean peninsula crises not involving "a direct military attack on Japan" ("U.S. may Get Wider Access in Emergency," *Daily Yomiuri*, January 12, 2006 [www.asianewsnet.net]).

9. It wants BMD funded from a basically flat defense budget rather than from a sizeable increase.

10. For a group of LDP Diet members and retired officials, "China is aiming . . . [at] . . . regional hegemony in Asia" so Japan needs "reciprocal diplomacy with China that is not overburdened by a reconciliation policy that is driven by dependence on the Chinese market . . . Japan–China disputes are not temporary aberrations, but are rather of [a] lasting nature . . . Japan . . . should resolutely deal with China without fear of temporary conflicts" (Study Group on Japan's Diplomacy for China 2005).

11. The importance attached to gaining a seat is suggested in Japan's threat to reduce U.N. contributions ("Govt. to Push for Cuts in U.N. Contributions," *Daily Yomiuri*, September 11, 2005 [www.asianewsnet.net]).

12. The Japanese public has reacted with shock and surprise to anti-Japanese riots in China, a reaction followed by support for assertive measures on the disputed energy reserves.

13. Meanwhile, the ROK energetically pursued conventional force modernization and an indigenous defense techno-industrial base (ROK Ministry of National Defense 2005, 171), increased defense spending, and gained peacetime command authority over its own forces.

14. ROK analyses had concluded that rapid reunification on the peninsula would be unacceptably costly and that, unless the DPRK got external economic help, there were unattractively high chances of a regime collapse into turmoil generating a flood of refugees or of it taking extreme military actions (Ministry of National Defense 2005, 297–308).

15. In mid-2002 Secretary of Defense Rumsfeld was reportedly briefed on an option to attack North Korea without consulting South Korea, a possibility supposedly then squelched by the secretary of state and the Commander-in-Chief, U.S. Pacific Command (CINCPAC).

16. Roh, elected in 2002, was not the United States' preferred candidate and campaigned on modifying the alliance. He led his Uri party to control of the National Assembly in 2004.

17. That was evident at the 2005 Roh–Koizumi summit. Annual bilateral defense ministerials have been held since 1994, and military personnel exchanges continue (Ministry of National Defense 2005, 117).

18. The ability to come to the defense of Taiwan using U.S. military capabilities based in the ROK is one element of the rationale for the basing changes the United States desires there; it is likewise an element in the argument for basing changes in Japan.

19. It is not clear to what extent funding for the initiatives would come from government budgets or, if parliamentary approval were necessary, whether the funding for them would receive it (J. Lee 2005a, 2005c, 2005d).

20. Chemical weapons intentions were signaled by Kim Il Sung's 1961 "Declaration for Chemicalization," and they and biological weapons were produced by 1990 (Ministry of National Defense 2005, 45).

CHAPTER FIVE

South Asia

Amit Das Gupta

No doubt an average newspaper reader in the summer of 2005 would have been left with the impression that the United States and India, whose relationship had, for decades, often been poor, finally had come to a fruitful and friendly level of cooperation. Prime Minister Manmohan Singh had undertaken his first state visit to Washington, which proved to be very successful. On July 18, he and President George W. Bush signed a joint statement announcing that the two countries had "reached a milestone in their strategic relationship by completing the Next Steps in Strategic Partnership (NSSP)" (U.S. Department of State 2005a).

The September 17, 2004, NSSP (U.S. Department of State 2005b), had been signed by Singh's predecessor Atal Behari Vajpayee, which was the more remarkable since Vajpayee, as head of a coalition frequently described as Hindu nationalist in the Western media, had initiated nuclear tests in Pokhran on May 11 and 13, 1998. Under the NSSP, the same prime minister was invited to cooperate in "civilian nuclear activities, civilian space programs, and high-technology trade." For India this was a major breakthrough, since it was the first country with nuclear weapons that had not signed the Non-Proliferation Treaty (NPT) to be welcomed into the nuclear club by the world's only superpower.

The only major commitment the Indian side made was to allow International Atomic Energy Commission (IAEA) control of many of its civilian nuclear plants, which hardly play any role in military capability. New Delhi will behave like the established members of the nuclear club without having had to sign the NPT—exactly what it long sought. George Perkovich, an expert on India's nuclear program, has summed up Washington's motives: "That the top priority should be balancing Chinese power, that strengthening U.S.–India relations is a promising way to do this, and that both of these objectives are more important than maintaining a rule-based nonproliferation regime. . . . India's exclusion as an accepted nuclear-weapons power is a historical anomaly that should be corrected" (Perkovich 2005).

The United States is likely also motivated by more global concerns. For example, it needs allies in the post–cold war world who are as interested as it in stability, free markets, and democracy. During the cold war, those sorts of allies were found among countries participating in the European integration process and Japan respectively — what was the G7. Now, in a world full of instability, failing states, and extremism, they are by far not enough. India is already a major political player and expected to gain even more importance as the twenty-first century progresses. Unlike the People's Republic of China (PRC), it is a stable democracy. It views itself as a status quo power without territorial claims and, thus, is concerned about stability and peace in Asia. By supporting India instead of China, the United States will not be throwing itself out of the frying pan into fire, as there is hardly a country on the globe that is less likely to become an open or imminent threat to the United States than India, except, perhaps, Israel, the other indispensable nuclear power in another explosive region.

Additionally India's bomb is an indigenous one, and over the past thirty years the country has proved that it is a responsible nuclear power. It has neither blackmailed opponents with open threats nor demonstrated interest in any proliferation of know-how or hardware. The militant rhetoric right after the nuclear tests was short-lived and aimed at provoking a Pakistani response (Bidwai and Vainak 2001, 57). That is why the Bush administration is trying to push through the new partnership despite massive resistance in the United States (Pant 2006).

Pakistan naturally has been less happy with U.S. foreign policy since 9/11. Being closely linked with the Taliban and to some extent with al Qaeda, it was forced to fall in line with Washington when the Bush administration decided to oust those groups from Afghanistan. Islamabad lost its safe hinterland against archenemy India. After five decades of a sometimes-close partnership with the United States, Pakistan knows that American interest in South Asia comes and goes and that often what Washington wants is not the same as what Islamabad wants. U.S. troops most probably will leave Afghanistan whenever their job of bringing peace and stability is done. Pakistan then will be sitting between the millstones of Afghanistan's and India's interests once again. Washington, on the other hand, knows pretty well that it is mostly dealing with symptoms in Afghanistan, which have their roots to some extent in Pakistan's inner instability, which breeds extremism and militant Islamism.

There are more problematic developments for the United States in South Asia. Nepal is bleeding because of a civil war between Maoists and the monarchy, which started in 1996 and escalated with the enthronement of the unpopular King Gyanendra in 2001 (Wolfe 2006). If the de facto toppling of the latter and the June 17, 2006, formation of a coalition government that includes the Maoists was a turning point has not yet been decided. Bangladesh is becoming another hotbed of militant Islamism. Bengali Muslims were not known as orthodox let alone extremist until recently. Massive sponsoring of madrassas and Islamist groups by Saudi Arabia and Pakistan, plus the need for a safe haven for Islamists after the ousting of the Taliban, has changed the pattern recently and a process of Islamization is taking place that is comparable to what took place in Pakistan in the 1980s (Ramachandran 2005). On August 17, 2005, the country was shocked by four hundred simultaneous bomb blasts, which did not create much damage but did demonstrate the existence of a highly efficient terrorist network.

Although there is reason to be concerned about developments in Nepal and Bangladesh, those are definitely not challenges to American hegemonic ambitions. Militant Islamism in Bangladesh seems to form a problem for India almost exclusively, which in the not-so-distant future could be facing serious security threats from a territory that is almost an enclave. As for Nepal, nowadays the United States regards Communist revolts as internal affairs; at least, so long as they take place in countries of little importance and are not sponsored from outside. What happens in Nepal is interesting to the United States mostly because it forms a buffer between the PRC and India (Wolfe 2006). Real challenges to U.S. hegemonic attempts in South Asia, however, only come from India openly and Pakistan indirectly.

Hegemony in General and in a South Asian Context

The United States is the most powerful country on the globe at the turn of the third millennium. While America's neoconservatives, such as Robert Kagan (2003), define hegemony mostly in military terms, military might does not automatically qualify a power as a hegemon. Even if it did, the United States would not necessarily qualify. It is true that only U.S. armed forces are able to strike any target on the globe, and today only Russia and the PRC would be able to retaliate on a limited scale. Additionally the United States is much ahead in exploring space, deploying satellites, and testing missile defense systems. However, 9/11 revealed the insufficiency of such armaments after the end of the cold war. The initial reaction of the Bush administration — to attack al Qaeda's base in Afghanistan — was rational, but its later behavior left the impression of a blind Polyphemus, causing much collateral damage but failing to get Ulysses (that is, Osama bin Laden). U.S. forces are able to occupy two countries simultaneously but are overstretched as soon as they are needed to guarantee peace, let alone create a stable order allowing a pullback. Therefore, it did not come as a surprise when the useless debate about a unipolar world was ended by Secretary of State Condoleezza Rice herself on January 18 and 19, 2006 (Weinstein 2006).

Paul Kennedy (1987) argues that there is no lasting hegemony without a strong economy. Economic power guarantees influence even without strong military muscle, as can be seen with Germany, the EU, and Japan. Would it be too much to say that George W. Bush has wasted the savings of the Clinton years and is ruining the U.S. economy to the same extent it was ruined during the war in Vietnam? The United States recovered then, but largely thanks to the support of Western allies, many of whom feel alienated from the United States today. To take it for granted that the U.S. economy sooner or later will be going through another cycle of regeneration is at best naïve. As far as the economy is concerned, there is no U.S. hegemony.

The military and economic powers of the United States definitely have visible limits, but the American way of life is spreading all over the globe. Barber (1996) calls it "McWorld"; others use the vague term "globalization." Antonio Gramsci's explanation of hegemony is still the best: according to him, "cultural hegemony" is achieved when a group gains long-lasting political control over others because it has been able to make its own values the common values of all (Kolakowski 1981, 3:264–68). This happened during the twentieth century, when democracy and open markets became standards together with many aspects of daily life seen as American.

All three aspects of U.S. hegemony are at stake in South Asia. Pakistan, on the one hand, forces us to question the usefulness and effectiveness of the U.S. military fighting a war against the Taliban, Islamabad's "own malignant creation" (Bidwai and Vainak 2001, xxi). Additionally we can see in the example of Pakistan how pursuing exclusively regional interests that do not align directly with American interests can have global repercussions. India, on the other hand, has challenged American hegemonic attempts for decades in a completely peaceful manner in all three fields and with growing success. As this volume concentrates on security factors in a more narrow sense, they will represent the focus of this investigation.

The Indian Response to the Bush Doctrine

Hindi–American Bhai Bhai — Indo–American Friendship?

The Bharatiya Janata Party (BJP) government under Atal Behari Vajpayee initially had wholeheartedly welcomed the Bush Doctrine. Having global ambitions itself, it was pleased that the new U.S. administration in such a document wrote about "India's potential to become one of the great democratic powers of the twenty-first century" (U.S. White House, Office of the President, National Security Strategy 2002). And it seemed to give India the justification to solve what had been one of its biggest security problems for more than a decade: the Pakistani-trained militants who were responsible for a massive and growing amount of bloodshed in Indian-controlled Jammu and Kashmir and who thereby forced New Delhi to station around half a million security forces there permanently.

"Preemptive strikes" in a "war against terrorism" were exactly what Indian hawks had long demanded.

Until 2002 India had not been able to do more than deal with the symptoms. In 1999, when Pervez Musharraf, then Pakistani chief of army staff, had probed limited warfare and sent a unit to cut off the Indian road connection through Jammu and Kashmir in Kargil, his Indian counterparts had not dared to retaliate across the Line of Control (LoC) (Perkovich 2002, 474). In 1965 India had responded to a Pakistani attempt to invade the region with a counterattack on Pakistan's homeland. In a nuclear South Asia this was now out of the question. Even when Pakistan-based terrorists attacked the Indian parliament on December 13, 2001, the Vajpayee government responded only with a massive military buildup along the LoC and the international border and verbal attacks. New Delhi went so far as to ignore open Pakistani threats of a nuclear strike.

Three months after 9/11 there were other surprising patterns of behavior to be seen, too. India, which had long backed the Northern Alliance (Rashid 2000, 95), welcomed the Afghanistan war. New Delhi openly offered to permit U.S. planes to refuel at Indian airports (Nayar and Paul 2003, 265), whereas a similar secret offer during the 1991 Gulf War was immediately revoked after it had become public (Kux 1994, 440–41). Commentators wrote of India's "exuberant acceptance of U.S. 'leadership' of the world" (Bidwai 2002). Pakistan had been weakened and had lost its "strategic depth," which, ever since the early 1980s, the military leadership had believed to be absolutely essential to every future conflict with India (Kux 2001, 282; Ahmad 1998). Therefore, despite significant domestic opposition, the Vajpayee government kept silent about the flawed selection process by which the United States made Hamid Karzai Afghanistan's president. In the past, any outside involvement in Asian affairs, and especially in a country in India's backyard, had always been opposed fiercely. This time pragmatism won out over principles.

Indian Critics

What sounds like the happy end of a Bollywood movie has resulted in more criticism than euphoria in India. Some of those voices cannot be taken seriously — for example, former prime minister Atal Behari Vajpayee and the BJP, who were those pushing for the rapprochement with the United States when in office. No matter what it be might saying right now, India's political right since independence has never had a problem with the United States or capitalism. Others argue against the new partnership with much more reason. First of all, the long tradition of Indian nonalignment seems to be in danger. Secondly, the nature of Indo–U.S. bilateral relations during the cold war has made Indian elites distrustful of Washington's motives. Thirdly, one has to take into account India's experiences in the fifteen years since the end of the cold war. And, finally, Indian elites already had had their rendezvous with the realities of the cons and pros of the Bush Doctrine as far as South Asia is concerned.

Nonalignment. Jawaharlal Nehru, India's first prime minister, opted for a non-aligned foreign policy, and he did so on the basis of a broad consensus at home. India could look back on a long history of being an advanced civilization, and there had been many powerful empires in India over the course of that history. Under the British, Indians proved to be good soldiers, administrators, scholars, and intellectuals. Colonial rule was thus seen as a humiliation (Cohen 2003, 50–54). During the struggle for independence Nehru had left no doubt that India was not fighting to become free in order to then immediately lose a part of its sovereignty by becoming a member of an alliance. The country should choose its position according to the individual case. Therefore, indigenous defense in-dustries were essential, and so New Delhi invested heavily into that sector (S. N. Singh 1986, 40), especially after India's 1962 military defeat in the Himalayas by the PRC. Help from outside was necessary, but India avoided becoming depen-dent on a single arms supplier.

Much of nonalignment was mere rhetoric. Nehru had his darkest hour when the Chinese People's Liberation Army (PLA) played havoc with Indian troops in 1962, because the latter had neither sufficient equipment nor powerful allies. India was better prepared when Pakistan attacked in 1965 partially because the Soviets did not stop arms deliveries to India, whereas the United States imposed an embargo on Pakistan. And the Bangladesh War in 1971 was won with Soviet diplomatic backing. None of the nonaligned countries supported India in any of these wars. Altogether it was an aligned rather than a nonaligned India carrying out a successful security policy. With the "peaceful nuclear explosion" (PNE) in 1974, however, India once again chose self-sufficiency. India has concentrated on nuclear armament and launching systems instead of on developing defense industries for conventional weapons comparable to other great powers.

For more than half a century India tried to stay independent in its decisions and opposed attempts of other powers to dominate the world and South Asia in particular. Partnerships are generally acceptable so long as New Delhi is not merely the junior partner. The new U.S. strategy to embrace the South Asian giant makes commentators uneasy. Close cooperation with the United States that serves India's national interests — that is, containing the PRC and Pakistan, fighting Islamist terrorism, and improving the country's global standing — keeps the traditions of Indian foreign policy alive, allowing India to exert influence, and therefore is most welcome. However, any obligation to follow U.S. foreign policy in other areas — for example, into wars like that against Iraq — would be totally unacceptable on principle. Even though there was a discussion in the Vajpayee government to join the coalition against Saddam Hussein (Noorani 2005), the debate was short-lived, as the BJP was fully aware that any decision that could be understood as a partial renunciation of complete sovereignty would cost public support (it is remarkable, however, that only in the United States and India does a majority of those polled believe that his removal has made the world safer [Pew 2005, 5]). Washington, too, revealed that it was well aware of the limitations of the strategic partnership by supporting the Japanese, but not the Indian, claim for a permanent seat in the U.N. Security Council (Cherian 2005). In both the Indian and the American concept of foreign affairs there is an element of unilateralism and zero-sum thinking. Given the background of different national interests, a longer lasting, close partnership is not an option either for Washington or New Delhi. However, this does not prevent India from taking advantage of the side effects of America's struggle for hegemony.

The Burden of History. From the very outset of India's independence India, the largest democracy, and the United States, the most powerful democracy, had high expectations of a fruitful cooperation. However, experiences during the cold war were mutually disappointing (Kux 1994). The United States did not support India's "just case" in Kashmir in 1948 but rather took account only of Western interests in Asia. Washington's military alliance with Pakistan in 1954 created a problematic constellation on the subcontinent. In its search for allies to contain Communism worldwide, the United States in fact gave Pakistan enough arms to make it a match for an India that was five times bigger, even though the latter proved to be the most stable democracy in the developing world. In a sort of chain reaction, the Soviet Union and the PRC mixed in South Asian affairs, too, which resulted in three interstate wars between 1962 and 1971 and a continuing arms race. Even the immediate American support India received following the Chinese attack in 1962 soon turned into a negative because the United States provided arms in only small amounts and because India was forced to engage in fruitless Kashmir talks with Pakistan. The latter's attack in 1965 was believed to be encouraged, at least unwittingly, by the steady influx into Pakistan of U.S. high-tech military equipment. And December 1971 almost witnessed an Indo–U.S. war, when Nixon sent the U.S. Seventh Fleet into the Gulf of Bengal in order to prevent the capitulation of Pakistani forces in what was to become Bangladesh, thereby engraving "an image of U.S. hostility into the Indian historical memory" (Kux 1994, 342).

Thereafter it was India creating further troubles. Indira Gandhi's leftist line in foreign and domestic affairs during the 1970s widened the gap between the two countries. The expulsion of American companies from India, the nationalization of Indian banks and insurance companies, and the 1972–75 state of emergency were topped by the peaceful nuclear explosion (PNE) in 1974 and the ambiguous attitude toward the Soviet invasion of Afghanistan in 1979. India was embittered, as well, when U.S. presidents Carter and, especially, Reagan decided to overlook Pakistan's nuclear program because it had become a new frontline state. Notwithstanding the remarkable sympathy for U.S. policy reflected in recent Indian opinion polls (Pew 2005), India's elites have been marked by the experience of having had to suffer through the regular fundamental turns in Washington's South Asia policy. During the cold war, the Unites States used the countries of the subcontinent mostly as pawns in more important political games on other chessboards and dropped them after they had served American purposes. The positive side effect was a massive influx of aid, the negative — from the Indian perspective — a highly militarized hostile nuclear neighbor. Neither for India nor for Pakistan had the United States proved to be a reliable partner.

India's Global Standing after the End of the Cold War. The decline of the Soviet Union initially meant a weakening of India's position in world affairs. Moscow had constantly backed India from 1963 on, and the mere existence of a second superpower had allowed New Delhi to maneuver between East and West. Rather unexpectedly India made the best of the Soviet collapse. After more than a decade of nearly complete insignificance in global affairs, it increased its diplomatic activity and was among the first to call for a polycentric rather than unipolar world. Since the early 1990s India has demanded a permanent seat in the U.N. Security Council with full veto-rights. Initially, India's request seemed to be mostly the rhetorical gesture of an already weak giant becoming ever weaker. But, because long-term Indian investments and economic reforms have begun to pay off, despite "an incompetent and heavy-handed state" (Das 2006), India now has the power to demand that it be taken seriously. India's soft power has grown steadily and it has become the leading country in software production. For decades the United States had learned to see the South Asian giant as a loan-hungry petitioner, but seemingly out of the blue India now has something to offer that is necessary to run the world economy. In other fields, too, Indian influence is no longer based just on sheer size combined with weakness. The country is a leader in high-tech medicine and among the few able to launch satellites.

The latter, of course, is inseparably connected to India's military missile program. The Chinese heartland lies within range of the midrange "Agni II," ensuring deterrence against any nuclear blackmail from Beijing. Indo–Chinese tensions eased during the 1980s. Both countries sought a modus vivendi so that they could make use of their limited resources for economic development. But there is still rivalry in many fields, mutual diplomatic attempts to contain the other's influence, and a race for dominance in the Indian Ocean, which is vital for oil imports (Bajpaee 2006). The PRC has adopted a more aggressive and successful containment policy toward India in recent years (Malik 2006). The prospects for another Indo–Chinese military conflict, however, are marginal. Beijing prefers to use Pakistan to keep India busy and locked up in South Asia, and it has massively supported that country's programs for bombs and missiles. Taking into account Pakistan's inner instability, this threat is much less calculable than the Chinese one. India's global standing has improved much — its immediate security hardly.

Over the past two decades major changes have taken place in Indo–U.S. relations. First, South Asia saw major Indo–Pakistani crises in 1987, 1990, 1998, and 2001–2003, several of which threatened to trigger a nuclear war. The second forced the United States to intervene diplomatically (Bidwai and Vainak 2001, 223). The third made President Clinton say that Kashmir is the most dangerous place in the world, while the fourth presented India as a victim of Islamist terror and resulted in its becoming a member of the coalition in the war on terrorism. Secondly, economic liberalization in India has made it a highly attractive market. Third, the collapse of the Soviet Union changed the constellation of power in South Asia. Pakistan ceased being a frontline state, and the decade-old American suspicion that India might be a potential surrogate for the Soviet Union dissolved, thereby also eliminating U.S. unwillingness to sell India dual-use technology (S. Gordon 1995, 254–55). India was seen increasingly as a responsible partner. Clinton started improving relations with the South Asian giant, signing an Agreed Minute on Defense Relations in January 1995. India's nuclear tests in 1998 caused no more than a small interruption in the improvement of its relations with the West. Many European countries did not even impose sanctions (Nayar 2001, 50), and American restrictions were short-lived. In fact, the economic sanctions imposed after the tests hurt Pakistan much more than India. And right from the beginning, the great names of American foreign and security policy from Henry Kissinger to Zbigniew Brzezinski showed understanding for the Indian tests (Nayar 2001, 46).

After the tests the United States started its first strategic dialogue with India. The talks between the U.S. deputy secretary of state, Strobe Talbott, and the minister of foreign affairs, Jaswant Singh, begun in June 1998 went on for two years (Talbott 2004). Although they did not lead to a consensus, let alone a joint statement, they were fruitful. Right after the 1998 Pokhran tests, India had made concessions, such as agreeing that it would not use nuclear weapons first against a nuclear power and would not use them at all against nonnuclear powers, which, had they been made during the talks, would have been praised as a major diplomatic breakthrough. The United States learned to appreciate India's security concerns in a hostile and unstable neighborhood as well as its stand against nuclear proliferation (Nayar 2001, 57–59). A number of reports about India produced by nongovernmental organizations (NGOs) and U.S. think tanks also suggested that India's security concerns needed to be taken seriously and that it was opposed to nuclear proliferation (Cohen 2003, 286–87). It became clear that India, on the one hand, never would accept its exclusion from the nuclear club, and that, on the other hand, it had the same interest as the United States in hindering others from developing nuclear capacities. The Kargil War in 1999 became a litmus test for the new Indo–U.S. relationship. India took a moderate stand whereas Pakistan played with fire. Washington "tilted" toward New Delhi and pressured Prime Minister Nawaz Sharif to pull back immediately, notwithstanding the massive loss of face that entailed for India (Kux 2001, 353). Clinton's visit to India in 2000—the first of an American president in twenty-two years—signaled U.S. acceptance of India's new status (Nayar 2001, 50).

Since the Republicans, concerned as they are mostly with China, were much more in favor of India than the Democrats, it did not come as a surprise when Clinton's successor followed this line of his policy. Since 2001 a number of joint maneuvers have taken place. The NSSP was topped by Prime Minister Manmohan Singh's visit to the United States in July 2005 and President Bush's visit to India in return in March 2006. The irritations about American demands to step back from nuclear cooperation with Iran (Kumaraswami 2005), which looked to India like the price Washington was asking it to pay in return for U.S. friendship, proved to be rather short-lived. Teheran's stubborn attitude and militant rhetoric made India move to the side of the majority of the international community. On February 4, 2006, India supported the decision of the IAEA to refer Iran's case to the United Nations Security Council (Varadarajan 2006), notwithstanding massive protests from the Indian political left that formed a part of the ruling coalition (*Prasad* 2006).

Indian Experiences with the Bush Doctrine. Even before the Bush Doctrine received its final shape, India had come to understand that the United States was claiming new rights for itself but denying them to others. This time it was not the old basic antagonism between a country that had traditionally believed in international institutions and rules and a superpower that invented those rules for others exclusively. After the terrorist attack on the Indian parliament, the Bush government intervened massively when New Delhi considered retaliating against terrorist training camps in Pakistan (Bedi 2002). India was threatening to get in the way of America's special treatment of Pervez Musharraf, who was believed to be the only guarantee of an ongoing pro-American official attitude in Pakistan and who therefore could not be pushed to give up Islamabad's second terrorist adventure in Jammu and Kashmir, lest he lose domestic public support completely. Further, during the Afghan war hundreds of Pakistani military advisers of the Taliban (as well as, in all likelihood, high-ranking members of the Taliban and al Qaeda) were flown out of Kunduz, in a U.S.-sanctioned airlift, before the troops of the Northern Alliance were allowed to attack (Hersh 2002). Pakistan had to end its engagement in Afghanistan, but it is well known as a safe haven for leaders of the Taliban and al Qaeda, some of whom also figure prominently in the network of Islamist organizations responsible for the ongoing fighting in Jammu and Kashmir. American pressure on Musharraf after the attacks on the Indian parliament resulted in a timely house arrest of some extremist leaders, but their organizations have simply been renamed and are as active as they used to be (Maher 2003).

The situation in Jammu and Kashmir has calmed down, but that owes more to the earthquake of October 8, 2005, leaving most of Pakistani Azad Kashmir literally in ruins, than to a thawing of Indo–Pakistani relations. A durable political solution is as far away as ever. Although the Bush administration has stepped up its rhetoric against terrorism in Kashmir in recent months, that has not brought about any results. Remembering earlier American statements about neutrality in the Kashmir dispute, while the U.S clearly supported Pakistan's case behind closed doors, India is left with the impression of double-talk once again.

The Bush Doctrine and India's Current Foreign and Defense Policy

American dominance has in fact made India more active on the global level. Parallel thinking has even brought it together with Beijing and Moscow on occasion, although this Indian–Chinese–Russian triangle promoted in Vladivostok in early June 2004 is mostly wishful thinking. It is almost unthinkable that these three rivals would be able to pursue a common policy. There was more substance in India's claim for a permanent seat in the Security Council. Because it was demanding a permanent seat along with Brazil, Germany, and Japan, even if the initiative never had a chance of approval, it nonetheless boosted New Delhi's image as part of a group of responsible, prosperous, and influential democracies. It is not surprising that its bid was supported by Russia, the UK, and France. Still, despite the fact that India has become more involved in international affairs, at best only one member of the G4, Japan, is a strategic partner for it, because they share a similar interest in containing the PRC. Moreover, Japan remains India's most important donor. Brazil and India share hardly any common interests; Germany is busy with internal problems and the development of a Common Foreign and Security Policy (CFSP) for the EU. The latter understands that India could be an important partner even though it has not yet become very active (Das Gupta 2006).

The continuity of the country's defense policy shows that the Bush Doctrine has had very limited impact on it. India has its own arms industries and demonstrated its self-confidence with the nuclear tests in 1998, followed by the draft nuclear doctrine of August 17, 1999 (National Security Advisory Board 1999). Between 1974 and 1998 governments had pursued a policy of nuclear ambiguity: they hesitated to claim openly to be members of the nuclear club because they feared economic sanctions. It was for this reason that the Rao government stopped test preparations in 1995 (Perkovich 2002, 353–77). The soft reactions of the Western world in 1998 proved that, as the BJP thought, India's improved standing had created more leeway. The draft doctrine declared the necessity of a "credible minimum nuclear deterrence" to allow further peaceful Indian development. First use was excluded but an "adequate retaliatory capability" was declared to be necessary in case deterrence should fail. Indian restraint in the Kargil War immediately before the publication of the doctrine won Vajpayee some respect, given that the BJP had quite often adopted an aggressive attitude toward Pakistan. In his first policy statement the new prime minister, Manmohan Singh, declared that he would follow the lines of the doctrine (M. Singh 2004). In addition, after the meeting with Bush in July 2005, he confirmed once again that the country would continue with its nuclear arms program.

The Indian bomb has a practical as well as a more symbolic function. Notwithstanding the massive doubts of prominent Indian critics about its rationale (Bidwai and Vainak 2001, 55–57), it provides deterrence against its nuclear neighbors, Pakistan and the PRC, and is seen as the entrance ticket into the club of the great powers. India does not accept the exclusiveness of that club — not only has it not signed the NPT but it also has not signed the Comprehensive Test Ban Treaty (CTBT). But the de facto recognition of the nuclear-power status of India by President Bush is at the same time highly problematic for the established nonproliferation system, as it encourages others not to give up their nuclear programs. If India's bomb has turned into a good one in American eyes, the United States could decide in the future that bombs of other countries are acceptable as well. However, the nonproliferation issue is trumped by the U.S. need for allies in Asia, and India offers not only military muscle but also democracy, a market economy, and stability. In fact, India has taken a rather passive stand, reacting to American initiatives rather than introducing its own; the United States had no option except to accept Indian nuclear developments and make the best out of the inevitable (Carter 2006).

India's security policy concerning conventional arms has also been little affected by the Bush Doctrine. Reacting to ever-growing Chinese power and Beijing's recent successes in gaining bases in Myanmar, opposite the Indian missile test site at the Gulf of Bengal, New Delhi is planning to create a blue water fleet.

The navy will receive at least two carriers enabling it to act further from the Indian homeland. As a first step in 2004 India paid U.S. $1.5 billion for the Russian carrier *Gorshkov*. The Indian Air Force is going to buy around 150 modern fighter jets in the coming decade. New Delhi can finance parts of this program of a regional power with higher ambitions thanks to economic growth rates of around 8 percent over the past fifteen years. Whether or not the recent Indo–U.S. statements will finally persuade India to buy American military equipment is uncertain. In July 2005 New Delhi at least ruled out the purchase of a missile defense system offered by the United States. Following its long-term policy, India wants to develop its own system.

However, no one can ignore the imbalance between Indian ambitions and resources. Upgrading the conventional arsenal will create a heavy financial burden; establishing a triad of nuclear arms is likely to lead to a budgetary disaster similar to the one created by the Ogarkov revolution in the Soviet Union. Finally, an Indian missile defense system in the foreseeable future is pure fiction. Those plans are at best blueprints — perhaps inspired by the American example.

India shows a greater sense of reality in its cooperation with Israel. The BJP government was among the staunchest supporters of Ariel Sharon's military attacks against the Palestinians. Since 1992 India and Israel have developed a close partnership in defense production and intelligence sharing. Israel has become India's second biggest arms seller, and India Israel's best customer in that field (Voll 2005, 323–25). This partnership also has an Indo–American component. In 1998, immediately after the Pokhran nuclear tests, Washington made major but fruitless protests against a large Israeli sale of advanced electronic equipment to India (Naaz 2000). Five years later the Bush administration gave Israel the go-ahead to export the sophisticated early airborne radar system Phalcon to India (BBC News 2003a). The long-standing common interest and cooperation of Tel Aviv and New Delhi in fighting Islamic extremism has now also found American approval within the context of the war on terrorism. Thanks to parallel national interests, a dominating position in their respective regions, and mutual self-confidence, Indo–Israel ties do not need to find favor with the United States in order to be operative.

Where the Indian military is involved in fighting — namely, Jammu and Kashmir — its tactics have changed in recent years. The artilleries of Pakistan and India had been firing over the LoC in Kashmir on a daily basis. To date India has launched no preemptive air or missile strikes against terrorist camps. Plans for such strikes were torpedoed by the United States, but they cannot have been realistic anyway, since a preemptive strike against Pakistan, a nuclear power, would be enormously risky (Rajagopalan 2005) and would not have much effect on India's problems in Kashmir — and in 1999 in Kargil Pakistan proved that limited warfare leads to nothing. In the new millennium India continues to resort to fighting terrorists with security forces and services — obviously with some support from outside — as well as through a détente with Pakistan. There is a new perspective that Pakistan could be a much friendlier neighbor, if it had a chance of an internally stable and prosperous future — the Indian success since 1991 has won the country friends among the average people in Pakistan (Das Gupta 2004a).

Summing up current Indian strategy, one can see heavy investments in armaments, armaments that are meant more to boost the country's status than to satisfy immediate security needs. On the other hand, India understands that it has made its way toward great-power status by successful economic development. The old problems with Pakistan and the PRC cannot be completely solved, and they can definitely not be solved by military force. India won two military engagements with Pakistan and helped divide the country into two parts in 1971. This separation of East Pakistan (now Bangladesh) from what was West Pakistan has not produced peace; not even a complete incorporation of Pakistan into India would ever lead to a lasting peace. Regardless of which party will rule China in the coming decades, the rivalry with India will continue, since it is not based on the differences of the political systems but on national interests. Therefore New Delhi is trying to combine a containment policy with peaceful diplomatic and economic cooperation to the benefit of all. This is much more a European than an American approach to dealing with international problems.

Pakistan

In Pakistani eyes the Bush Doctrine and its effects are a nightmare. President Musharraf criticizes the United States but with great reluctance. In late 2004 he told CNN that the war against Iraq was a mistake because it had stirred anti-American feelings in the Muslim world (CNN 2004). In another interview in May 2005 (Musharraf 2005) he warned against a preemptive strike against Iran, although he admitted that his country had sold nuclear know-how and equipment in the knowledge that Teheran was after the bomb. Musharraf cannot afford to provoke Washington further. In almost all terms Pakistan is a rogue state and the linchpin in the axis of evil, which without Pakistan is no axis at all. Abdul Qadeer Khan, the "father" of Pakistan's bomb, who buys and sells nuclear know-how and hardware for and from countries that are seen as major threats to U.S. security, is the only link among North Korea, Iran, and Libya (Braun 2004). To make things worse, Pakistan had incubated the Taliban in its madrassas and later supported their regime, which closely cooperated with al Qaeda through military advisers and the secret service Inter-Services Intelligence (ISI). That the leaderships of al Qaeda and the Taliban obviously survive in the Pakistani–Afghan border region says much about the Pakistani willingness to cooperate as does the fact that Khan and his helpers have not been sent to Pakistani or American prisons (Hersh 2004). Both of the major threats that the Bush administration tries to fight could and can be located in Pakistan: nuclear proliferation and international terrorism. It should not be forgotten that the Clinton administration gave similar importance to the fight against the production and trade of narcotics and that Pakistan today is a hub for both (Kukreja 2005, 191–225).

India can live with the Bush Doctrine, although it is openly questioning potential U.S. hegemony in the world. Pakistan offers assistance, but it is the real challenge for the doctrine. There has been much criticism of U.S.–Pakistani cooperation (Hadar 2002). For a number of reasons, however, it would be difficult to put Pakistan on trial. It has never threatened Washington directly and, in fact, has enjoyed a rather close relationship with the United States for fifty years (Kux 2001). The United States also can hardly blame Pakistan for developing the first "Islamic" bomb, since it had a number of chances to stop Pakistan's nuclear program but chose not to act on them. When the Dutch authorities in 1975 came into possession of evidence that Khan stole secret information, the CIA intervened in order to prevent his imprisonment (*Trouw* 2005), Secretary of State Henry Kissinger also ignored State Department reports about Pakistan's nuclear ambitions (Kux 2001, 219). The Carter administration was much tougher on the issue and an interagency group even suggested an attack against the Kahuta uranium-enrichment facility (Kux 2001, 240). Nothing happened, because the United States needed Pakistan as a base once again after the Soviet invasion of Afghanistan. For the same reason the Reagan administration did everything to avoid the Pressler Amendment, which stated that aid to Pakistan could be continued only if the U.S. president certified annually that Pakistan did not possess nuclear weapons and that was scheduled to come into force in 1984 (Kux 2001, 275–79). Between 1985 and 1988 Reagan certified that Pakistan had no explosive nuclear devices, and in 1989, Bush also certified as much, although both administrations were aware Pakistan was enriching uranium beyond weapons-grade level. By 1990, when Bush announced he was unable to certify that Pakistan possessed no explosive nuclear devices, the damage had been done.

The story of the Taliban is not much different. The CIA mostly left it to its Pakistani colleagues to decide which resistance group fighting the Soviets in Afghanistan should be supported. Not surprisingly the ISI chose what was best for Pakistan. Washington at first had no major problems with the Taliban, which brought stability to Afghanistan, burned opium fields, and started negotiations on pipeline projects with U.S. companies (Rashid 2000, 292–93). Altogether, it would be strange to punish a country for actions that were well known and quite often even agreed to by Washington.

Pakistan enjoys much less leeway at present. One side effect of the developments in Afghanistan is that Pakistan has become even more fragile than it used to be. It has been described as "anti-India" because the logic behind its creation was simply to establish a country that was not India. Even today Pakistan lacks a positive national identity (Thornton 1999, 171). It has experienced numerous ethnic and religious conflicts since 1947; before the dictator Gen. Zia-ul-Haq came to power in 1977, power had been exercised by secular elites — either politicians or military men. Under Zia, orthodox Islam became a new factor in the political game and today forms the third power within Pakistan, along with the secular politicians and the military. The other two have regularly tried to make use of it — not only in Afghanistan and Kashmir — but have lost control (Kumar 2000). The Islamists have infiltrated the higher ranks of Pakistan's army and enjoy support in the ISI leadership (Hersh 2004). Violence in Pakistan itself has increased massively, and the frontlines have become less and less clear (Kukreja 2003, 179–85). There is no need for military intervention; rather what is required is patient nation building. The United States is not known for success in this area, and the Bush Doctrine, with its military focus, does not offer any answers here either. The best Washington can do at the moment is to secure the survival of Musharraf, who himself only recently underwent a Pauline conversion from being the general responsible for the Kargil adventure and the toppling of Prime Minister Sharif to the pro-Western president looking for détente with India.

Pakistan plays a double game — supporting the war on terrorism in Afghanistan (at best half-heartedly) and sponsoring terrorism and extremism directed against India at the same time. Terrorists can count on intelligence and logistics — the same intelligence and logistics that made possible the highly provocative attacks against the parliaments in New Delhi and Srinagar right after 9/11. Whether or not Musharraf is sympathetic to the ongoing attacks in India, he has to work with the extremists and leave them one battlefield at least if he does not want to see their energies directed against his own government.

Pakistan's obvious interest in protecting the remnants of the Taliban and al Qaeda creates headaches for the United States, too. The military leadership and ISI tell the CIA only what they believe to be necessary. Once the pressure from Washington becomes too strong, Islamabad will have to start a fruitless expedition in the border areas or imprison second-rate terrorists like Ramzi bin-al-Shib (Maher 2003). Recently the U.S. Army has been striking in Pakistan's border region (Knowlton and Gall 2006), which says a lot about the credibility of Islamabad's own efforts. These forays have been undermined by Islamabad. The decision of the Musharraf regime to withdraw Pakistani forces from the Afghan border and to consign the security of this region to local chiefs essentially permits Taliban and al Qaeda elements to operate freely in Afghanistan. Western forces cannot pursue either into Pakistan. Unless the border is closed, the likelihood of defeating either the Taliban or eliminating terrorist enclaves in Afghanistan is slim. The Musharraf government has apparently bet on these groups as a hedge against the loss of Afghanistan by the United States and the West.

The Afghanistan question is far from being settled, and the Taliban are back in the south and the east. Kashmir has not generated much interest in Washington. As noted above, prominent extremist leaders were placed under house arrest for a couple of months after the attack on India's parliament, but their organizations were simply renamed once they landed on the U.S. list of terrorist organizations. The future will show whether Pakistan is able and willing to cure its inner disease, stay away from the Jihad concept in its foreign policy (Kukreja 2003, 173–75), and accept its just or unjust borders together with its status as only the second strongest power in South Asia. The role of the United States and the Bush Doctrine will be marginal in such a process.

Conclusions

South Asia has never asked for an outside hegemon, although Pakistan has regularly sought U.S. support in its ongoing struggle with India, and neither the end of the cold war nor the changes after 9/11 have enabled the United States to play that role. Throughout the cold war, Washington had demonstrated only a casual and occasional interest in that part of the world — for example, during the Soviet occupation of Afghanistan. The long-term impact of the terrorist attacks has brought the United States back to the region again, although one is tempted to say for another short-term visit that will not yield decisive results.

No doubt U.S. influence in South Asia is strong, especially where American soft power is concerned. Pakistan is more dependent on American aid than ever. India, however, is developing into a partner, since it is doing much better in the world economy today (though the Indian business community knows very well that the latter fundamentally depends on the health of the U.S. economy). The pattern changes when we talk about hard power, that is, hegemony in military terms. Both India and Pakistan are nuclear powers, and neither is willing to cooperate with Washington on the latter's terms: New Delhi resists openly and Islamabad silently. Contemporary Asia has often been described as a balance-of-power system with a number of great powers. The United States today is simply one of them and requires partners and allies. Once again it has opted for both the rivals, one to bring peace to Afghanistan, the other to contain the PRC. This strategy failed half a century ago (Das Gupta 2004b) and will likely fail again.

The weakness of the American position is clearly visible in the new Indo–American "friendship" since this is, as we have seen, a partnership on Indian terms. Washington can have no doubt that India is also a potential rival in the long-term. New Delhi is outspoken against the idea of a unipolar world in any form and insists that there be rules and regulations that apply to everybody, including the United States. Bilaterally, it is after no less than a partnership of equals. Anything less would conflict in principle with a long-established self-image and confirm critical judgments India came to make during the cold war about U.S. aims in general. New Delhi has benefited from the Afghanistan war and needs backing in the face of growing Chinese power, but it sees the old double standard in the Kashmir dispute. Still, the Bush administration has opted for close cooperation, which requires abandoning the nuclear regime to which it was committed for decades. Obviously it feels too weak to contain the PRC solely with its established allies in the region.

It might seem as if it should be much easier for the United States to control Pakistan. Musharraf was forced to undertake a fundamental shift toward the United States after 9/11 and ever since has attempted to play the role of the trustworthy ally. However, the way he was treated during Bush's visit to South Asia in spring 2006 signaled clearly that Washington knows that Pakistan, in fact, is less an ally than it is a hatchery for all that fundamentally endangers the United States today. It is breeding militant extremism; it has sold nuclear know-how and hardware; it plays a major role in the international narcotics trade. Whether its own nuclear weapons will remain under central control is an open question; it is a country that shows many signs of being both a failing and a rogue state. As long as Washington needs partners like Pakistan, described as "the most dangerous country for the United States now" (Hersh 2004), there is no basis for the idea that the United States has established a global hegemony.

CHAPTER SIX

Southeast Asia

Joseph Chinyong Liow
and See Seng Tan

That no singular perspective today adequately describes how Southeast Asians view America should come as no surprise to seasoned watchers of the region. Regional perceptions of the United States appear to be marked by an underlying tension rooted in a traditional reliance on the part of most Southeast Asian governments on a sustained U.S. security presence in a region that is increasingly being met by a growing anti-Americanism in some segments of civil society.[1] Moreover, this apparent ill will toward the United States arose amid democratic transitions within the region, a development that is compelling affected states to rearticulate, if not recalibrate, the traditional terms of their relations with the United States. This is not to imply those states are seeking to balance U.S. power or revise the international status quo, no matter how self-righteous, hypocritical, and heavy-handed they perceive America to be (Walt 2005, 125). What it does mean, however, is that the state of U.S.–Southeast Asian relations in the foreseeable future will likely be shaped not only by how ably Southeast Asians manage those tensions but also by how Washington responds to them.

According to François Heisbourg, the following visions of America more or less comport with European perceptions of the United States in the post–cold war era: benign hegemon, rogue state, trigger-happy sheriff, and keystone of world order (Heisbourg 2000). Arguably, the more odious of these might not have applied to how member countries of the Association of Southeast Asian Nations (ASEAN) viewed America during the cold war period. The image of the United States then held by many in non-Communist Southeast Asia, though by no means a pristine one, was still relatively generous (Kwa and Tan 2001, 97). The same certainly could not be said of the view Southeast Asia takes of the United States in the post–cold war period, much less the post-9/11 period. If anything, regional circumspection over U.S. foreign policy, already on the rise during the Clinton years, has patently increased since the advent of George W. Bush's presidency, particularly in reaction to Washington's perceived proclivity for a unilateralist foreign policy, which in itself had pre-9/11 origins.[2] Tradition-ally regarded as the region's stabilizer and "honest broker"—a view still held by a not insignificant number of specialists of Southeast Asian security—the United States nevertheless has had to make do with unflattering characterizations of its identity and behavior. As Samuel Huntington (1999, 42) observed, "While the United States regularly denounces various countries as 'rogue states,' in the eyes of many countries it is becoming the rogue superpower . . . the single greatest external threat to their societies."[3]

This surfeit of antagonism against the United States has often been linked to the rise in religious militancy within Southeast Asia, and while that is a factor, the backdrop against which the growth of anti-American attitudes and behavior have burgeoned, notably, the ongoing albeit uneven process of democratic transition within the region, which has received considerably less attention, is also impor-tant. Our aim here is neither to revisit the controversial debate on democratiza-tion and conflict, nor to hold the democratization process as primarily account-able for the rise of anti-Americanism in Southeast Asia.[4] At most, we allow that democratic transitions, especially in weak states reacting against an illiberal past, tend to be unstable as long as democratic consolidation has not been achieved (Bush 2005).

What does seem apparent, however, is that the tension stemming from the traditional dependence on a robust U.S. presence and a contemporary revision of that stance in view of mounting domestic pressure is most palpable today in Southeast Asian countries that have experienced democratic transition but not necessarily consolidation, notably, Indonesia, the Philippines, and Thailand. Such tensions are not, however, restricted to weak developing democracies but are also discernible in developed semidemocratic countries with fairly substan-tial Muslim populations, such as Malaysia or even Singapore.

This clearly has serious ramifications for the Bush administration's policy of re-gime change. If, in the U.S. president's words, the "survival of [America's] liberty" is increasingly dependent on "the success of liberty in other lands" (Bush 2005), and given that opposition to such a policy (and possibly to the United States it-self) is most virulent in societies where political liberalization has transpired, not least in Southeast Asia, then just how might a program of democratic expansion to "other lands" ensure America's liberty?

With these concerns in mind, we begin by outlining the traditional areas of collaboration between the United States and Southeast Asian partners during the cold war and after. The second section traces the changing geopolitical en-vironment and the concomitant shift in American priorities as the democratic expansion agenda gained pace as well as Southeast Asian responses to U.S. pres-sures. It also describes the changing regional context as societies within the region democratized — quite apart from Washington's plan to export democracy abroad. A third section looks at regional responses to the war on terror. A final section explores U.S.–Southeast Asia relations against the backdrop of longer-term geostrategic considerations, namely, the rise of China and its influence on this relationship.

Traditional Bastions of Collaboration

Few would dispute the fact that following World War II the United States occupied a unique place in history, being one of only two truly "global" superpowers whose actions would influence every other state in the world. In the case of Southeast Asia, the United States would figure largely in the security of the region during the cold war years. For anti-Communist regimes, Washington would prove the main guarantor of security while posing a threat at the same time to Soviet and Chinese-supported regional Communist governments. American interests in the region during that period were primarily strategic — Southeast Asia was a major theater of operations for Washington's cold war policy that pursued a global containment of the spread of communism (Gaddis 1982). This role entailed the commitment of U.S. security forces as a counterweight against Communist expansion in the region and took the form of bilateral and multilateral alliance agreements with regional governments prepared to align their interests with Washington's. American commitment was most tellingly demonstrated in its involvement in the Vietnam War, which cost the United States tens of thousands of U.S. dead and wounded (69th Armor Page, http://www.rjsmith.com/kia_tbl .html). U.S. obligations to the security of Southeast Asia during the cold war were chiefly built around a series of bilateral alliances (Tow 2001, 1–11). Washington committed itself to the security of Thailand and the Philippines through the Manila Pact, a Southeast Asian collective defense treaty signed on September 8, 1954, which was initiated by the United States in order to shore up the Geneva Agreement on the status of Indochina in July that year. The Manila Pact took on institutionalized form in February 1955, when it anchored the creation of the Southeast Asia Treaty Organization (SEATO), a collective security body that was premised on American political and diplomatic weight and underwritten by U.S. military power. Because of the understanding that the United States would bear the larger share of risks and costs of security management in the region, SEATO members also accepted American primacy on matters of strategic importance, not least of which were decisions surrounding the commitment of SEATO forces. This would eventually cause friction among members, particularly with the non–Southeast Asian allies Britain and France, and led to the demise of the organization in 1971.

While not signatories of explicit defense pacts with the United States, states such as Malaysia, Singapore, and post-Sukarno Indonesia, by virtue of their opposition to Communism and close political and economic relations with Washington, did nonetheless enjoy the fruits of the American security umbrella, which provided much-needed stability and formed the backdrop of economic growth and an influx of investments (Stubbs 1999). In return, Malaysia, Singapore, Thailand, and the Philippines provided facilities for the American war effort in Indochina. Aside from its military power, American political, economic, and diplomatic support also proved critical to the anti-Communist governments of Southeast Asia given the strident domestic political and security challenges posed by belligerent Soviet and China-backed local Communist parties to the legitimacy of capitalist regimes (Ang 2001).

The American cold war security presence in Southeast Asia was not without its drawbacks. American primacy was not something that was either palatable or acceptable in the eyes of pro-Communist regimes. In fact, the United States was at various times viewed as a threat to the security of a number of Southeast Asian states. This was certainly the case with the Hanoi government of the Democratic Republic of Vietnam (DRVN), which was engaged in conflict with the United States and its South Vietnamese ally until the fall of Saigon in 1975. Under President Sukarno, Indonesia, too, was wary of American intentions in a region where it viewed itself as the natural leader (Leifer 1983). These suspicions appeared to be corroborated with the capture of Allen Lawrence Pope on May 18, 1958, while the American pilot was flying combat missions against Jakarta during the 1957–58 regional rebellions in Sumatra and Sulawesi, popularly known as the Revolutionary Government of the Indonesian Republic (PRRI)/Permesta Rebellion.[5] Even in the case of established allies such as the Philippines and Thailand, the existence of strident nationalist elements meant that the American security presence became a routine issue of national debate as nationalist lawmakers and left-wing politicians leveraged residual anticolonial sentiments by playing up the issue of American-led neocolonialism.

The withdrawal of American troops from what looked like an increasingly unwinnable Vietnam War in 1973 marked the start of a diminishing U.S. security role in the region. Following the fall of Saigon and Phnom Penh two years later, non-Communist Southeast Asia rallied around ASEAN at the Bali Summit in 1976. It was at Bali that the leaders of Indonesia, Malaysia, Thailand, the Philippines, and Singapore adopted the Zone of Peace, Freedom, and Neutrality (ZOPFAN) as the principle of regional order. ZOPFAN was a corporate vision of regional autonomy cobbled together in a 1971 foreign minister's meeting that was premised on a regional resilience that would derive from the noninterference of major external powers in Southeast Asia (B. Singh 1992).

The Vietnamese occupation of Cambodia in 1978 saw ASEAN embark on a global diplomatic initiative to rally international support to condemn the Vietnamese occupation. While Washington lent its diplomatic weight to this initiative, it did little else to allay regional concerns that Soviet-backed Vietnamese aggression would turn to Thailand, ASEAN's frontline state, and from there threaten the existence of non-Communist archipelagic Southeast Asia.[6] Eventually, it was the reduction in Soviet support, a consequence of a deterioration of the Soviet economy and polity itself, which led to the introduction of elections under the auspices of the U.N. in 1993 and, finally, to Vietnam's withdrawal from Cambodia. Notwithstanding pretensions of regional security management, the question of how to sustain the U.S. security umbrella continued to weigh heavily on Southeast Asian minds through the final years of the cold war (Leifer 1989). These concerns would take on greater salience with the geostrategic uncertainties that confronted the region at the end of the cold war.

While the collapse of the Berlin Wall and the end of the cold war was lauded in Europe as heralding a new era of peace, in Southeast Asia it heightened regional anxieties regarding an increasingly uncertain security climate. Two interrelated issues fixated the region's policy makers and analysts and dominated post–cold war regional security discourse — the possible withdrawal of the United States, on the one hand, and the rise of China, on the other.

Throughout the cold war, the United States was viewed by non-Communist Southeast Asia as a balancer against the Soviet Union and China. Concomitantly, despite residual nationalist reservations about American interference, which in any case were effectively dealt with through mostly repressive measures undertaken by Washington-supported authoritarian regimes, such concerns were supplanted by the more pressing issue of the need for a bulwark against communism. Given its preoccupation with its global strategic rivalry with the Soviet Union, and to a lesser extent China, Washington was for the most part also prepared to make this commitment.

With the end of the cold war, a major pressing challenge was that of gauging and ascertaining American commitment to the region in the absence of a clearly defined enemy. Domestic political and economic developments in the United States did little to assuage these insecurities. Since 1990, American policy circles have been given to intense debates over post–cold war security commitments, particularly in East Asia. In 1990 the Department of Defense under the administration of George H. W. Bush announced its East Asia Security Initiative (EASI), which laid out plans for a gradual and modest reduction of American military presence from Southeast Asia, while at the same time introducing a security strategy based on "low-profile bilateral arrangements . . . worked out in memoranda of understanding with various ASEAN member countries" (Emmerson 1996, 109).

Disengagement from the region was hastened by closure of the last remaining American bases in Southeast Asia — the eruption of Mount Pinatubo in the Philippines in 1991 rendered Clarke Air Force base too costly to repair, and the Philippine Senate voted to oust American forces from Subic Bay in 1992. With the election of Bill Clinton in 1992, the American people had chosen a president who was seen to have little interest or aptitude for foreign affairs, certainly not for international politics that concerned Asia. And insofar as Asia featured at all, it was Northeast Asia, where American attention was fixated on the Korean Peninsula, the restructuring of the U.S.–Japan Alliance, and the rise of China.

At issue for Southeast Asia's policy makers was the security vacuum that they perceived would naturally materialize in the aftermath of a U.S. withdrawal and the likelihood that a resurgent China might choose to fill that vacuum (M. Richardson 1992). It was this concern that sparked Singapore, with which the United States has arguably the strongest relationship in the post–cold war era, to immediately offer to facilitate the relocation of American naval forces from Subic Bay by offering the U.S. naval logistics facilities. Even Vietnam, which was only just recovering from a decade-long military confrontation with the United States, received the possibility of a U.S. withdrawal with much consternation. Despite residual hostility toward the United States, especially on the part of an older generation of Vietnamese who had participated in the Second Indochina War, Vietnam has a longer tradition of bilateral antagonism and rivalry with China that only recently manifested itself in the Third Indochina War. Here, Vietnamese leaders are concerned that the absence of a countervailing U.S. presence might well embolden Beijing to the detriment of Vietnam's security. In this respect, the marked improvement in U.S.–Vietnam relations in the 1990s was telling, even if it was predicated mostly on trade and economic issues that took center stage when ties were normalized in July 1995.[7]

The ramifications of uncertainty surrounding American security obligations were brought out into greater relief in February 1992, when China restaked its claim on the South China Sea islands and declared its right to use force to protect "China's islands" (Emmers 2005, 6). Washington's response to the South China Sea imbroglio was to carefully distance itself from it. While proclaiming freedom of navigation through the sea a matter of U.S. interest, Washington skirted a potential diplomatic confrontation with China by endorsing ASEAN's calls for the peaceful settlement of the disputed claims. It was clear from the U.S. position on the South China Sea that, much to the dismay of its old allies in Manila and old foes in Hanoi (both of whom were counterclaimants to some of the South China Sea islands), it was not prepared to bring its political or diplomatic weight to bear on the issue.

Given the perception that regional security was being compromised by Washington's "benign neglect" and, flowing from that, expectations that the basis for strong bilateral ties premised on the presence of American troops on Southeast Asian soil would gradually weaken as a consequence, ASEAN sought to supplement existing bilateral security arrangements with a web of multilateral organizations. The most significant of these organizations was the ASEAN Regional Forum (ARF), formed in 1994 under the auspices of ASEAN. A key raison d'être of the ARF, as many scholars have observed, was to keep the United States "in" the region (Leifer 1996).

Washington's immediate reaction to the ARF was one of apprehension. Despite shifting priorities and military deployments, the United States still preferred bilateral modes of security management even as it prepared to scale down its overall commitments to the region. Washington viewed multilateral initiatives with caution because of their tendency to stymie action. This fear was quickly mollified when it became increasingly clear that a multilateral arrangement such as the ARF in fact provided a complementary means of security management, allowing the United States to continue playing a role in the shaping of the regional security environment without forcing it to incur expensive and expansive military commitments or sacrifice existing bilateral alliances (Leifer 1998, 5–6). Another major factor in the recalibration of attitudes toward the ARF and multilateralism in general on the part of American policy makers was the need to deal with the resurgence of China. Neorealists are given to the grim view that the greatest challenge to U.S. global dominance in the near future will come from China (Brzezinski and Mearsheimer 2005). Indeed, the question of China warrants deeper discussion and will be addressed later in this chapter. Suffice for now to note that for some, Southeast Asia was seen as one probable arena where Sino–U.S. rivalry would play out (Friedberg 1993–94). To be sure, this view was echoed by many within the Southeast Asia policy establishment.

Washington's Democracy Conundrum in Southeast Asia

Southeast Asian concern over American security commitments did not foreclose the emergence of new disagreements between the United States and the region. The end of the cold war also marked the resurgence of democracy and human rights as major foreign policy priorities. While not irrelevant during the cold war, these issues were nevertheless overshadowed by the more pressing security challenge of "rolling back" the tide of Communism across Southeast Asia. After the cold war this emphasis on human rights and democracy took on an intellectual veneer in the form of the "Asian Values" debate that sparked academic and popular interest both in the region as well as in the United States in the early 1990s. Other issues such as Jakarta's policy toward East Timor, ASEAN's admission of Myanmar into its fold, and Washington's annual human rights report, which catalogues abuses in Southeast Asian countries, posed minor problems for relations.

The East Asian financial crisis of 1997–98, however, tempered regional reactions to the United States to much greater effect. During the crisis, the United States was perceived to have exercised its leverage over international financial regimes such as the International Monetary Fund (IMF) and World Bank in order to exploit fragile Southeast Asian economies, force open hitherto closed markets, and restructure political economies in the region (Beeson 2002). American arrogance was epitomized by Vice President Al Gore's public snub of his Malaysian host at the 1998 Asia-Pacific Economic Cooperation (APEC) Summit in Kuala Lumpur. Not surprisingly, Washington's economic policies toward Southeast Asia during the crisis were met with widespread resentment and anti-U.S. protests throughout the region (Hewison 2001). Malaysia used the opportunity to critique the Western world's monopolization of global trade and finance and with Chinese support rekindled talk of a "genuine" East Asian economic and financial regionalism that would keep the United States at arm's length.[8]

As was suggested earlier, the spread of democracy had since the end of the cold war become a major facet of Washington's foreign policies, though some have argued that it had antecedents long before that (Kristol and Kagan 1996). Even so, the democratization drive undoubtedly gained greater pace and purpose during the second Bush administration. This was made abundantly clear when the policy was given substantive expression in America's military campaigns in Afghanistan and Iraq, both of which had regime change and the introduction of "free and fair elections" as their primary declaratory objective. Though Washington has been careful to reassure its Southeast Asian counterparts that the means of regime change it has exercised thus far, namely the use of force, need not be a matter of concern, it remains adamant that democracy promotion continues to inform much of its policy toward the region (Rieffer and Mercer 2005). Indeed, Deputy Assistant Secretary of State Eric John indicated as much when he testified before the House International Relations Committee in 2005 that insofar as Southeast Asia was concerned, "the most important and encouraging trend in recent years has been the strengthening of democracy." Given the primacy of this objective, it is telling too that later in similar testimony John intimated that "ASEAN has not done all it could or should to promote democracy" (U.S. Department of State 2005c).

These seemingly contradictory statements capture the longstanding frustration that Washington policy quarters have felt toward Southeast Asian states that continue to resist American pressures to democratize even as they reap the fruits of Washington's commitments to the region. At least one reason for this complicated picture is the fact that the democratic transition process is taking place in what are essentially weak states in the region but states that are also home to the most virulent public expressions of anti-Americanism in Southeast Asia.

American unilateralism and regional anxieties aside, the Southeast Asian region has undergone a prolonged yet incomplete period of democratic transition whose origins date back to the so-called Third Wave of Democratization (Huntington 1992) — "people power" in the Philippines in 1986 and the bloody street demonstrations of Thailand in May 1992. These movements continue to this day, most emphatically in Indonesia since the downfall of Suharto. The rise of participatory democracy in these ASEAN societies should not be underestimated, not least the growing involvement (or "intrusion") of civil society actors and social movements in domains that traditionally were the exclusive preserves of Southeast Asian governments (Acharya 2003; Lizee 2000; Neher 1996). What is discernible is the vitriolic anti-American rhetoric that is often associated with democratic societies in Southeast Asia. In the Philippines, a cloud has been cast over the return of American troops under the auspices of the Visiting Forces Agreement (VFA) signed in 1998, ostensibly to strengthen the capacity of the Armed Forces of the Philippines in their fight against Communist and separatist rebels, by recent allegations of the involvement of American servicemen in a gang rape of a local woman. The groundswell of discontent that surfaced as a result of these allegations erupted into street protests in Manila as well as several cities in Mindanao (Cerojano 2006). American reluctance to hand over the suspects to Filipino authorities further hardened anti-U.S. resentment and pressured the Arroyo administration into taking a tougher stand against Washington. Similarly, the Thaksin administration in Thailand was besieged by large anti-U.S. demonstrations in Chiang Mai and Bangkok in January in opposition to free trade negotiations between America and Thailand. Indeed, these anti-American protests in Thailand reached a level not seen since nationwide student protests in the mid-1970s against the presence of American military bases.

A key point to stress here is that insofar as the nexus between democratization and anti-Americanism is concerned, it is somewhat telling that Southeast Asian societies in which these trends registered most prominently had (with the exception of Malaysia) relatively weak governance and poor state capacity. For instance, Indonesia and the Philippines stood out as weak states with incomplete administrative coverage over their extensive territories where law and order were concerned, hampered by an excessive legalism created to prevent the possibility of authoritarian reversals — in comparison to the strong, well-resourced states of Singapore and Malaysia (Almonte 2003). Sharing this view, Sheldon Simon

(2003, 16) made the observation that "the two Southeast Asian states where terrorist movements are strongest, Indonesia and the Philippines, are weak states unable to enforce basic law and order, with the political and economic marginalization of large portions of their populations despite the fact that both are functioning democracies."

The lack of central governmental coverage over its remote southern part suggested that Thailand might in some respects demonstrate elements of state weakness as well (Liow 2004). In this respect, while some analysts were quite right to be concerned with the detrimental effects of excessive state controls and potential repression of Southeast Asian societies in the war on terror, the opposite extreme might have been equally inimical, namely, the rise of virulent anti-American attitudes and behaviors that, if left unchecked, could prove highly destabilizing to the region (Jones and Smith 2002; Tan and Ramakrishna 2004). Already, there are signs of such instability surfacing in the region.

That said, a lesson drawn from the recent controversy involving Danish cartoons depicting the Prophet Mohammad was that states with significant Muslim constituencies themselves might not be above using such events as opportunities for their politically repressed populations to vent their grievances — as long as their vitriol is reserved for targets other than their own governments. In this regard, the proclivity of most governments in the Southeast Asian region — with Singapore perhaps the sole exception — to engage in "the politics of scapegoating" unfairly turned America into an alternative target of distrust and hostility (Wright-Neville 2003, 6). Both the democracy conundrum and the "politics of scapegoating" were to assume greater salience in U.S.–Southeast Asia relations in the context of the American-led global war on terror.

The War on Terror and Southeast Asian Responses

At first glance, Washington's relations with Southeast Asia appeared to undergo a major shift in the immediate aftermath of the tragic terrorist attacks of 9/11. After decades of "benign neglect," the era of the global war on terror saw Southeast Asia designated its "Second Front" by influential quarters of the Washington policy establishment when the October 2002 Bali attacks in Indonesia put the region back on Washington's security radar (Gershman 2003). This translated into several substantive initiatives as security relations experienced a new lease on life. U.S. military forces returned to the Philippines under the VFA. Long-standing bilateral alliances with Thailand and the Philippines were enhanced as these states were upgraded to "Major Non-NATO Ally." Security relations with Singapore and even Malaysia, a regular critic of American policy, were also strengthened in the wake of 9/11.

Washington's "return" to Southeast Asia has also paradoxically created new fault lines and widened old ones within the region, fueling domestic debates over U.S. activism and hegemony. Because of the Bush administration's binary reading of the war on terror, where the international community had basically to choose to be "with us or against us," states in Southeast Asia perceived that they were confronted with a fait accompli as the policy appeared to give little choice to smaller and weaker states that were expected to either comply or risk some sort of retribution (Goh 2003).

Another problem for Southeast Asia was the way the region's vast Muslim community regarded the war on terror. The exertions of American diplomats and politicians have done little to convince the vast majority of the Muslim world that the U.S.-led war on terror is not a war against Islam. Indeed, as Richard Betts (2002, 26) bluntly warned, despite strident efforts of several American leaders to divorce the two, "U.S. leaders can say they are not waging a war against Islam until they are blue in the face, but this will not convince Muslims who already distrust the United States." The perception has informed much of Southeast Asia's response to the American counterterrorism effort. In Thailand and the Philippines, where ethnic separatist movements are active in mobilizing Islamic motifs and metaphors to legitimize their resistance, governments try to downplay their security relations with the United States. Even Singaporean leaders have exercised caution by engaging their Muslim minority in dialogues geared toward explaining why it was strategically necessary for the city-state to cast its lot with the United States. Apprehension toward the U.S.-led war on terror, however, gained greatest currency in Indonesia, home to the largest Muslim population in the world, and Malaysia, current chair of the Organization of Islamic Countries (OIC) and, ironically enough, arguably Washington's most indispensable ally in the counterterrorism campaign.

To be sure, leaders of Indonesia and Malaysia were quick to offer their sympathy, both private and public, to the United States after the 9/11 attacks. Indonesian President Megawati Sukarnoputri was among the first foreign heads of state to visit the White House after the terrorist attacks. Malaysian Prime Minister Mahathir Mohamad turned his characteristically caustic verbal attacks, often reserved for American leaders in particular but also more generally for the "West," on Islamic militants as well as Muslim governments that had created the domestic political, economic, and social conditions that gave rise to them. Given the numerous diplomatic tussles between his administration and Washington over the years, the red-carpet treatment accorded to Mahathir on the occasion of his visit to the United States in May 2002 certainly suggested that U.S.–Malaysia relations had turned a corner.

Muslim Southeast Asia's sympathy for the United States was, however, short-lived. Support soon turned to frustration and anger in the wake of Washington's hasty and ill-considered reprisal. The invasion of Afghanistan was greeted with caution in both Indonesia and Malaysia. In Indonesia, massive student and civil society demonstrations against the war in Afghanistan took place in Palau, Makassar, East Java, and Jakarta, and local militant Muslim groups, such as Laskar Jihad (Jihad Army) and Front Pembela Islam (Islamic Defender's Front), threatened retaliation against U.S. citizens if Washington proceeded with aggression against their Muslim brothers.[9] The Indonesian government's response was encapsulated in the comments of a legislator: "I am deeply concerned over the U.S. attack against Afghanistan. It is a terrorist act. Terror should not be confronted with terror. The United States should make efforts to end terrorist acts without creating new terror."[10] More recently, the Indonesian government has been particularly incensed by Washington's reluctance to hand over Hambali aka Ridzuan Hishammudin, a major terror suspect believed to have been the mastermind behind the Bali attack of October 2002 who was captured in a joint CIA–Thai intelligence operation in the Thai city of Ayutthaya on August 11, 2003, to Indonesian security forces for interrogation.

The Afghanistan campaign sparked similar reactions in Malaysia, where the government condemned the attack and orchestrated protests.[11] Relations took a further turn for the worse following the invasion of Iraq. Both Kuala Lumpur and Jakarta challenged the legality of Washington's twin objectives of the destruction of weapons of mass destruction (WMD) and regime change, which they saw as a matter of Iraqi internal politics. The profound irony that democratization was being "forced" on Muslim lands by an alien Western government that in any case was never intent on ascertaining the will of the local people they claimed they were "rescuing" from the grip of tyranny was certainly not lost on either political leadership or popular opinion across Muslim Southeast Asia. The Malaysian government was especially proactive in orchestrating condemnation of the U.S. war on Iraq at both international and domestic levels. Prior to the outbreak of hostilities, Malaysia was already actively involved in marshaling international diplomatic opinion in opposition to U.S. policy. Then–prime minister Mahathir took advantage of Malaysia's position as chair of the Non-Aligned Movement to formulate a resolution rejecting a U.S.-led attack on Iraq without the sanction of the U.N. The Malaysian government also led the OIC in protest against U.S. military action. At home, the Malaysian Parliament unanimously adopted a motion condemning the unilateral military action against Iraq by the United States and its allies. Leaders of both government and opposition parties orchestrated a joint demonstration outside the U.S. Embassy on March 25, 2003. This followed a massive, state-organized antiwar demonstration at the Merdeka Stadium that was attended by fifty thousand people, including the entire cabinet. Elements within government, the opposition, and civil society further mobilized support for a national peace movement (*Aman Malaysia*) that sought to lobby the United Nations to investigate the "war crimes" of America and its allies and bring the "perpetrators" to court.

At the heart of popular discontent in Southeast Asia toward the United States also lies a perception of American hypocrisy manifested in a major policy disconnect between the Bush administration's purported pursuit of democracy and freedom and its support of undemocratic practices and human rights violations in some Southeast Asian countries. For example, criticisms of the Internal Security Act (ISA) and other forms of legislation deemed authoritarian violations of human rights that have regularly been leveled at several Southeast Asian regimes from the corridors of power in both the White House and Capitol Hill have been conspicuously silent in recent years. Instead, the fledgling Indonesian democratic system has been taken to task for not putting in place terrorism laws that in effect amount to surveillance. Likewise, the use of the ISA in Malaysia and Singapore, so often a point of contention for the United States as far as forming ties with them went, is today tolerated, if not tacitly encouraged, by Washington as it is mobilized as part of counterterrorism campaigns.[12] This disconnect is not lost on large segments of civil society and popular opinion in the region, with many viewing it as an example of American hypocrisy. The American conduct of the war on terror deepened skepticism on the part of a public that was already concerned about the fact that Washington's purported objective of democracy was being pursued in an "undemocratic" fashion via a unilateral use of force that undermined the sovereignty of the targeted state.

In order to appreciate Muslim Southeast Asia's responses to the war on terror and American policy, one needs to understand the complex domestic political forces at play that inform the framing and conduct of foreign policy, particularly in Jakarta and Kuala Lumpur. Since the fall of President Suharto in 1998, the advent of democracy has facilitated the reemergence of political Islam in Indonesia. This has taken the form not only of a plethora of Muslim political organizations and parties that have emerged and have become part of the mainstream political process but also the form of a number of popular radical Islamist groups that had flourished and that have since been at the forefront orchestrating anti-U.S. demonstrations throughout the country. Because of the increasing weight of Islam in Indonesian politics, populist leaders often seek to court the Muslim vote by aligning themselves in the public eye with these radical groups. In the case of Malaysia, the politicization of Islam can be traced further back to the early 1980s with the emergence of the Islamist opposition party, the Pan Malaysian Islamic Party PAS (Parti Islam Se-Malaysia), and the consequent "Islamization race" between it and the incumbent United Malays National Organization (UMNO)-led regime. As a result of this contest, politicians from both parties have regularly burnished their Islamic credentials in order to enhance their popularity and support base.

Yet despite strident rhetorical broadsides in both directions, post-9/11 relations among the United States, Indonesia, and Malaysia have in truth been much more ambivalent. The United States continues to play a critical role in the counterterrorism calculus of regional states. While Jakarta and Kuala Lumpur constantly engage in megaphone diplomacy toward the United States, cooperation on defense and security matters has not ceased. On the contrary, certain aspects of cooperation such as intelligence sharing and collaboration against terrorist financing have increased over recent years. At Washington's request, Malaysia created a regional center for counterterrorism to conduct training for various state security forces from Southeast Asian countries.[13] Defense ties enjoyed by both Malaysia and Indonesia remain solid, and in the latter case a temporary halt on U.S. security cooperation in protest of the Indonesian military's human rights abuses in East Timor has just been lifted. To be fair, Washington, too, has wisely chosen to tread carefully in the implementation of counterterrorism policy in Southeast Asia. While adamant that its own national security justifies unilateralism and preemption at any cost, the United States is slowly demonstrating more sensitivity and sophistication in its dealings with Muslim regimes and constituencies throughout the region. Consequently, the United States has trodden diplomatic and political minefields carefully by assuming what has largely been an auxiliary role in Southeast Asia's war on terror, only offering support on request (such as the case in the Philippines); it has also limited tangible cooperation chiefly to bilateral arrangements, which take on a lower profile and are more manageable. In this regard, Secretary of State Condoleezza Rice's March 14–15, 2006, visit to Indonesia captured much of this apparent readjustment in U.S. strategic thinking vis-à-vis Southeast Asia. During the course of the visit Secretary Rice emphasized America's desire to strengthen its "strategic relationship" with Indonesia. Clearly in the corridors of power in Washington there has been a realization that Indonesia, as the politico-diplomatic heavyweight in Southeast Asia possessing a Muslim-led government that is increasing its gravitas in the Muslim world, will prove an important ally on issues such as Chinese assertion of regional hegemony as well as American policy toward Palestine and Iran.

The China Factor in U.S.–Southeast Asia Relations

Notwithstanding the difficulties that the Bush administration's post-9/11 war on terror-era foreign policy positions have posed for Southeast Asia's relations with the United States, particularly the states with significant Muslim populations, regional policy makers continue to stress the age-old mantra that American commitment to the region is vital to regional security. This reluctance to distance themselves from Washington despite domestic pressures reveals the magnitude of longer-term geostrategic concerns for Southeast Asian leaders. To that end, one question dominates and fixates — how to deal with China if and when it becomes a major power — if indeed it is not already a problem.

Put simply, a major consideration for Southeast Asia's calibration of policy toward the United States for the foreseeable future will be the arid strategic reality posed by the rise of China. It bears noting here that while terrorism poses an immediate threat that is not likely to dissipate anytime soon, it is the potentially destabilizing challenge that a powerful and activist China might pose in the future that looms large in the thinking of Southeast Asian policy makers and will lead them to finesse any overt expression of anti-American sentiment, popular opinion notwithstanding.

The emergence of China as a major power has occupied much of the international security literature. Likewise, Washington's policies toward the broader Asia region, particularly the manner in which it has strengthened relations with Japan, Indonesia, and India, indicate that the United States has been read in several quarters as adopting a "containment policy" of sorts toward Beijing.[14] Along those lines, recent visits by Secretary of State Condoleezza Rice and Secretary of Defense Donald Rumsfeld to Southeast Asia indicate that Southeast Asia too appears to feature in this policy. Our objective here is not to debate the veracity of claims that Washington is indeed embarking on a containment policy vis-à-vis China. More important for current purposes is consideration of how the question of China may or may not animate U.S.–Southeast Asia relations.

The fact that the rise of China has major strategic, not to mention economic, implications for Southeast Asia is already a given. Of immediate concern for the region is how to read China's policies even as it develops its economic potential and military capabilities. To be sure, Chinese foreign policy positions toward Southeast Asia appear to have undergone a transformation since the end of the cold war. While previously suspicious of ASEAN and concerned that the regional organization would throw its weight behind a United States that was intent on "keeping China down," the past decade has seen Beijing undertake what scholars have termed a "charm offensive" toward Southeast Asia. This has included conciliatory gestures such as restraint (to some extent) in its claims to South China Sea territories, heightened economic and trade relations with Southeast Asian economies, active diplomatic and political support for ASEAN initiatives such as the ARF and the newly formed East Asian Summit (EAS), and an important decision not to devalue the renminbi during the height of the regional financial crisis. Most recently, China has gained accession to ASEAN's Treaty of Amity and Cooperation, a document that governs relations between ASEAN member states, spelling out the terms of regional security management, such as the non-use of force to settle disputes, and which external parties are allowed (and in some instances encouraged) to accede. Already impressive in comparison to the long history of mutual suspicion between China and Southeast Asia, the positive net effect of these initiatives is further amplified when they are juxtaposed to Washington's relations with the region over the past decade, which, as this chapter has labored to describe, has been plagued by a range of issues.

There is little doubt that as a result of its "charm offensive" over the past few years, China is gradually dispelling some of the public suspicion that regional states harbored about its hegemonic intentions in the wake of several diplomatic altercations contesting territorial claims in the South China Sea (primarily in 1992, 1995, and 1997). In private, however, policy makers continue to hedge against the possibility of a non–status quo China in the future (Johnston 2003). Three issues in particular stand out as matters of concern for the policy community in Southeast Asia. First, despite its support of "joint exploration" initiatives and the fact that it is a signatory to the South China Sea Declaration of 2003, China has not renounced its claims to the South China Sea Islands. Second, the Chinese establishment continues to maintain that while its objective is peaceful reunification with Taiwan, it would be prepared to use force against a Taiwanese government that unilaterally declared independence. While the outbreak of hostilities across the Taiwan Straits is not likely to spill over into Southeast Asia, regional governments harbor deep reservations and anxieties about potential conflict and worry that it might have a dire impact on the regional, if not global, economy. Moreover, given Taiwan's intimate relations with the United States, Southeast Asian leaders have often expressed candidly that they do not want to find themselves having basically to choose sides. Finally, China–Japan relations continue to vacillate between periods of hostility and accord. Here again, regional states are confronted with the same trepidation of the dire economic impact on the region, on one hand, and the potential political and diplomatic costs of being caught in the middle of a conflict between two major regional powers, on the other.

It is through these lenses that Southeast Asia's policy makers from Vietnam — which continues to harbor historical suspicions of Chinese hegemony — to Indonesia and Malaysia — who are wary of American unilateralism and foreign policy rhetoric — view the United States as a strategically important countervailing force vis-à-vis an increasingly assertive China. That said, Southeast Asian states, including Washington's traditional allies, have been reluctant to pursue overt balancing strategies toward China, conscious of the danger that such a policy might inadvertently "will" a hostile China into being, and hence raised concerns at the discourse of strategic competition that the Bush presidency engaged in at the onset of its tenure.

Conclusions

In sum, if American engagement with the region since the Vietnam War seemed somewhat distracted, if not disinterested, relative to its involvement in other regions, then U.S.–Southeast Asian ties under George W. Bush have only confirmed regional suspicions that the ASEAN region is but a distant concern of Washington's, one that matters only where international terrorism and democratization are concerned (Acharya and Tan 2006). When prodded by the regional media during his maiden visit to Southeast Asia as Bush's first assistant secretary of state for Asia and the Pacific, the sum total of James Kelly's terse comments on the region was that Southeast Asia was "always a problem for the United States."[15] And while the post-9/11 period might have been marked by heightened U.S. attention toward and engagement with the region — strengthening ties with and providing military assistance to regional allies and growing cooperation in counterterrorism and intelligence exchange, calls for greater attention to democracy in the region, the ongoing effort to establish bilateral free trade agreements with Asian states (the first of which was signed with Singapore) — the perception within the region that all this merely reflected Washington's parochial preoccupation with its war on terror rather than any genuine concern for the well-being of Southeast Asians proved perdurable. On the other hand, the Pentagon's Global Force Review, which called for a strategic reorientation from maintaining permanent forward bases to keeping so-called "lily pads" and "warm bases," fueled perennial regional anxieties (unsubstantiated) about a possible U.S. military disengagement from the region.[16] More recently, the decision by Secretary of State Condoleezza Rice to skip last year's ARF meeting and the gaping silence in the latest edition of the Pentagon's *Quadrennial Defense Review* (released in February 2006) regarding U.S. priorities vis-à-vis Southeast Asia only served, unfairly or otherwise, to reinforce the sense of marginalization.

Whether Southeast Asian states can successfully reconcile the tension between a traditional reliance on the U.S. security presence and virulent anti-Americanism within their populations remains uncertain. Southeast Asian leaders clearly need to do better at managing the sense of relative deprivation and blame displacement that, among other things, has engendered much ill will toward the United States. While democratization has significantly broadened the political (or at least electoral) process in ASEAN states, cultural and religious enfranchisement remains woefully inadequate in some of those societies — such is the case for Muslims in southern Thailand, for example.

On the other hand, that tension has also been tied to how the United States has exercised its foreign policy. Clearly, anti-Americanism in the contemporary era did not begin strictly as a rejoinder to the second Bush administration's neoconservative agenda (Katzenstein and Keohane 2006). But the manner in which Bush's unilateralist foreign policy has been received and reviled in certain quarters of Southeast Asian societies raises important questions regarding the alleged intentions, if only imagined, behind that policy. To paraphrase Herman Melville's *Billy Budd,* if handsome is as handsome does, then how America is perceived by Southeast Asians and others most certainly has something, if not everything, to do with what America does (or is perceived to have done). In this respect, anti-U.S. attitudes and behaviors are but the price the United States is paying not just for its current global position but also for the specific ways in which the Bush administration has employed American power (Walt 2005). In the words of a Taliban official, "We are not against America or Americans. We are against the arrogance of intimidation. . . . I like America. I like Americans. I just don't like American foreign policy." [17] For all intents and purposes, this sentiment is one shared even by democratic societies that are allies and strategic partners of the United States. As President George H. W. Bush once reportedly said, "I will never apologize for the United States of America — I don't care what the facts are."[18] If Washington is indeed serious about engaging the world with (in the president's words) "purpose without arrogance," then a generous measure of strategic restraint in the foreign policy of the world's sole superpower is sorely required.

Notes

1. Anti-Americanism has earned sufficient attention by international relations scholars to justify an entire volume on the topic (Katzenstein and Keohane 2006). That said, the Katzenstein and Keohane volume focuses primarily on anti-U.S. currents in Europe, whereas this paper deals with similar phenomena in the Southeast Asian region.

2. As Stewart Patrick (2000) observed, despite its purported advocacy for an "assertive multilateralism," the Clinton administration "demonstrated a growing willingness to act alone and to opt out of multilateral initiatives."

3. And as Indian author Arundhati Roy has put it, "American foreign policy has created a huge, simmering reservoir of resentment" (quoted in Walt [2005, 68]).

4. On the link between democratization, belligerent nationalism, and war, see Mansfield and Snyder (1995, 2002). In much the same vein, a report on China recently released by the Australian Strategic Policy Institute noted: "An authoritarian China has been highly predictable. A more open and democratic China could produce new uncertainties about both domestic policy and international relations" (quoted in Eyal [2006]).

5. For a detailed study of this episode, see Doeppers (1972).

6. Nor did Washington share the concern of ASEAN states that Vietnamese aggression against Thailand might drive Bangkok into Peking's sphere of influence, thereby facilitating the southward expansion of Chinese influence.

7. That is not to say that Washington's relations with Hanoi did not have their fair share of irritants. Differences continue to this day, for instance, over export tariffs, and on its part the United States has persisted in criticizing Vietnam's poor record on human, religious, and labor rights.

8. In 1990, Malaysian prime minister Mahathir Mohamad had planted the idea of an East Asian trade bloc following the U.S.-led creation of North American Free Trade Agreement (NAFTA). In a deliberate affront to the United States and Australia, Mahathir defined this trade bloc in exclusivist terms—Washington and Canberra were identified as powers that would be omitted from it. The trade bloc would be known as the East Asian Economic Group (EAEG). In the course of deliberation within ASEAN, Singaporean and, in particular, Indonesian reservations resulted in the concept being diluted into the East Asian Economic Caucus (EAEC), which was defined as a caucus that would operate within APEC.

9. "Assault on American Politics: Indonesians Demonstrate Against U.S.," *Financial Times*, September 29, 2001.

10. "U.S. is Creating New Terror, Not Ending It," *Antara*, October 8, 2001.

11. "Malaysian Islamic Leader Vows Support for Afghanistan," *Dow Jones International News*, September 24, 2001.

12. In the case of Malaysia, it is quite clear that the ISA has also been manipulated by the incumbent regime for political purposes (Liow 2004b).

13. Having said that, Malaysia was careful to ensure that the center was not identified with American interests and initiatives and hence rejected offers from quarters in the U.S. establishment to provide expertise to it.

14. See for instance, Bobrow's chapter in this volume.

15. For a good discussion of U.S.–Southeast Asian ties under Kelly's watch, see Limaye (2004).

16. Most analysts see the ongoing reorientation in terms of a slight adjustment of the U.S. military footprint in Asia with no significant change for the foreseeable future (Cossa 2005; Camroux and Okfen 2004).

17. From Mohammad Sohail Shaheen, who represented the Taliban government in Pakistan ("At Home with the Taliban," *Salon*, October 10, 2001, www.salon.com/news/feature/2001/10/10/taliban/index.html).

18. Quoted in "Overheard," *Newsweek*, August 15, 1988; cited in Walt (2005, 93).

EUROPE AND CENTRAL ASIA

CHAPTER SEVEN

Europe

Trine Flockhart

> We are engaged in a deadly standoff with the axis of evil.
> You know who I am talking about: Iran, Iraq, and one
> of the Koreas . . . and don't forget France!
>
> —WILL FERRELL (as G. W. Bush) on *Saturday Night Live*

The epigraph is comedic and should be seen as just that. Yet political satire contains an element of truth, and the inclusion of France in the "axis of evil" shows a change in how the United States views some of its European allies. From the other side of the Atlantic, there is a growing concern over American foreign policy in general and particularly over the war in Iraq and its subsequent bloody peace and the misconduct by some American forces notably in Abu Ghraib and at the massacre in Haditha. Added to that are concerns over the disregard of human rights at Guantánamo and disquiet over the Bush administration's repudiation of a series of multilateral agreements such as the Kyoto Protocol, the Antiballistic Missile (ABM) Treaty, the Comprehensive Test Ban Treaty (CTBT), the International Criminal Court (ICC), and the Protocol to the Biological Weapons Convention as well as references in the *National Security Strategy* to act preemptively in using force against another state. The result is that the European discourse on the transatlantic relationship has gone in a negative direction and that cooling transatlantic relations have led to a change in European foreign and security policy aspirations.

The issue is not European opposition to America as a hegemonic power. American hegemony has been widely accepted and welcomed in Europe since the end of World War II. Rather Europe is concerned about its own security in an era in which the United States affords Europe less priority and, above all, about the way the United States is perceived to *manage* its position as global hegemon. The way the United States manages its relations with the European states is perceived to have gone from being based on consensus achieved through patient argument and persuasion to a form of brute power and a take-it-or-leave-it bargaining strategy. If it is really the case that Europe objects to American claims of hegemony under the Bush Doctrine rather than simply disagrees over substantive policy issues, then the problem in the transatlantic relationship concerns the fundamentally important question of how value-based relationships such as the Euro-Atlantic community are maintained and secured. The problem therefore is not that "Europeans are from Venus and Americans from Mars" (Kagan 2002), but that the relationship between them is no longer being managed in a way that engenders trust and shared core values and organizational principles. If the trust in a value-based relationship is undermined and the values and identities of the entities that make it up change and go in different directions, the core foundations of the relationship will be at risk. This chapter, therefore, tries to discover whether the crisis in the transatlantic relationship is merely "squabbles among friends" or if it should be seen as symptomatic of the much more serious problem of fundamental ideational changes with repercussions for the level of trust and legitimacy between its members.

The Euro-Atlantic Security Community

It is frequently stated that the relationship between the United States and Europe is cemented through shared values, which have compensated for the two sides' different strategic interests and unequal military strength. Although this problem, known as NATO's "nuclear dilemma" (Schwartz 1983), was widely acknowledged as a problem without a solution, it has nevertheless been solved throughout NATO's history by the parties to it engaging continuously in processes of persuasion and consensus building (Bertram 1983) that have been based on an informal understanding of the United States as primus inter pares. In most cases the consensus-building method has worked because the Europeans, albeit grudgingly, eventually have been persuaded to at least not obstruct the consensus-building process.[1]

Consensus building through continuous dialogue and persuasion has been a key factor for alliance cohesion by creating knowledge and understanding between the military and foreign policy elites on both sides of the Atlantic and thereby cementing the shared values and principles underpinning the Euro-Atlantic community. It is precisely such processes that are regarded as necessary conditions for establishing and maintaining a Deutschian security community, because the primary "glue" of a security community is shared values, mutual trust, and collective identity (Adler and Barnett 1998, 38).[2]

To emphasize values within the discourse on security communities does not mean power within security communities is unimportant. In fact, power and hegemonic ideas are central concepts for understanding how security communities develop and are maintained over the long term (Adler and Barnett 1998, 39), as the powerful members are likely to assume a hegemonic position within the security community by setting agendas and acting as role model for the rest. The hegemony exercised within a security community is a hegemony based on consensus, where the hegemon's ideas are accepted by the nonhegemonic members of the community, not because they are enforced but because they are perceived to be right and to constitute appropriate action. This stands in opposition to the traditional conception of hegemony as one state having a "preponderance of resources" (Keohane 1984) that enables the hegemonic state to force the nonhegemonic states to accept new norms.[3] In the alternative conception of hegemony, hegemony is founded on moral, cultural, and intellectual leadership and is based on consent among the secondary states who accept the legitimacy of the hegemon's authority. Crucially, the hegemon can only maintain its hegemony through socialization and continuous efforts to preserve its legitimacy.

Power within the security community may be understood as the authority to determine what constitutes the shared values underpinning the security community (Adler and Barnett 1998, 39). In practice this means that the strong center performs an educational role through socialization whereas the less powerful members undergo a process of social learning. Socialization and social learning are all the more necessary in times of change, when values must be reinforced. Therefore, one of the essential tasks of the leader of a security community is to ensure that the values and the identity of the security community remain shared, even during times of change and crisis.

In the discussion here on European responses to the Bush Doctrine, the question is whether the United States, faced with crisis and large-scale international change, has altered its conception of leadership from one based on consent to one based on "a preponderance of force" and therefore has abandoned the crucial process of socialization through persuasion. If so, then the problem of the current Atlantic crisis relates more to the fundamental challenge of maintaining the security community during significant international change when persuasion and socialization processes are crucial than to particular disagreements over particular policies.

European Views on American Announced and Operational Foreign and Military Policies

Although European consternation over American foreign policy only really came to the fore following the election of George W. Bush, entering into free fall in the run up to, and aftermath of, the war in Iraq, the change in the transatlantic relationship cannot be wholly attributed, as Michael Cox (2005, 207) suggests, to just "one controversial president or one unfortunate war." Rather, the change in the transatlantic relationship is the result of a gradual process that was set in motion by the Clinton administration, particularly by policy differences between the Clinton administration and Europe over how to handle the war in the former Yugoslavia and in Kosovo. In both cases the United States displayed a degree of (understandable) impatience and exasperation over the European inability to act decisively in the face of growing tragedies. By the time of the Dayton accord, key personnel within the Clinton administration had decided that the Europeans could simply not cope with the Bosnian crisis and that the Americans had to take the lead role (M. Cox 2005, 212; Holbrooke 1998) to resolve it. As a result the Europeans were left playing second fiddle to the Americans in managing a problem that was decidedly a European rather than an American priority. Similarly, when the crisis in Kosovo escalated during the winter of 1998 and the diplomatic effort failed to stop yet another tragedy unfolding within southeastern Europe, it was again the United States that led allied forces. The Europeans, who on this occasion contributed extensive forces to NATO, found that they could not participate actively in the air campaign because of inadequate military capabilities. While it is fair to say that the Kosovo campaign was a success in the sense that NATO went to war (out of area) as an alliance for the first time in its history and decisively defeated Serbian forces, the way the war was carried out led the United States to declare it would never again conduct a "war by committee."

The Balkans crises cannot be said to have led to a crisis in the transatlantic relationship. The disagreements were largely limited to corridor grumblings among security policy makers and academics. However, they highlighted the differences in the two sides' typical modus operandi. The Europeans prefer diplomacy and political pressure, while the Americans prefer to use military force at a much earlier stage. The Yugoslav experience led to a change, albeit subtle, in the way the United States behaved toward Europe. Americans became less concerned with NATO and took the Europeans less seriously. This change in attitude was clearly resented within NATO circles.[4]

The accusation of military weakness was, however, accepted within European policy circles, giving rise to renewed efforts within the European Union (EU) to establish a European Security and Defense policy (ESDP) with the implied purpose of being able to act both independently of, and more effectively alongside, the United States. But a subtle shift in the relationship had occurred: the Europeans had to come to terms with no longer being the main security concern of the Americans, and the Americans in turn seemed less concerned with maintaining consensus within the alliance through traditional consensus-building processes.

George W. Bush and "Winds of Change" in Transatlantic Relations

With the election of George W. Bush, European security concerns increased significantly, although at first these new security concerns were mostly related to Europe's worry about the withdrawal of the United States and the shift in American foreign policy interests from Europe to Asia. The concerns seemed to be vindicated by the initial, rather limited, foreign policy plans of the new administration in which the newly elected Bush talked about doing less rather than more abroad (M. Cox 2005, 214). However, it soon became evident that the new Bush administration's foreign policy plans were more "active" than the reference to "doing less" suggested, as "doing less" seemed to amount to repudiating (without consulting or negotiating with European allies) a string of multilateral agreements that were regarded as politically very significant in Europe. Even before the attacks on Washington and New York in 2001, Europeans were already deeply concerned that the new administration was making significant changes to both the content of foreign policy and the way of doing business with its allies. They detected what seemed to be a fundamental shift from bargaining based on mutual respect and multilateralism to unilateralism and a disregard for the long-established tradition of a negotiated order (Ikenberry 2001). The crisis seemed deeper than those that had come before and perhaps deeper than the crisis that might have been caused by the U.S. repudiation of just one of the international agreements. As suggested by Elizabeth Pond (2004, x), crises in the past had tended to be over single issues — not over a whole range of issues. These issues taken together constituted a significant departure from what had until then been "normal" foreign policy (Flockhart 2004).

It was within this acute sense of transatlantic crisis that the attacks of September 11 took place. As suggested by Michael Cox (2005, 215), Europe both expressed a heartfelt compassion for those affected by the attacks and sincere shock and revulsion by the atrocity as well as an opportunity to repair some of the damage in transatlantic relations. Within only a day of the attacks, NATO members invoked article 5 of the Atlantic Treaty for the first time in the history of NATO. European support for the now-declared "war on terrorism" remained firm, despite dislike of the term, as the United States began attacks (without NATO) on Afghanistan in October 2001, leading to the defeat of the Taliban government a month later. At this point Germany and France declared their explicit support for the U.S. response and offered military contributions to the effort in Afghanistan, offers that were rejected by Washington (Wallace 2002, 113).

Had this chapter been written at the end of November 2001, it would probably now have proceeded at this point to express a cautious optimism on the prospects for reestablishing the transatlantic relationship on a more healthy footing. The Europeans would have acknowledged that they had to do more to improve their military capabilities and transatlantic cooperation to prevent terrorism, and the United States might have been willing to accept that what the Europeans lacked in decisive military action they compensated for with their ability to "pick up the bill" for postconflict reconstruction (Hill 2004b, 149). Even if such an outcome had been possible following the fall of Kabul, the Europeans would have once again been worried by American rhetoric when in the 2002 State of the Union address in early 2002, the president referred to Iran, Iraq, and North Korea as an "axis of evil"—rogue states sponsoring terrorist organizations and oppressing their own people. Not only did Europeans recoil from the language employed, but most European terrorist experts would have rated states such as Yemen, Pakistan, Algeria, and Chechnya (Hill 2004b, 151) well above the three the president named as comprising the "axis of evil," at least as far as sponsoring terrorism was concerned. If the issue was domestic oppression, the list seemed remarkably short and not particularly logical. The former French minister of foreign affairs, Hubert Védrine, denounced the characterization as simplistic and suggested that the Americans had fallen into precisely the trap set by the terrorists—to start a "clash of civilizations" (Holm 2004, 484).

The crisis deepened further over the summer of 2002, when the administration increasingly alluded to preemptive strikes as a general means of dealing with threats to U.S. national security and as a specific means of dealing with Saddam Hussein. By the time of the publication of the *National Security Strategy* in September 2002, preemption was already a priority option of the evolving American security policy, which Europeans regarded as a serious breach of previously accepted approaches to diplomacy and a grave undermining of traditional patterns of U.S.–European dialogue and discourse. As the document contained no promise of negotiations about the circumstances under which preemptive power would be used, John Peterson (2004, 624) concluded that it seemed "to spell the end of the negotiated international order."

The transatlantic relationship then faced probably its most serious crisis ever, mirrored by an equally serious crisis within the EU itself. The crisis was caused by profound differences in threat perceptions between some Europeans and the Americans. France, Germany, Belgium, and other NATO and EU members did not share the American assessment that Iraq constituted a clear and present danger that warranted forced regime change. They argued that the weapons inspections should be given more time to assess whether Iraq possessed WMD and that the presence of inspectors would limit the threat (Terriff 2004, 423). This position was opposed to that of the United States and Britain and a number of other European states, characterized by Washington as "new Europe." These

European states agreed with the United States that the terrorist threat over the long term could only be addressed through regime change, a regime change that if necessary would have to be achieved through force.

The Iraq War and a Deepening Transatlantic Crisis

The Bush administration's relentless drive to carry out a war against Iraq without U.N. or allied approval or support brought European disunity over American foreign and strategic policy into the open. In early February 2003 the political dispute within NATO spilled into the public domain as France, Germany, and Belgium refused authorization for advanced NATO military planning to help defend Turkey in the event of war in Iraq. This essentially amounted to a refusal to honor article 4 of the Atlantic Treaty, which states that "NATO members will consult together whenever, in the opinion of any of them, the territorial integrity, political independence or security of any member country is threatened" (Terriff 2004, 440). Although Turkey was eventually furnished with antiair Patriot missiles, airborne warning and control system (AWACS) surveillance aircraft, and chemical and biological defensive units (B. Park 2004, 510), the dispute caused "fear and loathing" in NATO (Terriff 2004, 420). An unnamed NATO diplomat is reported to have described the incident as "a near death experience" and U.S. secretary of state Colin Powell raised the specter of NATO breaking up as a consequence (B. Park 2004, 510).

The drive toward war also resulted in a serious crisis within the EU. The refusal by France, Germany, and Belgium to release NATO forces for the defense of Turkey raised the question of just how dependent the ESDP might be on the goodwill of Turkey. Turkey, a full NATO member and EU applicant, appeared to hold considerable power in deciding when and if to release its NATO forces for use within the ESDP. The crisis within the EU was brought to a head when it became clear that the EU's claim to speak and act with one voice through its Common Foreign and Security Policy (CFSP) was simply void in practice. With the publication of the "letter of eight" led by Prime Ministers Jose Maria Aznar of Spain and Tony Blair of Britain and the subsequent Vilnius letter in which ten accession and prospective member states joined the five EU and three soon-to-be EU states in supporting the U.S. line, it was clear that the fifteen EU members and the ten accession states held profoundly different views on the question of support for the United States and the war in Iraq. The EU Commission under Romano Prodi of Italy, along with France, Germany, Luxembourg, Sweden, Austria, Finland, Slovenia, and Cyprus, opposed the war, while Britain, Denmark, the Netherlands, Spain, Portugal, Italy, Poland, Hungary, Estonia, Latvia, Slovakia, Bulgaria, Czech Republic, and Romania saw no other option than to support the United States. A smaller group of EU and accession states chose fence-sitting, including Ireland, Belgium, Lithuania, and Malta as well as Greece, which as EU president had to remain neutral. At the emergency European Council Meeting in February 2003 and at the routine spring council in March the leaders of the major EU countries could barely bring themselves to speak with each other. The only accord possible was an agreement on the fundamental role of the United Nations in resolving the Iraq crisis. This elegantly papered over the fact that individual EU member states were busily pursuing fundamentally different and opposing policies (Allen and Smith 2004, 96).

Turkey, as a nonmember of the EU but on the brink of EU accession negotiations and as a neighbor with friendly relations with Iraq, warranted special attention. Clearly the issue of Iraq held geopolitical implications that were far more profound for Turkey than for any European state (B. Park 2004, 494). Geographic proximity to Iraq and Kurdish separatism within Turkey posed a threat both to regional stability and to Turkey's own territorial integrity (B. Park 2004, 498). The issue was brought to a head in July 2002 when Paul Wolfowitz during a visit to Ankara left little doubt that U.S. plans involved ground attacks to be launched from Turkish territory. In September 2002, the United States began putting intense diplomatic pressure on Ankara, which was mirrored by steadily increasing Turkish opposition to the war, at the same time that Turkey was engaged in political efforts to achieve accession status to the EU. The question of whether Turkey should allow attacks on Iraq from Turkish territory provoked a parliamentary crisis that resulted in the refusal of the Turkish National Assembly to permit U.S. troops to use Turkish territory in the attack on Iraq (B. Park 2004, 494). This led to recriminations from Wolfowitz, who suggested that Turkey should apologize for refusing entry and chided Turkey's military leaders for failing to exercise leadership (B. Park 2004, 195), causing a political uproar in Turkey and further fueling already growing anti-Americanism. Hence even in the case of Turkish–American relations, warmed by unwavering American support for Turkish EU membership and by Turkey's obvious strategic importance for the United States, a transatlantic chill had set in as a result of the war in Iraq.

Throughout the Iraq crisis Javier Solana's attempts to preserve unity by brokering innocuous joint statements were undermined by the actions of individual member states (Allen and Smith 2004, 95). Following the publication of the "letter of eight" and the Vilnius letter the conflict between "old Europe" and "new Europe" even threatened the impending enlargement of the EU. Jacques Chirac linked the issues in chiding prospective members of the EU for having "missed a good opportunity to shut up," adding that if Romania and Bulgaria really had wanted to "diminish their chances to join the European Union, then they couldn't [have found] a better way of doing it."[5] As hostilities erupted in Iraq, the EU was deeply divided, raising doubts whether it would be able to develop its own foreign and defense policy and whether the divisions would prove permanent (A. Menon 2004, 631).

The split in the EU makes it decidedly impossible to speak of a particular "European response" either to the Iraq crisis itself or to American use of power under the Bush Doctrine more generally. Both issues have in effect become intertwined. Support for the United States and the war in Iraq has come to be seen as an expression of support for the United States as leader of the Euro-Atlantic community; the question of the ethics of invading a sovereign state, albeit one with a disagreeable regime, is seemingly moot. It seems safe to say that Europeans, being "Venutians," would prefer to use diplomacy until all other avenues have been exhausted and then only invade with explicit U.N. support, suggesting that those European states that supported the United States, either rhetorically or practically by actually contributing to the coalition, did so for the sake of the transatlantic relationship.

The crisis has continued, but following the initial bitter exchanges of 2003, most EU leaders have judged silence to be the best strategy for at least drawing back from the brink. Furthermore, with changes of government in Spain (2004), Germany (2005), Poland (2005), and Italy (2006), there has been a subtle shift of position in Europe. In particular, Angela Merkel has returned to a much more traditional German foreign policy that puts greater emphasis on the transatlantic relationship (though not without criticizing, e.g., the existence of Guantánamo), and she had a slightly less cozy relationship with Chirac than did Schroeder. However, the changes in government have also emphasized the vulnerability of the coalition in Iraq, as several European coalition members have withdrawn (Spain, Hungary, the Netherlands, Portugal, Bulgaria, Ukraine and Italy) and a long string of coalition countries plan withdrawal of their troops during 2007 and 2008. There is no doubt that as the situation in Iraq becomes bleaker and bleaker and as casualties in national coalition contingents escalate the fragile public support for participation in the coalition is weakening. Indeed, a Pew Research Center poll (June 13, 2006) showed people in Great Britain, France, and Spain saying the U.S.-led war in Iraq is a greater danger to world peace than the governments of Iran or North Korea (*USA Today* June 21, 2006).

Since the reelection of George W. Bush, a change has, however, occurred on the other side of the Atlantic. Bush has gone out of his way to project a different kind of tone when talking about Europe. In his first press conference after reelection, the president talked about "the importance of working with partners and friends," mentioning specifically both NATO and the EU. He cited them again in his inaugural address (Steinberg 2005), suggesting that the second G. W. Bush administration would be in the business of mending fences and would be dropping the "tone" it had adopted during the first term. This was a message that was reiterated in Condoleezza Rice's first visit to Europe as secretary of state, in February 2005, when she declared at the Institut d'Etudes Politiques in Paris that "it is time to turn away from past disagreements and to open a new chapter in our relationship and a new chapter in our alliance." The president reiterated the message during his Europe trip in February 2005, which was widely perceived to be conciliatory, bringing with him a "new Rumsfeld," who no longer spoke badly about "old Europe," and the apparent determination to reforge a new cooperative relationship with Europe. However, the substantial outcome of the European trips must be said to have been limited, as except for the symbolic pledge made by NATO to train one thousand Iraqi security forces a year, the Europeans were not willing to extend their support in Iraq.

Still, since the reelection of George W. Bush, disagreements in the transatlantic relationship have mellowed and there has been a substantial rapprochement from both sides of the Atlantic. Disagreement does persist over Iraq, Guantánamo, and the forceful rendition of suspected terrorists to their home countries, but at least Washington has changed its language. For example, the president conceded that he would like the prison camp closed (*USA Today* June 21, 2006). Also, the two sides now seem to agree about Iran and North Korea. They also agree that the Palestinian Hamas-led government must recognize the right of Israel to exist and that it has to accept the provisions of the "road map" for peace in the Middle East, which calls for the creation of a Palestinian state that would exist side by side in peace with Israel (*Timesonline* January 31, 2006). In relation to Iran, the United States agreed in March 2005 to the EU approach of using diplomacy and incentives in the form of a possible World Trade Organization (WTO) membership although the EU conceded that a tougher approach should be adopted if the diplomatic negotiations failed. With the election of the ultraconservative Mahnoud Ahmadinejad as president of Iran, the EU broke off negotiations and has since reevaluated the threat posed by Iran (Malmvig and Jakobsen 2006, 4). At the EU summit in Vienna in June 2006, Bush and leaders of the EU said they are past their disputes over Iraq and are united against Iran's nuclear ambitions and North Korean missile tests. All in all, therefore, the two sides of the Atlantic appear to have moved closer to one another.

Changes in European Foreign and Military Policies

Despite the recent rapprochement, the crisis in the transatlantic relationship has had repercussions for policy making in Europe and has led to European soul searching on how Europe should proceed within NATO and the EU. According to Chris Patten, the commissioner for external affairs, the Iraq issue had "blown apart Europe's ambitions to be a global player" and "the handling of the Iraq issue has been seriously damaging for the CFSP" (*The Independent* March 10, 2003). In NATO a similarly gloomy state of affairs prevailed, indicated by the crisis over Turkey and frustration over the apparent American downgrading of the alliance following the two campaigns in the Balkans as well as especially by the stinging rejection of NATO's offer of help in Afghanistan following the invocation of article 5 in 2001. It seemed that although NATO had appeared extremely successful in forging a new post–cold war role, especially in relation to enlargement, its practical difficulties in operating alongside the United States on the battlefield negated what had been achieved and launched the alliance into a deep crisis of confidence.[6] That American disregard for NATO was not imagined by the Europeans was indicated by the reportedly popular internal Pentagon slogan on NATO: "NATO—keeping the myth alive" (*Washingtonpost.com* July 5, 2004).

Policy Responses in the EU

EU policy responses to the events and perceived changes in the transatlantic relationship have occurred within all three EU pillars, the CFSP, the ESDP, and Justice and Home Affairs (JHA), in connection with the EU's attempt following 9/11 to strengthen cooperation to prevent international terrorism. The story is not all doom and gloom as suggested by Chris Pattern and as suggested by perceptions on both sides of the Atlantic. In fact it could well be that the shocks encountered over the last half decade may have constituted a wake-up call for European member states to address the gaps and weaknesses of the collective system (Hill 2004b, 144). Indeed, Anand Menon (2004, 631) ponders whether the ESDP may in fact emerge strengthened from the traumas experienced during the transatlantic crisis.

As suggested earlier, the tragedy in the former Yugoslavia and the inability of the Europeans to solve the Balkan crises without U.S. involvement, leading to American leadership in the strategic and military thinking that guided the Balkan wars, has had profound effects on policy making in Europe. Both conflicts clearly exposed European military deficiencies in coping with violent conflict on the EU's doorstep. They also exposed a difference in approach between the Europeans and Americans. Americans preferred high-tech and high-altitude warfare — and to leave the reconstruction and ground war to the U.N.-mandated forces in Bosnia and Kosovo. The question that will probably always haunt Europeans is whether the genocide at Srebrenica could have been prevented with better equipped or more numerous forces on the ground. Certainly the tragedy of Srebrenica could never have been prevented by air strikes. This fact led Europe to realize that for it to have a military role, it must have real deployable forces able to prevent such a massacre from happening again in Europe.

The immediate policy response to the experience in Bosnia and later reiterated by the experience in Kosovo was a British and French rapprochement on the necessity for the development of ESDP. The meeting between Tony Blair and Jacques Chirac at St. Malo, France, in December 1998 cleared the political blockage between Europeanists and Atlanticists and opened up the possibility of embarking on the road toward the security and defense integration that had been politically introduced in the Treaty of Amsterdam. Almost immediately following St. Malo, the situation in Kosovo started to deteriorate rapidly, thereby underlining both the need for ESDP and the growing gap in capabilities between the Europeans and the Americans. The result was a rapid succession of decisions, the first one made as early as the June 1999 European Council in Cologne, which committed the EU to gaining the "capacity for autonomous action backed by credible military force." At the December 1999 Helsinki Council, the member states undertook in the so-called Headline Goal to have sixty thousand troops at the union's disposal capable of carrying out all the Petersburg missions by 2003. At the December 2001 Laeken European Council the Belgian EU presidency declared the ESDP operational.

Apart from giving the EU the impetus to undertake the operational development of the ESDP, it could also be argued that the transatlantic crisis motivated it to develop a strategy as well, the result of which was the EU's first-ever security strategy paper. With the 2003 EU adoption of its European Security Strategy (ESS), the EU added a clear strategic element to its security program. The ESS reflected the consternation of European capitals over the Bush administration's *National Security Strategy*. The main author of the ESS, Robert Cooper, had previously declared that "if the Europeans do not like the US National Security Strategy, they should develop their own rather than complain from the sidelines" (Cooper 2003, 165). The document contains a number of specific policy objectives concerning conflict prevention, rogue states, nuclear proliferation, and particularly preventive (as opposed to preemptive) military action. As Christopher Hill suggests, the ESS was produced partly in order to adapt to new circumstances but also "to convince the Americans that Europe was not totally mired in delusional 'soft power' thinking" (Hill 2004a).

Following the events of September 11, a number of political and diplomatic initiatives were taken in the EU to show support for the United States in its fight against terrorism. The extraordinary European Council of September 21, 2001, stated that it would fight terrorism in all its forms and that "the fight against terrorism will, more than ever, be a priority objective of the European Union." Within only a couple of days of the attacks, the EU tabled proposals for a "European

Arrest Warrant" to more effectively be able to combat cross-border terrorism (Hill 2004b, 147). Also in recognition of the international aspect of terrorism, it was decided at the June 2002 European Council in Seville to increase the union's involvement in the fight against terrorism through a coordinated approach embracing all union policies, including the CFSP and ESDP.

All in all up until when Washington began linking the war on terrorism with war in Iraq, the political and diplomatic response within the EU was characterized by collective action and a high degree of support for the United States. Political and diplomatic support from both the EU and NATO remained firm as the United States embarked on its "war on terror" with a military campaign in Afghanistan, even though in general Europe is cautious about taking military action. Despite the disagreements among member states over Iraq, the EU has since 2003 engaged in a growing number of military, civilian, and police operations under the auspices of the ESDP, in some cases using NATO assets under the Berlin Plus arrangements. These moves suggest that the EU is now an organization with a clear military and security dimension. Although the initial impetus for this security and defense dimension undoubtedly was the Yugoslav tragedy, it seems that the transatlantic crisis has in fact provided further political incentive for particularly those member states that traditionally have belonged to the Atlanticist camp within the EU.

Policy Responses in NATO

In NATO the events in the Balkans also prompted a flurry of activity independently of its attempts to enlarge itself and its attempts to establish a European Security and Defense Identity (ESDI) as part of its relationship with the EU. For purposes here, the two policy categories that specifically warrant, albeit brief, attention are "out of area" and capabilities — two areas that have increasingly become intertwined.

The issue over NATO's actual ability to conduct military missions successfully was brought to a head in the campaign against Serbia in Kosovo, where the disparity between American and European (as well as Canadian) military capabilities raised serious questions about the relevance of NATO as a military organization (Terriff 2004, 424). Of course "burden sharing" has always been a recurring problem within NATO, and the related problem of the capabilities gap was already being addressed as the Kosovo campaign unfolded when the alliance met in Washington in April 1999 to celebrate its fiftieth anniversary. At the Washington Summit, NATO agreed on the Defense Capabilities Initiative (DCI), which called for alliance members to ensure the interoperability and common capabilities of national forces needed to perform the roles and missions outlined in NATO's New Strategic Concept— (also agreed to at the Washington Summit). As the Kosovo campaign unfolded, the importance of the DCI became crystal clear, suggesting that the gap between U.S. power-projection capabilities and those of Europe was particularly striking in modern and transport aircraft and in smart weapons. Furthermore, European capabilities were seen as lacking in strategic lift, intelligence, command, control, and communications. The lesson drawn by the Americans from the campaign in Kosovo was that the European members of NATO simply did not possess the capabilities that would enable the two sides to fight on the same battlefield.

It could be said that if Kosovo was a wake-up call for the EU to improve its defense and security dimension, so the Kosovo campaign was a brutal awakening for NATO on the extent of its capability gap. However, it was also clear that the political environment was not conducive to large-scale increases in defense spending, especially given European electorates that traditionally have been unwilling to favor "guns over butter." Because very little had been achieved in meeting target goals, NATO ended up abandoning the DCI at the Prague Summit in November 2002 and formed the Prague Capability Committee as well as made a commitment to establish the NATO Response Force (NRF). These are supposed to furnish NATO with the ability to rapidly dispatch military forces into deteriorating security situations wherever they may arise. By introducing the NRF, NATO was simultaneously able to address the inherent problem of capabilities, as the NRF was seen as a lever for developing European military capabilities, as well as the problem of being able to operate on the same battlefield as the Americans.

The lesson from Kosovo clearly stuck with the Americans. When the attacks on the Pentagon and World Trade Center prompted the Europeans to invoke article 5 of the North Atlantic Treaty, not only was this remarkable show of sympathy and solidarity rejected by the American administration, but the rebuff of help was generally seen as representing a fundamental shift in U.S. strategy. As Donald Rumsfeld's article in the *New York Times* suggested, "this war will not be waged by a grand alliance. . . . Instead it will involve floating coalitions of countries . . . the mission will define the coalition— not the other way around" (*New York Times* September 27, 2001). The European feeling of having been dismissed was cemented, as the Pentagon repeatedly stated that it would not allow itself to be bound by the alliance and as that claim was followed up in practice as the United States fought the Taliban without involving NATO. American strategy thus highlighted the severity of the crisis in the Atlantic Alliance and underscored American disdain for its traditional allies.

By committing to involvement in Afghanistan through the 2001 article 5 invocation, the Europeans indicated their willingness to move NATO not only "out of area" but also to move the alliance "out of region." Although the alliance did not participate in the war against the Taliban, it did enter the scene following the defeat of the Taliban government through the International Security and Assistance Force (ISAF). The role of the alliance within ISAF has grown steadily since then, with NATO taking the command of ISAF in August 2003 and expanding into the unstable southern and eastern regions during 2006.

The mission in Afghanistan is NATO's first major out-of-region role, clearly reflecting a very real understanding that success in Afghanistan will be a major determinant for the future of the alliance. The importance of the success of the NRF should not be underestimated. It is designed precisely for NATO to be able to participate at short notice in Afghanistan-like situations, where a collection of NRF "niche capabilities" could match and be compatible with those of U.S. forces (Terriff 2004, 431). At least on paper it seems that NATO has overcome the important historical aversion to going out of area, while the futility of aiming for capabilities that can match American capabilities across the board seems to have been grasped, leaving the much more realistic goal of having a collective military capability of approximately twenty thousand to twenty-two thousand personnel for specific crisis situations. However, as Elizabeth Pond notes, the lingering legacy of the Iraq debacle has eroded European trust in Washington's judgment and leadership and at the same time has led Washington to question Europe's solidarity with American global strategy (Pond 2005, 55). The sense of purpose that seems present in the EU's drive toward improving its security and defense dimension simply seems absent in NATO, where the Europeans appear to comply with American wishes without enthusiasm and out of residual fear that the United States might still choose to abandon Europe or undermine its security interests.

Conclusions

The transatlantic relationship has always been delicate, prone to crisis, and not always characterized by logical behavior or rationality. This is essentially because the relationship is a political relationship based on shared ideas and values and a commitment to mutual assistance. As a result trust and a commitment to shared values play a key role in maintaining the relationship, which has traditionally been located within the institutional framework of NATO. The apparent U.S. reassessment of NATO following the campaigns in the Balkans seemed to Europeans to suggest that the essential negotiation processes of the institutional order had come to an end (Ikenberry 2001). In this connection, it is of little comfort that the relationship appears unchanged with respect to economic relations, as these policy areas historically have been based on an entirely different tradition of fierce competition but noncoercive conflict relations. Therefore, since U.S.–European trade and economic relations do not underpin the security and ideational foundations of the Euro-Atlantic community, their relatively healthy state makes little difference to the overall stability of the value-based relationship.

The health of the transatlantic relationship depends on strategic policy and foreign policy because it is within these policy areas that the essential socialization and persuasion processes of the Euro-Atlantic community have been located. Here it is essential to distinguish between two different categories of policy change. On the one hand, the Europeans have responded to the changed structural conditions following the end of the cold war and, on the other, they have reacted to the perceived change in American global policy, particularly with respect to its European allies, that started during the wars in the former Yugoslavia and accelerated with the election of George W. Bush and the publication of the Bush Doctrine. Both are important for the transatlantic relationship but in different ways because the two sides of the Atlantic have a different idea as to what constitutes the most major change in the international system. For the Europeans, the important recent "critical juncture" (Finnemore and Sikkink 1998) is the end of the cold war, which fundamentally challenged the whole way Europeans approach their own security. This is not the case for the Americans. For them, the end of the cold war symbolized a victory and a reinforcement of existing ideas on how security and strategic issues should be approached. Apart from minor changes of emphasis and urgency, the end of the cold war did not lead to any specific U.S. policy changes vis-à-vis Europe, except to make it less important. The opposite is true of September 11, which most certainly has constituted a critical juncture on the American side of the Atlantic but not for the European side, since terrorism has always been a real threat in Europe.

This is not to downgrade the atrocity of the violence. Rather just as the United States did not fundamentally change its foreign policy after the end of the cold war whereas Europe did, so too Europe did not radically change its foreign policy after 9/11, seeing it as presenting a change in the *degree and scale* of terrorism but not in its fundamental character. As Andrew Moravscik (2003, 76) observes, for the Europeans, the fall of the Berlin Wall is the defining moment of the contemporary era whereas for the United States, it is the fall of the Twin Towers. For that reason policy changes in Europe following 11/9 (1989) have a different significance and role from policy changes following 9/11 (2001). This is a view that President Bush showed he understood at the June 2006 EU summit in Austria when he stated that "for Europe, September the 11th was a moment, for us, it was a change of thinking" (*USA Today* June 21, 2006).

Following the official end of the cold war and the collapse of the Soviet Union, European responses to the now widely accepted structural condition of unipolarity were to further strengthen efforts at establishing in practice the goals set out in the Treaty on European Union (TEU) for a CFSP and an eventual framing of a common European defense policy as well as to create extensive frameworks within both NATO and the EU for managing relations with Central and Eastern Europe (CEE), preparing CEE for EU membership and other forms of association. The changed structural relations also led to more urgent calls for an independent European defense capability within the EU, as the specter of diverging interests between Europe and the United States and abandonment by Washington seemed less implausible given that the strategic environment was now one in which Europe was no longer the prime concern of the only remaining superpower.

European responses to the perceived changes in U.S. management of its hegemony are completely different in character from its responses to the structural changes in Europe brought about by the end of the cold war and have led to widespread confusion and disagreement on how to proceed because the Europeans have not been guided in their policy making by a significantly changed threat perception. They certainly do not agree with the United States that terrorism is the major threat to security in the global system. They differ also on the matter of how the problem should be solved. Europeans are more concerned with the causes of terrorism, which they see as essentially a question of justice and global distribution of wealth and therefore not a problem that can be solved by declaring war on it.

The problem for the transatlantic relationship is therefore compounded by the fact that change has come in several guises. First, there was a major change in American policy *content* as the new Bush administration abandoned its commitment to a number of multilateral agreements. Second, Washington adopted a fundamentally changed foreign policy as a result of 9/11. Third, the administration also altered *the way* it conducts foreign policy. The changes introduced by the Bush Doctrine and by changes in U.S. power projections have generated a level of disunity among both EU and NATO countries, which for the moment does not seem to be healing. The dynamism in NATO of the 1990s seems to have vanished. The EU is also in limbo following the rejection of the Constitutional Treaty. It is paralyzed by growing popular anti-American sentiments as a result of the war in Iraq and atrocities at Abu Ghraib and Guantánamo and what to do about them. A unified European response to the changes in American foreign and security policy seems long off in the distance. Yet if the value-based relationship between Europe and the United States is not nurtured through negotiation and persuasion, a vital part of the proper maintenance of consensual security communities will have been neglected. That could have repercussions that for the moment can only be guessed at but that certainly could potentially unravel the Euro-Atlantic community.

Notes

1. There are of course several examples of consensus not being reached. France in 1967 is probably the prime example, but there is also Denmark's so-called footnote policy during the 1980s and the ongoing stalemate between Turkey and Greece.

2. The concept of a security community was developed by Karl Deutsch and his colleagues in the late 1950s.

3. The realist form of hegemony was used by the Athenians against the Melians in the Peloponnesian War. According to the supposedly "archrealist" Thucydides (Lebow and Kelly 2001), such hegemony is based on control and force, which will ultimately end in rebellion.

4. The resentment was remarked on in interviews conducted by the author with NATO officials on a number of occasions between 2001 and 2005.

5. Chirac's comments came on February 17 after the Extraordinary European Council Meeting.

6. Information culled from interviews by the author with NATO officials in Ohrid, Former Yugoslav Republic of Macedonia (FYROM), September 2004.

CHAPTER EIGHT

The Russian Federation and the CIS

Maria Raquel Freire

The 9/11 terrorist attacks in the United States changed the international security landscape and revealed that terrorism, already a large-scale and immeasurable phenomenon, had gone transnational and could cross any boundary. Washington took the lead in the global fight against terror, at first with broad international support — as evinced in the military operations conducted in Afghanistan — but under growing criticism as time passed, with the invasion of Iraq probably representing the height of dissension.

Russia immediately offered its support to the United States after September 11, showing its solidarity with the American people over a tragic reality with which the Russians are all too familiar. Moscow likened the terrorist acts in the United States to those perpetrated during the Chechen separatist movement and was prepared for active involvement in the global fight against terror. But problems began to develop in the U.S.–Russian relationship, particularly after the unilateral assertiveness of Washington regarding Iraq and its presumptuous posture of "going it alone." Nevertheless, despite friction, neither side finds it strategically sound to neglect the other. The relationship has thus been marked by many ups and downs, underlined by a continuous dialectical discussion concerning multilateralism and unilateralism, cooperation versus hegemonic behavior, multivector policies and unidirectional approaches.

Adding to these difficulties, the western Commonwealth of Independent States (CIS), in particular the Slavic triangle formed by Russia, Ukraine, and Belarus, seems increasingly disjointed. In the face of the threat of global terrorism and U.S. hegemony, the relationship between these states and Washington and among themselves has been ambivalent. The three Slavic countries, traditional historical and cultural allies, have pursued distinct paths. Immediately after the disintegration of the Soviet Union the three took the lead in the creation of the CIS. However, gradually this jointure gave place to animosity, the result largely of Moscow's assertiveness within the CIS. While Belarus regarded the CIS as an opportunity for almost a decade, Ukraine soon viewed it as an obstacle. And this misalignment had repercussions that have required adjustments in the formulation of internal and external policies to the present day. Russia's leading role has increasingly been challenged, the union between Russia and Belarus has flagged, and the Ukraine's inclination to align itself with the West has been reinforced. The result has been a change in the traditional pattern of relations of these states with Moscow — of almost subservience from Belarus and of resignation from Ukraine. However, there are common bonds of an historical, cultural, and particularly economic nature that cannot be overlooked and that characterize the interrelationships among these states. This mix of cooperative versus competitive policies suggests questions about (dis)jointure within the Slavic triangle.

In the face of the interdependence of regional and global security, the fight against terrorism has assumed a leading place in international agendas, particularly in Washington, which has embraced it as an endeavor to pursue at any cost, through unilateral and hegemonic policies that are crowned by U.S. military might. This chapter focuses on the Russian, Ukrainian, and Belarusian responses to the announced and operational strategic military policy of the United States and asks whether these states understand it as a window of opportunity or, rather, as a threat to their own perceived interests. It looks at the issue not only through the separate lenses of each of these republics but also through the CIS as an integrating mechanism led by Moscow, underscoring the complex links within this institutional framework that affect the ways Ukraine, Belarus, and Moscow behave toward each other and toward the United States. The fight against terrorism exemplifies how the Bush administration has used the moral obligation to conduct a war on terror as a pragmatic means of intervening and involving itself in the affairs of other countries, which has been the source, in many instances, of foreign irritation. The relationship of the United States with Russia, as well as with Ukraine and Belarus, obviously denotes this foreign policy orientation. Whether this causes restraint, resentment, disengagement, bandwagoning, insulation, or supportive responses is another issue this chapter explores.

Although rhetoric has often called for and pragmatism often required cooperation between the United States and Russia, both rhetoric and pragmatism have in many instances been overruled by purely realistic considerations of hard power, economic domination, and strategic superiority by the political establishments in Washington and Moscow. As for Ukraine and Belarus, their independent status has not shielded them from often being treated in a cold war style. The general pattern resulting from this situation has been that, when the relations between Kiev and Minsk and Moscow are particularly good, they get little attention from Washington; conversely, when relations are poor, Washington's interest is piqued. In the same vein, when there is tension between Washington and Moscow, both Belarus and Ukraine, but particularly Ukraine, attempt to play off the disagreement to their maximum benefit. This imbalanced balance, based on policies of competition and self-interest, renders difficult the discovery of common approaches in the fight against terror that might frame a sound, coordinated policy. By looking at this complex triangle — one that is surely not equilateral — this chapter aims to reveal the patterns of state change in Russia, Ukraine, and Belarus and how they define the strategic policy and behavior these countries adopt in reaction to U.S. military dominance.

Russia: A Regional Power Searching for Affirmation

Vladimir Putin came to power in Russia during a time of great instability. To redress the anarchic state of Russian politics, Putin applied a tough hand and reaffirmed the preeminence of his presidential power over elitism and powerful lobbying groups, proclaiming as goals domestic stability and growth and a co-operative stance in foreign policy. Since his election in March 2000 his politics have, nevertheless, increasingly assumed an undemocratic tone. The illusion of democracy has dissipated in a country where the centralization of power, the control of the media, and the manipulation of electoral processes have proceeded side by side with economic recovery, the end result of which has been wide popular support for these policies. In fact, the Russian president managed to achieve a great degree of popularity in the midst of the fighting of a war against the Chechens and in the struggle against the power of corrupt officials and the oligarchs. Building on the "passionately nationalistic" (Mishler and Willerton 2003, 114) character of Russian society, Putin managed to gather substantive support for his politics.

The three main foreign policy documents adopted by Putin at the beginning of his first term as Russian president point to a multilateral approach in foreign policy, to the CIS as an area of strategic importance, and to the Asia-Pacific region as a relevant region in Moscow's external policy (Russian Security Council 2000; Russian Defense Ministry 2000; Foreign Policy Concept 2000). The Russian Defense Ministry Military Doctrine document ends by stating the Russian goal of achieving a "balanced, equitable, multipolar world." This goal is recalled in Russia's Foreign Policy Concept, where it acknowledges the trend toward a "unipolar structure of the world with the economic and power domination of the United States," notes its potential destabilizing role, and underlines the relevance of a multipolar system of international relations. The United States deserves, therefore, particular attention, with the document stating that, despite disagreement over a number of issues, "Russian–American interaction is the necessary condition for the amelioration of the international situation and achievement of global strategic stability." Thus, preserving this long-standing relationship requires that each country take a pragmatic look at both problems and opportunities.

The terrorist attacks of September 11, 2001, in the United States had wide repercussions. Facing similar threats on its own territory, Russia promptly offered its support, understanding the antiterrorist campaign as an opportunity to garner international support for its increasingly repressive interventions, particularly in Chechnya. This campaign gained further legitimacy in the face of the violent terrorist attacks within its borders, such as the siege of the Moscow theater in 2002 and the Beslan school tragedy in the fall of 2004. "Russia's own experience with urban terrorism rendered 9/11 an overseas instance of the same phenomenon they themselves faced: 9/11, in short, was domesticated in Russia as a 'global Chechnya'" (O'Loughlin, Ó Tuathail, and Kolossov 2004, 7).

Western criticism of Russian actions in Chechnya has diminished to virtual silence, and Putin has managed to transform the language used to describe the situation so that it is no longer represented in Russia or in the West as a war against rebels demanding independence but instead as a fight against terrorism that menaces order and stability within the Russian Federation and the world beyond. The identification of a common enemy between Russia and the Western powers was critical in enhancing their relationship. Taking advantage of the close rapprochement with the United States after September 11, Russia sought to close the influence gap between itself and the United States internationally, despite many adverse conditions and disagreement over fundamental issues with its overseas partner.

Russia and the United States are united in the promotion of common goals, at least on paper, such as the fostering of democratic political systems, the protection of individual rights, and the consolidation of economic benefits. They also share concerns, particularly in the security realm, regarding the fight against terror and organized crime, the proliferation of weapons of mass destruction (WMD), and crisis management. These common interests resulted in the signing of the Moscow Declaration on the New Strategic Relationship in May 2002, the aim of which is to achieve stability, security, and economic integration and to counter global challenges and resolve regional conflicts jointly. Ensuing collaboration led Putin to state that "in some areas, such as the fight against terrorism, the United States is a consistent and reliable partner for Russia," adding, nevertheless, that he disagreed with the U.S. unilateralist course with respect to Iraq (Yasmann 2003). In addition, Moscow shut down some cold war military facilities, amply supported the U.S. campaign in Afghanistan, and gave its consent on the stationing of American military forces in Central Asia, showing a cooperative stance (Blagov 2004). In response it received recognition as a market economy, full membership in the G8 group, and support for its accession to the World Trade Organization (WTO).

However, competing interests have overshadowed shared concerns and collaborative approaches. Hot topics, particularly in the political and economic domains, elicited mutual accusations in a relationship often said not yet to have overcome the cold war legacy. Russian economic and financial support to Saddam's Iraq and technical aid to the Iranian government have caused discontent in Washington. Moscow's involvement in the development of the Iranian Busheer nuclear plant is understood by the United States to have conferred on Russia added power over Eurasian regional security. However, the Iranian nuclear program and the tough stance adopted by President Ahmadinejad, including suspension of voluntary cooperation with the International Atomic Energy Agency (IAEA) in February 2006, as well as Washington's geostrategic goals in the Middle East, have suggested the need for conciliation with Moscow, which has put forward guidelines for negotiation. Tension remains and diplomatic activity has so far prevailed, but Washington views the Russian–Iranian relationship with much concern. The official confirmation of a deal between Moscow and Tehran for the sale of Russian air-defense missile systems to the Islamic republic in early February 2007, and the continuous challenges of Iranian authorities to U.S. demands, have been reducing the opportunities for dialogue. Thus an issue that has been a source of tension between the United States and Russia is currently yielding some form of rapprochement between the two, but mistrust persists.

Adding to difficulties, Russia is critical of NATO's expansion policies and the deployment of military forces close to its borders, revealing its persistent fear of Western institutions. Nevertheless, Putin took a soft line on the enlargement of NATO, which elicited inflamed reactions at home. Gen. Anatolii Kvashnin, chief of the general staff, has defined the NATO–Russia Basic Act as "an informational cover" under which cold war thinking persists in the West (Kvashnin cited in O'Loughlin, Ó Tuathail, and Kolossov 2004, 13). Agreement over the creation of the NATO–Russia Council in a new format under the name "NATO at 20," which refers to the nineteen current members plus Russia, wherein Russia would have equal status in decision making regarding European security (NATO 2002), diminished the voices of discontent, although it did not silence them. From time to time the traditional image of the "enemy," a remnant of the cold war, is recovered along with the fact that because the geostrategic context changed at Russia's expense, Russia must remain vigilant. This image is extended to politico-military issues ranging from arms control treaties to the war on terrorism.

Russia was disappointed by the U.S. announcement of its intention to withdraw from the Antiballistic Missile (ABM) Treaty in 2001, a move to some extent counterbalanced by the signature of a new treaty in May 2002, the Strategic

Offensive (Arms) Reduction Treaty (known as SORT), aimed at reducing the number of long-range nuclear weapons. It is a cosmetic document that some see as clearly favoring the United States over Russia and as representing an overt move by the United States to contain possible proliferation of weapons and related technologies in Russia (Utkin 2002, 48; Rogov 2002, 53). In the words of Aleksandr Shabanov, deputy chair of the Duma's Foreign Affairs Committee, "the United States has always followed its own political course and has such a dominant position in the world in every way. How can you have equal relations with such a supreme power? Of course it's impossible. We shouldn't have illusions and even think about it. Present-day Russia and its elite have to accept it" (Buckley 2003, 37).

Washington's military projects, particularly the development of the national missile defense shield, have also elicited adverse reactions in Moscow. In reply the Kremlin announced the adoption of a preemptive military doctrine following in the footsteps of Washington as well as the development of a new nuclear missile system to ensure Russia's security. Adding to the discord, Russia has also criticized the West for meddling in its internal affairs by complaining about governing practices in the country from human rights to the war against terror, the latter of which, according to Russia, the West "attempts to classify" as "'ours' and 'theirs,' as 'moderate' and 'radical'" (RFE/RL 2004a). In addition, certain American actions have reinforced the suspicions of some Russians that the United States is seeking to parlay the war against terror into a war for control of oil, gas, and pipeline routes (Foglesong and Halin 2002, 11). Thus, for them, the political and economic issues are directly linked, making the relationship between the two countries even more delicate.

The initiation of war in Iraq (March 2003) clearly marked the lowest point in Russian–U.S. post–cold war relations. The gathering in St. Petersburg for the celebrations of the city's three hundred years at the end of May 2003 made clear the underlying differences between Moscow and Washington. "Putin had reestablished links with his neighbors near and far and put Russia's relationships on a more sober, realistic footing. But there was also a new assertiveness, as he demonstrated that he might not be a pariah but neither was he a lackey of the West. It was a relationship of realpolitik, a balance of forces and economic interests far more than it was a true meeting of minds or values" (Jack 2004, 296). The rules of the game became clearer, too, with pragmatism and a realist look leading the Kremlin's policy formulation. Russia pursued its own course, disagreeing with the United States when necessary, but maintained diplomacy and certainly took a circumspect approach. Underlying problems persist, smoothed over by behind-the-scenes diplomacy and implicit conditionality and bargaining, although such trade-offs of political-military assistance for economic gains are always denied by the parties.

From 2003, after an initial grace period, Putin came under fierce criticism. At home increasing protests over excessive intervention and social and economic sacrifices, as well as the protracted conflict in Chechnya, have subjected the president to intense pressure. "The seemingly all-powerful president has become hostage to his inflexible system, and the over-concentration of control has made the system unable to alter the set course," the result being that Russia has turned inward and backward (Baev 2004, 11). The weathering of the president's strong image might demonstrate that, while seemingly powerful, his power may not be so real. More authoritarianism does not necessarily mean more power, in the sense of being politically untouchable.

In external affairs Russian foreign policy has been constrained, since Putin wishes full integration into Western institutions, particularly in the economic domain. Efforts at integration in the WTO and the hosting of the G8 meeting in July 2006 demonstrate Putin's commitment to this endeavor and the desire to avoid exclusion. But the ambiguities inherent in the Kremlin's policies are many, because it often adopts irreconcilable positions — such as when it agreed in international forums to abide by international norms and principles while dismissing these compromises at home and justifying the dismissals internationally by claiming that other countries' interpretations of Russian developments were distorted. This demonstrates how internal factors affect external options, with Russia appearing to be "a colossus with feet of clay" (Aslund 2005).

Therefore, Washington should base its policies toward Russia on "mutual interests, not the expectations of mutual values," as Trenin (2005b) argues. It is increasingly clear that each country's underlying values are different, as are their interpretations of democracy. Vladimir Putin has been cautious in the formulation of this relationship. While Russia needs Western support for its effort in the fight against terror, he does not want an enlarged Western presence in its neighborhood, where Russia has vital strategic and economic interests.

Russia's Multilateral Approach: Balancing U.S. Unilateralism

As then–Russian foreign minister Igor Ivanov put it in 2003, "Multipolarity, the way we see it, means above all close interaction of all states and regions on the basis of equality, democracy, and constructive partnership. It is, essentially, about the need to resolve international problems through multilateral cooperation, taking into account the interests of all states" (34).

Russian foreign policy objectives include as a first goal the promotion of the CIS as an area of vital interest to Russia. The area's vast natural resources push Moscow to assert control of pipeline routes and infrastructures as a way of both maintaining influence over local governments and profiting from these economic assets. But although several accords have been ratified on political-security and economic matters within the CIS, most of these have not been fully implemented, either because of language the countries find restrictive or due to disagreement over interpretation. "[T]here is very little sense of common identity within the CIS. . . . Instead, there are divergent processes of state formation, nation building, economic diversification, and foreign policies in constant uncomfortable interaction with one another" (Sakwa and Webber 1999, 379). In addition to this geostrategic, political, and economic puzzle, most of the agreements do not involve all CIS members, thus resulting in an asymmetrical game, where the conjugation of different interests and demands has rendered the organization's functioning almost impossible.

This has resulted in Russia's assuming the bulk of the tasks pertaining to the CIS: it has sought a prominent role, securing a vital sphere of influence, and has managed conflict and prevented international involvement in the area. In this regard, commonwealth politics have since its inception been overshadowed by Russian politics and goals. The lack of sustainable decision making and the nonexistence of supervision mechanisms raised suspicions that Russia's interventionist practices through the CIS serve Russia's own interests. For example, the Treaty on a Single Economic Space (SES), signed in September 2003 by Russia, Ukraine, Belarus, and Kazakhstan ("The Four"), is apparently a demonstration of the coming together of the Slavic triangle. However, it has been embedded in ambiguity since Ukraine approved it under the condition that the accord abide by Kiev's strategic goal of European integration, which means that there would be substantial limits to its involvement. The SES has been accused of being a vehicle for hidden Russian ambitions—"part regional ambition, part explicit hegemonism, and even part anti-globalism" (Sushko 2004, 129). It also appears to be a pragmatic move toward the East, meaning an attempt to solidify the Eastern dimension in Russian politics by fostering closer ties with the Central Asian states.

Regional integration processes in the former Soviet space have suffered from a simple malaise: usually they are regarded as pro- or anti-Russian, which renders their existence and meaning difficult to sustain. Russia's attempt to secure regional influence and leverage, along with the bearing that attempt has on Russia's relations with its neighbors, has been a source of disagreement between it and the United States. The persistent paradox in Russia's relations with Belarus and Ukraine has been that Moscow's every effort at building ties with the two has signified a step taken not toward the West but away from it. Thus, the Russian commitment to multilateralism, with all the limits it entails, is a part of the Kremlin's strategy to balance U.S. hegemonic ambitions by keeping control, or at least maintaining sufficient leverage, in the former Soviet area. By trying to gain a margin of maneuverability in political-diplomatic and economic terms,

Moscow pursues simultaneously the goal of keeping this area as a special area of influence and of counterbalancing and having a say regarding the U.S. presence in the region. This balancing has encompassed, therefore, contradictory tendencies of jumping on the U.S. bandwagon with regard, for example, to the stationing of troops in Central Asia, but also of restraint as to the extent and quality of this presence.

Ukraine: Looking West while Not Overlooking Its Eastern Neighbor

Since regaining statehood in 1991 post-Soviet Ukraine has pursued an independent course, although its location has conditioned to a great extent the contours of its foreign policy. Ukraine's multivector policy has been understood in Western circles as a mask for covering up elite maneuvers in the pursuit of personal profit via both Western assistance and Russian friendship. This unreliability in terms of foreign policy goals has not played in favor of the country's integration into the West.

As Russia's neighbor, Ukraine has been playing a game of national affirmation, restraint, and bandwagoning that has been shaped by Moscow's position and its own chosen path. Sometimes, however, what it wants is directed or to some extent conditioned by external pressures, such as the reduction or disruption of oil and gas supplies from Russia. Despite the settling of the gas dispute with Moscow in January 2006, it has been a recurrent source of pressure from the Kremlin. And despite hopes to the contrary, the Yanukovich administration, in power since August 2006, has not managed to obtain compensation for transporting Russian gas to Europe at the level it hoped for. Ukraine has nevertheless reached a gas deal with the Kremlin for 2007, ensuring that there will not be a repeat of the crisis of the previous year.[1] Ukraine relies on Russian energy resources and on Russia as a major commercial partner (after the 2004 enlargement, the European Union (EU) became the number one trading partner), which confers on its so-called independence a sense of dependence. Nevertheless, Moscow recognizes the relevance of good neighborly relations with Kiev, because of the country's strategic location, growing market, and presence of a large Russian minority, and this recognition works to counterbalance Ukraine's dependence.

Russian–Ukrainian relations suggest low-key pragmatism, in which protracted bargaining is likely over interests that are often difficult to reconcile (Allison 2001, 452). At home politics are changing and rapprochement with the West has been a stated priority. The cabinets since the Orange Revolution, while pursuing a resolute course in the fight against illicit practices along with the promotion of democracy, have been cautious in their foreign policy formulations, adopting a pragmatic posture of economic development and political consolidation in order not to create unnecessary friction. In fact, while rapprochement with the West is very much valued, relations with Russia remain a central pillar in the Ukrainian foreign policy construct — thus, Ukraine looks west, while not overlooking its neighbor to the east. In its multivector foreign policy it has been following the dictum, "To Europe with Russia," apparently trying to reconcile the Eastern and Western vectors in Ukrainian foreign policy orientation. The words are clear: "the priorities will be the same — that is European and Euro-Atlantic integration, meaning EU, NATO. Certainly we will continue to pay adequate attention to our neighbors and, among neighbors to strategic partners, that is Russia and Poland, and certainly the United States" (Krushelnycky 2004). However, despite continuity in policies, the gas crisis with Moscow settled in January 2006 served as a pretext for the voting of a nonconfidence motion against Prime Minister Yekhanurov's government, with the parliamentary elections on March 26, 2006, leaving the country in a delicate political situation. The results sent a message about growing disenchantment with the poor outcomes of the Orange Revolution more than a year after the fair and free runoff election of President Yushchenko brought the protests to an end, with economic difficulties, political mishandlings, and social problems pointed out as serious shortcomings. Dragging on for almost six months, institutional paralysis — a result of the inability to form a new government after the balloting — demonstrated the difficulties in the post-Communist transition course. Domestic instability together with the management of a multivectoral foreign policy reveal the complementarity of the internal and external dimensions in Ukraine's foreign relations. Agreement over the establishment of an anticrisis coalition and the nomination of Viktor Yanukovich as prime minister on August 3, 2006, put an end to this long period of uncertainty in Ukrainian politics. President Putin immediately congratulated Yanukovich on his new post. This shift might play to the interest of Ukraine but it could also represent a retreat in the consolidation of Ukrainian statehood, with the bargaining between concessions and demands in the relationship with the Kremlin leading to further Ukrainian dependence on its Russian neighbor. Yanukovich has, nevertheless, noted the relevance of the European vector in the country's foreign policy, showing his intention not simply to bow before Russian demands.

The 2004 presidential elections, very much disputed and a matter of great controversy, translated in a symbolic way this ambivalence inherent in the U.S.–Russian relationship. Put simply, the crisis came to be equated with a dispute between a Western-oriented Ukraine led by Viktor Yushchenko and an Eastern-inclined Ukraine under Viktor Yanukovich. This labeling, despite the similarity in the political programs of both governments, was reinforced by both international and national media and by the meddling of foreign governments. Putin's support for Yanukovich garnered much international criticism and raised questions about possible Russian neoimperialist aspirations. Former secretary of state Colin Powell criticized Putin for his financial and political support of Yanukovich (Warner 2004), while the Kremlin responded with similar criticism regarding U.S. support for Yushchenko. Putin criticized the U.S. involvement in Ukraine as an attempt to isolate Russia; at the same time he referred to the U.S.–Russia relationship as more than "partnership," as an "alliance" (RFE/RL 2004b)—contradictory statements such as these are increasingly common in the policy-making discourse of post-Soviet Russia.

In the wake of the September 11 terrorist attacks in the United States, Russia and the West developed a closer relationship, thus preventing Ukraine from playing its card as the in-between power. In addition, by the end of 2002, cooperation between Kiev and Washington suffered a blow with the public release of tapes containing information about corruption and other criminal acts involving President Kuchma and close collaborators. As a direct consequence of the arms scandal, also known as the Kolchuga affair, President Kuchma was disinvited from the 2002 NATO summit, a gathering where he, nevertheless, made an appearance. For the first time in the organization's history, the seats were arranged according to the French names of member countries, which ensured that Ukraine and the United States would not end up sitting side by side and left Ukraine with the last seat in the row. Moreover, the usual annual Ukrainian–U.S. summit did not take place. These snubs caused humiliation and put on hold the announced Ukrainian intention to join NATO and the EU.

As a way of minimizing the damages caused by the Kolchuga scandal, Ukraine sent to Iraq a sixteen-hundred-person military force in the summer of 2003 (the last troops returned home in December 2005), a gesture welcomed in Washington. Moreover, in the aftermath of the December 2004 Orange Revolution, Ukraine's looking westward seems on track again. Yushchenko's first moves were directed at regaining Western confidence without putting into jeopardy collaboration with Russia. This approach is based on the understanding that the European and Russian vectors in the country's foreign policy are complementary, but that Ukraine's integration into European structures still requires the implementation of deep reforms.

The EU acknowledges Ukrainian intentions to join it, although membership is not on the agenda. The strategic partnership between the EU and Ukraine framed within the principles of the Partnership and Cooperation Agreement (1998) and the Common Strategy (1999) and the inclusion of Ukraine in the European Neighborhood Policy (from 2003) all aim at promoting harmonious relations and thereby facilitating economic and political cooperation. The negotiation of a free trade zone is on the table, on the condition that Ukraine joins the WTO (which the Ukrainian authorities hoped would come to pass in the first quarter of 2007, with support from both the EU and the United States, but did not). Ukraine's bid to join NATO, on the other hand, has generated much discord.

Ukraine has been pursuing a differentiated policy regarding its integration into NATO and the EU. The governing leaders have adopted a so-called step-by-step approach toward NATO, while taking a more direct approach with the EU. It has opted to take a more cautious approach to NATO because the balance it seeks in its foreign options will be hard to achieve given the objections Russia has to its becoming a member of the Atlantic Alliance. But its circumspection has been interpreted in Washington as a sign of weakness and an uncompromising attitude. Still, Washington realizes that Ukraine is an important partner in the region and that it might serve as a check on Russia, whose role and position is uncertain (Kubicek 2003, 4). Therefore, the United States has offered support for a reform course toward a working democratic system and market-oriented economy. This support is not given without conditions, however: there is a trade-off between U.S. support for membership in the WTO and NATO and progress on Ukraine's part in democratization and market reform. The United States has concentrated on economic aspects, pushing for agreement over a system of preferences and trade benefits, recognition of Ukrainian market economy status, and normalization of trade relations (Kramer 2006; Dobriansky 2005).

Energy is also an issue at the top of the agendas of both the United States and Europe, not to mention Russia, with routes for pipelines coming from the Caspian Sea and Russia to Europe through Ukraine. The country could take advantage of this strategic transit position, but Russia has not been cooperative and instead has used oil and gas as a political tool to pressure the authorities in Kiev. The Odessa–Brody pipeline could benefit Ukraine, but constructive engagement with a difficult Russia is essential. Thus, Ukraine remains dependent on Russian goodwill, leaving Kiev in an uncomfortable position. In addition, the Kremlin has adopted a more assertive stance in trying to get Ukraine back into its sphere of influence, playing with the pro-Russian orientation of the new government. The resignation of Foreign Minister Tarasyuk in January 2007, one of the few remaining pro-Western key figures in the government, was immediately praised in Russia as a further step away from integration with the West. These ups and downs in Ukrainian politics have been exploited by the Russian authorities and have made it hard for Ukraine to keep an equal distance from Brussels and Moscow.

Delicate issues such as border delimitation, the status of Crimea and of the Russian population in Ukraine, the division of the Black Sea Fleet, the construction of pipelines in Ukrainian territory, and the destiny of Soviet military equipment have been objects of discord. Despite the fact that most of these problems have already been overcome, their resolution has not resulted in an improvement in the relationship between the two. This is evident in the conditions Ukraine has set on its integration into the CIS, the CIS being seen by the Ukrainian authorities as an obstacle to its integration into European structures, in particular the EU.

The SES established within the CIS is irrelevant in Ukrainian political-economic dealings, as its limited involvement and commitment make clear. Kiev has obtained market economy status from the EU and is close to negotiating a free trade area with it, and it is also getting support for accession into the WTO. In addition, since the Ukrainian parliament has not yet ratified the CIS charter, Ukraine is technically not a member of the CIS (Kuzio 2003), giving it some leverage over Moscow. "The Russians are considering SES to be not only a shape for the multi-national in-depth cooperation, but also as a tool for achieving regional international stability on the most suitable basis" (Parakhonsky 2004; see, also, Trenin 2005a and Khokhotva 2003). This goal is not compatible with full Ukrainian independence or with the Ukrainian idea that "the CIS [is] . . . a means of civilized 'divorce,' not . . . the basis for a new integration" (G. Simon 2001, 75).

The relationship between Ukraine and Russia seems to have evolved from the personal one introduced by presidents Yeltsin and Kuchma to a moderately pragmatic one, where complex and time-consuming negotiations seem to underline interests that are increasingly difficult to reconcile. In fact, Ukraine was one of the founding members of GUUAM (Georgia, Ukraine, Uzbekistan, Azerbaijan, and Moldova), an alternative to the Russian efforts at integration that benefits from U.S. support. Uzbekistan left the organization in 2002, following a rapprochement with Russia and a clear backing away from the West. With the problems that the CIS faces and the "color" revolutions in Georgia, Kyrgyzstan, and Ukraine, new life has been breathed into GUUAM as a promoter of cooperation in the area of energy and transportation as well as on security matters. In May 2006, the four members agreed to rename the group the Organization for Democracy and Economic Development (ODED)—its new name clearly indicating the desire to move closer to the EU and NATO. Russia has responded in part by strongly voicing its opposition to the Ukrainian bid to join NATO, leading the latter to retreat from its efforts on this front. Russian defense minister Ivanov has stated that a decision by Ukraine to join the Atlantic Alliance will "inevitably" affect bilateral relations (RFE/RL 2006). This pressure demonstrates the permanence of old ghosts from the Soviet era, particularly among the military establishment in Moscow, and a resurgence of myths that have remained useful in slowing down the Ukrainian westward course. But the Kremlin's discourse simultaneously plays to the West by repeating that Russia sees no problem in NATO's enlargement and that the relationship institutionalized so far with the Atlantic Alliance has produced fruitful cooperation. These changes in discourse and contradictory arguments make it difficult to grasp Russia's real ambitions and intentions regarding NATO. But, despite statements such as "[w]e never saw NATO as a hostile organization. It's another matter that we believed — and we continue to hold this belief — that simply expanding NATO will not answer the challenges of the present day" (Putin 2005), the national security document as well as many other documents and statements make it clear that the NATO issue is not an easy matter for Russia (see also Polyakov 2002, 175).

Thus, Ukrainian policy toward Russia swings continuously among dependence, independence, and reciprocity. Both countries have a vital interest in maintaining a cooperative relationship, and both acknowledge at the same time the difficulties in coping with their differences. The cards are on the table, and it remains for the new political establishment in Ukraine to implement the announced reforms. Whether it will be successful is still to be seen, but what seems to be certain is that "[h]enceforth, Ukraine will not be ignored by Europe [or the United States,] or be a client state of Russia" (Lavelle 2005).

Belarus: Insulating from East and West

Aleksander Lukashenko was elected president of the Republic of Belarus in July 1994, after a democratic electoral process described as free and fair by international observers. Since then Lukashenko has been engaged in a process of reinforcing his power. In November 1996, after a contested referendum, the president of Belarus introduced a new Constitution and dissolved the 13th Supreme Soviet, appointing loyal members of the latter to the renamed Chamber of Representatives. Lukashenko also established full state control of politics and economics, still in force today. And, in fact, in an observation about the centralization of power in the hands of the president, it is wryly noted that "one day Lukashenko will get bored of being a president and say 'the crowning will be tomorrow.'"

These changes in the national decision-making and executive structures of the country generated controversy. Tension grew, aggravated by the repressive measures the Belarusian authorities took toward opposition members, eliminating voices of discontent, obstructing free broadcasting, and impeding demonstrations in favor of political change. Internally the political situation is, therefore, one of authoritarianism, and Belarus usually described as a repressive and nonfree state (Karatnycky 2000, 195).

Despite Belarus's affirmation of cooperation with the West, it refuses to acknowledge the existence of problems. Mainly, Belarus finds Western criticism of its policies and reforms intrusive, arguing that the national authorities know well how to proceed toward democracy. "Recipes and medicines that are more dangerous than illnesses are being imposed on us," said the Belarusian Deputy

Prime Minister (Latypov 2000). According to Lukashenko the West puts pressure on Belarus because it has not allowed the West to set up a hostile Baltic–Black Sea corridor around Russia and because the Belarusian leadership "stands against the international political monopolism and hegemony of one state [the United States]" (RFE/RL 2001). These political accusations have clearly led to a cooling in relations with the United States, aggravated by the contested referendum in 1996 reinforcing presidential powers. Since then, and particularly after September 11, mounting criticism has been giving place to concrete measures of disapproval.

In December 2001 Belarus described its relations with Washington as "worsening," and talks between the two countries had come to "a complete standstill," according to President Lukashenko (Kuzio 2002). In the context of growing encirclement and isolation, brought about in part by the U.S.–Russia partnership in the fight against terrorism and the establishment of the NATO–Russia Council as well as by Ukraine's increasingly westward drift, Belarus realized the limits of insulation. In the words of Lukashenko (Kuzio 2002), "we must take the current situation into account, adjust our policy, and get used to this reality." Fighting against isolation, Belarus approached NATO and participated for the first time in a NATO military exercise in 2002. Belarus thus attempts to carry out a paradoxical policy of independence and dependence by affirming the country's choices while at the same time coordinating these with much needed international cooperation. The result has been contradictory arguments and positions, which make it difficult to guess whether Lukashenko truly believes he might obtain benefits from cooperation with the West or whether his moves are just a strategic hit to counter isolationism.

Belarus criticizes Washington's unilateral policy based on the precept "with us or against us," arguing that it is merely a way for the United States to hamper and meddle in others' policies and exert pressure over governing options of foreign countries. This meddling and hampering is reputedly evidenced in the listing of Belarus as a rogue country described as an "outpost of tyranny" by Secretary of State Condoleezza Rice. Lukashenko (J. M. 2004) commented that if the country was "moving in the wake of the U.S. policy, [it] should face no criticism. Since Belarus has ventured to conduct independent foreign and domestic policies this boldness is punishable." The Bush administration reported close contacts between the Belarusian regime and Saddam Hussein's Iraq, claiming that Belarus had engaged in secret weapons and military equipment sales to Baghdad along with the laundering of funds in exchange for oil and large sums of money. But despite this problematic relationship, the West acknowledges that it is counterproductive to isolate the country, since if Belarus did become enough like a rogue state, making deals with well-funded criminal groups, it could become a safe haven for terrorism-related activities, with serious consequences for security and stability at the doors of Europe.

Clearly Russian leverage over Belarusian policies is much greater than that of Western governments. The Russian Federation as a privileged partner, and a powerful one, is the country most suited to pressure Belarus into reform and most likely to have a moderating effect on Lukashenko's authoritarian policies. "A preventive regime change is Moscow's best chance of defusing a western-oriented revolution in Belarus" (Trenin 2005c) and of avoiding anti-Russian or confrontational attitudes unfavorable to Russia. Therefore, Putin should pursue a more proactive policy toward Belarusian politics.

By pressuring both the national authorities and the opposition groups to reach an acceptable agreement over representation and a functioning multiparty system, Russia could eventually contribute to eliminating domestic tension in Belarus. At the same time, however, Russia aims at preventing strong ties between Belarus and the West, particularly in the face of NATO's expansion eastward in admitting countries from the former Soviet Union and the Eastern bloc. This results in ambivalence in the intricate relationship between the authorities in Moscow and Minsk. As a noted Russian analyst has put it, "To many among the Russian political elite, the west (whether seen as NATO or the EU) is still a potential adversary, the Baltic states are virulently anti-Russian, and Ukraine is in the process of being taken over by the west and turned into a buffer state against Russia. Within such a context, a friendly Belarus is virtually priceless; and no concession is enough to keep it that way" (Trenin 2005c).

The Russian desire for Belarusian policies oriented in its favor has been a goal since President Lukashenko came to power in 1994. The Russian Federation did not contest the 1996 referendum or the new constitution but rather strengthened ties with its neighbor. The two countries ratified the Treaty on the Formation of the Belarus–Russia Community on August 26, 1996, which was upgraded in December 1999 to a Union State Treaty. This is a union based on the principles of sovereignty and equality, the goal of which is to form a deeply politically and economically integrated community — that is, it is, simply put, a new federal state formation, according to which the national legislation of Russia and Belarus should be subordinated to the Union's law. Despite acknowledged advantages, the disparate economic, social, and political evolution of the two countries might render these goals impracticable. Belarusian state monopolistic socialism contrasts with Russia's still flawed but nonetheless functioning market capitalism. In addition, the reconfiguration of political goals and strategies in both countries has been creating differences between them. Although many in Belarus acknowledge the importance of Russia as a political, economic, and commercial partner, there are fears about growing interference of Moscow in Belarusian affairs, with many citing Russia "as the greatest threat to Belarusian independence" (Marples 2004, 40).

Increasing dissension between Russia and Belarus has thus been based on the contradictory expectations underpinning collaboration. While Lukashenko had expected that the collaboration would allow him to run for president of Russia in the election for Yeltsin's successor (an expectation that did not generate a response in Moscow), Russia looks at Belarus as a small and poor neighbor, eligible for no more than the status of autonomous republic — the ninetieth — within the Russian Federation. Lukashenko classified this proposal as an "insult" (Trenin 2005c) to Belarus (but which in practice would mean the loss of power and authority for Lukashenko himself). Thus, since 1999 Belarus and Russia have taken several gigantic steps backward in the construction of the Union State, undoing the small steps forward they had taken before that time. Integration has effectively been displaced by distancing.

September 11 has contributed to the shaping of a different world order and has directly affected Belarus's relationship with Russia as well as that with the United States. The immediate U.S.–Russia rapprochement following the terrorist acts in the United States compelled Lukashenko to refigure Belarus's relationship with Moscow. In the face of a distant Russia Minsk opted not to support the CIS and its integration course. It chose instead to delineate an alternative policy centered on the preservation of the country's independence in political and economic terms and, thus, to downgrade the importance of the Russia–Belarus Union, which at the time was already an unconvincing integration mechanism. In addition, the relationship has been strained by the increase in the price of Russian oil to Belarus, igniting a new energy crisis in early 2007. Although there are some similarities between Belarus's dispute with Russia over oil prices and Ukraine's quarrel with Russia over gas prices, the disagreement between Russia and Belarus has assumed different contours. Despite much wrangling and numerous retaliatory moves, with Minsk imposing a transit fee on Russian oil across Belarus and threatening to charge Russia for the two military bases it is using on Belarusian territory, as well as for the land it is using under the Yamal–Europe pipeline, the issue goes much further than simple price calculations. Russia's formal explanation for price increases is that the WTO requires domestic prices to reach world market levels by 2011, but Russia is also trying to pressure Belarus economically so as to keep the Belarusian regime closely tied to Moscow. Simply put, Moscow wants to have options regarding Belarus. However, this game has not been welcomed by Lukashenko, who in his usual rhetorical style commented that "Russia is trying to disregard the former Soviet republics, thinking they won't go anywhere and they will remain hooked to the Russian Federation. This is a misguided position." In addition, Lukashenko has been waving the European flag at Moscow, in a defiant move. And in fact it has not been any more than that—defiance. Europe is concerned about the reliability of Russia as an energy supplier but showed surprise at the claim of the Belarusian president that "Europe has suddenly turned its attention to Belarus and understood that without Belarus it is difficult to ensure Europe's energy security" (RFE/RL 2007). It seems that the danger of a disruption in supplies has been overcome, but it has had a negative effect on Russian–Belarusian relations.

Lukashenko's relations with the United States and Russia are thus increasingly complex. The Belarusian president referred to this in his speech commemorating ten years in power, when he said, "we do not choose east and west or east or west—we choose Belarus!" Simultaneously, Lukashenko recognizes the importance of not being isolated, commenting that Europe is a "strategic neighbor" and adding that "our brothers are not NATO or the west. These are our brothers—the Russians" (cited in Kudrin 2004). All of this represents a reversal in discourse, a mix-up in policies, and reflects unclear goals, all of which render Belarus politics an intricate set of sayings, at times difficult to interpret.

Russian and the Other Western CIS Responses to U.S. Unilateralism: An Assessment

The U.S. global strategy in the fight against terrorism, that of pursuing a unilateral strategic military policy, has encountered many obstacles, particularly at the level of implementation. This has elicited different reactions in Russia, Ukraine, and Belarus, whose chosen courses have led to quarrels among them and have become increasingly hard to reconcile.

The complex U.S.–Russia relationship is marked by a "give-and-take" policy consisting of concessions and demands. This ambivalence demonstrates U.S. acknowledgement of Russia's significance as a strategic player in the fight against terrorism and shows how friendly relations with the United States are important for Russia. Moscow, which faces terrorism and separatism within its borders, is a particularly sensitive actor in the global fight against the menace of terrorism because it directly affects its own security and territorial integrity. The tightening of various political, bureaucratic, and legal procedures in the wake of the terrorist acts in the United States in 2001 was seen as an opportunity in Moscow and as conferring legitimacy on its actions, particularly regarding Chechnya. But it is not an opportunity without difficulty. Russia has been seeking symmetry in a clearly asymmetrical relationship. Still, although the Russian desire to be seen as an equal is not realistic, the U.S. tendency to behave in a paternalistic way, treating Russia as a "junior partner," is likely to have repercussions (Kortunov 2002, 38), since Russia enjoys greater power and influence than the United

States in the former Soviet area in addition to commanding important economic and nuclear potential. But, if Washington's discourse and practice has fluctuated between rapprochement and distancing, Russia also appears to have followed a similar path, despite its diminished power.

Russia supports the United States to the extent that it finds legitimacy for its actions, but tries to counteract it when it perceives its interests might be threatened. The American intervention in Afghanistan was very much welcomed in Moscow since it had the potential to eliminate a dangerous source of instability close to its borders. As for the former Soviet republics, which represent an area of strategic interest for Russia, American involvement there is more problematic. Nevertheless, Putin is pragmatic and allowed U.S. troops to be stationed in the area in the hope that he might be able to reap economic and political benefits in return. Moscow has reemphasized its commitment to multilateralism, a foreign policy approach already visible in Russian official documents prior to September 11, severely criticizing American intervention in Iraq without a U.N. sanction. However, the Russian posture might in some instances be compared to that of the United States. When it feels its interests are at risk, Moscow is willing to go it alone, to contravene international resolutions and even block decision making in international bodies. Thus, Moscow has been pursuing a strategy of cooperation when possible and one of competition when necessary, making an already complex relationship even more complex.

Despite dissension, both sides acknowledge mutual gains from cooperation even in the midst of accusations. The war on terrorism, the push for nonproliferation, and Russia's integration into the international economy are three main matters the two can agree on that might bring mutual rewards. However, questions arise regarding underlying motives and the strategies chosen. While Americans are troubled primarily by the danger of being a prime target of terrorist attacks, which requires a firm response, Russians worry that radical Islam could weaken neighboring states or even endanger their country's territorial integrity. The two different perspectives, the U.S. outsider view versus that of the Russian insider, when combined with the multilateral versus unilateral debate, renders the development of harmonized policy options difficult for the two countries. Nevertheless, there are simple moves that could make a difference.

Changes in the format and style of communication between the United States and Russia are necessary in order to minimize the perception among Russians that the United States regards Russia as a second-rate country, which Moscow cannot accept. In addition, counterterrorism cooperation might be pursued through intelligence sharing, the development of joint threat assessments, and the implementation of confidence-building measures through, for example, active collaboration with Russia and other states on border security and antitrafficking. These are sensitive matters for Russia, particularly the matter of its and others' involvement in the near abroad.

Belarus is a small country, authoritarian in style and inward looking, with a domestic political strategy meant to keep Lukashenko's power untouched. Minsk pursued integration with Russia until President Lukashenko realized that that policy would not give him more power, at which point he replaced a policy of rapprochement with Russia with one of independence for Belarus. This has resulted in Belarusian isolation and its labeling as a rogue state. Its relations with the United States are quite limited, often assuming an assertive tone, which, given the current status quo, might render small Belarus a big obstacle in the fight against terrorism.

Ukraine has pursued a more diversified foreign policy. During his ten-year reign, President Kuchma simultaneously played the EU, NATO, and Russia cards. Although Russia has substantial influence over Ukrainian politics, particularly regarding the country's dependence on energy resources, this has not impeded Kiev from opting for a multivector external policy that incorporates both an Eastern and Western dimension. The impact of September 11 as well as the internal scandals of the Kuchma administration over Iraq and allegations over human rights violations resulted in a distancing between Ukraine and its Western partners. These tensions were, nevertheless, gradually eased, with the 2004 Orange Revolution crowning the efforts of those who favored the Western path. This has shown that while good relations with Russia, a huge country on its borders, cannot be disregarded, Western assistance in economic growth and regime change is also fundamental. While Ukraine sees cooperation with the United States as a window of opportunity, Belarus feels it as a threat to the regime's perpetuation, and Russia balances itself between the two. This results in a mixed picture within the Slavic triangle regarding relations with the United States. It also denotes disagreement within the triangle among the three states, adding complexity to the geopolitical game in the area.

Conclusions

The three Slavic countries, Russia, Ukraine, and Belarus, are immediate neighbors of Europe and NATO and serve as a bridge between East and West. This makes them especially relevant to the geostrategic political-economic puzzle of the fight against terrorism, to the push for democratization, and to the economic dealings in the area. Serious setbacks on any of these fronts, particularly in Russia and Ukraine, could destabilize the region. Russia is to some extent an actor that is difficult to interpret, since its loud promotion of democratic ideals is not translated into effective democratic policies. Belarus is even more problematic and a cause of concern because of its isolationist course.

Therefore, the stakes are high for the United States. It is not just a question of trading some benefits for support in the fight against terrorism. It is a deeper question of helping to reform structures and procedures and to change attitudes. The United States should attempt to push these states toward democracy, a long-term effort promising long-term benefits. It should be done in such a way that gaps in political, institutional and economic standards might be narrowed, allowing the sharing of development goals in a positive, collaborative sense. The United States understands the priority of support for these states, although it cannot take the same approach to all three countries. The "Slavic brotherhood," which could have constituted an opportunity for integration, has proven to be inadequate to this task. The CIS, which could have served as a convergence mechanism, has also revealed divergent perspectives that have resulted in deadlock.

Internal rivalry and competition, along with fears of Russian domination, have prevented further cooperation within the Slavic triangle. Fears regarding U.S. dominance have also arisen. Explicit U.S. dominance might become a factor that compels the three countries to distance themselves from the United States, with overall negative consequences for Washington and negative repercussions for international stability. Therefore, the White House should pursue a careful and balanced approach, keeping in mind that a course of action based on the imposition of U.S. views — which both Ukraine and Belarus have been subject to for a long time — will not produce the expected positive results of a cooperative nature. Moreover, Russia has already made clear it will counterbalance U.S. military power whenever its interests might be at risk. Therefore, imposition should give place to dialogue and dialogue to cooperation. The ambiguous nature of these relations demands concrete approaches and firm commitment. Although achieving genuine dialogue will present a difficult challenge, it is also a goal worth fighting for, since further collaboration between the United States and the western CIS—Russia, Ukraine, and Belarus—could prove to be a valuable asset in the fight against terror.

Notes

1. In 2007, Ukraine is paying Russia $130 per one thousand cubic meters of gas, while Belarus's rate is $100. Moldova and Georgia pay more — the former $170 and the latter the much higher price of $235.

CHAPTER NINE

The Balkans to Turkey and the Northern Tier

Gülnur Aybet

The so-called Bush revolution in foreign policy is a quest for a global order that rests on two anomalous premises (Kanet 2005; Daalder and Lindsay 2003)—American exceptionalism and the symbiotic relationship between power and norms. Exceptionalism justifies the freedom a superpower enjoys from the multilateral constraints that bind other states through the rules and regulations of international organizations. The symbiotic and interdependent relationship between power and norms, by contrast, ensures that each justifies the other. Power and norms correspond to the material and subjective dimension of the Bush administration's vision to reform the global order. The symbiosis of power and norms means that power alone does not legitimize military power projection.[1] The morality of spreading the American system of democratic governance and free-market economies legitimizes the use of power to achieve this end.

However, the availability of power determines and justifies the undertaking of the Bush administration's mission to revamp the global order. This can be seen in references in Bush's speeches to the "opportunity" that this particular time of unprecedented American power presents. Therefore, power and norms justify each other. Another complicating factor is the almost unchallenged feature of these norms and their ownership by the United States. As Edward Kolodziej points out, the normative power of U.S. hegemony "serves and secures a universal public good." After all, who would deny that "freedom, democracy, and free enterprise" are malignant? (Kolodziej 2007; Kolodziej, chapter 1; and U.S. White House, Office of the President 2002).

American exceptionalism, although not a new concept, has, under the Bush administration, given the term "superpower" a new meaning. During the cold war, when the term "superpower" itself emerged, it directly connoted the quantity of power possessed by a country. Today, "super" in "superpower" does not necessarily mean merely quantitatively "more" powerful. The meaning of the word is tied rather to the structure of the international system. In this sense, its force goes beyond the parameters of traditional realism. The superpower does not see itself in terms of where it "stands" in the international system or its "place" in the international system. Whereas traditional European powers in the Machiavellian sense have always had a sense of "place" in the international system, the superpower sees itself and the world as two distinct entities; it is not concerned about its "place" in it. There is, on the one hand, itself and then, on the other, there is the world. Therefore, in terms of the structure of the international system, it is not a player in the classical realist sense but an orderer.

This premise can be challenged by adopting a wider view, one that goes beyond the peculiarities of a unipolar international system. The question that needs to be asked to go beyond the peculiarities of a lone superpower's coming to grips with norms and power is whether the United States itself is simply reacting to an inevitable change in the global order. The *National Security Strategy* of 2002 undoubtedly constitutes a blueprint for a grand design, but is it really a testament to the ultimate power of the United States as an orderer? Before we can make any assessments about regional reactions to the hegemon, we need to question to what extent the hegemon itself is reacting to changes in the global order rather than taking its power as a given and assuming that its place in the international system is as an "orderer" of things.

This is particularly relevant when looking at the vast regional scope of the Balkans from Turkey to the Northern Tier. What needs to be asked is whether reactions to U.S. hegemony are indeed "reactions" or whether they represent states and actors trying to "fit" into the world in a global era of transition, pretty much in the same way the hegemon is trying to "fit" itself into the same changing international system. The fact that the United States may not see itself as a "player" in that system in the traditional Machiavellian sense may also be because refusing that conception of itself represents a useful coping mechanism for dealing with a new world with the tools of a system created in 1945. One coping mechanism employed by the superpower itself in this time of transition may be the coalitions of the willing. But if the Bush doctrine rests on the symbiotic relationship between norms and power, then this leads to the question of to what extent coalitions of the willing can replace established multilateral channels legitimately.

If multilaterism is in crisis, it is not so much because the United States has undermined it as that the system of ownership of international organizations is still stuck in a 1945 groove (M. Brown 2006, 1). In an era of growing predominance of intrastate wars, terrorism, rising medium-size nuclear powers, changes in regional balances of power, and the instability of regions that source long-term oil and gas supplies, the post-1945 framework of international organizations is no longer adequate. For example, it will not be possible to deal with North Korea's nuclear ambitions without the help of other Northeast Asian countries. The U.N., as the main organization for collective security, finds itself trying to keep up its missions to cope with these new demands, none of which bear any semblance to the challenges envisaged for global peace and security at the time of drafting the U.N. Charter in 1945. Therefore if the United States operates on the logic that multilateral arrangements created to serve a different time ought not to impede its mission of delivering the public goods of democracy, freedom, and free enterprise, this suggests that those arrangements are not being weakened by a preconceived American design. Rather, those arrangements are being weakened because they are challenged by new demands of a different era, to which they need to adjust. The deliberate choice of the United States to use the symbiotic relationship of norms and power as a launching pad for global dominance is also a reaction to these changes, not because of a preconceived design. Therefore, a lot rests on a world coming to grips with a new world and with new demands and, for the present, being forced to face these demands with the tools of a different era. The post-1945 liberal international order has not been altered because it has not been challenged, and if anything it has vanquished every other order that posed a challenge to its premises. Yet being a victor creates its own problems in that being unchallenged by another system is not synonymous with not being out of date.

This has a direct bearing on Turkey as a pivotal point between the Balkans and the Northern Tier because so much of what could be termed as a "reaction" to U.S. hegemony in the region in fact rests on the power relations vested there after 1945. The so-called Northern Tier was a favorite terminology of the early days of the cold war. Similarly, Turkish–U.S. relations fundamentally rest on the strategic relationship established after 1945. What is interesting in the peculiar configuration of this region is that the western Balkans remain a unique regional entity wherein U.S. power projection has been implemented on a "clean slate" through military intervention and the establishment of a networked presence of both international governmental and nongovernmental organizations (NGOs). A "clean slate" because domestic and state institutions, as well as traditional parameters of normative relations with peripheral powers, were jettisoned after the breakup of Yugoslavia. This peculiarity is relevant for the western Balkans, on which this paper will dwell. The conditionality of European Union (EU) membership has clearly been a stabilizing factor in Central and Eastern Europe (CEE), but this has not been achieved to the same degree in the western Balkans. This is because U.S. dominance in the region, a direct result of military intervention as a tool of conflict management, has made it difficult for regional organizations to draw the states of the western Balkans in, with the exception of the cases of Bulgaria and Romania. Turkey, on the other hand, oscillates between the United States and the EU in reformulating its foreign policy from an "issue-based" compartmentalized one founded on strategic relationships fostered during the cold war to a comprehensive one that reconciles domestic and international priorities in accordance with EU criteria. Turkey's relations with the Northern Tier are going through a transition from a cold war framework to a new regional balance-of-power configuration based on natural resources and continuing strategic partnerships with the United States and Europe.

In the case of the Balkans and Turkey in particular, two factors emerge that are important when analyzing reactions to U.S. hegemony. The first is that an *intrastate level of analysis* seems to be far more relevant and crucial when analyzing actor reactions to U.S. hegemony in this region. In the case of the western Balkans we see this in terms of the problematic internalization of externally imposed norms by regional civil societies. In the case of Turkey, internal reactions to the United States are checked and balanced by internal reactions to the EU. In this sense, Turkey's "Western" orientation whether as a component of its Western identity or as a policy agenda tends to drift from accepting U.S. hegemony, to promoting Turkish geographical "exceptionalism," to expressing its frustrations with the EU.

The second factor that is relevant to both the Turkish and Balkan cases is the fact that their reactions to U.S. hegemony cannot be divorced from the dynamics of transatlantic relations. For the purposes of the Balkans and Turkey, Europe cannot be classified as merely another "region." For the structural and normative elements of the transatlantic relationship shape the acquiescence of the hegemon's norms by regional actors. The paradox here is that while the transatlantic relationship is crucial for the transformation of the Balkans and for keeping Turkey on board with the alliance, the United States sees Europe as just another "region" because of the structural vision it has of itself and the "world" as two distinct entities.

The disparity among European reactions to U.S. hegemony does not go very far to help solve this dilemma either. If anything, they justify the Bush administration's idea that Europe is no different from other regions. At the same time, this disparate reaction on the part of Europe to American hegemony is confusing to the Balkans and to Turkey, for different reasons. European reactions, particularly during the buildup to the war in Iraq, oscillated among poking the superpower in the eye, quiet diplomacy, a wavering between the two, or quiet disagreement. The EU high representative Javier Solana has commented on this lack of unity in the EU: "of course, it's a problem, we are not a country."[2] A post–cold war Europe, free of the superpower squeeze but not entirely free of "entrapment" by the United States, and certainly not unified in its foreign policy, is bound to display such differences of opinion. The paradox in a unipolar world of not being able to "balance against" an ally as Europe was traditionally used to being able to do presents an awkwardness that the European states have never had to encounter before that also contributes to their differences of opinion.

However, differing European reactions to U.S. hegemony are not the only paradoxes in the transatlantic relationship, for there is an anomaly in the U.S. global mission itself. The concepts of "consensual" and "coercive" hegemony as put forward by Kolodziej correspond to the concepts of "material incentives" and "substantive beliefs" as put forward by Kupchan and Ikenberry. While a transformation in substantive beliefs seems to be the end goal of the Bush administration (that is, a desire to shape and reestablish the normative base of the international order), the means for achieving this are purely based on material incentives (that is, economic inducements and military power projection), followed by threat or use of force. It is the consensual aspect of the Bush administration's design for global order and the coercive method by which it is trying to achieve this global order that present an anomaly. In this sense, hegemony can either be consensual or coercive; it cannot be both. In the same way, Kupchan and Ikenberry argue that socialization or the acquiescence of normative ideals put forward by the hegemon can be achieved either by offering material incentives or by attempting to change substantive beliefs via normative persuasion. Gramscian concepts of hegemony take this argument further by interrelating the socioeconomic, ideological, and political structures that enable the hegemony to claim legitimacy (Ikenberry and Kupchan 1990, 284; Kanet 2005; and R. Cox 1987). This distinction between coercive/material and consensual/substantive beliefs does not sit comfortably with the notion of a "balance of freedom" implicit in the Bush doctrine, where there is supposedly a "growing convergence of common values across cultures and nations" (Kolodziej, chapter 1).

The Balkans and Turkey are crucial to the transatlantic relationship and the U.S. administration's global mission because of the implications they have for other regions such as the Black Sea, the Caucasus, and the Middle East (Asmus and Jackson 2004; Teft 2005; R. Menon 2003; and Asmus et al. 2005). This paper dwells on the impact of the geographical stretch from the Balkans to Turkey on the Northern Tier not only because of the proximity of the Balkans and Turkey to the Northern Tier but also because of the impact of reforms and their links with Western institutions on their neighboring countries. The Balkans, although still rife with unfinished business from the matter of what is to become of Kosovo to Bosnia and Herzegovina and Albania's development into functioning states, are nevertheless seen as a stepping stone to further reforms in the neighboring countries of the Black Sea and the Caucasus. Most significant will be how the region receives EU and NATO conditionality, which can be gauged by looking first at the case of the western Balkans. Some analysts have suggested that Turkey could be a role model for the Broader Middle East, not only because it is a living example of an Islam-democracy synthesis but also because of the impact the EU-induced reforms have had on the country. Turkey's progress in this area could be held up as an example of what political and economic reform can achieve in the Middle East (Taspinar 2005, 37).

The Western Balkans: Different Stages of Socialization

Today the western Balkans is probably one of the few places about which Europe and America see eye to eye. The given common interest of projecting stability in a near but tough neighborhood and bringing organized crime under control keeps the transatlantic relationship in healthy fusion. Therefore the mission of the United States and that of the EU become interlinked in the case of the western Balkans. The business of transferring international norms to this region in order to project stability rests on the three key norms of free-market economics, democratic governance, and human rights. The issue in the region is not so much whether U.S. hegemony is seen as a good or a bad thing, but how these norms exported from the outside are internalized, whether by elites or civil society. The problem in the western Balkans is one of socialization of hegemonic norms in developing societies. Here the most significant level of analysis for the reaction of regional actors to hegemonic policies is *intrastate*. This is because internal governance and domestic regimes are still largely at a developmental stage and interstate relations are largely determined by the inducements and still-lingering coercive measures of the international community. However, the internalization of external norms at the level of civil society is proving to be more problematic than the direct enforcement of rules and institutions from above. Because the Bush administration's global mission is so dependent on the internalization of these norms by regional societies, the Balkan transformation case could present serious obstacles to the materialization of that mission elsewhere — especially if the western Balkans are to be used as a shining example of transformation yet to come in the Black Sea region and the greater Middle East or, in cold war parlance, the Northern Tier. Another problem with regard to the Balkans is the disparity between the countries and the different stages of conditionality and development.

The region is unique because, for example, in the case of Bosnia and Herzegovina, we have a sovereign state that at the same time continues to be an internationally administered territory. This alone creates an anomaly regarding the norm of democracy that is being imposed "top-down" by the United States and its allies in the region, since "trusteeship and sovereignty are mutually exclusive concepts" (Caplan 2005, 465). On the other hand the internationally administered protectorate of Kosovo is short of being a state but without any official recognition or admission of secession from Serbia.

While Kosovo's ultimate fate has yet to be determined, its future rife with obstacles, the split between Serbia and Montenegro brings a new configuration. While Bulgaria and Romania have made it into the EU, neighboring Former Yugoslav Republic of Macedonia is also relatively stable by virtue of the international community's efforts in holding up the Ohrid Agreement of August 2001, which was brokered by the United States and the European Union after the outbreak of violence between ethnic Albanians and Macedonians in February 2001. While the peace was first kept by NATO and later EU peacekeeping forces, it was taken over by an EU-led police mission in 2003. While the present government upholds the Ohrid agreement, there is still the looming possibility instability might be imported from neighboring Kosovo with its large ethnic Albanian population.

In the cases of Bosnia and Kosovo, in particular, old institutions, procedures, and norms were jettisoned with the collapse of communism and the breakup of Yugoslavia, and a "top-down"-imposed peace settlement followed on the heels of a military intervention led by the United States. In this sense, nation building within the postconflict areas of the western Balkans started on a "clean slate." A good example is the Bosnian Constitution, which is, in effect, Annex 4 of the Dayton Peace Agreement. Article 12 states that the "Constitution shall enter into force upon signature of the General Framework Agreement as a constitutional act amending and superseding the Constitution of the Republic of Bosnia and Herzegovina" (General Framework 1995). However, according to the old Bosnian constitution, any amendment to the constitution had to be drafted by the Assembly and presented to the public for discussion and then adopted only if two-thirds of the total number of the deputies of every chamber in the Assembly voted in favor of it. So although Bosnia and Herzegovina had existing domestic structures and regulations regarding amendments to its constitution, these rules and structures preceded Bosnia's achievement of its sovereignty and were subsequently ignored under the Dayton Agreement. This is a very good example of how the norms imported by a U.S. hegemonic presence in the region are working on a "clean slate" that leaves little room for "reaction" in the rational sense. The sense of alienation in these civil societies further impedes the internationalization of imposed "top-down" norms. In Bosnia and Herzegovina, 62 percent of the young population wish to emigrate, and those who can, do. In fact one of the most crucial impediments to building a future in Bosnia is the brain drain (U.N. Development Program 2002). But whether this alienation can be seen as a reaction to U.S. hegemony is unclear simply because of the "clean slate" situation. There are very few existing local norms and practices that can form a reaction to externally imposed hegemonic rules, whether in the form of acquiescence or rejection.

Similarly, it is hard to say whether the "clean slate" situation is a result of U.S. hegemonic designs in the region. If anything U.S. involvement in the western Balkans happened more by default than by design. In 1989 the senior Bush administration's directives on U.S. policy toward Yugoslavia were given to Warren Zimmermann, the last U.S. ambassador to Yugoslavia. This policy consisted of two points: first, as a consequence of the demise of the Warsaw Pact and the impending end of the cold war, Yugoslavia no longer enjoyed the geostrategic significance it had held for the United States during the cold war. Second, the United States supported the unity and territorial integrity of Yugoslavia. However, this second point also had an anomalous condition attached to it—that the United States could only support unity in the context of democracy and would be opposed to force being used to impose unity. Aside from these conditions, the initial U.S. policy toward the western Balkans at the end of the cold war was one of noninvolvement (Zimmermann 1995).

Therefore the one place where the United States has unprecedented power to impose international norms through military intervention and a multilaterally enforced peace is in fact an unintended result of the shifts resulting from the end of the cold war era. The "clean slate" on which the U.S. vision of nation building occurs in the western Balkans, at least, is a consequence, not a result of "ordering." It may well be the direct experience of this unimpeded "ordering" in the western Balkans that prompted the Bush revolution to be bold and to try to repeat the experience of the western Balkans in the greater Middle East. If the United States proclaimed "ordering" as an agenda, it did so only after falling into the role of an "orderer" consequentially as a result of changes in the intrastate make up of the western Balkans. But this consequential role that the United States has played in the Balkans has not been so straightforward, even though in the beginning the military enforcement succeeded to a certain extent, because, as noted earlier, civil society has had trouble internalizing international norms as they have been handed down by international community institutions. Second, the processes of peace building in the western Balkans, without which dissemination of norms and nation building could not take place, have occurred at different stages of the socialization process.

If we take the case of Bosnia and Herzegovina and the differences between the EU and NATO peace-building missions, we can see that each corresponds to a different phase of socialization, that is, the internalization of norms imposed by the hegemonic power conceived here as a U.S.–European coalition. In the Bosnian case the socialization process starts with internal reconstruction based on the export of hegemonic norms via the enabling power of international institutions. In the next stage the enabling power follows with coercive or material inducements; this corresponds to the phase of the Implementation Force (IFOR) peace-enforcement mission. Next the Stabilization Force (SFOR) mission serves as a tool of transition from external coercive inducements to normative persuasion. Normative persuasion as opposed to norm imposition is the presence of conditionality whereby norm change occurs through an internalization of norms by local elites. This results in policy change. The EU mission, which took over from SFOR in 2004, is, therefore, more integrated with the principles of conditionality than coercion, while SFOR as a mission serves as a transition from one to the other. In this sense, both the EU and NATO serve different stages of this spectrum (Ikenberry and Kupchan 1990).[3]

While Kupchan and Ikenberry's model is useful, their overreliance on the internationalization of externally imposed norms by the regional elite make their thesis in this respect inapplicable to the western Balkans. This is because in particular with the states like Bosnia and Herzegovina the elite are more international than local. The newly emerging transatlantic consensus that accords the EU a greater role in the western Balkans does not alleviate the problem of lack of local leadership that can internalize externally imposed norms (International Commission on the Balkans 2005).[4] Here, conditionality and "club rules" do not have quite the same meaning as they did for the CEE states, for the simple reason that Bosnia and Kosovo were not states to begin with, but creations of the international community. At this juncture the top-down imposition of hegemonic norms such as democracy, free-market economies, and human rights is accomplished through a coercive/inducement mechanism, namely, the legitimate authority and economic and military force of international organizations. However, these norms translate into little meaning at the local grassroots level, because the internalization of these norms by local elites is still not taking place. Even beyond the unique cases of Bosnia and Kosovo, the problem in the western Balkans in general is a sense of alienation at the local level. The concept of "if the country does well, I do well" that existed in pre-EU accession CEE is seriously lacking in the western Balkans from Kosovo and Macedonia to Albania. The geographical proximity of these countries to Bulgaria and Romania, who joined the EU in 2007, and Greece, the only EU-member state in the Balkans, makes the disparity of intrastate perceptions of international norms all the more problematic.

Turkey: Somewhere Between the Transatlantic Divide?

Turkey's relationship with and reaction to U.S. hegemony is totally different from that of any other region or country. This is because Turkey, first of all, is far more sympathetic to the concept of U.S. exceptionalism than are its European allies or Middle Eastern neighbors, owing to the fact that there is such a thing as "Turkish" exceptionalism. While not as grand in scale as American exceptionalism, which encompasses the globe, it is nevertheless a national security-driven regional and geographical exceptionalism. In the Turkish Ministry of National Defense White Paper of 2000 Turkey's immediate neighborhood is listed as a prime determinant of Turkish security and foreign policy. This geographical determinism not only shapes Turkey's security policy but also shapes its political processes (Bilgin 2005, 186). Exceptionalism is not confined to civilian-military elite discourse but is also shared by general public opinion, according to the survey *Transatlantic Trends* (German Marshall Fund of the United States and Compagnia di San Paolo 2004, 21–22). The survey shows that the Turkish public support for the use of military force is much higher than in other European countries. It also showed that 71 percent of the population agreed that, if it were in the vital interests of the country, it would be justified to bypass the United Nations, in contrast to 44 percent in Europe.

Secondly, Turkey's relations with the United States cannot be analyzed at an intra- or interstate or transnational level because how Turkish reactions to U.S. hegemony evolve is linked to where Turkey stands in the transatlantic divide. In this sense Europe is not just another region that can be manipulated or deconstructed by the United States. The crude reference to "old" and "new" Europe is not sufficient to explain the complexities of Turkey's "Western" policy, given its aspirations to the join the EU, its continuing frustration with the policies of EU member states, and its deteriorating but remarkably solid strategic relationship with America. As a Balkan, European, and Middle Eastern country, Turkey straddles many regions and its role as a regional player also affects U.S. policies in these regions. While both Europe and America see eye to eye when it comes to presenting Turkey as the "benign" face of the West looking toward the East, Washington and Brussels in fact view Turkey in remarkably disparate ways. This makes it hard for Turkey to reformulate its "Western" foreign policy with an eye to both Europe and America. Furthermore, Turkish policy planners are somewhat skeptical about Turkey's place as a "role model" for the Middle East given that it is a predominantly Muslim democracy. However, there are also intrastate challenges that interestingly enough are more reactive to the EU than to the United States. The initial anti-U.S. sentiments, which were much more predominant in the wake of the Iraq war and its immediate aftermath, have been taken over by repeated disappointments with the European Union, despite the fact that accession talks with the Union began in October 2005.

Given the difficulties of practical issues related to the accession process, which include Cyprus's relations with Greece, the rise in nationalism and the growing opposition to Turkey's EU membership within European political ranks as well as from the public, there has been a loss of interest in the European Union within

Turkey; popular support for the EU dropped by 10 percent to 63 percent between December 2004 and April 2005 (EurActiv 2005). This indicates that deteriorating relations with the United States during the war in Iraq have been paralleled by a growing disillusionment with the EU. This is why in the Turkish case, reactions to U.S. hegemony cannot be divorced from the issue of transatlantic relations and Turkey's relationship with the EU. Another factor linked to the transatlantic relationship concerns the disparate ways with which the United States and Europe deal with Turkey. These intrastate tensions that lead Turkey to oscillate between reacting to the EU and the United States are followed with closer scrutiny in the United States than they are in Europe.

Bruce Jackson (2005), addressing the Senate Committee on Foreign Relations, observed that Turkey found itself in a "national and geopolitical identity crisis" and that "Turkey may be entering a difficult and problematic stage." Jackson concluded that Turkey has become "unhelpful." American observations are critical because they relate to the concern over anti-Americanism in Turkish public opinion, especially since the outbreak of the Iraq war. European observers are less concerned about evident cultural anti-Europeanism in Turkey, although a recent survey of Turkish public opinion toward Europe and America found that Turkey's thermometer reading toward the EU was 53 degrees, in comparison to a European average of 70 degrees and a U.S. reading of 62 degrees. The same survey found that 91 percent in Turkey did not favor the Iraq war and 47 percent found U.S. leadership in world affairs undesirable (German Marshall Fund and of the United States and Compagnia di San Paolo 2004, 21).

Turkey's relationship with the United States has traditionally been termed a "strategic partnership." During the cold war it was obvious that this referred to a NATO country sharing a border with the Soviet Union. But what has it really meant since the end of the cold war? For former secretary of state Madeleine Albright, the strategic partnership still means "the NATO relationship and the strategic location of Turkey itself" (Albright 2005, 49). In fact, it is the very cold war parameters of the strategic relationship with Turkey that still determine U.S. policies. The problem, not just for Turkey but also for U.S. policy makers, is that it is no longer sufficient for the United States to formulate its policies toward Turkey through a governing elite. The undersecretary for defense policy, Douglas Feith spoke to this very problem in early in February 2005. Feith stated in an interview to the Turkish press that the United States would have preferred to have seen its efforts in Iraq to be better understood and appreciated by the general public in Turkey and that this was a matter of grave concern for the United States (Sedat 2005; Yetkin 2005a, 2005b).[5]

Yet, policy makers in Washington were at odds concerning how they had not foreseen the result of the Turkish parliamentary vote blocking the transit of U.S.

troops through Turkey to open a second front in northern Iraq. During the cold war the strategic partnership between the United States and Turkey rested on the relationship that U.S. policy makers had with the Turkish government and particularly with the Turkish General Staff. Prior to the Gulf War of 1991 it was the Turkish Parliament that passed an extended war powers bill on January 17, 1991. The role that is played by the Parliament at times of crisis has always been evident. Despite this, policy makers in the United States were baffled when the Turkish Parliament voted against the stationing of and transit of U.S. troops through Turkish territory on March 1, 2003. Deputy Defense Secretary Paul Wolfowitz stated that the U.S. government was surprised that "for whatever reason, the Turkish military did not play the strong leadership role we would have expected" (cited in Taspinar 2005, 29). Other U.S. analysts have commented that it is time for a new strategic relationship with Turkey, one not based on engaging "Turkey's traditional security policy makers alone" (Lesser 2004). Even Turkey's accession into the EU is, for the United States, a matter of strategic concerns — a perspective that is not always shared by EU member states, which do not see the primary role of the EU as strategic or military. For the United States, Turkey's EU membership would enhance political stability in Turkey but also ensure a strong democracy on the doorstep of the Middle East and Central Asia. For this reason, those in the U.S. government most supportive of Turkey's EU membership have usually come from the defense and security establishment (Abramowitz et al. 2004).

If "reading Turkey" was difficult in the run up to the Turkish Parliament's 2003 decision, it can also be attributed to the "muddling through" foreign policy adapted by the Justice and Development Party that came into power in 2002. Turkey had reverted through this decision to its cold war foreign policy on the Middle East that advocated noninvolvement in regional crises and separation of its Middle Eastern policies from that of its policies toward Europe and NATO (Aybet 1994). But this was not a deliberate policy choice made at the outset of the crisis. In fact the Turkish government did not have a clear policy on the issue. Before the parliamentary vote had been taken, the government had given signals of approval to the U.S. requests.

The decision by the Turkish Parliament and the attitude of the Turkish government prior to that decision can be seen as exemplifying the transition from the cold war foreign policy of separating Middle Eastern–regional policies from those of "Western" and NATO policies. It is hard to see this transition as a reaction to U.S. hegemony. Rather it seems more a coping mechanism for the crisis Turkey faces in its own foreign policy as it adjusts to the requirements of the post–cold war era. Turkey has traditionally maintained a foreign policy of exceptionalism based on its geostrategic position. This has been accompanied by a separation of its foreign policy toward the "West," largely driven by its NATO membership, from its regional policies, particularly its relations with the states of the Middle East. Turkey has also separated the sensitive issues of internal security challenges, such as Kurdish separatism and Islamic fundamentalism, from its external security relations based on a state-centric relationship embedded in the NATO framework. Since 1991 Turkey has been going through a transition from a cold war compartmentalized foreign policy to a more comprehensive strategic one that bridges Turkey's "Western" NATO policies with its Middle East and Northern Tier ones. The decision of March 2003, which prevented U.S. troops access through Turkish territory into Iraq, is a symptom of this, not a reaction to U.S. hegemony.

This transition process is the source in the misunderstanding experienced by U.S. policy makers in March 2003. While the Turkish Parliament's vote to block the transit of U.S. troops through Turkey displeased Washington, it was also a demonstration of a healthy democracy at work—the very thing that the United States is trying to promote in the Middle East. The United States dealt with this awkward issue by evaluating it as a strategic-military concern. Just as Turkey has been dealing with the transition of "fitting in" to a new world order, the United States has treated Turkey in the same way, by dealing with it within the parameters of the U.S.–Turkish cold war relationship.

Relations between Turkey and the United States deteriorated after the parliamentary decision of March 1, 2003. Both sides also firmly believed that in the long term the strategic partnership had to be amended and salvaged. For Turkey the strategic partnership with the United States is vital both for its security and its economic interests. U.S. support cannot be dismissed lightly.[6] For the United States, Turkey's geostrategic location is as important as ever; in particular, it wants access to the Incirlik airbase close to Adana in southeast Turkey. Moreover, Turkey's role as a predominantly Islamic democracy and a member of Western institutions is seen more and more as a vital asset for promoting democracy in the greater Middle East by the Bush administration (Yetkin 2005c).

Two further developments in the aftermath of the war exacerbated the decline in Turkish–American relations, particularly in terms of Turkish public perceptions of the United States. The first has been the reluctance of the United States to deal with the presence of the Kurdistan Workers' Party (PKK) in northern Iraq, despite Turkey's insistence about the gravity of the situation. The second was the detention of a small number of Turkish special forces near the northern Iraqi town of Suleymaniye in July 2003 by the U.S. Army (*Hurriyet* 2003; Yetkin 2005b).

Despite these setbacks, damage limitation has been sought on both sides. After the parliamentary vote denying U.S. troops transit for a second front, the Turkish government softened its approach by offering to station peacekeepers in Iraq. Although the United States welcomed Turkey's offer, it was rejected by the Kurdish and Arab leaders in Iraq, and the United States at this precarious juncture did not see the point of pressuring the local leaders on whose cooperation it depended (Goktas 2003). Perhaps the most significant development in mending relations was the approval by the Turkish government for the use of the Incirlik airbase by the United States as a logistics hub in May 2005. Under the agreement reached between U.S. and Turkish authorities, Incirlik would be used for the transfer of logistics and supplies exclusive of lethal supplies such as weapons and explosives. The logistical support is destined for ongoing operations in Iraq and Afghanistan.

The visit by U.S. congressmen to the Turkish Republic of Northern Cyprus in May 2005, despite the protests of the Cypriot government, was an example of a small gesture of good will on the part of the United States. However, two crucial issues were as yet unresolved during Prime Minister Recep Tayyip Erdogan's visit to Washington in early June 2005. These were, first, Turkey's request for U.S. support in dealing with the PKK threat still present in northern Iraq and the Security Council's approval of the U.N. Secretary General's report of May 28, 2004, calling for an end to the isolation of Northern Cyprus. While the Bush administration stressed Turkey's vital role in the greater Middle East during the visit, it seems that Turkey's insistence on receiving support over Cyprus and ousting the PKK from northern Iraq did not receive the response that Turkish officials expected from the United States (Yetkin 2005d; Wright 2005a; Knowlton 2005; Sammon 2005). Whatever the outcome of these deliberations, the fact that the U.S. government has dragged its feet for so long about these issues has done little to mend the damage in Turkish–U.S. relations.

Overall, the United States structures its relations with Turkey within the cold war parameters of its strategic relationship, and Turkey defines its relations with the United States within the same parameters. While doing so, it tries to reconcile its internal and external policy challenges and its "Western" policies that relate to Europe and the United States with those that have a broader regional dimension.

The Northern Tier and Turkey in the Post–Cold War Era

In comparison to the western Balkans and Turkey, there is probably more regional reaction specifically directed against U.S. hegemony from an *interstate* perspective in the region referred to as the Northern Tier or the greater Middle East. Given the complexities of the region itself, reactions are widely disparate and difficult to measure in a regional context. Nevertheless, this section explores some aspects of what was termed the "Northern Tier" during the cold war in the context of relations with Turkey and its transition from relative stability to gross instability.

The term "Northern Tier" was used frequently in the early stages of the cold war, particularly after the globalization of containment. While curbing Soviet designs in the region commenced with the Truman Doctrine, it was the short-lived 1955 Baghdad Pact that gave a geographical meaning to the term "Northern Tier." The British-backed plan was to prevent Soviet expansion in the area by promoting a pact of Western-friendly Middle Eastern states — not that dissimilar from the Bush administration's Broader Middle East project (Asmus et al. 2005). The pact was created by Britain, Iran, Iraq, and Pakistan, with the aim of absorbing Jordan and Syria. Britain's involvement in the Suez crisis in 1956 and riots in Jordan against the pact diminished its credibility. Finally, the overthrow of the kingdom in Iraq in 1958 by the pro-Soviet Baathist party resulted in the name and structure of the original Baghdad Pact being changed. The remaining members continued the organization under the name of the Central Treaty Organization (CENTO). It was modeled on NATO, but hardly shared any of its features. In particular, it lacked an integrated military structure.

CENTO failed to materialize as an effective regional organization, and the 1979 Iranian revolution brought about its final demise (Khalilzad 1979/80). Regional reactions to U.S. hegemony throughout the cold war were balanced by alignments with the Soviet Union or a strict policy of nonalignment in the region. These interstate factors continued to affect regional responses to the United States after the fall of the Shah in Iran and the Soviet invasion of Afghanistan in 1979. For the United States, this spelled the opening of a new era that demanded an increased focus on Southwest Asia. Despite attempts to formalize NATO "out-of-area" cooperation under the Carter and subsequent Reagan administrations, resistance by NATO allies to formalizing military cooperation with the United States in the region put an end to these plans (Aybet 2001).[7]

The collapse of the Soviet Union and the emergence of the newly independent states (NIS) in the Caucasus and Central Asia proved to be a turning point for interstate relations in the region. It was only in the aftermath of the 1991 Gulf War that we can see the United States as a factor in the region, provoking reactions that have direct bearing on its policies. This is because reactions to U.S. hegemony in the context of the geographical changes brought on by the collapse of the Soviet Union can be said to be minimal, as interstate relations for the most part were driven by regional power considerations checked by the regional role of Russia (Sayari 1994, 108). In the aftermath of the war the undefined status of northern Iraq became a further source of tension in Turkish–Iranian relations. Since the war both Iranian and Turkish armed forces have carried out incursions into bordering northern Iraq for purposes of "self defense." During this period, one analyst observes, "U.S. policy toward the Middle East . . . included support for the expansion of Turkey's role and the isolation of Iran in the region — a policy that . . . served both to sharpen the competitive edge and to constrain the cooperative aspects of Turco–Iranian relations" (Calabrese 1998, 93).

Meanwhile, Turkey's border with Armenia has remained closed since 1993. There will be increasing pressure to open the border, especially given that since 2004, Armenia has figured within the European Neighborhood Policy (ENP) (Gorvett 2005; Commission of the European Communities 2004). This is likely to exacerbate nationalist tendencies especially where there is sympathy with Azerbaijan, which remains opposed to the opening of the Turkish–Armenian border. If anything, the ENP is largely complementary to the U.S. vision for the Broader Middle East. This was spelled out in the EU Security Strategy (ESS), which states that "our task is to promote a ring of well-governed countries to the East of the European Union and on the borders of the Mediterranean with whom we can enjoy close and cooperative relations" (Council of the European Union 2003).

Another country in the region that is part of the EU's ENP is Georgia. The successful Rose revolution of November 2003 saw that country on its way to becoming a model of democracy in the region. However, two intrastate conflicts with Abkhazia and South Ossetia, which started in the 1990s, have not subsided. If anything, the conflict with South Ossetia, in particular, was exacerbated in the summer of 2004. The peace brokering of the United Nations and the Organization for Security and Cooperation in Europe (OSCE) has shown limited success. While Russian-led peacekeeping operations in both conflicts have been criticized by Tbilisi, the Russian military still lingers as a result of the unresolved implementation of the Conventional Forces in Europe (CFE) Treaty. Of course the main significance of Georgia in the region relates to the Baku–Tbilisi–Ceyhan oil pipeline, which will, once completed, transport Caspian energy sources to Turkey's Mediterranean coast. The first stage of the construction was undertaken in May 2005 and the pipeline was completed a year later (Lynch 2006).

It was the issue of energy in the region that prompted the visit of deputy commander of U.S. European Command (EUCOM), Gen. Charles Wald, to Ankara in January 2006. The significance of this high-level military visit was its linkage to the nuclear crisis over Iran. With the possibility of sanctions looming after Iran's referral to the U.N. Security Council, alternative energy supplies within the region gained an unparalleled significance. Turkey's role with regard to the nuclear crisis in Iran has become pivotal. This was made evident by the visit by National Security Advisor Stephen Hadley, followed by that of then–director of the CIA Porter Goss, to Turkey in September 2005 (Yetkin 2006). Unless the United States goes so far as to take military action against Iran, Turkey will have no choice but to adhere to sanctions if these are passed in a U.N. Security Council resolution. Turkey's reluctance to adhere to sanctions against Iran increases the tension in the already strained U.S.–Turkish relationship. Meanwhile, as the internal turmoil in postwar Iraq exacerbates, Turkish–Iranian–U.S. interests could converge in the effort to stabilize Iraq, particularly if the United States can see the value of Iranian influence over the Iraqi Shia population. On the other hand, some analysts predict that if Iran goes nuclear, this may draw Turkey closer to the U.S. strategic partnership rather than to the EU (Lesser 2006).

At the same time Afghanistan remains far from stable since the U.S.-led intervention to oust the Taliban regime in 2001 following 9/11, despite the recent expansion of the International Security Assistance Force (ISAF). Operation Enduring Freedom has continued in the south of the country for the past four years. The only point of comparison between the western Balkans and the Northern Tier is the heavy military intervention by the United States followed by a multilateral postconflict nation building process in Iraq and Afghanistan. Unlike in the western Balkans, neither Iraq nor Afghanistan has enabled the United States to commence nation building on a "clean slate." This is because the conflict in both countries is far from over, and yet nation building is occurring simultaneously. Furthermore, as Gen. Mark Kimmit, the deputy director of U.S. Central Command (CENTCOM), noted: "We cannot garrison the region like we garrisoned in Europe after World War Two." The United States will need to reduce its military presence in the region to a fraction of what it is today; otherwise there would be no avoiding a "culture of dependency" and the image of occupation.[8] This requires a normative transformation in the region, not just military enforcement. Yet while coercion and transfusion of norms has worked with a mixed degree of success in the western Balkans, it is hard to see the same model applied to the Northern Tier. Conditionality and club rules instigated by European institutions still have some meaning for the populations of the western Balkans, albeit to a much lesser degree than for those of CEE, while in the Northern Tier old power politics at the interstate level still dominate and Western norms are far more alien to civil societies than in the western Balkans. The transformation from coercive enforcement to internalization of the norms of free markets, democratic governance, and human rights may be difficult to achieve.

Conclusions

It would seem that in the case of the Balkans and Turkey, the intrastate level of analysis is far more relevant in measuring reactions to U.S. hegemony and the norms that it tries to export than transnational levels of analysis. Oscillation between anti-Americanism and anti-Europeanism is the main intrastate factor within Turkey. Within the Balkans, U.S. and EU hegemony on the other hand are perceived as one and the same thing, although they each serve different stages of socialization of hegemonic norms at the regional level. In the Northern Tier interstate factors dominate as old power politics centering on regional rivalry and energy supplies determine the outcome of relations between states. Intrastate conflicts persist but mostly as a means of manipulation among regional power players. While Iraq and Afghanistan constitute the only two cases of U.S. military power projection leading to nation building, this exercise is by no means carried out on a near "clean slate" as in the western Balkans, as the conflict in both countries is ensuing, and the turmoil of the aftermath of U.S. military intervention is far from over.

While the insurgency in Afghanistan and Iraq is clearly a reaction to U.S. hegemony, reaction of this sort is harder to pinpoint in the Turkish–Iranian–U.S. triangle over Iraq. Here, there could be a convergence of interests over stabilizing the region, regardless of differences over Iran's nuclear program. Therefore, regional power politics played with and against the United States do not take merely the form of reaction to the coercive and normative presence of the United States in the region.

From the Balkans through Turkey to the Northern Tier it is hard to measure reactions to U.S. hegemony because the power of U.S. hegemony is not the only factor that elicits these so-called reactions. As discussed in the introduction to this chapter, there are limits to the power of the United States, and the hegemon is by no means the architect of a preconceived design. If the so-called Bush revolution in American foreign policy entertains a symbiotic relationship between international norms of "oughtness" and "goodness," on the one hand, and naked power projection, on the other, it does so as a reaction to a changing world order, which is undeniably out of date but as yet unchallenged by another would-be hegemon. This is the core of the contradictory trajectory in which U.S. foreign policy finds itself, torn between being a "consensual" and a "coercive" hegemon. Therefore, if the United States challenges multilaterism, it is not because it has a preconceived design, but again, because it is reacting to the out-of-datedness of the post-1945 order. The unchallenged nature of that order by another is at the heart of the unilateral bullishness of U.S. foreign policy.

The only place in the region from Turkey to the Northern Tier where the United States has had power in imposing international norms through military power projection, largely unhampered, has been, as we have seen, the western Balkans. In the case of Bosnia, U.S. state building was almost started on a "clean slate." Despite this grandiose U.S.-driven project to reshape the former Yugoslavia in the aftermath of the Bosnian and Croatian wars, U.S. involvement in this region was a far cry from being the intended result of a preconceived strategy. If anything, U.S. foreign policy toward the western Balkans at the end of the cold war was one of noninvolvement. Its subsequent intervention was the unintended result of the shifts occurring at the end of the cold war. The western Balkans, apart from pockets of Serb resentment, have by and large been "reactionless," but this is by no means because the United States possesses the monocausal hegemonic power of an orderer.

In Turkey, reactions to U.S. hegemony are tempered by reactions to the EU, but in both cases, these are not just simply "reactions" to the United States or the EU, but also the way Turkey is coping with the same transition with which the United States is dealing. Therefore, it is not really a matter of who is reacting to whom; rather it is more a matter of a world coming to grips with a new world. In the case of Turkey, it is going through a transition from its compartmentalized cold war foreign policy to a more comprehensive one based in a long-term strategic vision. So far this goal has eluded Turkey, and it is still muddling through, trying to reconcile internal policy challenges with external ones as it makes the steep climb up the path to EU membership. On another level, Turkey is also trying to move away from its traditional cold war foreign policy of keeping its policies toward the Middle East separate from those toward the West within the context of NATO. This has proved harder to do since the first Gulf War of 1991, and the United States has at times found it difficult to read Turkey as it deals with this transition. The United States copes with this unreadability by operating within the cold war parameters of the strategic partnership between itself and Turkey. This has the effect of inhibiting Turkey's search for a place in the emerging new-era transatlantic partnership.

Although the Broader Middle East is to some extent a blueprint for a grander American design for the region of the former Northern Tier, U.S. involvement in the power politics of the Northern Tier is a manifestation of a superpower "fitting in" with changing times by using the tools of a bygone era. It is a moment of transition, as it is for the key players in the region, Iran and Turkey included. The makings of this grand design are more embedded in rhetoric than in a concrete agenda for regional change. This is because such a grand design depends heavily on a joint transatlantic agenda, which at the moment, is lacking in substance. Overall, regional reactions from the Balkans through Turkey to the Northern Tier do not so much represent an opposition to the power of U.S. hegemony as a coping mechanism for dealing with a changing global order.

Notes

1. I also refer here to the difference between the Bush administration's justification for the use of force and the Athenian logic in the Melian Dialogue, see Kolodziej, chapter 1.

2. Interview with Javier Solana, Brookings Institution, Washington D.C., April 2004.

3. This adaptation of the Kupchan and Ikenberry's model of socialization and hegemonic power is based on an earlier paper, "U.S.–EU Cooperation in the Balkans? The Case of Peacekeeping in Bosnia and Herzegovina" (South East European Studies Program, St. Antony's College, Oxford University, February 2005).

4. The international panel recommends that the region as a whole move from the stage of being protectorates to the stage of acceding to the EU. Under this transatlantic approach, the EU would play a much bigger role in the region. For example, the panel recommends that in Bosnia the Office of the High Representative OHR be replaced with an EU negotiator and that Bosnia and all the other non-NATO countries join the Partnership for Peace (PFP) as soon as possible.

5. Feith also stated later on at a lecture at the Council on Foreign Relations that the U.S. government was trying very hard to explain the importance of its relations with its allies and partners to Congress and the American public. This was not, he said, being reciprocated by allied governments, referring to Turkey.

6. During the cold war, U.S. support of Turkey, which shared a border with the Soviet Union, was evidently important. But since the end of the cold war, the United States has at times been more sensitive to Turkey's regional concerns, such as over the threat of WMD, than to those of its European allies. Economically, as Turkey entered its worst financial crisis in 2001, it was the IMF bailout of U.S.$39.5 billion that saved the day, although the Bush administration, at the time, was against any IMF bailouts. This can be seen as a signifier of Turkey's strategic importance for the United States (see Taspinar 2005, 19).

7. The Carter administration had proposed a Rapid Deployment Joint Task Force that would rely on forces assigned to NATO in times of a crisis in the region.

8. Brigadier Gen. Mark Kimmitt, deputy director of plans and policy, U.S. Central Command, "America's Future Military Involvement in the Middle East" (lecture, RUSI Transatlantic Forum, RUSI, March 2, 2006, London).

NORTH AFRICA, THE MIDDLE EAST, AND AFRICA

CHAPTER TEN

North Africa

Badredine Arfi

Is the United States implementing a hegemonic agenda in North Africa (Morocco, Algeria, Tunisia, Libya, and Egypt)? That the United States has in the post-9/11 era paid more strategic attention to, and been actually involved in, the region is not in doubt. Likewise, that U.S.–North African relationships are by and large driven by the latter's domestic political concerns — perhaps reinforced but not driven by U.S. post-9/11 global interests — is also not in doubt. There indeed is a confluence between, on the one hand, U.S. interests in fighting a global war on international terrorism, globally constructing a corresponding military infrastructure and deploying a strategy to that effect, pursuing a new democratization agenda in the Greater Middle East and seeking to counter the proliferation of nuclear weapons to the region and, on the other hand, the domestic concerns of North African regimes. Some might interpret this confluence of various factors as evidence that the United States is seeking to play the role of a hegemon in the region. This supposed U.S. drive for hegemony is then confronted by resilient traditional European security and economic concerns; political, economic, and cultural interests; and ebbs and flows of regional/domestic politics in North Africa. This, however, is far from the whole story.

What is happening in North Africa is that the region is actively participating in the construction and deployment of an emerging global discursive framework — the discourse on the global war on terrorism (GWOT). That the United States has played a decisive role in initiating this new discourse in the immediate aftermath of 9/11 is not in dispute. Yet, as the case of North Africa demonstrates, the qualifier "global" does mean what it should — the discursive framework has indeed become global, not only in the sense that its scope is global but also in that constructing, sustaining, and deploying this discourse is a globally decentralized process, with no power in control of it. What we have is the hegemony of a discourse and not (not even a nascent) U.S. hegemony in the conventional (military/economic or imperialist/neoimperialist) meaning of the term. The case of North Africa evidences that states and regions that are much less militarily and economically powerful than the United States are not only effective participants in constructing this new discursive hegemony but are also as essential as is the United States itself in enacting it. President Bush promised in the 2002 *National Security Strategy* document that "in leading the campaign against terrorism, we are forging new, productive international relationships and redefining existing ones in ways that meet the challenges of the twenty-first century" (U.S. White House, Office of the President 2002, 7). This paper raises the question of whether this is really the case (at least in the North African region). The answer is that although the Bush administration is perceived, and perceives itself, as trying to do so, the end result has been the construction of a new hegemony of the discourse on the GWOT, which is enthralling the world, including the most powerful state on the planet.

North African states had been looking forward to a closer relationship with the United States, even before the end of the cold war. The U.S. penetration of the region has in effect remained a one wished for rather than achieved. Post-9/11 has only provided the discursive context for that wished-for penetration to become more visible. Whereas the Moroccan king and his entourage and the Egyptian state leaders have sustained strong and friendly relations with their American counterparts for decades, the Algerian, Tunisian, and, more recently, Libyan leaders had been looking forward to improved and more closer relations with the United States. The obstacle was that the Americans were reluctant to engage them and, hence, trespass the Europeans' self-designation of North Africa as their exclusive sphere of influence. However, the new U.S. foreign policy discourse has provided more instruments for the local governments to further reinforce their respective domestic agendas, the major element of which is how to surmount a resilient legitimacy deficit that transpires in the persistence of a simulacrum of democratic governance compounded with worsening, if not already dismal, socioeconomic conditions with booming populations.

This chapter explores how the North African states responded to the U.S. post-9/11 policies regarding the war on terrorism, weapons of mass destruction (WMD), and democratization and shows that the governments in North Africa seem to agree with the United States on these policies not because the United States is behaving as a hegemon but rather because the U.S. discourse with which they agree reinforces what these governments have been doing or have sought to do anyway for years. The image or potential of "U.S. hegemony" is a tool that the North African states have appropriated as another way to cover up their lack of legitimacy and commitment to true and comprehensive democratic reforms.

U.S. Strategy in the GWOT

The U.S. self-declared GWOT has become a defining general framework for the discourse of its foreign policy. The Bush administration is actively working on and succeeding in incorporating North Africa as a major component of this enterprise. The local governments are strongly forthcoming in adhering to the new U.S. strategy and concomitant infrastructural and military changes. The North African states joined the United States to construct a more internationally acceptable self-image for what these states have themselves been doing in their self-styled war against domestic and sometimes regional terrorism since the 1990s. Algeria, Egypt, Tunisia, and, belatedly, Morocco had been embattled in their own wars on terrorism well before September 2001. The U.S. reaction to the 9/11 event thus quickly provided to the presidents of Algeria, Egypt, and Tunisia — respectively, Abdelaziz Bouteflika, Hosni Mubarak, and Zine el Abidine Ben Ali — a window of opportunity through which to seek international acknowledgment for their continuous crackdowns on opposition Islamists. They also hoped to get as a by-product of this commitment to the GWOT a good amount of Western support to boost their respective military arsenals.[1]

North African regimes quickly and unequivocally condemned the 9/11 attacks and agreed to be part of the antiterrorism coalition led by the United States. The Algerian government felt vindicated in its decade-long position that terrorism is global in nature and that global terrorism had indeed the capacity to threaten states. Algerian leaders argued that they had been at the forefront of the war against terrorism and that they had been fighting it without having received much in the way of help from the outside world, including the United States and most of Europe. They blamed the United States, Canada, and Europe for having sheltered Islamist individuals and members of groups like the Groupe Islamique Armé (GIA) to which the Algerian government attributes responsibility for the conflict that ravaged Algeria for some ten years following the cancellation of December 1991 national elections.[2] However, while supporting the U.S. efforts to build a coalition of states, the Algerian government also called for a military coalition under the U.N. umbrella that would not be expected to target "a country, a religion, a people, a culture, or a civilization" (*El Moujahid* September 22, 2001). Both the president and the armed forces made it clear that Algeria would not participate in any military coalition not under U.N. control (*El Watan* 2001).

As a gesture of good will and commitment, the Algerian authorities provided the United States with a first list of some 350 Algerian citizens in Europe and the United States whom the Algerian government described as terrorists or connected to al Qaeda. The Algerian government also forwarded another list of some 1,000 Algerians whom it described as Islamist militants active in the West (Mills 2004). In return, Bush invited Bouteflika to Washington on November 5, 2001, following the third U.S.–Africa Business Summit, sponsored by the Corporate Council on Africa, held in Philadelphia on November 2. Less than a week prior to Bouteflika's visit, Bush had already called on African states to ratify the summer 1999 Algiers Convention on Terrorism, a ratification that most African countries had not been willing to carry out before 9/11. Bouteflika's visit to Washington opened the door for much more cooperation between the two countries on the war against terrorism. Williams Burns, U.S. assistant secretary of state for Near East affairs, stated, as he was ending a visit to Algiers on December 9, 2002, to sell the country military equipment to fight the Islamists, that the agreement was aimed at "intensifying the security cooperation between the two countries," since "Washington has much to learn from Algeria on ways to fight terrorism" (Tremlett 2002; James 2002). Prior to this agreement, the United States held joint military exercises with the Algerian navy and had been helping to train Algeria's military and security forces to fight the Islamist militants (Lugar 2005).

In general, North African officials have been forthcoming with the United States on security and intelligence matters. For example, U.S. delegations representing a number of U.S. intelligence services (such as the FBI, the CIA, and the National Security Agency [NSA]) visited with their Algerian counterparts (Department of Intelligence and Security [DRS] and the National Popular Army [ANP]) in the framework of antiterrorism security cooperation (*Le Quotidien* 2003). Algeria allowed the United States to create a four-hundred-man-strong special-operations military base in the extreme south in the region of Tamanrasset as a communication center to monitor "terrorism chatter" in Sub-Saharan Africa (Benkaci 2005). The Algerian military and U.S. military also play "war games" together in the Algerian desert to prepare themselves to carry out joint war campaigns against terrorism in the region.[3] This is part of a larger plan of action named the Trans-Saharan Counterterrorism Initiative (TSCTI) that seeks to massively support Algeria, Chad, Mali, Mauritania, Morocco, Niger, Senegal, Nigeria, and Tunisia in their antiterrorism wars (Zouaoui 2005). Given Algeria's recent history, the United States expects and encourages Algeria to play a central role in this initiative.

In 2002, the Bush administration advanced the Pan Sahel Initiative (PSI) as a means of strengthening the region's armed forces against terrorist threats. The PSI was effectively implemented in mid-January 2004 as a means of stopping al Qaeda and affiliated/supportive groups thereof from penetrating Mali, Niger, Algeria, and Mauritania. The Bush administration has also increased its funding for U.S.-based training of Algerian military officers under the international military education and training (IMET) program.[4] Similarly, in 2003 the United States gave Morocco some sixty million dollars as assistance for fighting terrorism as well as for development programs. On June 3, 2004, the United States bestowed on Morocco the status of "major non-NATO ally" thereby making Morocco eligible for priority delivery of defense material, enabling it to take part in research and development programs related to defense, and allowing it to become a beneficiary of U.S. government loan guarantee programs that it can use to purchase military matériel (Tyson 2005).

An important component of the U.S. war on international terrorism since September 11, 2001, has been to detain larger numbers of people in various parts of the world from whom it hopes to acquire more intelligence on terrorism-related issues. In this pursuit the United States has resorted to using "extraordinary rendition" (Center for Human Rights)—the secret transfer of individuals from one country to another—for the sake of interrogation. The destination country may use coercive tactics and torture on these rendered prisoners if they are commonly used in that country, notwithstanding the "diplomatic assurances" U.S. officials may receive from the country that "torture" will not be used.[5] Numerous reports and off-the-record statements made by various U.S. government officials do strongly indicate that the United States did indeed practice rendition after September 11 (Chandrasekaran and Finn 2002; Mayer 2005; Scheuer 2005; Shane, Grey, and Williams 2005).[6] Two North African states in particular, Morocco and Egypt, have participated in U.S.-ordered rendition. This is not surprising, as these two governments have often used torture as a means of gathering information from dissenting elements in their countries. Hence, answering the call from the United States was just part of the normal politics of "stabilizing" the regime that the North African regimes often engage in.

In sum, North African states have been more than happy to join the United States in countering international terrorism in the region for a number of reasons: partly as a continuation of their own respective efforts in eradicating the (violent and otherwise) Islamist opposition that refuses to be co-opted by the governments and partly as a strategy whereby they can reap the benefits for being on the right side of the U.S. self-styled GWOT, benefits such as favors from the U.S. government in the form of military equipment, economic benefits, prestige, and image remaking. The U.S. discourse on the GWOT found a fertile ground in North Africa not as the result of U.S. drive toward hegemony but rather because the North African states had already been deploying similarly self-styled discourses on terrorism before 9/11.

The U.S. Strategy on Countering the Proliferation of WMD

The Bush administration, in line with its predecessors, has made the issue of WMD, especially nuclear weapons, a central concern of its national security agenda. In addressing the WMD threat, the Bush administration advocates reliance not only on a strong nonproliferation policy but also a vigorous counterproliferation agenda, the purpose of the latter being to address proactively and preemptively any effort by a nonnuclear state or by any group to acquire WMD. The United States never strongly raised the WMD issue with the North African states, except of course with Libya. Although Algeria and Egypt entertained some thoughts about pursuing research on nuclear power (for civilian as well as military purposes), they never considered it as forcefully as did Libya. Egypt had a nuclear weapons research program from 1954 to 1967 and Algeria conducted some research on subcritical mass nuclear reactors in the late 1980s and early 1990s. But the fact is that Algeria, Egypt, Morocco, and Tunisia have signed the nonproliferation treaty as nonnuclear states and are abiding by its stipulations.

On June 28, 2004, Libya was taken off the U.S. State Department's list of rogue/terrorist states and states that sponsor terrorism and reestablished diplomatic ties with the United States after a twenty-four-year break. Soon thereafter, on September 19, 2004, President Bush released some $1.3 billion in frozen Libyan assets and on September 24 Secretary of State Colin Powell met with Libyan foreign minister Abdel-Rahman Shalqam (*Washington Post* September 24, 2004). All this occurred after Libya abandoned its WMD programs and allowed U.S. and British inspectors to verify the claim. A post-hoc cursory reading (or rewriting) of the history of the events that led to Libya's giving up its WMD program might lead one to conclude that the Libyan case is a sign of success of the Bush administration's stated and actively pursued PSI strategy. The Bush rhetoric on the "axis of evil" and the administration's publicly declared willingness to start a new page of history in the post-9/11 world as well as the immediate intelligence cooperation between the Libyan and U.S. services on lists of suspected Arab and Muslim militants in the United States and Europe have very likely encouraged or, at least, opened up a window of opportunity for the Qaddafi regime to seek reconciliation with the United States and the West in general on various lingering issues (the negotiations on the resolution of the Pan Am 103 bombing issue of course being ongoing in the background). However, careful attention to how the events that led to Libya abandoning its WMD ambitions unfolded clearly shows that neither forceful Bush rhetoric nor even the 2003 invasion of Iraq and subsequent toppling of the Saddam regime and occupation of Iraq played decisive roles in Qaddafi's change of heart on WMD.[7]

Libya had been seeking to give up its WMD programs for about a decade before September 2001 (St. John 2004). The elder Bush administration rejected informal Libyan overtures in 1992, and so did the Clinton administration. Libya was ready to entertain a complete renunciation of terrorism and the abandonment of WMD programs if its Western counterparts would in return engage Libya in serious talks about ending sanctions and normalizing relations. Eventually the Clinton administration began to negotiate with the Libyans on how to resolve once and for all the Pan Am 103 issue but rejected an expansion of the agenda to the other issues raised by the Qaddafi regime. The 2000 presidential campaign forced the Clinton administration to stop negotiating with the Libyans, fearing that this might become public and hurt the Democratic candidate.

The Pan Am 103 issue was resolved in May 2002 and the case was finally closed in September 2003 with Libya accepting responsibility for the actions of Libyan agents in the bombing and agreeing to pay each of the victim families ten million dollars. At the same time the Bush administration kept up its heat on the Qaddafi regime during 2002–3, accusing Libya of having active biological, chemical, and nuclear weapons programs, all the while the Pan Am 103 issue was being resolved and the Libyan intelligence services were actively cooperating with their U.S. counterparts on various aspects of the war on terrorism.

In March 2003, Musa Kusa, the chief of Libyan intelligence, conveyed to officials in the British intelligence service that his government was interested in initiating serious talks with Britain and the United States on how to end its WMD programs. This eventually led to negotiations among the three parties that lasted some nine months and that were ultimately successfully concluded in December 2003. The Qaddafi government announced on December 19, 2003, that it would dismantle its WMD programs and open the country to immediate and comprehensive verification inspections. Libya pledged that it would eliminate all elements of its nuclear weapons programs, declare all nuclear activities to the International Atomic Energy Agency (IAEA), accept international inspections to ensure its complete adherence to the Non-Proliferation Treaty (NPT), and sign the Additional Protocol. It promised to eliminate all chemical weapons stocks and munitions and accede to the Chemical Weapons Convention (CWC). It also committed itself to eliminating ballistic missiles beyond a three-hundred-kilometer range with a payload of five hundred kilograms. Libya has indeed fulfilled all these commitments and has fully cooperated with the United States and Britain and the nonproliferation international institutions (DeSutter 2004).

It seems to be an established fact that the North African region is WMD-free (especially nuclear weapon-free) and that the incumbent regimes do not seem to entertain WMD ambitions for the future. This is not necessarily the result of a post-9/11 U.S. drive for hegemony in the region for at least two reasons. First, the United States has persistently sought a North African WMD free zone without seeking to be a hegemon in the region, partly as a show of respect for the European self-declared position that North Africa is a European sphere of influence. Second, even in the case of Libya, the Bush administration cannot claim to have convinced the Libyan regime since the process of negotiations started during the Clinton administration. The Bush administration can be credited for having advanced the notion of a "new page of history" in the GWOT, which opened up a window of opportunity for Qaddafi to cooperate with the United States on intelligence matters. To put it differently: it is the discursive framework of the GWOT, the preemption subdiscourse being an integral part of it, that made the Libyans come forward and express their willingness to abandon WMD ambitions. Bolton's rhetoric against Libya and the debates about invading Iraq un-doubtedly (if only to a certain extent) contributed to shaping Qaddafi's change of heart. It is far-fetched to argue that it is the Bush strategy on countering WMD based on preemption that resulted in the final outcome. What the Libyan regime did is exactly what its Algerian counterpart also did — join in the construction of a new hegemonic discourse that not only creates a rapprochement with the United States but also relegitimizes the Libyan regime itself, all the while obtaining a discursively legitimated license to continue to eradicate the Islamist opposition to the regime, which in fact amounts to eliminating all political opposition that could pose a threat to the rite of passage of Qaddafi's son Saif al-Islam to the "throne" (Ronen 2005).

The U.S. Discourse on Democratization of the Broader Middle East

The discourse on democratization of the Greater Middle East is part of the Bush *National Security Strategy* of September 2002 and has become a constant theme of the official discourse of the administration, especially after it was definitely es-tablished that the two major reasons for justifying the invasion of Iraq were "dead wrong," that is, Iraq had no WMD programs and had no links with al Qaeda. The Bush administration anchors its policy of democratization on three hypotheses. First, fostering democracy in the Middle East would create more freedom and hence potential terrorists, even rank and file extremists, might be more inclined to use nonviolent means to express their views. This would deprive terrorist orga-nizations of a recruiting pool of frustrated and dissatisfied young people. Second, spreading democracy would create a zone of peace in the Middle East since "de-mocracies do not go to war with one another," a claim that represents a buying into of the policy implication of the democratic peace argument. Third, the Bush administration also believes that economic liberalization would promote more democratic reforms, and so it calls for free trade agreements with Arab govern-ments in the hope of creating a Middle East free trade area by the year 2013.

Overall, the United States has been promoting democratization in the Arab Middle East since 2001 in three different ways (Dalacoura 2005). First, the United States formulated a number of policy initiatives delineating clusters of projects through which it would support civil society organizations and push for a reform of state institutions to encourage democratic change (USAID 2002). A major step in this respect was the Middle East Partnership Initiative (MEPI) (U.S. De-partment of State 2002), announced in December 2002, which by and large was based on the U.N. Development Program Arab Human Development Report of 2002 (U.N. Development Program 2003). The MEPI strategy was expanded to the Broader Middle East and North Africa (BMENA) Partnership Initiative in June 2004 at the G8 summit in Atlanta (G8 Summit 2004). Both the MEPI and the BMENA Partnership Initiative aim to encourage reforms in political, social, cultural, and economic areas, with the former targeting countries of the Middle East as a whole and the latter targeting Pakistan and Afghanistan as well (U.S. Department of State, Office of the Spokesman 2004a; 2004b). Second, the U.S. administration relies on public diplomacy as a means of encouraging democratic reforms in the Middle East and pressuring the incumbent governments to be more responsive to such calls.[8] Third, the United States justifies post hoc its occupation of Iraq as a way of democratizing the country, arguing that a democratic Iraq would become a beacon of democratic reforms in the Arab world.

Notwithstanding these policies, there is a widespread belief in the Arab world that democracy for the U.S. administration is a secondary goal and the primary goals are related to vital security interests such as fighting the war on terrorism and countering the spread of WMD. This belief is confirmed by neoconservatives (in and outside the U.S. government) who have on many occasions argued that the United States should commit financial and human resources in support of democratization only when American vital interests are at stake. The lack of credibility of a U.S. policy promoting democracy in the Arab Middle East was evidenced in the negative response with which the Arab world received the announcement of the MEPI and BMENA Partnership Initiative, despite U.S. efforts to foster a more positive image of itself in the Arab mind (Powell 2002; Pew Research Center 2004; 2005). This image problem is reflected in the serious drop in the numbers of people from the Gulf coming to study in U.S. universities and colleges, although MEPI is constantly working to organize visits and exchange programs between the United States and Arab countries (U.N. Development Program 2004, 21).

A superficial reading of these U.S. efforts might suggest that the North African states are under strong pressure to engage in serious political reforms to achieve more democratization. This obfuscates a much more complex reality. It is in fact an undeniable truth that the most important goal for the United States and the European Union (EU), at least in the short term, is to secure regime stability in the North African region, even when this means contravening the policy of supporting democratization. The North African states understand this and hence make it a cornerstone of their strategic responses to calls for more democratization. In the post-9/11 era it is easy for the North African regimes to use the card of fighting terrorism as a justification for why they must repress the strongest opposition and resistance to regime co-optation — the Islamist opposition (Entelis 2005) — through a variety of means ranging from physically eliminating dissidents (through jailing or execution) or exiling them to restricting Islamist- and neutrality-leaning free press. Playing the card of fear of Islamist takeover thus legitimizes a rhetoric that justifies a very high level of repression as well as the failure to achieve true progress in the implementation of social and political reforms toward democracy. The United States and EU in turn play their share of the game by pretending not to be pretending and thus buying into the argument of fighting the Islamist threat as part of the GWOT.

To hide the true nature of the democratic simulacrum unfolding in North Africa the governments make a variety of formal gestures that look democratic, including allowing various political parties to participate in regularly held elections, as long as these elections never truly pose a threat to the true power holders (Entelis 2005). The regimes justify the simulacrum of democratization in a number of ways. First, should Islamist opposition be allowed to hold power in North Africa the outcome would be much less democratic than what results under the currently existing regimes. Second, the current governments do have a level of popular legitimacy that they sustain through distributive social welfare. Third, the incumbent regimes are working to incorporate their national economies into the global liberal economy and argue that this will eventually improve the socio-economic conditions in the countries, a fact that would undermine the popular appeal of the Islamist cause. Fourth, in spite of all that is happening the situation is steadily improving, as evidenced by the regularly held elections and pluralist multiparty systems in Morocco, Algeria, Tunisia, and Egypt. That elections are routinely rigged, that parliaments are denied a truly independent political role, that any media that is not clearly proregime is strictly monitored, controlled, or marginalized, that economic power is steadily being concentrated in the hands of the power holders—the king in Morocco, the army in Algeria, the security apparatus in Tunisia, and the everlasting president in Egypt—do not seem to matter. For example, the lack of true progress toward democratization and a de-politicization of the military did not prevent the United States from sponsoring Algerian requests for loans and credits from the World Bank and the International Monetary Fund (IMF).

U.S. support for the Moroccan regime has been continuous and strong, dating back to the cold war era. Because King Hassan II positioned himself in the Western camp of the cold war he enjoined good relations with the United States and Europe in general (particularly France) throughout the cold war, which resulted in it being well treated by international financial institutions. The situation remains much the same under his son's rule, King Mohammed VI. The king tightly controls the decision-making processes in the realm of security, defense, foreign policy, and judiciary, thereby curtailing the powers and prerogatives of the cabinet members and parliament. The economy is for all practical purposes under the control of the IMF and the World Bank whose officials follow rigorous neoliberal policies (Daoud 1999). The king also endeavors to strongly co-opt all political parties that are legally allowed to exist, with the king reserving for himself the prerogative to resolve issues on which the parties cannot reach a consensus. These seemingly pluralistic features notwithstanding, the king has no intention of turning the absolute monarchy into an effectively constitutional one.[9]

The Bush administration is thus rhetorically pushing its democratization agenda for the Middle East and North Africa, and the Middle East and North Africa are rhetorically acceding to it. For example, although the United States always hails elections as a breakthrough, these elections in no way reduce or check the power of the leaders in place and often tend to put back the same people in office (such as the presidents of Egypt and Tunisia), and if not this, then the real power holders of the regime remain outside the purview of elections (such as the Algerian army and the Moroccan king). What elections do is to open up a contrived political space without truly affecting the status quo. Rather than genuinely institutionalizing freedom of speech, association, and pluralistic political practices, incumbent regimes are still using the same survivalist strategies that are meant to reinforce, not change, their robust authoritarian nature (Entelis 2005). The governments are still resorting to the same strategies of "manipulating, coopting, or coercing civil society's most politically potent organizations — mass-based political parties both secular and Islamist" (Entelis 2005).

Egypt, which enjoys the best relationship with the United States among the North African states, has consistently responded to calls for more democratization through a mixed strategy that in the end does not threaten in any way the semiauthoritarian nature of the Mubarak regime. Reform initiatives, such as creating a Human Rights Council, making changes in the National Democratic Party (NDP) (the president's ruling party that wins an overwhelming majority in the parliament at every election), or, recently, allowing multiple candidate presidential elections, do not weaken Mubarak's strong hold on state power. Nor do provisions for open expression of political dissent and critiques of the regime lead to any meaningful changes. The fact that these led to the emergence of informal Tahrir and Kefaya movements, which organized antiregime protests in 2003 and 2004–5 respectively, or that the country's professionals, including its judges, call for reforms does not matter much. In sum, what the Mubarak regime does is to keep deferring making a difference in the existing status quo rules of the game of politics, while at the same time instrumentally using (inconsistent) U.S. overt pressure for changes as a means to mobilize popular support by portraying the U.S. calls as foreign infringement on Egypt's sovereignty. For example, when the proposal for the BMENA initiative was leaked to the press prior to its official release in June 2004, President Mubarak stated he was "furious" about being dictated to by others (*New York Times* June 6, 2004). Likewise, in March 2005,

Foreign Minister Aboul Gheit in slamming President Bush for his extolling of democratization in the Arab world stated that "the pace will be set by Egypt and the Egyptian people and only the Egyptian people. The Egyptian people will not accept what we call trusteeship" (*Washington Post* March 10, 2005).

Libya is unique when it comes to U.S. calls for more democratization in North Africa. Before the Qaddafi regime decided to abandon its WMD program, the United States simultaneously promoted two goals there — achieving democratic reforms and containing the threats of terrorism sponsorship and WMD programs. When Libya gave up its WMD goal in December 2003, however, U.S. attention to domestic reforms withered away. The situation in Libya is summed up by Qaddafi's son Saif, allegedly being groomed as the "heir," who stated to the press that "we don't need Mr. Bush to teach us a lesson in democracy. . . . [W]e are not the students, and America is not the teacher" (*Afrol News* January 17, 2006). Repression of dissenting voices persists unabated as illustrated by the arrest of Fathi El-Jahmi, a Libyan bureaucrat imprisoned after he acknowledged that reforms required free speech and democracy at a 2002 People's Conference (Rosett 2004). That Al-Jahmi was released subsequently and that George Bush praised the regime for his release on March 12, 2003, was all for nought since the same person was reincarcerated within two weeks of his release. This occurred two days after a visit on March 24, 2003, by Assistant Secretary of State William Burns to Libya. Nor did this prevent a number of U.S. diplomats and members of the Congress from meeting subsequently with Qaddafi.

The North African regimes and the other Arab states have also used the medium of the League of Arab States to respond to U.S. calls for more democratization. The League of Arab States is a weak and ineffective organization, a fact that nobody can deny, including the leaders of the Arab states themselves. Yet the league does provide a forum for the Arab leaders to debate issues of common interest and to compete with one another and posture on the framing of these issues. The league has thus always been a tool that state leaders have sought to steer one way or the other in pursuing not only self-serving agendas but also to define the agenda for the Arab nation as states and as a people. Although the era of Gamal Abdul Nasser during which he skillfully used the league as a discursive tool to pursue his agenda, sometimes with force, above the heads of opposing/reluctant Arab leaders, has long passed, the league and the forum that it provides are still an arena with much rhetorical and posturing value. The latter is indeed an important weapon that the Arab states are using to keep their distance from what they perceive as a threatening Bush discourse on democratization.

Put differently: the Arab leaders use the rhetorical and symbolic space of the Arab nation as reflected in the league to resist a seemingly hegemonic U.S. discourse on democratization. This resistance is nuanced and multifaceted. Instead of rejecting outright the discourse on democratization, a very hard sell both internationally and domestically given the widespread rhetorical and popular acceptability of democracy as THE most preferred twenty-first-century system of domestic governance, the resistance seeks to capture the democratization discourse only to subvert it and undermine its foundations and any chance of success it might have of radically transforming the incumbent regimes. The Arab leaders thus highjack or control the debates on democratization, a strategy in part encouraged by U.S. mixed messages, only to derail them and redeploy them as a way of reinforcing their strong grip on the state institutions and their citizens, all the while posturing before the international community that they are not against change per se and that "good" change will eventually occur in due time and under the right conditions.

Thus, for example, the Arab League Summit of May 2004 did refer to political reforms in its Tunis Declaration but only as a preemptive move against the then-imminent G8 summit at which the BMENA Partnership Initiative for democratization was scheduled to be introduced. Not surprisingly, the league declaration was lukewarm and lacked any serious reference to monitoring mechanisms (Blanford 2004). Likewise, the various Arab governments highjacked regional meetings bringing together nongovernmental organizations (NGOs) (Wright 2005b), with the meetings ultimately producing general statements in favor of reforms while avoiding specifics that would offer concrete and useful recommendations for change.[10]

To summarize: the Bush administration calls for more democratization in North Africa have not been heeded not only because the regimes in place see the calls as a threat to their going on existing as they are — that is, as authoritarian regimes that amount to a simulacrum of democratic institutions. The calls were also contrived by the Bush administration itself to subordinate democratization to other goals of the war on international terrorism and to preserve the instrumental roles that the regimes in place play in this war in terms of fully adhering to it as if the war was theirs — and indeed they preceded the United States in this respect — and in terms of providing many logistical contributions to the counterterrorism forward strategy that the administration has opted for.

This situation was compounded by the EU's goal of democratizing North Africa. The EU does not fare better than its American counterpart either in consistency or authenticity. It responded to the 2004 American democratization policy with a European Neighborhood Policy (ENP) in 2004 meant to revitalize Euro–Mediterranean cooperation on security. The EU strategy sought to include the current regimes irrespective of whether they were authoritarian or democratic. The 2004 EU new policy was a "preemptive" move seeking to shape, if not undermine, the 2004 U.S. Middle East initiative. The EU acted quickly based on the publication in the UK-based *al-Hayat* newspaper in February 2004 of a draft of the U.S. Broader Middle East initiative and managed to present its new policy in May 2004 right before the United States was to make its case at the G8 summit in June.[11]

The North African states hence find themselves given an opportunity to navigate their ships in waters the flow of which both the EU and the United States seek to redirect. The North African regimes therefore sometimes play the EU game, at other times the U.S. game, and still at other times they either simultaneously play both games in a mutually reinforcing manner or against one another or hide from both games altogether (such as in hiding from the democratization initiatives). Yet the bottom line remains that the regimes channel these games to ultimately preserve and reinforce their authoritarian (or cosmetically semiauthoritarian) character. The United States is not going to give up its agenda for influencing the region, nor is the EU about to abandon its self-styled declaration that North Africa is its historic sphere of influence. But neither will the North African states become completely subordinated to either power or be forced to change their nature.

This complex dynamic has received a mixed response in North African societies, in spite of the fact that the societies are in general in favor of democratization and economic growth. That nonstate actors have been playing different roles in the shaping of the responses to U.S. policies in North Africa is well established. Responding to the various U.S. strategies is considered to be part of "high politics" in North Africa — that is, the top leaderships in the regimes give to themselves an exclusive right to address it. Not surprisingly then, despite many and diverse vocal nonstate responses on many issues related to the U.S. role in the region and the Greater Middle East, nonstate actors are simply not allowed to be part of "high politics." The effort of the governments to minimize the importance of the U.S. democratization policy and its true character has not been the only factor in the mixed response from the population at large in North African states. The harsh critique of Islam and the Islamic world by neoconservative elements within the U.S. administration (and beyond) compounded by the pressure from the Christian right on the administration to open the Islamic countries for their missionaries (and of course the occupation of Iraq and ongoing bloody insurgency therein) reinforced a widespread belief that the United States was using democratization and the GWOT as a smokescreen to hide its true intentions of establishing an undisputed hegemony in the Arab world, the purpose of which was to control its oil resources and promote the interests of Israel at the expense of the Palestinians, the Arab nations, and Muslim Ummah.

That the Arab world wants political and economic reforms is a fact that is widely recognized in the written as well as spoken press and evidenced by the mushrooming of free and frank debates (Ibn Khaldun Center for Development Studies 2004). These forums not only allow for the critique of authoritarian regimes but also seek to establish the broad contours of the way to solve many lingering issues. For example, Arab writers, intellectuals, and political activists organized a conference on Arab Reform in Alexandria in March 2004 in which they called on Arab states to implement reforms that should include the abolition of "the state of emergency" rules prevailing in much of the Arab world. Likewise, in June 2004 over one hundred thinkers and politicians from various Arab countries adopted a Doha Declaration for Democracy and Reform at the close of a conference in Qatar.[12] Most political forces are engaged in these debates, including the Islamist movements (Ibn Khaldun Center for Development Studies 2004). For example, the (banned) Egyptian Muslim Brotherhood responded to the American proposal by unveiling of its reform strategy in March 2004 that called for more democratization and the lifting of emergency law that has been in place since the early 1990s (Muslim Brotherhood 2004). The Egyptian regime tolerated this move by the Muslim Brotherhood much like many other countries in the Arab world do — not only because the move fits well within the Islamist paradigm of opposing the strategies the United States has adopted toward the region but also because it most importantly benefits the incumbent regime, contributing as it does to the impression that there is a certain level of political freedom in the region. However, this is always within predefined and strictly enforced limits.

In North Africa, the Islamists are allowed to express their views as long as they pose no serious threat to the regimes or to primordial U.S. interests in the region — that is, those interests that the United States would not jeopardize for the sake of pushing for more democratization in the Broader Middle East, which include fighting the war on terrorism, stabilizing oil supplies, and standing firm with Israel. Conversely, the United States does not help its call for more democratization as its support is clearly inconsistent in the case of antigovernment opposition in North Africa — whenever the suppressed or oppressed groups and individuals are not Islamists the United States goes ahead and calls the government to task (Agence France Presse 2006). On the other hand, the United States has consistently remained silent when the governments arrest hundreds of Islamists of all brands, even those who do not advocate violence, as soon as they go against the existing system.

Even when it looks like the United States is seeking to support nongovernmental efforts (e.g., human rights NGOs) as a way of encouraging the construction of a civil society, such as through democracy projects implemented by the U.S. Agency for International Development (USAID) and MEPI or by providing technical assistance to legislatures and the judiciary, this does not amount to much. These civil society efforts are weak and do not address wider societal concerns for the most part.[13] Nor do parliaments and judges enjoy real powers to check the power of the executive. This dilemma is illustrated in the case of calling for women's rights. The fact that individual programs calling for women's rights might make some difference is very unlikely to weaken the power of the executive on women's issues. The North African governments go as far as letting NGOs provide many state services that the regimes fail or decide not to provide, with the proviso that the regimes retain ultimate control over these services and knowing very well that increasing the number of these small organizations would ultimately turn them into rivals competing for resources and legitimacy, thereby undermining any potential confluence against the regime.

Whereas Morocco, Algeria, Tunisia, and Egypt effect a simulacrum of democratic reforms, the story in Libya is very different. The regime is very oppressive and does not allow even a co-opted opposition to exist, in contrast with the rest of North Africa. Given the ongoing rapprochement with the United States and the West in general, Qaddafi finds his relationship with the United States on the rise for the better. He thus does not even feel pressured to play a game of corrupted democratization. He has been playing the "Islamist danger" card (and cooperating on intelligence issues with the United States) to show Libya is a good repentant after having been a rogue state for more than two decades. It does not bother Qaddafi that Libyan exiles espouse the U.S. democratization call whereas he does not. His firmly and well-established records of being anti-Islamist are good enough for Washington to throw its lot behind him rather than behind an opposition that has fully espoused the democratization program, especially given that the opposition is more or less Islamist oriented, thereby undermining the U.S. rhetoric on seeking to spread democracy to the Middle East.[14]

The Islamist card is thus posing a huge challenge both to the incumbent regimes in North Africa and to the United States, which are calling for more democratization in the Broader Middle East. The only social and political movements in the North African countries that are very popular and are insisting on democratic reforms, regime accountability, the rule of law, transparency, and civilian authority are nonviolent Islamist groups. They are able to challenge the semiauthoritarian character of the states, both rhetorically and through their societal welfare programs. Yet no North African state allows an Islamist movement to come to power, except for those that have been co-opted and even then these are usually made subordinated minority partners when they participate in the governments or hold seats in elected legislatures. In spite of the fact that this undermines the U.S. project of democratization the Bush administration does accept the choices made by the states as part of prosecuting the war on terrorism and preserving the stability of incumbent regimes. By the same token, North African leaders have used the fear of "Islamist threat" to warn the United States not to push for democratic reforms too fast, which, they argue, will most likely bring the Islamists to power and, hence, Iranian-type regimes in many parts of the Arab world.

What emerges from these maneuvers is a stronger consolidation of the incumbent regimes and no serious attempt to genuinely democratize existing political systems. The irony is that when nonstate actors seek to voice their responses to U.S. policies, and at times very strongly, they end up contributing to a resilient absence of true democratic governance in the region. The dilemma is that the Bush discourse on liberty, democratization, and reforms encourages nonstate actors to seek change to the status quo. These efforts are then highjacked and manipulated by the incumbent regimes that seek to undermine any serious change to their authoritarian nature. The strategies that the Bush administration has been following in prosecuting its self-declared GWOT conflict with one another — that is, it cooperates with corrupt governments to establish a free trade region and to apprehend suspected terrorists while at the same time calling for democratizing these very regimes that would ultimately undermine them. The United States ends up stopping short of being faithful to its rhetoric on democratic reforms, thereby tacitly agreeing with the incumbent regimes that they should persist.

Hegemony of the Discourse on the GWOT

Is the United States seeking to project a hegemonic relationship with North Africa? The answer is simultaneously "no" and "yes." It is "no" in the sense that not so much has tangibly changed in or been forced on North Africa that would suggest that the incumbent regimes have submitted to U.S. directives or wishes. What has happened was not unprecedented in the region; it had happened before. Nor was it the result of any U.S. pressure or even action. The answer is "yes" in the sense there indeed is an important change, if of an intangible nature. The North African region has fully espoused the new discourse on how to play the game of world politics, on what counts as world politics, a discourse the first stage of which was launched by the United States immediately after 9/11.

What has the G. W. Bush administration done — on the ground — in North Africa that is radically different from what previous administrations did, especially since the end of the cold war? What seems to have changed but remains mostly invisible to the gaze of mainstream international relations discipline is that the Bush administration has been successful in initiating the deployment of a new discursive framework within which world politics is unfolding. What the United States has thus done post-9/11 is launch a new hegemonic discourse of global politics that friends and foes alike have intentionally or unintentionally but, in almost all cases, willingly and freely espoused and deployed in pursuing their own agendas or in reinforcing the U.S. agenda from which they would also benefit.

Even seemingly perennial problems such as the Israeli–Palestinian conflict and the Chechen and Kashmiri problems that have resisted resolution for decades have been recast to fit the new hegemonic discourse — the GWOT. The latter has thus become an "empty" signifier, by which I mean a signifier without any specified meaning attached to it and around which other meanings and signifiers are organized, promoted, repressed, erased, and so forth. The empty signifier — the GWOT—has steadily become a surface of discursive inscription wherein international actors (especially, governments) are inscribing and enacting a wide range of foreign and domestic policy demands, views, attitudes, and practices. This discursive framework began to be articulated immediately after 9/11 when President Bush started making reference to the "axis of evil" and so on. The articulation was put on firmer ground in his June 2002 speech at West Point Academy and then put in writing in the September 2002 *National Security Strategy* document. The articulatory discourse has since become a set of principles and beliefs that the Bush administration is defending (e.g., preemption and counterproliferation) and within which it is enacting certain practices (preparing small military bases for the sake of rapidly intervening in weak states to chase suspected terrorists or redress rogue governments). Even those who oppose U.S. hegemony enacted through unilateralism, preemption, and the formation of coalitions of the willing end up framing their resisting discourse within the hegemonic discourse that the empty signifier — GWOT—sustains. Borrowing from French psychoanalyst Jacques Lacan, we can say that the GWOT has indeed become a master signifier that defines what world politics are and the actors that play this global game.

Lest I be misunderstood, I do not mean to imply that the Bush administration has won the hearts and the minds of people (the leaders and the led) around the world. Nor am I implying that the U.S. policies are not alienating most of the world. Nor should it be concluded that U.S. post-9/11 policies in the Greater Middle East have not weakened U.S. soft (and, some would argue, hard) power or jeopardized U.S. interests in the region. All of this might be happening or not happening, depending on what perspective one assumes in looking at the "facts" or in analyzing them. Rather, my point is that we are in a new discursive era that is affecting everybody, including the United States itself as well the Bush administration.

Conclusions

There is no U.S. hegemony (even in an emerging form) in North Africa — that is, no more than what had already existed between the end of the cold war and September 11, 2001, and even before. Yet there is a far-reaching transformation taking place around the world — the revolution of the hegemonic discourse of the global war on undergirding world politics. This discourse is projected and sustained by democracies and authoritarian regimes alike. The United States still enjoys a prominent place and role in this discursive framework but does not dominate it. In fact, this new world discourse is working better for semidemocracies like Russia and the North African states than for the United States itself owing to the character of domestic politics in these states. Whereas it is becoming increasingly harder for the Bush administration to sustain good domestic support for its foreign policies, the North African regimes have benefited quite well from the discursive framework of the GWOT, thereby consolidating even further their democracy-lacking forms of governance.

Notes

This paper was first presented at the Challenges to U.S. Global and Regional Hegemony and Implications for the Post–Cold War International System conference, March 20–22, 2006, Chicago, Illinois, organized under the auspices of the Center for Global Studies at the University of Illinois at Urbana-Champaign. I thank Jonathan Jones (graduate student at the University of Florida, Department of Political Science) for research assistance.

1. A few days before 9/11 the United States had agreed to deliver sophisticated antiguerrilla equipment — the kind used to detect troop movements — to Algeria, with the proviso that these technologies would not be used against Algeria's neighbors (*Le Quotidien d'Oran*, November 6, 2001).

2. Groupe Islamique Armé was added to the State Department list of terrorist organizations after September 11, 2001.

3. A recent example is the operation code-named "Flintlock 2005" in which some eight hundred U.S. troops and two thousand African troops participated in summer 2005 ("Les armées à l'épreuve du terrorisme," *Le Quotidien*, July 2, 2005).

4. Some $600,000 was provided for such training in 2003, which is much more than $30,000 provided in 2002 (U.S. Department of State, Bureau of Democracy, Human Rights, and Labor, Middle East and North Africa, in *Supporting Human Rights and Democracy: The U.S. Record 2003–2004* [Washington, D.C.: USDS, 2004], 170–71, 185–87).

5. Mayer (2005) estimates that approximately 150 people have been subjected to extraordinary rendition since 2001.

6. For a general discussion, see the Committee on International Human Rights of the Association of the Bar of the City of New York and Center for Human Rights and Global Justice, 2004, Torture by Proxy: International and Domestic Law Applicable to "Extraordinary Renditions" (New York: ABCNY and CHRGJ, New York University School of Law, 2004) (www.nyuhr.org/docs/TortureByProxy.pdf), and "Rendering unto Caesar," *Economist*, February 7, 2005, 376.

7. By late September 2003, that is, three months before Saddam was captured, the Qaddafi government had decided to abandon its WMD ambitions and thus invited U.S. and UK inspectors to visit suspected Libyan weapons sites.

8. See remarks by the president at the twentieth anniversary of the National Endowment for Democracy ("President Bush Discusses Freedom in Iraq and Middle East," October 16, 2003) (http://www.ned.org/events/anniversary/20thAniv-Bush.html) and U.S. Department of State, Bureau of Democracy, Human Rights and Labor, Supporting Human Rights and Democracy: The U.S. Record, 2003–4 and 2004–5 at http://www.state.gov/g/drl/rls/shrd/2003 and http://www.state.gov/g/drl/rls/shrd/2004.

9. Interview in *Le Figaro*, September 4, 2001.

10. The final thirteen-point statement linked political reforms in the Arab states to a just settlement of regional conflicts, in particular the Israeli–Palestinian conflict (El-Naggar, 2004).

11. G8–Greater Middle East Partnership, working paper circulated prior to the June 2004 G8 Summit, Sea Island, Ga. Available at www.al-bab.com/arab/docs/international/gmep2004.htm.

12. The Doha Declaration is available at the Ibn Khaldun Center for Development Studies, http://www.eicds.org/english/publications/books/reforminitiatives/doha8.htm.

13. In Egypt, advocacy NGOs constitute four-tenths of one percent of the total number (see Shahin 2005, 7).

14. The recent overwhelming Hamas victory in the Palestinian parliamentary elections has made the dilemma for the United States even starker.

CHAPTER ELEVEN

Middle East

Jacob English

The events of September 11 turned the world's focus, once again, to one of the most dynamic regions in the world, the Middle East. The nationality of the hijackers involved in the attacks seemed to matter little. More important than their nationalities was that they were Muslims and Arab. This is important because of the region's long history of conflict with the West over the perceived or real intentions of the West in its relations with the Islamic and Arab worlds. In the days and years following September 11, U.S. foreign policy has become mired in the Middle East. American national security and defense policy specifically targets the Middle East as a strategically critical region where the global war on terror will be lost or won.

As the introduction to this volume states, the purpose is to assess regional responses to U.S. power and their implications for regional and global order. No region has been more important or in the public eye more than the Middle East and the larger Islamic–Arab world. Furthermore, at no point in history has a state wielded the amount of coercive and economic power as the United States does now. As Edward Kolodziej states in the introduction to this volume, "It is the only state capable of projecting its military power around the globe. No other state or group of states . . . can defeat the United States in a direct military clash." American military forces have had a profound effect on the Middle East, shaping to a large extent how it responds to U.S. power and presence in the Islamic–Arab world.

Indeed, there has been concern within the Middle Eastern region regarding the growing power, presence, and intentions of the United States. Some have argued that the United States is intent on ruling the region, essentially on "resurrecting empires" (Khalidi 2005). Still others believe that the United States is a beacon of freedom and that its intentions are purely good and "express the deep humanitarian instincts of the American people."[1] There are varying explanations for why both sides feel as they do, yet few have ventured very far to try to determine why the United States has acted or been perceived to be acting in the manner in which it has.

This chapter presents a more probing and balanced explanation by answering three related questions pertaining to Middle East reactions to U.S. primacy in the post-9/11 era. First, how do the major states in the Middle East view U.S. announced and operational strategic policy? As the other chapters in this volume show, U.S. policy is perceived as aggressive and idealist, and military strategy as much preventive as preemptive. The difference between preventive and preemptive is that the former connotes a campaign launched to stop an adversary from being able to launch a possible attack in the distant future, while the latter connotes a campaign launched to prevent an imminent attack in the immediate future. Second, what changes in announced and operational policies and strategies are emerging in the region? Here I show how the major Middle East actors have adjusted their own policies and strategies to meet the challenges from the United States. Finally, what are the principal factors explaining the regional responses? I address the first two questions in a combined section, looking at each major country (Egypt, Israel, Saudi Arabia, Iraq, and Iran) in subsections preceded by a regional overview where minor actors can be addressed. The third question will be addressed and related to the first two in the final section of the chapter.

Middle Eastern Responses to U.S. Policy

Until the middle of the last century the relationship between Americans and Middle Easterners was pacific and mutually satisfactory (Khalidi 2005, 31). But the relationship began to change in 1948 with the recognition of Israeli statehood and continued to change with the slow but steady increase in U.S. presence and power within the region leading to a drastic change in course on September 11, 2001. The region now has a different view of the United States, its power, and its presence.

Post-9/11 calls for democracy in the Middle East have not been sympathetically received. Regional powers were indignant. Egyptian president Hosni Mubarak complained that "we hear about these initiatives as if the region and its states do not exist, as if they had no sovereignty over their land" (Stevenson 2004, 157). In an effort to maintain control over their countries, leaders attempted to make it appear as if the United States was encroaching on their sovereignty, ignoring their own long-standing oppressive practices. This reaction has been consistent among the Middle Eastern countries. Despite reform debates and some modest progressive measures, the region remains politically moribund. Entrenched authoritarian governments well versed in absorbing political reforms without changing the fundamental elements of power persist. Arab governments are still, in light of U.S. policy pressures, unwilling to take serious steps toward democratic reform, even when it means heading off long-term troubles such as rising socioeconomic pressures or out-of-control population growth (Carothers and Ottaway 2005, 7).

There have been two primary responses to U.S. power and presence within the Middle Eastern region. First, Arabs fear being the "next victim" of U.S. aggression and thus feel a need to appease the United States by submitting to its pressure and demands. This submission has primarily taken the form of allowing U.S. troops on Arab soil, which terrorist organizations have objected to, and the faux running of elections to give the illusion of moving toward democracy in accordance with U.S. demands. Second, Middle Eastern leaders also continue to try to maintain dictatorial control over their societies while making sure they do not end up on the U.S. axis of evil list.

Israel presents a special case, as described below. Iran presents still a different case with its insistence on pursuing the nuclear option and gaining a greater hold on power within the Gulf region. Overall, however, the Middle East has gone through significant change since 9/11, proving again to be the planet's most dynamic region.

Israel

Israel's response to the Bush Doctrine has been distinct from the other major actors in the region. Israel has long been one of the United States' crucial allies in the Middle East but at the same time has been seen by those in the region as a source of regional conflict. Yet, Israel has arguably been the only functioning democracy in the Middle East and has thus been considered a vital part of U.S. strategy to promote open societies in the region.

This does not mean that Israel has openly accepted U.S. announced and operational strategy in the region. In fact, there has been some division between the allies over the years. The biggest point of contention between Israel and the United States, and the rest of the world, is the long-running Arab–Israeli conflict. Several rounds of wars, interminable negotiations, improvident and violated treaty signings, and repeated assassinations by both sides of rival leaders have kept the region in constant tension since 1948. However, since 9/11, Israel has become an even more critical partner of U.S. strategy in the Middle East.

The Bush Doctrine supports Israel's right to defend itself from terror. Washington accepts an Israeli-inspired two-state solution to the Israeli–Palestinian conflict but, in contrast to Israel, the *National Security* document does not allot a privileged status to specific Arab or Middle East states but rather refers only to "key Arab states." The sole exception is Iraq, which the Bush Doctrine singles out as a state where a stable democratic government must be created. In a region where perception plays a compelling psychological and political role and where historical narratives drive current and future relations, this tends to confirm Arab suspicions and bolster Israeli confidence about U.S. policies. According to Dennis Ross, "Peacemaking in the last decade [1989 to 1999] emerged from a historical context of deep-seated grievances and desire for justice on both sides. Arabs and Israelis each have a narrative that tells their story and interprets their reality, and these narratives are lurking in every discussion" (Ross 2004, 15). The Arab narrative is based on real or perceived past injustices committed by the West, while the Israeli narrative is based on both religious and communal group rights and longtime support of the West. By privileging Israel in current U.S. strategic policy the narratives are reinforced and serve to perpetuate long-standing beliefs, which have shaped Israeli responses toward U.S. policy.

Because the Bush administration has not fully grasped or attempted to understand the complexity of the Middle East conflict, the Bush Doctrine and defense strategy, as well as multiple statements by high-level U.S. officials, have tended to mirror Israeli policy in the region and support the actions of the Israeli government under the auspices of the "war on terror." The Bush Doctrine and increased assistance to Israel weakens many previous agreements to the effect that the borders of Israel should be drawn back to the pre-1967 borders by stating that "Israeli forces need to withdraw fully to positions they held prior to September 28, 2000," which is the start date of the al-Aqsa Intifada. No mention is made of the 1967 borders, suggesting they are lost forever, a further grievance Arabs can add to their narrative of Western- and, specifically, American-inflicted injury on Arabs and Muslims. This victims' narrative is given additional credence by reports that the 40 percent of the land that Israel plans to keep in its unilateral withdrawal from the West Bank is on privately owned Arab property.[2]

Israeli responses to U.S. power and policies are varied. They are driven principally by Israeli notions of the state's national interests. That means that some do not support U.S. preferences. Israel has grown bolder in pursuing its own policy objectives and has centered on a unilateral definition of its borders that, until recently, entailed the forced relocation of Israeli settlers. According to Naseer Aruri (2003, 198), "Bush shares Ariel Sharon's view that it [Israel's war with Palestine] is simply a defensive war to dismantle the terror infrastructure of the Palestinians." The attacks of 9/11 have, according to some Israeli analysts, produced an "undoubtedly greater understanding of Israel's struggle" (Sneh 2005, 69). The alleged Jenin refugee camp massacre of April 2002 was portrayed by media and human rights groups as clear-cut evidence of Israel's aggression against the Palestinians, while the Bush administration viewed the incident as a lesson in how to conduct the war on terrorism. According to Randy Gangle, executive director of the Center for Emerging Threats and Opportunities, accounts of the Jenin fighting "reflected everything that we have been saying for the last four years about the problems we are going to face in the urban battle space" (Aruri 2003, 47). Knesset member and Deputy Minister of Defense Ephraim Sneh (2005, 69) further confirms that the U.S. government officials "will also have a greater need to learn from the experience of our [Israel's] own struggle against Shiite and Palestinian terror, and thus will need to increase their cooperation with us." The practice of eliminating specific terrorist suspects, a practice referred to as "targeted killings," has sparked further violent reactions on the part of Palestinian groups. The unilateral Israeli development of the "Iron Wall" to keep terrorists out of Israel has been compared to the Berlin wall, but though the policy has been exceptionally controversial, initial reports from observers in Israel suggest that the wall has been effective in separating the two populations and improving Israeli security.

The policies of the United States and Israel often conflict on key issues. There have been disagreements on who exactly poses the greatest threat in the region — specifically, over which country is the biggest supporter of terrorism. While the United States until recently contended that Iraq is the biggest threat, Israel has been consistent in its belief that Iran poses the greatest threat to the region, a view that received more attention in the 2006 revision of the Bush Doctrine. Indeed, Sneh has stated that "the most salient strategic threat to Israel's existence is Iran" (Sneh 2005, 55). This perceived threat dates back much further than 9/11, as remarks made by Sneh and Rabin in 1993 to the Knesset emphasizing the importance of eliminating the coming Iranian nuclear threat suggest. Rabin stated in January 1993 that "we must be concerned about the possibility that Iran will gain nuclear weapons. Perhaps in the middle and long terms the goals of Iran's rulers . . . may be even more dangerous than those of Iraq's ruler in his present diminished situation" (Sneh 2005, 55). To credit the consistency of Israeli policy over time, this concern with Iran has not diminished in any way. Some within Israel are pushing the United States to act on the Iranian threat. Israel's perception of Iran as the primary threat has been confirmed by the repeated actions and comments by Iran's leadership over the years from slogans written on Shihab-3 missiles in the 1998 Revolution Day parade calling for the destruction of Israel to recent comments in November 2005 by Iranian Prime Minister Mamoud Ahmadenijad for the total annihilation of Israel (Sneh 2005, 60).

There was tension initially between the United States and Israel over Prime Minister Sharon's January 2004 decision to unilaterally withdraw from Gaza in August and September of 2005. This tension was caused primarily by Israel's intention to the use American aid in the form of U.S.-issued weapons to conduct the unilateral disengagement but also by the fact that Israel had made a unilateral decision without consulting the United States. The use of American weapons or other forms of aid for the purposes of forcibly removing people from their homes is a violation of the human rights guidelines of the U.S. Foreign Assistance Act.

Section 502B of the law states that a "principal goal of the foreign policy of the United States shall be to promote the increased observance of internationally recognized human rights by all countries" and that "no security assistance may be provided to any country the government of which engages in a consistent pattern of gross violations of internationally recognized human rights" (Klein 2005).

This tension was short-lived; on April 14, 2004, President Bush endorsed the withdrawal and noted that Israel should continue to follow the road map for peace. He stated the plan was "bold and courageous" and that "peace should be recognized by the realities on the ground" and the need for Israel to defend itself (Mark 2005, 5). The United States has, however, sought a number of safeguards to ensure that the move was not an effort to abandon the road map (Kessler 2004, 16). Such safeguards were deemed necessary given the attitude of senior Israeli advisors to Sharon. Dov Weisglass, for example, stated that "the significance of the disengagement plan is the freezing of the peace process. And when you freeze that process, you prevent the establishment of a Palestinian state, and you prevent a discussion of the refugees, the borders, and Jerusalem" (Shavit 2004). Yet, because of U.S. support for unilateral withdrawal from some occupied territory, the perception on the part of the Palestinians and others in the Arab world is that the Palestinians will be forced to comply with something contrary to their interests. On May 18, 2005, the *Mideast Mirror* stated that the United States would likely try to force Palestinian prime minister Mahmoud Abbas to accept the Israeli plans at a time when he could neither reject nor accept them.[3] This was partly confirmed with the 2005 victory of Hamas in the Palestinian elections, in which the radical group won a clear majority of the vote. Since the elections the Palestinians have not been able to create a stable government.

Hamas's victory, which highlights the strength of radical Islam, has led to a significant change in policy on both the Israeli and U.S. sides. The ascendancy of Hamas also illustrates the weakness of the Bush Doctrine and its inability to deal with the prospect of radical groups claiming power through democratic means. Israeli policy has remained remarkably consistent by holding that it will not negotiate, deal with, or tolerate terrorists in any form and by maintaining its right to exist. Despite international criticism Israel has not given up its policy of "targeted killings" of suspected terrorists.

A final point of tension has emerged between Israel and the United States over U.S. strategic military policy. Israel has routinely objected to the close military relationship the United States maintains with Egypt and Jordan and the large sums of aid and military technology it affords these states (R. Williams 2001). For much of the post–cold war era and specifically the post-9/11 era, the relationship between Israel and its Arab neighbors has been chilly. For the United States its relationship with the Arab states that surround Israel has been vital to its strategic interests, and the United States has been a primary source of financial and military assistance to these Arab states. For Israel, until recently, Egypt was the principal Arab military threat owing to its being the second largest recipient of U.S. aid after Israel at roughly an annual rate of $1.3 billion (Turner 2001, 19–25). Since much of this aid is tied to maintaining peace with Israel, many believe that Arab states like Egypt will only remain peaceful as long as aid continues to flow. Jordan has also received an increase in U.S. aid as a result of 9/11. In 2002 Congress, at the request of the Bush administration, doubled assistance to Jordan to $448 million (of which $198 million would take the form of military aid), making Jordan the fourth largest aid recipient (Qadamani 2002). In 2003 Jordan received $450 million in aid and over $1 billion in a supplemental to help Jordan deal with added expenses resulting from the war on terror and the war in Iraq (Prados 2005).

This tension between the United States and Israel over American aid to other Arab states was played out in December of 2001, when Israel and its U.S. Congressional allies objected to a routine arms deal between Egypt and the United States. Under the sale Egypt would purchase $1.34 billion in U.S. arms and military equipment (Jerusalem Institute for Western Defense 2002). Many pro-Israeli groups with ties to powerful U.S. legislators feared that Egypt would likely plan to use these weapons against Israel, a concern that spearheaded the anti-Egypt campaign (Jerusalem Institute for Western Defense 2002). However, much of the aid Egypt has been receiving since 9/11 has been conditional on Egypt's progress toward democracy, a key element of the Bush Doctrine. It is a condition that has been more often ignored than not. Although the Bush administration and policy-making circles maintain a strong commitment to Israeli security, economic and other security interests induce them to also fund and provide arms and equipment to Israel's neighbors who are willing to join the United States in the war on terrorism.

The Bush Doctrine has given the Israeli leadership a mandate to crack down hard on terrorism. Strong U.S. support, evidenced in the Israeli war against Hezbollah in Lebanon, has created the perception in Arab capitals and in the Arab street that Israel has been given a green light to be more bold and aggressive in its own responses to terrorism. The Bush administration understands, as a result of 9/11, what life is like under the constant threat of attack, and thus, U.S. strategic policy, which accents preventive and preemptive war, has led to a tacit approval of offensive Israeli policy. There have been few major policy changes in Israeli policy toward the Palestinians, though Israel's unilateral withdrawal from Gaza and some of the occupied territories and the split within the Likud party that led to the formation of the new "Kadima" party signal important internal developments in the post-9/11 era. These moves have had the unexpected result of hardening Palestinian opinion against a two-state solution defined by Israel, a resistance that contributed to the electoral victory of Hamas in the fall 2005. This is a case where greater democratic rule has led to more, not less, violence between Israel and the Palestinians.

Egypt

Egypt has long been considered the United States' top Arab ally in the Middle East. This pre-9/11 relationship is now at perilous risk as a consequence of changes in U.S. Middle East policy and the Iraqi intervention. Before 9/11 Hosni Mubarak, Egypt's unopposed head of state, had been viewed by successive Washington administrations as a source of stability in the region. With the Bush Doctrine's dual and conflicting goals of fighting terrorism and spreading democracy, the tight relationship between the United States and Egypt has been placed on shaky ground.

Egypt, along with other Arab states in the region, has taken two approaches to the post-9/11 U.S. policy in the region. On the one hand, Mubarak is comfortable receiving U.S. aid and in supporting the war on terror to suit the regime's domestic agenda of controlling its opponents. On the other hand, disingenuous Egyptian gestures toward democracy in the form of contested elections proved a dumb show, as President Mubarak was reelected by a large majority in an election where rival candidates and their supporters were intimidated and in some instances incarcerated. Mubarak has taken strong measures to ensure that he remains in power by restricting civil liberties. As Badredine Arfi describes in his chapter in this volume, Washington has had little difficulty accepting stability over democratic reforms, periodic calls for democratization of Egyptian practices to the contrary notwithstanding. This interesting paradox explains a lot about Egypt's response to U.S. regional power and presence.

In 2004, Egypt received $575 million in economic grants and $1.3 billion in military grants from the United States (Sharp 2005). This is the annual tribute made to Egypt for recognizing Israel as a consequence of the Camp David accords signed under President Jimmy Carter between the two states. Washington also values Egypt's role as a leader of the Arab world. Further, it trades on Cairo's active opposition to terrorism and welcomes Egyptian influence in convincing other Arab states to cooperate in the war on terror (Sharp 2005), evidenced by Egypt's long-standing fight against the Muslim Brotherhood and Mubarak's attempts to keep it powerless and its leadership in prison. According to former American ambassador Edward Walker, providing bountiful aid to Egypt gives Mubarak a pass on democratic reforms and human rights. U.S. policy here highlights the contradiction that follows from trying to fight terrorism and spread democracy across the region at the same time (Levinson 2004).

The movement toward democracy in Egypt is a double-edged sword. Any movement toward democracy, as the Hamas example illustrates, has the potential to bring to power Muslim extremists who are opposed to Washington and are more the problem then the solution to regional terrorism. A move to democratic reform might well topple the Mubarak regime and lead to the ascendancy of the Muslim Brotherhood and associated Muslim groups bent on destroying Israel and extending terrorism to the shores of the United States.

In a number of public speeches, Mubarak has raised objections to the Bush Doctrine, particularly to the war in Iraq. In March 2003, Mubarak publicly proclaimed his opposition to the coming war in Iraq, claiming that it would "produce a thousand bin-Ladens" where few if any existed before (Stevenson 2003, 157). In 2004 he stated that the Bush Doctrine threatens the sovereignty of states in the Middle East (Stevenson 2004, 157). However, Mubarak's opposition to U.S. policy is in practice largely rhetorical, stopping well short of directly opposing U.S. policies in the region.

To placate the United States Mubarak announced on February 26, 2005, that the Egyptian electoral system would be reformed to allow secret ballot voting and to permit multiple candidates to run for office (Youssef 2005). At first this appeared to be a major victory for the U.S. policy goal of spreading democracy. Egypt seemed to be moving toward contested elections, a key requirement of a functioning open society and government. As the year went on, Mubarak and members of his party made numerous promises to hold free and fair elections. The government even went so far as to change article 76 of the Egyptian Constitution to allow for the first-ever multicandidate presidential elections (Dean 2005). However, the free and fair presidential elections appeared anything but free and fair when Mubarak proclaimed victory with 88.6 percent of the vote in an election day marred by claims of fraud, cheating, and poll abuse.

The parliamentary elections of October and November 2005 proved much freer and fairer than the presidential elections and the much-feared and officially banned Muslim Brotherhood won a significant number of parliamentary seats.[4] With the win the Muslim Brotherhood candidates and leadership proclaimed their commitment to moving toward democracy. They insisted that "no political, religious, social, or cultural group should be excluded from Egypt's political life" (Howeidy 2005). Therefore, it may be possible that Egypt is adopting, though very slowly, democratic reforms. However, many argue that Mubarak has no real intentions of moving toward democracy, but that he is instead grooming his son Gamal Mubarak for succession in the near future. It does seem that for the time being and with minimal U.S. resistance Egypt has satisfied the U.S. policy goal of taking steps toward democracy and has thus avoided being "next" on the list of states earmarked for regime change as the United States carries out its global war on terrorism.

The second Egyptian response to U.S. policy has been to dampen public enthusiasm, raised provisionally by the limited experience of a contested presidential election, for Western-style democracy. Within Egypt the National Democratic Party (NDP) and President Mubarak have sent clear (and coercive) messages to opponents that he intends to maintain the status quo by enforcing its authority. Since 2002 Cairo has been responding to public protests and anti-Mubarak rallies with a tough law-enforcement crackdown (Stevenson 2003, 165). Tens of thousands have been jailed; thousands of protesters have been beaten by military and police; and in one incident, in May 2005, a group of Egyptian women were sexually assaulted and abused by members of the police, military, and NDP supporters that were present (Halawi 2005). Voter registration for both elections was limited only to those who registered by December 2004, prior to the changes in the election laws, thereby guaranteeing a limited voting body, evidenced by the low voter turnout to eligible ratio in September 2005 (Pan 2005).

The Egyptian government dissuades participation in the political process by arresting opposition candidates, by condoning police beatings, and by stationing military and police at polling stations to impede voter turnout where opposition support is strong. The NDP and Mubarak have made it clear to opponents that democracy will not happen under Mubarak's rule (Parsowith 2005). Thus the Egyptian government has responded to American demands for democratic reforms by proclaiming and holding seemingly contested elections while frustrating the public's ability to realize that democratic ideal. Appeasing U.S. policy by showcasing steps toward democracy and by being tough on terrorism but at the same time blocking public participation in the political process is a pattern reproduced among other authoritarian allies of the United States in the Middle East, notably Saudi Arabia.

Saudi Arabia

The United States has had a long relationship with Saudi Arabia, dating back at least to before World War II. Since 1990, Saudi Arabia has been the top U.S. arms customer, the Pentagon having delivered more than $39.6 billion in arms over a little more than a decade (Federation of American Scientists 2002). This close-knit military relationship has been heavily strained in the post-9/11 world, in part because of the extreme forms of Islam, specifically Wahabism, practiced in Saudi Arabia and exported abroad by way of support for fundamentalist education in regional madrassas, the government's publicized human rights abuses, the existence of multiple terrorist organizations within Saudi Arabia or of Saudi origin, and the current thrust of U.S. foreign policy that is perceived, in Riyadh, as threatening the regime.

For years the United States has based thousands of military personnel and equipment inside Saudi Arabia, which has been a major complaint of both the Saudi public and the terrorist organizations alike (Prados 2003, 1).[5] There have been many attacks on U.S. military personnel and contractors. One such attack was launched against the compound of American defense contractor Vinnell Corporation in May 2003, in which thirty-four were killed and numerous others wounded (CNN.com 2003). Such attacks have not diminished, and on a number of occasions the United States has accused the Saudi government of withholding evidence hindering these and the 9/11 investigations.

It has been known or suspected that many Saudi citizens provide funds to extremist and terrorist organizations, the most prominent of which is al Qaeda (Federation of American Scientists 2002). There remain two questions regarding the U.S. relationship with Saudi Arabia. First, why has the United States preserved its close relationship with Saudi Arabia when there is such a clear hostility to U.S. presence? Second, how has Saudi Arabia responded to the 9/11 attacks and subsequent U.S. policies, including the extended deployment of American military forces to the Middle East? The answer to the first question is simple. Saudi Arabia is a major player in the oil industry, accounting for the largest percentage of oil production of all oil suppliers. The answer to the second is that the United States wants to keep U.S. troops in a convenient strategic location for future operations as they become necessary. This solution, however, of retaining U.S. power in the region so as to ensure the flow of oil is itself a problem, since Saudi Arabians do not appreciate the military presence. How this balancing act impacts on Saudi Arabia is a complex story.

Saudi Arabia poses several dilemmas for U.S. policy. While it is the protector of most sacred Muslim holy sites and hosts the annual Hajj, it also spawned most of the 9/11 terrorists, following a Saudi policy of exporting terrorist plots to maintain home security. Complementing this Saudi strategy at odds with American security interests is its continued support of madrassas within the Muslim world, which teach hatred of the West and, specifically, the United States. Saudi Arabia also has one of the most oppressive human rights records in the world, again largely as a result of the extremist forms of Islam practiced by the regime.

Saudi Arabian leadership and the public at large oppose any U.S. military presence within the borders of Saudi Arabia. In fact, ridding Saudi Arabia of the U.S. military is one of the stated central goals of numerous terrorist groups, radical organizations, the Saudi public, and many within the royal family. RAND's Mary Morris commented at a Saudi–American Forum in 2004 that "public opinion in Saudi Arabia and the Middle East are currently more anti-American than at any time in history, due to both the U.S. invasion of Iraq without international validation and the lack of a strong U.S. support of an unbiased settlement of the Israeli–

Palestinian conflict" (Morris 2004). Little has changed since Morris made that observation. Saudi concerns are rooted in religious fears of Western domination and fundamentalist beliefs opposed to non-Muslim occupation of Islamic lands. While the Saudi government allowed a U.S. military presence in Saudi Arabia during the first Gulf War (1991) and, afterward, to enforce the U.N.-mandated no-fly zone, following 9/11 Saudis have expressed significantly greater resistance to U.S. military presence than ever before.

Several members of the royal family rejected the U.S. war against Iraq. Speaking at the 2002 Arab Summit in Beirut, Crown Prince Abdullah embraced the Iraqi second-in-command and "articulated the view that Saudis would prefer to see the departure of the American troops permanently deployed in Saudi Arabia since the Gulf War" (Stevenson 2003, 160). In July 2002, Saudi foreign minister Prince Saud al-Faysal said that the government "does not want allied forces to use Saudi grounds for any attack on Iraq," and on March 19, 2003, the day of the U.S. attack against Iraq, King Fahd stated that Saudi Arabia "will not participate in any way in a war against Iraq" (Prados 2005, 5).

Although the Saudis verbally oppose U.S. strategy and policy, it is also noteworthy that Saudi Arabia has resisted a break that would alienate the United States and undermine its long-standing relationship. Since 2001, Saudi Arabia has taken possession of $4.7 billion in U.S. arms deliveries with another $3.8 billion in arms transfer agreements still pending (Langton 2005, ix–x). The economic-military relationship between the United States and Saudi Arabia has remained relatively intact.

Riyadh has also taken a number of steps to check the financing of terrorist organizations. In December 2001, the Saudi government required all Saudi banks to have anti-money-laundering units and charity oversight programs to monitor the bank accounts of prominent Saudi businessmen. In October 2002, the Saudi government announced several more steps that would be taken to stop terrorist financing. Any bank account with suspected terrorist ties would be frozen. The Saudis also agreed to implement U.N. Security Council resolutions related to terrorist financing. All charities would be audited and measures would be taken to prevent terrorist use of "legitimate charitable groups." All charities dealing outside Saudi Arabia must report activities to the Saudi Foreign Ministry. Finally, in August of 2003, the Saudi government agreed to establish a joint U.S.–Saudi task force to investigate sources of terrorist funding (Prados 2003, 1–5). Despite these modest examples of cooperation and the continued vital importance of the oil connection, U.S.–Saudi relations are not as stable now as they were prior to 2001. This is primarily because of changes to U.S. policy under the Bush Doctrine regarding the spread of democracy as an antidote to terrorism and its steadfast support of Israel and Israeli policies to suppress Hamas in Palestine and Hezbollah in Lebanon.

If Saudi Arabia has begun to crack down on terrorism, its record on democratic reforms has scarcely materialized. From February to April 2005, Saudi Arabia held its first-ever municipal elections to appease U.S. leaders. The elections were virtually meaningless (Reuters 2004). Despite being touted by U.S. officials, Saudi leaders, and Western media as a "first concrete political reform in [an] absolute monarchy" and as a "giant step" toward reform, the election of one-half of the municipal local assembly seats amounted to little tangible political gain in open democratic practices (MSNBC 2003; BBC News 2003b).[6] The municipal assemblies possess almost no local power and little to no influence at the state level. The election process itself was far from free and fair. Even in the postelection era the Economist Intelligence Unit ranked Saudi Arabia as 2.80 on a 10-point democratic scale, tying with Syria for second to last, and even falling below Iran, which scored 3.85 (BBC News 2005a).

During the Saudi elections, unlike during the Egyptian elections, international observers were allowed to man polling stations and several civilian organizations were allowed to monitor polls according to international norms (BBC News 2005c). While some criticisms were reported regarding election-day practices, few compared to Egypt's brutal treatment of voters and widespread fraud, although the fact that women were banned from voting virtually eliminated any democratic legitimacy that may have been gained from holding elections. Many proreformers were jailed prior to the elections (MacFarquhar 2005; BBC News 2005b). The exercise confirmed the view that low-level municipal elections were little more than a ruse to placate U.S. political leaders pressuring Riyadh for democratic reform.

Egregious human rights violations continue to occur in Saudi Arabia. Hundreds of arrests of suspected religious activists and government critics are reported to have been carried out, often on persons who have no terrorist links and are essentially being held as political prisoners (Amnesty International 2002). They remain in custody without formal charges being filed against them nor are they afforded speedy trials to determine their fate. Torture of men and women prisoners, flogging of children, and public executions continue in the post-9/11 era. Like Egypt, Saudi Arabia has finessed U.S. demands for reform, eliminating the possibility of any serious threat of U.S. action against Saudi Arabia for not falling in line with the Bush Doctrine. There is little fear in Riyadh of "being next" on Washington's hit list of regimes earmarked to undergo revolutionary democratic changes to suit U.S. political ideals. The Bush administration also missed a chance to push its program of reform with the death of King Fahd in August

2005. The installment of new leadership in King Abdullah opened a small window of opportunity for change that the United States could have taken advantage of but didn't (MSNBC 2005).

The August 2003 withdrawal of most U.S. forces was a welcome event inside Saudi Arabian borders and alleviated public pressure within it over the presence of U.S. troops on Saudi soil. Still, if the U.S. democratic experiment in Iraq succeeds, Saudi Arabia then has to worry about the potential of democracy spreading within its own borders. On the other hand, Saudi Arabia has real fears of a deteriorating situation to its north. If the situation in Iraq fails, then ensuing chaos and civil war invites domestic upheaval and foreign intervention, notably from rival, Shiite-dominated Iran. Saudi Arabia would need to worry about a potential Shiite alliance between Iraq and Iran. Such an alliance would give Iran unfettered access to Muslim holy sites within Iraq and allow it to vie for a greater role in Islamic leadership. A large Shiite community, geographically situated athwart some of Saudia Arabia's largest oil reserves, adds to Western and Saudi concerns.

Iraq and Iran

Immediately following 9/11 Iraq became one of two focal points in the war on terrorism. Afghanistan was the other. Following the successful campaign in Afghanistan to unseat the Taliban, the Bush administration launched a campaign to convince the Americans and international public opinion that the Hussein regime was at the cusp of producing nuclear weapons and had close links to al Qaeda. The dual threat of nuclear weapons and those weapons falling into the hands of terrorists proved a volatile cocktail, a mix that justified preemptive war against Iraq and forceful regime change. The American campaign placed Saddam Hussein on the defensive. He perversely pursued a self-defeating strategy of defiance to U.S. pressures seeking open inspection of possible sites producing weapons of mass destruction (WMD) although none existed, a self-destructive strategy that fueled fears that the Hussein regime might well be building such weapons and, worse, have links to the terrorists implicated in the 9/11 attack.

The U.S. military easily defeated the Iraqi military in the spring of 2003 and subsequently dismantled the Hussein regime. The conventional war quickly morphed into an unexpected and prolonged insurgency that at this writing is progressively eroding into a full-scale civil war. The principal beneficiaries of the American invasion have been Iran and its Shiite allies in Iraq. The United States removed its principal regional rival, Saddam Hussein, at no cost to Teheran, which appears to be actively seeking a nuclear weapons capability. The inconclusive Israeli–Hezbollah war of summer 2006 has further reinforced Iranian influence in the region. Anti-American sentiment is widespread, even among

Sunni governments allied with Washington. The Shiite-dominated Iraqi government, the product of general elections, resulted in the ironic outcome of more democracy in Iraq producing increased resistance to American policies and military presence in Iraq.

Iraq embodies Middle East fears of U.S. military power in the region. The war has been transformed into an intractable insurgency and may expand into a civil war that has the potential to become a regional conflict. Little can be written here regarding Iraq that has not already been contained within the pages of the hundreds of articles and books published since the beginning of the 2003 war. However, there are a few points worth underlining because of their important implications for regional stability. First, Iraq has become a test of the Bush Doctrine and of American aspirations in the Middle East, notably in its efforts to democratize the authoritarian states now ruling the region. Failure of the American intervention will arguably have a long-term negative impact on U.S. influence and interests and economic well-being. The erosion of American power is also likely to have a damaging effect on U.S. allies, Arab and Israeli, as Iran and Syria and Muslim extremists gain the upper hand in shaping the region to their liking.

Second, it is also important to remember that Iraq has the second largest oil reserves in the world. The importance of reliable, accessible, and affordable oil to fuel the U.S. and Western economies prompts many in the Arab world, including Iran, to conclude that the 2003 war was not just about terrorism. The war reinforces the widely held view that the central issue of the U.S. invasion was the control of Iraqi oil, since it has been proven that there were no ties between the Saddam Hussein regime and terrorist organizations. The new Iraqi constitution, guided by the strong hand of Paul Bremer's Coalition Provisional Authority (CPA), allows a major role for foreign oil companies, giving them the chance to exploit Iraqi oil. These concessions further confirm suspicions that the war was fought for oil[7] (Rubin 2003). Skepticism is deepened by the secrecy surrounding the U.S. Energy Task Force, by its continued reliance on Middle East oil despite the deteriorating situation in Iraq, and U.S. Agency for International Development (USAID) reports of favorable contracts being given to U.S. corporations to ensure American energy security (Muttitt 2005). According to one USAID report, "Using some form of [production sharing agreement] with a competitive rate of return has proved the most successful way to attract [international oil company] investment to expand oil productive capacity significantly and quickly" (BearingPoint 2003, 50). Such reports and the fact that many Iraqis still lack basic services only serves to fuel the insurgency and bolster beliefs that the United States seeks to use its military might in conjunction with calls for regime change and democratic reforms to ensure access to Middle East oil (Pickering, Schlesinger, and Schwartz 2005, 160–61).

Third, the initial euphoria experienced by most Iraqis with the overthrow of the Hussein regime quickly gave way to anguish and resentment over the occupation of their country by a non-Muslim, Western power. The insurgency that ensued in the wake of the cessation of "major combat operations" has claimed thousands more lives than the war itself. If Iraq was not a terrorist recruiting ground before, it certainly is now. Whereas the Hussein regime discouraged terrorists from operating within Iraq, the democratically elected Iraqi government has been helpless to prevent Iraq from becoming a breeding ground for foreign and domestic terrorists and sectarian militias able to operate freely with fatal consequences for the vulnerable populations on whom they prey.

While the insurgent forces were initially small, consisting mostly of the remaining Iraqi Republican Guard, some Hussein loyalists, and some foreign fighters, insurgent forces grew exponentially in the years following the war. One major contributor to the size of the insurgency was the decision of CPA administrator L. Paul Bremer to disband the entire four-hundred-thousand-plus Iraqi military with almost no benefits rather than retain and retrain them to form the initial new Iraqi military force. Regular military and junior officers were to get one month's severance pay, while senior officers were summarily dismissed with no severance. Another fifty thousand plus Baathists were banned from all future government activity (L. Diamond 2005, 35).

Despite warnings of a serious backlash, Bremer and the Bush administration dismantled the Iraqi security system. As one U.S. official remarked, "that week we made 450,000 enemies on the ground in Iraq" (Rieff 2003, 72). In that time, the insurgency expanded from a small number of hardcore loyalists to thousands of angry, trained, but unemployed, military personnel determined to undermine the American occupation and efforts to install an effective and freely elected central government. Many in the region see the insurgent war and rising civil war in Iraq as destabilizing forces; they fear the failure of the Iraqi experiment may well turn into a larger, regional conflict and lead, ironically, to a true terrorist state. Spreading democracy may have the unwitting effect of overturning dictatorial regimes, uneasily allied with the United States, and of ushering in populist and radical Islamist regimes, like Hamas and Hezbollah, inimical to American interests and values.

Fourth, the escalating civil war and lack of legitimate rule in Iraq have created an enlarging power vacuum in the region. Many fear the growing power of Iran, bolstered by the stalemate war between Israel and Hezbollah, which acted as the surrogate of the Lebanese government. The elected Iraqi government, dominated by the Shiites, is more sympathetic to Tehran than Washington, as evidenced by the support of its partisans for Hezbollah and their vocal opposition and mass demonstrations against the United States and Israel. The balance of power between Iraq and Iran has tilted decisively in Iran's favor, an outcome quite the reverse of Bush Doctrine aims and expectations. Informed observers expect an Iraqi-Iranian Shiite alliance in the event of a U.S. withdrawal. There is now a distinct possibility of an Iraqi civil war among the Kurdish north, the Sunni center, and the Shiite south. Such a war would almost certainly incite foreign intervention and become a regional conflagration. It is no secret that the Iraqi Kurds in the north wish to establish an independent Kurdistan. The Iraqi election results in 2005 revealed the ethno-religious divisions of the country, evidencing how prone to civil war Iraq would be should the United States precipitously withdraw.[8]

If the U.S. plan for democracy in Iraq fails, others in the region are not likely to continue with reforms, however tentative and feeble their form at present. Conditions in Iraq have not improved under U.S. occupation and human rights violations are mounting, according to multiple reports. Kidnappings and civilian killings are daily occurrences; water and electricity are sporadic at best; and multiplying instances of torture at the hands of insurgents [as well as the United States] have gravely disrupted normal life and impeded, or even often eroded, recovery efforts (CNN.com 2006). Continued unrest in Iraq has exposed the region to threats from Iran, which has been engaging in nuclear activity, and increasingly hostile anti-Western commentary. The United States has tacitly recognized the security threat the Iranian nuclear program poses and has modified its original unilateral approach, pursuing instead multilateral cooperation with allies in Europe, as well as Russia, and China.

Conclusions

This chapter has sketched in broad strokes the responses of major Middle Eastern states to U.S. policy and military doctrine. Perceptions in the Middle East are that the United States is a highly aggressive and threatening state and that aggression is directed at the Islamic world in response to the September 11, 2001, World Trade Center and Pentagon attacks. The close U.S.–Israeli relationship continues to strain U.S. relations with its Middle East Arab allies. It has seriously damaged its role as an honest broker in siding with little or no effective qualification of Israel's coercive policies to suppress Palestinian and Hezbollah terrorism. Recent fighting in Gaza (July 2006) and the new cross-border conflict between Israel and Hezbollah have reinforced the perception in the Arab streets that the United States, and Israel as its proxy, are the principal destabilizing forces in the region and the central obstacle to the realization of Arab political aims. This incendiary mix has now been made even more volatile with election of President Mahmoud Ahmadenijad in Iran. His denial of the Holocaust, calls for the elimination of Israel, and pursuit of nuclear power and, presumably, nuclear weapons make the Middle East ripe for civil and interstate wars on terms that do not favor U.S. military might, as the failure of the occupation to stanch the Iraqi insurgency abundantly demonstrates.

Much of the response of U.S. Arab allies in the region has been an effort to appease the Bush administration's demands for democratic reforms while at the same time continuing to oppress their populations and intimidate and incarcerate, even murder, their opponents. The result has been an increase in human rights abuses in states like Egypt and a tightening of authoritarian rule in Saudi Arabia. In Iraq, the elected government has been unable to control the level of violence that is greater at this writing than at any time since the American intervention in 2003. Its preference for Tehran over Washington is as palpable as it is unnerving to American officials who expected at least some thanks for having toppled Saddam Hussein and for having brought the Shiites to power. Iran and Syria have until now been the big winners in the struggle to define order in the Middle East. Israel as the only true democracy in the region battles opponents on all fronts and is unable either to deter or put a quick end to attacks on its citizens and cities. Israel's policy of trading land for peace, linked to its withdrawal from Lebanon and Gaza and its call for a two-state solution to the Palestine question, is a shambles. A divided Israeli population, pondering the failure to disarm Hezbollah and to achieve its announced objectives in attacking Lebanon, have never been more embattled nor bereft of a strategy that could ensure without serious qualification the security of the Israeli state and people. Israel's increased vulnerability underlines the failure of American policy and the Bush Doctrine in the Middle East.

The Middle East will continue to be unstable for the foreseeable future. The existence of the Israeli state is only part of the source of conflict. U.S. Arab allies sit on volcanic forces, and pawing efforts at democratization have only served to further undermine their legitimacy and power to rule. Muslims are now engaged in a long-term struggle to define the path that the region will take: whether toward modernization and harmony — which is not, frankly, very likely — or toward internal Muslim sectarian war in which intracommunal struggles like those of the Shiite and Sunni militias in Iraq will dominate. In this inflamed setting, the traditional struggles for power of the principal regional states, with a rising Iran in the forefront, will ensure sustained and lethal conflict. And lurking in the wings to fuel these flames is the spread of nihilistic terrorist groups, decentralized, self-styled, and bent on their own destruction and that of their victims. The United States evidences limited power to control these forces. Indeed, it appears more led by them than leading them.

Notes

1. Testimony of Andrew Natsios before the Senate Appropriations Committee, Subcommittee on Foreign Operations, May 8, 2001, http://www.usaid.gov/press/spe_test/testimony/2001/ty010508.html.

2. *New York Times*, November 21, 2006.

3. "Bleak Future for Palestinians," *Mideast Mirror*, May 18, 2005.

4. There were still reports of widespread election violations, including the use of police to block polling stations and physically abuse voters.

5. In August 2003 the United States withdrew nearly all of its military forces from Saudi Arabia.

6. The remaining municipal assembly seats were appointed by the government.

7. See http://www.geocities.com/nathanbrown1/interimiraqiconstitution.html.

8. Iraq is 65 percent Shiite and 20 percent Kurdish; Sunnis boycotted the 2005 election (CIA *World Factbook* 2005, https://www.cia.gov/cia/download2005.htm, and Electionworld, http://www.electionworld.org/iraq.htm).

CHAPTER TWELVE

Sub-Saharan Africa

Kevin C. Dunn

Presidential candidate George W. Bush infamously quipped that the United States had no vital interests in Africa. During its first eight months the Bush administration paid very little direct attention to the African continent. In keeping with the long-standing tradition of U.S.–African engagement, senior policy makers treated the continent as marginal at best, while mid- and lower-level bureaucrats shaped and implemented various policies (Schraeder 1994). But in the wake of September 11 and the declaration of the Bush Doctrine, Africa seems to have achieved a relatively more pronounced place in the worldview of Bush and his administration. This chapter investigates the ways in which Africa currently fits into the Bush administration's global vision and how African governments have navigated the various expressions of American power.

At the outset it should be stressed that the United States is not a unified actor, but speaks to African governments with multiple voices. Primary among those voices are the White House, the State Department, the Pentagon, the U.S. Agency for International Development (USAID), which sometimes speaks with a voice distinct from State, the Commerce Department, particularly working through the World Bank and the International Monetary Fund (IMF), and private economic and humanitarian aid actors. The multiplicity of actors often means that the United States engages with the African continent in varied and, at times, conflictual ways. It also means that there are multiple avenues for the exercise and manifestation of U.S. power and hegemony.

In this chapter I understand the concept of hegemony to refer to not only coercive and consensual expressions of power but also the ability to create and shape dominant discourses. As Badredine Arfi notes in his chapter on North Africa, a major element of American hegemony under the George W. Bush administration is its ability to articulate and circulate a dominant discourse — *the global war on terror* — that frames conversations and practices within world politics. This new discourse in world politics, one of the primary components of the Bush Doctrine, provides a frame for how the United States engages with African states and societies. Africa appears on the American agenda in four ways: as a potential battlefield in its global war on terror; as an alternative oil producer to the Middle East; as a potential beneficiary of the liberal peace agenda, which incorporates both democratization and economic neoliberalism; and as a recipient of humanitarian aid, in particular, assistance for managing the AIDS crisis. In the second section of the chapter I examine the ways in which African political elites have responded to American foreign policy under Bush. Admittedly, generalizing across the entire African continent is largely a futile exercise, given that it will inevitably raise more questions than answers. But such are the pitfalls of a venture as this one.

U.S. Interests in Africa

In his discussion of U.S. cold war foreign policy toward Africa, Peter Schraeder (1994, 2) claims that American policy makers "tended to ignore the African continent until some sort of politico-military crisis grab[bed] their attention." But one should be careful not to overstate the case. The United States was kept occupied with maintaining African cold war allies like Mobutu Sese Seko in Zaire and with trying to undermine Marxist–Leninist regimes in places like Angola and Mozambique as well as with managing the devastating impacts of Structural Adjustment Programs (SAPs) imposed on much of the continent by American-directed International Financial Institutions (IFIs) and the more complex effects of American private economic actors, particularly regarding commodities like oil, gold, diamonds, coffee, and tea.

With the end of the cold war it seemed as if the African continent slipped further off the agenda of American senior policy makers. The formal apparatus of American power seemed less interested in Africa, but private economic actors remained active on the continent as emerging markets in minerals like coltan joined long-standing interests in oil and diamonds. As a result of the ideological shift caused by the 1994 Republican Revolution, USAID and the State Department became less engaged with Africa than they had been during the cold war. Cold war allies, such as Mobutu in Zaire and Jonas Savimbi in Angola, lost favor in Washington and were left to suffer the consequences of their actions alone. After a perceived disastrous defeat in Somalia the United States swore off direct military engagement with the continent, turning a blind eye to horrifying post–cold war political catastrophes, such as the 1994 Rwandan genocide, as well as the slow implosion of the former Zaire and the subsequent civil war in the renamed Democratic Republic of Congo, which has claimed more than four million lives since the 1990s.

The presidency of George W. Bush initially seemed to offer Africans very little. Salih Booker (2001) argued that the Bush administration was "bad news for Africa" because of its benign neglect, misguided priorities, and failure to address the root causes of Africa's problems. But the events of 9/11 affected the relationship between the United States and Africa. Or, more to the point, Africa became a more pronounced feature in the rhetoric of the Bush administration's foreign policies. The 2002 *National Security Strategy* contained a full two pages relating directly to Africa. Within this articulation of the Bush administration's foreign policy vision for the future, the United States dedicated itself to promoting "liberty, peace, and growing prosperity" by working with European allies to "help strengthen Africa's fragile states, help build indigenous capability to secure porous borders, and help build up the law enforcement and intelligence infrastructures to deny havens for terrorists" (U.S. White House, Office of the President 2002, 9).

Importantly, where the rest of the *National Security Strategy* downplayed the importance of multilateral institutions and approaches, the section on Africa expressly championed working with others. The report claimed that the Bush administration would employ three "interlocking" strategies in its policy toward the region: that of working with regional powers like South Africa, Nigeria, Kenya, and Ethiopia, coordinating with "European allies and international institutions" for conflict mediation and peace operations, and strengthening "Africa's capable reforming states and sub-regional organizations" (U.S. White House, Office of the President 2002, 10). Informing the Bush administration's engagement with Africa was a continued commitment to the liberal peace agenda — the belief that liberal democracies and free-market economies would provide peace, stability, and development for all. As the report stated, "ultimately the path of political and economic freedom presents the surest route to progress in Sub-Saharan Africa, where most wars are conflicts over material resources and political access" and are "often tragically waged on the basis of ethnic and religious difference" (U.S. White House, Office of the President 2002, 10).

Rhetorical flourishes of the Bush Doctrine aside, the Bush administration has four primary goals in Sub-Saharan Africa: combating terrorism, securing African oil and other material resources, fostering the liberal peace agenda, and combating AIDS. The degree to which each of these four goals is an actual priority for the Bush administration and the ways it has pursued them is discussed below. Part two of the chapter addresses how African states have responded to the Bush Doctrine and its policies.

Africa as a Potential Site for Terrorism

First and foremost, the Bush administration is concerned about Africa as a potential site for terrorism. Part of this concern is well founded. Three years before the events of 2001 terrorists bombed the U.S. embassies in Dar es Salaam and Nairobi, killing 224 (including 12 Americans) and injuring 4,574. The United

States is also concerned that African states will become a breeding ground for terrorists. For example, in her November 2001 testimony to the U.S. Congress, former Clinton assistant secretary of state for Africa Susan Rice stated that "Africa is unfortunately the world's soft underbelly for global terrorism" (House Committee 2001).

What makes Africa the supposed "soft underbelly" is the existence of weak states. As the 2002 *National Security Strategy* noted, "weak states . . . can pose as great a danger to our national interests as strong states. Poverty does not make poor people into terrorists and murderers. Yet poverty, weak institutions, and corruption can make weak states vulnerable to terrorist networks and drug cartels within their borders" (U.S. White House, Office of the President 2002, 2). This view was echoed by Gen. Jeffrey Kohler, director of plans and policy at U.S. European Command (which has responsibility for much of Africa), who stated, "what we don't want to see in Africa is another Afghanistan, a cancer growing in the middle of nowhere" (quoted in Mills 2004, 159).

For U.S. policy makers, Sub-Saharan Africa contains a potentially dangerous mixture of forces — weak and failing states, poverty, political repression and alienation, and social disintegration — that lends itself to radicalism and the emergence of terrorism. Indeed, in combating al Qaeda, the United States has become aware of the numerous ways that organization has already exploited the political and social crises that have gripped several African states. For example, al Qaeda reportedly worked with the governments of Burkina Faso and Liberia to buy diamonds from the rebels operating in Sierra Leone and Liberia during the civil wars that destroyed the region during the late 1990s. Moreover, there is evidence that al Qaeda marketed gems through East African networks and has been taking advantage of the ongoing war in the Democratic Republic of Congo (Lyman and Morrison 2004, 83–84).

In responding to these concerns the United States has focused primarily on the Horn of Africa because of the Horn's proximity to the Middle East, its predominant Muslim population (Africa has 250 million Muslims, compromising 40 percent of the continent's population), and the fact that Somalia has long been regarded as the poster child for failed states. For these reasons, the Bush administration — particularly the Pentagon — has designated the greater Horn of Africa as part of the front line in its global war against terrorism. There was concern that al Qaeda would relocate to Somalia after the collapse of the Taliban in Afghanistan. This did not occur, but the Bush administration continues to watch closely activities in Somalia and throughout the region in general. While analysts have no doubt that terrorist and extremist groups are present in Somalia, it is unclear how strong and numerous they actually are, given the complexity of Somalia's political fragmentation.

Evidence of Africa's more pronounced place (at least rhetorically) on the U.S. foreign policy agenda came in 2003 with President Bush's visit to Africa. In July the president paid visits to Senegal, South Africa, Botswana, Uganda, and Nigeria. Visits by sitting American presidents to Africa are very rare occurrences, and Bush's trip made him the first sitting Republican president to undertake the trip. As Greg Mills rightly observes, it is doubtful that Bush would have ever visited Africa had it not been for September 11: "At the very least, the September 11 attacks added urgency to his visit" (Mills 2004, 158).

In 2003 President Bush also announced a $100 million commitment to help fight terrorism in Africa. Some justifiably scoffed at the insignificance of this amount. But the Bush administration has increased the level of American military engagement in Africa, the cornerstone of which is the Horn of Africa, again largely because of its proximity to the greater Middle East, the focal point of U.S. geopolitical strategy (see Bacevich 2005, esp. chapter 7). The U.S. military's involvement in the Horn is primarily coordinated through the Combined Joint Task Force–Horn of Africa (CJTF-HOA) program. The CJTF-HOA covers the airspace and land of Djibouti, Ethiopia, Eritrea, Kenya, Somalia, Sudan, Tanzania, Uganda and Yemen as well as the coastal waters of those countries in the Horn that border the Red Sea, the Gulf of Aden, and the Indian Ocean. At the center of this presence is Camp Lemonier in Djibouti, which by the spring of 2004 was home to over eighteen hundred U.S. personnel. Camp Lemonier is the only true military base that the United States maintains on the African continent, but in 2004 it established a "forward base" called Camp United in Ethiopia near Hurso.

CJTF-HOA is part of an overarching diplomatic/military program, one aspect of which is the working with and training of the militaries of the Horn and East Africa. Brig. Gen. Samuel Helland, commander of CJTF-HOA, was quoted in an AP interview as saying that "we've got forces now in almost every country and we've got representation in every country" except Somalia. He observed that the U.S. task force was averaging one civilian-military operation every three days to promote antiterrorist cooperation (quoted in Grey 2006, 128). The Pentagon has made similar arrangements with the militaries in North Africa, West Africa, and the Sahel, focused primarily on providing training to military personnel in these areas but also arms and supplies (Grey 2006, 130). There have been prospects initiated to establish a base similar to CJTF-HOA in West Africa, possibly in Nigeria. Meanwhile, the Pentagon has identified several key African countries where austere camps or airfields could be established to which Europe-based U.S. troops would rotate, greatly improving the U.S. military's ability to deploy quickly into African trouble spots (Mills 2004, 164). There are also reports of interest in a U.S. naval base in the Gulf of Guinea and on the southern tip of South Africa (Hentz 2004, 23–24). In 2002 the African Crisis Response Initiative (ACRI) was replaced by the African Contingency Operations Training and Assistance (ACOTA) program, which trains special military units from several African states as well as provides arms and equipment to these forces. While these programs are limited and relatively minimal, they have impacted the military landscape in Africa, reflecting a greater reliance among African militaries on American training and equipment. In a major development, in February 2007, President Bush approved a Pentagon plan for a new command center in Africa (to be known as AFRICOM) to oversee U.S. military activities on the continent, which should be in place by the end of 2008 (currently responsibility for the continent is divided among three other regional commands: European, Central, and Pacific).

African Oil and Other Resources

On September 19, 2002, the *Washington Post* observed: "Africa, the neglected stepchild of American diplomacy, is rising in strategic importance to Washington policy makers, and one word sums up the reason — oil" (quoted in Hentz 2004, 23). There are substantial reserves of oil in Nigeria and Angola, which to date make up around 15 to 16 percent of America's imports. This is a relatively small amount when compared to the imports coming from the Middle East, but Nigerian and Angolan oil exports to the United States are growing significantly. Further, the United States hopes to double its imports of Nigerian oil from 900,000 barrels per day to around 1.8 million barrels daily in the next five years.

There have also been recent discoveries of substantial oilfields from Equatorial Guinea in the Gulf of Guinea through Chad and into Sudan. These oil reserves offer the United States an attractive alternative to Middle East oil. As Lyman and Morrison (2004, 83) observe, "in the past decade, new discoveries of oil off the coast of West Africa have more than doubled estimates of the region's reserves to more than 60 billion barrels. By 2015, West Africa may provide a quarter of U.S. oil and is likely to acquire an increasingly high strategic profile. The region is home to almost 130 million Muslims, yet it exhibits little grass-roots support for terrorism." Indeed, it is estimated that in the coming decade Africa is expected to supply as much as 25 percent of U.S. oil imports, becoming the United States' second-most important supplier of oil, and possibly natural gas, after the Middle East (Abramovici 2004; Hentz 2004, 23–24; Volman 2003).

The rising importance of African oil has shaped America's strategic engagement with the continent. The proposed U.S. naval bases in the Gulf of Guinea and on the southern tip of South Africa reflect an American desire to secure an uninterrupted flow of African oil. Strategic thinking focuses on the Chad–Cameroon pipeline, the Higleig–Port Sudan pipeline, and a proposed Chad–

Sudan pipeline. Indeed, desire for access to Sudanese oil has impacted America's relationship with the Islamist regime in Khartoum. Once a major adversary of the government, even supporting the rebels in the south during the Sudan's long civil war, Washington has dramatically increased its interaction with Khartoum. The United States was directly involved in negotiating a temporary halt to the long-running civil war in the south. As Gerard Prunier (2005, 89) notes, the main factor pushing the Khartoum government in the peace process was American pressure rather than "any inner conviction that peace should actually be negotiated." But the Bush administration's closer connection with the Sudanese government has meant that the United States has been notably muted in its response to the violence in Darfur and Khartoum's horrendous human rights record.

The United States has not focused its attention exclusively on African oil but also on the continent's natural gas reserves, its diamonds, and its metal resources — including manganese, cobalt and chrome vital for alloys, vanadium, coltan, gold, antimony, fluorspar, and germanium (see Abramovici 2004). The primary focus, however, is African oil. As Assistant Secretary of Defense for African Affairs Walter Kansteiner declared in 2002: "African oil is of strategic national interest to us" (quoted in Grey 2006, 131).

Africa and the Liberal Peace Agenda

According to the Bush Doctrine, American interest in Africa is also motivated by a desire to foster a "liberal peace." In Africa, as elsewhere, such a project is theoretically a two-pronged affair: spreading liberal democracy and encouraging free-market capitalism via economic neoliberalization. With regard to the latter goal, the 2002 *National Security Strategy* pronounces "the United States will stand beside any nation determined to build a better future by seeking the rewards of liberty for its people. Free trade and free markets have proven their ability to lift whole societies out of poverty — so the United States will work with individual nations, entire regions, and the entire global trading community to build a world that trades in freedom and therefore grows in prosperity" (U.S. White House, Office of the President 2002, 2). Elsewhere in the document the claim is made that "including all of the world's poor in an expanding circle of development — and opportunity — is a moral imperative and one of the top priorities of U.S. international policy" (U.S. White House, Office of the President 2002, 16–17).

Yet, the White House has seemingly done very little to meet the goals set by its rhetoric. Under President Bill Clinton the primary focus of U.S.–African relations was the creation of the African Growth and Opportunity Act (AGOA), which claimed to give African products greater access to the U.S. market. President Bush pledged to continue that policy, signing the AGOA Acceleration Act in July 2004, although the utility and success of AGOA remains questionable (Adebajo

2003). Bush also pledged his support for the Millennium Challenge Account (MCA), an initiative to distribute aid to those states pursuing economic neoliberal policies. Yet, in 2004 Bush asked for only $1.3 billion for the MCA, $300 million less than originally promised (Booker, Minter, and Colgan 2003, 198). With regard to encouraging African development, the Bush administration has also heralded the work of New Partnership for Africa's Development (NEPAD), ostensibly an African partnership to combat the sources of poverty and create a new aid/development regime for the continent but more accurately regarded as a self-imposed structural adjustment program with questionable chances for success (see Taylor 2005).

While heralding its support for these initiatives, the United States has also pursued unilateral engagement with African governments on issues of trade and aid. The Bush administration's proclivity for unilateral action has meant that it has minimized America's traditional participation in multilateral efforts for dealing with the continent's development issues. This unilateral approach has also meant that each African government has had to compete with other African governments in negotiating its relationship with Washington and its access to resources and trade concessions (Booker, Minter, and Colgan 2003, 198). Yet, perhaps ironically, U.S. economic power is best expressed through and its economic interests still best realized through multilateral international financial institutions (IFIs), such as the World Bank and the IMF. As James Hentz (2004, 30) has correctly observed, "IFIs continue to be an important proxy for U.S. interests in Africa." It is through the IFIs and their structural adjustment programs that American power continues to be exerted upon African political elites to open their markets, cut back on social programs, privatize public services and goods, and facilitate the integration of local economies into the global capitalist system, often at debilitating costs to the average African.

With regard to the second aspect of establishing a "liberal peace"—promoting liberal democracies—the Bush administration also seems prone to making grand rhetorical pronouncements on which it has made no move to act. The 2002 *National Security Strategy* claims "the United States will use this moment of opportunity to extend the benefits of freedom across the globe. We will actively work to bring the hope of democracy, development, free markets, and free trade to every corner of the world" and spreading democracy is framed in terms of promoting trade and development (U.S. White House, Office of the President 2002, 2). In practice, however, the U.S. engagement with democratization is driven by self-interested political consideration, echoing its cold war disregard for African interests and grassroots struggles. As Robert Grey notes, "the United States has not seemed to make a major bilateral commitment to promoting African democratization. Moreover, America's limited commitment to African democratization began to clash with what were increasingly seen as intense and growing American strategic concerns, the war on terrorism and access to African oil" (Grey 2006, 124). Thus, while African economies continue to be restructured along the lines dictated by global capitalism, Washington's support for democratization has been mostly empty rhetoric.

Combating AIDS in Africa

According to the Bush administration, its fourth goal with regard to Africa is combating AIDS. As the 2002 *National Security Strategy* states, "We will also continue to lead the world in efforts to reduce the terrible toll of AIDS and other infectious diseases" (U.S. White House, Office of the President 2002, 2). Yet, like its commitment to democratization in Africa, the Bush administration's actions have fallen far short of its rhetoric. For example, the Bush administration has failed to deliver the financial assistance it promised so that the Global Fund to Fight AIDS, Tuberculosis, and Malaria received only a fraction of the resources needed. In February 2003 the White House attempted to thwart a move by Congress to provide an additional $150 million from the budget for this fund (Booker, Minter, and Colgan 2003, 197).

In a much-heralded move the Bush administration pledged $10 billion in 2003 for new "emergency" funds to fight AIDS in Africa. Yet, although the Bush administration promised that the additional funds were for Africa, the budget proposal actually counted all the money spent worldwide for HIV/AIDS toward that pledge (Adebajo 2003, 183), so that the United States was not in fact supplying more money. Further, part of the funding it did provide came from cutting nearly $500 million from international child health programs (Booker, Minter, and Colgan 2003, 197).

U.S. efforts to combat HIV/AIDS were further stymied by congressional interference. According to a mandate from Congress at least a third of U.S. money to prevent the spread of AIDS worldwide must be devoted to sexual abstinence and fidelity programs. Yet, according to the U.S. Government Accountability Office this ideologically based insistence by Republican congressional leaders is actually undercutting comprehensive and widely accepted aid models, further exacerbating the struggle to combat HIV/AIDS (Dugger 2006). Thus, U.S. efforts to combat AIDS in Africa have been undercut by underfunded promises and the enforcement of policies that may have made the situation worse.

African Responses to American Power

This section examines the numerous ways African governments have negotiated American power as exercised within the context of the Bush Doctrine. As always, it is hard to generalize about the behavior of several dozen governments, particularly when American power is expressed and employed in multiple dimensions, from military initiatives of the Pentagon to White House pronouncements to economic conditionalities enforced via international financial institutions. When encountering American power African political elites employ a wide array of strategies, suggesting that there exists a continuum between bandwagoning and balancing (see Walt 1987) rather than a stark dichotomy. As the following discussion illustrates, many African governments occupy a murky middle position, simultaneously bandwagoning while resisting and/or appropriating American power. Badredine Arfi's chapter on North Africa provides the theoretical lens for understanding this situation: the American discourse of the "global war on terror (GWOT)" is functioning both as a master signifier and an empty one. Thus, across Sub-Saharan Africa, as in North Africa, political elites often embrace the discourse while at the same time recast it for their own domestic purposes.

In expressing their support for American policies (and power), African political elites are generally driven by one or more of four possible motivations. First, many African governments are hoping to extract favors (such as increased aid, improved trading relations, and so forth) from the United States for their support. Second, several African governments are hoping that improved relations with the United States will help them navigate the regional insecurity complexes in which they find themselves. Third, a handful of African states hope to use closer ties with the United States to balance the continuing power and influence of their former European colonial powers. Finally, many states willingly embrace the Bush Doctrine and the GWOT in an attempt to redefine their own domestic conflicts within this new hegemonic discourse. In addition to embracing, exploiting, and appropriating the GWOT, some African states have also resisted expressions of American power for various reasons.

Embracing

While most African leaders expressed horror at the events of September 11, 2001, only a handful have openly embraced the Bush Doctrine and backed the U.S. invasions of Afghanistan and Iraq. Both Ethiopia and Eritrea were quick to join the "coalition of the willing" and supported the U.S. invasion of Iraq. Later both Uganda and Rwanda joined the coalition as well. In their own ways, both Sudan and Djibouti sought to ingratiate themselves with the Bush administration. In all, only seven African governments have formally joined the global war on terror (Djibouti, Egypt, Eritrea, Ethiopia, Kenya, Morocco, and Uganda). As of 2004 only five (Botswana, Ghana, Kenya, Mali, and Sudan) had signed all twelve international conventions and protocols relating to terrorism (Mills 2004, 163).

Cooperating with the United States offers the possibility of direct financial benefits for some African states. Perhaps the biggest beneficiary in these terms has been Djibouti, which currently hosts the only true U.S. base on the continent. In January 2003 Djibouti president Ismael Omar Guelleh was invited on a state visit to Washington during which Bush promised to reopen the USAID office in Djibouti and pledged eight million dollars in American education grants (Economist Intelligence Unit 2003, 41). This was a significant boost for the small, impoverished, but strategically located African country.

Other states have been able to increase the amount of military aid and assistance they receive by cooperating with the United States and its various antiterrorism initiatives. Reflecting the overarching concern of the United States for the geopolitical situation in the greater Middle East, most of these programs — and the African beneficiaries — have been located in East Africa and the Horn. For example, the Bush administration's East Africa Counter-Terrorism Initiative has provided Djibouti, Eritrea, Ethiopia, Kenya, Tanzania, and Uganda with important resources to improve their police and judicial capabilities. This program includes training and equipment for these countries as well as support for senior-level African decision makers to draft legislation on terrorist financing and money laundering (Mills 2004, 166). In June 2003 President Bush announced a $100 million package of counterterrorism measures to be spent in the Horn over fifteen months. Around $50 million was earmarked for coastal and border security programs to be administered by the U.S. Department of Defense, while $10 million was pledged to the Kenyan Anti-Terror Police Unit and around $14 million for Muslim education in an apparent "hearts and minds" campaign (Lyman and Morrison 2004, 77).

While the United States has mainly focused on East Africa and the Horn, other African governments have also profited from the increased military assistance that comes from working with the United States, such as the Nigerian military, which, significantly, has been a primary beneficiary. ACOTA, which provides military training and standardized attack equipment (such as assault rifles, machine guns and mortars), is linked to the training centers of the Joint Combined Arms Training System (JCATS). The first JCATS was opened in Abuja, in Nigeria, on November 25, 2003. Nigeria joins Canada as the only other country with JCATS software (Abramovici 2004).

In addition to ACOTA, over forty African militaries are also taking part in an officer training program called the International Military Education and Training (IMET) program, which provided training for more than fifteen hundred officers in 2002. Moreover, the Africa regional peacekeeping program provides training in offensive tactics and, more importantly, the transfer of military technology. In many ways these programs represent a return to cold war–era practices, according to which African political elites pledge support to the superpower in return for military assistance, training, and technology.

For these reasons almost all African leaders find it useful to cooperate with the Bush administration. In addition to whatever innate benefits these military links provide, such as helping to maintain the security of the existing regime, they are only one part of the complex web of connections between the United States and Africa. As noted at the outset, American power on the continent is expressed in multiple ways and through multiple channels. And as Robert Grey notes (2006, 130–31), "African leaders may perceive participation in these military programs as the price they must pay for continued American support of the other, nonmilitary programs."

Sudan represents an important example of an African government that has been able to parlay its support for the Bush administration into substantial assets. Long considered a threat to American interests in the region given the nature of the Islamist regime in Khartoum and its support for international terrorism, Sudan now enjoys a privileged position in the region. After the events of September 11, 2001, the Khartoum government decided to embrace the U.S. war on terror and moved to improve its relations with the United States, which was interested in reciprocating for reasons having to do with antiterrorism and oil. The Bashir government, with U.S. backing, moved to negotiate an end to the long-standing civil war in the south and also implemented various antiterrorist operations. The rapprochement had begun as early as 2000, with the commencement of an intensive counterterrorism dialogue between the two governments, but after September 11 the United States promised to improve relations further if Sudan cooperated fully and quickly, which it did. The conflict in the Darfur has threatened to further tarnish the Sudan's international reputation, but, significantly, Washington has been reluctant to punish Khartoum for its gross human rights record and continues to work for a resolution of the conflict that would largely benefit the Bashir regime. In fact, President Bush intervened in the peace negotiations, offering the rebel groups a personal guarantee that the plan would be implemented (BBC 2006). In the face of rising domestic pressure, Bush signed the Darfur Peace and Accountability Act, which imposes sanctions against individuals (as opposed to the Sudanese government) accused of genocide, freezing their assets and denying them entry to the United States. At the same time he appointed Andrew Natsios, the former head of USAID, to act as his special envoy to Sudan in September 2006.

Yet, as several East African countries learned, support for the Bush administration and its war on terror can come at a cost. In Kenya a Mombasa tourist hotel was attacked in November 2002, and an Israeli airliner narrowly escaped a terrorist's surface-to-air missile. Reflecting a growing belief that it was unsafe to travel to Africa, in 2003 the United States and United Kingdom both announced travel alerts for Kenya and Tanzania. On May 15, 2003, British Airways announced a travel ban to Kenya for security and safety reasons. Ironically, while the travel ban to Kenya was in effect, British Airways announced that it would be the first European airline to land in Baghdad, Iraq. The travel alerts proved highly damaging, undermining the recovery of the region's tourist trade. The Kenya Tourist Board reported that the country's tourist sector had lost more than $30 million due to the ban (*The Monitor* 2003). The bans also raised questions in Nairobi and Dar es Salaam over the wisdom of partnering with Washington (Lyman and Morrison 2004, 78).

Exploiting and Appropriating

Several African states have supported America's war on terror in hopes of enlisting the United States as an ally for their own purposes. Often, African political elites hope that by embracing American power they will find it easier to negotiate their own regional insecurity complexes. This can be most clearly seen in the cases of Ethiopia and Eritrea. The countries are locked in a seemingly intractable border dispute that has cost both dearly. As Grey (2006, 125) points out, both Ethiopia and Eritrea "seemed to think that its declaration of support might make America more sympathetic to its claim in their mutual border conflict." To that end Eritrea even went so far as to offer the United States the use of its Red Sea naval facilities. Neither country has been successful in drawing the United States into its camp over the border dispute. Or, perhaps more accurately, because they have both embraced American power, they have negated the other's "superpower trump card."

While some African governments have tried to use closer ties with the United States to strengthen their hand in regional politics, others have used closer ties to the United States as a way of decreasing their dependence on former colonial powers. This was a standard practice during the cold war. African governments would gravitate toward the United States or the Soviet Union in an attempt to counterbalance Europe's continuing influence. The Mobutu regime was quite adept at this, and its successors in the renamed Democratic Republic of Congo have continued the practice in the post–cold war era (see Dunn 2002 and 2003). Currently, it seems no state is having greater success with this move than Djibouti, which had long been regarded as part of France's traditional zone of influence, given the colonial ties and continuing French military presence. Having few, if any, valuable resources, the extremely poor country enjoys a significant strategic position, jutting out into the Red Sea where roughly a quarter of the world's oil production passes by. The influence that France previously had over the country has been virtually eclipsed by that of the United States, the latter's permanent military base at Camp Lemonier greatly contributing to the power it wields there (Abramovici 2004). While the White House has often been reluctant to get pulled into regional power games or to step overtly on the toes of Europeans interested in maintaining their African zones of influence, the Pentagon continues to increase its level of engagement with African militaries. Thus, African militaries are working more closely with the United States than ever before — often more closely than are their statehouses.

Yet the U.S. "war on terror" has proved useful for African political elites, as they attempt to recast their own domestic conflicts within this new discursive framework. Terrorism, broadly conceived, has long been a tactic of African guerrilla armies, warlords, and repressive regimes. But those struggles, even during the cold war, were local and regional in nature, disconnected from global terrorist networks. With the Bush administration's declaration of war on "terror," several African governments have attempted to reframe their domestic problems as part of this internationally sanctioned struggle.

For example, Ugandan president Yoweri Museveni frequently situates his government's war with the Lord's Resistance Army (LRA) within the larger "war on terror" context. The war, which has virtually destroyed northern Uganda, has been waged for almost two decades, but the Museveni government has repeatedly sabotaged any attempts at diplomatically resolving the conflict, continuing to believe that the conflict can be won through military force. While there are certainly questions about whether or not the Museveni regime is really interested in resolving the conflict, framing the LRA war within the U.S.-sanctioned "war on terror" clearly enables Museveni to continue the military option while dismissing any and all peace initiatives (see Dunn 2004).

Museveni is not alone in trying to frame uprisings within the "war on terror" framework. Nor do he and other African political elites stop there. Museveni, like many other African leaders, has sought to appropriate the rhetoric and practices of America's "war on terror" as a means of dealing with their own domestic opposition. In the fall of 2005, Uganda's main opposition leader, Kizza Besigye, was arrested and charged with treason under post-2001 inspired antiterrorist legislation. Though he was eventually released and allowed to campaign (unsuccessfully) against Museveni, his arrest is one example of the growing militarization of Ugandan politics that is explicitly justified by the struggle against "terror."

Ethiopia and Eritrea, two other primary allies of the United States, have also used the rhetoric and practices of the U.S. "war on terror" to justify repressive measures against their domestic oppositions. The government of Eritrea, which has offered the United States two sites for military bases, has accused the exiled Alliance of Eritrean National Forces (AENF) dissidents of being connected to al Qaeda. The Ethiopian government has branded opposition members in Oromo as international terrorists and has arrested hundreds of opposition leaders on the grounds of combating "terrorism." Even then-exiled Liberian leader Charles Taylor appropriated the "war on terror" rhetoric. He established the Antiterror Unit (ATU) that rather ironically included former members of the Revolutionary United Front (RUF) in addition to his Liberia fighters. Taylor repeatedly referred to his domestic opponents as "terrorists" and justified the detention of dissidents by claiming they were "unlawful combatants" (Adebajo 2003, 181).

The ongoing power struggles in Somalia have also been shaped by these discursive opportunities. Political rivals attempt to portray each other as terrorists who may have ties to al Qaeda and Islamists. In an attempt to garner American support, opponents of the Somali Transitional National Government (TNG) initially claimed that it had strong links to terrorists and Islamic fundamentalist groups, a charge TNG officials denied (Maclean 2001). The situation became more complex when the Union of Islamic Courts (UIC), a group established by local businessmen to restore order, made rapid gains in 2006, eventually establishing complete control of Mogadishu. The UIC was a collection of numerous groups, including the remnants of al Ittihad, which neighboring Ethiopia has claimed was a terrorist organization. Despite the lack of concrete evidence connecting al Ittihad to Islamic terrorist groups like al Qaeda (see Dagne 2002, 67), the U.S. State Department placed the group on its terrorist list, assisted the Ethiopian military in its strikes against it, and aided and armed local warlords against it (Wax and DeYoung 2006). Al Ittihad was virtually defeated, but its forces have become a dominant element within the UIC, which is led by former al Ittihad leader Sheikh Hassan Dahir Aweys. After the success of the UIC, Ethiopia threw its support behind the TNG (who it had originally claimed was itself supported by terrorists and Islamic fundamentalist). Eritrea, Ethiopia's regional adversary, has responded by supporting the UIC and charging the TNG (and Ethiopia) with terrorist proclivities. At the end of 2006, Ethiopian forces joined the TNG to drive the UIC out of Mogadishu and surrounding areas. With the defeat of the Islamists, who brought calm and order to Mogadishu for the first time in over a decade, the capital has been plunged back into insecurity and violence.

The act of reframing domestic struggles within this new global discourse has been repeated across the continent, which points up a serious concern for observers of African politics, namely, that the "war on terror" will subsume all other issues, such as development, democracy, and human rights. Importantly, at a gathering of over one hundred African ministers at an AGOA forum — a group interested in trade and development — Condoleezza Rice focused on Africa's role in the American war on terror: "Africa's history and geography give it a pivotal role in the war on terrorism. Nevertheless, some Africans have expressed concerns that U.S. attention and resources devoted to Africa will be shorted in favor of the Middle East and South Asia. This should not be the case under any circumstances. Africa is critical to our war on terrorism" (quoted in Hentz 2004, 37). But James Hentz (2004, 38) correctly notes the irony here, namely, that the "problem now is not that Africa will be ignored, but rather that what attention it gets will be framed by the American 'war against terrorism.'" Certain African political elites make that possibility more likely by exploiting the various opportunities that the embrace and employment of this new framing discourse offers.

Resisting

African political elites have also engaged in open resistance to American power. For example, in the lead-up to the invasion of Iraq the three African states on the U.N. Security Council at that time, Guinea, Angola, and Cameroon, resisted intense American pressure, while other states worked actively to prevent the attack on Iraq. The African Union even produced a resolution opposing any decision to go to war against Iraq without U.N. authorization.

Some African political elites were quite outspoken in their opposition to the expression of American power. In January 2003 former South African president Nelson Mandela called on the world to "condemn both Blair and Bush and let them know in no uncertain terms that what they are doing is wrong." Mandela argued "what I am condemning is that one power, with a president who has no foresight, who cannot think properly, is now willing to plunge the world into a holocaust. Why does the United States behave so arrogantly? . . . Who are they now to pretend that they are the policeman of the world?" (Swarns 2003). Current South African president Thabo Mbeki also warned an African Union meeting that war in the Persian Gulf could trigger an economic meltdown in Africa and set development back more than three decades (Booker, Minter, and Colgan 2003, 196).

The South African case is an interesting one because of the concerted effort of the postapartheid governments to play a greater role in international affairs. They have sought to establish themselves not only as a stable regional power but also as an impartial international mediator and a champion for global development issues (Van der Westhuizen 1998). This has meant that they have explicitly refused to support actions that might make it seem like they are a proxy for other major powers, namely the United States. Publicly promoting multilateralism and critiquing the U.S. war in Iraq and other aspects of the Bush Doctrine, South Africa can be seen as directly countering U.S. power in an attempt to increase its global standing as an impartial and principled international power.

African political elites have also attempted to raise other issues within the American-authored "war on terror" discourse. Some have tried to restructure the discourse to include issues of development and social justice. Nelson Mandela has been prominent in this regard, suggesting that a war on terror needs to address the economic and social roots of terrorism. Other African leaders have also attempted to equate the war against terrorism primarily with the war to end poverty—sometimes in hopes of securing greater financial assistance from Western countries but mostly to appropriate the terror discourse for a development agenda. As Tanzanian president Benjamin Mkapa argued, "it is futile, if not foolhardy, to think there is no link between poverty and terrorism" (quoted in Mills 2004, 159–60).

African leaders have also been wary of engaging with the United States, given Washington's track record on the continent. Across the continent there remains a latent hostility to Western powers over colonial policies as well as over destructive postcolonial policies carried out during the cold war. As Greg Mills (2004, 162) notes, the situation "is further complicated in an environment where wars of liberation have left a certain residue of ambiguity about the distinction between terrorists and freedom fighters and a latent hostility toward the West over colonial and postcolonial policies."

Recent actions by the Bush administration in Africa have further undermined its ability to win the trust of African governments. In November 2001, the United States decided to freeze the assets of Somalia's largest financial company, al-Barakaat, because of its alleged association with al Qaeda. This move endangered the welfare of thousands of Somali families who were dependent on remittances from the Somalia diaspora that were transferred via al-Barakaat. The measure proved hugely damaging to the reputation of the United States in the Horn, precisely what the White House has been trying to avoid (Omaar 2004).

The administration fumbled again in 2003. Prior to Bush's visit to Africa significant pressure was mounting on the United States to do something to help resolve the destructive civil war ripping apart Liberia, historically an American protectorate / quasi colony. On the verge of his African tour Bush raised the possibility of American military intervention but then immediately backed away on his return to the United States. His bungling badly damaged U.S. credibility across the continent, suggesting that the United States was only interested in extracting what it wanted from Africa and was not prepared to get its hands dirty doing so (no matter to what extent it was complicit in the development of Africa's problems).

Conclusions

In conclusion, I would like to offer two observations. First, the current geopolitical situation in which African leaders find themselves is not that different from the cold war one. In the Bush administration's "war on terror" African allies are again protected and strengthened, regardless of their democratic credentials. African leaders can again exploit opportunities provided by the geopolitical concerns of the (now lone) superpower. Again, as was the case during the cold war, the goal for these elites is primarily securing and entrenching their own hold on power. And with the "war on terror" there is a renewed emphasis on confrontation with a global enemy, much like there was during the cold war. As Adekeye Adebajo (2003, 177) notes, "an important concern of America's post–cold war policy toward Africa is that a 'green menace' (the color of Islam) may be replacing the 'red peril' of the cold war." Again, the United States grants more prestige and resources to those it deems important and trusted allies in its global struggle, regardless of their domestic (il)legitimacy.

Second, despite its attempts to express its power in Africa and its strengthened ties to various African militaries, the United States is a limited hegemon at best, its ability to shape events in Africa being very much constrained. But with regard to the Bush Doctrine, there is an irony at work. The Bush Doctrine, in both word and deed, promotes American unilateralism over multilateral cooperation. Yet the United States is most effective in its ability to express its power in Africa when using multilateral institutions like the IMF and World Bank. This is the nature of hegemony; it works best when expressed as consensual power via multilateral institutions (see Gill 1993). Perhaps, ironically, the Bush Doctrine's strategy for expressing American power will have the unintended consequence of weakening that power. Undoubtedly, such a process will provide African political elites opportunities to further embrace, exploit, appropriate, and resist that power for their own ends.

|||||||||||||||||||||||||||||||||||||||
LATIN AMERICA

CHAPTER THIRTEEN

Latin America

Remonda B. Kleinberg

A symbol of often conflicting U.S. policy, Latin America continues to provide the test case of nations thriving (or not) under a hemispheric power that also remains the undisputed global hegemon. Clearly successful, if one looks at regional shifts to democratization and trade and economic deregulation and at the emergence not only of democratic grassroots movements but also of a rising middle class capable of shaping democracy in its own image. At odds with the transition toward "liberal institutionalism," however, are the enormous social gaps that persist throughout Central America and the Andean region. Indeed, there is growing discontent — discontent that has been historically stifled by the presence of authoritarian regimes and that has increased as the United States confronts a growing security dilemma on its own soil. Latin American governments and civil society have historically defined their relationship with the United States as one based on its meddling and intervention, and confrontational tactics. Resentment and opposition have often colored responses to the hemispheric giant, particularly throughout the cold war. But in the post-9/11 era, in the face of the expanding scope of U.S. national security and hegemony, Latin America appears to be waging a counterhegemonic backlash, clearly evident in the size and number of demonstrations greeting George W. Bush on his 2007 visit to the region.

Interestingly, alongside the consolidation of democratic institutions, economic reform policies, and free trade agreements, there has been a reemergence of populist ideologies guiding politics; or perhaps it is because of these factors that a string of left-leaning politicians have taken office in Chile, Bolivia, Peru, Venezuela, Argentina, Uruguay and Brazil. Although highly polarized during the 2005 presidential elections, Mexico has an equally strong contender from the Left. Some have suggested that South America, in particular, is moving to the democratic Left, as a new generation of leaders vent opposition to both security and economic policies backed by the George W. Bush administration. Indeed, throughout the region, grassroots movements, opposition leaders, and governments themselves are seemingly rejecting U.S. leadership, and there is an emerging consensus that U.S. hegemony is not benevolent but rather malevolent.

Clearly a new wave of rebellion and reformism is tightly gripping Latin America and the Caribbean. The election of indigenous farmer Evo Morales as president of Bolivia on December 18, 2005, reflects this wave, particularly as it mobilizes the poor and the historically disenfranchised and excluded groups in regional politics. And so did the kidnappings and assassinations that drove pre-election Haiti into panic and chaos — its then-interim government paralyzed to stop it, and the U.S.-supported democracy-building group nowhere to be found, its strategy clearly a failure. Campaign politics and their aftermath in Mexico have clearly shown an increasing polarization between the Left and the Right, intensifying social unrest and threatening newly consolidated, but fragile, democratic institutions (Council on Hemispheric Affairs 2006a).

The trend is visible and potent, the questions — and the answers — as to why are not. Is the resurgence of resistance and a shift to the left in domestic politics a response to the wider and more intense reach of a so-called malevolent hegemon? Or is it a response to the consolidation of democratic institutions and the impact of domestic reform policies, most of which were implemented in the 1980s and 1990s?

A "Limited" Hegemon and Democratic Peace Theory

Latin America has been subjected to American hegemonic influence, containment strategies, and attempts to impose stability longer than any other region on the planet, and at a great cost socially and politically. Contradictory cold war policies often guided U.S. political and economic strategies, risking long-term damage to U.S.–Latin American relations and stunting social progress. To be sure, engagement and confrontation reflected the delicate balance that strained hemispheric relations throughout the cold war era — and to some extent beyond. At the same time, the effects of colonialism, Fascism, and Communism in the region have been defeated, and the largest ongoing challenge remains economic instability, which has mobilized several governments to adopt reform policies with mixed results, particularly since the Free Trade Area of the Americas (FTAA) remains dormant.

But, while the United States remains unrivaled in its power capabilities, hegemony, in the author's view, is limited under the present administration. In essence, a limited hegemon is one that has (undisputed) global power and influence but cannot exert its will in all endeavors. The limited hegemon must pursue alliances, out of both practical necessity and for purposes of securing credibility; this applies to both economic and military aspects of policy. That the United States is not the global hegemon — or, "Empire," that some have made it out to be — is also demonstrated in the lack, as Robert Kagan (1998) has pointed out, of any of the balancing behavior that international relations theory predicts would be undertaken by all the other global powers to counter the hegemon. There can be only two explanations for this. Either the United States is less of a threat to the other major actors than they are to each other—an implicit vote for democratic peace theory (DPT)—or the United States simply isn't the global empire that critics claim it to be.[1] Indeed, these limitations are inherent in all the policy strategies outlined in the Bush administration's *National Security Strategy of the United States of America* (U.S. White House 2002). These limitations are also apparent in a wide variety of security and trade alliances and arrangements with NATO members, Latin American states, Pacific Rim nations, and even (economic) arrangements with China. U.S. actions are paradoxically also constrained by multilateralism and the resultant institutions that the United States itself created at and beyond Bretton Woods.[2]

According to DPT, both the United States and all stable democracies will benefit from democracy and economic liberalization. Indeed, and in line with DPT, consolidated democracies, or what some scholars consider "mature" democracies, do not conquer other states or engage in warfare with other democracies (Owen 2005).[3] While the cold war period had a spotty record with respect to the implementation of DPT, the long-term success potential of U.S. foreign policy is better illustrated by the recently emerging results of the U.S. DPT-driven efforts in Latin America.[4]

The G. W. Bush administration has made a point of promoting both democratization and morality as "world values" (McFaul 2004/5)—ones worth fighting for. Promoting democracy has become a cornerstone of U.S. foreign policy but, as the United States finds itself without a viable or immediate exit strategy in Iraq, increasingly criticized. Strategies for democracy promotion are vigorously debated in official and academic circles, particularly whether military force is justified to advance democracy.

However, the United States, as the most powerful actor in the international system, can promote or impede democratic development and has played a pivotal role in making the advancement of democratic values a legitimate foreign policy objective—particularly in the last century. According to Michael McFaul, democracy has become an international norm and is far stronger now than it ever has been. Moreover, democracy as an ideal system of government has "near-universal appeal among people of every ethnic group, every religion, and every region of the world." The international community has increasingly accepted democracy promotion as a foreign policy goal (McFaul 2004/5).

But, while in Latin America autocratic and military regimes have successfully civilianized and democratized, the region views U.S. military intervention in Iraq as a reminder that U.S. hegemony can be forcefully applied, paradoxically, to promote its enlightened vision. Indeed, moral arguments for democracy become mired in the methods used to attain it — a dilemma faced by the Bush adminis- tration, as it increasingly enters into wider and more intense trade and economic relations with a progressively more hostile region.

The Argument

Political stability, institution building, and the promotion of investments and eco- nomic orthodoxy, all of which have encouraged interventionism, have long char- acterized U.S. hemispheric concerns in the region. Indeed, U.S. foreign policy has shifted between engagement and confrontation, both before and during the cold war.[5] That U.S. policies toward Latin America are still mixed reflects re- gional relations, particularly as leftist governments are democratically elected in more and more Latin American countries, but this paper posits that U.S. hege- mony has worked more to stabilize the region and provide the groundwork for coherent and simultaneous economic and political reforms, particularly in the post–cold war era. The elimination of anti-Communism as the guiding principle of U.S. foreign policy has broadened the spectrum of U.S.–Latin American rela- tions and has allowed for engagement, which has aided democratic transition and economic development in Latin America. However, while U.S. foreign pol- icy has fundamentally changed, the effects of liberalization have been inconsis- tent and often disparate, thereby giving fuel to the governments of Hugo Chavez, Evo Morales, and others, who now pose an enormous challenge to these reforms and who are implementing alternative polices. Hemispheric free trade has been halted as individual nations and the region at large face ongoing social disparities and confront some of the negative effects of structural adjustment.

That the region is turning to leftist leadership for answers appears at the out- set a clear indication of disenchantment with reform policies and a vote against hemispheric meddling. I suggest that this trend is also rooted in the consolidation of democratic institutions and civil society voting against corruption, not just a result of malevolent hegemony squeezing the regional powers into compliance. Moreover, while economic reform policies have had a positive impact on the growing export sectors, they have not yet helped the already disenfranchised. However, the potential does exist for more cooperation. U.S. policy in the region can have a positive effect in the region as a whole in the longer term, particularly in those countries where governments have implemented progressive internal economic and social policies.

U.S. policy is, in fact, less focused on micromonitoring Latin American govern- ments and domestic politics in a post–cold war Bush administration and more fo- cused on security concerns. While the foreign policy during the Bush administration's first term in office reflected regionalism alongside a multilateral approach in hemispheric relations, counterterrorism as a top national security concern has replaced political stability as the dominant objective in U.S.–Latin American relations. Moreover, U.S. national security policy is more far-reaching, and the Latin American region now appears to take a slight back seat to the Middle East and West Asia in terms of threat potential, leaving many officials to believe that other vital Latin American interests are being neglected. Clearly, Latin American governments continue to face daunting challenges, including poverty, economic inequality, urban violence, and massive displacement, all of which need to be addressed by domestic policies that the United States will support.

In post 9/11 hemispheric relations, security, however much it continues to be redefined, is focused on narco-trafficking and indigenous and foreign insurgent groups and cells, known as the Grey area phenomenon (GAP).[6] Still, free trade and hemispheric integration have not been completely undermined by the new security environment. At the same time a series of Latin American administrations in the post-military era turned corrupt, as Latin America attempts to consolidate once-fragile democracies and economic reform policies negatively impacted several social sectors.

In order to show the multiple transitions in U.S. foreign policy and its hegemony in Latin America, I will first briefly look at the basis of historic U.S. interests in the region and the cold war policies that focused on both economic and military initiatives in South and Central America and the Caribbean and that made political stability, even under military regimes, an end goal. Indeed, U.S. national security evaluations in its hemisphere were almost exclusively concerned with assessing leftist political movements, popular organizations, and guerrilla forces. Here, the role of Southern Command (SOUTHCOM) in carrying out U.S. interests plays an important role. Hence, confrontation and engagement reflected the often contradictory policies in Latin America until the mid-1980s, when Central America became militarized and both neoliberal reform policies and strategies for democracy promotion were implemented as the military juntas in South America started to fall. By the 1980s the recession and the crash of Latin American economies necessitated significant economic reforms and structural adjustment — all formulated and guided by the International Monetary Fund (IMF) and the World Bank.

Secondly, I will examine the post–cold war Clinton era, which focused almost solely on economic reforms, trade, and institution building in the region and internationally. It was then that Latin American leaders began to pursue integration policies with the United States. However, responding to the 1989 Defense Authorization Act, SOUTHCOM during the 1990s gradually began redefining its mission to include defense against what were described as "emerging" and "nontraditional" security threats — that is drug trafficking. But it is also during this time that constructive engagement under both Clinton and Bush created the basis for smooth democratic transitions and the consolidation of economic and political reforms as well as for revived and new trade agreements.

Another shift in U.S. foreign policy focus occurred after 9/11 when Washington implemented the National Security Strategy of the United States, otherwise known as the Bush Doctrine, which made counterterrorism as part of its "global war on terrorism" its top security concern rather than political stability. At the same time, however, democracy promotion has allowed for the continued and somewhat peaceful electoral transitions in Latin America and the Caribbean as well as for the uninterrupted economic and trade arrangements within the Americas at large and with the United States in particular, suggesting that engagement, not confrontation, reflects hegemonic efforts in the region.

U.S. Policy in Latin America — Political Instruments of Pax Americana: Engagement and Confrontation

A Brief Historical Analysis

Indeed, the extent and limitations of hegemony are nowhere better reflected than in the U.S. relationship with Latin America. In a speech to Congress on December 2, 1823, President James Monroe outlined three points that were later to become foreign policy doctrine: the United States would not permit the hemisphere to be colonized; any attempt by European powers to colonize would be considered a danger to the peace and security of the Americas; and the United States would not get involved in wars of the Europeans with each other. Ever since the enunciation of the Monroe Doctrine the United States has regarded the Western Hemisphere as its own domain. Clearly the intent of this foreign policy doctrine was to prevent foreign powers from exercising influence that might challenge the U.S. stake in Latin America and the Caribbean. While the policy effected economic development and political progress in the region for over a century, the tenets of the Monroe Doctrine also ensured that the Western Hemisphere remained a militarily secure region (J. Richardson 1907, 287).

Policies confirming entrenched U.S. political and economic interests reflected U.S.–Latin American (and Caribbean) relations from the Platt and Taft Amendments of the early twentieth century through the containment policies of the Truman Doctrine (1947) and the cold war — that is, Gunboat and Dollar Diplomacy continued to vie for the position of top-agenda item. U.S. forces protected American interests in 1904 in the Dominican Republic; in Cuba from 1906 to 1909; in Honduras in 1907, 1910, 1911, and 1912; in Nicaragua in 1910; and in Cuba again in 1912. Between 1913 and 1920 U.S. troops occupied Haiti and Nicaragua and intervened in Cuba, the Dominican Republic, Honduras and Mexico — to name a few (Landau 2005). Countering confrontation, however, were strategies of engagement that suggested a new model of constructive hemispheric relations, such as Franklin D. Roosevelt's Good Neighbor Policy of the 1930s, John F. Kennedy's Alliance for Progress, and certain aspects of the policies of both the first Bush and Clinton administrations. But it was in the post–World War II environment that the United States developed more intense strategic concerns in Latin America.

Cold War Tensions: Tools of Interventionism

While the intent was otherwise, U.S. policy in Latin America during the cold war appeared at the outset to be an obstacle to economic, political, and social progress. Confrontation, rather than engagement, characterized the policy tools utilized by American administrations during the "long peace." The East–West conflict defined U.S. relations and national security interests in the region, and the pursuit of political stability continued to be a top priority in U.S. foreign policy. Clearly the Cuban Revolution in 1959 set the stage for the United States to engage a series of policy tools that would further shape and intensify a more confrontational rather than constructive relationship. At the same time, U.S. officials recognized that the development gap between the poorer Latin American and Caribbean nations and the United States could (and did) strengthen the resolve and position of both socialist leaders and movements in the region, a trend that had not abated since the ousting of Jacobo Arbenz in 1954 in Guatemala. Insisting on providing an alternative to the increasingly popular Cuban model, John Kennedy announced an "Alliance for Progress" in 1961 to develop the Latin American infrastructure and build democracy. Kennedy described it as "a vast cooperative effort, unparalleled in magnitude and nobility of purpose, to satisfy the basic needs of the American people for homes, work and land, health and schools — techo, trabajo y tierra, salud y escuela" (John F. Kennedy Library and Foundation 2001). The initiative focused on establishing and maintaining democratic governments, creating industrial and agricultural development projects, and effecting a more equitable distribution of wealth.[7]

At the same time, however, that Washington was implementing economic initiatives, it was also engaging in confrontational policy tactics — for example, the Bay of Pigs Operation and the Cuban Missile Crisis in 1961 and 1962. These incidents were the impetus for establishing what would become an entrenched national security policy focused on anti-Communism in the Caribbean, Central America, Mexico, Brazil and all of Spanish America — particularly the Southern

Cone nations of Argentina, Chile, Uruguay and Paraguay. In its hegemonic pursuit of political and regional stability, the United States immediately isolated and sanctioned Cuba and gave its support to the anti-Communist (and mostly military) leadership in the region at large.

Southern Command: In Defense of U.S. Security Interests

With the consolidation of Communist Cuba in the Caribbean and Western Hemisphere came the consolidation of various military operations under SOUTHCOM in June 1963. U.S. military operations shifted their emphasis from the Caribbean to Central and South America.[8] During the cold war SOUTHCOM saw its mission as conducting "military operations and promoting security cooperation to achieve U.S. strategic objectives." Its first operation was in 1963, when Marines were sent to Panama to protect the railroad and the Panama Canal project, an operation that was sustained through the decades.[9] But its main role has been to defend U.S. security interests in and around Latin America. This was particularly the case during and after World War II, and it is now again in the wake of the September 11 terror attacks.[10]

Inter-American organizations such as the Conference of American Armies (CAA), created in 1960 by the American Armies, the Inter-American Naval Conference (INC) and the System of Cooperation among the American Air Forces (SICOFAA) as well as the Organization of American States (OAS) all provided the security policy tools to ensure cooperation and coordination within the hemisphere and under the auspices of its hegemon.[11]

SOUTHCOM's mission reflects several major points of U.S. foreign policy. First, its emphasis on U.S. strategic and security objectives illustrates U.S.-centric policy implementation. Second, it demonstrates the U.S. assumption that it is what guarantees security to all of Latin America as well as to its surrounding waters. However, though SOUTHCOM attests to U.S. military power and presence in the region to be sure, it draws heavily upon cooperative agreements, information sharing, and joint multinational operational exercises and deployments to achieve these mutual security goals.

Still, the extent to which the United States was committed to democratic values and human rights was intensely debated as collective security organizations supported often-brutal authoritarian military regimes, from Branco in Brazil in 1964 to Pinochet in Chile and Bordaberry in Uruguay in 1973 and to Videla in Argentina in 1976. The entire Southern Cone was under military rule until at least the mid-1980s, suggesting that U.S. hegemony and its confrontational anti-Communist policy tools had undermined more "popular" paths to democracy. Moreover, military operations centered on counterinsurgency, political stabilization and counternarcotics intensified in Central America and the Caribbean throughout the 1980s under the Reagan and, later, first Bush administrations. Indeed, the militarization of Central America between 1981 and 1989 compelled Washington to send more U.S. military advisors to the region to address the growing number of insurgent groups emerging in El Salvador and Guatemala after the successful revolution in Nicaragua in 1979. A thousand more troops (adding to the ten thousand already permanently stationed there) were sent to Panama in 1988 and 1989 during a period of instability there and as pressure grew for its military leader, General Manuel Noriega, to resign.

By the late 1980s and the early 1990s, as military regimes were allowing for democratic or at least civilian transitions and the cold war was coming to an end, security was focused on counternarcotics and the Andean Initiative, established by the first Bush administration. Military assistance was provided to the region to combat the increasing drug trade in Colombia, Bolivia, and Peru (Collier 1993). By 1995 SOUTHCOM had replaced bilateral exercises with multilateral ones focused more on post–cold war activities such as peacekeeping, humanitarian assistance, and counter-narco-trafficking (SOUTHCOM 2005b). Enlargement, alongside other modifications, continued through 2006 under the second Bush administration, where up to three thousand military and civilian personnel were permanently assigned to over twenty-six locations throughout the region, including bases and operation centers spanning Florida, Guantánamo Bay, Cuba, Puerto Rico, Honduras, and Arizona (SOUTHCOM 2006).[12]

U.S. hegemony in the region, as illustrated by the goals of its military instrument, demonstrates a tension between security goals, on the one hand, and adherence to democratic principles, human rights, security, and partnerships with regional states, on the other. And by including the states as participants and partners in its overarching security efforts, the United States has managed to entrench the tools of constructive engagement and confrontation in the hemisphere.[13]

On one level these aspects all reflect the underlying goals of security for the United States and its neighbors via the structures and mechanisms of DPT.[14] They further demonstrate that, on another, the United States is a limited hegemon, for as Thucydides' maxim has it, "The strong do what they can, and the weak suffer what they must" (Thucydides 1982). Inter-Americanism stands fairly solidly alongside Pax Americana in the historic neighborhood of the United States.

U.S. Policy Change in the Post–Cold War Clinton Era: Let's Talk Trade and Democracy

The strategic context of international relations has been radically transformed since the dismantling of the Soviet Union. Almost all the states in Latin America made the transition to democratic governance and increasingly embraced the free-market economic model. Structural adjustment programs, or SAPs, guided much of the initial reform in almost all countries of the region from the 1980s through the 1990s — many with mixed results, as noted above. The economic crisis of 1982 devastated the region and accelerated the external debts of these countries to upward of U.S.$500 billion in total (Kleinberg 1999, 3–5). Hyperinflation, balance-of-payments crises, spiraling debts, disequilibria in current accounts, and dwindling government coffers forced the governments of the region to seek massive amounts of external aid from international financial institutions (IFIs) such as the IMF and World Bank. SAPs that included deregulation, privatization, and trade liberalization, alongside inflation-fighting polices such as social programs and subsidies slashing, wage freezes, and fiscal austerity, formed the basis of the new economic model (Kleinberg 1999, 3–5).

With strong presidentialism replacing military juntas, privatization occurred at a rapid pace and by the late 1980s Latin America had privatized over U.S.$75 billion worth of assets and was still selling off some of its most strategic state-owned industries against the protests of the labor and popular classes (Kleinberg 1999, 6). Unilateral trade liberalization prepared the way for increased deregulation and privatization, with Mexico leading the region in its accession to the General Agreement on Tariffs and Trade (GATT) in 1986 and the North American Free Trade Agreement (NAFTA) in 1994. Regional trade accords were signed or rejuvenated. The Common Market of the South (MERCOSUR), the Caribbean Common Market (CARICOM), the Central American Common Market (CACM), and bilateral agreements as well as initiatives taken toward the FTAA required extensive trade liberalization measures and opened the region to the influx of goods and gave it access to cheap labor — with mixed results in the different capital and noncapital sectors (Kleinberg 1999, 6–7).

It is in this way, ironically, that Latin American protectionism and overt antipathy toward the United States gave way to expectations of a more positive relationship with it embodied in both former president George Bush's "Enterprise for the Americas Initiative" and the Clinton administration's effort at reversing military rule in Haiti. The Clinton administration effected a shift in U.S. policy under which it fast-tracked free trade, supported democratic civilian elections and governments, and discouraged the use of military regimes to restore order domestically. The Clinton administration was also the force behind the creation of the Inter-American Committee against Terrorism (CICTC) of the OAS. The First and Second Summit organized around this theme were to establish cooperation among member states in order to share and exchange information to "prevent, combat and eliminate terrorism" (U.S. Department of State, Bureau of Western Hemisphere Affairs 2002). In January 2004 the Bush administration merely proposed to amend the statute, suggesting that it saw no reason to shift radically the extant security policy (AG/RES.2051 2004).

However, trade and investment, or what Joseph Tulchin (1997) calls a "NAFTA-ization" of inter-American relations, which appeared to be the most important route toward political and economic progress in the post–cold war era of economic globalization, topped the foreign policy agenda in Latin America. Tulchin suggests that the new millennium saw several patterns emerging: first, a U.S. policy that focused more on Europe and that limited its concern with Latin America to trade and economic issues. There was also a reemergence of what Tulchin (1997, 35–36) considers a "U.S. policy of a Wilsonian urge to do good works on behalf of democratic capitalism teaching other nations how to behave and how to enjoy the benefits of the 'American way of life.'" He also states that the United States was experiencing a "Vietnam syndrome" during this period in that the United States did not get embroiled in international "adventures"—at least at that point. At the same time the post–cold war environment, including U.S. interests elsewhere, tended to elicit the reemergence of pre–cold war approaches to hemispheric relations. Washington was simply trying to preserve U.S. autonomy in the region in order to protect those global interests. As Tulchin (1997, 35–36) posits, this was "a hemispheric hegemon whose major preoccupations were elsewhere; one that would prefer not to get involved, if at all possible; and one that would like to view the region as a kind of preserve, a safety area that might be redefined as an economic bloc should that prove necessary."

Nevertheless, according to Richard Feinberg (2002, 129) Latin American actors were more responsible for initiating post–cold war strategies in the region than was the hegemon. As he suggests, "rarely is the drive toward regional integration perceived to be a bottom-up affair, in which the smaller, developing nations are a driving force in history. In reality by the early 1990s structural shifts in Latin American economies and polities and in Latin Americans' interpretation of their own interests had altered the region's traditional aversion to integration with the United States." Clearly Latin American leaders actively engaged the United States in negotiating a "strategic alliance," pursuing reciprocal hemispheric integration through an FTAA—the first time so many countries of varying sizes ever attempted such a feat (Schott 2005, 1). Between 1990 and 1997, U.S. direct foreign investment (DFI) in Latin America increased from $71 billion to $172 billion or 142 percent. At the same time a growing number of American investors have developed business and personal relationships with their Latin American counterparts, creating more of a convergence of interests within the region as a whole as well as more impetus for integration (Feinberg 2002, 132–33).

As Jeffrey Schott (2005, 50) notes, negotiations for an FTAA—started by the first Bush administration and continued through the Clinton and second Bush administrations—would be challenging at the best of times. The advent of financial crises and political turmoil in the region in the past ten years in conjunction with a post-9/11 security environment and the "prospective expiry" of U.S. trade promotion by 2007 has made the task even more onerous. Although many in the region looked to the European Union (EU) as a model, the FTAA was only meant to eliminate barriers to trade and investment in the thirty-four participating countries while providing a strategy for securing access to the U.S. market — beyond the several free trade areas (FTAs) in the region. The idea of politically ceding sovereignty to a supranational body would to many mean the entrenchment of U.S. hegemony in the Western Hemisphere.

In his first year in office G. W. Bush continued to push a regionalist agenda focused on development, trade, and investment and met with heads of state in the hemisphere twenty-six times. Bush spoke on the issue of U.S.–Latin American relations to the OAS and the World Bank. A "competitive liberalization strategy" informed much of Bush's discourse on the region at that point and responded to some of the key initiatives taken by Latin American leaders in the area of trade and economic policy, addressing in particular their role as an effective post–cold war strategy.[15] Bush went as far as drawing a link between trade and democracy, and with other heads of state he adopted a democracy clause at the Quebec Summit that "establishe[d] that any unconstitutional alteration or interruption of the democratic order in a state of the Hemisphere constitutes an insurmountable obstacle to the participation of that state's government in the Summits of the Americas process" (OAS 2001). By linking the two, and clearly taking cues from the European Union, Bush was clearly trying to garner more support for the idea that the region ought to be committed to the "collective defense of democracy," which became codified in the Inter-American Democracy Charter, signed on September 11, 2001 (OAS 2001).[16]

There has been less success, however, in breaking an impasse in negotiations for an FTAA. While a rough-draft text exists, negotiations to reduce barriers to market access for goods and services have not progressed since the Miami Ministerial meeting in 2003, the outcome of which prevented the collapse of the negotiations but exacerbated conflicting interests and resulted in differing levels of commitment.[17] Modest capacity-building initiatives advanced by the World Bank and national development agencies are, according to Schott (2005), the only positive outcome to date.

This "Century of the Americas" (Fauriol and Weintraub 2001) had within it several explicit and implicit elements of a growing U.S.–Latin American "partnership" that was guided by the United States but clearly had led to deeper interstate integration. Economic and political reforms had received considerable support throughout the region, as had the concept of going beyond NAFTA toward hemispheric integration. That a prosperous and democratic region could be a strategic asset to the United States is conceptualized by some scholars as "not based on an imperial vision of U.S. hegemony, but on a fairly harmonious and mutually beneficial sense of national relationships among states of the Americas" (Fauriol and Weintraub 2001). The strategic advantages and, by extension, the importance of an economically prosperous and democratic region have actually been underestimated because of the lack of any real threat to the United States from its Latin American or Caribbean neighbors (Fauriol and Weintraub 2001).

In summary, then, by 2001 constructive engagement based on economic and trade interests as well as the promotion and maintenance of democratic norms topped the agenda in U.S.–Latin American relations, even though an active campaign in counternarcotics continued to dominate the security agenda in the region overall.

9/11 and the Bush Doctrine

While globalization, democratization, and liberalization became the tenets on which the post–cold war system was based, the attacks on September 11 successfully shook it to its very foundation. Emerging from the ashes was a new global threat — packaged as both state and nonstate actors — that undermined the stability of a system grounded in complex interactions and interdependencies and, indeed, created a new world order that looked much like a "clash of civilizations." With this came a major paradigm shift in national security that affected all of the Pentagon's areas of command, placing the United States at the helm of a "global war on terrorism." The latter became the centerpiece of the national security strategy under the Bush administration, and policy was reconfigured in Latin America accordingly.

For its part, SOUTHCOM promptly integrated itself into this new security framework, bringing regional issues such as human and drug trafficking, narcotics production, document forging, money laundering, immigration flows, and guerrilla movements under the terror umbrella. Latin America suddenly appeared a potential haven for terror cells desiring eventual access to the United States. In addition intraregional military alliances among South American states has emerged independently of SOUTHCOM's institutional arrangements.

Although a shift in security strategy occurred within SOUTHCOM and within the region at large, Latin American nations have continued to consolidate leadership on issues of international trade, finance, and regional economic integration, showing that the region's economic platform has not been undermined. Clearly, the formation of the Group of 21 at the Fifth Ministerial of the WTO in Cancun in 2003 — with Brazil at its helm as trade "reformer" — suggests an even deeper commitment to an economic platform.

However, governments in the region continue to face corruption within their ranks along with overwhelming poverty, economic inequality, urban violence, and massive displacement. In their wake is a noted and rising popular militancy directed against traditional political parties and elected governments — several resulting in fatal clashes between protestors and security forces. Protests have focused more and more attention on to the failure of economic reforms — many implemented in the 1980s and 1990s — to alleviate worsening conditions or to "trickle" down economic improvements, as many economists suggested they would. Rather, one of the fallouts of SAPs has been economic polarization. SAPs tended to strengthen the export and private sectors and weaken the noncapital sectors. Power, wealth, and representation were concentrated in the hands of ever fewer — particularly in Mexico, where reforms were implemented above and beyond the austerity measures required by the IFIs. Regressive concentration of wealth occurred in tandem with a series of regressions in the social sectors. Between 1970 and 1990, the percentage of wage earners declined from 74 percent to 69 percent as the informal sector increased from 26 percent to 31 percent. At the same time, poverty alleviation programs were not a strong element of liberalization programs and scarce state entitlements were largely dismantled, immediately and negatively affecting poverty figures (Kleinberg 1999, 6–7). Alvaro Díaz suggests that "markets in social services are indifferent to social inequalities and they have numerous flaws and high transaction costs" (Díaz 1997, 42). The proportion of people living on less than one dollar a day has remained at 40 percent and, given the rise in the cost of living, reflects an increase in the number of people living below the subsistence level (Fauriol and Weintraub 2001).

Importantly, the legitimacy of the state under these conditions (always) remains at risk and any space earned "for crucial social compromise is jeopardized" (Diaz 1997). The erosion of state legitimacy is being played out through the forging of new social actors as rural and urban social movements are challenging free-market principles and the new economic arrangements that are in place (Kleinberg 1999, 8).

With little end in sight to persistent poverty and inequality, particularly as governments continue to vie for regional trade and the United States shifts its focus to the Middle East and Asia, popular sectors have voted for alternative "packages." The combination of economic reforms and revelations of corruption within the rank and file of governments in the region has led to what many choose to call a "Pink Tide" (Council on Hemispheric Affairs 2005) — bringing into power a string of leftist political parties and leaders, led in good part by Hugo Chávez of Venezuela and capped by the renewed popularity of former Sandinista leader Daniel Ortega of Nicaragua. But the movement to the left in a growing number of nations in the region does not just reflect deep opposition to political and economic policies advocated by the Bush administration but also attests to the consolidation of democracy after many tumultuous and oppressive years under military rule. Importantly, continued pressure by nongovernmental organizations (NGOs) to "conform to the region's developing democratic value system in a systemic and peaceful manner" has had positive effects in the region at large. Indeed, between 1970 and 2000 only one in eight regimes "suffered an unconstitutional breakdown, compared to one in two from 1930 to 1970" (Fauriol and Weintraub 2001).

Consolidation of Democratic Institutions and the Movement to the Left

That Condoleezza Rice attended the inauguration of Chile's new socialist president Michelle Bachelet and stood for a photo-op with Bolivia's Evo Morales in 2006 suggests that U.S.–Latin American relations have indeed achieved the level of partnership. The promotion of "freedom and democracy" in Latin America has taken root and the United States is no longer forcefully opposing electoral outcomes even if it is not in favor of them. Outgoing Chilean president Ricardo Lagos put it succinctly when he said that the string of leftist victories poses no threat to the United States and merely reflects widespread opposition to the status quo. Lagos, himself a populist who opposed Pinochet's rule, states that people "are looking for more democracy, rather than less" (Gallardo 2006). He also alluded to a "mature relationship" with the United States in which Chile could oppose U.S. policies (such as the invasion of Iraq) but still enter into a free trade agreement with the would-be hegemonic power. He stated, moreover, that U.S. values, including "democracy [and] markets in the areas where markets have a role and human rights," are harmonious with those of Chile.

Although a partnership may be developing more and more around those very values, there is rising discontent throughout Latin America over the Bush administration's "assumption of regional hegemony" (Carlsen 2005). Some suggest that there is little commitment by the United States to grapple with more immediate problems in the region, and policy is more "a series of reactions, punctuated by a few pet projects" (Venezuelanalysis.com). There is emerging consensus that the United States lacks an overall Latin American policy and that key political appointees have little background in Latin American issues (Carlsen 2005). President Bush's diplomatic mission to Latin America in March 2007 was meant to address this lack of policy in the region, but there are conflicting reports as to whether his visit served its purpose.

The U.S.–Venezuela Question: A Fly in the Oil?

It is at this juncture that Hugo Chávez, waving a clenched fist at the United States, has attempted to increase his own influence in Latin America as well as among nations within the nonaligned movement. Containing Chávez and his flagrant and confrontational left-wing rhetoric has been no small feat for the United States. Elected first in 1998 on an anticorruption platform, Chávez has exploited growing anti-American sentiment by openly chastising the Bush administration — indeed, demonizing Bush himself while maintaining that the "imperialist nation" to the north sought and supported a short-lived coup against his government in April 2002. While courting a close friendship with Fidel Castro, Chávez has ruthlessly and frequently denounced "U.S. imperialism and intervention in the region" and openly opposed free trade.[18]

On the economic front Chávez has fast-tracked trade initiatives and energy supply contracts with its southern neighbors and aggressively pursued deals with fast-growing economies such as China, whose potential (and enormous) level of consumption make it an alternative market to the United States.[19] Courting China marks a conscious attempt to lessen the Venezuelan economy's dependence on the U.S. market for its oil exports (Council on Hemispheric Affairs 2006b). At the same time it promotes a Castro/Chávez "model," a model supported by more and more governments in the region.

However, the Venezuelan economy is inextricably tied to the United States with the latter importing 68 percent of Venezuela's entire oil production and processing the majority of it in refineries owned by the Venezuelan petroleum industry, PDVSA. The refineries were built exclusively to convert Venezuelan heavy crude into a more usable form and have required a considerable amount of specialized technology paid for by Venezuelan investment (Council on Hemispheric Affairs 2006b). Deepening interdependence, moreover, is the sale of petroleum byproducts that flood the U.S. market as well as the widespread distribution of Venezuelan gasoline in more than twelve thousand Citgo stations throughout the United States. Indeed, at the Seventh Conference of Defense Ministers of the Americas, OAS Secretary-General José Miguel Insulza insisted that Venezuela had the best balance of trade with the United States in the hemisphere and that relations between the two would never stray too far from the norm (OAS 2006).

In many ways, present Venezuelan–U.S. relations encapsulate historic Latin American sentiments toward U.S. hegemony in the region, where complex economic and political ties are manifested in often-contradictory policy. Where U.S. strategy in the region is clearly one of engagement, as it accepts and embraces the democratically elected governments in the region, its Venezuela strategy is one of "qualified" containment (Venezuelanalysis.com 2005). U.S. policy toward Latin America including Venezuela is more multilateral in tone and puts more stress on working with the OAS to both support democracy in Venezuela and diminish Chávez's efforts to expand his influence (*Economist* 2006). Elected democratically, Chávez is nonetheless perceived as governing in an "illiberal" fashion. While this has provoked U.S. ire, it has limited its opposition efforts to convincing the OAS to "enact their Democratic Charter against Venezuela, an action that could entail economic and political sanctions" (Venezuelanalysis .com 2005).

The feeling that it shares its fate with Cuba has no doubt intensified Venezuela's strategic relations with the largely isolated island. This suggests to the United States that any transition process — or democracy promotion — that might occur after Castro's death may be slow in coming, particularly at its own hand or in its own image, given that, according to Julia Sweig (2006a), the United States has, as a result of the Helms–Burton Law that codified the embargo, undermined any role it may have in shaping Cuba's future politically. Indeed, as Sweig suggests, although the United States "is very good at helping to foment nationalism, or helping the leaders to foment nationalism . . . our policy options are very limited. [Moreover] the United States has limited intelligence, limited access, no one to call, very poor ties and very negative credibility on the island with the Cuban public." Ironically, the challenges posed by a post-Castro Cuba are consistent with the challenges the United States now faces in more and more countries in the region — promoting sustainable growth, equality, and political stability.

Conclusions

At the height of anti-Americanism, the United States is presented with a unique and timely opportunity to reassess its historic relationship with Latin America and to modify its policy of constructive engagement. If it chooses to support the new democracies in the region it can ease past resentment. In several ways, Secretary of State Rice's presence alongside Bachelet and Morales on March 11, 2006, was tacit acceptance of significant change in the region and proof that freedom and democracy are alive and well. Democracy promotion has been successful in the region, even in the wake of less successful economic policies — or rather economic policies that have had scattered and uneven results. According to the OAS, there were thirteen presidential elections between December 2005 and December 2006 alone, "the largest 12-month figure in the history of the Hemisphere" (OAS 2006). During the same period there were general congressional elections in many countries and numerous municipal and local elections and a number of nationwide plebiscites. In 2006, the OAS observed sixteen electoral processes in member countries and three presidential elections (OAS 2006).

However, while OAS Secretary-General José Miguel Insulza concedes that democracy has been "fully instituted" he maintains that the challenges of governance have yet to be addressed, including "continuous and sustainable economic growth, much more equitable distribution of wealth, elimination of poverty and discrimination, greater access to justice, full respect for human rights, better social services for all and increased security for them and their children." He added that "the stability of our democracies will depend upon our ability to correct this" (OAS 2006).

To be sure, economic reforms and free trade policies have yet to convince civil society that they benefit anyone other than the corporate elite in both Latin America and the United States. Indeed, Bush attempted to suggest otherwise in his mission to five nations in Latin America in March 2007. His own presence was clearly meant to show that the United States remains committed to long-term trade and economic relations as well as willing to address deepening social crises in the region by funding health care, particularly in rural areas, and education programs and by providing multilateral debt relief for some of the poorest countries in the region (U.S. White House, Office of the President 2007).

However, it was clear from the angry demonstrations in several of the countries he visited that civil society did not welcome Bush or his proposals — one of which pushed for closer ties with Brazil's ethanol industry, which along with the United States, controls two-thirds of the world's supply of biofuels (Council on Hemispheric Affairs 2007a).

Border security issues were also a point of contention between Bush and several nations in the area, including Mexico, Brazil, Colombia, and Guatemala. Post-9/11 policy failed to establish a more coherent guest worker program or establish alternatives for gaining citizenship for illegal immigrants living in the United States. Rather, stiffer immigration policies along with plans for constructing a seven-hundred-mile fence only angered and alienated Latin American policy makers (Council on Hemispheric Affairs 2007b).

U.S. efforts to help Latin American nations formulate appropriate domestic policies are imperative. If nothing else, accepting domestic policies that bend the rules of economic orthodoxy and trade liberalization would allow governments to address persistent poverty and despair and create a true partnership. A limited hegemon, benevolent or otherwise, has an obligation to guarantee the political and economic stability of the hemisphere — not just its own — and, critically, to be perceived by the latter as doing so. Importantly, while it is trying to guarantee security for the hemisphere, its support of consistent economic development in the region is perceived to be faltering in parallel with the fortunes of Latin American nations. While this represents a challenge to U.S. foreign policy, it also represents a golden opportunity for the United States to reaffirm regional stability in the economic realm and its own status in the role of hegemon.

Notes

I want to thank Howard G. Kleinberg, defense and national security analyst with the George C. Marshall Institute, for all his comments, some editorial suggestions, and his understanding of U.S. defense activities in the hemisphere and beyond.

1. According to Kagan (1998), it is certainly a better international arrangement than all realistic alternatives. To undermine it would cost many others around the world far more than it would cost Americans — and far sooner. Kagan agrees with Huntington's earlier stance that "a world without U.S. primacy will be a world with more violence and disorder and less democracy and economic growth than a world where the United States continues to have more influence than any other country shaping global affairs."

2. Limitations of U.S. power were also apparent in Operations Desert Storm, Enduring Freedom, and Iraqi Freedom (ongoing) with the United States needing assistance from other states to implement and maintain these operations and subsequent regime changes. Significantly, the United States does not retain control of militarily overturned states. Rather, it attempts to implement democratic institutions (based on DPT) in these states and maintains economic and political ties. As Robert Kagan suggests, "the benevolent hegemony exercised by the United States is good for a vast portion of the world's population."

3. A debate ensues, however, suggesting that immature, or emerging democracies, do go to war or are prone to conflict with other nations (see Owen 2005; Snyder 2000; and Mansfield and Snyder 1995).

4. See also, Gelpi and Griesdorf (2001), Mousseau (2005), Owen (1994), Mearsheimer (1990). See also democratic peace theory, http://en.wikipedia.org/wiki/Democratic_peace_theory.

5. The concept of engagement and confrontation is used by Wesley Fryer (1993).

6. Here the "Rice Doctrine" has reinforced elements of the Bush Doctrine but focuses on what is considered "transformational diplomacy" where national security interests (openly) work in tandem with development efforts and democracy building. Rice suggests that there will be a major shift in traditional recipients of U.S. diplomacy. Top diplomats would be reassigned from Europe to "global hot spots — including China, India, Africa, and Lebanon" — and work to "build and sustain democratic, well-governed states that will respond to the needs of their people and conduct themselves responsibly in the international system." This would occur alongside a shift in the structure and delivery of U.S. foreign assistance (R. Nolan 2006).

7. The program of industrial and agrarian development mirrored Operation Bootstrap in Puerto Rico. "By the summer of 1950 eighty new industrial plants were in operation and the hundredth was under construction. When the constitution of the new Commonwealth of Puerto Rico came into effect, on July 25, 1952, some 152 factories were in operation. The overwhelming majority were consumer goods industries: producers of textiles, wearing apparel, footwear, electronics equipment, electric wiring, drafting tools, artist's brushes, fishing tackle, artificial flowers, and other plastic and metal articles assembled in Puerto Rico for sale in the Unites States. They were 'labor intensive' industries, for they relied more heavily on labor than on machinery to supply the value added to the raw materials which they imported from the mainland" (John F. Kennedy Library and Foundation 2001).

8. Recommendations of the Joint Chiefs of Staff for a comprehensive system of military commands were approved by President Truman in December 1946. The plan was to "put responsibility for conducting military operations of all military forces in various geographical areas" in the "hands of a single commander." Thus, the principle of unified commands was established, and the Caribbean Command was one of them. Although the Caribbean Com-

mand was designated by the Defense Department on November 1, 1947, it did not become fully operational until March 10, 1948, when the old Caribbean Defense Command was inactivated (SOUTHCOM 2005a).

9. According to SOUTHCOM's information page, "military strength in the area was gradually rising and reached its peak in January 1943, when 68,000 personnel were defending the Panama Canal. Military strength was sharply reduced with the termination of World War II. Between 1946 and 1974, total military strength in Panama fluctuated between 6,600 and 20,300 (with the lowest force strength in 1959). From 1975 until late 1994 total military strength in Panama remained at about 10,000 personnel" (SOUTHCOM 2005a).

10. Indeed as its website states, "this mission has never been more critical than it is today, in the wake of the September 11, 2001, terrorist attacks on the United States. This mission has no more important focus than within our own hemisphere" (http://www.southcom.mil/ PA/Facts/Mission.htm).

11. The CAA was created for the stated "purpose of creating a debate forum for the exchange of experiences within the Armies of the American Continent" (http://www.redcea .org/HistoricalBackground.aspx?Language=1). The INC and the SICOFAA were counterpart organisms within the naval and air forces of CAA member countries.

12. More territory was added to SOUTHCOM's Area of Responsibility (AOR) in the following two years including the thirteen island nations of the Caribbean, several U.S. and European territories, the Gulf of Mexico and significant portions of the Atlantic and Pacific oceans (http://www.southcom.mil/AppsSC/pages/aoi.php).

SOUTHCOM lists four major strategic goals: supporting efforts to suppress drug production and smuggling; sustaining a negotiated peace settlement in El Salvador; promoting liberty in Panama; and finally, enhancing professionalism in the military forces of Central and South America (SOUTHCOM 2005c).

13. According to SOUTHCOM, "what distinguishes it from the other regional unified combatant commands is the nature of the theater and consequently the way in which military power is employed. Forces assigned to U.S.SOUTHCOM support U.S. and allied nations' law enforcement agencies for counter-drug operations, joint and bilateral/multilateral exercises, engineering and medical exercises, search and rescue operations, disaster relief operations, humanitarian and civic assistance operations, command post exercises, security assistance programs, personnel exchange programs, staff visits, conferences, and other foreign military interaction (military-to-military contact) programs" (SOUTHCOM 2005c).

14. One of the means by which SOUTHCOM claims to support democracy in the region is by encouraging the militaries to be supportive of civilian authority and respectful of human rights and the rule of law.

15. According to Richard Feinberg (2002, 130–38), "Bush White House aides report that he regularly [pushed] them to keep working on various Latin American issues of interest to him including the FTAA and his then–national security advisor Rice . . . beefed up her Latin American staff to keep pace with Bush's interest in hemispheric affairs."

16. As Feinberg (2002, 142) also suggests, the FTAA "became a tool of international political economy, a potential trade sanction to deter would-be authoritarians and to punish those . . . [who] violate democratic norms" (see OAS 2005).

17. The later failure of the WTO's meeting in Cancun in September 2003 put negotiators under a great deal of pressure to keep the FTAA alive. The United States and Brazil, cochairs of the FTAA process "produced a procedural compromise that allowed them to shake hands and promise to resume negotiations in 2004" (Schott 2005, 8).

18. Chávez went as far as to accuse the Bush administration of planning his assassination, adding to increasing tensions between the two nations ("Chavez and Foreign Minister Say U.S.–Venezuela Relations Can Improve," Venezuelanalysis.com, March 18, 2005).

19. Hugo Chávez joined Mercosur alongside Brazil, Argentina, Uruguay, and Paraguay at its July 20–21 meeting in Cordoba, Argentina ("The Opposition Finds a Leader," *Economist*, August 19, 2006).

CHAPTER FOURTEEN

Brazil

Monica Hirst

The U.S. presence as a superpower in Brazil has been a fact of life since the end of World War II. All through the second half of the twentieth century the United States was regarded by Brazilian elites as the most important power factor in world affairs. The strategic constraints imposed by a bipolar system compelled Brazil not to treat the United States as an adversary, although on many occasions Brazil expected much more in the realm of economic support from it. When anti-American sentiments were expressed in Brazil, they tended to be linked mostly to economic nationalism. Defense and military matters were rarely a source of contention.

Recently new international and domestic realities, such as the end of the cold war, financial and trade globalization, which has increased Brazil's economic exposure, and the growing importance of domestic public opinion as a consequence of the deepening of democracy, have reshaped perceptions in Brazil. In this context the consolidation of U.S. military superiority in world affairs has made political, bureaucratic, academic, business, and social organizations as well as the military in Brazil wary.

To the United States Brazil matters quite little in world politics and international security, especially when compared to crucial U.S. allies such as Canada and Great Britain or to other world powers such as France, India, and Russia. Yet, the reverse is not the case. Brazil keeps a permanent watch on the United States and what it does in world politics. In making its foreign policy decisions, Brazil always assesses the costs and benefits of convergence or conflict with the United States.

Brazil has become more cautious in the face of unipolar world politics, particularly since September 11, 2001. State-to-state political relations between the United States and Brazil primarily aim for prudent coexistence, possible collaboration, and minimal collision. While the United States moves ahead in its attempt to consolidate its increasingly contested power, Brazil searches for a secure and legitimate economic and political platform in South America.

In the context of an asymmetric power structure, Brazil's influence is constrained by its irrelevance to the American strategy of preserving its preeminent global position. Hence Brazil's marginality within the American foreign policy framework limits the importance of hard politics per se in the relationship between the two countries. Although the United States regards Brazil's stance on world politics to be irrelevant to its concerns, the same cannot be said of its view of Brazil's position in regional politics, particularly in South America. Even though this region has been a safe sphere of influence for the United States, Washington has very slowly acknowledged that Brazil is crucial to stability and peace in the area. Under post-1990 democratic rule Brazil has expanded its regional security role, even though Brasilia has repeatedly refused to let mutual interests between itself and Washington force it into a blank check alignment with the United States. Meanwhile, the United States has become more open to the idea that Brazil expects more than just a say in South American politics. In response Brazilian foreign policy has become more receptive to the positive aspects of the global presence of the United States as well as more accepting of the pros of hegemonic stability (Lins 2005).

Brazil's precondition for bilateral relations with the United States is that Washington recognize that the country has a unique identity and a promising future. Brazil has once again made explicit its expectation that the United States should acknowledge the country's distinctive identity both in South America and in the international system. Also the idea of the inauguration of "new eras," frequently applied to domestic politics, has been mirrored in Brazil's relationship with the United States. In this regard it is worth noting that both Brazil and the United States have expectations that have been unmet, even if in the past Brazil has more or less done what the United States has asked.

A very important point, particularly regarding the thesis of this book, is the fact that economic matters are more important in U.S.–Brazil relations than political and security matters. Brazilians express nationalistic sentiments that could push them to contest U.S. hegemony and/or cause them to adopt anti-American stances more in reaction to U.S. coercive trade policies and to U.S. pressure on local economic policies than to the prominence of the United States in world politics and international security. A strong explanation for this is that Brazilian elites and the state bureaucracy involved in shaping the country's foreign policy consider the country's external threats and risks to be primarily economic and not military (Hirst and Lima 2006, 22).

The Highs and Lows of Bilateral Relations

U.S.–Brazil relations have gone through different phases, oscillating from "good" to "cool" without ever breaking out into open hostility. These historical phases include "unwritten alliance" (1889–1940); "automatic alignment" (1942–74); "autonomy" (1975–90); "adjustment" (1990–2002); "affirmative relationship"

(2002–4) and more recently "respect and solidarity" (Hirst 2005, xviii).[1] In all periods a basic pattern has repeated itself in which both parties have ended up frustrated time and time again. Despite this pattern, the current Lula administration in Brazil initially adopted a foreign policy that took a more affirmative stance vis-à-vis the United States.[2]

At present the U.S.–Brazil relationship could once again take a downturn, with each country's expectations remaining unmet. Brazil and the United States have typically engaged in "constrained diplomacy," which, while it has always avoided open confrontation, has nevertheless resulted in frustrations on both sides that have long tainted their relations. But these mutual frustrations have not kept bilateral relations from playing a crucial role in Brazil's foreign affairs as well as in the U.S. hemispheric agenda.

The cause of the cyclical crises in U.S.–Brazil relations concerns erroneous calculations on both sides. At the end of World War II Brazil expected, but did not receive, special acknowledgment for having fought against the Axis. It was frustrated again in the early 1950s, when the United States did not grant the Brazilian government support for its economic development policies, and then yet again in the mid-1960s, when it did not receive economic compensation for having contained "domestic communist forces." In the mid-1970s, the United States first failed to upgrade Brazil to the status of a key country in U.S. foreign policy and then included Brazil among the target countries for U.S. nonproliferation and human rights policies. In the mid-1980s Brazil, together with other Latin American countries, decried the fact that the United States had not developed a political approach to deal with the debt crisis and, in the mid-1990s, criticized the United States for failing to provide support in a period of global financial turmoil.

Frustrations have also accumulated on the U.S. side. Ever since the 1950s, Brazil's nationalist economic policies have diverged from U.S. economic interests. The United States was also frustrated by Brazil's reluctance to align militarily with it during the Korean War in the early 1950s, the Vietnam War in the 1960s, the Central American struggles of the 1980s, and the Gulf War in the 1990s. Most recently, it has upset the Bush administration by its opposition to the attacks against Afghanistan and Iraq.

Though U.S.–Brazil relations have always been dominated by an intergovernmental agenda, nongovernmental actors have become more prominent in recent years. Military, economic, political, educational, and cultural interests have opened up the agenda, introducing a broader range of concerns and pressures. As a result, U.S.–Brazil relations are now more complex on both sides.

It is important to keep in mind that there is a striking difference between the bureaucracies involved with bilateral relations in Brazil and in the United

States. On the American side interstate relations are carried out by a bureaucratic mélange intercoordinated by the State Department, Defense Department (with a growing participation of the Southern Command [SOUTHCOM]), the National Security Council (NSC), and the U.S. Trade Representative (USTR). In Brazil, a bureaucratic mix comprising the presidency, the Foreign Ministry — referred to as "Itamaraty" — and the embassy in Washington, D.C., has always been responsible for the conduct of Brazil–U.S. relations. It is important to state that in Brazil the diplomatic corps plays a subordinate role to the Itamaraty, and its views take a back seat to those of the Itamaraty, which believes that if points of disagreement emerge between the United States and Brazil, they ought to be managed and conflict avoided. Accordingly, the Itamaraty would rather see Brazil expand its responsibilities and international prestige in the world arena than escalate tensions with the United States by arguing over conflicts in their agendas. In the Foreign Ministry the dominant view is that a multipolar world order would offer more opportunities and fewer constraints for Brazil than the currently contested unipolar order based on U.S. primacy.

In the United States foreign policy making is less centralized, and on many occasions that has facilitated independent negotiation processes, unlike in Brazil. Presidential diplomacy has also become an instrument for improving U.S.–Brazil political communications on global and regional matters.[3] Communications maintained between presidents Clinton and Cardoso in the 1990s and more recently between Bush and Lula have deepened the political dialogue and improved the "chemistry" between Washington and Brasilia (Lins 2005). Brazilian diplomats consider relations with the United States to have "finally achieved political maturity," meaning that bilateral communications have become more straightforward and pragmatic and that they avoid the most problematic areas, such as trade disputes, lest they contaminate the relationship as a whole. Further, there is a strong perception among local officials that the United States and Brazil have had more in common politically ever since Brazil's democracy was consolidated. Indeed, Brazilian diplomatic officials frequently note that an interdemocratic connection has now become the leitmotif of bilateral relations.

In defense matters, however, it has not been as easy to build new bridges. Nationalistic feeling among Brazilian military officials runs strong and only very gradually have they and their U.S. counterparts begun to establish closer relations. Regular bilateral military exercises and the creation of the Brazilian Defense Ministry (1998) have helped reestablish bilateral communications after more than twenty years of indifference.[4] After the inauguration of a Bilateral Working Group for Defense (1999), Brazil hosted and actively participated in the Fourth Defense Ministerial of the Americas (2000) as well as in the subsequent ministerial conferences at Santiago (2002) and Quito (2004).

The creation of the Brazilian Defense Ministry has helped facilitate communications between the United States and Brazil on security matters. At first Brazilian authorities strongly resisted the idea of creating a civilian-led defense ministry, which in the 1990s was at the top of the U.S. shopping list in security matters in its talks with Brazil. This resistance mainly came from the Brazilian army, which was reluctant to subordinate its forces to a single civilian authority. The creation of the ministry in 1998 led to an intense debate among academics, politicians, and the military regarding the future of Brazil's defense policy, a debate that resulted in the preparation of Brazil's first white paper. Even though the creation of the Ministry of Defense could be interpreted as a step forward in Brazil's military relations with the United States, it has not erased the anti-American sentiments in the Brazilian armed forces.

The main source of difficulty in U.S.–Brazil military relations at present stems from the growing U.S. military involvement in Colombia in combating drug traffickers and guerrillas, which Brazil regards as negatively affecting the security conditions in the Amazon area near its borders.[5] The Brazilian armed forces are particularly concerned with Colombia's future and the possibility that it has become tied to the deepening U.S. political and military presence in South America. Ever since 2000, when the U.S. Congress approved Plan Colombia to help fight drug trafficking, Brazil has become even more apprehensive.[6] Meanwhile, the Brazilian military and police forces are undertaking more defense initiatives against narco-guerrilla activities in the Amazon area, and their increased presence on the border with Colombia has enhanced the importance of defense policy in Brazil's regional agenda and has expanded budgetary needs, though the forces still face a dramatic lack of resources to meet those needs.[7] To deal with these shortages, therefore, the U.S. and Brazilian military and police have paradoxically begun cooperating more in defense initiatives in the Brazilian Amazon, in spite of Brazilian apprehensions about the American military presence there.[8]

Many members of the Brazilian Congress, from across the political spectrum, also take a nationalistic and anti-American stand, making it difficult to improve U.S.–Brazil negotiations over sensitive technology. This has been a taboo subject for both countries since the mid-1970s, when the United States opposed Brazil's nuclear agreement with Germany. More than twenty years later anti-American sentiments within the Brazilian legislative branch led it to reject an agreement that would have allowed U.S. companies to use an equatorial launching site at a base on the northeastern Brazilian coast. While this agreement would not have given Brazil access to technology, it would have given it the opportunity to participate in the international space market.[9] Negotiations with the United States were first carried forward at an intergovernmental level with the aim of dissipating Washington's concerns regarding the agreement Brazil had reached with

Ukraine whereby it would supply rocket technology to Brazil.[10] But in 2002 this became a lost cause for the Brazilian Foreign Ministry, and the agreement with the United States was buried. This is a clear example of a domestic difference in which the Itamaraty pushed for a cooperative agenda with the United States, while the military and the legislative branch maintained their strong nationalistic positions.

World Politics and Security

In the post–cold war world, international politics tend to follow a fragmented and less predictable pattern, particularly in the case of countries like Brazil, in which bandwagon diplomacy has been firmly avoided since the mid-1970s. Although it is harder now for Brazil to remain autonomous in its foreign policy, it still aspires to retain some level of independent capability to determine its moves in world affairs. Clear examples of such aspirations include South–South activism, particularly with other regional powers like India and South Africa, its leading initiatives in South America, the aim to become a permanent member in the U.N. Security Council, and its recent leading role in international and hemispheric trade negotiations. There has also been widespread and diverse support in Brazil for the idea that Brazil should be politically independent in world affairs as well as pressure for Brazil to make known that political independence.

In the interim Brazil has adapted to the fact of U.S. preeminence in post–cold war world politics and security. Though it would prefer a multipolar world order, Brazil has become less resistant to the unipolar structure of the contemporary international system. The combination of political changes in Brazil and more recent world events has broadened the range of convergence with the United States, particularly regarding political values and world peace efforts.

Brazil's reaction to the September 11 terrorist attacks on the United States emphasized its affinity for and attachment to Western political values. Brazil immediately voiced solidarity in grief as well as in broad-based efforts to combat terrorism. It also took the lead in the immediate call for an Organization of American States (OAS) conference, which was followed by the activation of the Inter-American Treaty of Reciprocal Assistance (IATRA). The United States did recognize Brazil's role in calling for the OAS meeting, though ever since it has expected Brazil to take more action regarding police and intelligence controls on terrorist suspects at its border zones. Subtle differences between Brasilia and Washington emerged as the United States made military preparations for operations in Afghanistan. At the time the Brazilian government emphasized the need to avoid irrational reactions and recommended caution instead of a precipitate military response. In fact, Brazil has discretely registered its opposition to U.S.

intervention in world and regional crises in a myriad of episodes such as the Gulf War (1991), the crisis in Haiti (1996), the Kosovo tragedy (1998), and the invasions of Afghanistan (2002) and Iraq (2003). In all cases the United States would have welcomed Brazil's support.[11]

Since the mid-1990s Brazil has been more willing to adopt a foreign policy that meets the international security expectations of the United States, particularly regarding adherence to international nonproliferation regimes. In 1994 Brazil joined the Missile Technology Control Regime (MTCR), and in 1997 it ratified the Non-Proliferation Treaty (NPT). Even though Brazil had to make major foreign policy changes to sign the NPT, new demands have been expressed on the part of the U.S regarding the country's nonproliferation commitments. Tension between Washington and Brasilia became noticeable when Brazil refused to comply with NPT expanded inspection procedures introduced by the 2004 Additional Protocol, not allowing the International Atomic Energy Agency (IAEA) to make a full visit to its uranium enrichment plant. U.S. concerns regarding Brazil's secrecy were that this could serve as a precedent to legitimate other and much more worrisome nuclear programs, such as those in Iran and North Korea. Memories of the last time the United States used coercive methods to deal with disagreements regarding Brazil's aims to access sensitive technology explain Brazil's defensive reaction to U.S. concerns, illustrating Brazilian touchiness when the United States acts indiscriminately to protect its general security interests and strategies. Another example of this kind of disagreement emerged in the U.N. Security Council when Brazil, together with other nonpermanent members such as Pakistan and Germany, tried to diminish the impact of U.S. antiproliferation initiatives that legitimized the imposition of unilateral sanctions on countries that did not adhere to the NPT.

Brazil is an active supporter of the enhancement of multilateral initiatives, particularly the expanded role of the United Nations in world politics, and its increased participation in U.N. peacekeeping operations has opened up a new area of commonality with the United States. Brazil participated in the U.N. Observer Mission in El Salvador (ONUSAL), in the U.N. Observer Mission in Mozambique (ONUMOZ), and in the U.N. Mission in Angola (UNAVEM), where it sent thirteen hundred soldiers, the largest military force it has sent abroad since World War II. Brazil also contributed police forces to the 1999 U.N. peace operation in East Timor and has assumed the military leadership of the U.N. Mission to Haiti (MINUSTAH) initiated in 2004. Working together, however, has not meant full-scale convergence. For example, although Washington has positively acknowledged Brazil's leading role in Haiti, it has insistently questioned the methods Brazilian troops use to control the country. Undoubtedly violence and turmoil in Haiti after the U.N. mission took over revealed the difficulties

MINUSTAH would face in attempting to stabilize the country politically and ensure the return of democratic rule.

For Brazil the reinforcement of the juridical and parliamentary structure of the U.N. system has become even more necessary given the present unipolar order (Amorin 1999). Brazil's active role in peacekeeping has not kept Brazil and the United States from holding different positions on a large share of U.N. General Assembly resolutions, particularly those concerning disarmament and human rights. Brazil has systematically taken a different position from the United States on human rights resolutions that are critical of China and Cuba. An illustration of the fragmented nature of U.S.–Brazil interstate relations can be observed in their voting patterns in different U.N. bodies. While their votes tend to coincide in the Security Council, they rarely do in the General Assembly. This is because in the General Assembly Brazil more often embraces Third World positions, which usually contrast with those of the United States and other great powers. Politics in the General Assembly basically reflect a North–South divide, and Brazil has long been a significant player in Third World politics. In the Security Council, however, where since the end of the cold war, Brazil has been elected a nonpermanent member four times (in 1989–90, 1993–94, 1998–99, and 2003–4), when resolutions are presented concerning crisis situations, Brazil rarely votes differently from the United States (U.N. Security Council, Reports of the Secretary-General).[12]

U.S. and Brazilian officials have also agreed on the need for broad institutional reforms within the U.N. system. The Brazilian government has made clear to the United States and other world powers its ambition to be one of the new permanent members of the U.N. Security Council if the number of seats increases.[13] Although Germany, France, and Russia have already endorsed Brazil's candidacy, the United States has been more cautious, as to endorse Brazil would mean it was indicating a regional preference, which could hurt the interests of other Latin American members, particularly Argentina and Mexico, who have not given up their candidacies in favor of Brazil. In 2005 Brazilian expectations regarding U.S. support for its aspirations were frustrated when Washington finally decided not to back an ambitious reform plan for the U.N. Security Council, supporting rather a "modest" expansion under which only two to three new permanent seats and two to three nonpermanent seats would be created. Another important and unexpected development of this matter for Brazil has been the convergence between the conservative stances of the United States and China regarding the reform issue, since Brazil had believed at first that it could count on Beijing to support its candidacy.[14]

After 9/11 Brazil developed a strategy to face the new global security threats, particularly those stemming from terrorism. In multilateral arenas, most notably the United Nations, it has insisted on the need for a conceptual revision of world institutional structures, evincing a special concern for the humanitarian impact of military action and emphasizing the importance of equilibrium between solidarity and globalization. It has also enforced concrete domestic measures intended to deepen control over money-laundering operations that could facilitate terrorist operations. At the same time, U.S. intelligence presence in Brazil was expanded to improve internal security. Two months after the September 2001 terrorist attacks, presidents Bush and Cardoso met to fine-tune bilateral relations on world politics.[15] Brazil adopted a rather difficult position; it granted support to the U.S.-led war against terrorism but declined to align itself wholesale with U.S. defense policy. For the United States the fact that Brazil did not offer military support for its war against terror has been an obstacle to deepening relations. Instead of offering full support for a global fight against terror, Brazil initiated a global campaign to fight poverty.[16] While for Brazil this is more a question of priorities, it also signifies a rejection of the militarized solutions adopted by the Bush administration to fight terrorism. At the same time the Lula administration has taken a cautious approach to Islamic terrorism and Middle East matters. It has condemned terrorists' claim that the use of violence to resist foreign occupation is justified — as many Arab countries have also done (*New York Times* 2005a) — but at the same time it seeks to increase its visibility in the Arab world, hosting to that end the 2005 Summit of South American and Arab Countries, to which it refused to invite the United States as an observer.

Regional Politics and Security

Improving communications with the White House via presidential diplomacy has become particularly important for dealing with South American crises. In recent years convergence and cooperation between Brazil and the United States facilitated the Ecuador–Peru peace process and the efforts to rescue Paraguay's democratic transition.[17] In October 1998 the governments of Ecuador and Peru signed a peace treaty in Brasilia, finally ending hostilities. The peace talks were coordinated during the 1997–98 period by the Brazilian government in permanent consultation with the United States, Argentina, and Chile (all of which have been formal mediators of the dispute since the first Ecuador–Peru war in 1942) (Herz and Nogueira 2002).

With regard to Paraguay, Brazil has consistently coordinated diplomatic measures with Argentina to contain authoritarian setbacks. Both countries have made use of the prerogatives offered by the democratic clause in the Common Market of the South (MERCOSUR) legislation to rein in antidemocratic movements in Paraguay. Tension reached its peak in 1996 when Brasilia, together with Buenos Aires and Washington, held back an attempt to overthrow the democratically elected government of Juan Carlos Wasmosy (1993–98). Communication between the United States and Brazil was also helpful in clarifying the different positions each country assumed regarding the status of democratic institutions in Peru during the electoral crisis in 2001 (Hirst 2005, 45). While Brazil adopted a more cautious approach, the U.S. government made explicit its support for the enforcement of the democratic procedures that had been put back in place.

Since the beginning of the twenty-first century South America has faced a new period of political instability, particularly in the Andean area. In the last six years major institutional breakdowns, massive popular protests, political violence, and local turmoil have brought down governments in numerous South American countries: Argentina (2001), Bolivia (2003), Ecuador (2000, 2003), Paraguay (1999), Peru (2000) and Venezuela (2002).[18] Regional and subregional instruments and regimes — such as MERCOSUR, the Andean Community, the Rio Group, the OAS, and the Iberamerican summits — have not been able to handle these crises, which appear to be both a cause and a consequence of the deepening of political fragmentation within the region. Nevertheless, in general, democratic institutions have remained intact, even if Washington does not see it that way. For example, SOUTHCOM officials have categorized some of the regional responses to these crises as "radical populism," which the United States considers to be an emerging threat in the inter-American environment.[19]

Brazil has refused to take a militarized approach and has expanded its political presence in the region, assuming new responsibilities by offering to mediate and to help bring about rule-based and democratic outcomes. The Lula administration has been particularly active in promoting political governability in South America, perceived in Brasilia not only as a means to enhance regional stability but also as a means to expand the country's presence in world affairs. This is probably the most important change that has been made in Brazilian foreign policy since the inauguration of the Lula administration, which had traditionally always been firmly grounded in the principle of nonintervention in the affairs of states.

The United States has been concerned that a more active Brazil could assemble South America into a single bloc that would destabilize Washington's preeminence in the hemisphere. If, as Brazil aims to become more active in regional affairs, it disagrees with the United States on regional trade and security issues, that could lead the United States to politicize hemispheric affairs. In fact, Brazil has been reluctant to support the U.S. drive to revitalize its inter-American leadership, and even though they both want to promote democratic values in South America, Brazil and the United States do not always agree on what the best method is for doing that.

More and more Washington is assuming an offensive posture toward populist democracies in South America, which may lead to a new chapter of discord between Washington and Brasilia. The countries in the region with which Washington feels political and ideological affinity are not the same countries Brazil favors. For example, relations between the Uribe government in Colombia and the Bush administration have been far more friendly and cooperative than those with Chávez in Venezuela, while exactly the opposite can be said of the Lula government's relations with these countries. Washington would welcome Brazilian involvement in the Colombian war against narco-guerrillas and would prefer that the Lula administration not maintain such friendly relations with Hugo Chávez. Washington became particularly concerned over the Venezuela–Brazil talks in which Brazil agreed to sell military equipment to Venezuela and in which both countries agreed to cooperate on developing nuclear programs.[20]

Brazil has also assumed a more active role in regional security matters. Concerns regarding the growing impact of the Colombian civil war led Brazilian officials in 2001 to participate with other international delegations as observers in the first open peace meeting held between the Colombian government and guerrilla organizations. Brazil also hosted a Latin American and Caribbean conference that focused on developing a regional approach to bring to the 2001 U.N. conference on illicit small-arms traffic, which deepened security cooperation in the region.[21] Further, ever since the Triple Border Security Plan was launched in 1998, which was followed by agreements facilitating extradition and joint police operations, Brazil and its MERCOSUR partners have fervently engaged in mutual antidrug operations. Special attention has also been given to the presence of money laundering and illegal arms trafficking in the area.

The Defense Ministerial Conferences of the Americas held in 2000, 2002, and 2004 brought changes in U.S.–Brazil relations owing to differences of opinion over how to ensure regional security. While caution has prevailed on both sides, Brazilian officials have made it clear that they are not willing to support U.S. security policies in South America, be it Plan Colombia or the more recent recommendations on how to fight terrorism in the area. Brazilian officials have been particularly critical of the concerns expressed by the U.S. Department of Defense regarding the threats posed by "ungoverned areas."

In fact, following the terrorist attacks of September 11 U.S. security interests in South America shifted and that inevitably affected relations with Brazil. The United States wishes to secure Brazilian support for its defense policies to ensure the equilibrium of its security policy in the Southern Cone, in which the ideal since the end of the cold war has been to combine military alliances with modest relationships (Shifter 2004). Since September 11, the United States has expected a higher level of response and commitment from its Latin American partners. The United States would, for example, like to strengthen intelligence cooperation and to develop a coordinated approach to handling new security threats in the region, effective counterterrorist strategies, and law enforcement and judicial measures to contain criminal activities. It would also like Latin America to deny any sort of support to governments that sponsor terrorism. According to the U.S. government, one-third of the terrorist groups spread around the world operate in Latin America.

The U.S. government has become particularly concerned with the need to improve intelligence and police control in the triple border area, between the cities of Puerto Iguazú (Argentina), Ciudad del Este (Paraguay), and Foz do Iguaçu (Brazil), which the FBI considers a sanctuary for Islamic terrorists. Tensions on this front emerged between the United States and Brazil at the Fifth Defense Ministerial (2002) in Santiago, as a consequence of U.S. expectations regarding antiterrorist security policies in the region. The United States proposed three ideas: (1) to increase cooperation among navies, coast guards, custom officers, and police forces to strengthen coastal defensive capabilities in the region, with special attention to the Caribbean area; (2) to develop regional peacekeeping initiatives among Argentina, Brazil, Uruguay, and Chile; and (3) to launch effective initiatives to enhance the control over ungoverned areas that could become havens for terrorist action, particularly the triple border area and Colombia.

More recently, the United States has negotiated a military agreement with Paraguay as part of its antiterrorist policies in the region, which has elicited a strong reaction from Brazil. This initiative has been interpreted by Brasilia as an unnecessary American intrusion into the MERCOSUR area, which could deepen even more the present difficulties the bloc faces in trying to improve Paraguayan relations with its partners. But Paraguay has its reasons for defecting, having for many years voiced major complaints about intrabloc economic asymmetries and the growing disadvantages of the bloc's ties with Brazil (Hirst 2005/6).

While there is still a gap between Brazil and the United States over antiterrorism measures, they are very much in agreement about the need to repress drug trafficking activities in South America. Formal collaboration has been framed in a bilateral narcotics agreement (1994), updated by a Memorandum of Understanding (1996) and the Mutual Legal Assistance Treaty (MLAT 1997).[22] In addition to these bilateral mechanisms, the United States and Brazil are cooperating in counternarcotics activities through multilateral arenas such as the U.N. Drug Control Program (UNDCP)—which Brazil joined in 1991—and the Organization of American States / Drug Abuse Control Commission (OAS/CICAD). The U.S. government has also acknowledged that Brazil has improved its police and legislative involvement in counternarcotics activities (U.S. Department of State, Bureau for International Narcotics and Law Enforcement Affairs 2006), and it praised the Brazilian government for approving anti-money-laundering and military air-interception legislation. Further, the U.S. government has provided equipment and personnel for Brazil's Antidrug Secretariat and has been working with this agency on antidrug and antiviolence educational programs.[23]

The United States still expects more progress in Brazil's drug trafficking controls, which would entail creating more legislation, enhancing the enforcement infrastructure of the existing legislation, and expanding counternarcotics programs.[24] The United States has been particularly concerned, as noted above, with Brazil's loose controls in the areas bordering its Andean neighbors (Passos 2005). U.S.–Brazil security collaboration has also increased at the triborder area where agents from the U.S. Department of Homeland Security have set up units to investigate and prosecute an array of financial crimes, including contraband smuggling and tax evasion (*New York Times* 2006). The Lula administration has also manifested a growing interest in expanding its presence in inter-American security matters, particularly within the OAS recently created Multidimensional Security Secretariat.

To a certain degree, the Lula government has presented the Bush administration with an opportunity to redevelop a positive relationship with Latin American partners after a period of relative neglect due to its post–September 11 security priorities. On Brazil's side, its intention to assume a more active role vis-à-vis political turbulence in the region has made it more interested in maintaining communications with the White House. Yet persisting U.S. misperceptions regarding regional political developments remain a source of tension between the countries, tension that could spoil such an opportunity.

Conclusions

Brazil's position vis-à-vis the United States is, in summary, typically defensive. Governmental and nongovernmental actors agree that the United States represents more a source of concern than of opportunity for the country, and that U.S. hegemony entails more costs than benefits. Yet Brazil has avoided and will continue to avoid confrontation with the United States, particularly in security and political matters. To "agree to disagree" has become one of the ways Brazilian officials have described relations with Washington (Pereira 2005).

As was mentioned at the beginning of this chapter, U.S.–Brazil differences are far more significant on economic issues, differences that, in recent years, have been exacerbated owing to regional and multilateral trade confrontations (Hirst 2005, 19–39). On the one hand, the long-standing negotiations of the Free Trade Area of the Americas (FTAA) have been affected by Brazil–U.S. disagreements regarding services, intellectual property, agriculture, and antidumping duties, while on the other, bilateral trade disagreements between the two have been inextricably linked to multilateral disputes carried out at the WTO. It seems that economics in bilateral relations is important to both sides, as a financial/monetary crisis in Brazil could threaten international markets. Further, policies Brazil might adopt that contest the dominant recipes prescribed by Washington based on multilateral credit institutions, particularly the International Monetary Fund (IMF), could pose risks for the United States.

The Brazilian media transmit a broad anti-American, nationalist message that expresses the views of different ideological groups. These sentiments are particularly voiced in nongovernmental circles and are especially visible within social movements and academic environments, where leftist and nationalistic political thinking prevail. At the same time, democratization and globalization have stimulated a new interest in international affairs in Brazilian politics. In Brazil, globalization and U.S. economic interests are frequently perceived as being synonymous and are viewed as being equally harmful. Brazilian apprehensions regarding U.S. post–cold war leadership are often linked to a critical vision of globalization (Fiori 2001). Brazil aspires to define its own democratic values, market economy rules, and national security interests, even though this aspiration collides with the interests of the United States. It is highly unlikely that anti-Americanism will dissipate in the near future. In fact, it has been magnified by the U.S.-led wars against Afghanistan and Iraq together with the expansion of unilateralism in U.S. trade policies.[25]

The international priorities established by the Bush administration in the wake of 9/11 have introduced new security variables that inevitably have had an impact on bilateral ties. As has already been mentioned, Brazil has maintained a cautious distance from Washington's war against terror. The United States has paid less attention to the aims identified as Brazil's foreign policy priorities such as economic development, environmental protection, expansion of multilateralism in world security, and the strengthening of democracy in the region, whether or not it involves a populist and nationalist discourse. Different priorities may not lead to collisions, but they certainly will not deepen convergence between the two countries in the near future. It would, however, be less costly and risky for Brazil if the Lula administration could realize its goal of expanding relations with other developing nations without negatively affecting its relationship with the United States.

The two countries' differences over U.S. global strategic priorities will not likely disappear and will in fact probably deepen. Brazil and the United States are much more likely to agree on regional matters, particularly in situations where democratic institutions face serious risk. Washington more and more addresses Brazil as a strategic partner and expects it to play a more active role in the region either by expanding its participation in U.N.-led peace operations or by using diplomacy to de-escalate state crises in the hemisphere, especially in South America.

Overall, in the coming years Brazil will probably move toward building a South American leadership position through which it will try to expand its global presence. However, Brazil will have to move cautiously in the region, since the expansion of its political involvement in local crises — together with growing trade and investment activities with South American neighbors — has not generated automatic acknowledgment of its regional leadership. If Brazil does not succeed in securing support and acknowledgment from it neighbors, the United States will be more hesitant to recognize its role as a regional leader. On the other hand, it will be Brazil's aim to build up such leadership in a way that does not make it seem like it is trying to compete with the United States. If Brazil succeeds, it could provide a new incentive for both countries to cooperate further. In other words, Brazil is not expected either to bandwagon or to contest U.S. global leadership. Its main goal will be to obtain Washington's recognition of its voice in global affairs.

Notes

1. Celso Amorim, the present foreign minister of Brazil, has defined the relationship with United States as one of "respect and solidarity" in which both countries share an interest in avoiding confrontation.

2. Brazilian ambassador Roberto Abdenur states that the relationship between United States and Brazil is and has always been characterized by its dynamism. In this context, Brazil and United States would have a "non-declared alliance" as Celso Amorim explained during his visit to Washington ("Parceira estratégica não declarada," *O Globo*, October 20, 2005).

3. Between 1995 and 2001 President Cardoso met President Clinton five times and President Bush two times.

4. Brazilian–U.S. military relations had been de facto frozen since 1977, when Brazil renounced its 1952 military agreement with the United States.

5. In August 2000 President Clinton traveled to Colombia to announce the Colombia Plan, a $1.3-billion-dollar aid package, and to reaffirm full support for the Pastrana government. Eighty percent of the aid package was designated for the formation of three one-thousand-men antidrug battalions, five hundred military advisers, and sixty helicopters. The plan was been renewed and expanded in 2005.

6. When referring to Plan Colombia at a joint news conference with Secretary of State Madeleine K. Albright, the Brazilian foreign minister at the time stated, "We do not have the same degree of commitment. We have no intention of participating in any common or concerted international action" (Larry Rohter, "Brazil Begins to Take Role on the World Stage," *New York Times*, August 30, 2000).

7. The Querari Operation, launched in 1999, became Brazil's largest military operation in the Amazon area. It comprised five thousand men who collaborated with the navy and the

air force and a special jungle brigade of specially trained indigenous soldiers. The government has also substantially increased the budget of the Calha Norte project in the Amazon area, which gives high priority to social work and infrastructure initiatives in areas inhabited by poor populations as well as indigenous communities.

8. The United States has contributed financially to Plan Cobra in the Amazon area, increased its aid to Brazil's federal police antidrug programs from $1.2 million dollars in 1999 to $15 million in 2002. In addition, American firms have been contracted to build the Sivan project, a monitoring program for the entire Amazon region (Narich 2003).

9. The world satellite-launching industry is expected to grow 20 percent a year. With the capacity for fourteen launchings a year, the Alcantara base in Brazil could bring the country an estimated thirty million dollars each year (Simon Romero, "Brazil is Allowing U.S. Companies to Use Launching Sites," *New York Times*, April 19, 2000).

10. That Washington had such concerns was mentioned in interviews the author conducted with Brazilian government officials in 1999–2000.

11. Brazil's opposition has not affected the development of Lula and Bush relationship. In fact of all the national leaders who opposed war in Iraq, Lula was the first to be invited to the White House.

12. Brazil was absent as a nonpermanent member from 1968 to 1988.

13. Brazil, Germany, Japan, and India (the so-called Group of Four [G4]) have been seeking worldwide support for the idea of enlarging the U.N. Security Council from fifteen to twenty-five members, which would involve the creation of six new permanent seats (besides seats for the countries mentioned above, two seats would be given to Africa). An alternate proposal called "United for Consensus" was put together by a group consisting of Pakistan, Argentina, Egypt, Italy, and others. It recommends the expansion of nonpermanent seats with periodic rotation.

14. In 2005 Wang Guangya met with John Bolton and agreed to block the G-4 plan because they believed it could divide U.N. members. China basically opposed a permanent seat for Japan and pleaded for increased representation for developing countries such as Africa. The United States, on the other hand, has not approved six new permanent seats but only two or three (Edith M. Lederer, "U.S. and China Unite to Block G4 Plan," Associated Press, August 4, 2005).

15. The meeting took place in the United States on November 8, 2001.

16. See U.N. campaign against poverty http://www.un.org/millenniumgoals.

17. Regarding the political crisis in Paraguay, a description of earlier coordination between the United States and Brazil appears in Arturo Valenzuela's "The Collective Defense of Democracy: Lessons from the Paraguayan Crisis of 1996" (1999), Report to the Carnegie Commission on Preventing Deadly Conflict, December, 32.

18. Arturo Valenzuela states that "the absence of a leadership at the State Department, combined with a waning interest in Latin American policy at higher levels of the administration, has contributed to a caretaker approach to hemispheric policy that failed to deal forcefully in 'crisis management,' particularly with respect to looming crises in Argentina and Venezuela" (Valenzuela 2004, 6).

19. In June 2006, Latin American countries refused a U.S. plan to establish a permanent committee of the OAS in order to monitor the exercise of democracy in the hemisphere

(Joel Brinkley, "Latin Nations Resist Plan for Monitor of Democracy," *New York Times*, June 6, 2005, A-1).

20. In the early months of 2006 the State Department vetoed a deal closed between Venezuela and Brazil under which Venezuela would have purchased of thirty-six Tucano aircraft produced by Brazilian Embraer because American technology had been used to make the planes (Jungblut and D'Ercole 2006).

21. The conference took place in Brasilia, November 22–24, 2000.

22. This treaty was signed by both countries during the 1997 Clinton visit to Brazil. Although the U.S. Senate approved the treaty in October 1998, it still awaited Brazilian congressional approval for several years.

23. The Educational Program for Resistance to Drugs and Violence deserves a special mention; it trains uniformed state military police drug education volunteers in seventeen of Brazil's twenty-six states.

24. Following its hemispheric policy, the White House Office of National Drug Control Policy (ONDCP) created a permanent connection with the Brazilian Antidrug Secretariat, while the U.S. Drug Enforcement Administration (DEA) has been invited each year to observe Brazilian federal police operations in the Amazon region.

25. Illustrative evidence of these feelings was provided by a poll conducted by the BBC on anti-American sentiments after the war against Iraq began. The poll surveyed eleven thousand people in eleven countries. Brazil was one of the countries in which a negative opinion toward the United States appeared to be the highest. According to the survey, in each country interviewed the percentage with negative opinions were: Jordan, 79 percent; Brazil, 66 percent; Indonesia, 58 percent; France, 51 percent; Australia, 29 percent; Russia, 28 percent; South Korea, 28 percent; Israel, 25 percent; England, 19 percent; and Canada, 16 percent ("O tamanho do antiamericanismo," *Revista Veja*, August 13, 2003, 59).

PART THREE

Limiting Reach to Grasp

CHAPTER FIFTEEN

From Superpower to Besieged Global Power

Edward A. Kolodziej

This chapter has three interrelated aims, each providing an ascending level of analysis and explanation of why the Bush model for reform of the international system and global politics was flawed both in aspiration and in application and why it has failed. The first section briefly summarizes what one respected and informed observer and longtime Pentagon watcher has termed the "fiasco" of the Iraqi invasion (Ricks 2006). It both draws on the mounting flood of criticisms of the war and supplements this converging assessment by analysts who otherwise hold rival political perspectives by identifying fault lines in the Bush strategy that have been either overlooked or slighted (Galbraith 2006; M. Gordon and Trainor 2006; P. Gordon 2006; and the belatedly repentant Fukuyama 2006. For counterpoint see Ajami 2005; Bremer 2006; Tenet 2007).

The second section, drawing on the regional chapters, widens and deepens this critique. In rich and reinforcing detail these chapters underwrite the argument of this volume: that a balanced understanding of American power, hard and soft, and the development of a workable strategy to advance American interests start with downsizing and ultimately discarding the notion of the United States as a superpower or hegemon. As a precondition for developing such a strategy, we need to realistically appraise the effectiveness and legitimacy of American power, policies, and purposes taking into account the perspectives and countervailing power of other peoples and states. American power must work through this resistant medium to get its way.

These perspectives, and the mutually contingent power relations with other peoples and states on which they rest, point to both the limits *and* (what is often overlooked) the opportunities that define the range of American power. Where constraints are intractable and cannot be wished away, American power is obliged to adapt to them if it is to avoid self-defeating strategies. Conversely, where U.S. and regional-national interests intersect, the impact of the United States on the global system can be positive and reinforcing, resulting in a virtuous circle, much like the use of American power after World War II that created a Western coalition that held together for over a half-century (something many esteemed observers of American foreign policy believed impossible) (de Tocqueville 1945; Kennan 1984; Lippmann 1947). That coalition, the real hegemon in international relations as Patrick Morgan reminds us, emerged ascendant with the collapse of the Soviet Union and the end of the cold war.

What we are witnessing today is a vicious circle in which American power and its projection abroad undermine American values and interests, weaken the Western coalition of open, market-oriented societies, and endanger the spread of the very ideals holding this coalition together — security, freedom, popular rule, human rights, and increasing material welfare for the populations of the coalition and those of the world, the stated but miscarried aims driving the Bush model.

The third section challenges several widely held notions among theorists about the patterns of power in international relations and global politics and their implications for global governance. The principal conclusion to be drawn from this section is that no actor, or alliance of actors, state or nonstate, is in control of global politics, viewed across the spectrum of the challenges confronting the world's populations: limiting violence, stanching the production and dissemination of weapons of mass destruction (WMD), assuring sustainable economic growth, and addressing man-made ecological catastrophes. Arguably, most daunting is the imperative to peacefully define a set of moral and political values and institutionalized rules that can be universally accepted by the world's contesting peoples to regulate their clashing values and aims and to create stable structures of power and set into motion the multiple political processes by which these accords can be implemented and perfected (Keohane and Nye 2001).[1]

The imperative for consensual accord across cultures, religions, and states at different stages of socioeconomic and political development has never been more urgent or necessary — nor arguably more problematic — than it is now. The decentralization of power, recounted by this volume, across six billion, interdependent peoples and the two-hundred-odd states they have created, within what is an emerging global society for the first time in the evolution of the species, poses a formidable challenge for humans everywhere, and how they cope with that challenge will determine whether they survive and thrive.[2] It remains an open question, which this volume poses but does not resolve, whether humans will be able to surmount their profound differences in order both to address their shared threats as well as to exploit the benefits of cooperation.

The jury is still out. The evidence of cooperation over the last century is impressive: the dismantling of empires, the defeat of Fascism, Nazism, and Communism as authoritarian solutions for global rule, the subsequent spread of popular governments and human rights as well as an enlarging global civil community linked in real time by instant communications and rapid transportation, accelerating scientific discovery, the rapid diffusion of technological innovation, and the unprecedented creation of global material wealth, estimated in excess of forty trillion dollars (and mounting).

Conversely, the global issues confronting an expanding world population — nine to ten billion by 2050, with growth occurring largely in the underdeveloped world — threaten the capacity of humans, not just Americans, to build on these achievements. The revolution in world politics prompts an update of Benjamin Franklin's cautionary advice about how the American revolution would be won: that is, either the world's populations hang together, or they will hang separately.

The Iraq "Fiasco": A Laboratory Test

The Iraqi invasion and occupation may be viewed as a laboratory test that falsifies the Bush model for global reform sketched in chapter 1.

First, Iraq has exposed as demonstrably untenable the proposition that American unilateral use or threat of force is sufficient to induce reticent allies, skeptical neutrals, and resolute opponents, either by consensus or coercion, to bandwagon on American power and policies. This constraint can be relaxed but not surmounted in an international system of diffused power, notwithstanding overwhelming American military prowess compared to any other state or coalition of states, as Patrick Morgan's chapter details. The precipitous defeat of the Taliban in Afghanistan and the rapid destruction of Iraq's more formidable military forces underscore this obvious imbalance in destructive power. What is also clear is the growing gap between the fighting capabilities of American forces and their capacity to address the actual security threats confronting the United States.

If it is arguably true that the United States can be viewed as a superpower in the limited sense of being able to defeat the militaries of other states in open combat, it is no less true that rational and sensible opponents will avoid engaging American forces directly. Rivals are resourceful enough to develop their own nuclear deterrents — witness Iran and North Korea — to frustrate prevailing U.S. security strategy. Where that option is unavailable, U.S. rivals can pursue a strategy of the weak, proven effective throughout the long period of decolonization. Iraqi insurgents, suicide bombers, Jihadists, and even those who are elected members of the new Iraqi parliament with their own private militias use a variety of means to undo the American occupation and Iraqi government: they set off improvised explosive devices (IEDs) of progressively increasing sophistication and destructive force, stage ambushes, assassinate Iraqis (e.g., interpreters, journalists, police, army, civil servants, and governmental officials) who collaborate with coalition forces, and intimidate the populace within which insurgents and terrorists are embedded to preclude cooperation with the American occupation and to demonstrate the inability either of American forces or of the American-forged Iraqi regime to provide for their security.

All of these tactics are classic components of an insurgency's tool kit in responding to the superior firepower of occupiers. Asymmetrical warfare balances all too well and lethally against American firepower. The Iraqi invasion and the subsequent insurgency and sectarian conflict have resulted in more than thirty-five hundred American deaths and over twenty-five thousand injuries, as chapter 1 recounts. These losses constitute the elimination of an American division in combat—a feat that Iraqi regular forces were unable to achieve.[3] Since the 2003 invasion tens of thousands more Iraqi civilians have died as a consequence of continuing hostilities, insurgent and Jihadist attacks, and rising sectarian conflict that is a civil war by any other name.[4]

From a political perspective of effectiveness, unprecedented American military power is itself insufficient to qualify the United States as a superpower within the understanding of this volume. The American Gulliver is hamstrung by countless domestic and foreign constraints that, taken together, reduce the United States to a much-beset global power. One would expect that in the strict sense conveyed by the term "superpower" the United States would be able to impose its will on others where its vital interests are at stake, much as the Bush administration assumed it could in rationalizing its unilateralist doctrine to remake global society in its image of American power and purpose.

Numerous and mounting published works have documented Bush administration miscalculations and witless blunders in its attempt to create a stable, economically reconstructed, and democratically governed Iraq. These errors of omission and commission need little elaboration here but can instead be summarized (see Ricks 2006; Galbraith 2006; M. Gordon and Trainor 2006; P. Gordon 2006; and Fukuyama 2006). The errors were two-fold. First was the rejection of a containment strategy to deal with the Hussein regime, which was the consensus view of the U.S. professional military corps of how to best manage the Iraqi threat (Ricks 2006, 12–28). Once war was inevitable and regime change was the order of the day, the Pentagon's civilian leadership then rejected the recommendation of military planners for an occupation force at least twice as large as the invasion army. As Michael Gordon and Bernard Trainor's detailed accounting shows (M. Gordon and Trainor 2006), the professional military's force projections were based on the lessons of Vietnam and, later, of the Balkan wars. With the inexplicable acquiescence of Secretary of State Colin Powell, the Bush Doctrine rejected the Powell doctrine that stipulated that overwhelming force was required not only to defeat an enemy but also to ensure security and hold territory once victory was accomplished.

The then–army chief of staff, Eric Shinseki, who had commanded NATO and American troops in Bosnia, extrapolated from the force deployments that had been required to contain the Balkan wars to estimate the number of troops needed to successfully occupy Iraqi territory and control the population. Shinseki informed Congress that several hundred thousand troops would be needed, double the invasion force, "'to maintain a safe and secure environment to ensure that people are fed, that water is distributed, all the normal responsibilities that go along with administering a situation like this'" (Ricks 2006, quoted by Ricks, 97). Deputy Secretary of Defense Paul Wolfowitz dismissed Shinseki's testimony as "outlandish" (Ricks 2006, 97). Bush administration officials, including Vice President Dick Cheney and Secretary of Defense Donald Rumsfeld, assured the Congress and skeptics that the Iraqi public would welcome U.S. forces. In wishing away the likelihood of an Iraqi insurgency as improbable, planning to address this very real contingency was shelved. Nor would economic recovery be any problem, Deputy Secretary of Defense Paul Wolfowitz told Congress. The elimination of state controls and corruption and the production of Iraqi oil yielding upward of twenty billion dollars annually would pay for Iraqi reconstruction (Ricks 2006, 98).

Coalition forces, which easily defeated Saddam Hussein's army, were too small and unprepared to ensure the security of Iraqi civilians, to protect Iraq's infrastructure, to prevent Iraqi military equipment and arms from falling into the hands of insurgents and criminals, much less to launch a massive rebuilding program of Iraq's economy, which had been ruined by years of Hussein regime predations and international sanctions.[5] Dismantling the Hussein government and its military forces and prohibiting former Baathists from serving in military and civilian positions facilitated the spread of the insurgency. Unemployed Sunni civil servants and lower ranking military personnel were ready recruits for rebellion, led by remnants of the defeated Hussein regime. These groups had little option other than resistance to improve their lots once cast to the margins of Iraqi society. Opposition to the U.S. occupation has since grown and now includes members of the elected Iraqi government who, like Moqtada al-Sadr, command militias capable of challenging American and governmental forces, even as Jihadists multiply, compounding Iraq's security problems and undermining the occupation and negating the vaunted claims of President Bush's surge strategy as his errant alternative to the Iraq Study Group's recommendation of a gradual drawdown of American troops from Iraq (Iraq Study Group 2006).

A second fundamental flaw in the Bush model of global reform is the notion that coercively induced regime change in the Middle East will produce democratic governments and ipso facto engender peace. After four futile years of pursuing this will-o'-the-wisp, the administration has been compelled to gradually accept the bankruptcy of its grand design, an acceptance that is reflected in its quiet abandonment of democratic rule as the primary aim of the occupation in favor of the lower standard of stability and order.[6] Facts on the ground provide little hope that the Bush design of a peaceful, Western-style democratic Iraq can be realized. Iraq's fragile, sectarian-based Shiite regime is at war with itself and with its Sunni rivals. It must rely for its survival on American military forces, a dependency that delegitimates its authority and renders empty its claim to represent a sovereign state. Iraq now breeds Jihadists and terrorist cells of all kinds that were previously destroyed or contained by an authoritarian, but secular, Hussein regime. Yet these disquieting facts have not fully shaken the administration from its state of denial that the Iraq it wants, one that if not friendly is at least not hostile to the United States, is beyond its power to realize. Pointedly rejected is the recommendation of the Iraq Study Group (Baker and Hamilton 2006) to draw down American forces and to shift the burden and responsibility of security to the Iraqi government. Instead, the administration, freed by the paralysis of a divided public and Congress, has been able to escalate the war by throwing more good troops at bad policy — a kind of Gresham's law of strategy — in a last-ditch assault to quell the insurgency, end the civil war, and defeat al Qaeda. The administration has continued to pursue this strategy even though such past surges failed to achieve these strategic aims.

As already noted, and as mounting casualty figures evidence, Iraq is in the midst of a civil war, contained by a thin line of American occupation forces. However much Iraqi officials must uneasily rely on U.S. forces to stay in power, the latter are still viewed as an occupation army and, even more threatening in some Iraqi circles, as the vanguard of a permanent presence to support American imperial expansion. American forces are thus easy targets, confronted by a wide array of armed and hostile opponents: suicide bombers, irreconcilable Jihadists, intransigent insurgents, and determined combatants engaged in rising sectarian conflict. The American occupation has, paradoxically, both contributed to the emergence of these disparate forms of civil violence and unwittingly placed American forces in their cross fire. The mounting toll of daily casualties, American and Iraqi, is slowly creating the conditions under which a "perfect storm" of an ungovernable Iraq, racked by civil war, threatens to engulf the entire region.[7]

As for regime change and the efficacy of democratic rule, the elected Iraqi and Afghan governments are too feeble to provide for the central function of a government — their own security and that of their populations. They can scarcely claim a monopoly on the use of legitimate violence, the standard definition of a successful regime in security terms. Conversely, elected regimes in Iran and in Palestine — however they may fall short of Western standards of free and fair elections — staunchly oppose the U.S. occupation in Iraq. They also refuse to accept the legitimacy of Israel and call for its destruction. The conflicting goals of fighting terrorism and spreading popular rule could not be more clearly, or painfully, evident.

The failed Iraqi invasion and flawed occupation have currently tipped the balance of power in the Middle East against the United States. Despite the deployment of 150,000 troops in Iraq, there is no clear exit strategy in sight. What popular government the United States may have provisionally created in Iraq is controlled by the ascendancy of a Shiite majority in the Iraqi parliament that works against American aims and interests. If the Iraqi government as it is presently composed can impose its will on insurgents, primarily Sunnis, defeat Jihadists, and rein in the Kurds in the North, it will still be a primarily sectarian-based, Shiite-dominated government, a far cry from a government that accepts the one person, one vote principle underlying American political practices and the Bush ideal of democracy.

The rise of Shiite power also enhances Iran's power and influence in the region. In the 2006 Hezbollah–Israeli war, Hezbollah reportedly received its arms from Iran and Syria. These included thousands of short-range missiles, which Hezbollah rained on Israeli cities. Further, the Iraqi Shiite community openly favored Hezbollah. In a visit to Washington during the war, the Iraqi prime minister, Nuri Kamal al-Maliki, addressed Congress to assure critics that the war in Iraq was being won, but he refused to support U.S. policy in the Lebanon crisis. The conservative news journal *Economist* titled its August 19–25, 2006, issue "Nasralla [Hezbollah] Wins the War." That may well be an exaggeration, reflecting the heady emotions of the time, but certainly Israel was not the winner even by Israeli standards. That the Israeli people did not regard Israel as having been triumphant was made clear by the resignation of the Israeli army chief of staff, the creation of a special Israeli commission to investigate the debacle, and calls for the resignation of the government over its alleged inept conduct of the war.

Adding to U.S. isolation (while implicitly undermining its pursuit of a democratic peace for the Middle East) has been the surprising extent to which the American-backed and democratically elected government of Lebanon has sided with Hezbollah against Israel and the United States. Too weak to stop Hezbollah from launching the war, it revealed its inability to execute the primary responsibility of a state, namely, to insure the security of its territory and population. Hezbollah, not the Lebanese government, commanded a force sufficient to deny the state's monopoly.

U.S. unconditional support of Israel and its air assault on Lebanese cities, notably Beirut, and the destruction of large segments of Lebanon's transportation and communication infrastructure had the added debilitating effect of voiding the time-worn and tattered but still discernibly viable broker's role that the United States had typically played over several decades of Middle East Arab–Israeli wars and armed exchanges. Two added signs of U.S. impotence were exposed when Washington, having been foiled in its expectation of a decisive defeat of Hezbollah by Israel, was compelled, lacking other options, to enlist the United Nations to authorize a peacekeeping force to separate Hezbollah and Israel and to engage the Europeans, notably the French who had been instrumental in cobbling together a U.N. resolution to stop the fighting, to supply troops to implement the cease-fire. With the loss of American legitimacy in brokering the Hezbollah–Israeli war and with U.S. troops tied down in Iraq, the United States was in no position to send American forces to Lebanon, nor would they have been welcome even if they had been available.

Despite this unexpected blow to American unilateralism, the administration still clings to the faded ideal of a democratic and peaceful Middle East and to the belief in the democratic peace as both the expected outcome of global social forces supported by American power and as the instrument and goal of American strategy to advance U.S. national interests.[8] As late as the Hezbollah–Israel war in July–August 2006, Secretary of State Condoleezza Rice, expecting a quick and decisive Israeli victory that did not materialize, asserted that the world was witnessing the "birth pangs of a new Middle East."[9] What was being born, presumably, was democratic governments throughout the region that would validate the Bush administration's embrace of the democratic peace as the basis for American and global order and peace. Popular movements, animated by exclusionary religious principles of political legitimacy, are clearly on the march in the Middle East. Also evident is that they are neither marching to a Washington drum nor to a liberal democratic human rights beat.

An equally damaging blow has been dealt to widely held notions across the American political spectrum, from right to left, from blue to red states, of American moral exceptionalism and superiority. As chapter 1 indicates, President Bush, like his predecessors, was able to draw on deeply embedded values and ideological certainties that are central components of the American psyche and American civic culture. Most states and peoples around the globe reject American self-approbation of its purportedly disinterested unilateralism in pursuit of its self-defined international security obligations under the U.N. Charter and its claim to the moral high ground. Majorities in all of the major European states of the European Union (EU) reject the Bush Doctrine and dismiss the administration's optimistic claims that Western societies are safer than they were before 9/11.[10] Confidence in American intelligence also rapidly evaporated when evidence of an Iraqi program of WMD and collusion with al Qaeda terrorists proved totally unfounded. These were administration fabrications, highlighted by a misleading and factually flawed presentation of the charges by a once-credible secretary of state Colin Powell before the United Nations in early 2003 (Ricks 2006).

The American invasion of Iraq has transformed the military from a liberating force into an occupying army. Its legitimacy rests primarily on force majeure, not the consent of the Iraqi public and government, both of which look forward to the eventual and timely withdrawal of American forces. Deepening the legitimacy crisis are the depredations committed by American forces against Iraqi citizens and widely publicized reports, circulating throughout the Muslim world, of desecrating assaults on Islamic practices and sensibilities. The incarceration of enemy combatants without determining their status as prisoners of war and, worse, the torture and, in some instances, the murder of prisoners in American custody eviscerate American claims of rendering justice superior to that which might be obtained by American observance of the Geneva Convention. The sophistic acceptance by the Bush administration of American obligations under the Geneva Convention (under current U.S. law the president alone determines what is consistent with the treaty) and its serpentine defense of torture, capped by photos beamed around the globe of American torture of Iraqi prisoners at Abu Ghraib, undermine American exceptionalism as a defensible moral claim.[11]

What is particularly difficult for Americans of all political stripes to accept is their complicity in these depredations. Those responsible for controlling American forces who could have precluded or stopped these gross violations of human rights enjoy presidential cover, owing to their effective insulation from removal until the next electoral test of their stewardship. The reelection of those in power who are responsible for initiating the Iraq war challenges the notion that the responsibility for the war and its disquieting strategic results and human rights abuses are the work solely of the Bush administration and its partisans in Congress. Paul Schroeder (2006, 51) makes a disconcerting case that "most Americans still seem to believe that anything done at home or abroad supposedly to make them safer from terrorists is fine regardless of legal niceties. Indeed, though it is not a matter of law, it is a frustrating sign of insularity and self-preoccupation that the American people should, now years later, still think that the only serious charge to be made against the administration with respect to the Iraq war is that it (perhaps inadvertently at the outset) misled the American people and Congress."

Until the recent shift in American global strategy under the Bush administration (see chapter 1), American exceptionalism assumed the positive form of multilateral cooperation. After the defeat of Germany and Japan and during the half-century after World War II, the United States could, indeed, claim superpower status. Without U.S. support and leadership, a United Nations charged with collective responsibility for international security, resting on the principle of great-power accord, would never have come to pass. American leadership and power were also principally responsible for the construction of the liberal trading order, institutionalized in the International Monetary Fund (IMF), the World Bank, and the General Agreement on Tariffs and Trade (GATT), which eventually became the World Trade Organization (WTO). Through the Marshall Plan, the United States played a key role not only in reconstructing Europe but also in setting the stage for the creation of the European Economic Community (ECC) that has now evolved into the EU. Other victor powers might well have divided Europe against itself and rejected any violation of the most favored nation (MFN) principle in economic exchanges between states. The United States did neither. It allowed violation of the MFN principle to permit the European states to privilege each other at the expense of the economic interests of other states, including the United States. Europe might well have never developed to its present level of socioeconomic and political integration, which, at least for the foreseeable future, has brought an end to centuries of armed conflict and civil war among its peoples — an aim of American foreign policy and a precondition for the formation of a united Western Europe to better fight the emerging cold war (Dinan 2004; Kolodziej 1974).

Regional Limits of American Power

As the review of U.S. policy toward the Middle East and, specifically, Iraq suggests, regional actors, state and nonstate, limit American aspirations for global dominance and check — and, in some instances, rollback — American power in their respective regions. In Lebanon, American security and foreign policy has been dealt a spectacular setback, delivered with surprising decisiveness by an embattled Hezbollah willing to trade disproportionate damage to Lebanon's infrastructure and loss of over a thousand lives to prevail in the face of the American-backed Israeli onslaught. The superiority of Israeli arms failed to achieve for Israel either a diplomatic victory over Hezbollah or a strategic advantage. The United States had to adapt to the muddled result of the war, the introduction of U.N. peacekeepers, who are not mandated to disarm Hezbollah. Their limited task is simply to separate the combatants, leaving the strategic balance between Hezbollah and Israel intact with the former remaining the principal gainer. The role of the United States in the region was outsourced to a weak U.N. secretary general and to the hazards of a divided Security Council. These are outcomes that scarcely square with the notion of Israel and the United States, respectively, as regional and global superpowers.

Western Europe, the EU, the Russian Federation,
and the Commonwealth of Independent States (CIS)

As the chapters of this volume reveal, other regions of the world also pose for-midable constraints on U.S. power. These are no less limiting than those in the Middle East, although they assume different forms and varying weight in check-ing American power and in thwarting the Bush Doctrine, depending on the re-gion and the actor mix under examination. Europe — EU, the Russian Federa-tion, and CIS — illustrates these frustrations of American aims and preferences. Some are self-inflicted. The campaign to divide Europe in the run-up to the Iraqi invasion and seek instead an illusive and unreliable "coalition of the will-ing" is among the most self-defeating tactics to emerge from the Bush Doctrine. As Trine Flockhart argues, the United States enjoyed strong and consistent Eu-ropean support during the cold war despite profound differences over American security policies and strategy. Pragmatism and deft practice managed these policy dilemmas until they might be relaxed or surmounted. During the struggle with the Soviet Union, the Europeans were willing to extend political capital and credit to Washington in joining the United States in balancing against Moscow and its East European satellites. Even so redoubtable a foe as Charles de Gaulle stood firmly in the American camp during the Cuban missile crisis. Nor did France's departure from the NATO military organization (but not the Atlantic Alliance) fundamentally shake U.S.–European collaboration.[12]

Patrick Morgan adds the crucial point that the real "hegemon" in international relations is not the United States, but a collective, namely, the combined re-sources of the U.S.–Western alliance. The Bush administration's decision to split that alliance between old and new Europe over the Iraq invasion departed from a half-century-long practice of negotiating cooperation among allies, reflected in the compromise reached between the United States and its West European al-lies over Washington's proposal to shift from a strategy of Massive Retaliation to Flexible Response. The U.S. commitment to Europe during the cold war, even at the risk of precipitating a nuclear exchange with the Soviet Union and its own destruction, was guaranteed by the presence of four hundred thousand American troops and their dependents in Europe, who were, in effect, hostages to American intent. Mindless application of the Bush Doctrine to Europe, aided and abet-ted by its partisans outside the government (Kagan 2002), undermined the real source of U.S. influence among allies — the trust it enjoyed as a consequence of its proven willingness to take into account the security interests of its partners and to bind itself to the negotiated agreements, rules, and institutional constraints of the Atlantic Alliance. A strong, united Western alliance was no longer prized by

Washington. Rejection of Europe's human and material resources and its collective diplomatic clout was a logical corollary of the Bush Doctrine and of the soon to be disproved assumption that the United States possessed enough power to get others, allies and adversaries, to adapt to U.S. preferences. The United States defected from what had been a winning strategy of using American power in ways that assured rather than threatened allied interests.

The assumed efficacy of a go-it-alone strategy was based, alternatively, on the delusionary notion that other states would either bandwagon on U.S. power or be marginalized or neutralized. The view was that these states were essentially irrelevant to American designs, that in fact eliciting their cooperation was a bother or a restraint on American discretion in deploying U.S. power. It was in this spirit that the Bush administration disavowed European assistance in the immediate aftermath of 9/11. Neither the military or especially the economic resources of the European allies nor the legitimacy they afforded by their unified stance in defense of U.S. and allied interests were valued as necessary for success in Afghanistan or Iraq or, more generally, in managing the conflicts of the Middle East or those of a globe full of ferment.

For many Europeans, the U.S. invasion of Iraq and its increasingly unconditional support of Israel's conduct of its armed struggles against Palestinians, notably Hamas, and of its war with Hezbollah threaten their security interests. Not only does unilateral use of American military power damage Europe's relations with the Middle East states and peoples, but it also undermines efforts to conciliate Europe's large Muslim minorities. An unchecked United States reduces confidence in Washington as a reliable partner, because profound European security interests are tributary to American initiatives beyond European control or influence. This parlous condition contrasts with the period of the cold war, when conflicting U.S.–European security interests were ultimately negotiated within a working Atlantic Alliance framework despite the frictions and distrust that arose among the parties as a result of those divergent interests. Current distrust on both sides of the Atlantic encourages defection from alliance solidarity with a resulting loss of overall Western power to guide, if not control, events in the Middle East and elsewhere to support their converging interests and values.

The erosion of American power in the Middle East and Washington's abdication of its brokerage role induced the Bush administration to belatedly acknowledge the leveraged power and legitimacy that alliance cohesion can dispose. Available to the alliance are a rich array of collective resources. These assets include the differential capacity of Western allies to gain access to Middle East states and leaders, access that may be foreclosed to the United States.

France, for example, has enjoyed long-standing relations with Lebanon and Syria, dating back to World War I when these states fell within the French sphere of interest. Its geopolitical position necessarily makes France a Mediterranean power (see Kolodziej 1974, chapters 9–10, 447–554). Further, France has four to five million Muslim inhabitants, which means that Paris has as much an interest in creating a peaceful Middle East as the United States (Giry 2006). Paris confronts a far more formidable domestic challenge than Washington, highlighted by the Muslim riots across France's cities in 2005. In contrast, the United States deals with a largely integrated Muslim community of some ten million in a population of three hundred million. Even if, partly for these reasons, French policies and security strategies are at odds with that of the Bush model, the two states as well as the other EU states have a converging interest in a stable Middle East. The U.N. peacekeeping role in Lebanon, supported by the Europeans and specifically by Italy, France, and Britain, the latter two as permanent members of the Security Council, illustrates the positive application of alliance power when it can be coordinated among its members.

There is, however, looming tension between the United States and the EU on several key fronts. While the United States supports Turkey's entry into the European Union, European opinion, particularly in France, is running against Turkey's request for accession. The Atlantic partnership is also strained by the differential postures toward the Hamas–Fatah coalition. Washington refuses to recognize the Palestinian government under Hamas rule until it renounces terrorism, recognizes Israel, and confirms previous agreements reached with Fatah, while the Europeans are more disposed to engage all Palestinian factions and to assume a broker's distancing stance in dealing with all of the dueling rivals.

In working out these and other differences, Europe's voice and bargaining position has been strengthened by its assumption of security responsibilities for a number of areas vital to U.S. interests: peacekeeping in the Balkans, particularly in Bosnia, which is divided by three irreconcilable sectarian communities; the dispatch of European forces under NATO auspices to lighten the American burden in Afghanistan; and strong French–British–German support to contain a nuclear-aspiring Iran. The posited Venus–Mars dichotomy between Europe and the United States in addressing regional conflicts — the Europeans pusillanimous, the Americans tough and militarily muscular — appears less persuasive than some commentators believed to be the case on the eve of the Iraqi invasion given the complex mix of hard and soft power and coordinated diplomacy needed to cope with these threats to the Western coalition (Kagan 2002).[13]

If the tensions in U.S.–Western European relations have eased somewhat since the sharp divisions within the alliance preceding the Iraqi invasion, U.S. policies toward most of the states of the former Soviet Union (the Baltic states excepted), notably the triangle of states covered in Maria Raquel Freire's evaluation of U.S. influence in the Russian Federation, Ukraine, and Belarus, have not enjoyed much success. Freire's detailed review (chapter 8) leads her to conclude that "Russia enjoys greater power and influence than the United States in the former Soviet area." The United States gained Russian support at the margin for the war on terror. This should come as no surprise, since the Putin government was quick to seize on Washington's globalization of the terror threat to justify its suppression of the Chechen revolt. Russia also assented to U.S. military presence in Central Asia and welcomed the Afghanistan invasion and the toppling of the Taliban regime. In addition, Ukraine sent a small contingent of forces to Iraq as a member of the American "coalition of the willing."

On most other issues, Russia has been a reluctant partner of the United States. Even before 9/11, it was an unwilling ally in ending the Balkan civil wars, in sanctioning Serbia, a long-term ally, and in agreeing to a Western-backed U.N. resolution to grant autonomy to Kosovo. It opposed the Iraqi invasion because the Security Council had not passed a resolution authorizing it. Multilateralism, not unilateralism, was the watchword. Moscow also resists applying sanctions against a nuclear-aspiring Iran, having actually aided Iran's nuclear program in the recent past. It also rejects U.S. objections to a proposed $700 million sale to Iran of an air defense missile system.

American pressure on Russia to open itself to democratic reform has been successfully resisted. The Putin government has increasingly centralized power in Moscow and has wrested control of the country's oil resources from the oligarchs who opposed him, stifled media criticism, and suppressed internal dissent. High oil prices have provided the regime the resources it needs to retain power and to contain a restive population. Its international posture is to resist American power while successfully enlisting U.S. support for its entry into the exclusive club of developed states, the result of which has been that the G7 has become the G8, positioning Russia for its eventual entry into the WTO. Russia would appear to have cleverly frustrated U.S. policy preferences, extended its sphere of influence over the CIS, and retained its economic leverage over Europe, thanks to the energy cards it holds in supplying gas and oil to members. The balance sheet shows U.S. influence in deficit in the CIS region, while Moscow's is in modest surplus.

Ukraine, Belarus, and the CIS largely remain within Russia's sphere of power and influence. The Orange Revolution that brought a Western and American-leaning regime to power in Ukraine has since been subdued and Ukraine brought back under Moscow's influence as a consequence of its control over Ukraine's access to oil and gas and also because of internal divisions within the ruling Ukrainian coalition and revelations of corruption that have weakened anti-Russian factions within the regime. Ukraine also withdrew its contingent of sixteen hundred troops from Iraq at the end of 2005. Belarus represents an even worse case scenario for Washington. Its pursuit of an isolationist, nationalist foreign policy raises the concern, as Freire observes, that Belarus may become a haven for terrorists if the price is right. The regime has until now successfully resisted U.S. pressures to democratize and has decomposed into an authoritarian state. Moscow's intimidation of Georgia over its support of separatist movements opposed to T'bilisi's rule exposes the inability of the United States to do much to aid these states.

Northeast Asia

Davis Bobrow paints a picture of Northeast Asian security and regional state relations that strikingly, if disquietingly, resembles that of Europe before World War I. Analogies of course limit themselves, but there are formidable forces afoot that, unless restrained by incentives for mutual cooperation, threaten the region's stability and security. On the one hand, economic interdependence has reached unprecedented levels among the principal market states in the region: Japan, South Korea, and China. Japanese investment in China grows apace. Thousands of Taiwanese businessmen reside in China so they can conduct their affairs there and exploit cheap Chinese labor. South Korea and Taiwan, Asian Tigers that emerged under the umbrella of U.S. security protection, are global exporters and keen competitors in former U.S.-dominated markets. China is among South Korea's principal economic partners after the United States. These interdependent trade and investment patterns — reflecting powerful but not necessarily determining incentives for cooperation — are reminiscent of the levels of economic activity across European state borders before World War I.

Economic interdependence, as World War I suggests, is not a decisive guarantee of peace in Northeast Asia. Nationalism is rising, not receding, despite the currently controlling interest of the major players — North Korea excepted — to preserve and extend the stunning economic gains of the past decades. Japan's neighbors oppose renunciation of the pacifist constitution imposed on Japan by the United States after World War II or any hint of a nuclear Japan. These attitudes are at odds with attempts by the United States, as early as the Nye–Armitage report under the Clinton administration, to induce an increasingly less reluctant Japan to assume a more active role in its own defense and to contribute to U.S.-led and U.N. peacekeeping operations (INSS Special Report 2000). Japanese noncombat naval and ground contingents have since been sent to Afghanistan and Iraq. Tokyo and Washington are already collaborating on antiballistic missile (ABM) systems. At an expenditure of 1 percent of GNP for its armed forces, Japan is among the major military powers in the world, a fact that is not lost on Japan's rivals in the region.

The tight U.S.–Japanese security alliance and increased likelihood of Japanese rearmament and renunciation of its pacifist defense posture worry Japan's neighbors. China, supported by other Asian states, opposes these trends. The shadow of past grievances between regional rivals, engendered by wars and colonial occupation, hangs heavy in negotiations over their differences. These open wounds seriously impede cooperation beyond issues of trade and investment. Nationalist sentiment, palpable among the rising generations of these states, impairs progress in negotiating a stable and mutually supported security regime for the region. Beijing specifically condemns former Japanese prime minister Junichiro Koizumi's visits to the Yasukuni shrine, which honors Japanese military who died in World War II, including convicted Japanese war criminals. China also insists that Japan apologize both for its invasion of Nanking in 1937 (in which thousands of Chinese were slaughtered by Japanese troops, Chang 1998) and more generally, for what the Chinese ambassador to the United States terms its aggression in World War II (Taube 2006). In dispute, too, are recent changes in Japanese history textbooks that, from the perspective of China and other Asian states, absolve Japan of wrongdoing during its imperial expansion in Asia. The hostility expressed by Beijing toward trends in Japanese security policies is echoed in Seoul and Pyongyang. Koreans harbor deep resentments against Japan, rooted in memories of its occupation of Korea between 1910 and 1945, during which it imposed military rule over the peninsula, suppressed the Korean language and culture, and coercively instituted Japanese culture as the dominant ethos.

China represents the long-run challenge to U.S. power. On the positive side of the ledger is the 1979 decision by Party Secretary Deng Xiaoping to adapt China to the Western market system, leading to its membership in the WTO. More recently, China's ruling party has for the first time passed legislation to protect important elements of private property, a clear departure from its Marxist and Maoist past. The spectacular economic development of China since that revolutionary decision was taken has generated double-digit annual rates of growth. China has become the workshop of the globe. It is second only to Japan in its holdings of U.S. debt and enjoys a steeply favorable balance of trade with the United States. While it remains inured to Washington pressures to revalue the Chinese yuan upward as a way to improve the trade balance with the United States or to address the issue of copyright violations by Chinese producers, it has been able to induce the United States to propose an expansion of the voting power of China and several other developing states within the IMF.

Conversely, China has not been very forthcoming in cooperating with Washington on a wide range of regional and global security issues. China supports oppressive regimes like that of Robert Mugabe's in Zimbabwe and sides with Sudanese president Omar Hasan Ahmad al-Bashir, who resists admitting U.N. peacekeepers to prevent further bloodshed in the civil war in Darfur, an improbable alignment forged by Chinese need for access to Sudanese oil. The quest for oil to drive the Chinese economy has also prompted Chinese officials to extend the same support for nonintervention to other African states, notably Nigeria, another oil supplier, as well as to tilt toward the regime of President Hugo Chávez in Venezuela, a move that appears calculated to produce favorable oil deals with Caracas. Concerns about oil also appear to partially explain China's resistance to imposing sanctions on Iran for its violations of the Non-Proliferation Treaty (NPT). More generally, China is at this stage of its modernization a status quo power opposed to regime change — certainly its own — and to the violation of state sovereignty. To preserve the regime's authoritarian rule, Beijing relies on traditional international principles of international law that limit interference in the domestic affairs of a state, precluding, for example, Chinese condemnation of oppressive regimes in Sudan and Myanmar.

The tepid U.N. sanctions voted by the Security Council in response to the North Korean nuclear test of October 2006 also revealed that the United States, which wanted more coercive measures to be taken against Pyongyang, was unable to get its way. It was obliged to abandon its preference for a more muscular approach to Pyongyang in deference to the limits set by Beijing and Moscow. This approach yielded modest results, yet they were more than would have been forthcoming if the United States had tried to maintain the pretended posture of a superpower that could simply impose its will on North Korea. Washington's diminished demands were shaped by the countervailing power of its reluctant non-Western Security Council partners who were prepared only to cobble together a weak and porous sanctions package that had the effect more of signaling discontent with Pyongyang than of containing or punishing the regime for exploding a nuclear device. Serious questions arise whether even these limited moves against North Korea will ever be implemented as both South Korea and China have reportedly notified Washington that they will continue to maintain economic relations with North Korea (*New York Times*, October 16, 2006).

What is particularly revealing about the weakness of the U.S. bargaining position in Northeast Asia and specifically in its efforts to staunch the North Korean nuclear program is the key role that China plays in the so-called Six-Party Talks. Absent Chinese leverage over North Korea, there is little likelihood of a slowdown or abandonment of Pyongyang's pursuit of nuclear weapons. The recent turnabout in the American negotiating posture that hitherto refused to negotiate directly with North Korea evidences Washington's dependency on Beijing as the principal arbiter of Northeast Asian security. The Bush administration, while still affirming its commitment to multilateral talks and coalitional pressure on North Korea, has agreed to supply energy and economic assistance to Pyongyang and to unfreeze North Korean assets in return for a promise from North Korea to shut down its Yongbyon reactor. The potentially modest success of these mutual concessions was achieved only because Washington relaxed the strictures of the Bush

Doctrine and implicitly shelved in this instance its assumption of superpower capacity to compel concessions.

What is striking is the contrast between Beijing's adjustment to an international system increasingly characterized by multiplying numbers of centers of power and Washington's resistance to adapting to these trends, as described in the final section of this chapter. The core interests and values of the Beijing regime are to remain in power, despite external pressures to democratize and to end human rights abuses, and to sustain economic growth, which it regards as the key to big-power status and domestic support for a regime bereft of a claim to political legitimacy. Beijing's strategy of protecting these core interests by conducting a subtle diplomacy of more carrots than sticks has had the effect both of increasing U.S. dependency on Beijing to support Washington's policies around the globe and of containing American power in the bargain.

Beijing has succeeded in strengthening its relations with Russia and India through a series of political and economic accords that have neutralized, offset, or arguably diluted the influence of the United States on these key Asian powers. South Korea has been increasingly drawn into the Chinese orbit; North Korea, of course, remains a petulant protectorate. China's "charm offensive" has quieted, if not quelled, fears among the Association of Southeast Asian Nations (ASEAN) states of its long-term hegemonic aspirations. Beijing's presence also extends to Central Asia where the Shanghai Cooperation Organization (SCO) includes Mongolia, India, Pakistan, and Iran as observers, a grouping of states that extends China's influence over South and West Asia. Africa and increasingly South America are within the scope of China's designs. The China–African Cooperation Forum is the vehicle by which China hopes to extend its interests on the continent. Reports of closer ties between Caracas and Beijing also herald China's emerging penetration of the Western Hemisphere, where American influence is either receding or irrelevant, as the chapters by Kleinberg and Hirst suggest.

Developing states in Africa and Latin America are attractive to China as producers of oil and gas, as potential markets for Chinese products, and as members of a loose alignment of states, including China, that checks American power in their regions. This enlarging alignment of states—witness Brazil's leadership of the Group of 21 within the WTO—bolsters the movement toward a multipolar system within which Chinese power presently plays a key role, foreshadowing its increasing influence as the system evolves at what appears to be accelerating speed toward the diffusion of power among state and nonstate actors.

At a global level, Communist China and liberal America have exchanged postures. China, presently a status quo power, no longer talks of a world Communist revolution, while the United States preaches the overthrow of authoritarian regimes around the globe. Beijing insists on the sovereignty of each nation and fully supports article 2 of the U.N. Charter that prohibits armed intervention in the domestic affairs of other states (the claims of the U.N. Secretary General of the right of the United Nations to monitor the human rights records of member states to the contrary notwithstanding, Annan 2001). Where Washington advocates regime change and the democratization of authoritarian states, Beijing rebuffs U.S. moves to intervene unilaterally to achieve these aims or to use the United Nations as the vehicle for such intervention; hence China opposed the Iraq war. As for human rights, China insists that the priority it assigns to economic development does more to advance human rights and welfare than Western demands for political freedoms. In any case, human rights are understood by Beijing as defined by national history and need — human rights with Chinese characteristics. Not without irony, the Bush Doctrine eschews the constraints of a rule-based international system, abandoning the leadership role that the United States decisively played in creating such a system after World War II, at the very time when the need for shared rules and norms of behavior in regulating relations between rivals and competitors has never been greater or more urgent, given the decentralization and diffusion of power within the global system.

What is disquieting is that this projection of rising Chinese power may be as much a chimera as the U.S. attempt to democratize the Middle East if neither is able to control the forces of globalization, unilaterally or even by cooperating. The Beijing regime depends on sustained economic growth to still domestic unrest, yet there is no assurance that another meltdown, like the Asian crisis of 1997, might not again occur. Or, worse, a global depression might well be set in train if Beijing and Washington fail to maintain a workable economic balance that currently is highly unstable as a consequence of receding U.S. competitiveness and rising trade and budget deficits. Given the shaky legitimacy on which Communist rule rests, a political upheaval greater than the threat to the regime posed by the Tiananmen Square demonstrations might well erupt. And as Li's chapter underlines, managing nationalism in Northeast Asia and the unresolved status of Taiwan in the face of overwhelming Chinese resolve to integrate the island under Beijing's rule and to bring closure to the Chinese civil war and foreign intervention into Chinese affairs are challenges that might well spin out of control. Against this grim background, it is not too much to argue that Northeast Asia is second only to the Middle East as the most unstable region of the globe.

South Asia

A surface reading of Indian and American values and interests would seem to predict a close partnership. India is a secular democracy, increasingly disposed to open-market practices, a progressive position responsive to American values and economic interests, holding out the prospect of increased U.S. penetration of Indian markets. Despite India's caste system New Delhi is working to improve the social and economic status of its citizens. The United States can also count on India's resistance to the expansion of the world's nuclear club, its fight against Muslim terrorists, and its growing global status. These converging U.S.–Indian interests define the objective strategic relation between the world's most populous democratic systems. They are the "realities" of India's domestic socioeconomic and political composition, realities that are contributing to its rising power as a global actor.[14] That said, India is still not for hire, as Indian officials repeatedly insist. There is no automatic transformation of the parallel interests between India and the United States into coordinated strategies or agreement on what means and policy instruments should be deployed to realize their overlapping interests or compromise their differences.

The United States comes to this region from a position of weakness; indeed its position is arguably weaker in South Asia than in any other region. It is now more *demandeur* than a determiner of strategic outcomes in South Asia. The United States gave more than it received in signing a nuclear accord with India. In agreeing to supply India with nuclear materials and technology to advance New Delhi's civilian energy program, the United States was in effect rewarding India for refusing to sign the NPT. India's nuclear reactors dedicated to military purposes will not fall under International Atomic Energy Agency (IAEA) inspection. The added nuclear materials and know-how supplied by the United States can be used to transfer some of the loads for developing civilian nuclear power to the Indian military sector. That is tantamount to American support for the spread of nuclear weapons, a paradoxical position for the United States, which has been so determined to stop proliferation to the members of the so-called axis of evil — Iraq, Iran, and North Korea. The long-run economic benefits of this nuclear accord are also problematic. Whether U.S. economic interests will be fostered will depend less on these concessions of nuclear know-how and materials than on the competitiveness of its goods and services and the attractiveness of its investment proposals. On these scores other states, particularly China, are formidable competitors.

Meanwhile, the Bush administration adds yet another to its growing list of international agreements that it has either renounced or, as in the Indian case, seriously weakened. If India can be rewarded for its nuclear intransigence, why can't other states be accorded variances from the NPT? North Korea is reported to have already insisted in talks with the United States that it should be treated as an equal to India and allowed to keep its nuclear weapons. Iran, which signed the NPT, is threatened with sanctions for insisting on pursuing a civilian nuclear program because it prohibits the IAEA from conducting full-scope inspections to preclude its militarization. As long as Iran does not renounce the NPT (following the U.S. administration with respect to other treaties), it incurs sanctions, while India does not. Double standards are being applied to both states, with India, which did not sign the NPT, enjoying rewards for its refusal to be party to the treaty. The U.S.–Indian deal also undermines European bargaining with the Iranians to forestall the development of an Iranian bomb. Russia and China, as erstwhile allies in the American-led effort to put pressure on Iran, have even less incentive than before to support the U.S. position, since the United States has abandoned its own antiproliferation policy.

The most damaging aspect of the Indian nuclear accord with the United States is that it threatens the integrity of the NPT. The underlying assumption of the treaty is that the threat to international security is nuclear weapons, not just those that have them. In contrast, the Bush administration has shifted the rationale for the NPT from controlling and eliminating these weapons to intimidating those states that it opposes that may have them or seek their acquisition. To further undermine the NPT regime that obliges nuclear states to seriously consider decreasing their arsenals on the road to nuclear disarmament, the Bush administration has embarked on the development of a new nuclear warhead to improve the U.S. nuclear stockpile. In an ironic sense, the administration has undermined the NPT to lay the groundwork for justifying its abandonment or neglect of its obligation to limit and decrease nuclear arms.

If George Perkovich's explanation of the U.S.–Indian accord, as quoted by Amit Das Gupta (chapter 5), is misguidedly optimistic about its capacity to strengthen "a rule-based nonproliferation regime," he is right and realistic when he sums up Washington's motives by saying "that the top priority should be balancing Chinese power." Expectations are out of joint with prospects of realization. The idea that an outdated nineteenth-century move to encircle China through the bait of nuclear concessions would render India a reliable partner is fanciful. The added notion, prompted by the visit of Secretary of State Condoleezza Rice to Japan and Indonesia on her way to India, that an incipient "entente cordiale" might be orchestrated to contain China, is no less illusory. India prefers to accommodate China, a posture reciprocated by China, rather than join the United States in a lame alignment stretching from Japan through Indonesia to check China. India's long history with Western colonialism, its record of nonalignment during the cold war, and the fierce nationalism of its elites across the Indian political spectrum preclude any enduring and reliable membership as a subordinate power within an American-led coalition of the willing.

Anyone with a casual knowledge of Indian history and domestic politics would scarcely find these observations surprising. Further evidence of the inability of

American power to draw India into its sphere of receding influence can be found in the internal debate within India over the nuclear agreement. Any constraint on Indian nuclear development, civilian or military, or even its sharing of nuclear materials and know-how with other states in the future, a core aim of the NPT, is ruled out by the Indian prime minister in response to domestic critics concerned about U.S. oversight.[15] A wide and powerful spectrum of Indian elite opinion — the nuclear scientific establishment, the military-industrial complex, and the Indian Left — insists on complete Indian autonomy in developing India's nuclear programs and unconditional exercise of its sovereignty. In an ironic twist, the American "yes" to the Indian bomb in the form of its lifting of sanctions and legitimation of the Indian nuclear programs may receive a "no" from the Indians. Even if the agreement goes through over the strong objections of domestic opponents in India, its implementation will be managed solely on Indian terms.

Whatever the doubtful reliability of India as an ally may be, the weakest link in the war on terrorism and in efforts to stop the spread of nuclear weapons, especially their acquisition by terrorist groups bent on attacking the United States and Western interests, is Pakistan. Until recently, the linchpin in the axis of evil has been Pakistan. As Amit Das Gupta observes, "Abdul Quadeer Khan, the 'father' of Pakistan's bomb, who sells nuclear know-how and hardware for and from countries that are seen as major threats to U.S. security, is the only link" to North Korea, Iran, and Libya (chapter 5, 110). The United States has little leverage over Pakistan's nuclear program, now even less so as a consequence of facilitating the expansion of India's nuclear capabilities. Washington claims that it has succeeded in pressuring the Musharraf government to rein in Khan by ostensibly placing him under house arrest. As a national hero, Khan is quite beyond the full powers of the state to punish him or his confederates in the Pakistani military and bureaucracy who have done so much to undermine the NPT. The reticence of the Bush administration to push Pakistan further on this issue is largely explained by Washington's need to rely on Islamabad and the Musharraf regime to fight the rising tide of the Taliban in Afghanistan and to help in the capture of Osama bin Laden and al Qaeda operatives, who reportedly remain under the protection of Pakistani tribes on Pakistan's western border.

The withdrawal of Pakistani troops from Pakistan's western borders and the agreement made by Islamabad with local tribal leaders to desist from attacking them reveal the internal weakness of the Musharraf regime. Now the Taliban can mount attacks on NATO forces in the south, and al Qaeda operatives and bin Laden himself are assured protection either against Pakistani- or Western-launched attacks. The Taliban is in no small part a creation of Pakistani intelligence services, initially encouraged by the United States in its efforts to oust the Soviets from Afghanistan. Pakistani intelligence and military ties are still strong, as evidenced by the cease-fire agreed to by Islamabad. It is a hedge against U.S.

withdrawal or the West's defeat in Afghanistan. In any event, efforts to employ the Pakistani army to defeat the Taliban or to capture bin Laden would likely incur major casualties and place the regime and specifically Musharraf at serious risk. Musharraf has survived several assassination attempts, including an apparent errant missile attack on an airplane carrying the prime minister in the midst of the crisis to reassert state control over Islamabad's Red Mosque, a center promoting extremist Islamic teachings. The military appears to be infiltrated by Taliban and Muslim extremist sympathizers, although how deeply they have penetrated remains a matter of speculation. Ethnic revolt, notably in Baluchistan, further weakens the Pakistan government.

Washington's pressures to democratize Musharraf's authoritarian rule could have the adverse and unwitting effect of bringing to power Islamic forces fiercely opposed to the United States. It also raises the ominous specter of these political forces controlling Pakistan's nuclear weapons, which, unlike Iranian aspirations to get the bomb, would be a clear and present danger to American and Western interests, opening the way to its risky use or threat of use by an extremist Pakistani regime or, worse, to the prospect that the regime might allow these weapons to fall into the hands of terrorists whose ideology encourages their use against the West.

Southeast Asia

Southeast Asia, composed of the ASEAN states, is also an important region for the United States, but largely of secondary priority when compared to South and Northeast Asia. As elsewhere, Washington must court these states and their diverse peoples for support of its policies. Most have resisted recruitment into Washington's coalition of the willing. None has sent forces to Iraq. Indonesia and especially Malaysia sharply criticize the U.S. interventions in the Middle East and Central Asia. These largely Muslim states are increasingly adopting the rhetoric of militant opponents of the United States who call for a global jihad against what they charge is an expansionist Washington warring on Islam everywhere. Washington's invasions of Afghanistan and Iraq have had the unintended effect of pushing the Muslim populations of these states, traditionally associated with a welcoming and moderate form of Islam, toward the extremist Muslim camp. In abandoning international norms by intervening in Iraq and occupying a Muslim state and in torturing and maltreating prisoners, depredations that are being widely reported in the Muslim media, the United States has unwittingly lost the moral high ground in the struggle against terrorism, relinquished too readily and heedlessly as this volume has detailed in its review of U.S. power.

U.S. relations with the other members of ASEAN than the predominantly Muslim states presents a mixed picture. The United States has a closer relationship with the Philippines and Singapore than it does with other ASEAN members. U.S. troops support Manila in its continuing war with Muslim insurgents, and the Philippines are portrayed as an integral, if marginal, battlefield in the global war on terror. Association with a corrupt Manila regime, on the other hand, scarcely lends much credibility to the United States commitment to open, transparent, and accountable democratic governance. Singapore's openness to cooperation with the United States, notably in offering a port of anchor after the loss of Philippine bases, is a plus for American planners. As a small city-state, Singapore cannot be the pivot for U.S. interests in the region, given the size, resources, and power of Singapore's ASEAN allies. It can be argued that this strategic relation benefits Singapore more than the United States, since Singapore can draw implicitly on U.S. backing in its negotiations with its more powerful ASEAN partners.

The recent coup d'état in Thailand brought to power a military junta, which runs counter to U.S. democratizing goals. The regime is also beset by militant Muslim insurgents who are demanding greater autonomy from Bangkok. There is not much that Washington can do about the overthrow of the elected Thai government, even if it had a will to try — which it clearly does not. On the contrary, it has incentive to desist from criticizing military rule, lest it weaken its capacity to cope with the Muslim insurgency.

Perhaps the only good news from this region is the closer economic and political ties that are beginning to develop between Vietnam and the United States after a generation of animosity that contributed to Pol Pot's rule in Cambodia and the "Killing Fields" that resulted in millions of Cambodians dead or reduced to destitution. Even these gains may be temporary; Beijing's influence, as Li's analysis of China's charm diplomacy in the region suggests, appears to be growing at the expense of the United States. Absent a real or perceived threat that is shared by the ASEAN states, which the Soviet Union and especially Maoist China had posed in the last half of the twentieth century, the presence of the United States in the region, while not resisted, is increasingly regarded as being of less value than during the cold war. What is certain is that these states cannot be counted as reliable partners of the United States except on a quid pro quo basis in competition with other states, particularly China, that are positioned to provide them with greater economic benefits and security guarantees than those on offer from the United States.

Central and South America

The Western Hemisphere, encompassing North and South America, has long been associated with American hegemony and superpower status. These terms could aptly be applied to the United States from the Spanish–American War on, when the United States replaced Britain as the dominant power in the region. Until that turning point, the success of American policy, embodied in the Monroe Doctrine, whose aim was to preclude European expansion into the Western Hemisphere, depended on British naval power, the Atlantic oceanic divide, and the preoccupation of the major European powers with managing their conflicts in Europe and with colonial expansion into Africa and Asia. The Roosevelt Corollary to the Monroe Doctrine self-legitimated U.S. intervention in the affairs of debtor states whose risky finances might induce Europeans to collect what was owed them by force. U.S. connivance with breakaway elements in Colombia led eventually to the construction of the Panama Canal. While the United States resisted intervening in Europe's wars except for the brief episode of World War I, it repeatedly intervened in Central and Latin American domestic politics, as Kleinberg recounts.

It can be argued that the United States maintained a hegemonic position in the Western Hemisphere through World War II and the cold war. The United States, no matter what administration was in power, was able to build a solid front against Soviet penetration, Castro's Cuba, an ongoing source of serious tension, notwithstanding. Washington had a hand in overthrowing leftist leaning regimes in Guatemala (1954) and Chile (1973). CIA intervention, highlighted by the Iran-Contra scandal of the Reagan administration in the 1980s, prevented regimes at odds with U.S. wishes from taking power in El Salvador and Nicaragua. Washington tolerated military regimes in Argentina, Chile, and Brazil as long as their anti-Communist credentials were intact. By and large, security trumped human rights and democratization concerns.

In the immediate aftermath of the end of the cold war, the United States was again able to assign a higher priority to the support of liberal economic and democratic regimes in Latin America. Its support for opening hemispheric markets grew apace. The influence it exerted through international financial institutions, like the World Bank and IMF, facilitated the integration of these states into the liberal trading system. The North American Free Trade Agreement (NAFTA) was one of the signal legacies of this era. The wave of democratization sweeping the region played again to American policy objectives once the threat of Communist influence, externally through the Soviet Union or internally through the socialization and nationalization of domestic economies, like Cuba and menacingly in Chile, had passed.

Times change. The chapters by Kleinberg and Hirst outline an entirely different rapport between the United States and its southern neighbors. Kleinberg's representation of the United States as a "limited hegemon" is little different from what the editors believe has been the transformation of the United States from a superpower and hegemon into a great power. Of course Washington gets some of its preferences registered in the policies of Latin American and Central American states whether on matters of security, economic exchange, the legitimacy of democratic regimes, or the protection of human rights. Conversely, its disappointments across these dimensions are many and growing and its expectations of the alignment of these states on U.S. preferences are currently being more frustrated than fostered, as President Bush's inconsequential March 2007 tour of Latin America and Mexico evidenced.

Brazil, a regional power and aspiring global leader, has consistently refused since World War II to align on U.S. security policies, demurring to assist militarily in the Korean, Vietnam, Afghan, and both Gulf wars as well as in a series of Central American struggles. If Brasilia has been keen to avoid a confrontation with the United States in the U.N. Security Council, its vote cannot be taken for granted in the General Assembly. In contrast to the Bush administration, which attacks the United Nations, Brazil supports the organization and participates actively in its peacekeeping operations. The American intervention in Iraq had little or no support across the Brazilian political spectrum. Meanwhile, Brazil ably leads the Group of 21 within the World Trade Organization as part of its thrust for enhanced global status as leader of the developing world. It is a keen competitor of the United States in agricultural exports, and it has successfully brought charges of unfair market practices against the EU and the United States. As Hirst concludes, Brazil neither balances nor bandwagons on U.S. power and preferences but pursues a strategy of managing its "discrepancies" with the United States, undermining its pretensions to being a hegemon and reducing its status to that of a great power that must bargain for what it wants and grudgingly accept compromises as a function of the countervailing power of rising middle powers like Brazil to advance their interests.

In the aftermath of the cold war, the United States was again positioned to champion democratization and liberal market principles in lieu of privileging security with the elimination of the Soviet threat to the United States and the hemisphere. What is not clear is whether the consolidation of democratic forces in Latin America was a function of U.S. policies or the evolutionary outcome of forces pressing for popular government both within the region and across the world. Kleinberg provides evidence that the spread of democracy can be attributed more to grassroots demands within each Latin and Central American state than to outside pressures exerted by the United States (Kolodziej 2003).

Whatever the final evaluation of the factors underlying the drive toward democratization in Latin America might be, what can be asserted more assuredly is that the Bush administration, as in the Middle East and elsewhere, is confronting regimes at odds with its security and economic policies. A leftist surge has recently swept through Latin America, engulfing some of its most popular and important countries. Affected states include Chile, Bolivia, Peru, Argentina, Uruguay, Brazil, Ecuador, and Venezuela. Venezuela's Hugo Chávez has been particularly caustic in his attacks on the Bush administration, dramatized in his U.N. address of September 2006 in which he attacked American imperialism and vilified President Bush as a "devil." If Washington resists accommodating the Chávez regime, it has pragmatically adjusted to the leftist tilt in other hemispheric countries while managing rather than combating the policy defections of these states from U.S. preferences. Closer to home, it faces a shaky right-of-center government in Mexico that is under great pressures from the Left, which charges it with having stolen the election. Further, whether the Right or the Left is in power in Mexico, the United States cannot count on its southern neighbor to solve the challenge of over eleven million undocumented immigrants in the United States. The erosion of U.S. influence in Latin America empties any force in the claim of those, like Richard Perle, quoted in the introduction to this volume, who champion the United States as a superpower, capable of indiscriminately using its power to get its way with other states.

North and Sub-Saharan Africa

A surface reading of the North and Sub-Saharan African chapters would appear to challenge the thesis of this volume: that the U.S. has been stripped of its superpower claims and lowered to the status of a besieged global power by the constraining capacity of states in the region and around the globe. Badredine Arfi argues (seconded by Kevin Dunn) that the Bush Doctrine's "discourse on terrorism" has had a systemic effect, much as one might expect of a superpower or hegemon. Nothing could be further from the truth on closer examination of what "facts on the ground" actually reveal. What the Bush administration failed to foresee was the perversion of its rhetoric by regional powers. They seized on the Bush Doctrine's "systemic" rhetoric to advance their domestic interests *at the expense of the war on terror.* Egypt, Algeria, Tunisia, Morocco, and a scattering of African governments aligned their announced policies with the U.S. war on terror to justify their suppression of domestic opponents. No less did President Putin become an early recruit to the war on terrorism to justify his crackdown on Chechnya and Georgia. The war on terrorism has become a club for authoritarian governments to marginalize or eliminate local rivals and frustrate social movements seeking greater regime transparency, democratic accountability, and human rights protections. These regimes co-opted a potentially estimable systemic force, embodied in the Bush Doctrine's call for a global war on terror, to service their parochial authoritarian interests. What could be more at odds with the Bush Doctrine's professed aims?

Conversely, the more the Bush administration presses for democratic reforms in the authoritarian regimes aligned in the war on terror, the greater the risk that those coming to power through the ballot box will be opposed to U.S. interests. Egypt, Algeria, and most especially Pakistan are likely to swing into an anti-American camp if Muslim parties gain state power. The United States has already experienced defections from a democratic Turkey, an ally of over a half-century, in the refusal of a Muslim-dominated Parliament to permit Turkey to be a staging and launching base for the attack on Iraq in the spring of 2003. President Musharraf of Pakistan can already be seen to be hedging his bets against the possible defeat of the West in Afghanistan to Taliban forces and the withdrawal of U.S. troops in Iraq by entering into agreements with tribal leaders along the Pakistani–Afghan border. Islamabad turns a blind eye to the safe haven that these areas, covering hundreds of miles of borders between the two states, provide the Taliban and al Qaeda.

Worse, popularly elected regimes might well spawn and harbor the very terrorists Washington is dedicated to defeating. The weak but democratically elected government of Lebanon cannot control its own territory, as Hezbollah is sufficiently powerful to have become a state within a state and to have intimidated the Beirut government to support its struggle against Israel. The Iranian government, however questionable its electoral practices, rests on a popular base. Teheran is squarely opposed to U.S. power and pursues nuclear weapons, a policy that appears to enjoy widespread domestic support, quite apart from the reported disenchantment of the public with the Mullah-run regime and President Mahmoud Ahmadinejad. In Venezuela, a majority of the electorate supports President Hugo Chávez, who attacks the United States as an imperial power and seeks alliances with other states in the Western Hemisphere and as far away as China to check U.S. power and influence. Hamas, whatever criticisms may be raised about its democratic credentials, did defeat the Palestinian Authority in a flawed but still open election.

There is no assurance that more democracy, as John Stuart Mill and Alexis de Tocqueville recognized almost two centuries ago, will necessarily yield peace and productive welfare policies. Sir Henry Maine, no friend of popular government, sharpened these concerns in stipulating that "there can be no grosser mistake [than] to have an impression that Democracy differs from Monarchy in essence. . . . The tests of success in the performance of the necessary and natural duties of a government are precisely the same in both cases" (Maine 1886, 60–61). Recent research suggests that newly created democracies are prone to armed conflicts (Mansfield 2005), a finding that qualifies the democratic peace proposition on which so many theorists and the Bush administration rely whether, respectively, for purposes of theory building or to justify coercive strategies to produce democratic regimes.

These lines of analyses are not designed to argue that efforts to defeat terrorism are futile, however difficult the challenge, or that the goal of creating more popularly based and democratic governments around the globe should be abandoned and authoritarian regimes simply supported to better cope with terrorism. Rather, it is important to recognize that declaring a global war on terror and advocating a world of democratic regimes raises as many problems as this solution to terrorism is intended to solve, as the Iraqi and Afghan cases testify. Given what social evolution has produced — the profound divisions of the world's populations into contending cultural, religious, national, ethnic, tribal, and linguistic identities — linking the automatic spread of democracy to the defeat of terrorism does not map with the constraints under which American power must act to advance these quite differentiated and often conflicting goals from one region of the world to another. Whether priority should be assigned to one goal over another will have to be scenario specific; that is the only way optimal results will be achieved in the trade-off between these estimable but competing aims, given a global society of peoples and states at sixes and sevens. If the United States is to successfully allocate its scarce power assets, it will have to acquire a deep, profound knowledge of local conditions and abandon sloganeering about the inevitable spread of democracy as well as vacuous crusades under the banner of a "global war on terror" — verbal legerdemain more effective, at least in the short run until reality rears its head, in mobilizing domestic voters than in defeating foreign enemies.

The Post–Cold War Global World: Some Trends and Challenges

What global parameters of power, viewed either as limits or as opportunities to exploit, confront American power and purposes? Despite this volume's contention that it has lost its superpower status, the United States remains a great power. It still retains enormous reservoirs of hard military and economic capabilities. It can rely on a resourceful and industrious population to build on these assets. Its soft power — notably the brilliance of its cultural creativity — has wide and deep positive impact on populations, particularly young people, around the globe. These cultural assets are offset by the precipitous fall in moral stature of the United States as a consequence of the errant policies recounted in this volume.[16] The Bush administration has mindlessly squandered the nation's hard-won power by refusing to enlist that power, as U.S. administrations had done in the past, in pursuit of a rule-based order that would regulate the contentious relations of states and peoples across the globe. Its wholesale defection from international norms and laws has galvanized allies and adversaries to oppose American power and preferences. Worse, other states and people have strong incentives to emulate the deviant American example. The deep divisions at home over American conduct of the Iraqi war and the untold self-inflicted damage done to America's power and moral standing abroad will not be undone soon, but it is not too late to try.

Chapter 16 sketches a new strategy for the United States. It rejects the notion that it is a failing power, the centerpiece of the spurious debate of the late 1990s (see Kennedy 1987). Nor does it put credence in the Bush Doctrine's stipulation that the United States has sufficient power and moral standing to pursue a unipolar hegemonic strategy capable of cowering adversaries and compelling others, friends and neutrals, to bandwagon on its vision of global order. It also parts company with those administration critics who would have it both ways, those who, on the one hand, condemn the Bush administration's management of American power but who, on the other hand, still insist on the primacy and special status of the United States, a conceit that implicitly consigns other great powers and rising local and regional states to a subordinate status.[17]

There is no doubt that the United States, like any power, large or small, must advance its self-interests and values, with force if necessary, and augment its influence to get the world it wants by aligning with peoples and states who share the same aims. Shaping the world society and its governance are necessarily shared challenges, not just discrete imperatives to be pursued by each actor without reference to the dependence by which each is constrained in seeking the cooperation of other state and nonstate actors to advance its policy agenda.

Developing new directions in American foreign and security policy requires not only drawing on the insights of the preceding chapters but also developing an understanding of the global, systemic constraints within which the power and policies of all states and peoples, not just Americans, now operate. It is important to recognize that all states as well as the diverse and divided peoples of the world are now entangled in a complex of self-sustaining and enlarging exchanges across all areas of human concern. Getting what actors want depends on them eliciting or coercing cooperation from other state and nonstate actors, many of whom are anonymous players on other continents.

From a systemic perspective, all actors are implicated in what has emerged as a world society for the first time in the evolution of the species.[18] What is meant here by a world society is simply the increasing interdependencies of the diverse and divided peoples and states of the world. The existence of this society does not imply some internal coherence — ruled out by the preceding discussion of the vast complexity and differentiations of regional politics. Nor does it suggest that the values of the world's populations will eventually converge.[19] There is no end to history as some self-regarding American intellectuals misguidedly contended by predicting the inevitable acquiescence of the world's populations to the alleged moral superiority of a liberal credo (Fukuyama 1992). As long as humans are free, as Rousseau recognized two centuries ago, they are at liberty to build their societies on edifying *or* debasing principles. (Greek philosophers whose discourses revolved around the creation of the best polity understood this human societal condition and problematic even earlier.) The power structures comprising the global society, including the decentralized distribution of violent capabilities across actors, the workings of global markets and the inequalities of wealth they produce, and the contesting loyalties of human groupings as social forces, generate incentives for actors to formulate their local and global strategies to suit their particular interests and to press for their favored global order, setting in motion a ceaseless process of global material and ideological conflict that manifests little sign of dissipating any time soon.[20]

From the perspective of what is now a global society, actors are confronted with two simultaneously interdependent constraints: to get what they want at the margin in their exchanges with other actors — say security, economic gain, or recognition of their identities as legitimate — they are also obliged, logically and objectively, to try to shape the global order they want on which these marginal exchanges depend for their realization. The scope of the interests of actors and the power they dispose now enable them to determine their preferred global order on which their marginal domestic and local interests ultimately depend. That states and their populations may well choose not to embark on efforts to shape the global environment to their liking — witness Switzerland that hides — does not negate the impact and constraints posed by an evolving and volatile global system on all actors.

Viewed from a global perspective, the Bush Doctrine and foreign policy can be understood as a response to the rise of a global society, though clearly a wrong step in the right direction. Specifically, it can be understood, as Gülnar Aybet observes, as a response to the crises in world order confronting Americans and populations everywhere. These crises have arisen from the very integration of global politics, driven by increased communications and connectedness, declining costs of transportation, markets fostering ceaseless technological innovation and economic development — Schumpeter's "creative destruction" — new, commonly shared ecological threats — man-made and natural — the spread of WMD, the resort to terrorism against civil populations by alienated groups, and the existence of a multitude of competing and contesting social identities, defined profoundly by culture, religion, national, ethnic and tribal loyalties, and language, each seeking privileged self-worth and legitimacy often at the expense of their competitors.

These forces and the social exchanges they generate comprise the global society. These illustrate but do not exhaust these mutually integrating and disintegrating forces. The Bush Doctrine is then a strategy, however flawed or fatuous, to control these forces for American advantage, as Washington interprets that imperative.[21] Bush policies respond both to what are perceived as the increasing incapacity of international institutions arising from the ashes of World War II to cope with the new forces unleashed by a global society *and* the perceived limits of domestic practices, party politics, and constitutional rules to advance the administration's use of American power in the service of its favored aims. These challenges are real and the administration must be credited with having helped to identify them. Lacking is a compelling understanding of their complexity and an appreciation of the limited power of the United States to discipline the forces unleashed by globalization.

The paradox of global politics today, and for the foreseeable future, is that, while actors and their agents have never been more connected and interdependent in real time, power has never been more fragmented and decentralized across these actors.[22] The impotence of actors to fully control the local and global environments within which they seek to realize their interests, aims, and values is universal, although obviously their capacity to partially surmount their impotence varies widely. The United States works on large measures and margins of power. It can afford to lose lots yet still have a lot of say about the global terms of its security, economic welfare, and moral standing. If the United States is constrained as a great power by the fragmentation and decentralization of power around the globe, held by actors with which it is compelled to negotiate, this imperative, perforce, can then be generalized and predicated of all actors.

This insurmountable condition of the rise of global society and the accompanying decentralization of power, hard and soft, across states and nonstate actors pose serious questions, as already noted, of conceptualizing international relations and global politics as state oriented and directed. This condition, actually long in evolution but only recently recognized as central to thinking about global politics, questions the reductionist habit of international relations scholars to speak in terms of superpowers and hegemons, as if these summary terms carried empirical referents that are readily described and explained. The editors of this volume, with some lapses to traditional thinking by contributors, prefer to induce a definition of a state power by its capability to get its way and say within what is a far more complex system of politics within a global society than understood by conventional international relations theory and practice.[23] The terms "superpower" and "hegemon" hide more than they reveal. The evidence advanced by this volume of the complexity of global politics, viewed from the vantage point of American power in play, raises serious doubts about the utility of hegemonic theory when all actors, big and small, state and nonstate, have some power to dispose to shape the global society to their liking or, as is more the case, to discover, along with American policy makers, that their best intentions and foreign and security aims go astray as a consequence of the uncertainties and unintended consequences of global politics today.[24]

What are the key dimensions of global fragmentation and power decentralization? Given the enlarging and deepening interdependencies that characterize global politics, no region's major axes of conflicts, however localized and intense, escape global notice and impact. Scan the horizon for evidence: the potential for nuclear war in South Asia; growing national tensions in Northeast Asia and the aberrant behavior of a nuclear North Korea; rising Muslim revolt in an arc from western Africa to Southeast Asia; struggles for power, bases, and resources in central Asia; chronic civil war, grinding poverty and disease, and episodic genocides in Africa; Balkan ethnic strife in Europe; Russian intervention in the states of the former Soviet Union and backsliding on economic and democratic reform; and leftist gains in Latin American that are at odds with the liberal Washington consensus and the stability of world markets. The Middle East needs little additional explanation as a source of global threats—the crucible of religious and culture clashes across states and peoples, a looming nuclear Iran whose influence extends throughout the region, and heightened competition among the developed states for access to the region's energy resources.

Adding to these regional divisions is the falling out of the great powers whose cooperation is a sine qua non of global stability. The U.N. Security Council is dysfunctional, scarcely a reliable guardian of international peace and security. The Hobbesian endgames taking place in Sudan and the Congo (not to forget Rwanda and the Balkans in the 1990s) testify to its indifference to these human catastrophes and its impotence in preventing or ameliorating their devastating effects. The U.S. solution of unilateralism to address the U.N.'s impotence has made matters worse, not better. Britain, now under Prime Minister Gordon Brown, no longer marches in lockstep with Washington as it did under Tony Blair, his predecessor. France, beset with its own domestic issues of Muslim unrest and better situated geographically since its formation as a Mediterranean power, may align with Washington on specific issues, as the current French president, Nicolas Sarkozy, professes, but is likely to continue to rebuff Washington's lead no matter who is president (Giry 2006).

China continues to ascend as an economic power. It has a favorable balance of trade, at the expense of its Western competitors. It pursues a focused nationalist policy and is cautious in supporting efforts to contain North Korean provocations, to stop genocide in Sudan where it has oil interests, or to vote sanctions against Iran. The uncertainties of its domestic stability—growing inequality between rich and poor, glaring regional imbalances, the widening disparity between the cities and countryside, rampant environmental degradation, widespread corruption, tens of thousands of officially recorded public demonstrations and riots against local and national authorities, and the absence of a popularly elected leadership to confer legitimacy on the regime in power and on the succession process — make the evolution of Chinese politics and governance at home a global concern. Yet outside actors, including the United States, which depend on Beijing's support for their economic and security policies, have a limited, arguably negligible, capacity to affect the resolution of these issues in ways that promote global stability.

The rise of middle and large regional powers complicates the global mix, reinforcing the fragmentation of power and its decentralization within the global society.[25] India, Japan, Brazil, Nigeria, and Germany have demonstrable power, albeit of varying weight, to shape regional and global politics to their liking. There can be no peace in the Middle East or at least an easing of tensions, in the absence of bringing Iran and Syria to the bargaining table, where they are conspicuously absent at this writing. What is clear is that whether they are in or outside a multilateral negotiating framework, they will have a say over regional stability and play a role in redefining the security of the Middle East. Those who argue that the United States should not negotiate with Tehran and Damascus unless preconditions are first met, such as Iran's affirmation of its NPT obligations, ignore Iran's and Syria's power assets already in play in the region.

Nationalist trends in Japan may lead to the revision of the Japanese constitution imposed on Japan by the United States after World War II, opening the way for enlarging its military capabilities and for a greater role assigned to force in Japanese diplomacy.[26] This trend does not bode well for stability in Northeast Asia or for the prospect that rivals will negotiate a mutually acceptable security regime for the region. Brazil has already carved out a greater regional and global role for itself in leading the Group of 21 that challenges Western control of the WTO. Venezuela and redoubtable Cuba defy U.S. power and preferences and attract left-leaning Latin American states to their parade.

Nonstate actors have risen, too, in importance, particularly because of the role they have played in the economic development of the world society. This volume, given space limitations, has said little about the workings of world markets. The liberal Western states have pursued an open-door economic exchange strategy since World War II that has produced unparalleled wealth for its citizens. This is largely not the case in the developing world where grinding poverty (2.5 billion people living on less than two dollars a day) and income inequality are chronic and growing problems as the population of the globe increases. Reinforcing these rising demands for economic equity and for global market reform are pressures from millions of blue- and white-collar workers in the developed world whose job security and incomes have been reduced as a consequence of market globalization.[27] They are thrust cheek to jowl with immigrants who are perceived as threatening their livelihoods and challenging their identities in what is a growing clash of classes and religious, cultural, and ethnic loyalties across states. A chorus of distinguished international economic leaders and scholars has highlighted the possibility of a backlash against the open exchange system unless some international accord to redistribute wealth and preserve job security is developed — and sooner rather than later (Rodrik 1998; Sachs 2005; Stiglitz 2006).

Absent some form of redistribution of wealth among states, particularly among the 20 percent of the world's population that controls 80 percent of the world's wealth, whereby they would tax themselves to fight global poverty and inequality, the market as a socially constructed system may falter and fall apart as it did between World Wars I and II. The immediate prospects of generating international cooperation to meet this challenge appear dim in no small part due to the fragmentation of power and interests across states and among peoples. The U.N.'s millennium goals to fight poverty, if not inequality, in the developing world have not been met except by a few Scandinavian countries, which have reached the level of foreign assistance called for at seven-tenths of one percent of their GDP.

The United States has essentially renounced its pledge. Its foreign assistance measures less than two-tenths of one percent of its GDP. Approximately half of that sum goes to two countries, Israel and Egypt, only one of which can be considered a developing state. The breakdown of the Doha trade talks because of the refusal of the United States and the EU to reform their protectionist trade policies in agriculture deepens skepticism about the likelihood sometime soon of bridging the global poverty/inequality divide.[28] The movement toward a global backlash can be seen, as noted in the chapters by Kleinberg and Hirst, in the leftist movements coursing through Latin America in response to widespread disillusionment with a global liberal exchange regime. The *Economist* (September 30–October 30, 2006), no friend of leftist economics or politics, concedes that Latin America is led not by the United States but by two competing Latin American leftist presidents, Luiz Inácio Lula de Silva of Brazil and Hugo Chávez of Venezuela.

Viewed from the rich states or top down rather than from the poor and bottom up, the market system is no less menaced by global financial imbalances.[29] The mounting trade and governmental debt of the United States and the accumulating foreign reserves of China, one of the principal consequences of U.S. economic policies, mutually contribute to the imbalance. China's trade surplus, only partially attributable to its undervalued currency, grows at an astonishing rate of more than $500 million a day. The United States is obliged to borrow $3 billion a day to cover its private and public spending, while China sits astride a foreign creditor balance of over $1 trillion at this writing. How long Chinese, Japanese, and other central banks as well as private investors will be willing to carry U.S. debt remains one of the great uncertainties threatening the stability of global financial markets. The memory of the Asian crisis of 1997 stokes fears of a much more dramatic run on the dollar that would have the effect of a financial tsunami because of the centrality of the Chinese and American economies to world economic stability and growth. The possibility that private investors might trigger a stampede cannot be ruled out, since the decisions of what Thomas Friedman (2000) aptly calls an electronic herd was instrumental in precipitating the 1997 crisis.

The more immediate and menacing nonstate actors are, of course, terrorist groups. Traditionally, these groups have been characterized as using terrorism as a political tool. Certainly this was true during the decolonization period in which weaker but politically more determined revolutionaries, like those in Kenya and Algeria, defeated successive colonial powers. However, there is a case to be made that terrorism has recently assumed a new and grimmer, nihilistic aspect. These forms of terrorism are carried out or inspired by charismatic leaders like Osama bin Laden, Abimael Guzman (Peru), Chamil Bsayev (Chechnya), Vellupillai Prabakharan (Sri Lanka), and Shoko Asahara (Japan). Many of these movements, animated by millennial visions, are inured to the typical coercive incentives of deterrence, retribution or revenge, and are not amenable to negotiation, compromise or corrupting blandishments — strategies that help to regulate state conflict and behavior and pacify domestic populations.

This new form of indiscriminate terrorism does not comfortably fit the conventional view that terrorism is the necessary strategy of the politically weak and that the actors using terrorism have clearly definable political ends. The forms of terrorism used by al Qaeda in destroying the World Trade Center, Bsayev in killing hundreds in the Beslan school attack, and Asahara in using Sarin gas against his fellow countrymen smack more of mindless murder than inspired and justifiable acts in pursuit of self-proclaimed and realizable political goals (B. Hoffman 2001; Pape 2006; L. Richardson 2006).

The Internet and accessible transcontinental transportation have provided nonstate actors with the tools and connections they need to empower them beyond their small numbers and to make them formidable adversaries. Individuals like Osama bin Laden can now influence the lives of billions in pursuing their destructive strategies while reinforcing the fragmentation of global power. Their ideological justifications recruit thousands to their cause. The decentralized organization of these terrorist organizations makes them particularly difficult to ferret out and defeat by any one state since they cross borders with relative ease. Failed states, like Somalia and Afghanistan, or candidates waiting in the wings in Africa provide bases and succor.

The occupation by terrorist groups of these failed states can also be partially explained as a response to a world society at sixes and sevens without universally acknowledged moral principles, international law norms, and accepted political practices. The fragmentation of national and global power affords space for the creation, survival, and flourishing of these groups. The multiplication of their number hinders substantially the ability of state police, intelligence, and military forces to cope with these new and rising threats to local and global security. To put the challenge in cold statistical terms, one-tenth of one percent of the world's six billion people yields upward of six million potentially alienated, aberrant individuals, many of whom might be prone to antisocial behavior with access to formidable forms of destructive power and, potentially, to WMD.

The Bush Doctrine in declaring a global war on terror has had the ironic effect of creating and multiplying terrorists and terrorist cells where none existed before, as in Iraq. As noted earlier, official national intelligence estimates conclude that the war in Iraq has swelled Jihadist recruitment and increased the number of terrorist groups bent on indiscriminately killing Americans and Westerners and attacking their vital economic interests around the globe. Terrorism as a phenomenon has many faces, and groups using these strategies have diverse and contradictory aims. A more nuanced strategy must be developed that responds to these complex challenges, which cannot be simplified by lumping all terrorists, whether politically conventional or nihilistic, in the same policy sack.

For U.S. strategy to effectively influence the global society and external environment within which American power works, it must take account of the divisions among states and among the world's diverse populations. Necessarily limited American power must either adapt to the countervailing power of rivals where they cannot be persuaded to accept U.S. policy goals or exploit splits among rivals to national advantage. As the French kings who assisted the American revolutionaries in the War of Independence recognized in signing the security treaty of 1778 with the Continental Congress to weaken British global power, security lies in dividing one's adversaries.[30]

Where possible, the integrative strategy that enlarges the coalition of liberal democratic states should be actively pursued. Certainly the Western coalition in its present form should not be divided against itself as the Bush administration was bent on doing in proposing to create shifting and unreliable coalitions of the willing. Nor should policy be based on the misleading and mischievous assumption of an inevitable clash of civilizations that risks becoming a self-fulfilling prophecy. It is useful to be reminded that the great civilizations of the world — Christian, Muslim, Hindu, Buddhist — are actually divided against themselves, as World Wars I and II made abundantly clear and as the struggle among Muslims to define themselves similarly evidences (Aslan 2005). This political rule of thumb segues the discussion to chapter 16, which outlines a new direction and strategy for the United States as a great power to make more efficient and effective use of its impressive but necessarily limited human and material resources.

Notes

1. Keohane and Nye describe these processes by which interdependence is negotiated in their pathbreaking volume.

2. The possibility of natural and man-made global catastrophes is now very much on the agenda of serious observers and scientists (see J. Diamond 2005; Rees 2003).

3. http://icasualties.org/oif/. These figures from private sources are close to those issued by the Pentagon.

4. There is considerable confusion and dispute over the number of Iraqi civilians who have died as a result of the invasion, but it is safe to say that the number is in the tens of thousands. For a start, consult the ongoing Wikipedia page, http://en.wikipedia.org/wiki/Iraq_Body_Count_project. See also chapter 1.

5. Even after three years of occupation, the U.S. military has not been able to gain control of arms in Iraq, as a Pentagon report noting that some five hundred thousand weapons were unaccounted for makes clear (*New York Times*, October 30, 2006).

6. See President Bush's justification for the Iraqi war in a speech commemorating the fourth anniversary of its commencement (*New York Times*, March 20, 2007).

7. A consensus report of governmental agencies released a National Intelligence Report, reviewed in the *New York Times* (September 24, 2006), found that the threat of terrorist attacks had increased as a consequence of the Iraq invasion.

8. See Condoleezza Rice, "The Promise of Democratic Peace: Why Promoting Freedom Is the Only Realistic Path to Security" (*New York Times*, December 11, 2005, B7).

9. Rice's boast of a new Middle East was widely published in the Arab world, much to the discredit of the administration (see *Al Jazeera*, http://english.aljazeera.net/English/Archive/Archive?ArchiveID=24662).

10. See the public opinion poll of Americans and Europeans, "Bush Doctrine on Terror Fails to Convince Public," *Guardian*, September 7, 2006.

11. See Jay Bybee, "Memorandum for Alberto R. Gonzales, Counsel to the President: Standards of Conduct for Interrogation under 18 U.S.C. §§ 2340–2340A." The argument for inherent executive power that purportedly justifies the claim that the president can define torture to be consistent with U.S. law is found in Yoo (2005). For a critique, see Cole (2005) and Schwarz and Huq (2007). For photos of Abu Ghraib, see http://www.antiwar.com/news/?articleid=2444.

12. This point is discussed at length in Kolodziej (1974).

13. Given European military intervention in the Balkans and Afghanistan, the Kagan argument that Europe is essentially pacific appears strained.

14. See, for example, the July/August 2006 issue of *Foreign Affairs* that features four articles under the banner of "The Rise of India."

15. See the analysis of Michael Krepon of the Carnegie Foundation, which also includes the full text of Indian prime minister Manmohan Singh's refusal to accept pending Congressional constraints on India's nuclear program. http://www.stimson.org/pub.cfm?id=322.

16. The Pew Foundation Global Attitudes project details the decline in global favorable attitudes toward the United States in 2005. http://www.pewtrusts.org/pdf/trends2005-global.pdf.

17. Although divided against themselves, partisans of the American primacy position include such strange bedfellows as Mandelbaum (2005), Walt (2005), and Yoo (2005). See also the editorial position of Thomas L. Friedman of the *New York Times*, who sides with them, and in particular with Michael Mandelbaum, who is often favorably quoted. The position of the editors of this volume is closer to that of Bruce Hoffman (2006) and Christopher Layne (2006a) in challenging the notion of the United States as a superpower.

18. I follow Michael Mann's view of society here (1986, especially 1–33).

19. On this score Marx and Kant agree although their endpoints of societal harmony radically diverge, respectively, on material and ideational grounds.

20. Kenneth Waltz correctly isolates the causal force of the political system, now globalized in the nation-state system, but unduly dismisses the power of open markets and social identities as equally powerful forces in determining human behavior. Sound theory in global politics requires attention to all three and their interdependent impact on each other in creating a system whole. Michael Mann (1986) does not make Waltz's mistake in stating the challenge of systemic analysis and theory building.

21. See also Renshon and Suedfeld (2007) for a parallel critique of the Bush Doctrine from a political psychological perspective that, like this volume, concedes its ambitious global scope but also finds it gravely flawed as a guide for the projection of American power.

22. James Rosenau (1990) was among the first to recognize the growing influence and power of individuals, although neither he nor others envisioned their malevolent aims and destructive impact on civil society and the state system.

23. See, for example, the chapter on transatlantic relations by Trine Flockhart, which casts the problem between the states on both sides of the Atlantic as largely a challenge of U.S. management of what Flockhart stipulates is its hegemonic position. What Flockhart in fact describes is American power and leadership in disarray, opposed by European public opinion and by distancing governments responding not only to their domestic publics but also to the threats posed for their nations by unchecked use of American military force. If the United States is a hegemon, then why is its lead either resisted, actively opposed, or just ignored by many of the European states?

24. See the discussion and critique of hegemonic theory in Kolodziej (2005, 227–58).

25. The *Economist*, September 16–22, 2006, contains a special report dedicated to these rising powers.

26. *New York Times*, September 25, 2006.

27. "Inequality and the American Dream," *Economist*, June 17–23, 2006, 13–14.

28. Even the *Economist*, a staunch defender of free markets, is worried by the breakdown of the Doha talks and the possibility of a global backlash (see "The Future of Globalisation," *Economist*, July 29–August 4, 2006, 11).

29. Joseph Stiglitz accents this problem in an op-ed article in the *New York Times* (October 3, 2006, A27), and in his recent book, *Making Globalization Work* (2006, 211–44).

30. Corwin (1916) makes this point quite nicely in explaining why a French monarch would enter into a security treaty with democratic rebels. His analysis also explains, conversely, why a democratic United States would enter informally into a security alliance with the Taliban, Muslim fundamentalists, to defeat the Soviet occupation of Afghanistan only to become the object of the Taliban insurgency.

CHAPTER SIXTEEN

American Strategy for Global Order

Roger E. Kanet

As the editors initially conceptualized the project that has led to this volume, they began with the assumption, widely held in the United States and abroad, that the United States is a superpower and hegemon of the international system. That assumption, a view that remains embedded in the thinking of both the Bush administration and its harshest critics, is not tenable.[1] What is implied by the terms "superpower" and "hegemon"—notions that gained increasingly concrete meaning as the conferences and countless exchanges among participants developed— is a power that can impose its preferences by eliciting, either through coercion or consent, the cooperation of other states and actors. This notion of superpower and hegemonic influence implies therefore, that the United States will always prevail over resistant factors and actors because of its overwhelming dominance.

What has emerged from the research and deliberations reported here is a realization that, regardless of the great discrepancies in military, economic and political capabilities between the United States and other regional and global actors and despite the commitment of U.S. leaders to attempt relentlessly to impose their views of global security and values on reluctant allies, as well as on resistant opponents, virtually all relationships between the United States and other states and actors are based on some form of bargaining, of give-and-take, not the simple imposition of U.S. preferences. The U.S. military can destroy conventional military opponents with relative ease, if they recklessly engage U.S. forces in open combat, but it is incapable of turning this advantage into a tool to ensure that the country's political objectives are achieved. That requires other capabilities that in both Iraq and Afghanistan, as well as elsewhere, have proven to be inadequate. Constraints on its military power and on its eroding economic power as well as declining legitimacy, at home and abroad, contribute to its inability to resolve regional and global problems to its satisfaction. In several regions, notably Latin

America, U.S. power appears less relevant than ever before to the concerns of those peoples and states.

The editors now conclude that both for reasons of conceptual accuracy and of policy-making effectiveness, it is best to regard the United States as doubtless a global power but not a superpower or hegemon. The sooner American policy makers jettison their unfounded assumptions of boundless American power, assumptions that have contributed so mischievously to the erosion of American prestige and influence around the globe, the sooner the United States will be able to use its necessarily scarce but still impressive human and material capabilities and reservoirs of moral authority, however damaged by the Bush administration, to ensure American security and welfare and to contribute positively to global order and the governance of the world's diverse and divided peoples.[2]

As one examines carefully the nature of recent responses of other states to U.S. policy initiatives, one finds extensive evidence of the absence of effective hegemony or credible superpower status. That is, these responses make clear that United States is not necessarily able to achieve objectives that it sets or gain substantial support for those initiatives, even from long-term allies, regardless of the immense differences between the United States and all other state actors in the world in terms of military, economic, and other capabilities. The war on terror is one case in which the United States has been successful in gaining support, but its partner states in this effort, such as Egypt, Algeria, and India, have often simply subverted U.S. policy goals associated with the war to advance their own interests at the very expense of the United States.

Edward Kolodziej's outline in chapter 15 of U.S. foreign policy in regions around the world and the reactions to it of other states that emerges from the case studies as well as his assessment of the realities of the global system together comprise the first of four components of the overall argument that the editors present in these final two chapters. This argument provides compelling evidence that, although the United States is a great global power, it is not, no matter the aspirations of its leaders to hegemony, a hegemonic power, nor does it actually exercise imperial control, as many have argued.[3] The limitations on the effective exercise of U.S. power are too great to permit it to function as a hegemon or imperial power.

The second part of the argument concludes that, under the Bush administration, U.S. policy has largely failed to adapt to these constraints and thereby surmount them. In all but a very few situations, the United States has exacerbated its overall security problems and contributed to its inability to realize legitimate foreign and security policy objectives by pursuing a self-defeating national security strategy.[4] Although the Bush administration has modified its tone and tactics in some policy areas, the core thrust of its policies has remained consistent, notwithstanding growing global resistance to them.

The third component of the general argument emerges directly from the fact that current U.S. foreign and security policy is not sustainable and cannot accomplish the objectives that have been set for it. The fourth part of the argument presents the outline of an alternative U.S. national security strategy that takes into account the realities of the global system, which include the very nature of the complex set of current and emerging challenges to U.S. and global security, the correlation among economic, political, and military forces that characterizes the global system, and the fact of limited U.S. capability to bend those realities to its liking. This entire argument is based on the proposition, already developed by Kolodziej and others throughout this volume, that the United States is but one of many state and nonstate actors that are able to influence regional and global security developments.

The Bush Doctrine's Failure to Adapt U.S. Policy to External and Internal Constraints

To what extent have the perceptions, the advice, and the criticisms of foreign statesmen and important domestic political figures, both those who have supported and those who have opposed U.S. policy, influenced that policy? Have American policy makers taken the positions and criticisms of others into account in assessing the success or failure of policy initiatives and in considering the possibility of modifying them? Briefly and bluntly, the answer is "no"—at least, until late 2006, a development about which we will elaborate later. Although there have been modulations in the tone of the official rhetoric as well as some shifts in tactics, the core elements of U.S. policy have remained stable. The United States in late 2006 was no more willing to commit itself to binding global institutional arrangements that might limit its freedom of action than it was in 2003, at the time of the invasion of Iraq, or in summer 2001, when the Bush administration was in the process of withdrawing from various existing and potential treaty commitments. U.S. policy in Iraq disregards the widespread domestic and international opposition to it and to the chaos and civil war that have resulted from the U.S. intervention and remains committed to "staying the course," even if the slogan of the day might imply a willingness to change tactics or allow greater flexibility in negotiating with adversaries. There is no evidence of a real reconsideration of how the United States might achieve the central goal that the administration has retroactively set for its Iraq policy — the creation of a stable, democratic, diverse, but unified, Iraq.

There is, however, a sense in which the Bush administration has reacted to both policy failure and to criticism — namely, by "outsourcing" to others responsibility for solving security problems with which it has been unwilling or unable to deal. For example, the Bush administration has until very recently refused to deal directly with North Korea — as part of the more general refusal to deal with all U.S.-defined "rogue states" — and has insisted that the group of states comprising Japan, China, Russia, and South Korea all must be present at negotiations with Pyongyang. In effect, the United States has delegated to China primary responsibility for dealing with North Korea.[5]

In a related development in the Middle East the Bush administration retreated from the long-standing U.S. role as a broker in the conflicts between Israel and its neighbors and instead assumed that the Israelis would effectively "take out" Hezbollah and thus weaken the role of Syria and Iran in the Middle East. This policy has contributed to the widely held view in the Middle East that the United States is engaged in a war against Islam.

Overall, U.S. refusal to deal directly with "enemies" has made any effective diplomatic initiative with Iran, North Korea, or the Palestinian Authority most difficult. In effect, in both East Asia and in the Middle East the Bush administration has abandoned constructive efforts to help manage conflict (Haass 2006; Schief 2006).

The current foreign policy of the United States as well as most of its domestic policy is based on strongly held, ideologically derived views that are not easily undermined by criticism or, for that matter, by empirical evidence. This aspect of George W. Bush's personality and of the "personality" of his administration has been emphasized by many analysts (Woodward 2006; K. Roberts 2005). Foreign policy decisions have been driven largely by the assumptions that undergird an assertive nationalist perspective, which, in turn, is tied to an approach to international affairs that emphasizes the role of coercive power.[6] Widespread criticism of his policies, including that from erstwhile domestic supporters (Fukuyama 2006), has not led Bush and his key advisors to deviate from the course that they assert is central to the ability of the United States to retain its dominant global position and to protect itself from threats to its security. They see power and security emerging mainly from the barrel of a gun, as Mao Tse-tung once said, not from collaboration through international institutions and treaties. As will be argued below, the Bush administration's assessment of the United States and its place in the world as well as its ideas about the most appropriate means by which to realize its national security objectives are based on a view of the effectiveness of military power alone and of the sustainability of the current American approach to the rest of the world that ignores the structural and regional constraints outlined in the preceding chapters—a view of the effectiveness of military power that is not limited to the political Right but cuts across much of the U.S. political spectrum.

One cannot ignore the fact that the assertive nationalist position of the current administration in Washington is an integral part of U.S. political culture and that some version of it is likely to continue to exert substantial influence on U.S. foreign policy in the future, although most likely in a less extreme version than that since 2001. It is important to recognize this fact as one attempts to understand current policy and the response to widespread domestic and foreign criticism or to clarify failures that have resulted from policy implementation, such as the growth of Islamic terrorist organizations and hostility toward the United States that U.S. invasion of Iraq has facilitated.[7] One must also recall this reality in considering the development of a new foreign and security policy and a new approach to relations with the rest of the world. U.S. society is deeply divided on issues related to foreign policy, with a very substantial portion of the population accepting the view of the United States as a global superpower that merits a privileged and primary role in global politics.[8]

There is anecdotal evidence to support the assertion that the Bush administration has in general not adapted its foreign policy in response to the reactions of other states. For example, as one examines U.S. relations with Europe since their confrontation prior to the U.S. invasion of Iraq in spring 2003, one does find that the United States has been displaying less overt animosity than it did earlier toward a number of countries and international institutions and treaties (above all the United Nations). No longer do Vice President Cheney and other administration officials denigrate European leaders openly, and the United States has, at least for the present, joined with the Europeans in attempting to deal diplomatically with Iran on the nuclear issue.[9] Secretary of State Rice has also made a number of trips to Europe designed, in part, to mollify European leaders. Yet, the substantive issues that have divided much of Europe from the United States—from U.S. policy in Iraq to an effective approach to the dangers of global warming and other serious environmental threats—remain largely unresolved. The July 2006 collapse of the Doha round of global trade negotiations resulted from the refusal of both the United States and Europe to look beyond narrow domestic interests to try to reach agreement with one another and with developing states on long-term trade issues, principally concerning agriculture.

In general, the United States is no more willing to commit itself to collective action to deal with serious global issues than it was at the outset of the Bush administration.[10] Recent policy decisions made in Washington to transfer U.S. troops and facilities from Germany and other locations in Western Europe to locations further east, motivated no doubt at least in part by logistical concerns related to the "war on terror," are also viewed by some in Europe as evidence that Washington is giving up on less reliable "old Europe" allies and replacing them with more pliable allies in "new Europe," where it can more easily carry out its global war against its opponents.[11]

Further east the attempted consolidation of U.S. military positions in Central Asia has emerged as one of a growing number of friction points in Russian–U.S. relations and has raised Russian as well as Chinese concerns (Kanet and Homarac 2007). It is evident that Russian President Putin's move away from democratization has been an important factor in the cooling since fall 2001 of U.S.–Russian relations. At the same time U.S. cooperation with Central Asian regimes has not been affected by considerations of democracy and human rights. Also important has been what the Russians perceive as a direct challenge to their legitimate "sphere of influence" in Central Asia and as an American effort to gain a hold in the natural gas– and oil-rich region along Russia's southern borders. There is no evidence that Washington is about to modify its commitment to establishing a base of operation in Central Asia, even though its position in the region is quite weak, or to change its policies concerning Iran or Iraq, where the Russian Federation and the United States are very much at odds.

In its relations with China the United States under George W. Bush has modified its aggressive and hostile rhetoric of early 2001 but has not really changed its overall approach to relations. Yet, the U.S. economy is increasingly dependent on the massive foreign investments that help to cover the two-billion-dollar-a-day U.S. trade deficit and, thus, the need for two billion dollars a day in foreign investment in the U.S. economy that this requires, with most of it coming from China and other East Asian and Middle Eastern states that are flush with surplus capital.[12]

When one looks at U.S. policy in Southeast Asia and the Middle East one does find another shift—associated with the emergence of India as a major power and the recent willingness of Washington to modify dramatically its longstanding opposition to nuclear proliferation in the attempt to solidify relations with Asia's second power.[13] Elsewhere in South Asia and the Middle East U.S. policy since the invasion of Iraq in spring 2003 has been overwhelmed by the insurgency in Iraq and has given full support to Israel in the ongoing struggle with its internal and external opponents. Attempts by regional states, as well as those in Europe and elsewhere, to influence a shift in U.S. policy have to date been more or less futile. With single-minded commitment the Bush administration has sought to reinvent the Iraqi political system — with no visible success to date.

Related to this has been the relative imperviousness of the administration to domestic and international criticism of the brutal and illegal treatment of prisoners in Afghanistan and Iraq, as well as in Guantánamo, and the restriction of civil liberties of both citizens and aliens at home. As one analyst has noted, "The torture, the illegal detentions, the unnecessary killings, the grisly prisons — not a single benefit has been shown from the tawdriness and moral depravity. It is likely to outlive its alleged purposes and brand its perpetrators forever" (Tirmain 2006). Ever since September 11, 2001, the "war on terror" has been the justification for policies, both foreign and domestic, that have generated widespread criticism and condemnation, not least because they contravene the international legal and domestic constitutional frameworks to which the United States has committed itself in the past. But there is little evidence that that criticism and condemnation have had any appreciable impact on Bush administration policies.

It is important to mention, in concluding this section, the argument of those who maintain that the Bush administration is backing off from its unilateral and hegemonic approach to accomplishing its foreign and security policy objectives. Such claims have become a standard component of news analysis since the U.S.-led invasion of Iraq in 2003 (Sanger 2006). Pragmatism, as some have argued (P. Gordon 2006) may be at work in influencing aspects of U.S. policy, but it is not eroding the core elements of a policy committed to ensuring U.S. dominance and to using U.S. capabilities to restructure the world in the interests of the United States. The Republican electoral defeats of fall 2006, growing evidence of the failure of U.S. policy in Iraq and Afghanistan, as well as toward Iran and North Korea, have resulted in some modifications of policy (Zakaria 2007), but the central idea that U.S. global dominance must be sustained remains stable.

The Unsustainability of the Bush Doctrine

The first two elements of the overall argument of this volume are now complete — that the United States has not been able to impose its will on the world in the manner to be expected of a superpower and hegemon and that the Bush administration has failed to recognize the constraints on the pursuit of key elements of its foreign and security policy and, in fact, continues to speak and to act as though its overall national security strategy will eventually succeed. Even after the midterm November elections in 2006, which most analysts believed represented a referendum on the Iraq war, the president still insists on "victory" in the face of impending defeat.

The third part of the argument treats the unsustainability of the current U.S. national security strategy. Many domestic critics of American foreign policy have noted that the unilateral and hegemonic approach to realizing foreign policy and security objectives is both counterproductive and prohibitively costly. Expenditures for the invasion and for the ongoing occupation of Iraq total more than $300 billion at the time of writing, with no end to the outflow of U.S. resources in sight.[14] Other aspects of U.S. policy, in particular the military component of that policy, which has involved the development of new weapons systems, have also generated astronomical costs.[15] Taken together the massive expenditure of U.S. resources to establish and maintain U.S. military domination represents a significant drain on the U.S. federal budget and on the economy as a whole.

The negative economic impact of a policy based on presumed hegemony and assertive nationalism is compounded by the fact that the Bush administration is ideologically committed to cutting dramatically the tax contributions of business corporations and the very wealthiest of private citizens. The most immediate effect has been immense, historically unprecedented budget deficits, accompanied by increasing cuts in commitments to the social and material infrastructure of the country both in order to cover a portion of the deficits and to appeal to the fiscal conservatives within the Republican Party.[16] Such a policy threatens to weaken further the already fragile foundations of the Social Security and health care systems, education, scientific research, and so forth, that in the past have characterized the opportunities provided by the American socioeconomic-political system and have been essential to the creation of the scientific and technological advantages that underlie U.S. economic and military power. Administration policies are simply not sustainable in the medium and longer term.

Besides the monetary costs, unilateralism and assertive nationalist policies entail other costs as well. Perhaps the most obvious one is the resistance that so many other countries and peoples have displayed toward key aspects of U.S. policy. Anti-American attitudes and behavior have expanded almost exponentially in response not to U.S. values, as President Bush would have one believe, but to U.S. behavior (Sweig 2006b). Just as important is the fact that most of the longer-term objectives that are central to U.S. interests simply cannot be accomplished alone. Any effective campaign to limit and eventually defeat the efforts of radical fundamentalists to blackmail the United States and the West through terrorist acts must be based on comprehensive cooperation among the target countries, as well as on efforts to reduce the appeal of anti-American attitudes that support terrorism in the first place. This campaign, contrary to current perceived wisdom in Washington, is not primarily a military one, as European allies have noted and as some of Bush's conservative domestic critics have also begun to point out (Will 2006). Other longer-term challenges to U.S. security — even those, such as global warming, that are not yet acknowledged by the administration — also require collaborative efforts, if they are to be managed.

"Soft power," based on the attractiveness of the American project of expanding liberty to its peoples and on the moral authority that the United States possessed throughout much of the twentieth century, has been a crucial instrument with which the United States has exercised influence in world affairs (Nye 2002).

Much of that moral authority has been lost — possibly irretrievably — as a result of the arrogance in the use of U.S. power, the torture of accused terrorists in U.S. prisons, the secret rendition of prisoners to other states where torture is the modus operandi, and the widespread disregard for the views and interests of other states and individuals that has characterized U.S. behavior in recent years.[17]

In sum, the unilateral and assertive nature of U.S. policy has brought with it high costs — it has been financially expensive, and it has led to a growth of hostility toward the United States and the weakening of collaborative relations essential to effecting important U.S. foreign policy and security objectives — objectives that, in most cases, coincide with those of other countries. Yet, the commitment to "go it alone" insofar as is possible and to base "cooperation" primarily on other state and nonstate actors, at home and abroad, acceding to American preferences essentially undermine the successful accomplishment of those goals.

The current attempt to pursue a policy based on U.S. dominance in world affairs is not sustainable, and the assertive and unilateral approach to pursuing its global interests cannot be maintained — if for no other reason than that the United States is overextended militarily and economically and simply cannot bear the costs required to persist in taking a unilateralist and assertive nationalist approach to the rest of the world. Several authors have developed the argument that the dominant role that the United States has played in recent decades has been essential to maintaining what limited stability there has been in the international system. Drawing on the assumptions of "hegemonic stability theory," they maintain that, absent any form of effective global governance, the United States and U.S. policy have been critical in helping to create and maintain the very institutions that have contributed to economic and political security.[18] This general argument about the importance of the United States in contributing to global stability does not run counter to the argument of this study — although, as will be agued below, the United States is not nearly as crucial to the process as many analysts would have it; other states and actors also are playing important, and in some instances indispensable, roles in establishing a more peaceful and prosperous global system. China and India, not to mention the European Union (EU), come readily to mind. In fact, the current assertive nationalist approach to dealing with the rest of the world undermines the very institutions that are essential to the type of global governance to which Mandelbaum (2005), Ferguson (2003; 2005), and others are referring.

The degree to which the United States is overextended is already visible in the economic sphere, where emerging economic giants in Asia are beginning to challenge U.S. dominance. But, even more important in the shorter term are the immense balance of payments and budgetary deficits that in fact are permitted only by massive foreign investments in the U.S. economy. The fiasco with the cancellation of the sale of port management to a Dubai firm in 2006 underscores the contradictions among different aspects of U.S. policy decisions.[19] On the one hand, the virtually unlimited commitment to free trade — at least to those aspects of trade likely to benefit large U.S. corporations — as well as the slashing of taxes, can only be realized if foreigners are willing to invest on an ever-increasing scale in the U.S. economy. Only in this way can the profligacy of the United States government and its people, including the costs of the war in Iraq and the "war on terror," be funded.[20] Yet, outraged cries of nationalist protectionism are heard when at least some of those foreigners attempt to purchase installations or firms viewed as central to U.S. security interests.[21] Similarly, the United States heavily subsidizes domestic agriculture, including competitive sections like grains, at the expense of producers in the developing world, who could be profitable if the price of products like cotton and sugar were not depressed by U.S. (and EU) supports that sustain inefficient agricultural practices. This, in turn, contributes to the flow of economic refugees to both Europe and the United States.

The goals of national control over the economy, unfettered foreign trade, and massive domestic tax cuts despite ballooning government budget and trade deficits are contradictory and self-defeating and cannot be pursued indefinitely. Unless policy is modified in one or more of these areas, the financial demands and their ensuing negative economic impacts on the U.S. economy will force a shift in policy — or accelerate the relative economic decline of the United States, which could cause a meltdown of global financial markets. Yet there is little evidence that the current administration is likely to make major changes in overall strategy on the basis of economic considerations. As the contributors to this study demonstrate, U.S. global strategic policy and the dominance of the United States over many aspects of global affairs have generated widespread opposition — ranging from efforts by friends and allies to persuade American leaders to modify their course to outright confrontation with the United States by others. To date, this criticism and opposition in most cases seems only to have galvanized the Bush security policy team's decision to "stay the course" — in Iraq, in the "war on terror," in a policy of preemption if deemed necessary by Washington, in pursuing a policy committed to regime change under the guise of democratization, and in its refusal to join with others in dealing with environmental and other important global issues if that would result in compromising Washington's sovereignty.[22] Even when the concerns and criticisms of others prove to be well-placed, as has largely been the case in Iraq, and it becomes evident that U.S. objectives cannot be achieved without a significant shift in approach — which is the case in an increasing array of areas from Iraq and Afghanistan to Haiti — Washington has been unwilling to reconsider its policies — at least until the November 2006 congressional elections greatly weakened its domestic political position.

Much of the argument about the rigidity of U.S. policy and the unilateral and assertive nationalist approach to dealings with the rest of the world applies specifically to the current Bush administration. One might conclude, therefore, that with the end of George W. Bush's current term in office in January 2009, there will be a return to the more balanced approach that the United States took in its relations with the rest of the world in the past. Yet the foundations of unilateralist and hegemonic thinking extend deeply in the American political psyche, as already noted above, and an assertive nationalist approach to the rest of the world commands widespread support domestically. Given the assertive nationalist orientation of so much of U.S. society and, even more importantly perhaps, the role of the military-industrial complex in the political process, it is highly unlikely that U.S. strategic policy will undergo a dramatic shift.[23] Yet, the harsh tone that characterized the first years of the Bush administration will likely be modified and modulated.

To sum up, the United States simply does not have the resources to impose its will on the rest of the world, even if that were desirable. Moreover, its relative position in the world, especially in economic and political terms, is declining and with it its ability to pursue the type of assertive nationalist policy that has characterized the first decade of the twenty-first century. This brings us, therefore, to the fourth and final stage of the concluding argument of this volume — the call for a new national security policy that both reverses the appreciable losses and damage of the recent past and effectively addresses the formidable obstacles in the way of advancing U.S. interests, aims, and values in a complex world of diverse and divided peoples and states.

A Revitalized National Foreign and Security Policy

The overwhelming military, economic, and political-diplomatic capabilities that the United States commands have not enabled it to achieve many of its current leaders' most cherished foreign and security policy goals in recent years. The Bush Doctrine has weakened the global position of the United States and exacerbated the challenges that it faces. The administration's persistent emphasis on keeping all options on the negotiating table — an unsubtle signal that military force is at the ready — is both crude and counterproductive. Experienced negotiators need no instruction that military force underpins negotiations between armed rivals. So why inflame and devalue talks at the outset by threatening force? That can only elicit the same response from adversaries and provoke defection by potential allies fearful of being placed in harm's way by aggressive U.S. initiatives.[24]

Changing U.S. national security policy requires first and probably most essentially that U.S. leaders recognize — not only rhetorically, but also in fact — that bluster and the threat of or the use of military power is not the appropriate solution to the vast majority of the security problems that face both the United States and the global community, including the threat of terrorism. Moreover, since most of the challenges facing the United States are global and involve other countries, collaboration is essential to their solution.

Closely associated with this point is the need to eliminate the sense of superiority, triumphalism, and disdain for others that has characterized recent U.S. behavior toward other countries and their leaders — the negative flip side of U.S. exceptionalism. Presenting others with nonnegotiable demands will not provide the foundation for a successful collaborative approach to working out problems. Even though virtually all current global problems require such a collaborative approach, in recent years the United States has often dealt with the rest of the world by presenting "solutions" or "demands" that others must accept or be castigated either as obstacles to resolution or, worse, as adversaries of the United States. Moreover, by simply refusing to deal with what the U.S. leadership terms "retrograde" or "rogue" regimes and by describing the conflicts with them and others as a global struggle between good and evil, the current U.S. administration has simply abandoned politics and rendered negotiated settlements virtually impossible.

From Assertive Nationalism to Collaboration

Before a discussion of the specifics of a revamped approach to national security is possible, the foundations of such a strategy must be clarified — foundations based on the reality of the U.S. position in the world that has been laid out in this study, not on some imagined global dominance that gives to the United States the right to dictate to others or the ability to impose its preferences on them. The United States is not a hegemon with a world empire, even though some of its leaders wish that it were and have pursued policies and committed themselves to actions based on the assumption that it is. The fifteen chapters that have preceded this one demonstrate the serious limitations on U.S. action, the degree to which other actors have been able to capture the attention and gain the support of the United States and even lay claim to its agenda, as well as the inability of the U.S. government to realize goals viewed as central to the national security of the United States. Thus, the assertive nationalists and neocons who have dominated policy making in recent years have greatly exaggerated the ability of the United States to go it alone in remaking the world in its preferred image.[25]

On the other hand, many of the critics of the current approach to U.S. foreign policy share the nationalists' and neocons' view of the centrality of the United States to virtually all that occurs in world affairs. This is evident in the work of those who criticize the aggressiveness and the unilateral nature of recent U.S. policy but argue that the U.S. simply must take *the* leadership position in world affairs lest the entire global community fall into complete disarray. In this argument the United States, and the United States alone, has the military and economic capabilities, the moral standing, and the vision of a better future to divert or control those forces that would destroy the emerging global order and community.[26] So even among those analysts who criticize an approach to the rest of the world based on efforts at domination and hegemony, there emerges a sense that the United States is the indispensable actor, the only one that can ensure the governance of an emerging world society divided against itself.[27]

What neither the advocates of U.S. empire nor many of the critics of a policy based on assertive nationalism recognize is the fact that the overwhelming discrepancies in military power between the United States and the rest of the world and the substantial capabilities available to it do not make it a hegemon that can simply impose its will on the rest of the global community. The hegemon, if one is even permitted to use the term, is the Western coalition of open, democratic, market societies and states. But even this coalition, assuming its ability to overcome its current internal problems, is not, and will not be, in a position simply to dictate to the other state and nonstate members of the global community. It will be essential for them to overcome their differences and develop a set of rules or standards of behavior and a collaborative strategy to deal with major threats to global security.[28] Their challenge is to preserve the ascendant position they still enjoy in what has devolved into a fractious and fractured global system and to enlarge the coalition of free, market states, dedicated not only to the welfare and human rights of their populations but also keen to extend these collective goods to other peoples. The example of the EU in setting conditions for democratic and market practices and in helping states meet these conditions for entry into the EU is a model that American diplomacy might well emulate, if it wishes to strengthen the Western project so challenged today and to advance American policy goals.

So, the first element of a new approach to a national security policy is a recognition by leaders in Washington that the United States will never be in a position to accomplish its legitimate foreign and security policy objectives alone and that it must collaborate with other states in real partnerships, messy and complicated though such partnerships might be, if it is to have a chance to advance its — and their — interests. In other words, the model of Western collaboration during the cold war must be revived and expanded. This will require, however, a major change in attitude among U.S. political elites.

In the same vein, U.S. political elites must also recognize that no state, including the United States, is in a position to impose its preferences for global order on other peoples and societies. Democratization via conquest, a sort of militant and muscular Wilsonianism, cannot succeed — the claims that the democratization of postwar Germany and Japan validate that approach notwithstanding. In fact, societies where socioeconomic development, political maturity, tolerance across ethnic and religious communities, and moral standards are alien to the contemporary Western ideal are ill-suited candidates for democratization. As is evident in Afghanistan and Iraq, such efforts are much more likely to turn out to have been an enormous waste of resources and to exacerbate the problems that were inherent in the country or region at the very outset. This line of analysis does not imply that the United States ought to abandon these states and peoples so much as it needs to lower its expectations regarding the prospects for the short-term reform of these societies, defined by their capacity to adopt a Western or, more specifically, an American model of modernization.

The third element of a new approach to a national security policy for Washington is the recognition that the social, environmental, and material infrastructure of the United States needs serious repair and revitalization. Current U.S. national foreign security strategy seems to have lost sight of the purpose of a national security strategy, namely, to protect and secure the core elements of what has made the United States a successful and attractive society and country — liberty, first of all, the protection and strengthening of the constitutional framework that guarantees that liberty, and the social and economic well-being of all of its citizens. The chaos within the federal government in responding to the disaster of Hurricane Katrina, the eroding performance of American schools in comparison with their global counterparts, the growing dependence of the country on imported energy, the national crisis in health care, the declining commitment of resources to scientific research and technological innovation, the gradual disintegration of the national transportation system, the widespread corruption of public officials, and the embarrassing breakdown in ensuring accurate vote counts in elections — these and a host of other issues evidence a serious decline in governmental competence. All of these problems challenge the very foundations of American society.

The watchword is domestic reform. Unless serious attention is given to rebuilding the nation's social, economic, and political infrastructure, the United States will find itself in an increasingly weakened position both domestically as a society and internationally in its ability to influence events of importance to its long-term interests. More specifically this means, first and foremost, that the government of the United States must return to the rule of law in domestic political affairs to counter the recent aggregation of power in the hands of what some have termed an imperial presidency; eliminate the corruption that is undermining the country's political and economic systems; modulate the strident ideologically based rhetoric that divides the American political system and cease using security concerns and security policy as tools to divide the nation in order to win elections and hold power; renew efforts to protect civil liberties; commit the resources needed to rebuild the country's educational system at all levels and to ensure its accessibility to all economic classes; and recommit itself to a principle of equity by recognizing that government is obliged to promote the welfare of all of its citizens without reference to economic class or social status. Measuring economic success solely in gross output terms or by GDP per capita, the usual measures in discussions of economic growth and well-being, ignores the gross economic discrepancies — and growing inequities — in the distribution of wealth and income and in the standard of living that have exploded in the United States during the past quarter century of increasingly unfettered laissez-faire capitalism. Addressing these issues, as Americans have before in solving the challenges of their times, is the proven recipe for forging the diverse peoples of the United States into the "more perfect union," envisioned by the Preamble of the Constitution. Rebuilding the social, political, and economic structures that made the United States a great society and country and that made it so attractive to other peoples of the world would, if successful, ensure the intellectual, scientific and skilled labor force that is essential, if the United States is going to remain competitive through the twenty-first century in an increasingly globalized economy. It would also reestablish the position of the United States as a model for those seeking ways to reform their own societies — as has been the case in the past. This project of reviving the infrastructure of U.S. society will be a long-term and expensive one, but one that is critical, if the country is to retain a prominent position in global affairs. Moreover, it will be much less expensive in the long term than the costs associated with the continued social and material decline of the country.

The United States must not only rebuild the foundations of domestic society to shape a new national strategy but must also address other issues generally viewed as essential for the future security of the United States and, for that matter, the broader world community:[29] (1) physical security against armed attack, whether the source is another country or a transnational movement such as al Qaeda and whether it is accomplished via conventional warfare or terrorist operations; (2) security against economic disaster and against the decline of those aspects of a national economy that enable an increasing percentage of the population to enjoy a comfortable standard of living without the fear that all may disappear over night; and (3) environmental and ecological security in the face of the dangers of global warming, potential global pandemics, and related concerns. The following pages will discuss briefly proposed approaches to each of these security concerns, recognizing, however, that the current political debate in the United States and the influence of ideologically and religiously based positions are likely to impede policy changes.

Military Security

Traditionally security against foreign attack has been the centerpiece of national security policy. It rested on two principles. Resources were committed to ward off or deter an aggressive attack by building a military establishment second to none and, what has been lost from sight in the Bush Doctrine, by embedding this formidable fighting force in alliances with like-minded and reliable allies to magnify the political influence of the United States in advancing its interests around the globe. The emergence of global terrorist organizations based, in part at least, in the target countries themselves, including the United States, changes quite dramatically the calculus of national security. Developing and maintaining traditional military capabilities remains important but is not enough, given the unconventional threat posed by al Qaeda and other terrorist organizations. Resources must be devoted to strengthening the military in ways that are relevant to its ability to carry out unconventional warfare against subversive and clandestine forces, as in both Iraq and Afghanistan, not used to fund the inordinately costly futuristic weapons systems that are designed to refight previous conventional wars or, worse, that are little more than "welfare" programs for the military-industrial complex.[30] Put more concisely, the massive funding provided for military security should be directed to current and likely future requirements, not to "pie-in-the-sky" projects that will siphon off the funding from where it is truly needed — to support real, on-the-ground, operations.

Second, the United States must work with key allies, beginning with NATO, to ensure that real collaboration exists in managing what are shared security threats. Since the greatest likely challenge to the physical security of the United States and its allies will be the acquisition of weapons of mass destruction (WMD) by terrorist organizations, emphasis must be placed on preventing such a development. To date the Bush administration has failed completely at preventing the spread of nuclear weapons to regimes that are potential sources of such weapons for terrorist groups.

To make radical terrorist organizations less attractive, especially in the Islamic world, it is essential that the United States reduce, even eliminate, the physical presence of its military forces from many of the areas of the world where they are now based and where, as in the Middle East, they contribute to the hostility toward the United States and help to fuel regional and global terrorist groups. This does not mean abandoning efforts to maintain stability in areas of interest and concern to the United States. But other states should be expected to play a more active role and the United States should focus its policy on developing forces to be injected into the region as a last resort in crisis situations from facilities in locations not likely to generate the type of hostility that now exists.

Third, the idea of a "war on terror," which overemphasizes the traditional military components of the current security challenge represented by al Qaeda and other groups, should be replaced by the recognition that intelligence and traditional policing activities are the crucial, even primary, components of the security struggle and that cooperation with other states, notably allies, in these areas is indispensable. Closely related to this, U.S. leadership should not exaggerate the degree of convergence of interests or methods and concerted cooperation among its regional and global opponents. In many cases they are as deeply opposed to one another as they are to the United States. By speaking and behaving as though all groups that oppose or disagree with the United States, terrorist and other, are part of an integrated global challenge, the U.S. government actually contributes to the emergence of greater cohesion among these groups. To repeat a point already made, solid intelligence (the acquisition of which would involve collaboration with U.S. allies), covert operations, and strengthening the security of the U.S. homeland are the best ways to combat terrorism.[31] This does not mean that conventional military operations will not play an important role in combating future security threats, just that a higher priority must be assigned than currently to these diplomatic and strategic initiatives against terrorists and insurgents.

The U.S. response to security threats, including those that emanate from terrorist organizations, overemphasizes the military instrument and makes no effective attempt to develop an integrated foreign and security policy response that draws on economic, political, and cultural resources, in addition to military capabilities. Such a strategy would recognize the importance of nonmilitary factors in the pursuit of national objectives. For example, the United States has virtually abandoned its once extensive programs, through the U.S. Information Agency (USIA), for example, to introduce foreigners to the United States and to American science, culture, and education. It spends more than five hundred times as much on its military than it does on broadcasting, education exchanges, and other programs combined that were an integral part of policy several decades ago.

Besides focusing its military resources directly on the types of threats that the United States and the world face in the twenty-first century (first and foremost the terrorist threat), assuring effective military cooperation with others and relying on others to take the initiative in situations where their interests are directly involved, the United States must do a much better job of managing its domestic security. Monies being poured into projects like the missile defense program or the pacification of Iraq would much better be used to upgrade the protection of port facilities, airports, nuclear installations, chemical plants, water supplies, and so forth in the United States (Flynn 2007).

Ensuring the protection of vital infrastructural installations is also directly relevant to the argument presented above about the need to rebuild the social and economic infrastructures of the United States to secure its ability to compete effectively in the global economy of the twenty-first century. To fulfill these aspirations, the political elite must abandon the negative attitude toward the role of government that recently has dominated the debate in the United States. Government can be, and has been, a force for good, not an evil conspiracy visited on a distracted public that should be starved to death. Only governing elites committed to the welfare of the country's population will be able to deal effectively with the broad domestic security needs of the American people, not those either determined to impose their ideological strait jackets on a trusting public or bent on defrauding the public treasury, Jack Abramoff–style, by promoting their own or their supporters' special interests.

An important element of military security that also cuts across economic security concerns refers to potential future challenges to U.S. interests that might arise from the efforts of a state to establish a dominant position in a region of the world of importance to the well-being of the United States and its key allies. The most important of these areas, at least so long as the industrialized world (led by the United States) remains addicted to petroleum and natural gas to fuel its economies, is the Middle East. For the foreseeable future, therefore, the United States and the rest of the industrialized world must be wary of the emergence of any regional power that might threaten to dominate the region and its natural energy supplies. In East Asia, following a policy of confrontation with a rising China rather than attempting to work with it and to help it to integrate into the global community is a recipe for disaster. The Bush administration has assumed a fundamentally contradictory stance toward China. On the one hand, it seeks to accommodate Chinese vital interests (by, for example, reaffirming a one-China policy) and to elicit support for its policies in Northeast Asia, the Middle East, and Africa. On the other hand, it undermines the nonproliferation treaty and mindlessly attempts an entente cordiale with India to contain China, even though India needs no instructions from the United States and, moreover, goes its own way to accommodate China. Such an approach to relations with China and overall policy in Asia appears doomed to failure on various fronts.[32]

Economic Security

We turn now to the second component of a new overall national security policy that focuses on ensuring the long-term economic well-being of the country and of all of its citizens. Of necessity, in the context of global economic interdependence, economic security depends on the United States taking a global perspective. The most important issue by far is related to decreasing American competitiveness in global markets, weighted down by a mounting federal debt that is estimated to be almost $10 trillion in an economy of $11 trillion in GDP. These constraints seriously impair the capacity of the United States to stay abreast of vigorous competition in the global economic system. As noted earlier in this chapter, the United States has been able to live beyond its economic means only because to date others (especially Japanese and Chinese central banks) have been willing to buy American securities. How long will this continue? When might the Chinese, for example, begin to balance their reserves in Euros as well as in dollar accounts, or when might Middle Eastern oil exporting countries decide that they want to denominate petroleum prices in Euros rather than dollars? Were one or both of these possibilities to occur, what would the impact be on the U.S. and world economy? So long as the U.S. economy and U.S. trade are completely out of balance and the country falls more and more in debt to the rest of the world, it will not be able to re-create the kind of financial and fiscal foundation for the future that is essential to preventing the long-term erosion of American capabilities and ensuring the welfare of its peoples.[33]

A broad, new U.S. foreign and security strategy, therefore, must begin by putting the fiscal house of the United States in order, as part of the program of rebuilding the social and economic infrastructure of the country. This will call for a leadership that is willing to lead, a leadership that will pursue policies that reverse the politically expedient tax policies of the recent past to pay off the massive federal debt and to prevent further erosion of U.S. scientific and technological capabilities. Savings from the current wasteful military budget, where so much flows into generally useless weapons systems or is lost to corruption, should also be used for these purposes.

This new strategy will also require a continued commitment to global cooperation in the development of open markets, but in a manner that does not limit the winners at both home and abroad to major corporations and those at the top economic levels of society. To date most of the vaunted benefits of globalization have bypassed large segments of society in both the United States and much of the rest of the world and have, in fact, contributed to the growing divisions and inequities that have generated opposition to globalization and stimulated anti-Americanism. Self-interest alone advises those who have reaped the rewards of global markets to share their gains with those less advantaged to preserve public support at home and abroad for a global free-exchange system and to resist pressures to adopt self-defeating protectionist policies.

It is also imperative that the United States recognize that real economic and political development in large portions of the developing world, including in the Islamic world, is essential for the emergence of stable societies that will not in the future serve as the breeding grounds for the disaffected who are ready recruits of terrorist organizations. Economic, social, and political development from the bottom up is a more likely long-term contribution to the solution to the problem of global terrorism than is the attempt to impose so-called democratic reforms from outside.

The challenges related to rebuilding the overall economic foundations of the United States are immense. The point to be made here is that answering these challenges should be central components of any medium- and long-term national security strategy of the United States.[34]

Environmental/Ecological Security

In addition to attending to issues associated with traditional military security and long-term economic well-being, the United States must also, in developing a new security strategy, address environmental and ecological concerns about the impact that the United States and other countries have been having on the very world in which they live as well as the impact potential pandemics could have on their societies. Although the current U.S. administration continues to question aspects of the scientific evidence that underscores these threats and, even more important, opposes any collaborative means to deal with them that would limit U.S. freedom of action or impact negatively on the profits of U.S. corporations, the reality is that global warming, air and water pollution, the depletion of fish stocks in the seas, and a host of other problems threaten the future of the entire human race.[35]

This is not the place to discuss the specifics of the environmental and ecological challenges facing the human community in the twenty-first century. It is enough to point out that, absent greater human cooperation to address these threats to the global commons, the prospects for a sustainable world are placed at serious risk. From the perspective of a new U.S. national security strategy, one must emphasize the obvious point that these efforts require broad collaboration across the global community. The defection of key states, such as the United States, from combined efforts undermines the possibility of coping with the formidable and forbidding threats to the very existence of humans on the planet.

Addressing some of the problems associated with global warming would have the added benefits of helping reduce the dependence of the American people on imported oil and helping revitalize of the U.S. economy. To date the U.S. government has simply avoided political responsibility by refusing to develop a national energy policy that emphasizes increased energy efficiency — for example, by fiscal intervention — and provides real incentives for the development of sources of energy to replace hydrocarbons.

Conclusions

In the course of this project and the writing of this book the editors (and other authors) have traveled a long distance. They recognize that U.S. foreign policy in recent years has been fatally flawed by the assumption that because of its formidable power the United States can simply command the world to change, and it will change. The overall military capabilities of the United States remain immense and are significantly greater in virtually all fields than those of any other state or movement, but they are finite and not always prepared to accomplish the goals abroad that American leaders set. This means that, like other states at other times, the United States must interact politically with both its friends and its opponents in its attempts to maintain security and realize other objectives important to its interests. Negotiation and compromise — in other words, diplomacy — are essential tools to political interaction. Interaction must also be coupled with deterrence to defend the United States against other states whose interests and goals may conflict with its own. Simple confrontation, the refusal to sit down and talk with "enemies," or the attempt to dictate the terms of any discussion are all more likely to exacerbate differences and preclude progress on the solution of problems.

Just as important as the reorientation of the external components of U.S. security policy away from unilateralism, assertive nationalism, and an overreliance on military instruments is the need for renewed concern about the domestic political and social environment. As Michael Lind (2006, 252) puts it: "The purpose of the American Way of Strategy is to defend the American way of life by means that do not endanger the American way of life." The government must expunge from the security policy of the United States those elements of it that have led to the abrogation of civil liberties, the abandonment of constitutional controls on the executive branch, and the redefinition of the U.S. commitment to both domestic and international law on issues such as the use of torture.[36] The United States must return to a policy based on cooperation with other states and peoples in attempting to create a world that is not torn by the divisions and conflicts of the recent past and that has a greater ability to adequately confront the challenges to humankind, whether they are economic, environmental, or humanitarian in nature. Only through such cooperation that builds on the efforts of the second half of the twentieth century but also draws in a larger percentage of the world's states and peoples, will the future remain bright for both the citizens of the United States and the peoples of the world.

Notes

The author wishes to express his sincere appreciation to Trine Flockhart, Heinrich Vogel, and, especially, Edward A. Kolodziej for their critical comments on earlier versions of this chapter, which have helped to clarify the argument.

1. All the major assessments of current U.S. foreign policy, whether supportive or critical, are grounded in the assumption that the United States is the central actor in contemporary global affairs (see Ferguson 2004; Johnson 2004; R. Kagan 2003; Krauthammer 2004; Mandelbaum 2005; Nye 2002; Walt 2005; and most contributors to *Foreign Affairs*).

2. In a perceptive recent review essay, Stanley Hoffmann (2006) comes to quite similar conclusions.

3. Arguing from quite different theoretical perspectives a number of noted analysts have maintained that a commitment to hegemony and empire have been essential elements of U.S. policy, even though they were tempered during the cold war by the realities of the confrontation with the Soviet Union and in earlier periods by the limited overall power capabilities of the United States. For the most recent development of this argument, see Layne (2006b). For similar conclusions, though based on quite different theoretical assumptions, see Bacevich (2002), Johnson (2004), and Gaddis (2004).

4. The 2006 version of *The National Security Strategy of the United States* (U.S. White House, Office of the President) advocates the very same approach to security as did the preceding versions, despite the evident failure of the approach.

5. With growing evidence of the chaos in Iraq and the failure of the threats against both North Korea and Iran to compel them change their policies on the development of nuclear capabilities as well as the takeover of both the Senate and the House by the Democratic Party in January 2006, the Bush Administration has modified its approach on a series of key foreign policy issues. As commentator Fareed Zakaria (2007) has noted, however, it is basically "too little, and too late."

6. The term *assertive nationalist* characterizes a broad range of analysts and policy makers who do not always fully agree among themselves on specifics (Kanet 2005). They do agree that, based on its dominant position in global politics, the United States should use its power to restructure the world for its own benefit. They allow that this restructuring can be done in collaboration with other states if possible but that it must always remain under U.S. leadership. If collaborators cannot be found, then the United States should act alone. Because of the overwhelming predominance of U.S. power, other states — even those strongly opposed initially to U.S. initiatives — will fall into line, if for no other reason than the fact that they are unable to resist. Where these analysts diverge is on the degree to which "assertive Wilsonianism," or creating democratic polities through coercive intervention if necessary as a means to extend and stabilize the U.S. global position, should be an essential element of U.S. policy. This general position was stated quite clearly as early as 1997 by the Project for the New American Century (Soros 2004, 5–7) most of whose members, in fact, became the foreign policy establishment of the new Bush administration in 2001. Influential policy analysts and publicists who belong to this group include Max Boot (2003), Charles Krauthammer (2002/3; 2004), Robert Kagan (2003), and William Kristol, editor of the conservative publication, the *Weekly Standard*.

7. A classified report from the combined U.S. intelligence organizations completed in April 2006 indicated that the Iraq war and U.S. treatment of prisoners at Abu Ghraib and Guantánamo Bay had "made the overall terrorism problem worse" and had "stoked the jihad movement" (Mazzetti 2006).

8. In his important study of American nationalism Anatol Lieven (2004) demonstrates that a broad spectrum of U.S. society, including large segments of the political elite, embrace this idea.

9. This willingness to join with EU states in dealing with Iran has, no doubt, been influenced by the Bush administration's refusal to engage in direct discussions with the governments of those that it views as "rogue states."

10. However, as part of the "new approach" to policy issues since the fall 2006 U.S. congressional elections, the administration has recognized the relevance of global warming and spoken in general terms about the need to initiate action—seemingly with the purpose of precluding action by others rather than initiating joint efforts.

11. There is evidence of European countries, especially new NATO member states, having cooperated with the U.S. policy of "rendition," the euphemism used for transferring terrorist suspects to undisclosed locations for interrogation that can involve torture ("Report Rendered," *Economist*, June 10–16, 2006, 49). The report of the investigation headed by Swiss Senator Dick Marty on behalf of the Council of Europe is available on line (Council of Europe 2006). The public recognition by President Bush in early September 2006 that the U.S. did, in fact, have secret prisons, revived the political immediacy of the issue.

12. The U.S. foreign trade deficit is now running at roughly $600 billion per year. Approximately two-thirds of that deficit has been financed by foreign governments' investments in the U.S. economy in recent years (Economic Policy Institute 2004; U.S. Department of State, Bureau of International Information Programs 2001).

13. It is important to note that the commitment of President Bush to supporting the development of India's nuclear industry contravenes U.S. treaty commitments under the Non-Proliferation Treaty (NPT) as well as domestic law in the United States. It is but another example that the U.S. government does not see itself as bound by international agreements. Even though it does represent a shift in U.S. policy toward India, it does not break with the overall disdain for international obligations or international law that characterizes current U.S. policy. Establishing good relations with India, which is viewed as a potential long-term friend, is seen as more important than adhering to international law or international institutional commitments (Cirincione 2006). The commitment to support India is also evidence of the concern about the rise of China as a major global power and is an attempt to secure an ally in Asia whose interests, at least as they relate to China, are likely to coincide with those of the United States (Center for Arms Control and Non-Proliferation 2006).

14. In late September 2006 the National Priorities Project (2006) estimated that the cost of the war in Iraq to date was greater than $318 billion.

15. It is extremely important to note that much of the money expended on the development of weapons systems has little to do with the war in Iraq or the "war on terror," since these weapons systems are more suited to managing the now-ended cold war confrontation with the Soviet Union than the threat posed by al Qaeda and other possible terrorist organizations. Domestic politics, including the immense political influence of the U.S. armaments industry and private military contractors, has more to do with to explaining these costs than the ongoing security challenges to the United States.

16. The Bush administration has cut deeply into social programs meant to support the poor, education, health care, scientific research, and so forth while simultaneously and repeatedly cutting taxes for the very wealthiest of U.S. citizens (*Boston Globe* 2006; Weisman 2004). In addition to dramatically cutting domestic programs, the United States has virtually abandoned its once extensive programs aimed public diplomacy on the grounds that they cost too much. The total outstanding public debt of the United States as of June 28, 2007

was $8,812,996,583,375.20 ($8.81 trillion). The annual debt in recent years has been running more than $500 billion per year (U.S. National Debt Clock 2007).

17. On the loss of U.S. legitimacy related to the issue of torture see the letter that former secretary of state Colin Powell (2006) sent to Senator John McCain during the U.S. Senate debates on the issue of torture in fall 2006.

18. See, for example, Mandelbaum (2005) and Ferguson (2004). On the issue of "hegemonic stability theory" see, for example, Ikenberry (2001).

19. The furor surrounding the sale of the management of various U.S. port facilities to a Dubai-based company finally ended when the company decided to sell its holdings to an American owner (Weisman and Graham 2006).

20. It is important to note that of the estimated $530 billion expended as of late September 2006 on the war on terror, the vast majority has been siphoned off by the war in Iraq ($316 billion), while $88 billion has gone to the war in Afghanistan and an additional $126 billion has gone to the Department of Homeland Security (Moreau, Yousafzai, and Hirsh 2006).

21. Even those authors who argue that the U.S. "imperial" role is essential to ensuring the stability of the international system, such as Niall Ferguson (2004), question the ability and willingness of the American people to fund that role. Michael Mandelbaum (2005) seems to downplay this concern in his assessment of the benefits of U.S. global dominance.

22. The most recent March 2006 version of *The National Security Strategy of the United States* (U.S. White House, Office of the President 2006) makes clear, for example, that, despite the failure to date of externally imposed efforts at democratization in the Middle East, the United States remains committed to pursuing this policy.

23. These attitudes toward the outside world are closely associated, as Lieven (2004) and others have demonstrated, with the religious fundamentalism that has gained such strength in recent years.

24. For a major recent proposal for a revitalized U.S. national security policy that still, however, views the United States as the dominant global actor, see Ikenberry and Slaughter (2006).

25. See the arguments of Bacevich (2002), Johnson (2004), Layne (2006b), Soros (2004), and others. Recent efforts to deal with both Iran and North Korea make it most clear that overwhelming military power does not necessarily provide the United States with the tools to accomplish its objectives.

26. This assumption is embedded in the arguments presented by Michael Mandelbaum (2005) and Niall Ferguson (2004). In a similar vein, during the Clinton administration Secretary of State Madeleine Albright regularly referred to the United States as "the indispensable nation" (Nordlinger 1999). See, also, the proposals of the Princeton Project on National Security (2006).

27. Joseph P. Nye Jr. (2006) comes very close to arguing this position in a number of his publications. In a recent policy piece, for example, he concluded that a new U.S. strategy "should look to the long-term evolution of world order and realize the responsibility of the international system's most powerful . . . country . . . to produce global public or common goods." This perspective also infuses Stephen M. Walt's incisive criticisms of George W.

Bush's foreign policy. Walt (2005) and others simply assume that the United States must and will lead in any global "partnership." For a recent critique of this aspect of Nye's views see Layne (2006c, 7).

28. In a superb recent study, in which he argues that Europe and the United States need to coalesce in facing the serious challenges to themselves and the entire global community, Timothy Garton Ash (2004) develops this argument most persuasively.

29. The approach to security taken here is based on the broad interpretation of security that defines it as encompassing more than military challenges, a view that has been developed by Buzan, Waever, and de Wilde (1998).

30. Billions of dollars have already been expended on the missile defense system (approximately ten billion dollars a year currently and estimated to double by 2013). Massive outlays of funding have also been made to permit production of outdated or unwanted aircraft and other expensive equipment solely to placate political supporters in the defense industry.

31. For a discussion of growing collaboration in resisting the West, including Israel and the United States, see "Coalitions of the Unwilling," *Economist*, October 21–27, 2006, 25–28.

32. For a series of articles on China and its foreign policy, see Zheng Bijian (2005), David Zweig and Bi Jianbai (2005), Wang Jisi (2005), and Kishore Mahbubani (2005).

33. As of early October 2006 the annual interest payments on U.S. foreign debt reached more than $220 billion and will reach $270 billion in 2008. For "the first time in more than 90 years the United States is paying more to foreign creditors than it receives from its investments abroad" (*New York Times*, editorial, "Deeper and Deeper," October 5, 2006, A30).

34. Stephen E. Flynn (2004, 23) argues that the Bush administration has failed to give serious attention to the security needs of the infrastructure of the U.S. economy. He argues that "This myopic focus on conventional military forces at the expense of domestic security even extends to making the physical security at U.S. military bases a higher budget priority than protecting the nation's most critical infrastructure."

35. This was the message of a largely buried report commissioned by the Department of Defense (Schwartz and Randall 2004).

36. Orenstein and Mann (2006) note the degree to which the U.S. Congress has simply failed to perform its constitutionally mandated oversight function in the foreign policy area since 2001.

References

Abramovici, Pierre. 2004. United States: The New Scramble for Africa. *Le Monde Diplomatique*, July 7.

Abramowitz, Morton D., Richard D. Burt, Donald K. Bandler, Frances G. Burwell, William Drozdiak, and Eric Melby. 2004. Turkey on the Threshhold: Europe's Decision and U.S. Interests. *Atlantic Council Policy Paper*, August. http://www.isn.ethz.ch/pubs/ph/details. cfm?lng=en&id=13480.

Acharya, Amitav. 2003. Democratization and the Prospects for Participatory Regionalism in Southeast Asia. *Third World Quarterly* 24: 375–90.

Acharya, Amitav, and See Seng Tan. 2006. Betwixt Balance and Community: America, ASEAN, and the Security of Southeast Asia. *International Relations of the Asia-Pacific* 6: 37–59.

Adebajo, Adekeye. 2003. Africa and America in an Age of Terror. *Journal of Asian and African Studies* 38 (2–3): 175–91.

Adler, Emmaneul, and Michael Barnett, eds. 1998. *Security Communities*. Cambridge, U.K.: Cambridge University Press.

Advisory Group on Defense Issues. 1994. Higuchi Report. *The Modality of the Security and Defense Capability of Japan: The Outlook for the 21st Century*. Tokyo: Defense Agency, August.

AG/RES, 2051 (XXXIV-O/04). 2004. Support for the Work of the Inter-American Committee against Terrorism, June 8. http://www.oas.org/XXXIVGA/english/docs_approved/ agres2051_04.asp.

Agence France Presse. 2006. Egypt–U.S. Free Trade Deal at Risk: U.S. Official. January 18.

Ahmad, Eqbal. 1998. What after 'Strategic Depth'? *The Dawn*, August 23.

Ajami, Fouad. 2005. *The Foreigner's Gift: The Americans, the Arabs, and the Iraqis of Iraq*. New York: Free Press.

Albright, Madeleine. 2005. America, Turkey and the World. Inaugural Sakip Sabanci lecture, May 3. Washington, D.C., Brookings Institution, Center on the United States and Europe.

Alexander, Gerard. 2007. International Relations Theory Meets World Politics. In *Understanding the Bush Doctrine: Psychology and Strategy in an Age of Terrorism*. Ed. Stanley A. Renshon and Peter Suedfeld, 39–64. New York: Routledge.

Allen, David, and Michael Smith. 2004. External Policy Developments. *Journal of Common Market Studies Annual Review* 42: 95–112.

Allin, Dana H., and Steven Simon. 2004. Bush's World: America's Predicament. *Survival* 46 (4): 7–30.

Allison, Roy. 2001. Russia and the New States of Eurasia. In *Contemporary Russian Politics: A Reader*. Ed. Archie Brown, 443–52. Oxford, U.K.: Oxford University Press.

Almonte, Jose T. 2003. Enhancing State Capacity and Legitimacy in the Counter-Terror War. In *After Bali: The Threat of Terrorism in Southeast Asia*. Ed. Kumar Ramakrishna and See Seng Tan, 221–40. London: World Scientific.

Amnesty International. 2002. Saudi Arabia. *Amnesty International Annual Report 2002*. http://web.amnesty.org/web/ar2002.nsf/mde/saudi%20arabia!Open.

Amorim, Celso, 1999. Entre o desequilíbrio unipolar e a multipolaridade: O conselho de segurança da ONU no período pós-Guerra Fria. In *O Brasil e as novas dimensões da segurança internacional*. Ed. Gilberto Dupas and Tullo Vigevani. São Paulo: Editora Alfa-Omega.

Andreani, Gilles. 2004. Bush's World: The "War on Terror": Good Cause, Wrong Concept. *Survival* 46 (4): 31–50.

Ang, Cheng Guan. 2001. The Domino Theory Revisited: The Southeast Asia Perspective. *War and Society* 19 (1): 109–30.

Annan, Kofi. 2001. Nobel Lecture. Nobel Peace Prize Award Ceremony, December 10. Oslo, Norway. http://nobelprize.org/nobel_prizes/peace/laureates/2001/annan-lecture.html.

Aruri, Naseer. 2003. *Dishonest Broker: The U.S. Role in Israel and Palestine*. Cambridge, Mass.: South End Press.

Ash, Timothy Garton. 2004. *Free World: America, Europe, and the Surprising Future of the West*. New York: Random House.

Aslan, Reza. 2005. *No God but God: The Origins, Evolution, and Future of Islam*. New York: Random House.

Aslund, Anders. 2005. The Perils of Putin. *Weekly Standard*, January 11.

Asmus, Ronald, Larry Diamond, Mark Leonard, and Michael McFaul. 2005. A Transatlantic Strategy to Promote Democratic Development in the Broader Middle East. *Washington Quarterly* 28 (2): 7–21.

Asmus, Ronald, and Bruce Jackson. 2004. The Black Sea and the Frontiers of Freedom. *Policy Review* 125 (June/July): 17–26. http://www.hoover.org/publications/policyreview/3437816.html.

Aybet, Gülnur. 1994. *Turkey's Foreign Policy and its Implications for the West: A Turkish Perspective*. London: Royal United Services Institute.

———. 2001. *The Dynamics of European Security Cooperation 1945–1991*. Basingstoke, U.K.: Palgrave.

Bacevich, Andrew J. 2002. *American Empire: The Realities and Consequences of U.S. Diplomacy*. Cambridge, Mass.: Harvard University Press.

———. 2005. *The New American Militarism: How Americans are Seduced by War*. Oxford, U.K.: Oxford University Press.

Baev, Pavel. 2004. The Evolution of Putin's Regime: Inner Circles and Outer Walls. *Problems of Post-Communism* 51 (6): 3–13.

Bajpaee, Chietigj. 2006. The Emerging Cold War on Asia's High Seas. *PINR*, February 20. http://www.pinr.com/report.php?ac=view_printable&report_id=439&language_id=1.

Baker, James A. III, and Lee H. Hamilton. 2006. *Iraq Study Group Report.* New York: Vintage.

Barber, Benjamin R. 1996. *Jihad vs. McWorld. How Globalism and Tribalism are Reshaping the World.* New York: Ballantine Books.

Barfield, Claude, and Jason Bolton. 2005. Korea, the U.S., China and Japan: The Rise of Asian Regionalism. *Pacific Focus* 20 (1): 179–255.

Barnett, Thomas P. M. 2004. *The Pentagon's New Map: War and Peace in the Twenty-first Century.* New York: G. P. Putnam's Sons.

BBC Monitoring. 2006. U.S. again Urges Taiwan Leader to Avoid Sovereignty Issue. October 1.

BBC News. 2003a. U.S. Clears Israel–India Radar Deal. August 12. news.bbc.co.uk/2/hi/south_asia/3145301.stm.

———. 2003b. Middle East Desk. Saudis Announce First Elections. October 13. http://news.bbc.co.uk/2/hi/middle_east/3188310.stm.

———. 2005a. Middle East Desk. Q&A: Saudi Municipal Elections. February 9. http://news.bbc.co.uk/2/hi/middle_east/4230685.stm.

———. 2005b. Middle East Desk. Reformists Jailed by Saudi Court. May 15. http://news.bbc.co.uk/2/hi/middle_east/4548849.stm.

———. 2005c. Middle East Desk. Index Ranks Middle East Reform. November 18. http://news.bbc.co.uk/2/hi/middle_east/4450582.stm.

———. 2006. Main parties sign Darfur Accord. May 5. http://news.bbc.co.uk/2/hi/africa/4978668.stm.

BearingPoint, Inc. 2003. Options for Developing a Long Term Sustainable Iraqi Oil Industry. Sector Study report to the U.S. Agency for International Development, 19 December.

Bedi, R. S. 2002. Bush Doctrine of Pre-emptive Strikes. Why Deny the Same Right to India? *Tribune* (Chandigarh), November 11.

Beeson, Mark. 2002. Southeast Asia and the Politics of Vulnerability. *Third World Quarterly* 23 (3): 549–64.

Benkaci, Rafik. 2005. Une base militaire U.S. installée dans le Sud. *Liberté*, August 1.

Bertram, Christoph. 1983. Defense and Consensus: The Domestic Aspect of Western Security. *Adelphi Papers* 183.

Betts, Richard K. 2002. The Soft Underbelly of American Primacy: Tactical Advantages of Terror. *Political Science Quarterly* 117 (Spring): 19–36.

Bidwai, Praful. 2002. On the Margin, Behind the U.S. *Frontline*, January 4, 114. http://www.hinduonnet.com/fline/fl1826/18261130.htm.

Bidwai, Praful, and Achin Vainak. 2001. *South Asia on a Short Fuse. Nuclear Politics and the Future of Global Disarmament.* New Delhi: Oxford University Press.

Bijian, Zheng. 2005. China's "Peaceful Rise" to Great-Power Status. *Foreign Affairs* 84 (5): 18–24. http://www.foreignaffairs.org/20050901faessay84502/zheng-bijian/china-s-peaceful-rise-to-great-power-status.html.

Bilgin, Pinar. 2005. Turkey's Changing Security Discourses: The Challenge of Globalization. *European Journal of Political Research* 44 (1): 175–201.

Bilmes, Linda, and Joseph E. Stiglitz. 2006. The Economic Costs of the Iraq War; An Appraisal Three Years after the Beginning of the Conflict. *NBER Working Paper* 120554. National Bureau of Economic Research, Graduate Center of the City University of New York. http://www2.gsb.columbia.edu/faculty/jstiglitz/download/2006_Cost_of_War_in_Iraq_NBER.pdf.

Binnendijk, Hans, ed. 2002. *Transforming America's Military*. Washington, D.C.: National Defense University Press.

Blagov, Sergei. 2004. Russia views NATO Expansion as a Strategic Threat. *PINR*, May 5. http://www.pinr.com/report.php?ac=view_report&report_id=166&language_id=1.

Blanford, Nicholas. 2004. The Arab League and Political Reform: A Vague Commitment. *Arab Reform Bulletin* 2 (6): 7–8. http://www.carnegieendowment.org/publications/index.cfm?fa=view&id=1557&prog=zgp&proj=zdrl#league.

Blum, John Morton. 1956. *Woodrow Wilson and the Politics of Morality*. Boston: Little, Brown.

Bobrow, Davis B. 2005a. International Public Opinion: Incentives and Options to Comply and Challenge. *Ridgway Center Working Papers* 16. http://www.ridgway.pitt.edu/docs/working_papers/13.%20Bobrow%20-%20Intl.%20Public%20Opinion%2011-22-05.pdf.

———. 2005b. Anti-Americanism and International Security: Indications in International Public Opinion. *Anti-Americanism Working Papers*. Center for Policy Studies, Central European University. http://www.ceu.hu/cps.

Booker, Salih. 2001. Bush's Global Agenda: Bad News for Africa. *Current History* 100 (May): 195–200.

Booker, Salih, William Minter, and Ann-Louise Colgan. 2003. America and Africa. *Current History* 102 (May): 195–99.

Boot, Max. 2003. What Next? The Bush Foreign Policy Agenda Beyond Iraq. *Weekly Standard*, May 5.

Boston Globe. 2005. Editorial, "Shanghai Warning." July 11.

Braun, Chaim, and Christopher F. Chyba. 2004. Proliferation Rings: New Challenges to the Nuclear Non-Proliferation Regime. *International Security* 29 (2): 5–49.

Bremer, L. Paul. 2006. *My Year in Iraq: The Struggle to Build a Future of Hope*. New York: Simon and Schuster.

Brinkley, Joel. 2005. Latin Nations Resist Plan for Monitor of Democracy. *New York Times*, June 6, A-1.

Brown, Christine P. 2005. Korea's Trade and Investment: Trends and Prospects. *Korea's Economy 2005* 21: 43–47.

Brown, Mark Malloch. 2006. United Nations Chief of Staff. The United Nations in the 21st Century. British Council Annual Lecture, Institution of Royal Engineers, March 9, London. http://www.britishcouncil.org/home-press-british-council-annual-lecture-2006.doc.

Bryce, James. 1924. *The American Commonwealth*. 2 vols. New York: Macmillan.

Brzezinski, Zbigniew. 1997. *The Grand Chessboard: American Primacy and Its Geostrategic Imperatives*. New York: Basic Books.

———. 2004. *The Choice: Global Domination or Global Leadership*. New York: Basic Books.

———. 2007. *Second Chance: Three Presidents and the Crisis of American Superpower*. New York: Basic Books.

Brzezinski, Zbigniew, and John J. Mearsheimer. 2005. Clash of the Titans. *Foreign Policy* 146 (1): 46–49.

Buckley, Mary. 2003. Russian Foreign Policy and Its Critics. In *Realignments in Russian Foreign Policy*. Ed. Rick Fawn, 29–46. London: Frank Cass.

Bukovansky, Mlada. 2002. *Legitimacy and Power Politics*. Princeton, N.J.: Princeton University Press.

Bull, Hedley. 1977. *The Anarchical Society: A Study of Order in World Politics*. London: Macmillan.

Bush, George W. 2005. President Bush Sworn-In to Second Term, January 20. http://www.whitehouse.gov/news/releases/2005/01/20050120-1.html.

Buzan, Barry, Ole Waever, and Jaap de Wilde. 1998. *Security: A New Framework of Analysis*. Boulder, Colo.: Lynne Rienner.

Bybee, Jay. 2002. Memorandum for Alberto R. Gonzales, Counsel for the President, Application of Treaties and Laws to al Qaeda and Taliban Detainees, January 22. Department of Justice. http://www.washingtonpost.com/wp-srv/nation/documents/012202bybee.pdf.

Calabrese, John. 1998. Turkey and Iran: Limits of a Stable Relationship. *British Journal of Middle Eastern Studies* 25 (1): 75–94.

Camroux, David, and Nuria Okfen. 2004. Introduction: 9/11 and U.S.–Asian Relations: Towards a New "New World Order"? *The Pacific Review* 17 (2): 163–77.

Caplan, Richard. 2005. Who Guards the Guardians? International Accountability in Bosnia. *International Peacekeeping* 12 (3): 463–76.

Carlsen, Laura. 2005. Bush Administration Must Reassess Relations with Latin America. Americas Program, Interhemispheric Resource Center (IRC), January 24.

Carothers, Thomas, and Marina Ottaway. 2005. *Uncharted Journey: Promoting Democracy in the Middle East*. Washington, D.C.: Carnegie Endowment for International Peace.

Carter, Ashton B. 2006. America's New Strategic Partner? *Foreign Affairs* 85 (4): 33–44. http://www.foreignaffairs.org/20060701faessay85403/ashton-b-carter/america-s-new-strategic-partner.html.

"Casualties — U.S. vs NVA/VC." http://www.rjsmith.com/kia_tbl.html.

Center for Arms Control and Non-Proliferation. 2006. U.S.–Indian Nuclear Deal: Proliferation Risks and Costs. March 2. http://www.armscontrolcenter.org/archives/002248.php.

Center for Human Rights and Global Justice. 2005. Torture by Proxy: International Law Applicable to "Extraordinary Renditions." All Party Parliamentary on Extraordinary Rendition Briefing Paper, December. New York: New York University School of Law. http://www.chrgj.org/docs/APPG-NYU%20Briefing%20Paper.pdf.

Cerojano, Teresa. 2006. Filipinos Protest U.S. Refusal on Marines. *Washington Times*, January 17.

Chandrasekaran, Rajiv. 2006a. GOP Loyalty Dictated Who Would Rebuild Iraq. *Seattle Times*, September 17. Reprinted from the *Washington Post*.

————. 2006b. *Imperial Life in the Emerald City: Inside Iraq's Greeen Zone*. New York: Knopf.

Chandrasekaran, Rajiv, and Peter Finn. 2002. U.S. Behind Secret Transfer of Terror Suspects. *Washington Post*, March 11.

Chang, Iris. 1998. *The Rape of Nanking: The Forgotten Holocaust of World War II*. New York: Penguin.

Chen, Rosalie. 2003. China Perceives America: Perspectives of International Relations Experts. *Journal of Contemporary China* 12 (35): 285–97.

Cherian, John. 2005. A Long Way to the High Table. *Frontline*, September 9. http://www.flonnet.com/fl2218/stories/20050909001805000.htm.

Choi, Jin Wook. 2005. The Second Term Bush Administration and the North Korean Nuclear Crisis. *Pacific Focus* 20 (Spring): 157–84.

Christopher, Warren. 1994. My Trip to Beijing Was Necessary. *Washington Post*, March 22.

Chu, Shulong. 1996. National Unity, Sovereignty and Territorial Integration. *The China Journal* 36 (July): 98–102.

Cirincione, Joseph. 2006. O, Canada! *Proliferation News*, March 13.

CNN.com. 2003. U.S. Defense Contractor a Target in Saudi Attacks. May 13. http://www.cnn.com/2003/WORLD/meast/05/13/saudi.vinnell/index.html.

————. 2004. Musharraf: Iraq War Has Made World "Less Safe." December 6. http://www.cnn.com/2004/US/12/05/musharraf.cnn.

————. 2006. Human Rights in Iraq "Much Worse." January 18. http://www.cnn.com/2006/WORLD/meast/01/18/humanrights.iraq.

Cohen, Stephen P. 2003. *India: Emerging Power*. New Delhi: Oxford University Press.

Cole, David. 2005. What Bush Wants to Hear. Review of *The Powers of War and Peace: The Constitution and Foreign Affairs After 9/11* by John Yoo. *New York Review of Books* 52 (18): 12.

Collier, Ellen C. 1993. Instances of Use of United States Forces Abroad, 1798–1993. Congressional Research Issue Brief for Congress IB931007, October 7. Washington, D.C.: Congressional Research Service. http://www.fas.org/man/crs/crs_931007.htm.

Commission of the European Communities. 2004. Communication from the Commission. *European Neighbourhood Policy Strategy Paper* COM 373, May 12. http://ec.europa.eu/world/enp/pdf/strategy/strategy_paper_en.pdf.

Conetta, Carl. 2006a. Pyrrhus on the Potomac: How America's Post-9/11 Wars Have Undermined U.S. National Security. *Project on Defense Alternatives Briefing Report* 18, September 5. http://www.comw.org/pda/0609br18.html.

————. 2006b. Fighting on Borrowed Time: The Effect on U.S. Military Readiness of American's Post-9/11 Wars. *Project on Defense Alternatives Briefing Report* 19, September 11. http://www.comw.org/pda/0609br19.html.

Cooper, Robert. 2003. *The Breaking of Nations: Order and Chaos in the Twenty-First Century*. London: Atlantic Books.

Corwin, Edward S. 1916. *French Policy and the American Alliance of 1778*. Princeton, N.J.: Princeton University Press.

Cossa, Ralph A. 2005. U.S. Security Strategy in Asia and the Prospects for an Asian Regional Security Regime. *Asia Pacific Review* 12 (1): 64–86.

Council of Europe. 2006. Committee on Legal Affairs and Human Rights. *Alleged Secret Detentions and Unlawful Inter-State Transfers Involving Council of Europe Member States*, Draft Report — Part 2, June 7. http://assembly.coe.int/CommitteeDocs/2006/20060606_Ejdoc162006PartII-FINAL.pdf.

Council of the European Union. 2003. *A Secure Europe in a Better World: European Security Strategy*, December 12. Brussels: The European Union Institute for Security Studies.

Council on Hemispheric Affairs. 2005. 2005: Another Terrible Year for U.S. –Latin American Relations, January 2. http://www.coha.org/2006/01/02/2005-another-terrible-year-for-us-latin-american-relations.

———. 2006a. Flirting with Danger: Mexican Presidential Campaign Grows Tense, June 6. http://www.coha.org/NEW_PRESS_RELEASES/New_Press_Releases_2006/COHA%20Report/COHA_Report_06.13_Mexican_Election_Danger.html.

———. 2006b. Caracas and Washington: Though Politically Divorced, the Economic Union Goes on, August 22. http://www.coha.org/2006/08/22/caracas-and-washington-though-politically-divorced-the-economic-union-goes-on-despite-worries-of-oil-production-decline.

———. 2007a. Bush Pays a Visit to Brazil, March 12. http://www.coha.org/2007/03/12/bush-pays-a-visit-to-brazil.

———. 2007b. Bush's Latin America Trip: Understanding the Protests and Criticisms, March 14. http://www.coha.org/2007/03/14/bush%E2%80%99s-latin-america-trip-understanding-the-protests-and-criticisms.

Council on Security and Defense Capabilities. 2004. *The Council on Security and Defense Capabilities Report: Japan's Visions for Future Security and Defense Capabilities*, October.

Cox, Michael. 2005. Beyond the West: Terrors in Transatlantia. *European Journal of International Relations* 11 (2): 203–33.

Cox, Robert W. 1987. *Production, Power and World Order*. New York: Columbia University Press.

Cristiani, Dario. 2006. China and Iran Strengthen Their Bilateral Relationship. *PINR*, October 6. http://www.pinr.com/report.php?ac=view_report&report_id=566&language_id=1.

Crossette, Barbara. 1996. China Outflanks U.S. to Avoid Scrutiny of Its Human Rights. *New York Times*, April 24.

Cumings, Bruce. 1997. *Korea's Place in the Sun*. New York: W. W. Norton.

———. 2003. *North Korea: Another Nation*. New York: New Press.

Daalder, Ivo H., and James M. Lindsay. 2003. *America Unbound: The Bush Revolution in Foreign Policy*. Washington, D.C.: Brookings Institution Press.

Dagne, Theodros. 2002. Africa and the War on Terrorism: The Case of Somalia. *Mediterranean Quarterly* 13 (4): 62–73.

Dalacoura, Katerina. 2005. U.S. Democracy Promotion in the Arab Middle East since 11 September 2001: A Critique. *International Affairs* 81 (5): 963–79.

Daoud, Z. 1999. L'alternance a l'epreuve des faits. *Le Monde Diplomatique*, April 29, 541.

Das, Gurcharan. 2006. The India Model. *Foreign Affairs* 85 (4): 2–16. http://www.foreignaffairs.org /20060701faessay85401/gurcharan-das/the-india-model.html.

Das Gupta, Amit. 2004a. Indiens Blick in die Zukunft. Bericht zur Konferenz [India and the Global Order: Security and Diplomacy in the 21st Century]. *Südasien* 24 (1): 17–20.

———. 2004b. The Role of the Superpowers in South Asia. *Asian Affairs*. 26 (4): 5–43.

———. 2006. India's Role in the Planning of European Foreign and Security Policy. In *Rising India—Europe's Partner?* Ed. Klaus Voll et al., 235–40 Berlin: Weissensee Verlag.

Davis, Anthony. 2003. Thailand Faces up to Southern Extremist Threat. *Jane's Intelligence Review*, October 1.

Davis, Lynn, J. Michael Polich, William M. Hix, Michael D. Greenberg, Stephen D. Brady, and Ronald E. Sortor. 2005. *Stretched Thin: Army Forces for Sustained Operations*. Santa Monica, Calif.: RAND.

Dean, John. 2005. Will Changing the Egyptian Constitution's Election System Really Foster Democracy?: Why Egypt-Watchers Don't Think So. *FindLaw*, March 25. http://writ.news.findlaw.com/dean/20050325.html.

Deng, Yong. 2001. Hegemon on the Offensive: Chinese Perspectives on U.S. Global Strategy. *Political Science Quarterly* 116 (November): 343–65.

DeSutter, Paula A. 2004. Completion of Verification Work in Libya. Report prepared for the Subcommittee on International Terrorism, Nonproliferation, and Human Rights, September 22. http://www.state.gov/t/vci/rls/rm/2004/37220.htm.

de Tocqueville, Alexis. 1945. 2 vols. *Democracy in America*. Trans. Henry Reeve and Francis Bowen. Ed. P. Bradley. New York: Knopf.

Diamond, Jared. 2005. *Collapse: How Societies Choose to Fail or Succeed*. New York: Viking.

Diamond, Larry. 2005. *Squandered Victory: The American Occupation and the Bungled Effort to Bring Democracy to Iraq*. New York: Times Books.

Díaz, Alvaro. 1997. New Developments in Economic and Social Restructuring in Latin America. In *Politics, Social Change and Economic Restructuring in Latin America*. Ed. William C. Smith and Roberto Patricio Korzeniecz. Miami, Fla.: North–South Center.

Dinan, Desmond. 2004. *Europe Recast: A History of European Union*. Boulder, Colo.: Lynne Rienner.

Dobriansky, Paula J. 2005. The Orange Revolution: One Year Later. Remarks to the American Enterprise Institute, December 5, Washington D.C. http://www.state.gov/g/rls/rm/2005/57802.htm.

Doeppers, Daniel F. 1972. An Incident in the PRRI/Permesta Rebellion of 1958. *Indonesia* 14 (October): 183–95.

Donohue, Laura K. 2006. Pentagon Spies Are Watching You. *Los Angeles Times*, May 18.

Drohan, Thomas A. 1999. The U.S.–Japan Defense Guidelines: Toward an Equivalent Alliance. *IIPPS Policy Paper* 238E, November. Tokyo: Institute for International Policy Studies.

Dugger, Celia W. 2006. U.S. Focus on Abstinence Weakens AIDS Fight, Agency Finds. *New York Times*, April 5.

Dunn, Kevin C. 2002. A Survival Guide to Kinshasa: Lessons of the Father, Passed Down to the Son. In *The African Stakes of the Congo War*. Ed. John F. Clark, 53–74. New York: Palgrave.

———. 2003. *Imagining the Congo: The International Relations of Identity*. New York: Palgrave Macmillan.

———. 2004. Killing for Christ? The Lord's Resistance Army of Uganda. *Current History* 103 (May): 206–14.

Dwor-Frecault, Dominique. 2005. North Korea's Economic Integration and Diplomatic Normalization. *Joint U.S.–Korea Academic Studies* 15: 137–55.

Economic Policy Institute. 2004. Foreign Governments Finance a Growing Share of U.S. Trade Deficit. *Economic Snapshots*, September 14. http://www.epinet.org/content.cfm/webfeatures_snapshots_09142004.

Economist. 2006. A Partnership Constrained. October 5.

Economist Intelligence Unit. 2003. Country Report: Djibouti. *The Economist*, March.

Economy, Elizabeth. 2005. China's Rise in Southeast Asia: implications for the United States. *Journal of Contemporary China* 14 (44): 409–25.

Eisenman, Joshua, and Joshua Kurlantzick. 2006. China's Africa Strategy. *Current History* 105 (May): 219–24.

El Watan. 2001. General-Major Mohamed Touati, Presidential Advisor. September 27.

Emmers, Ralf. 2005. Maritime Disputes in the South China Sea: Strategic and Diplomatic Status Quo. *IDSS Working Paper* 87. Singapore: Institute of Defense and Strategic Studies.

Emmerson, Donald. 1996. U.S. Policy Themes in Southeast Asia in the 1990s. In *Southeast Asia in the New World Order: The Political Economy of a Dynamic Region*. Ed. David Wurfel and Bruce Burton, 103–27. New York: St. Martin's Press.

Entelis, John P. 2005. The Democratic Imperative vs. the Authoritarian Impulse: The Maghrib State between Transition and Terrorism. (Northern Africa). *The Middle East Journal* 59 (4): 537–59.

EurActiv. 2005. EU Fervour Cooling in Turkey. April 13. http://www.euractiv.com/en/enlargement/eu-fervour-cooling-turkey/article-137645.

European Commission. Directorate General External Relations. 2002. EC Country Strategy Paper India. *India: Country Strategy Paper 2002–2006*, September 10. http://ec.europa.eu/comm/external_relations/india/csp/index.htm

Ewens, Michael. 2005. Casualties in Iraq. *BBC*, July 19. http://www.antiwar.com/casualties/.

Eyal, Jonathan. 2006. Democratic China "May Pose More, Not Less, Danger." *The Straits Times*, March 4.

Fallows, James. 2006. *Blind into Baghdad: America's War in Iraq*. New York: Vintage.

Fauriol, Georges A., and Sidney Weintraub. 2001. The Century of the Americas: Dawn of a New Century Dynamic. *Washington Quarterly* 24 (2): 139–48.

Fawn, Rick, ed. 2003. *Realignments in Russian Foreign Policy*. London: Frank Cass.

Federation of American Scientists. Arms Sales Monitoring Project. 2002. *U.S. Arms Client Profiles — Saudi Arabia*, March. http://www.fas.org/asmp/profiles/saudi_arabia.

Feigenbaum, Evan A. 2001. China's Challenge to Pax Americana. *Washington Quarterly* 24 (3): 31–43.

Feinberg, Richard E. 2002. Regionalism and Domestic Politics: U.S.–Latin American Trade Policy in the Bush Era. *Latin American Politics and Society* 44 (4): 127–51.

Feldman, Noah. 2006. Our Presidential Era: Who Can Check the President? *New York Times Magazine*, January 6, 5.

Ferguson, Niall. 2003. Hegemony or Empire? *Foreign Affairs* 82 (5): 154–61. http://www .foreignaffairs.org/20030901fareviewessay82512/niall-ferguson/hegemony-or-empire.html.

———. 2004. *Colossus: The Price of America's Empire.* New York: Penguin Press.

———. 2005. Opinion Journal, "The End of Power." *Wall Street Journal*, June 21.

Finnemore, Martha, and Kathryn Sikkink. 1998. International Norm Dynamics and Political Change. *International Organization* 52 (4): 887–912.

Fiori, José Luis. 2001. 60 lições dos 90. *Record*, Rio de Janeiro.

Flockhart, Trine. 2004. Trans-Atlantic Relations after the War in Iraq: Returning to — or Departing from — "Normal Politics"? *Perspectives on European Politics and Society* 5 (3): 395–417.

Flockhart, Trine, ed. 2005. *Socializing Democratic Norms; The Role of International Organizations for the Construction of Europe.* Basingstoke, U.K.: Palgrave.

Flynn, Stephen E. 2004. The Neglected Home Front. *Foreign Affairs* 83 (4): 20–33. http:// www.foreignaffairs.org/20040901faessay83504/stephen-e-flynn/the-neglected-home-front .html.

———. 2007. *The Edge of Disaster: Rebuilding a Resilient Nation.* New York: Random House.

Foglesong, David, and Gordon Halin. 2002. Ten Myths about Russia: Understanding and Dealing with Russia's Complexity and Ambiguity. *Problems of Post-Communism* 49 (6): 3–15.

Folha de Sao Paulo. 2005. Os EU são contra reforma da ONU. July 13.

Foot, Rosemary. 2000. *Rights Beyond Borders: The Global Community and the Struggle over Human Rights in China.* Oxford, U.K.: Oxford University Press.

———. 2003. Bush, China and Human Rights. *Survival* 45 (2): 167–86.

Foreign Policy Concept. 2000. *The Foreign Policy Concept of the Russian Federation*, June 28.

Freedman, Lawrence. 1998. The Revolution in Strategic Affairs. *Adelphi Paper* 318. Oxford, U.K.: Oxford University Press.

———. 2006. The Transformation of Strategic Affairs. *Adelphi Paper* 379. London: International Institute for Strategic Studies.

Friedberg, Aaron. 1993–94. Ripe for Rivalry: Prospects for Peace in a Multipolar Asia. *International Security* 18 (3): 5–33.

Friedman, Thomas. 2000. *Lexus and the Olive Tree.* New York: Anchor.

Fryer, Wesley A. 1993. Defining and Refocusing U.S. Policy in Latin America. http://www .wtvi.com/wesley/uslapolicy.html.

Fukuyama, Francis. 1992. *The End of History and the Last Man.* New York: Free Press.

————. 2006. *America at the Crossroads: Democracy, Power, and the Neoconservative Legacy.* New Haven, Conn.: Yale University Press.

Fukuyama, Norihisa, and Douglas F. Ramsey. 2003. Whither the Japanese Defense Industry. *Japan Economic Currents* 36 (September): 4–6.

Gaddis, John Lewis. 1982. *Strategies of Containment: A Critical Appraisal of Postwar American National Security Policy.* New York: Oxford University Press.

————. 2004. *Surprise, Security, and the American Experience.* Cambridge, Mass.: Harvard University Press.

Galbraith, Peter W. 2006. *The End of Iraq: How American Incompetence Created a War without End.* New York: Simon and Schuster.

Gale, William G., and Peter R. Orszag. 2004. *The Budget Outlook: Updates and Implications.* Washington, D. C.: Brookings Institution Press.

Gallardo, Eduardo. 2006. Chilean President Says Leftists No Threat. *Guardian Unlimited,* February 28.

Garfield, Andrew. 2006. Succeeding in Phase IV: British Perspectives on the U.S. Effort to Stabilize and Reconstruct Iraq—Executive Summary. *E-Notes Foreign Policy Research Institute,* September 8. http://www.fpri.org/enotes/20060908.military.garfield .britishperspectiveiraq.html.

Garver, John W. 1997. *Face Off: China, the United States, and Taiwan's Democratization.* Seattle: University of Washington Press.

G8 Summit. 2004. Partnership for Progress and a Common Future with the Region of the Broader Middle East and North Africa, June 9, Sea Island, Georgia. http://www .g7.utoronto.ca/summit/2004seaisland/partnership.html.

Gelpi, Christopher F., and Michael Griesdorf. 2001. Winners or Losers? Democracies in International Crisis. *American Political Science Review* 95 (3): 633–47.

The General Framework Agreement for Peace in Bosnia and Herzegovina. 1995. Annex 4: The Constitution of Bosnia and Herzegovina, art. XII. http://www.ohr.int/dpa/ default .asp?content_id=380.

George, Alexander, L. 1979. Case Studies and Theory Development: The Method of Structured, Focused Comparison. In *New Approaches in History, Theory and Policy.* Ed. P. G. Lauren, 43–68. New York: Free Press.

George, Nirmala. 2005. India, China Agree to Form "Strategic Partnership" in Major Shift in Relations between Asian Giants. Associated Press, April 11.

German Marshall Fund of the United States and Compagnia di San Paolo. 2004. *Transatlantic Trends.* http://www.transatlantictrends.org/trends/index.cfm?year=2004.

Gershman, John. 2002. Is Southeast Asia the Second Front? *Foreign Affairs* 81 (4): 60–74. http://www.foreignaffairs.org/20020701faessay8520/john-gershman/is-southeast-asia-the-second-front.html.

Gill, Stephen. 1993. *Gramsci, Historical Materialism and International Relations.* Cambridge, U.K.: Cambridge University Press.

Gindin, Jonah. 2005. Democracy Behind Closed Doors: Regional Body Elects Leader U.S.-Style. Venezuelanalysis.com, May 4.

Giry, Stéphanie. 2006. France and Its Muslims. *Foreign Affairs* 85 (5): 87–105. http://www
.foreignaffairs.org/20060901faessay85508/stephanie-giry/france-and-its-muslims.html.

Goh, Evelyn. 2003. Hegemonic Constraints: The Implications of September 11 for American Power. *Australian Journal of International Affairs* 57 (1): 77–97.

Goktas, Lutfullah. 2003. Interview with Celal Talabani. NTV–MSNBC, July 21.

Goldstein, Steven. 1999. Terms of Engagement: Taiwan's Mainland Policy. In *Engaging
China*. Ed. Alastair Iain Johnston and Robert S. Ross, 57–86. London: Routledge.

Gordon, Michael R., and Bernard E. Trainor. 2006. *Cobra II: The Inside Story of the Invasion and Occupation of Iraq*. New York: Pantheon Books.

Gordon, Philip H. 2006. The End of the Bush Revolution. *Foreign Affairs* 85 (4): 75–86.
http://www.foreignaffairs.org/20060701faessay85406/philip-h-gordon/the-end-of-the-bush-
revolution.html.

Gordon, Sandy. 1995. *India's Rise to Power in the Twentieth Century and Beyond*. Basingstoke, U.K.: Macmillan.

Gorvett, Jon. 2005. Turkish Drive towards EU Increases Possibilities for Change in the
Caucasus. *Eurasianet.org*, June 1. http://www.eurasianet.org/departments/insight/articles/
eav010605a_pr.shtml.

Graebner, Norman A., ed. 1964. *Ideas and Diplomacy*. Oxford, U.K.: Oxford University
Press.

Gray, Colin S. 2005. Transformation and Strategic Surprise. *Monograph of the Strategic
Studies Institute*. Carlisle, Pa.: U.S. Army War College. http://www.strategicstudiesinstitute
.army.mil/pubs/display.cfm?PubID=602.

Grey, Robert D. 2006. Africa. In *The Bush Doctrine and the War on Terrorism*. Ed. Mary
Buckley and Robert Singh, 121–35. London: Routledge.

Haass, Richard. 2006. The New Middle East. *Foreign Affairs* 85 (6): 2–12. http://www
.foreignaffairs.org/20061101faessay85601/richard-n-haass/the-new-middle-east.html.

Hadar, Leon T. 2002. Pakistan in America's War against Terrorism: Strategic Ally or Unreliable Client? *Policy Analysis*, August 13, 1–22.

Halawi, Jailan. 2005. Women in Black. *Al-Ahram Weekly*, June 2–8.

Halberstam, David. 2002. *War in a Time of Peace: Bush, Clinton, and the Generals*. New
York: Touchstone.

Hartz, Louis. 1955. *The Liberal Tradition in America*. New York: Harcourt, Brace.

Hassig, Ralph C., and Kongdan Oh. 2005. The Dilemma of Security Cooperation in Northeast Asia. *Joint U.S.–Korea Academic Studies* 15: 157–69.

Hayashi, Tadashi. 2004. Looking at China: A Japanese Business Perspective. *Japan Economic Currents* 48 (September): 1–3.

Heisbourg, François. 2000. American Hegemony? Perceptions of the U.S. Abroad. *Survival*
41 (4): 5–19.

Hentz, James J. 2004. The Contending Currents in United States Involvement in Sub-
Saharan Africa. In *Africa in International Politics*. Ed. Ian Taylor and Paul Williams,
23–40. London: Routledge.

Hersh, Seymour M. 2002. The Getaway. *New Yorker*, January 28. http://www.newyorker
.com/archive/2002/01/28/020128fa_FACT.

————. 2004. The Deal. *New Yorker*, March 8. http://www.newyorker.com/archive/2004/03/08/040308fa_fact.

————. 2006. The Iran Plans. *New Yorker*, April 17. http://www.newyorker.com/archive/2006/04/17/060417fa_fact.

Herz, Mônica, and João Nogueira. 2002. *Ecuador vs. Peru: Peacemaking amid Rivalry*. Boulder, Colo.: Lynne Rienner.

Hewison, Kevin. 2001. Nationalism, Populism, and Dependency: Old Ideas for a New Southeast Asia? *Southeast Asia Research Centre Working Paper Series* 4. Hong Kong: City University of Hong Kong. http://www.cityu.edu.hk/searc/WP4_01_Hewison.pdf.

Hill, Christopher. 2004a. Britain and the European Security Strategy. *German Foreign Policy in Dialogue: A Quarterly E-Newsletter on German Foreign Policy* 5 (13): 24–31.

————. 2004b. Renationalizing or Regrouping? EU Foreign Policy Since September 11, 2001. *Journal of Common Market Studies* 42 (1): 143–63.

Hiroshi, Nakanishi. 2005. Middle Ground. *Japan Journal* 2 (August): 15.

Hirst, Monica. 2005. *The United States and Brazil: A Long Road of Unmet Expectations*. New York: Routledge.

————. 2005/6. As relações Brasil-Paraguay: baixos incentivos no latu e strictu sensu. *Política Externa* 14 (3): 11–21.

Hirst, Monica, and Maria Regina Soares de Lima. 2006. Brazil as an Intermediate State and Regional Power: Challenges and Opportunities. *International Affairs* 82 (1): 21–40.

Hitoshi, Chiba. 2005. "Peace" and Peacekeeping. *Japan Journal* 2 (June): 6–11.

Ho, Chung Jae. 2005. The "Rise" of China and its Impact on South Korea's Strategic Soul Searching. *Joint U.S.–Korea Academic Studies* 15: 1–11.

Hoffman, Bruce. 2001. *Re-thinking Terrorism in Light of a War on Terrorism*. Santa Monica, Calif.: RAND.

Hoffman, Frank G. 2006a. Lessons From Lebanon: Hezbollah and Hybrid Wars. *Foreign Policy Research Institute E Notes*, August 29. http://www.fpri.org/enotes/20060824.military.hoffman,hezbollahhybridwars.html.

————. 2006b. Changing Tires on the Fly: The Marines and Postconflict Stability Operations — Executive Summary. *Foreign Policy Research Institute E-Notes*, September 10. http://www.fpri.org/enotes/20060910.military.hoffman.marinespostconflictstabilityops.html

Hoffmann, Stanley. 2003. America Goes Backward. *New York Review of Books* 1 (10): 74–80.

————. 2006. The Foreign Policy the U.S. Needs. *New York Review of Books* 53 (13): 60–64.

Holbrooke, Richard. 1998. *To End a War*. New York: Random House.

Holm, Ulla. 2004. The Old France, the New Europe and a Multipolar World. *Perspectives on European Politics and Society* 5 (3): 469–92.

Howeidy, Amira. 2005. Who's Afraid of the Brotherhood? *Al-Ahram Weekly*, November 24–30.

Hughes, Christopher W. 2004. *Japan's Re-emergence as a "Normal" Military Power*. International Institute for Strategic Studies. Oxford, U.K.: Oxford University Press.

————. 2005. Japanese Military Modernization: In Search of a "Normal" Security Role. In *Strategic Asia 2005–06: Military Modernization in an Era of Uncertainty*. Ed. Ashley J.

Tellis and Michael Wills, 105–34. Washington, D.C.: National Bureau of Asian Research.

Huntington, Samuel P. 1981. *American Politics: The Promise of Disharmony.* Cambridge, U.K.: Cambridge University Press.

———. 1992. *The Third Wave: Democratization in the Late Twentieth Century.* Norman: University of Oklahoma Press.

———. 1999. The Lonely Superpower. *Foreign Affairs* 78 (2): 35–49. http://www.foreignaffairs .org/19990301faessay966/samuel-p-huntington/the-lonely-superpower.html.

Hurriyet. 2003. Derhal Ozur Dileyin. July 6.

Hwang, Jin Hwoan. 2005. The Dynamics of U.S. Defense Transformation and Its Policy Implications for the ROK's Security. *Journal of East Asian Affairs* 19 (1): 1–41.

Ibn Khaldun Center for Development Studies. 2004. 2004, Year of Reformation Initiatives in the Middle East. http://www.eicds.org/english/publications/books/reforminitiatives/ main.htm.

Ignatieff, Michael. 2001. *After Victory.* Princeton, N.J.: Princeton University Press.

———. 2004. *The Lesser Evil: Political Ethics in the Age of Terror.* Princeton, N.J.: Princeton University Press.

Ikenberry, John. 2001. Getting Hegemony Right. *The National Interest* 63 (Spring): 17–24.

Ikenberry, John, and Charles Kupchan. 1990. Socialization and Hegemonic Power. *International Organization* 44 (3): 283–315.

Ikenberry, John, and Anne-Marie Slaughter. 2006. Forging a World of Liberty under Law: U.S. National Security in the 21st Century: Final Report. The Princeton Project on National Security, Princeton Project Papers, Woodrow Wilson School of Public and International Affairs. http://www.wws.princeton.edu/ppns/report/FinalReport.pdf.

INSS (Institute for National Strategic Studies) Special Report (Armitage-Nye Report). 2000. The United States and Japan: Advancing toward a Mature Partnership, October. Washington, D.C.: Institute for National Strategic Studies, National Defense University. http:// www.ndu.edu/inss/strforum/SR_01/SR_Japan.htm.

Institute for the Study of International Migration. Iraq: The Human Cost of War. Panel discussion on the humanitarian situation in Iraq, March 21, 2007, Georgetown University, Washington, D.C.

International Commission on the Balkans. 2005. The Balkans in Europe's Future. Report of the International Commission on the Balkans, April 12. Sofia, Bulgaria: Centre for Liberal Strategies.

International Herald Tribune-Asahi Shimbun. 2004a. Draft Pushes Easing of Weapons Export Ban. November 20–21.

International Herald Tribune-Asahi Shimbun. 2004b. Hosoda: Security Treaty Will Maintain Vital "Far East" Clause. October 21.

International Institute for Strategic Studies. 2006. U.S. Options Against Emerging Nuclear Threats: the Challenge of a Denial Strategy. *Strategic Comments* 12 (3): 1–2.

Ismail, Zaidi Isham. 2004. ASEAN, China to Complete Talks by June. *Business Times,* March 30.

Ivanov, Igor. 2003. A New Foreign Policy Year for Russia and the World. *International Affairs: A Russian Journal of World Politics, Diplomacy, and International Relations* 49 (6): 33–38.

Jack, Andrew. 2004. *Inside Putin's Russia*. London: Granta Books.

Jackson, Bruce Pitcairn. 2005. Testimony before the Committee on Foreign Relations, Subcommittee on European Affairs. The Future of Democracy in the Black Sea Region, March 8.

James, Barry. 2002. U.S. Enlists Algeria in Terror Battle. *International Herald Tribune*, December 10.

Japan Defense Agency. 2005. 2005 Defense of Japan. Tokyo: Inter Group Corp.

Jerusalem Institute for Western Defense. 2002. *Cairo Times, Egypt, December 6–12, 2001: Summary of Report*, January. http://www.westerndefense.org/articles/Egypt/jan02.htm

Jervis, Robert. 2005. *American Foreign Policy for a New Era*. New York: Routledge.

Jisi, Wang. 2005. China's Search for Stability with America. *Foreign Affairs* 84 (5): 39–48. http://www.foreignaffairs.org/20050901faessay84504/wang-jisi/china-s-search-for-stability-with-america.html.

J. M. 2004. ". . . and has sour words for the United States." RFE/RL Newsline, December 7.

John F. Kennedy Library and Foundation. 2001. New Exhibit Celebrates JFK's Alliance for Progress. *John F. Kennedy Library and Foundation Newsletter* (Summer): 13. http://www.jfklibrary.org/NR/rdonlyres/2832AA57-8E75-48DD-B2FB-E9A022026265/20255/Summer2001Newsletter.pdf.

Johnson, Chalmers. 2004. *The Sorrows of Empire: Militarism, Secrecy, and the End of the Republic*. New York: Henry Holt.

Johnston, Alastair Iain. 2003. Is China a Status Quo Power? *International Security* 27 (4): 5–56.

Jones, David Martin, and Michael Smith. 2002. The Perils of Hyper-Vigilance: The War on Terrorism and the Surveillance State in South-East Asia. *Intelligence and National Security* 17 (4): 31–54.

Joo, Sang-min. 2005. USFK Incidents Prompt Korean Protest. *Korea Herald*, July 18.

Joshi, Vijay. 2004. Southeast Asia Adopting Sweeping Pacts to Create Pan-Asian Bloc with China, India. Associated Press, November 28.

Jungblut, Cristiane, and Ronaldo D'Ercole. 2006. Embraer: Lula pode recorrer a Bush sobre veto. *O Globo*, January 20.

Kagan, Donald. 2003. *The Peloponnesian War*. New York: Viking.

Kagan, Robert. 1998. U.S. Dominance: Is It Good for the World?: The Benevolent Empire. *Foreign Policy* 111 (Summer): 24–35.

———. 2002. Power and Weakness. *Policy Review* 113 (June/July): 1–26.

———. 2003. *Of Paradise and Power. America and Europe in the New World Order*. New York: Knopf.

Kanet, Roger E. 2005. The Bush Revolution in U.S. Security Policy. In *The New Security Environment: The Impact on Russia, Central, and Eastern Europe*. Ed. Roger E. Kanet. Aldershot, U.K.: Ashgate.

Kanet, Roger E., and Larisa Homarac. 2007. The U.S. Challenge to Russian Influence in Central Asia and the Caucasus. In *Russia: Reemerging Great Power?* Ed. Roger E. Kanet. Basingstoke, U.K.: Palgrave.

Kang, Choi. 2005. A View of America's Role in Asia and the Future of the ROK-U.S. Alliance. *Joint U.S.–Korea Academic Studies* 15: 217–33.

Kaplan, Fred. 2006. Hunkering Down: A Guide to the U.S. Military's Future in Iraq. *Atlantic Monthly* 297 (5): 34–37.

Karasaki, Taro. 2004. Great Expectations: the SDF Dispatch to Iraq has Made Clear that Japan will Share the Risk and Stand by the United States. *International Herald Tribune-Asahi Shimbun*, October 11.

Karatnycky, Adrian. 2000. A Century of Progress. *Journal of Democracy* 11 (1): 187–200.

Katzenstein, Peter J., and Robert O. Keohane, eds. 2006. *Anti-Americanism in World Politics*. Ithaca: Cornell University Press.

Kennan, George F. 1984. *American Diplomacy: 1900–1950*. Chicago: University of Chicago Press.

Kennedy, Paul M., ed. 1979. *The War Plans of the Great Powers, 1880–1914*. London: Allen and Unwin.

———. 1980. *The Rise of the Anglo-German Antagonism 1860–1914*. London: Allen and Unwin.

———. 1987. *The Rise and Fall of the Great Powers: Economic Change and Military Conflict from 1500 to 2000*. New York: Random House.

Keohane, Robert. 1984. *After Hegemony*. Princeton, N.J.: Princeton University Press.

Keohane, Robert, and Joseph S. Nye. 2001. *Power and Interdependence*. 3rd ed. New York: Longman.

Kessler, Glenn. 2004. U.S. Seeks Safeguards for Israel's Gaza Pullout. *Washington Post*, February 18, sec. A.

———. 2005. Both Sides Bend to Restart N. Korea Talks. *Washington Post*, July 14.

Khalidi, Rashid. 2005. *Resurrecting EMPIRE: Western Footprints and America's Perilous Path in the Middle East*. Boston: Beacon Press.

Khalilzad, Zalmay. 1979/80. The Superpowers and the Northern Tier. *International Security* 4 (Winter): 6–30.

Khokhotva, Ivan. 2003. Dead on Arrival. *Transitions*, September 29.

Kim, Hi-hyun. 2005. East Asia Summit: A Step toward Community? *Korea Herald*, December 12.

Kim, Jinwung. 2004. Ambivalent Allies: Recent South Korean Perceptions of the United States Forces Korea (USFK). *Asian Affairs* 30 (4): 268–85.

Klein, Aaron. 2005. Gaza Withdrawal Violates U.S. Law? *World Net Daily*, March 28.

Klein, Rick. 2006. Deep Cuts Sought for Social Programs. *Boston Globe*, February 7. http://www.boston.com/news/nation/washington/articles/2006/02/07/deep_cuts_sought_for_social_programs/?page=1.

Kleinberg, Remonda Bensabat. 1999. *Strategic Alliances and Other Deals: State-Business Relations and Economic Reforms in Mexico*. Durham, N.C.: Carolina Academic Press.

Knowlton, Brian. 2005. Praise and Chill in Turkey Meeting. *International Herald Tribune*, June 9. http://www.iht.com/articles/2005/06/09/news/prexy.php.

Knowlton, Brian, and Carlotta Gall. 2006. Pakistanis Protest Airstrike by U.S. *International Herald Tribune*, January 16. http://www.iht.com/articles/2006/01/15/news/pakistan.php.

Ko, Shu-ling. 2006. Chen Vows to Deliver on Constitution. *Taipei Times*, September 29.

Kogan, Eugene B. 2005. Pyongyang Palliative is Bush's Bitter Pill. *Japan Times*, September 11.

Kolakowski, Leszek. 1981. *Die Hauptströmungen des Marxismus*. 3 vols. Munich: Pieper and Co.

Kolodziej, Edward A. 1966. *The Uncommon Defense and Congress*. Columbus: Ohio State University Press.

———. 1974. *French International Policy under De Gaulle and Pompidou: The Politics of Grandeur*. Ithaca: Cornell University Press.

———. 2005. *Security and International Relations*. Cambridge, U.K.: Cambridge University Press.

———. 2007. The World Society and Global Governance. Paper presented at the annual meeting of the International Studies Association, February 28–March 4, Conrad Hilton Hotel, Chicago.

Kolodziej, Edward A., and Roger E. Kanet, eds. 1989. *The Limits of Soviet Power in the Developing World*. Baltimore: Johns Hopkins University Press.

———, eds. 1996. *Coping with Conflict after the Cold War*. Baltimore: Johns Hopkins University Press.

Korea Herald. 2006. S. Korea's Roh Raps Japan on History. March 2.

Kortunov, Sergei. 2002. Russian–American Partnership: A Chance to Open a New Page. *International Affairs: A Russian Journal of World Politics, Diplomacy and International Relations* 48 (3): 23–39.

Kramer, David. 2006. Deputy Assistant Secretary of State for European and Eurasian Affairs. Speech at the Woodrow Wilson Center, March 21. Washington, D.C.

Krauthammer, Charles. 2002/3. The Unipolar Moment Revisited. *The National Interest* 70 (Winter): 5–17.

———. 2004. *Democratic Realism: An American Foreign Policy for a Unipolar World*. Washington, D.C.: American Enterprise Institute for Public Policy Research.

———. 2005. The Truth about Torture. *Weekly Standard*, December 20, 7.

Kristol, William, and Robert Kagan. 1996. Toward a Neo-Reaganite Foreign Policy. *Foreign Affairs* 75 (4): 18–32. http://www.foreignaffairs.org/19960701faessay4210/william-kristol-robert-kagan/toward-a-neo-reaganite-foreign-policy.html.

Krushelnycky, Askold. 2004. Interview with Borys Tarasiuk, Yushchenko's Foreign Policy Adviser. RFE/RL News and Analysis Ukraine, December 30

Kubicek, Paul. 2003. U.S.–Ukrainian Relations: From Engagement to Estrangement. *Problems of Post-Communism* 50 (6): 3–11.

Kudrin, Alyaksandr. 2004. Belarus: A Decade with Lukashenko. *Transitions*, July 26.

Kukreja, Veena. 2003. *Contemporary Pakistan: Political Processes, Conflicts, and Crises.* New Delhi: Sage.

Kumar, Satish. 2000. Militant Islam: The Nemesis of Pakistan. *Aakrosh* 3 (6): 17–38.

Kumaraswami, P. R. 2005. India's Interests Collide over Iran. *PINR*, October 28. http://www.pinr.com/report.php?ac=view_report&report_id=389&language_id=1.

Kux, Dennis. 1994. *Estranged Democracies. India and the United States 1941–1991.* New Delhi: Sage Publications.

———. 2001. *The United States and Pakistan 1947–2000: Disenchanted Allies.* Washington, D.C.: Woodrow Wilson Center Press; Baltimore: John Hopkins University Press.

Kuzio, Taras. 2002. Belarusian President Lukashenko Warms to NATO. *RFE/RL Newsline,* July 29.

———. 2003. Ukraine and Euro-Atlantic Integration. *Kyiv Post,* January 16.

Kwa, Chong Kuan, and See Seng Tan. 2001. The Keystone of World Order. *Washington Quarterly* 24 (3): 95–103.

Lampton, David M. 1997. China and Clinton's America: Have They Learned Anything? *Asian Survey* 37 (12): 1099–1118.

———. 2001. *Same Bed, Different Dreams: Managing U.S.–China Relations.* Berkeley: University of California Press.

Landau, Saul. 2005. The Good Neighbor Policy and Other Political Amusements Bolivian Democracy and the U.S.: A History Lesson. *ZNET* Latin America, December 22.

Langton, Christopher, ed. 2005. *The Military Balance: 2005–2006.* International Institute for Strategic Studies. London: Routledge.

Latypov, Ural. 2000. Deputy Prime Minister, Minister for Foreign Affairs Answers Questions. *Belarus Magazine,* June.

Lavelle, Peter. 2005. Analysis: Ukraine, Russia Start Anew. *Washington Times,* January 12.

Layne, Christopher. 2006a. Impotent Power? Re-Examining the Nature of America's Hegemonic Power. *The National Interest* (September/October): 42–48.

———. 2006b. *The Peace of Illusions: American Grand Strategy from 1940 to the Present.* Ithaca, N.Y.: Cornell University Press.

———. 2006c. The Unipolar Illusion Revised: The Coming End of the United States' Unipolar Moment. *International Security* 31 (2): 7–41.

Lebow, R. Ned, and Robert E. Kelly. 2001. Thucydides and Hegemony: Athens and the United States. *Review of International Studies* 274 (October): 593–609.

Lee, Joo-hee. 2005a. 7-point Economic Aid Offer to N.K. Devised by Seoul. *Korea Herald,* June 29.

———. 2005b. N. Korea Returns to Nuke Talks in July. *Korea Herald,* July 10.

———. 2005c. Rice Calls on N. Korea to Dismantle Nuc Weapons. *Korea Herald,* July 14.

———. 2005d. Debate Brews over Seoul's Expenses for N. Korea. *Korea Herald,* September 22.

———. 2005e. S. Korea Prepares "Korean Peninsula" Peace Initiative. *Korea Herald,* October 31.

———. 2005f. U.S. Envoy Says No End to Sanctions on N. Korea. *Korea Herald*, December 8.

———. 2006. U.S. Wants N. Korea to Avoid New Conditions in Nuke Talks. *Korea Herald*, January 5.

Leifer, Michael. 1983. *Indonesia's Foreign Policy*. London: Allen and Unwin.

———. 1989. *ASEAN and the Security of Southeast Asia*. London: Routledge.

———. 1996. The ASEAN Regional Forum: Expanding ASEAN's Model of Regional Security. *Adelphi Paper* 302. London: International Institute of Strategic Studies.

———. 1998. The ASEAN Regional Forum: A Model for Cooperative Security in the Middle East. *Research School of Asian and Pacific Studies Working Paper* 1. Canberra: Australian National University, Department of International Relations.

Le Quotidien. 2003. Visite d'une mission Américaine à Alger. Le FBI, la CIA et la NSA sollicitent le DRS. February 10.

Lesser, Ian O. 2004. Turkey in the EU: A New U.S. Relationship. *Insight Turkey* 6 (4).

———. 2006. Turkey and the United States: From Geopolitics to Concerted Strategy. *Sakip Sabanci International Research Award Paper*, May 23. Washington, D.C.: Brookings Institution.

Levi, Michael A., and Michael E. O'Hanlon. 2005. *The Future of Arms Control*. Washington, D.C.: Brookings Institution Press.

Levin, N. Gordon, Jr. 1968. *Woodrow Wilson and World Politics*. New York: Oxford University Press.

Levinson, Charles. 2004. $50 Billion Later, Taking Stock of U.S. Aid to Egypt. *Christian Science Monitor*, April 12.

Lieven, Anatol. 2004. *America Right or Wrong: An Anatomy of American Nationalism*. New York: Oxford University Press.

Limaye, Satu P. 2004. Minding the Gaps: The Bush Administration and U.S.–Southeast Asia Relations. *Contemporary Southeast Asia* 26 (1): 73–93.

Lin, Limin. 2005. Dangqian zhongguo zhoubian anquan huanjing pingxi [Assessment of China's Current Security Environment in the Surrounding Areas]. *Dangdai Shijie* [Contemporary World] 4: 4–6.

Lind, Michael. 2006. *The American Way of Strategy: U.S. Foreign Policy and the American Way of Life*. New York: Oxford University Press.

Lins, Carlos Eduardo. 2005. La Casa Blanca y el Planalto: respeto y solidaridad. *Foreign Affairs en Español* 5 (1): 19–26.

Liow, Joseph Chinyong. 2004a. The Security Situation in Southern Thailand: Towards an Understanding of Domestic and International Dimensions. *Studies in Conflict and Terrorism* 27 (6): 531–48.

———. 2004b. The Mahathir Administration's War against Islamic Militancy: Operational and Ideological Challenges. *Australian Journal of International Affairs* 58 (2): 241–56.

Lippmann, Walter. 1947. *The Cold War*. New York: Harpers.

Liu, Hongwu, and Luo Jianbo. 2001. Zhong fei guojian ershiyi shiji xinxing zhanlue huoban guanxi de teshu yiyi [Special Implications of the Construction of Sino–African New

Strategic Partnership in the Twenty-first Century]. *Guoji Guancha* [International Perspectives] 6: 50–60.

Liu, Qingjian. 2005. Er shi yi shiji chu zhongguo yu fazhan zhong guojia guanxi de tedian [Characteristics of Relations between China and the Developing Countries at the Beginning of Twenty-first Century]. *Xiandai Guoji Guanxi* [Contemporary International Relations] 6: 1–7.

Livishin, Sergei. 2006. 2006: The Year of Russia in China. *Far Eastern Affairs* 34 (1): 1–13.

Lizee, Pierre P. 2000. Civil Society and Regional Security: Tensions and Potentials in Post-Crisis Southeast Asia. *Contemporary Southeast Asia* 22: 550–69.

Lugar, Richard. 2005. Algerian National TV, 19:00 GMT, August 18.

Lyman, Princeton N., and J. Stephen Morrison. 2004. The Terrorist Threat in Africa. *Foreign Affairs* 83 (1): 75–86. http://www.foreignaffairs.org/20040101faessay83108/princeton-n-lyman-j-stephen-morrison/the-terrorist-threat-in-africa.html.

Lynch, Dov. 2006. *Why Georgia Matters. Chaillot Paper* 86. Paris: EU Institute for Security Studies.

Mabry, Marcus. 2006. Feeling Blue? *Newsweek*, November 10. http://www.msnbc.msn.com/id/15667442/site/newsweek.

MacFarquhar, Neil. 2005. Asterisk Aside, First National Vote for Saudis. *New York Times*, February 10.

Maclean, Williams. 2001. U.S. Forces Welcome to Deploy in Somalia. *Reuters*, December 16.

Mahbubani, Kishore. 2005. Understanding China. *Foreign Affairs* 84 (5): 49–61. http://www.foreignaffairs.org/20050901faessay84505/kishore-mahbubani/understanding-china.html.

Maher, Brian. 2003. Will Musharraf Take Decisive Action Against Internal Militants? *PINR*, November 6. http://www.pinr.com/report.php?ac=view_report&report_id=107&language_id=1.

Maine, Sir Henry. 1886. *Popular Government.* New York: Henry Holt.

Malik, Mohan. 2006. China's Strategy of Containing India. *PINR*, February 6. http://www.pinr.com/report.php?ac=view_report&report_id=434&language_id=1.

Malmvig, Helle, and Martin Fernando Jakobsen. 2006. Stadig et trekantsdrama? Europæisk og amerikansk sikkerhedspolitik i Mellemøsten siden Irak-krigen. *DIIS Brief*, April. Copenhagen: Danish Institute for International Studies.

Mandelbaum, Michael. 2002. *The Ideas That Conquered the World: Peace, Democracy, and Free Markets in the Twenty-First Century.* New York: Public Affairs.

———. 2005. *The Case for Goliath: How America Acts As the World's Government in the 21st Century.* New York: Public Affairs.

Mann, James. 1999. *About Face: A History of America's Curious Relationship with China, from Nixon to Clinton.* New York: Alfred A. Knopf.

Mann, Michael. 1986. *The Sources of Social Power: A History of Power from the Beginning to A.D. 1760.* Vol. 1. Cambridge, U.K.: Cambridge University Press.

Mansfield, Edward D., and Jack Snyder. 1995. Democratization and War. *Foreign Affairs* 74 (3): 79–97. http://www.foreignaffairs.org/19950501faessay5039/edward-mansfield-jack-snyder/democratization-and-war.html.

————. 2002. Democratic Transitions, Institutional Strength, and War. *International Organization* 56 (2): 297–37.

————. 2005. *Electing to Fight: Why Emerging Democracies Go to War*. Cambridge, Mass.: MIT Press.

Mark, Clyde R. 2005. *Israel's Proposal to Withdraw from Gaza*. Congressional Research Service Report to Congress, February 2.

Marples, David. 2004. The Prospects of Democracy in Belarus. *Problems of Post-Communism* 51 (1): 31–42.

Mastanduno, Michael. 1999. Preserving the Unipolar Moment: Realist Theories and the U.S. Grand Strategy After the Cold War. In *Unipolar Politics*. Ed. Ethan B. Kapstein and Michael Mastanduno, 138–81. New York: Columbia University Press.

Mayer, Jane. 2005. Outsourcing Torture. *New Yorker* 81 (1): 106–12.

Mazzetti, Mark. 2006. Spy Agencies Say Iraq War Worsens Terrorism Threat. *New York Times*, September 24, 1, 8.

McBeth, John. 2003. Taking the Helm. *Far Eastern Economic Review*, October 16.

McFaul, Michael. 2004/5. Democracy Promotion as a World Value. *Washington Quarterly* 28 (1): 147–63.

Mearsheimer, John J. 1990. Back to the Future: Instability in Europe after the Cold War. *International Security* 15 (1): 5–56.

Medeiros, Evan S. 2006. Strategic Hedging and the Future of Asia-Pacific Stability. *Washington Quarterly* 29 (1): 145–67.

Menon, Anand. 2004. From Crisis to Catharsis: ESDP after Iraq. *International Affairs* 80 (4): 631–48.

Menon, Rajan. 2003. The New Great Game in Central Asia. *Survival* 45 (2): 187–204.

Mikheev, Vasily. 2005. Multilateral Approaches to Peace Building in Northeast Asia. Paper presented at the nonngovernmental Six-Party Talks on Cooperation, October 6–7, Seoul.

Mills, Greg. 2004. Africa's New Strategic Significance. *Washington Quarterly* 27 (4): 157–69.

Mishler, William, and John Willerton. 2003. The Dynamics of Presidential Popularity in Post-Communist Russia: Cultural Imperative Versus Neo-Institutional Choice? *The Journal of Politics* 65 (1): 111–41.

Monitor (Kampala, Uganda). 2003. Britain Lifts Flights Ban to Nairobi. June 27, 1–2.

Moon, Chung-in. 2005. After Beijing Breakthrough, What Next? *Korea Times*, September 23.

Moravcsik, Andrew. 2003. Striking a New Transatlantic Bargain. *Foreign Affairs* 82 (4): 74–89. http://www.foreignaffairs.org/20030701faessay15406/andrew-%20moravcsik/striking-a-new-transatlantic-bargain.html.

Moreau, Ron, Sami Yousafzai, and Michael Hirsh. 2006. The Rise of Jihadistan. *Newsweek*, October 2, 24–30.

Morgan, Patrick M. 2003. *Deterrence Now*. Cambridge, U.K.: Cambridge University Press.

Morris, Mary E. 2004. At a Crossroads: American Foreign Policy and the Middle East. Paper presented at the Saudi–American Forum, January 22, California State University, San

Bernardino. http://www.arabialink.com/Archive/GWPersp/GWP2004/GWP_2004_01_29 .htm

Mousseau, Michael. 2005. Comparing New Theory with Prior Beliefs: Market Civilization and the Democratic Peace. *Conflict Management and Peace Science* 22 (1): 63–77.

MSNBC. 2005. Saudi Arabia's King Fahd Dies at 84. August 1. http://www.msnbc.msn .com/id/8782793.

Musharraf, Pervez. 2005. Interview. Who Is Fighting al-Qaida. *Spiegel*, May 28.

Muslim Brotherhood. 2004. Muslim Brotherhood Initiative, January 13, Cairo, Egypt. http://www.eicds.org/english/publications/books/reforminitiatives/muslimbrothers.htm.

Muttitt, Greg. 2005. Crude Designs: The Rip-Off of Iraq's Oil Wealth. *PLATFORM Report*. Oxford, U.K.: Seacourt Press. http://www.carbonweb.org/showitem.asp?article=57&pare nt=4&link=Y&gp=3.

Naaz, Farah. 2000. Indo–Israel Military Cooperation. *Strategic Analysis* 25 (5): 969–98. http://www.ciaonet.org/olj/sa/sa_aug00naf01.html.

Naggar, Said El-. 2004. The Alexandria Statement. *Al-Wafd*, April 25.

Nakamura, Yuichiro. 2006. Seoul, Tokyo Agreed to "Cover Up" Abduction. *Daily Yomiuri*, February 6.

Nakano, Tamotsu. 2004. Observations on the Relationships Between Japan, China, and the United States. *Japan Economic Currents* 50: 3.

Nakash, Yitzhak. 2006. *Reaching for Power: The Shi'a in the Modern Arab World*. Princeton, N.J.: Princeton University Press.

Nardulli, Bruce R., and Thomas L. McNaugher. 2002. The Army: Toward the Objective Force. In *Transforming America's Military*. Ed. Hans Binnendijk, 101–28. Washington, D.C.: National Defense University Press.

Narich, Richard. 2003. Traditional and Non-Traditional Security Issues in Latin America: Evolution and Recent Developments. *Geneva Centre for Security Policy (GCSP) Occasional Paper Series* 42.

Nasr, Vali. 2006. *The Shia Revival: How Conflict within Islam Will Shape the World*. New York: W. W. Norton.

Nathan, Andrew J., and Robert S. Ross. 1997. *The Great Wall and the Empty Fortress*. W. W. Norton.

National Priorities Project. 2006. Cost of War. National Priorities Project: Turning Data into Action. http://nationalpriorities.org/index.php?option=com_wrapper&Itemid=182.

National Security Advisory Board. 1999. *Draft Report of the National Security Advisory Board on Indian Nuclear Doctrine*, August 17, New Delhi, India. http://www.indianembassy .org/policy/CTBT/nuclear_doctrine_aug_17_1999.html.

NATO. 2002. NATO–Russia Relations: A New Quality. Declaration by Heads of State and Government of NATO Member States and the Russian Federation, May 28, Rome, Italy.

The Nautilus Institute. 2006. *DPRK Briefing Book*. The Nautilus Institute at the Center for the Pacific Rim, University of San Francisco. http://www.nautilus.org/DPRKbriefingbook/ index.html.

Nayar, Baldev Raj. 2001. *India and the Major Powers after Pokhran II.* New Delhi: Har-Anand Publications.

Nayar, Baldev Raj, and T. V. Paul. 2003. *India in the World Order: Searching for Major-Power-Status.* Cambridge, U.K.: Cambridge University Press.

Neher, Clark D. 1996. *Democracy and Development in Southeast Asia: The Winds of Change.* Boulder, Colo.: Westview Press.

Nelson, John. 2003. Social Memory as Ritual Practice: Commemorating Spirits of the Military Dead at Yasukuni Shinto Shrine. *Journal of Asian Studies* 62 (2): 443–67.

New York Times. 2005a. South American, Arab Leaders Hold Summit. May 11.

———. 2005b. Text of Joint Statement from Nuclear Talks. September 19.

———. 2006. Homeland Security to Soon Help Brazil. March 23.

———. 2006. Editorial, Deeper and Deeper. October 5, A30.

Noh, Hoon. 2005. South Korea's "Cooperative Self-reliant Defense": Goals and Directions. *KIDA Papers* 10.

Nolan, Janne E. 1999. *An Elusive Consensus: Nuclear Weapons and American Security After the Cold War.* Washington, D.C.: Brookings Institution Press.

Nolan, Robert. 2006. The Rice Doctrine: A Look at "Transformational Diplomacy." *Foreign Policy Association Global News,* February 16. http://www.fpa.org/newsletter_info2583/newsletter_info.htm.

Noonan, Michael P. 2006. The Quadrennial Defense Review and U.S. Defense Policy, 2006–2025. *E-Notes Foreign Policy Research Institute,* March 9. http://www.fpri.org/enotes/20060309.military.noonan.qdrdefensepolicy.html.

Noorani, A. G. 2005. Volte-Face on Iran. *Frontline,* November 18. http://www.flonnet.com/fl2223/stories/20051118006700400.htm.

Nordlinger, Jay. 1999. Albright Then, Albright Now: Secretary of State Madeleine K. Albright. *National Review,* June 28.

Nye, Joseph S., Jr. 2002. *The Paradox of American Power: Why the World's Only Superpower Can't Go It Alone.* New York: Oxford University Press.

———. 2005. The Rise of China's Soft Power. *Wall Street Journal Asia,* December 29.

———. 2006. Progressive Realism. *Project Syndicate: An Association of Newspapers around the World,* August. http://www.project-syndicate.org/commentary/nye36.

Oberdorfer, Don. 2001. *The Two Koreas: A Contemporary History.* New York: Basic Books.

———. 2005. Dealing with the North Korean Nuclear Threat. *E-Notes Foreign Policy Research Institute,* June 8. http://www.fpri.org/enotes/20050608.asia.oberdorfer.northkorean-nuclearthreat.html.

O'Loughlin, John, Gearóid Ó Tuathail, and Vladimir Kolossov. 2004. A "Risky Westward Turn"? Putin's 9/11 Script and Ordinary Russians. *Europe–Asia Studies* 56 (1): 3–34.

Omaar, Rakiya. 2004. Peace-Building and Democracy: The Lessons of Somalia and Somaliland. In *Global Challenges and Africa. Royal United Services Institute for Defense and Security Studies (RUIS) Whitehall Paper* 62. Ed. Richard Cobbold and Greg Mills, 83–92. http://www.thebrenthurstfoundation.org/Files/Tswalu_Reports/TSWALU_Dialogue_2004.pdf.

Orenstein, Norman J., and Thomas E. Mann. 2006. When Congress Checks Out. *Foreign Policy* 85 (6): 67–82.

Organization of American States. 2001. Third Summit of the Americas. Declaration of Quebec City, April 22, 1. http://www.oas.org/36AG/english/doc_referencia/Cumbre AmericasQuebec_Declaracion.pdf.

———. 2006. Insulza: The People Expect Benefits of Democracy, October 2.

Osamu, Sawaji. 2005. Serving the High Cause. *Japan Journal* 2 (July): 6–11.

Osgood, Robert E. 1953. *Ideals and Self-Interest in America's Foreign Relations*. Chicago: University of Chicago Press.

Owen, John M., IV. 1994. Give Democratic Peace a Chance? How Liberalism Produces Democratic Peace. *International Security* 19 (Autumn): 87–125.

———. 2005. Iraq and the Democratic Peace. *Foreign Affairs* 84 (6): 122–27. http://www .foreignaffairs.org/20051101fareviewessay84611/john-m-owen-iv/iraq-and-the-democratic-peace.html.

Packer, George. 2005. *The Assassin's Gate: America in Iraq*. New York: Farrar, Straus and Giroux.

Pan, Esther. 2005. Egypt: Elections. Council on Foreign Relations, August 31. http://www .cfr.org/publication/8744/egypt.html.

Pant, Harsh V. 2006. The U.S.–India Nuclear Deal: The End Game Begins. *PINR*, January 27. http://www.pinr.com/report.php?ac=view_printable&report_id=428&language_id=1.

Pape, Robert A. 2006. *Dying to Win: The Strategic Logic of Suicide Terrorism*. New York: Random House.

Parakhonsky, Boris. 2004. Present Challenges for Ukraine–Russia Bilateral Relations. *Ukrainian Monitor Policy Papers* 14.

Park, Bill. 2004. Between Europe, the United States and the Middle East: Turkey and European Security in the Wake of the Iraq Crisis. *Perspectives on European Politics and Society* 5 (3): 493–516.

Park, Juhyun. 2005. Medium-Term Expenditure Framework and Year 2005 Defense Budget. *KIDA Papers* 9.

Parsowith, Sara. 2005. Women Voters Kept from Polling Stations in Egypt Elections. *Jurist Legal News and Research*, December 7. http://jurist.law.pitt.edu/paperchase/2005/12/women-voters-kept-from-polling.php.

Patrick, Stewart. 2000. America's Retreat from Multilateral Engagement. *Current History* 99 (December): 430–39.

Paul, T.V. 2005. Soft Balancing in the Age of U.S. Primacy. *International Security* 30 (1): 46–71.

Pereira, Merval. 2005. Relacão ambígua. *O Globo* (Rio de Janeiro), March 6.

Perito, Robert M. 2004. *Where is the Lone Ranger When We Need Him?: America's Search for A Postconflict Stability Force*. Washington, D.C.: United States Institute of Peace Press.

Perkovich, George. 2002. *India's Nuclear Bomb: The Impact on Global Proliferation*. New Delhi: Oxford University Press.

———. 2005. Faulty Promises: The U.S.–India Nuclear Deal. *Carnegie Endowment for International Peace Policy Outlook*, September. http://www.carnegieendowment.org /files/ PO21.Perkovich.pdf.

Peterson, John. 2004. America as a European Power: The End of Empire by Integration? *International Affairs* 80 (4): 613–29.

Pew Research Center. 2004. Pew Report: A Year after the Iraq War, March 16. http:// peoplepress.org/reports /display.php3?ReportID=206.

———. 2005. Pew Report: U.S. Image up Slightly, But Still Negative, June 23. http:// pewglobal.org/reports/display.php?ReportID=247.

Pickering, Thomas R., James R. Schlesinger, and Eric P. Schwartz, eds. 2003. Iraq: The Day After. *Task Force Report* 43. New York: Council on Foreign Relations Press.

Pincus, Walter. 2006. Growing Threat Seen in Afghan Insurgency. *Washington Post*, March 1.

PIPA (Program on International Policy Attitudes). 2007. World View of U.S. Role Goes From Bad to Worse. Washington, D.C.: World Public Opinion: Global Public Opinion on International Affairs. http://www.worldpublicopinion.org/pipa/articles/brglobalmulti-regionra/306.php?nid=&id=&pnt=306&lb=brglm.

Pollack, Jonathan D. 2005. The Strategic Futures and Military Capabilities of the Two Koreas. In *Strategic Asia 2005–06: Military Modernization in an Era of Uncertainty*. Ed. Ashley J. Tellis and Michael Wills, 137–72. Washington, D.C.: National Bureau of Asian Research.

Polyakov, Leonid. 2002. Current Russian–Ukrainian Rapprochement: Forward or Backward? A Rejoinder. *Security Dialogue* 33 (2): 171–76.

Pond, Elizabeth. 2004. *Friendly Fire: The Near-Death Experience of the Transatlantic Alliance*. Washington D.C.: Brookings Institution Press.

———. 2005. The Dynamics of the Feud over Iraq. In *The Atlantic Alliance under Stress*. Ed. David M. Andrews, 30–55. Cambridge, U.K.: Cambridge University Press.

Powell, Colin. 2002. Middle East Partnership Initiative: Building Hope for the Years Ahead. Speech to the Heritage Foundation, December 12, Washington, D.C.

———. 2006. Letter to Senator John McCain, September 13. http://graphics8.nytimes. com/packages/pdf/politics/PowellLetter.pdf.

Prados, Alfred B. 2003. Saudi Arabia: Current Issues and U.S. Relations. Congressional Research Service Issue Brief for Congress IB93113, September 15. Washington, D.C.: Library of Congress. http://www.fas.org/sgp/crs/mideast/IB93113.pdf (February 24, 2006, version).

———. 2005. Jordan: U.S. Relations and Bilateral Issues. Congressional Research Service Issue Brief for Congress IB93085, April 13. Washington, D.C.: Library of Congress. http:// www.fas.org/sgp/crs/mideast/IB93085.pdf (April 26, 2006, version).

Prasad, K. V. 2006. Let Parliament Debate Iran Issue: Left. *The Hindu*, February 6. http:// www.hindu.com/2006/02/06/stories/2006020613470100.htm.

Princeton Project on National Security. 2006. Final Report of Princeton Project on National Security: Forging a World of Liberty under Law. http://www.princeton.edu/ppns/ report/FinalReport.pdf.

Prunier, Gerard. 2005. *Darfur: The Ambiguous Genocide*. Ithaca: Cornell University Press.

Przystup, James J. 2005. U.S.–Japan Relations: Progress toward a Mature Partnership. *Institute for National Strategic Studies Occasional Paper* 2, June. Washington, D.C.: National Defense University.

Putin, Vladimir. 2005. Interview with Radio Slovenko and the Slovakian Television Channel STV. Information and Press Department, Minister for Foreign Affairs of the Russian Federation, February 22.

Qadamani, Issam. 2002. White House Seeks to Double Aid to Jordan. *Jordan Times*, February 5.

Qian, Qichen. 1993. Speech at the 48th General Assembly of the United Nations. *Beijing Review* (October): 11–17. http://www.nti.org/db/china/engdocs/qian0993.htm.

Rajagopalan, Rajesh. 2005. *Second Strike: Arguments about Nuclear War in South Asia*. New Delhi: Viking.

Ramachandran, Sudha. 2005. The Threat of Islamic Extremism to Bangladesh. *PINR*, July 27. http://www.pinr.com/report.php?ac=view_report&report_id=334&language_id=1.

Rashid, Ahmed. 2000. *Taliban: Afghanistans Gotteskrieger und der Dschihad*. Munich: Droemer.

Rees, Martin. 2003. *Our Final Hour: A Scientist's Warning: How Terror, Error, and Environmental Disaster Threaten Humankind's Future in This Century — One Earth and Beyond*. New York: Basic Books.

Renmin Ribao [People's Daily]. 1991. Yang Shangkun speech, October 10.

Renshon, Stanley A., and Peter Suedfeld, eds. 2007. *Understanding the Bush Doctrine*. New York: Routledge.

Reus-Smit, Christian. 2004. *American Power and World Order*. Cambridge, U.K.: Cambridge University Press.

Reuters. 2004. Saudi Arabia To Hold First Elections Next Year. MSNBC, September 11. http://www.msnbc.msn.com/id/5970996/

Revista Veja. 2003. O tamanho do antiamericanismo. August 13, 59.

RFE/RL. 2001. Lukashenko slams West, Opposition in Election Campaign Address. *RFE/RL Poland, Belarus and Ukraine Report*, September 12.

———. 2004a. Putin Accuses West of Double Standards on Terrorists. *RFE/RL News and Features on Russia*, September 18.

———. 2004b. Russia: Putin Defends Reforms, Condemns "Revolutions." *RFE/RL News and Features on Russia*, December 23.

———. 2006. Russia Warns Ukraine against Joining NATO. *RFE/RL News and Features on Ukraine*, December 7.

———. 2007. Belarus: Lukashenka Wants to Go His Own Way. *RFE/RL News and Features on Ukraine*, February 7.

Rice, Condoleezza. 2005. Remarks. Sophia University, March 19, Sophia, Bulgaria. http://www.state.gov/secretary/rm/2005/43655.htm.

Richardson, James D., ed. 1907. *Compilation of the Messages and Papers of the Presidents*. Vol. 2. New York: Bureau of National Treasure and Art.

Richardson, Louise. 2006. *What Terrorists Want: Understanding the Enemy, Containing the Threat*. New York: Random House.

Richardson, Michael. 1992. Southeast Asia Burying the Cold War. *International Herald Tribune*, January 22.

Ricks, Thomas E. 2006. *Fiasco: The American Military Adventure in Iraq*. New York: Penguin.

Rieff, David. 2003. Blueprint for a MESS: How the Bush Administration's Prewar Planners Bungled Postwar Iraq. *New York Times Magazine*, November 2.

Rieffer, Barbara Ann J., and Kristan Mercer. 2005. U.S. Democracy Promotion: The Clinton and Bush Administrations. *Global Society* 19 (4): 385–408.

Roberts, Kimberley. 2005. Values-Based Foreign Policy: The Administrations of President Jimmy Carter and President George W. Bush. PhD diss., University of Miami.

Roberts, L. Kathleen. 2003. The United States and the World: Changing Approaches to Human Rights Diplomacy under the Bush Administration. *Berkeley Journal of International Law* 21 (3): 631–61.

Rodríguez, Sifuentes, Emma. 2006. The U.N. Security Council and the Notion of International Security in the Nineties. PhD diss., University of Miami.

Rodrik, Dani. 1998. Globalisation, Social Conflict and Economic Growth. *The World Economy* 21 (4): 143–58.

Rogov, Sergei. 2002. The Bush Doctrine: Outlines of United States Strategy in the Twenty-first Century. *Russian Politics and Law* 40 (6): 47–61.

Rohde, David. 2006. Afghan Symbol for Change Becomes a Symbol of Failure. *New York Times*, September 5.

ROK (Republic of Korea). Ministry of National Defense. 2005. *2004 Defense White Paper*.

Ronen, Yehudit. 2005. Libya's Rising Star: Saif al-Islam and Succession. *Middle East Policy* 12 (3): 136–44.

Rosenau, James N. 1990. *Turbulence in World Politics*. Princeton, N.J.: Princeton University Press.

Rosett, Claudia. 2004. Are We Keeping Faith? *Opinion Journal*, March 24.

Ross, Dennis. 2004. *The Missing Peace: The Inside Story of the Fight for Middle East Peace*. New York: Farrar, Straus and Giroux.

Rozman, Gilbert. 2002. Japan's Relations with the U.S. and Its North Korean Option. *E-notes Foreign Policy Research Institute*, December 3. http://www.fpri.org/enotes/asia.20021203.rozman.japanusrelationsnorthkorea.html.

Rubin, Barry. 2005. English Interpretation of the New Interim Iraqi Constitution. *The Middle East Review of International Affairs* 9 (3): .

Russian Defense Ministry. 2000. *Russian Military Doctrine*, April 21.

Russian Security Council. 2000. *National Security Concept of the Russian Federation*. January 14.

Sachs, Jeffrey. 2005. *The End of Poverty: Economic Possibilities for Our Time*. New York: Penguin.

Sakwa, Richard, and Mark Webber. 1999. The Commonwealth of Independent States, 1991–1998: Stagnation and Survival. *Europe-Asia Studies* 51 (3): 379–415.

Sammon, Bill. 2005. Bush Won't Help Turkey with Kurds. *Washington Times,* June 9.

Samuels, Richard J. 1994. *Rich Nation, Strong Army: National Security and the Transformation of Japan.* Ithaca: Cornell University Press.

Sanger, David E. 2003. North Korea Says It Has Material for Atom Bombs. *New York Times,* July 15.

———. 2005. U.S. and Seoul Share a Goal but Not a Strategy on North Korea. *New York Times,* November 17.

———. 2006. In Global Shift, Bush Rethinks Going It Alone. *New York Times,* March 13, A1, A6.

Saunders, Philip C. 2000. China's America Watchers: Changing Attitudes towards the United States. *China Quarterly* 161: 41–65.

Sayari, Sabri. 1994. Turkey, the Caucasus, Central Asia. In *The New Geopolitics of Central Asia and its Borderlands.* Ed. Ali Banuazzi and Myron Wiener, 175–96. London: I. B. Tauris.

Schedler, Andreas. 1998. What is Democratic Consolidation? *Journal of Democracy* 9: 91–107.

Scheuer, Michael. 2005. A Fine Rendition. *New York Times,* March, 11, A23.

Schiff, Ze'ev 2006. Israel's War with Iran. *Foreign Affairs* 85 (6): 23–32. http://www.foreignaffairs.org/20061101faessay85603/ze-ev-schiff/israel-s-war-with-iran.html.

Schott, Jeffrey J. 2005. Does the FTAA Have a Future? Institute for International Economics, November. http://www.iie.com/publications/papers/schott1105.pdf.

Schraeder, Peter J. 1994. *United States Foreign Policy toward Africa: Incrementalism, Crisis and Change.* Cambridge, U.K.: Cambridge.

Schroeder, Paul. 2006. Mirror, Mirror, on the War: The Dreyfuss Affair and the Iraq War Compared. *The National Interest* 1 (Spring): 41–53.

Schwartz, David N. 1983. *NATO Nuclear Dilemma.* Washington, D.C.: Brookings Institution Press.

Schwartz, Peter, and Doug Randall. 2003. *An Abrupt Climate Change Scenario and its Implications for United States National Security.* Oakland: Global Business Network. http://www.gbn.com/ArticleDisplayServlet.srv?aid=26231.

Schwarz, Federick A. O., Jr., and Aziz Z. Huq. 2007. *Unchecked and Unbalanced: Presidential Power in a Time of Terror.* New York: New Press.

Scobell, Andrew. 2003. *China's Use of Military Force: Beyond the Great Wall and the Long March.* New York: Cambridge University Press.

Sedat, Ergin. 2005. Interview with Douglas Feith. *Hürriyet,* February 3.

Sengupta, Somini, and Howard W. French. 2005. India and China are Poised to Share Defining Moment. *New York Times,* April 10.

Seo, Dong-shin. 2005. Joint Statement of Nuke Talks a "Linguistic" Minefield. *Korea Society Quarterly* 4 (1): 20–21.

Seymour, James D. 1998. Human Rights in Chinese Foreign Relations. In *China and the World.* 4th ed. Ed. Samuel S. Kim, 217–38. Boulder, Colo.: Westview Press.

Shahin, Emad el-Din. 2005. Political Islam: Ready for Engagement? *La Fundación para las Relaciones Internacionales y el Dialogo Exterior (FRIDE) Working Paper* 3, February.

Shambaugh, David. 2004. China Engages Asia: Reshaping the Regional Order. *International Security* 29 (3): 64–99.

Shane, Scott, Stephen Grey, and Margot Williams. 2005. CIA Expanding Terror Battle under Guise of Charter Flights. *New York Times*, May 31, A1.

Shanker, Thom. 2005. Rumsfeld and South Korea Defense Chief Agree to Keep Status Quo. *New York Times*, October 22.

———. 2006. A New Enemy Gains on the U.S. *New York Times*, July 30.

Shanker, Thom, and Scott Shane. 2006. U.S. Military Placing Crack Teams Overseas. *International Herald Tribune*, March 9.

Sharp, Jeremy M. 2005. Egypt–United States Relations. Congressional Research Service Issue Brief for Congress IB93087, June 15. Washington, D.C.: Library of Congress. http://www.fas.org/sgp/crs/mideast/IB93087.pdf.

Shavit, Ari. 2004. Top PM Aide: Gaza Plan Aims to Freeze Peace Process. *Haaretz*, October 6. http://www.jfjfp.org/thinkpieces/tp3_A5_weisglass.pdf.

Shen, Bian. 2003. New opportunity for China–ASEAN Trade. *Beijing Review*, May 1.

Sheng, Lijun. 2001. *China's Dilemma: The Taiwan Issue.* Institute of Southeast Asian Studies.

Shifter, Michael. 2004. The U.S. and Latin America through the Lens of Empire. *Current History* 103 (February): 31.

Simon, Gerhard. 2001. Russia and Ukraine Ten Years after the Fall of the Communist Regimes: Similarities and Differences. *Russian Politics and Law* 39 (6): 74–79.

Simon, Sheldon W. 2003. U.S. Policy and Terrorism in Southeast Asia. In *Fighting Terrorism on the Southeast Asian Front. Asia Program Special Report* 112, 16–21. Washington, D.C.: Woodrow Wilson International Center for Scholars.

Singh, Bilveer. 1992. ZOPFAN *and the New Security Order in the Asia-Pacific Region.* Subang Jaya: Pelanduk.

Singh, Manmohan, Prime Minister. 2004. Address to the Nation, June 25. http://www.indianembassy.de/English/pmaddress.htm.

Singh, S. Nihal. 1986. *The Yogi and the Bear. A Study of Indo-Soviet Relations.* New Delhi: The Riverdale Company.

Smith, Michael J. 1998. Humanitarian Intervention: An Overview of the Ethical Issues. *Ethics and International Affairs* 12 (1): 63–79.

Smith, Tony. 1994. In Defense of Intervention. *Foreign Affairs* 73 (6): 34–46. http://www.foreignaffairs.org/19941101faessay5149/tony-smith/in-defense-of-intervention.html.

———. 2007. *A Pact with the Devil: Washington's Bid for World Supremacy and the Betrayal of the American Promise.* New York: Routledge.

Sneh, Ephraim. 2005. *Navigating Perilous Waters: An Israeli Strategy for Peace and Security.* New York: Routledge Curzon Press.

Snyder, Scott. 2005. South Korea's Squeeze Play. *Washington Quarterly* 28 (4): 93–106.

Soros, George. 2004. *The Bubble of American Supremacy: Correcting the Misuse of American Power.* New York: PublicAffairs.

SOUTHCOM (Southern Command). 2005a. Facts and Figures: U.S. Southern Command History. http://www.southcom.mil/pa/Facts/History.htm, December 19.

———. 2005b. Facts and Figures: Operational Overview. http://www.southcom.mil/pa/Facts/OpOverview.htm, December 29.

———. 2005c. Facts and Figures: U.S. SOUTHCOM's Theater Strategy. http://www.southcom.mil/pa/Facts/Strategy.htm, December 29.

———. 2006. U.S. Southern Command (SOUTHCOM) Overview. http://www.milnet.com/pentagon/southcom.htm.

———. 2007. U.S. Southern Command. Theater Security Cooperation, June 29. http://www.southcom.mil/AppsSC/pages/theaterSecurity.php.

Stevenson, Jonathan, ed. 2003. *Strategic Survey 2002/3.* International Institute for Strategic Studies. London: Oxford University Press.

———, ed. 2004. *Strategic Survey 2003/4.* International Institute for Strategic Studies. London: Oxford University Press.

Stiglitz, Joseph E. 2006. *Making Globalization Work.* New York: W.W. Norton.

St. John, Ronald Bruce. 2004. Libya Is Not Iraq: Preemptive Strikes, WMD and Diplomacy. *The Middle East Journal* 58 (3): 386–402.

Stubbs, Richard. 1999. War and Economic Development: Export-Oriented Industrialization in East and Southeast Asia. *Comparative Politics* 31: 337–55.

Study Group on Japan's Diplomacy for China. 2005. *Policy Recommendations on Japan's Diplomacy for China.* Tokyo: Tokyo Foundation.

Sullivan, Andrew. 2005. Abolition of Torture. *New Republic,* December 19, 7.

Sushko, Oleksandr. 2004. The Dark Side of Integration: Ambitions of Domination in Russia's Backyard. *Washington Quarterly* 27 (2): 119–31.

Sutter, Robert G. 1995. *U.S. Policy toward China: An Introduction to the Role of Interest Groups.* Lanham, Md.: Rowman and Littlefield.

Suzuki, Miwa. 2004. Japan Defence Shake-Up Bound to Unsettle Asia. *Daily Times,* October 10.

Swarns, Rachel L. 2003. Threats and Responses: South Africa; Mandela Rebukes Bush Over Crisis With Iraq. *New York Times,* February 1, A11.

Sweig, Julia E. 2006a. After Castro: The Future of United States-Cuba Relations. Council on Foreign Relations, Conference Proceedings, August 24, Washington, D.C.

———. 2006b. *Friendly Fire: Losing Friends and Making Enemies in the Anti-American Century.* New York: PublicAffairs Books.

Talbott, Strobe. 2004. *Engaging India: Diplomacy, Democracy, and the Bomb.* Washington, D.C.: Brookings Institution Press.

Talmadge, Eric. 2006. Japanese City Rejects U.S. Navy Relocation. *Forbes,* March 12.

Tan, See Seng, and Kumar Ramakrishna. 2004. Interstate and Intrastate Dynamics in Southeast Asia's War on Terror. *The SAIS Review of International Affairs* 24: 91–105.

Tangredi, Sam J. 2002a. Assessing New Missions. In *Transforming America's Military.* Ed. Hans Binnendijk, 3–30. Washington, D.C.: National Defense University Press.

———. 2002b. Globalization and Sea Power: Overview and Context. In *Globalization and Maritime Power.* Ed. Sam J. Tangredi, 1–24. Washington, D.C.: National Defense University Press.

Taspinar, Ömer. 2005. Changing Parameters in U.S.–German–Turkish Relations. *AICGS Policy Report* 18. Washington D.C.: American Institute for Contemporary German Studies.

Taylor, Ian. 2005. *NEPAD: Toward Africa's Development or Another False Start?* Boulder, Colo.: Lynne Rienner.

Teft, John F. 2005. Deputy Assistant Secretary of State for European and Eurasian Affairs. The Future of Democracy in the Black Sea Area. Testimony to the Senate Foreign Relations Committee, Subcommittee on European Affairs. March 8.

Tenet, George. 2007. *At the Center of the Storm: My Years at the CIA.* New York: Harper-Collins.

Terriff, Terry. 2004. Fear and Loathing in NATO: The Atlantic Alliance after the Crisis over Iraq. *Perspectives on European Politics and Society* 5 (3): 419–46.

Thornton, Thomas Perry. 1999. Pakistan: Fifty Years of Insecurity. In *India and Pakistan: The First Fifty Years.* Ed. Selig S. Harrison et al., 170–88. New York: Cambridge University Press.

Thucydides. 1982. The Melian Conference. In *The Peloponnesian War.* Trans. Richard Crawley. New York: Random House.

———. 1993. The Melian Dialogue. In *International Relations Theory.* Ed. Paul R. Votti andMark V. Kauppi, 84–90. New York: Macmillan.

Tirmain, John 2006. Three ways (Out of 100) that America is Screwing up the World. *AlterNet,* 15 August 2006. http://www.alternet.org/module/printversion/40175.

Tow, William T. 2001. *Asia-Pacific Strategic Relations: Seeking Convergent Security.* Cambridge, U.K.: Cambridge University Press.

Traub, James 2006. The World According to China. *New York Times Magazine,* September 3. http://www.nytimes.com/2006/09/03/magazine/03ambassador.html.

Tremlett, Giles. 2002. U.S. Arms Algeria for Fight against Islamic Terror. *Guardian,* December 10.

Trenin, Dmitri. 2005a. Russia after Ukraine. Carnegie Endowment for International Peace, January 24.

———. 2005b. A Russia beyond Putin's Russia. *Taipei Times,* April 11.

———. 2005c. Moscow's Relations with Belarus: An Ally without a Handle. Carnegie Endowment for International Peace, June 8. http://www.carnegie.ru/en/pubs/media/72720.htm.

Trouw. 2005. Lubbers: CIA wilde atoomspion laten gaan. August 10.

Tsuchiyama, Jitsuo. 2004. Why Japan is Allied? Politics of the U.S.–Japan Alliance. In *Global Governance: Germany and Japan in the International System.* Ed. Saori N. Katada, Hans W. Maull, and Takashi Inoguchi, 71–85. London: Ashgate.

Tucker, Nancy Bernkopf. 2001. *China Confidential.* New York: Columbia University Press.

Tulchin. Joseph S. 1997. Special Issue: U.S.–Latin American Relations. *Journal of Interamerican Studies and World Affairs* 39 (Spring): 34.

Turner, Mandy. Arming the Occupation: Israel and the Arms Trade. *Defense News, Campaign against Arms Trade,* November 19–25, 2001.

Tyler, Patrick E. 1996. As China Threatens Taiwan, It Makes Sure U.S. Listens. *New York Times,* January 24.

Tyson, Ann Scott. 2005. U.S. Pushes Anti-Terrorism in Africa. *Washington Post,* July 26.

———. 2006. Beyond the War Zones. *Washington Post National Weekly,* May 1–7.

U.N. Development Program. 2002. *Human Development Report 2002: Deepening Democracy in a Fragmented World.* New York, N.Y.: Oxford University Press.

———. 2003. *Arab Human Development Report 2002: Creating Opportunities for Future Generations.* New York: United Nations Development Program, Arab Fund for Economic and Social Development.

———. 2004. *Arab Human Development Report 2003: Building a Knowledge Society.* New York: United Nations Development Program, Arab Fund for Economic and Social Development.

U.N. Security Council. *Reports of the Secretary-General.* http://www.un.org/Docs/sc.

U.S. Agency for International Development (USAID). 2002. *Foreign Aid in the National Interest: Promoting Freedom, Security, and Opportunity.* http://www.usaid.gov/fani/Full_Report—Foreign_Aid_in_the_National_Interest.pdf.

U.S. Congress. House Committee on International Relations. 2001. *Africa and the War on Global Terrorism: Hearings before the Subcommittee on Africa of the Committee on International Relations.* 107th Congress, 1st session.

———. House Committee on Ways and Means. 2005. *Communication from the Board of Trustees. Federal Old-Age and Survivors Insurance and Disability Insurance Trust Funds.* April 5.

U.S. Department of Commerce. Bureau of Economic Analysis. 2005. *2005 Annual Revision of the National Income and Product Accounts,* June 29. http://www.bea.gov/newsreleases/national/gdp/2005/gdp205a.htm.

U.S. Department of Defense. 2005. *The National Defense Strategy of the United States of America.* http://www.dami.army.pentagon.mil/offices/dami-zxg/National%20Defense%20Strategy%20Mar05-U.pdf.

U.S. Department of Defense. 2006. *Quadrennial Defense Review Report,* February. http://www.defenselink.mil/pubs/pdfs/QDR20060203.pdf.

———. Chairman of the Joint Chiefs of Staff. 2004. *The National Military Strategy of the United States of America.* http://www.defenselink.mil/news/Mar2005/d20050318nms.pdf.

———. Office of Force Transformation. 2003. *Military Transformation: A Strategic Approach.* http://www.oft.osd.mil/library/library_files/document_297_MT_StrategyDoc1.pdf.

———. Office of International Security Affairs. 1995. *United States Security Strategy for the East Asia-Pacific Region,* February 27. http://stinet.dtic.mil/oai/oai?&verb=getRecord&metadataPrefix=html&identifier=ADA298441.

———. Office of the Secretary of Defense. 2006. *Annual Report to Congress: Military Power of the People's Republic of China.* http://www.dod.mil/pubs/pdfs/China%20Report%202006.pdf.

U.S. Department of State. 2005a. *United States and India Successfully Complete Next Steps in Strategic Partnership,* July 18. http://www.state.gov/p/sa/rls/fs/2005/49721.htm.

———. 2005b. *United States–India Joint Statement on Next Steps in Strategic Partnership,* September 17. http://www.state.gov/r/pa/prs/ps/2004/36290.htm.

————. 2005c. *The United States and Southeast Asia: Developments, Trends, and Policy Choices*. Statement before the House International Relations Committee, Subcommittee on Asia and the Pacific, September 21, Washington D.C.

U.S. Department of State. Bureau for International Narcotics and Law Enforcement Affairs. 2006. *International Narcotics Control Strategy Report*, March. http://www.state.gov/p/inl/rls/nrcrpt/2006/vol1/html/62106.htm.

U.S. Department of State. Bureau of International Information Programs. 2001. Foreign Trade and Global Economic Policies. In *An Outline of the U.S. Economy*, February. http://usinfo.state.gov/products/pubs/oecon/chap10.htm.

U.S. Department of State. Bureau of Western Hemisphere Affairs. 2002. *Inter-American Committee against Terrorism: Fact Sheet*, January 30.

U.S. Department of State. Office of the Spokesman. 2004a. *Middle East Reform Forum Accomplishments: Fact Sheet*, December 11. http://usinfo.state.gov/mena/Archive/2004/Dec/12-452580.html.

————. 2004b. *State Department's Mideast Partnership Funds over 100 Programs: Fact Sheet*, March 9. http://usinfo.state.gov/mena/Archive/2005/Mar/09-625548.html.

U.S. Department of State. Security Consultative Committee Document. 2005. *U.S.–Japan Alliance: Transformation and Realignment for the Future*, October 29. http://www.mofa.go.jp/region/n-america/us/security/scc/doc0510.html.

U.S. Department of the Treasury. Federal Reserve Bank of New York. 2005. *Report on Foreign Portfolio Holdings of U. S. Securities*, June. http://www.treas.gov/tic/shl2005r.pdf.

U.S. National Debt Clock. http://www.brillig.com/debt_clock.

U.S. White House. Office of the President. 1993. Report to Congress Concerning Extension of Waiver Authority for the People's Republic of China. In *Public Papers of the Presidents: William Jefferson Clinton — 1993*. 2 vols. 1: 772–76. Washington, D.C.: U.S. Government Printing Office. http://frwebgate.access.gpo.gov/cgi-bin/getpage.cgi?position=all&page=772&dbname=1993_public_papers_vol1_misc.

————. 2002. *The National Security Strategy of the United States of America*, September. http://www.whitehouse.gov/nsc/nss.pdf.

————. 2006. *The National Security Strategy of the United States of America*, March. http://www.whitehouse.gov/nsc/nss/2006/nss2006.pdf.

————. 2007. *Advancing the Cause of Social Justice in the Western Hemisphere*, March. http://www.whitehouse.gov/infocus/latinamerica.

Utkin, Anatolii. 2002. America: Imperial Ambitions Rekindled. *International Affairs: A Russian Journal of World Politics, Diplomacy and International Relations* 48 (5): 43–54.

Valenzuala, Arturo. 1999. *The Collective Defense of Democracy: Lessons from the Paraguayan Crisis of 1996*. Report to the Carnegie Commission on Preventing Deadly Conflict, December, 32.

————. 2004. Democracy and Trade: U.S. Foreign Policy towards Latin America. *Real Instituto Elcano Working Paper* 30. Madrid, Spain: Real Instituto Elcano De Estudios Internacionales y Estratégios.

Van der Westhuizen, Janis. 1998. South Africa's Emergence as a Middle Power. *Third World Quartely* 19 (3): 435–55.

Varadarajan, Siddharth. 2006. India Backs Resolution. *The Hindu*, February 5. http://www
.hinduonnet.com/thehindu/thscrip/print.pl?file=2006020512100100.htm&date=2006/
02/05/&prd=th.

Vatikiotis, Michael. 2006. The Architecture of China's Diplomatic Edge. *Brown Journal of World Affairs* 12 (2): 25–37.

Voll, Klaus. 2005. *Globale asiatische Grossmacht? Indische Aussen-und Sicherheitspolitik zwischen 2000 und 2005.* Berlin: Weissensee Verlag.

Volman, Daniel. 2003. The Bush Administration and African Oil. *Review of African Political Economy* 30 (98): 573–84.

Wallace, William. 2002. American Hegemony: European Dilemmas. In *Superterrorism: Policy Responses.* Ed. Lawrence Freedman, 105–18. Oxford, U.K.: Blackwell.

Walt, Stephen M. 1987. *The Origins of Alliances.* Ithaca: Cornell University Press.

———. 2005. *Taming American Power: The Global Response to U.S. Primacy.* New York: W.W. Norton.

Wang, Jiang Yu. 2005. The Legal and Policy Considerations of China–ASEAN FTA: The Impact on the Multilateral Trading System. In *China and Southeast Asia: Global Changes and Regional Challenges.* Ed. Ho Khai Leong and Samuel C. Y. Ku, 42–79. Singapore: Institute of Southeast Asian Studies.

Wang, Vincent Wei-cheng. 2005. The Logic of China–ASEAN FTA. In *China and Southeast Asia: Global Changes and Regional Challenges.* Ed. Ho Khai Leong and Samuel C. Y. Ku, 17–41. Singapore: Institute of Southeast Asian Studies.

Wang, Yiwei. 2005. China Conceives Big Moves in Diplomacy [Zhongguo waijiao yunyu "da shou bi"]. *Policy Research and Exploration*, September.

Warner, Margaret. 2004. East-West Divide. *Online NewsHour*, December 14.

Wax, Emily, and Karen DeYoung. 2006. U.S. Secretly Backing Warlords in Somalia. *Washington Post*, May 17, A1.

Weinstein, Michael A. 2006. Condoleezza Rice Completes Washington's Geostrategic Shift. *PINR*, February 1. http://www.pinr.com/report.php?ac=view_report&report_id=431&language_id=1.

Weintraub, Sidney. 2000. *Development and Democracy in the Southern Cone: Imperatives for U.S. Policy in South America.* Washington, D.C.: CSIS Press.

Weir, Fred. 2003. Budding Allies: Russia and China. *Christian Science Monitor*, June 4.

Weisman, Jonathan. 2004. Cuts in Domestic Spending on Table. *Washingtonpost.com*, May 27. http://www.washingtonpost.com/wp-dyn/articles/A58762-2004May26.html.

Weisman, Jonathan, and Bradley Graham. 2006. Dubai Firm to Sell U.S. Port Operations. *Washingtonpost.com*, March 10. http://www.washingtonpost.com/wp-dyn/content/article/2006/03/09/AR2006030901124.html.

Will, George F. 2006. What Problem Has Been Solved? *Miami Herald*, August 15, 17A.

Williams, Richard Lt. Col. (ret.). 2001. Bright Star: Almost Business As Usual. *PolicyWatch* 574, October 15. Washington Institute for Near East Policy. http://www.washingtoninstitute.org/templateC05.php?CID=1452.

Williams, William Appleman. 1970. *The Shaping of American Diplomacy.* 2nd ed. Chicago: Rand McNally.

————. 1991. *Tragedy of American Diplomacy.* New York: W.W. Norton.

Wilson, Peter A., and Richard D. Sokolsky. 2002. Changing the Strategic Equation. In *Transforming America's Military.* Ed. Hans Binnendijk, 283–308. Washington, D.C.: National Defense University Press.

Wolfe, Adam. 2006. Nepal's Instability in the Regional Power Struggle. *PINR,* February 3. http://www.pinr.com/report.php?ac=view_report&report_id=433.

Woodward, Bob. 2002. *Bush at War.* New York: Simon and Schuster.

————. 2006. *State of Denial: Bush at War, Part III.* New York: Simon and Schuster.

Wright, Robin. 2005a. Turkey Calls for Help On Rebels—Premier to Meet with Bush Today. *Washington Post,* June 8.

————. 2005b. U.S. Goals Are Thwarted At Pro-Democracy Forum: Demand by Egypt Derails Middle East Initiative. *Washington Post,* November 13. A24.

Wright-Neville, David. 2003. Prospects Dim: Counter-Terrorism Cooperation in Southeast Asia. In *Fighting Terrorism on the Southeast Asian Front. Asia Program Special Report* 112, 5–10. Washington, D.C.: Woodrow Wilson International Center for Scholars.

Xia, Liping. 2005. North Korea's Nuclear Program and Asian Security Cooperation. *Joint U.S.–Korea Academic Studies* 15: 171–201.

Xinhua News Agency. 1997. Sino–Russian Joint Declaration Regarding a Multi-polar World and the Establishment of a New International Order. April 23.

————. 1998. Pursuing Power Politics in the Name of Human Rights [Ming wei renquan, shi wei qiangquan]. March 2.

————. 2003. China, India Sign Declaration on Bilateral Ties. June 24.

————. 2004. The Record of U.S. Human Rights in 2003 [2003 Nian meiguo de renquan jilu]. March 1.

————. 2005. Sino–Russian Joint Declaration Regarding the International Order in the 21st Century,. July 1.

Yan, Xuetong. 2000. Post–Cold War Continuity. *Zhanlue yu Guanli* [Strategy and Management] 1: 3.

Yang, Zhong, Jie Chen, and John M. Scheb II. 1997. Political Views from Below: A Survey of Beijing Residents. *PS: Political Science and Politics* 30 (3): 471–82.

Yardley, Jim and Chris Buckley. 2005. U.S. Reassures North Korea at Opening of 6-Party Talks. *New York Times,* July 26. http://www.nytimes.com.

Yasmann, Victor, comp. 2003. Putin Touts U.S.–Russia Relations. *RFE/RL Reports,* June 11. http://www.rferl.org/reports/securitywatch/2003/06/23-110603.asp.

Yetkin, Murat. 2005a. Ankara ve Washington'da Soru Ayni: Bu Nasil Iliski? *Radikal,* February 5.

————. 2005b. ABD ile Gerilim Yönetilebilirmi? *Radikal,* February 20.

————. 2005c. Incirlik Izin Bekliyor. *Radikal,* March 19.

————. 2005d. Diyalog Zorunlu. *Radikal,* June 10.

————. 2006. ABD ile Iliskilerde Iran Bahari. *Radikal,* January 19.

Yoo, John. 2005. *The Powers of War and Peace.* Chicago: University of Chicago Press.

Youssef, Maamoun. 2005. Egypt's Mubarak Orders Election Reform. Associated Press, February 27.

Zakaria, Fareed. 2007. Right Ideas, Wrong Time. *Newsweek*, March 13, 36.

Zhang, Guihong. 2005. Mei yin zhanlue huoban guanxi yu Zhongguo: yingxiang he duice [U.S.–Indian Strategic Partnership and China: Impact and Response]. *Dangdai ya Tai* [Contemporary Asia-Pacific Studies] 5: 28–34.

Zhou, Qi. 2005. Conflicts over Human Rights between China and the U.S. *Human Rights Quarterly* 27 (1): 105–24.

Zimmermann, Warren. 1995. The Last Ambassador: A Memoir of the Collapse of Yugoslavia. *Foreign Affairs* 74 (2): 2–20. http://www.foreignaffairs.org/19950301facomment5021/warren-zimmermann/the-last-ambassador-a-memoir-of-the-collapse-of-yugoslavia.html.

Zouaoui, Mouloud. 2005. L'Algérie, noyau central au Maghreb. *Le Jeune Independent*, March 29.

Zweig, David, and Bi Jianbai. 2005. China's Global Hunt for Energy. *Foreign Affairs* 84 (5): 25–38. http://www.foreignaffairs.org/20050901faessay84503/david-zweig-bi-jianhai/china-s-global-hunt-for-energy.html.

Contributors

Badredine Arfi is an assistant professor in the Department of Political Science at the University of Florida. His research interests include international relations, international security, politics of the Middle East and North Africa, Islamic politics, game theory, and the application of mathematical modeling and fuzzy logic methods to the study of politics. He is the author of *International Change and the Stability of Multi-Ethnic States* (Indiana, 2004). His other research has appeared in *International Studies Quarterly, Security Studies, Political Analysis, Democratization, Physical Review Letters, Physical Review B,* and in edited volumes.

Gülnur Aybet is lecturer in the Department of Politics and International Relations at the University of Kent at Canterbury. Her major publications include A *European Security Architecture after the Cold War: Questions of Legitimacy* (Macmillan, 2000) and *The Dynamics of European Security Cooperation, 1945–1991* (Macmillan, 1997; 2nd Edition, 2001). She is also the author of two monographs: NATO's *Developing Role in Collective Security* (SAM Papers 4, 1999, Strategic Research Centre, Turkey) and *Turkey's Foreign Policy and Its Implications for the West* (Royal United Services Institute for Defence Studies, 2004). She has published several journal articles on issues relating to European security.

Davis B. Bobrow is professor emeritus of political science and international affairs at the University of Pittsburgh. His research interests have focused on international security affairs, international political economy, public policy, information and decision making, and East Asia. His recent publications include "A Changing American World Role?" *Zeitschrift fur Politikwissenschaft* (2002); "Visions of (In)Security and American Strategic Style," *International Studies Perspectives* (2001); "American Views of Asia-Pacific Security: Comprehensive or Military," in James C. Hsiung, ed., *Twenty-first Century World Order and the Asia Pacific: Value Change, Exigencies, and Power Realignment* (Palgrave, 2001); *Policy Analysis by Design* (coauthor, Pittsburgh, 1987); *Dezain shiko-no Seisakubunseki* (Showado, 2000); *Prospects for International Relations: Conjectures about the Next Millennium* (editor and coauthor, Blackwell, 1999); and "Hegemony Management: The U.S. in the Asia-Pacific," *The Pacific Review* (1999).

Amit Das Gupta is scientific collaborator in the Institute for Contemporary History of the Ministry of Foreign Affairs of Germany. His research concentrates on the foreign, security, and development policy of Germany and on South Asia since the independence of India and Pakistan in 1947. His publications include *Handel, Hilfe, Hallstein-Doctrine. Die bundesdeutsche Südasienpolitik unter Adenauer und Erhard 1949 bis 1966* (Trade, Aid, Hallstein Doctrine: The South Asia Policy of the Federal Republic of Germany under Adenauer and Erhard, 1949 to 1966), in the series Historische Studien (Matthiesen Verlag, 2004), and numerous articles that have appeared in *Südasien, Magazine of the Südasienbuero, Internationale Spectator,* and elsewhere. He previously held the position of senior researcher at the Germany Institute of the University of Amsterdam.

Kevin C. Dunn is assistant professor of political science at Hobart and William Smith Colleges. He is the author of *Imagining the Congo: The International Relations of Identity* (Palgrave, 2003) and the editor of *Africa's Challenge to International Relations Theory* (with Timothy Shaw, Macmillan, 2001); *Identity and Global Politics: Theoretical and Empirical Elaborations* (with Patricia Goff, Palgrave, 2004); and *African Insurgencies: Raging against the Machine* (with Morten Boas, under contract with Lynne Rienner). He also has numerous book chapters and articles in such journals as *Third World Quarterly, Journal of Third World Studies, Geopolitics,* and *Millennium.*

Jacob English is communications project manager and analyst for the Middle East and North Africa at Intermedia: Global Research, Evaluation, and Consulting in Washington, D.C. His research interests include international affairs, international security, military strategy, international communications, Middle East relations, and Islamic studies. He is a veteran U.S. Marine Corps infantryman with extensive travel, education, and work experience in the Middle East, North Africa, and South Asia. His publications include the *Encyclopedia of International Security Studies* (Congressional Quarterly Press, 2007).

Trine Flockhart is senior researcher and head of the Research Unit on Defence and Security at the Danish Institute for International Studies. Her research interests include the process of socialization of new norms (she is currently developing a structural framework for explaining norm change across different cases) and the process of Europeanization both in its current form and historically. She is currently working on an edited volume on socializing democratic norms in the new Europe and a monograph on the Europeanization of Europe. Her publications include *From Vision to Reality: Implementing Europe's New Security Order* (Westview Press, 1998); "Democracy, Security and the Social Construction of Europe," *Perspectives on European Politics and Society* (2001); and "Masters and Novices — Socialization through NATO's Parliamentary Assembly," *International Relations* (2004). She is the editor of *Socializing Democratic Norms: The Role of International Organizations for the Construction of Europe* (Palgrave, 2005).

Maria Raquel Freire is an assistant professor in the Department of International Relations at the University of Coimbra. Her research focuses on conflict and security issues and the role of international organizations in Europe and the former Soviet Union. Her publications include "The Search for Innovative Procedures: The OSCE Approach to Conflicts in the Former Soviet Area," in Howard Hensel, ed., *Sovereignty and the Global Community: The Quest for Order in the International System* (2004); "Poland at the Crossroads: The Impact of Post–Cold War Globalization Processes in the Country's Post-Communist Transition" (with Teresa Gomes), *Canadian American Slavic Studies* (2005); *Conflict and Security in the Former Soviet Union: The Role of the OSCE* (Ashgate, 2003); "The Multi-Dimensional Approach of the OSCE in Estonia: Assessing the Organization's Preventive

Diplomacy Role," in Howard Hensel, ed. *The United States and Europe: Policy Imperatives in a Globalizing World* (2002); and "Crisis Management: The OSCE in the Republic of Moldova," *Journal of Conflict, Security, and Development* (2002).

Monica Hirst is executive director of the Fundación Centro de Estudos Brasileiros and professor in the Program on International Relations at the Latin American Faculty of Social Sciences at the Universidad Torcuato di Tella, Buenos Aires. She has published extensively on Brazilian foreign policy and on Brazilian–U.S. relations, including *Brazil–Estados Unidos na trasicao democratica* and *The United States and Brazil* (Routledge, 2004) as well as on MERCOSUR and broader security issues in Latin America. She was a Robert F. Kennedy Visiting Professor of Latin American Studies at Harvard University in spring 2000.

Roger E. Kanet is professor of international studies at the University of Miami and professor emeritus of political sciences at the University of Illinois at Urbana-Champaign. He has edited and contributed to twenty books on security and foreign policy issues, including several books coedited with Edward Kolodziej: *The Limits of Soviet Power in the Developing World: Thermidor in the Revolutionary Struggle* (Macmillan/Johns Hopkins University Press, 1989); *The Cold War as Cooperation: Superpower Cooperation in Regional Conflict Management* (Macmillan, 1991); and *Coping with Conflict after the Cold War* (Johns Hopkins University Press, 1996). He also served as editor of *Resolving Regional Conflicts* (University of Illinois Press, 1998) and is the author of more than two hundred articles that have appeared in scholarly journals and edited books.

Remonda B. Kleinberg is associate professor of international and comparative politics/international law at the University of North Carolina at Wilmington. Her research interests include international trade and security issues, international law, and terrorism. She is completing an LLM degree in international law and in addition to several articles, her publications include a volume edited with Janine Clark entitled *Economic Liberalization, Democratization, and Civil Society in the Developing World* (St. Martin's Press, 2000) and *Strategic Alliances and Other Deals: State-Private Sector Relations and Economic Reform in Mexico* (Carolina Academic Press, 1999).

Edward A. Kolodziej is research professor of political science emeritus and director of the Center for Global Studies at the University of Illinois at Urbana-Champaign. He has written or edited fourteen books on security and foreign policy, including *The Uncommon Defense and Congress: 1945–63* (Ohio State University Press, 1966); *French International Policy under De Gaulle and Pompidou: The Politics of Grandeur* (Cornell University Press, 1974); and *Making and Marketing Arms: The French Experience and Its Implications for the International System* (Princeton University Press, 1987). He has coedited several books with Roger Kanet, including *The Limits of Soviet Power in the Developing World: Thermidor in the Revolutionary Struggle* (Macmillan/Johns Hopkins University Press 1989); *The Cold War as Cooperation: Superpower Cooperation in Regional Conflict Management* (Macmillan, 1991); and *Coping with Conflict after the Cold War* (Johns Hopkins University Press, 1996), and is editor of a volume entitled *A Force Profonde: The Power, Politics, and Promise of Human Rights* (University of Pennsylvania Press, 2003). His most recent publication is *Security and International Relations* (Cambridge University Press, 2005), a critique of prevailing schools of security theory.

Li Mingjiang is assistant professor at the S. Rajaratnam School of International Studies of Nanyang Technological University, Singapore. His research interests include the rise of China in the context of East Asian regional relations and Sino–U.S. relations, China's diplomatic history, and the domestic sources of China's international strategies. He has published and presented papers on China's domestic politics and foreign policy.

Joseph Chinyong Liow is associate professor and Head of Research at the Institute of Defense and Strategic Studies at the S. Rajaratnam School of International Studies, Nanyang Technological University, Singapore. His research interests include the international politics of Southeast Asia, Muslim politics in Southeast Asia, and the domestic politics and foreign policies of Malaysia. He has published on Malaysian politics in numerous international peer-reviewed journals and is the author of *The Politics of Indonesia–Malaysia Relations: One Kin, Two Nations* (RoutledgeCurzon, 2005) and editor of *Order and Security in Southeast Asia: Essays in Memory of Michael Leifer* (RoutledgeCurzon, 2005). His latest publication is *Muslim Resistance in Southern Thailand and Southern Philippines: Religion, Ideology, and Politics* (East–West Center Washington Policy Studies 24), and he is currently working on two book manuscripts — one on Muslim politics in Malaysia, the other on Islamic education in Thailand.

Patrick M. Morgan is Tierney Chair of Peace and Conflict Studies in the Department of Political Science at the University of California, Irvine. He concentrates his research primarily on national and international security matters — deterrence theory, strategic surprise attack, arms control, American military strategy, and related subjects. He has a longstanding interest in theoretical approaches to the study of international politics. Currently he is involved in projects on the theory and practice of deterrence in the post–cold war era, security strategies for global security management, and security in Northeast Asia. His most recent publications include *Deterrence Now* (Cambridge University Press, 2003) and articles in *Contemporary Security Policy* and the *Journal of Strategic Studies*.

See Seng Tan is the deputy head of studies at the S. Rajaratnam School of International Studies, Nanyang Technological University, Singapore. He also directs the school's research center on multilateralism and regionalism. He is the editor or coeditor of the following anthologies: *Asia-Pacific Security Cooperation: National Interests and Regional Order* (M. E. Sharpe, 2004); *After Bali: The Threat of Terrorism in Southeast Asia* (Institute of Defence and Strategic Studies, 2003). He is the author of *The Role of Knowledge Communities in Constructing Asia-Pacific Security: How Thought and Talk Make War and Peace* and is currently writing a book on Asia-Pacific international relations theory (under contract). He has contributed to various anthologies and to refereed journals such as *International Relations of the Asia-Pacific*, *International Peacekeeping*, *Journal of Asian Studies*, *Pacific Review*, *SAIS Review of International Affairs*, and *Washington Quarterly*.

Index